LETTERS OF
CHARLES O'CONOR
OF BELANAGARE

LETTERS OF CHARLES O'CONOR OF BELANAGARE

A Catholic Voice in Eighteenth-Century Ireland

❧

Edited by
Robert E. Ward, John F. Wrynn, S.J., and
Catherine Coogan Ward

The Catholic University of America Press
Washington, D.C.

Previously published by University Microfilms International in a two-volume edition entitled *The Letters of Charles O'Conor of Belanagare, I: 1731–1771; II: 1772–1790*. To permit publication of this edition in one volume, the editors have summarized a number of the letters which appeared in full in the earlier edition.

Copyright © 1988
The Catholic University of America Press
All rights reserved
Printed in the United States of America

LIBRARY OF CONGRESS CATALOGING-IN-PUBLICATION DATA

O'Conor, Charles, 1710–1791.
    Letters of Charles O'Conor of Belanagare : a Catholic voice in eighteenth-century Ireland / edited by Robert E. Ward, John F. Wrynn, and Catherine Coogan Ward.
       p.   cm.
    Bibliography: p.
    Includes index.
    1. O'Conor, Charles, 1710–1791—Correspondence. 2. Historians—Ireland—Correspondence. 3. Catholics—Ireland—Correspondence. 4. Ireland—History—18th century. 5. Ireland—Social life and customs—18th century. I. Ward, Robert E. II. Wrynn, John F., 1940– . III. Ward, Catherine Coogan. IV. Title.
DA908.7.O34A4   1988
941.507'092'4—dc19   87-32563
ISBN 0-8132-0645-6

For the O'Conor Family

The Late Reverend Charles O'Conor Don, S.J.
The Late Miss Josephine O'Conor
Mrs. Gertrude O'Conor Nash
The Late Mrs. Helen O'Conor Sweetman
Mrs. Eva O'Conor Staunton
Mr. Pyers O'Conor Nash
The Late Mrs. Alice Hufstader of New York

CONTENTS

Preface ix

O'Conor's Correspondents xi

Subjects Covered in the Letters xiii

Acknowledgments xv

Manuscript Sources xvii

Abbreviations xix

Introduction xxi

LETTERS 1

The Known Works of Charles O'Conor 505

Bibliography 509

Index 513

PREFACE

This edition of letters came about because a need existed for information about the lives of Irish Catholics in the eighteenth century, a subject which, for the most part, has been unresearched. This edition for the first time brings together as many of Charles O'Conor's letters as the editors have been able to find. These letters are dispersed throughout Ireland, England, and the United States. After O'Conor's death, a grandson, the Reverend Charles O'Conor, D.D., took many of the letters and books and fifty-nine of O'Conor's Gaelic manuscripts with him when he became librarian at Stowe for the Marquis of Buckingham, George Grenville, who had twice been Lord Lieutenant of Ireland and whose wife was a Roman Catholic. Dr. Charles O'Conor was both the librarian for the Marquis and the confessor for the Marchioness. Later, when the Stowe collection was sold, Lord Ashburnham bought the O'Conor material, which now resides at the Royal Irish Academy. Dr. Charles O'Conor's brother Matthew, who was also an author as well as a practicing attorney, obtained the largest number of O'Conor's letters and took them to his estate at Mt. Druid. There he wrote in 1813 *History of the Irish Catholics* . . . , using O'Conor's letters to Dr. John Curry as a basis for his book. These letters, approximately 285, are now in the private collection at Clonalis House, County Roscommon, Ireland. The Clonalis letters are the largest single collection.

Thirty other letters, written to Joseph C. Walker, author of *Historical Memoirs of the Irish Bards*, concern O'Conor of Belanagare's relationship with Carolan, the harper. These are in the Gilbert Collection in the Pearse Street Public Library in Dublin. Donal O'Sullivan, Carolan's biographer, wrote that a 209-page manuscript, discovered in a coal bin in Rathmines, appeared for auction in the nineteenth century. Sir John T. Gilbert bought this manuscript. The British Museum bought another group of letters from O'Conor to the Chevalier Thomas O'Gorman in France. A notation on the cover of the British Museum additional MS. 21121 states, "Purchased at Dr. Nelligan's sale, 1 August 1855, one lot £259." The Egerton collection, also in the British Museum, contains eight letters to George Faulkner, the Dublin publisher of the first collection of Jonathan Swift's works. Faulkner's replies to O'Conor are in the Ashburnham Collection at the Royal Irish Academy.

A notation on a first-draft letter in the Royal Irish Academy led the editors to the final draft of a letter to Edmund Burke in the Sheffield City Library in England. Finally, three letters of O'Conor of Belanagare, his Gaelic diaries, and much information on Dr. Charles O'Conor are in the Henry Huntington Library in California.

Once the editors knew the whereabouts of the various caches of letters, they could begin to transcribe them. They worked with the originals at Clonalis House, Pearse Street Public Library, and the Royal Irish Academy, spending four years checking their typescripts with the originals. Microfilms or machine copies were used in all other cases.

Because the editors wanted to make the material in these letters as accessible as possible, modern spelling, capitalization, and punctuation are used throughout. A Conference on Editorial Problems at the University of Toronto in November 1978 indicated that authorities are sharply divided on the issue of modernization. In the case of this publication, readability won out over absolute reproduction of the originals. Only book titles, place names, and ancient Irish names are in O'Conor's spelling. Also, farewell salutations and signatures are omitted without the use of ellipsis.

O'Conor dated his letters sometimes at the beginning, other times at the end, using month, day, year. For standardization the editors have placed all dates at the beginning of the letter in the upper right hand corner, using day, month, year. Unless otherwise indicated in a footnote, a bracket around a date means that O'Conor had placed the date at the end of the letter. When an omission occurs between paragraphs, ellipsis points appear at the beginning or at the end of the paragraph that contained the deleted material. Sometimes phrases or sentences are quoted from the letters in a summary. In that case, the source of the quoted material will be indicated.

The full letters and abridgments are printed in larger type, the summaries in smaller type.

ROBERT E. WARD
JOHN F. WRYNN, S.J.
CATHERINE COOGAN WARD

O'CONOR'S CORRESPONDENTS

1731–1740	John Fergus	1
1741–1750	Michael Reilly	1
1751–1760	John Curry	62
	Denis O'Conor	6
	George Faulkner	3
	Hugh Stafford	3
	Miscellaneous	4
		78 letters
1761–1770	John Curry	89
	George Faulkner	11
	Archbishop John Carpenter	5
	Denis O'Conor	4
	Sylvester O'Halloran	4
	Lord Lyttleton	3
	Hugh Stafford	1
	Thomas O'Gorman	1
	Miscellaneous	9
		127 letters
1771–1780	John Curry	46
	Denis O'Conor	39
	Archbishop John Carpenter	16
	Charles Vallancey	10
	Charles Ryan	6
	Charles O'Conor (grandson)	1
	Miscellaneous	14
		132 letters
1781–1790	Thomas O'Gorman	37
	Joseph C. Walker	23
	Denis O'Conor	22
	Archbishop John Carpenter	5
	Charles O'Conor (grandson)	3
	John Pinkerton	3
	Charles Ryan	2
	Charles Vallancey	2
	Miscellaneous	14
		111 letters

SUBJECTS COVERED IN THE LETTERS

1731		Evidence of O'Conor's first interest in purchasing old Gaelic manuscripts.
1750–1770	1756–1763	Formation of the first Catholic association.
	1756–57	Catholic Registry Bill in the Irish Parliament.
	1756	O'Conor's brother Hugh files a Discovery Bill, which is in the courts for the next twenty years.
	1761–1762	Agrarian disturbances in Munster and Ulster—Whiteboys and Oakboys.
	1765	Militia Bill and surreptitious entry of Catholics into the armed services.
1770–1790		A record of the Irish Catholic response to the American Revolution. O'Conor hoped that the English would win and grant Maryland to the Irish Catholics.
		O'Conor's lawsuit continues. O'Conor is held under house arrest in 1779. Irish Volunteers are formed. The letters give a firsthand description. First Catholic Relief Bill is passed. Detailed records of O'Conor's attempts to acquire higher education abroad for his grandsons and to place them in good positions.
		Linguistic research in correspondence with Vallancey.
		References to Carolan in correspondence with Walker.
		Attempts to produce an accurate Irish history from O'Conor's annals.

ACKNOWLEDGMENTS

The editors owe a debt of gratitude to the O'Conor family members who allowed us access to materials in their possession. A special acknowledgment is made to the late Miss Josephine O'Conor, archivist of the O'Conor Don Collection at Clonalis and sister of the late O'Conor Don, Father Charles O'Conor, S.J., for her encouragement during the project and her hospitality during the summers we worked at Clonalis. Since Miss O'Conor's death this role has been filled by her nephew, Pyers O'Conor-Nash, the present resident at Clonalis. Thanks also go to the late Mrs. Alice Hufstader of New York, an American descendent of Charles O'Conor, for allowing us to photograph and publish her portrait of Charles O'Conor.

To Maurice O'Connell of Fordham University, editor of the *Correspondence of Daniel O'Connell*, we owe a profound debt of gratitude. His suggestions helped us formulate our editorial principles in the early stages of the edition. He shared his experience as an editor with us, and his advice helped us to present a work we feel will be an important contribution to Irish studies. Another American expert whose advice we followed is Professor William Griffin of St. John's University and archivist for the American Irish Historical Society in New York City. Thanks should go also to Professor John Armstrong of the Celtic Department, Harvard University, for his help in transcribing and translating Gaelic phrases in the letters. A member of the Western Kentucky University community who deserves our thanks is Miss Fannie Holland, a retired Latin teacher at University High School. She diligently translated the Latin quotations that abound in Charles O'Conor's correspondence.

Many Irish librarians and scholars helped us gain access to materials. Mrs. Brigid Dolan, Librarian for the Royal Irish Academy, deserves special thanks. She and her assistants made available to us the O'Conor of Belanagare papers in the Ashburnham Collection. Furthermore, she acquainted us with books relating to O'Conor of Belanagare and the O'Conor family. Without her help the O'Conor letters from the Irish Academy would have remained unpublished. Mr. R. J. Casey, Deputy City Librarian of Dublin, made available the letters from the Gilbert Collection of the Pearse Street Public Library. He machine-copied the letters from O'Conor to J. C. Walker for us. Reverend Kevin Kennedy, Archivist of the Dublin Diocesan Archives at Holy Cross College, Dublin, allowed us access to the Diocesan Archives.

Acknowledgment is made to the university presses, the libraries, and the private collections that allowed us to reproduce materials from their books and manuscripts. Fourteen lines of "The First Epistle of Horace" are from the *Satires and Epistles of Horace,* trans. Smith Palmer Bovy (Chicago: University of Chicago Press, 1959; Phoenix Books, 1963). The letters of Charles O'Conor to George Faulkner were first printed in Robert Ward's *Prince of Dublin Printers, The Letters of George Faulkner* (Lexington, KY: University Press of Kentucky, 1972). The editors also thank the following libraries for permission to publish manuscript materials: the letters of O'Conor in the Ashburnham Collection, Stowe MS., and Catherine Sheehan's "Charles O'Conor of Belanagare," both by permission of the Royal Irish Academy, Dublin; the letters of Charles O'Conor to Joseph C. Walker, Gilbert MS. 203, by permission of the Dublin Public Libraries, Central Branch, Pearse Street; Charles O'Conor to Edmund Burke, Wentworth-Woodhouse Muniments, Bk. 1/43, by permission of Earl Fitzwilliam, his trustees, and the Director of the Sheffield, England, City Libraries; the letters of Charles O'Conor to George Faulkner, MS. Egerton 201, ff31–61, and Additional MS. 21121, and the letters of Charles O'Conor to Chevalier Thomas O'Gorman, both by permission of the British Library, Department of Manuscripts; miscellaneous letters of Charles O'Conor, MSS. STO 887–892, 1346, by permission of the Henry Huntington Library and Art Gallery; the letters of Charles O'Conor to John Curry, M.D., Denis O'Conor, and others, by permission of Mrs. Gertrude O'Conor Nash and the Trustees of the O'Conor Don papers, Clonalis, Castlerea, Co. Roscommon, Ireland. The Henry Huntington Library also granted permission to republish four letters previously published by the Rev. Charles O'Conor, D.D., in the *Memoirs of the Life and Writings of the Late Charles O'Conor of Belanagare.* Since the letters of Charles O'Conor in the Clonalis House manuscript collection are now cataloged by Professors Gareth and Janet Dunleavy of the University of Wisconsin at Milwaukee, we wish to acknowledge the use of their catalog numbers. We found the Dunleavy catalog, *The O'Conor Papers, A Descriptive Catalog and Surname Register of the Materials at Clonalis House,* an invaluable tool for its arrangement and listing of the Clonalis materials, for its overall view of the O'Conors and their place in Irish history, and finally for its help in tracing links among the O'Conor correspondents.

MANUSCRIPT SOURCES

Castlerea, County Roscommon, Ireland. Clonalis House, The O'Conor Don Papers.
Dublin. Dublin Public Libraries, Central Department, Pearse Street. Gilbert Library, MS. 203.
Dublin. Royal Irish Academy. Ashburnham Collection, Stowe MSS, Bi_1, Bi_2, Bi_1a, Bi_2a; Sheehan, Catherine. "Charles O'Conor of Belanagare," MS. 12W36.
London. The British Library, Department of Manuscripts. Egerton MS. 201, ff. 31–61; Additional MS. 21121.
San Marino, California. The Henry Huntington Library and Art Gallery. MSS. STO 887–892 and 1346.
Sheffield, England. Sheffield City Libraries. Wentworth-Woodhouse Muniments, Bk. 1/43.

ABBREVIATIONS

BDIF	*Biographical Dictionary of Irishmen in France*
BM	British Museum
BMCPBCE	*British Museum Catalogue of Printed Books*—Compact Edition
BP	*Burke's Peerage*
Burke	*The Correspondence of Edmund Burke*, ed. Thomas W. Copeland
Concise *DNB*	Concise *Dicionary of National Biography*
CtY	Yale University, Beinecke Library
CFmH	The Henry Huntington Library and Art Gallery
CuL	Cambridge University Main Library
DJ	*Dublin Journal*
FJ	*Freeman's Journal*
GM	*Gentleman's Magazine*
HBC	*Handbook of British Chronology*
HJ	*Hibernian Journal*
Ia U	University of Iowa Library
ICN	The Newberry Library, Chicago
IU	University of Illinois Library
KU	University of Kansas, Spenser Research Library
LCOC	*The Letters of Charles O'Conor of Belanagare*
OCD	The O'Conor Don Collection at Clonalis House, Castlerea, Co. Roscommon. Cataloged by Gareth and Janet Dunleavy, *The O'Conor Papers*
PSPL	Pearse Street Public Library
RCHM-8a	Royal Commission on Historical Manuscripts, *Appendix to the Eighth Report*
RIA	Royal Irish Academy
RIA Stowe MS	Royal Irish Academy, Ashburnham Collection, Stowe Manuscripts
SCL	Sheffield City Library
UMI	*The Letters of Charles O'Conor of Belanagare*, eds. Catherine Coogan and Robert E. Ward

INTRODUCTION

The historian's task is to pass on the story of society's past from one generation to the next. In traditional Irish society this was highly revered and was entrusted to *aos dána*, "the people of the gift." However, the assaults that this society suffered in the sixteenth and seventeenth centuries also threatened to smother the voices of the historians who had chronicled its triumphs and disasters, both great and small, for nearly a millennium. This suppression threatened Irish society with the most thorough form of oblivion—forgetfulness of its own past.

Charles O'Conor, the author of the correspondence presented in this volume, enjoyed, among the members of one of the oldest families of the western world, the sobriquet, "the Historian." The eighteenth-century historian was both more and less than his professional descendant of today. Seldom did he have either the luxury or the inclination to devote all his time to history; on the other hand, he was invariably master of many more vocations than one. The reader will note the variety of his many interests and undertakings. But Charles O'Conor was more than the gentleman historian of his century who dabbled in history as it suited him or paid his pressing creditors; he was conscious of being part of the living but embattled tradition of the nation and religion to which he belonged. And he also knew that his post could only be defended by the frail weapons of learning, tact, and circumspection. And it was so armed he spent his long life.

Family

Charles O'Conor (Ó Conchabhair) was born on land held by his family at Cnoc Mór, Cill Mac Trannaigh, on the border of Roscommon and Sligo ón 15 January 1710.[1] On his father's side he was de-

---

1. Robert E. Ward and Catherine Coogan Ward. *The Letters of Charles O'Conor of Belanagare.* 2 vols. (Ann Arbor: University Microfilms International, 1980), no. 159; hereafter *UMI* with the number of the letter.

scended from the O'Conor kings of Connacht and on his mother's from the O'Rourke kings of Breifne.[2] His paternal granduncle and grandfather had fought for the losing side in the Williamite wars and had died, in prison and in exile respectively. By a technicality of the law the family retained the use, if not the ownership, of considerable portions of its holdings because they had been mortgaged to Protestant neighbors, the Frenches of French Park, Co. Roscommon. Hence the family holdings were no longer the O'Conors' to lose in the general confiscations of the 1690s and the early 1700s.[3] As part of a settlement Charles's father Donncha Lia (Denis the Gray) had to surrender the "fee of Belanagare" in 1720 to John French and held his several hundred acres in "base tenure" for a rent of around £80 per annum.[4]

Education

Charles was the first of six sons and three daughters who survived infancy and was educated by a series of instructors in the locality of his birth rather than being sent abroad, though there were family connections enough on the continent for him to have been sent there. The boy's maternal uncle, Dr. Tadhg Ó Ruairc, O.F.M., "titular" and often fugitive bishop of Killala, Co. Mayo, appears to have maintained a supervisory role in his education by this series of hedge school masters. It was also thanks to this uncle that Charles inherited a manuscript copy of the *Annals of the Four Masters* that had been property of his great-grandfather Fearghal Ó Gadhra, the patron of Micheál O Cléirigh and his fellow chroniclers.[5]

By 1727 it was decided that Charles should leave Belanagare, where the family had finally settled in the mid-twenties, and go up to Dublin to attend an academy illegally and therefore discreetly kept by an elderly priest, Mr. Walter Skelton. Charles's stay in Dublin in the late twenties provided him with the chance of making contact with the circle of the Ó Neachtain family whose "school" or "court" of Irish poetry flourished at the time. We can conclude from Charles's copying

---

2. For the O'Conors see Charles Owen O'Conor Don, *The O'Conors of Connaught;* for the O'Rourkes, various numbers of *Breifne,* the Journal of the Cumann Seanchais Bhreifne (the Leitrim-Cavan historical association) esp. 2, 5 (1962): 50–79; 2, 8 (1966): 441–54; and 4, 14 (1979): 225–54.

3. J. G. Simms. *The Williamite Confiscations in Ireland, 1690–1703.* (Westport, CT: Greenwood Press, 1976), p. 181.

4. *UMI* no. 282. In no. 169 O'Conor refers to 800 acres and in no. 399 to 700. See also no. 446.

5. Ibid., no. 13. See no. 186. This copy of the Four Masters is now in the Royal Irish Academy, MS. c iii 3.

sections from a manuscript of the Book of Ballymote at this time in the possession of the Uí Neachtain that he had already acquired that interest in Irish antiquities for which he would later become so justly renowned.⁶ To round off his education Charles had the exceedingly good fortune of occasional tuition from the best known composer in the Gaelic tradition of his day, Toirdhealbhach Ó Cearbhulláin (Turlogh Carolan, 1670–1738). Ó Cearbhulláin's harp is part of the collection of O'Conor memorabilia kept at Clonalis House, Castlerea, Co. Roscommon.⁷

Charles O'Conor "The Historian"

O'Conor was in his mid-thirties when the idea of turning from his private scholarship to write history for the larger English-speaking public of Ireland and beyond became a real possibility. Toward the end of 1731 he had married Catherine Hagan and with his bride settled in a homestead of their own. But in addition to farming and raising a family, Charles continued to build up his library.⁸ After bearing five children Catherine O'Conor died on 11 November 1741, and one of her children, Marc, followed her in less than a year.⁹ Shortly afterward, the young widower, on the invitation of one of his neighbors, Oliver Goldsmith's uncle, The Reverend Thomas Contarine, began collaborating with Henry Brooke (1703–1783) and Richard Digby, an in-law of the latter, on the production of a fictionalized history of Ireland to be called the Ogygian Tales. For reasons that are somewhat obscure the partnership broke up.¹⁰ But the material garnered by O'Conor proved useful in the preparation of his *Dissertations on the Antient History of Ireland*, a series of historical essays published

---

6. Charles O'Conor, S. J. *The Early Life of Charles O'Conor (1710–1791) of Belanagare. The Beginning of the Catholic Revival in Ireland in the Eighteenth Century.* (M.A. Thesis, University College, Dublin, 1934), pp. 464–66; hereafter O'Conor, S. J., Thesis.

7. Ibid., p. 467–68; Gearóid MacEoin, ed. Edward O'Reilly, *A Chronological Account of Nearly Four Hundred Irish Writers* (Dublin: Iberno-Celtic Society, 1820; rpt. New York: Barnes and Noble, 1970), pp. 227–29; Donal O'Sullivan, *Carolan, the Life, Times, and Music of an Irish Harper.* 2 vols. (London: Routledge and Kegan Paul, Ltd., 1958), pp. 53–64.

8. *UMI* nos. 426 and 446.

9. Síle Ní Chinnéide "Dhá Leabhar Nótaí le Séarlas Ó Conchubhair." *Galvia* 1 (1954): 35.

10. *UMI* no. 84. See Dr. Charles O'Conor, D.D. *Memoirs of the Life and Writings of the Late Charles O'Conor of Belanagare, Esq., M.R.I.A.* (Dublin: J. Mehain, 1796), pp. 189–93, for a dramatic account of the difficulties that emerged among this editorial team; O'Conor, S.J., Thesis, 19–20; Seán F. Gallagher, *The Life and Works of Henry Brooke (1703–1783).* (Ph.D. Dissertation, National University of Ireland, 1966), pp. 150–63.

anonymously in 1753. It was this work that eventually established O'Conor's reputation as an authority on Irish antiquities.

The sort of history represented by the first edition of the *Dissertations* is in many ways a typical eighteenth-century "philosophical history." In it O'Conor displays his familiarity with the thought of Newton, Montesquieu, Toland, and Temple and pursues topics of interest to thinkers of the time, such as the evolution of the constitutional state and the development of the use of writing. An Introduction to the *Dissertations* traces the generally accepted lines of Irish history as contained in the medieval annals from the first settlements of Ireland to the Norman invasion. In this survey Charles O'Conor shows special interest in the growth of an integral Irish constitution comparable to the English one, unwritten yet entailing a consensus of the commonwealth to a political procedure. Very much under the influence of Montesquieu, whom he cites repeatedly in the *Dissertations,* O'Conor criticizes this pre-Norman constitution on the grounds of its failure to conform to current views of separation and balance of powers and finds it particularly defective because of the weakness of its executive. O'Conor persists in seeing squabbles over the kingship of Ireland as dynastic revolutions against the "Hy-Niall" house.[11]

The body of the *Dissertations* begins with a series of essays on various themes: language, politics, religion, arts and sciences, topography, and so on. Regarding the pre-Christian religion of the Irish, O'Conor maintained that Ireland was "the seat of our Celtic Religion," and accepted the existence of a struggle of pure "natural religion" to assert itself against the superstition of Druidism, a view maintained earlier in the century by his countryman, John Toland (1670–1722).[12]

Throughout the *Dissertations* O'Conor insists on the existence of writing in Ireland before the coming of Christianity. This concept is important for the historian in him; it is needed as a guarantee for the veracity of the Irish annal tradition on which he, much more than Anglo-Irish historians, relied. O'Conor was convinced that some of these, like Archbishop James Ussher (1581–1656) and Sir James Ware (1594–1666), by calling into question the existence of writing in pre-Patrician Ireland, had done irreparable damage to Irish historiography and had lent credence to the prejudice that before the coming of Christianity the Irish were savages. Later on O'Conor would moder-

---

11. See [Charles O'Conor,] *A Vindication of a Pamphlet* (Dublin: P. Lord, 1755), pp. 48 and 50 for similar thoughts on the constitution.
12. Charles O'Conor. *Dissertations on the History of Ireland* (Dublin: G. Faulkner, 1766), pp. 91–105. UMI nos. 193, 194, 198. See Stephen H. Daniel, *John Toland, His Methods, Manners, and Mind.* (Montreal: McGill–Queens University Press, 1984), p. 92.

ate his own claims for the antiquity of Ireland's written sources.[13] In his efforts to introduce what he viewed as the latest results of historical science into the Irish historiography, he applies Sir Isaac Newton's *Chronologia Universalis* to this material, and proudly asserts a remarkable agreement.[14]

In discussing his more recent predecessors in Irish historiography O'Conor declares himself most indebted to "the accurate Mr. O'Flaherty" (Ruairí Óg Ó Flathartaigh, 1629–1718). On the other hand, he is very severe on Dr. Seathrún Céitinn (G. Keating, c. 1570–c. 1643) for his "injudicious collection . . . degraded by the fabulous," which is further "debased by many vulgarisms in language," the final results of which "ought never to be published."[15]

In addition to topics from the history of Ireland O'Conor includes in the *Dissertations* an Appendix on the settlement of what he persists in calling North Britain (i.e., Scotland), settled by Irish *Scoti* in the early Middle Ages.[16] In the second edition published in 1766 by his friend George Faulkner (1699–1775), this subject is considerably expanded in consequence of James MacPherson's (1736–96) "translations" from Ossian that began appearing earlier in the decade.[17] To O'Conor must go the credit for being one of the earliest critics to challenge the historicity of MacPherson's Ossianic tales.

Nothing of equal scope to O'Conor's history had appeared since the works of Keating, Ware, Lynch, and O'Flaherty in the previous century. O'Conor's historical interests, though centering on Irish antiquity, were not confined to it, and in later life he seems to have contemplated addressing modern problems in Irish historiography in yet another edition of the *Dissertations*. Nothing ever came of this plan but an outline of several pages has been preserved at Clonalis House.[18]

In the same year in which the first edition of the *Dissertations* appeared, Charles O'Conor also edited and wrote the Preface to the *Memoirs* of James Touchet, the second Earl of Castlehaven (1617?–1684). One of the burning issues of history-writing in the eighteenth

---

13. *UMI* nos. 402, 407, 417, 418, 437.
14. O'Conor. *Dissertations*, pp. 15–16, 17–34. See *UMI* no. 12 for his dispute with an early friend and patron, Dr. John Fergus of Dublin, on this use of Newton.
15. O'Conor. *Dissertations*, p. x; *UMI* no. 127, O'Conor warns Ferdinando Warner that Céitinn is "not to be trusted in a single line where he was not supported by our old Annals."
16. O'Conor. *Dissertations*, pp. 182–217.
17. See *UMI* no. 147.
18. Gareth Dunleavy and Janet Dunleavy. *The O'Conor Papers, A Descriptive Catalog and Surname Register of the Materials at Clonalis House*. (Madison, WI: University of Wisconsin Press, 1977), no. 8.4.219.

century was still the civil war which had opened in Ireland in 1641. Assuming the guise of a reasonable Protestant, which he often adopted in his pamphlets, O'Conor compares the civil war in Ireland with that in the late Roman Republic. There "the best ... [were] butchered by the worst." But he sees the two wars as also dissimilar; for while Sulla and Caesar triumphed over the republic, history "even in their own days triumphed over them...."[19] It was O'Conor's hope that what he considered an impartial historical account of the wars would disqualify the claims the two religious communities in Ireland used to justify their positions as combatants or historians of the combat by appeals to religion.

Unfortunately O'Conor was to be disappointed throughout his life by the failure of even friends like Dr. Thomas Leland (1722–1785) and Dr. John Curry (c. 1720–1780) to write the recent history of Ireland without "giving good Names to bad Things and Causes the most laudable to effects the most wicked...."[20] O'Conor, nonetheless, never seemed to have abandoned his hopes for the production of a truly impartial history of his country. Writing in a periodical series launched in the mid-eighties by Charles Vallancey, which later became the *Transactions* of the Royal Irish Academy, he observed that religious confrontation in public life was being replaced by "unanimity in one creed of politics and in a profession of civil faith abundantly sufficient for every purpose of political salvation."[21]

In his later years O'Conor began to question the reliability of his sources for the chronology of Ireland's ancient past. Here he had relied on the chronicles of the Middle Ages and their early modern successors, like the Four Masters and Roderick O'Flaherty. The historiographical researches necessitated by his confrontation with James MacPherson and the school of modern Scottish historians (people like Thomas Innes [1662–1744], David Hume [1711–76], and William Robertson [1721–93]) led O'Conor to moderate his claims on behalf of the antiquity and reliability of his Irish sources and even to abandon to some extent his much admired "Mr. O'Flaherty."[22]

19. [Charles O'Conor, ed.] *The Earl of Castlehaven's Memoirs* (Waterford: J. Calwell, 1753), pp. iii–iv.
20. Ibid., p. vii; *UMI* no. 247; Walter Love, "Charles O'Conor of Belanagare and Thomas Leland's 'Philosophical' History of Ireland," *Irish Historical Studies* 12 (1962).
21. Charles O'Conor. "Reflections on the History of Ireland during the Times of Heathenism" *Collectanea de rebus hibernicis* 3 (hereafter *Coll. Hib.*) (1786): 245; *UMI* no. 407, "we are ... all *good Protestants in politics*" (emphasis O'Conor's). However, see Walter Love, "Edmund Burke and an Irish Historiographical Controversy," *History and Theory* 2 (1962): 183–187, for an account of the antagonism among the contributors to this publication.
22. Charles O'Conor, ed. Roderic O'Flaherty. *The Ogygia Vindicated* (Dublin: G. Faulkner, 1775), p. xxiv, and *Coll. Hib.*, 228–29.

Still he always maintained the authenticity of dates in the Irish annals from "seven generations before our vulgar aera" onward (c. 250 B.C.), and insisted on the pre-Patrician use of writing of some sort. To this end he supported, perhaps with more fervor than faith, the claims made by his friend and benefactor, Charles Vallancey, to have discovered a close connection between Phoenician and Irish, a claim that would of course assure the Irish of the early possession of an alphabet.²³ In the end, O'Conor found himself defending a historiographical position from two opposing assaults. On one side were arrayed the "enlightened" critics like Hume and O'Conor's own countrymen, Edward Ledwich and Thomas Campbell, who viewed medieval sources as all equally unreliable; but on the other side stood enthusiasts of an early romantic cast, like O'Halloran, who faulted O'Conor for contradicting "all the antiquities of his country."

An Apologist for the Catholic Cause

As early as the accession of George II (1727), attempts had been made by Irish Catholics to present a declaration of their allegiance to the new king that might have the effect of improving their civil and economic conditions within the kingdom. Dissention among the Catholics, however, arose because of the unacceptable language in the declaration regarding the papacy and the theory of the pope's power to depose princes.²⁴ Through most of the century the problem of presenting a united front was to hobble the work of Catholics interested in improving their relations to the state.

Longer than his career as a historian was Charles O'Conor's work as a publicist on behalf of the relaxation of the penal laws. To ensure himself of the widest audience O'Conor published his works in this area anonymously and in many instances he was at pains to create the impression that it was a Protestant who was writing.²⁵ Moreover O'Conor confessed to his friend John Curry that he had never been a fervent Jacobite like his mother, but embraced the common political creed, which he felt should unite all Irish.²⁶

In 1756 O'Conor found himself in a leading position in the newly founded Catholic Committee formed to present an Address of Loy-

23. Charles O'Conor. *Ogygia Vindicated*, p. xxiv, and *Coll. Hib.*, 213–14.
24. Patrick J. Corish *The Catholic Community in the Seventeenth and Eighteenth Centuries* (Dublin: Helicon Limited, 1981), p. 118; Edith Mary Johnston, *The Eighteenth Century*, The Gill History of Ireland, Vol. 8 (Dublin: Gill and Macmillan, 1974), p. 22.
25. See *UMI* no. 217 where his true identity is inadvertently betrayed, and Catherine Coogan Ward and Robert E. Ward, "The Catholic Pamphlets of Charles O'Conor (1710–1791)," *Studies* 68 (Winter 1979): 259–64.
26. *UMI* no. 407.

alty to the Speaker of the Irish Commons on behalf of Catholics. Both the fact and the form of this declaration displeased Catholics of the old stamp. Richard Lincoln, the Catholic Archbishop of Dublin, particularly irritated O'Conor, who regretted the "schism" in the Catholic ranks. O'Conor taxes the "Hyper-doctor," as he calls him, for criticizing the Committee's work without presenting an alternative formula.[27]

When George III succeeded his grandfather the next year, a new address was drawn up and Charles O'Conor was more than a passing observer in this process. He had sent the draft of an address to the Committee through Curry and had personally secured the adherence to the address of a group of notables in his neighborhood.[28] On this occasion it was the old Catholic nobility under Lord Trimleston who spiked the efforts of the Committee and ended by presenting their own separate address to the new monarch.

During the Whiteboy disturbances in rural Munster in the early sixties, O'Conor drafted a letter urging upon Lincoln a five-point "Exhortation" to be read at all Sunday Masses in the capital, reminding Catholics of their duty to entertain sentiments of loyalty and gratitude toward the king, to pray and fast for him and the royal family, and to remember that it was not the Hanoverians but the Stuarts, in the person of Queen Anne, who bore responsibility for the penal code.[29]

Charles O'Conor was not, however, ready to encourage cooperation with the regime at all costs. His response to the Registry Bills of 1756 and 1757 illustrates the limits of his willingness to oblige the government.[30] This proposed legislation would have replaced the virtually unenforceable act of 1704 requiring popish clergy to register with the local authorities. O'Conor rightly saw that the new bill was aimed against the authority of Catholic bishops to maintain some control over their subordinate clergy and that it sought to curtail the number of priests who would be licensed to serve in the country. But here, too, his answer to this threat was not the circumspect silence of the past, but a public declaration of principles and of loyalty.[31] Clearly O'Conor thought that Catholics would never earn the place they sought without a frank statement of what and whom they stood for.

However, O'Conor's main interest was not the political but the

27. Ibid., nos. 63–65. As an illustration of the lengths to which the archbishop was willing to go in exercising restraint on his flock, see his threat of excommunication in no. 64, n. 4.
28. Ibid., nos. 78–80; W. E. H. Lecky, *A History of Ireland in the Eighteenth Century*, 5 vols. (London: Longmans, Green, 1892; rpt. New York: AMS Press, 1969), 2: 183.
29. *UMI* no. 95.
30. Lecky, p. 113.
31. *UMI* nos. 33–34.

economic status of Catholics in Ireland. It is difficult to say whether Charles O'Conor saw economic improvement as more easily attainable in his day or whether he perceived, as so many on the opposite side did, that full economic equality would inevitably lead to political power. In any case during the nearly three decades he devoted himself to the cause his plea was principally for the freedom of Catholics from the economic disadvantages of the penal code. In the area of land tenure, especially, O'Conor saw the penal laws acting to "tie up the hands of industry and cooperation" in the country.[32] In several places O'Conor suggested that Catholics "ought to deem" their exclusion from political power "no great Hardship."[33] Not the fear of a real political threat, but "resentment of former injuries, when Protestant and Papist . . . contended about the mighty stake of power and property" was the real reason behind these laws.[34] O'Conor criticized these benighted policies because they drove enterprising Catholics and their capital abroad, accounted for the failure to develop marginal or poor land on the model of The Netherlands, and nurtured an ethos of slothfulness and neglect among the majority of Ireland's farmers. He repeatedly claimed that whatever reasons existed for refusing conformity to the ecclesiastical establishment, Catholics by the mid-eighteenth century embraced, in common with their fellow subjects, "civil faith" in the constitution, the work of their own ancestors before the Reformation. In his frequent reviews of the history of penal legislation in these pamphlets, his hero in moderation and tolerance is the "late immortal King William III," while the present debilitating laws, he points out, were enacted under Queen Anne, who was "tinctured . . . *deeply* and fatally, with all the Ductility and Irresolution of the *Stuart*-Race."[35]

O'Conor thought the penal laws not only crippled the Irish economy, but morally corrupted the Irish people because they fostered occasional conformity, "the Womb of Irreligion and sooner or later the Bane of Liberty."[36] Their corruptive potential was to be dramatically illustrated in his own experience. Though the penal laws, as is now generally maintained, were never as draconian in practice as they appeared on paper, the possibility always remained that they could be invoked to the ruin of innocent individuals and their families. Their

32. Ibid., no. 218.
33. See, for instance, *A Vindication*, p. 47.
34. [Charles O'Conor]. *Observations on the Popery Laws*. (Dublin: T. Ewing, 1771), p. 17.
35. [Charles O'Conor]. *The Case of the Roman Catholics of Ireland*. (Dublin: P. Lord, 1755), p. 44–5 (emphasis O'Conor's).
36. Ibid., p. 59.

arbitrary nature became clear to the elderly and respected man of letters and learning that Charles O'Conor had become by 1777, when his youngest brother, Hugh, who had conformed, sued for possession of the family property. The litigation dragged on for nearly eight years and, though the case was finally settled out of court, it amounted to a considerable expense in material resources and mental preoccupation. At one point O'Conor was even placed under house arrest in Dublin. Hugh eventually returned to the Catholic faith.[37]

The Preservation of Irish Antiquities

Antiquities, as we have seen, occupied the center of O'Conor's intellectual attention since his youth. His earliest historical work dealt with this portion of Irish history, and, though he often expressed interest in more recent history to Dr. Curry and others, his linguistic skills and the private collection of manuscripts he had built up pointed him in the direction of Ireland's ancient past. The growing fascination in Ireland for antiquities in the 1760s and 70s created a broader audience for O'Conor's work both in the country and abroad but especially in the capital. The Dublin printer George Faulkner, with his wide circle of friends, was largely responsible for this audience.[38]

In 1763 O'Conor had written to Dr. Francis Sullivan, Senior Fellow of Trinity and lecturer in law, proposing to edit for publication the college's manuscript of the *Annals of the Kingdom of Ireland* (the Four Masters). Sullivan's initial response was enthusiastic. But O'Conor, relieved a few years before of the responsibility of maintaining Belanagare, still did not have the leisure that Sullivan seemed to presuppose. Sullivan, for his part, lacked the knowledge of Irish required to do his share of the work, and the collaboration, a "chimerical idea," came to an end.[39]

O'Conor's collaboration with another Trinity Fellow, Dr. Thomas Leland, proved more profitable and led to professional respect and personal friendship. Leland was an enthusiastic ferreter of manuscripts for the college library and secured for O'Conor permission to use that library.[40] Another contact made through Faulkner was a military engineer with a penchant for ancient languages, Charles Val-

---

37. See Index: O'Conor, Charles: discovery suit.
38. See Robert E. Ward, *Prince of Dublin Printers, the Letters of George Faulkner* (Lexington, KY: University of Kentucky Press, 1972).
39. *UMI* nos. 124, 125, 130, 131, 351; T. Ó Raifeartaigh, *The Royal Irish Academy: A Bicentennial History, 1785–1985*. (Dublin: The Royal Irish Academy, 1985), p. 4.
40. *UMI* no. 186.

lancey. Through General Vallancey, O'Conor and his good friend Archbishop John Carpenter, a successor of the "Hyper-doctor," were invited in 1773 to become corresponding members of the Select Committee of the Dublin Society for Irish Antiquities.[41] It was this body that sponsored O'Conor's edition of O'Flaherty's *Ogygia Vindicated*.[42] In the 1780s O'Conor contributed several articles on pre-Christian Ireland to Vallancey's *Collectanea de Rebus Hibernicis*. When the "Mount Callan Ogham" became the fad, people wrote to him seeking his opinion.[43] O'Conor regularly supplied encouragement and material to anyone entering the lists against James Macpherson on the question of the comparative antiquity of Scotland and Ireland.

We have already noted the help offered by O'Conor to Leland on his *History of Ireland* as well as on his earlier refutation of Macpherson. Besides Leland, many others solicited O'Conor's help with their historical research: Dr. Silvester O'Halloran of Limerick; Dr. Ferdinand Warner of Surrey; the British poet, politician, and man of letters, George Lord Lyttleton; O'Conor's long-time friend, Dr. John Curry of Dublin; Joseph Cooper Walker, the antiquarian; the Scottish historian John Pinkerton, who eventually entertained such a low estimate of the Celts; Irish emigrés like the Chevalier Thomas O'Gorman and the Abbé Jacques McGeoghegan; and Charlotte Brooke, the daughter of his old associate in both historical research and propaganda for the Catholic Association. In addition to this O'Conor, who had been taught the special scribal hand as a youngster by his various tutors, often obliged librarians and private collectors by training scribes and copyists.

As his reputation for historical and antiquarian studies increased, O'Conor was duly recognized in the society of the capital, where he had come to spend more and more time since his retirement. In 1785 Vallencey nominated him for membership in the newly formed Irish Academy (which received its royal charter a year later). Though O'Conor sometimes complained of the burdens imposed on him because of his reputation by "mere holiday readers" and by Irish emigrés ambitious for an impressive family tree that would secure them preferment at foreign courts, he continued to the end to respond with generosity.[44]

41. Ibid., nos. 240–43; Charles O'Conor, S.J., "Origins of the Royal Irish Academy," *Studies* 38 (1949): 330.
42. Ó Raifeartaigh, p. 7.
43. *UMI* no. 385.
44. Ibid., no. 221, and also nos. 124 and 126 for his work on a disputed Irish title.

Death and Legacy

Just as his father had given Belanagare to O'Conor in his own lifetime, Charles turned over the estate to his eldest son Denis in 1760. (This was, no doubt, to avoid the uncertainties posed by the Gavelkind Law, which was not repealed till 1778 and which provided that the land of deceased Catholics be divided among all children equally.) But unlike his own father, O'Conor moved out of the big house and built himself a fine dwelling nearby which he referred to in correspondence as "my Hermitage."[45] There, surrounded by his books and manuscripts, he spent the last three decades of his life except for his increasingly prolonged sojourns in Dublin. It is those sojourns that are responsible for the amount of correspondence with his eldest son who, as the close friends of O'Conor's generation died, became more and more the confidant of his father.

One of Denis's sons, Charles, who became a priest, inherited his grandfather's interest in manuscripts and the distant past they told of. Deep gratitude came from the grandfather when he heard that Vallancey was proposing the young man's name to the Royal Irish Academy in 1788. That same year Vallancey secured the prospect of a pension for his old friend from the Lord Lieutenant, the Marquis of Buckingham, in exchange for the promise that O'Conor's library after his death be given to the Academy.[46]

For years O'Conor's letters echo a growing crescendo of complaint about the discomforts of increasing age. Yet he lived well into his eighty-second year. At the age of seventy-four he was confined for a time to bed and was assured by his physician that "I shall never be reestablished." And indeed his scholarly activity lessened considerably from then on. The new history of Ireland that he had been laboring on with encouragement from Vallancey and others was still unfinished when he died. He had left instructions that if unfinished it be destroyed, and so it seems to have been.[47]

On the 1st of July 1791 O'Conor died at Belanagare and was buried with his ancestors near the ruins of the great O'Conor stronghold of Ballintober Castle. Despite the agreement that had been made regarding the conveyance of his papers to the Academy, it was to the Marquis himself that they eventually went. These were kept by none other than O'Conor's grandson, the Reverend Charles O'Conor, D.D.,

---

45. See Ibid., no. 159, for the daily routine there in the mid-sixties.
46. Ibid., no. 439.
47. Ibid., no. 382.

who was appointed chaplain to the Marchioness (a Catholic) and librarian at Stowe Castle in England.[48] There they were kept till the middle of the nineteenth century and eventually in 1883 the collection reached the destination for which it had been meant.[49]

Charles O'Conor of Belanagare seemed almost destined for his life's work by his ancestry and by the education he received, which was unique to the generation, class, and religious community to which he belonged. As a writer of history himself, he combined in good measure a reverence for his material tempered with a critical eye that sometimes scandalized more enthusiastic contemporaries.[50]

Though he was principally engaged in recording as much as he could of the ancient past of the nation, he was not disinterested in the events of the recent past and encouraged others to deal with this subject.[51] Indeed his own personal experiences from childhood onward made the history of Ireland since the Civil War and the surrender of Limerick a living reality in his own life. And yet it may also have been fear of what the consequences would be for a descendant of the ancient aristocracy that characteristically kept him from publicly acknowledging his own works dealing with Ireland's recent past. But in a real sense we may view the corpus of O'Conor's apologetic writings as his own personal contribution to modern history. These consist not merely of a polemicist's appeal to emotion or logic; they rest upon his ample knowledge of and judgments on the recent history of Ireland.

Charles O'Conor lived and wrote at a crucial stage in the history of Ireland's Catholic community. In the second half of the eighteen century acceptance of Irish Catholics as equal participants in the political and economic life of the nation would not have been possible without unacceptable concessions on their part. Yet O'Conor had the vision to realize that the ambiguity of the clergy regarding loyalty to the Stuart pretender and the discreet silence of the Catholic peers of Ireland would hardly serve to allay the suspicions of the government and the establishment. The good eighteenth-century concept of the *common civil faith* in the Irish constitution (a constitution to which O'Conor devoted so much space in his *Dissertations*) would have to be the first step in the anticipated reconciliation.

Perhaps it was a stroke of genius, perhaps just a reflection of his

---

48. See Giovanni Costigan, "The Tragedy of Charles O'Conor, An Episode in Anglo-Irish Relations," *American Historical Review* 49 (October 1943–July 1944): 32–54 for the strange and tragic history of this man.

49. See the Preface to this edition for the history of these manuscripts.

50. [Sylvester O'Halloran] *A General History of Ireland*, 2 vols. (London: A. Hamilton, 1778), 1: 122–23.

51. *UMI* nos. 162, 166, 167.

class interest, but the removal of the property disqualifications was for him the essential start in the dismantling of the pernicious system of the penal code. The recognition of his own personal vulnerability as displayed in the Discovery Suit brought by his brother would have reinforced these motives. In any case O'Conor's personal and confessional interests were direct links with the continued fortunes of his people, which stretched from the remote past of the invasions of Ireland to the high tide of the Protestant Nation. For Charles O'Conor—the Historian—it was one continuous unfolding.

To the Westerner that Charles O'Conor was by birth, Dublin would always be the city where he spent two years of his youth learning French and science with Mr. Skelton, and also where he met Dr. Fergus and discovered the amount of Gaelic scholarship that still survived in the land of the *Gall*. As he came to spend more and more of each winter in Dublin, he found a growing interest in Ireland's history even among those whose own ancestors had not participated in that history. As the Irish establishment became more independent in spirit from the Westminster government in the last quarter of the eighteenth century, it is not difficult to see why its members would lay claim to more than the present of the country they had come to settle. They wanted to be part of its past as well. To all who were curious about Ireland's past O'Conor was generous with his knowledge and his encouragement. As the pre-Romantic fascination for Europe's Celtic past spread out from the whirlwind that followed the extravagant Ossianic claims of Macpherson in the 1760s, O'Conor received inquiries even from beyond the confines of Ireland.

As so often happens, the true promise of Charles O'Conor's life and his work—religious emancipation, historical research, and cultural revival—had to wait for another century before it came to full fruition. But already, in his century of cultural assault and political and religious bigotry, this man, as an individual and as the mentor of a generation, was at work in a modest but substantial way, doing justice to the past, making suggestions to the people of his generation, and responding with courtesy and deference to the great and small, to those from near and far, who were anxious to do justice to the complex reality of Ireland.

LETTERS

1. To Dr. John Fergus[1]

Memoirs of the Late Charles O'Conor

[10 October 1731]

This first letter already indicates O'Conor's interest in Gaelic manuscripts. He asks his friend John Fergus, M.D., to purchase the manuscripts of John Conry from a certain Charles O'Neal,[2] who is otherwise unknown. O'Conor also asks about manuscripts in the Navarre Library in Paris and stresses Ireland's civilizing influence on Europe in the past.

1. When he died in 1763, John Fergus was known as the most knowledgeable collector of old Irish manuscripts in Dublin. Fergus, a Roman Catholic, was active in trying to save Gaelic manuscripts from destruction. It would appear that Fergus met Charles O'Conor during the latter's student days in Dublin in 1727–1728. John T. Gilbert, "The Streets of Dublin," *Irish Quarterly Review*, 3 (September 1853), 610.
2. Bishop Nicholson thought Conry's collection one of the two best "in any private hands here in Dublin." See *The Irish Historical Library* (1724), 243.

2. To Civicus [Michael Reilly][1]

Memoirs of the Late Charles O'Conor

[28 October 1749]

Your hints are friendly and demand many thanks, but I am by no means interested, nor is any of our unfortunate people in this affair of Lucas[2] into which we are dragged by violent and wanton malevolence; I have even some disgust to Lucas on account of his *Barber's Letters;* a true patriot would not have betrayed such malice to such unfortunate slaves as we. . . .

1. The rest of O'Conor's reply to Michael Reilly, O'Conor's cousin in Dublin and his factotum, concerns the uproar caused by O'Conor's pamphlet, *A Counter-Appeal to the People of Ireland against the Appeal . . . of Sir Richard Cox.* While O'Conor had little use for Charles Lucas, who wrote the anti-Catholic *Barber's Letters,* he defended Lucas' right to speak about the liberty of Conscience in a Whig-controlled city like Dublin.

Sean Murphy, Dublin genealogist, has suggested that this letter is a fabrication by O'Conor's grandson, Rev. Dr. Charles O'Conor. Murphy has written an unpublished article that attempts to show that Dr. Charles took a letter *to* Charles O'Conor and falsely attributed it as being *from* O'Conor "in order to minimize his grandfather's support for Lucas." Even though Murphy has questioned the authenticity of Letter 2 and has supported his point, the editors have retained this letter in the collection in an abridged form.

2. Reilly had written on 12 October 1749 after the publication of the pamphlet:

Your inflammatory *Counter Appeal* has been roared about the streets here all this day and so inflaming it is that Walter Harris, the historian, told the printer Kelbourne he would be summoned to the bar of the house and sent to Newgate; for that it is of a more dangerous tendency than all Lucas' papers together. The best of it is that Kelbourne himself cannot guess the author; some say he is Brooke, others Lucas himself; but let them guess on while you are safe; you must guard against all Sir Richard's friends; he is not only warm but malicious against Lucas.

3. To Denis O'Conor[1]

OCD, 8.3 SE 028

[1751][2]

Postscript to Denny

I am proud of the account given of you by my Cousin Reilly.[3] In reading Virgil and Horace you might consult with profit Sanadon and Davidson,[4] but you ought to seek the flowers of those authors by some industry of your own; many such will occur which the best of critics and commentators pass by. You should observe the same rule with regard to Cicero, the best and ablest prose writer of antiquity. A thorough acquaintance with such authors will form the genius which Nature gave you and qualify you to judge of those works in the English language which are written with a true Classical Spirit. My own taste, such as it is, was vitiated much by reading too indiscriminately, all owing to the worst of an academical education. I now begin to reform a little, though too late in life when other avocations engross me. Your handwriting is stiff and uncouth and, though a point of the least consideration, it should by no means be neglected. Pray write to me every post, as it may be an exercise for forming your epistolary style and as an account of the manner of your spending time is to me very interesting; it must be much more so to yourself as you must lay in a fund of merit to set off or supply the deficiencies of fortune. Let your religious duty supersede every other, and the happiness is that every other is compatible with it. May our Divine Master, Jesus Christ, give your endeavors (in a boisterous, way-laying world) His benediction....

1. Charles O'Conor's eldest son, died 1804.
2. Undated. In another hand is written, "My father's letters to me in the year 1751."
3. Michael Reilly, O'Conor's business agent in Dublin.
4. Davidson's Horace. See *DJ*, 1–4 October 1748.

4. To Charles O'Conor[1]

OCD, 8.3 SE 028

[17 November 1751]

I neither heard of you nor from you since Luckey[2] arrived, what I must attribute to Denny's neglect (if you be not in Dublin yourself). I am very uneasy about you and him. I, therefore, request a particular account of the motions of both of you since your departure home. I lately got a letter (directed to you) from Count Dan O'Rourke,[3] and I would send it you if I thought it worth while. He begins with a compliment in answer to another of yours of the 25th of October, then informs you that Capt. O'Conor[4] wrote in favor of Mr. Hugh O'Conor[5] (who is with me this night and sets off on Wednesday next for Dublin) to his friends in Spain. He solicits Capt. MacDonough[6] (not yet arrived here) to remit some succor to his brother William Hesdin, just enough to bear his charges to Spain, where he thinks his exile will be more tolerable or his fortune more favorable. This is all I have for twenty pence. I have nothing new with regard to our affairs here to inform you of, and I think it needless to burden you with my thoughts about your future conduct till I receive some light from events which are now remote and of which I will expect a faithful narrative from yourself when any material ones occur. May God take you into His Holy Protection.

P.S. to Denis

If your uncle[7] departed from Dublin, you should inform me of the time and manner and give a history of your own plan of life and study as you know how much I am now a stranger to both and how much I have the proper conduct of both at heart. Every minute of your time is precious and any you give to indolence or vice (which may God keep you from) is a storage for future and often fruitless sorrow. I sent drafts by Mr. Barlow for £80.8. Why should I be so long a stranger to the fate of these papers? I had one in Elphin every post day those ten days in expectation of some intelligence. Remember me most affectionately to Cousin Michael Reilly, whose handwriting I expect to see soon. You may chance to meet Dr. Fergus in your way. If you do, pray challenge his friendship and give him my service. Let me know of your reception with Judge French and give me a detail of it, if you can, of the subject of conversation with him. You ought also to send your observations of incidents as will occasionally affect you most, for such an exercise will be useful in forming your epistolary style, which you will (if you live) have sundry occasions for hereafter. Let your narrative be plain and unaffected, your periods clear of all obscurity and rising one out [of] another in an order which Nature will direct if you consult her and her alone. Choice of words and good construction will set you more hard and must be the work of time and close observations. I am your most affectionate friend.

17 November 1751

    1. Charles of Mt. Allen, O'Conor's younger son, studying in Dublin.
    2. A servant.
    3. O'Conor's mother was the sister of Bishop Thadeus O'Rourke and the daughter of Colonel Tiernan Count O'Rourke. Her mother, the Countess O'Rourke, lived at Belanagare until her death on 22 December 1760. Dan O'Rourke is O'Conor's cousin. Sir John T. Gilbert, "Correspondence and Ms. of Charles O'Conor of Belanagare, Co. Roscommon—The O'Conor Don, D.L., Clonalis, Co. Roscommon," in *Appendix to the Eighth Report* (London: Royal Commission on Historical Manuscripts, 1881), p. 442. Hereafter referred to as *Appendix*.
    4. Perhaps Thomas O'Conor, later Brigadier O'Conor, uncle to Hugh O'Conor.
    5. Hugh O'Conor, the younger brother of the O'Conor Don of Clonalis.
    6. The MacDonoughs and O'Conors were also close. Charles's great uncle, Major Owen O'Conor, served with Major Owen MacDonough against the English abroad. Charles's mother was the niece of the lawyer, Terence MacDonough, who helped gain the lands of Belanagare for Charles's father. The MacDonoughs were a branch of the MacDermot clan of Sligo. Thus Captain MacDonough is a distant cousin to O'Conor.
    7. Daniel O'Conor.

5. To Denis O'Conor, High Street, Dublin

OCD, 8.3 SE 028

[17 November 1751]

I this day received your letter by Tully.[1] Be a little diffuse; you give me no account of your reception with Judge French[2] nor of Mr. Reilly,[3] my particular friend. Give Mr. Fagan[4] my thanks for his friendship and civility. I wish I may merit the favors he bestows on you. I will at least merit them by gratitude. Do you merit them by yours and by your proficiency also. I wrote to you lately by post; pray take notice of the few instructions I give you; the conscience of behaving well will not suffice in sight of the world, whatever it may do in the sight of God; and there is a certain distinction of conduct which Nature will point out and experience teach without [corrupt] Virtue itself will be only like a candle in a dark lantern. You live now in a busy, elbowing scene; if you have any sagacity, you will make reflections on every incident and reap instruction and, whatever it be, strive to adapt it to the rank you are to fill hereafter: that of a Roman Catholic in a Protestant country, that of one in a low way, obnoxious to the laws. A wise man will derive advantages even from that situation in which bounds are set to all hopes and fears. It is, indeed, a condition of life more eligible than our dull brethren can imagine or benefit by. Be it your task to rise above their low conception; of all things may the Holy Spirit speak inwardly in you and through you; its consolations, dear Denny, will render any incident (except such as is connected with vice) a means of some instruction and therefore of some happiness. . . .

17 November 1751

    1. A servant.
    2. Robert French, Judge of the Court of Common Pleas, died 1770. Uncle of O'Conor's landlord, Arthur French of French Park. *BP*, p. 705.
    3. Michael Reilly.
    4. John, Denis's teacher.

6. To Bryan O'Conor of Kerry[1]

Memoirs of the Late Charles O'Conor

[*c*.1754]

    The etymon of Kerry is *Cahir riaghta,* the kingdom of Chair, son of Fergus, King of Ulster, from whom the O'Conors Kerry are descended. From this ancient family the northern part of that country is still called *Riaght ui Chonchabhair,* O'Conor's kingdom. But though these are matters to which you will undoubtedly pay every attention, you are not to forget that the MacCarthy Mores were the most eminent by far of all the noble families there and sovereigns of all that part of Ireland including the greatest part of the county of Cork. . . .

    But I beg you will not overload your subject with too much matter. It is disgusting in the highest degree to see how heavily people enter into barren pedigrees, skeletons without meat and bodies without soul. Let us have the spirit of our ancient families transfused into the pens of their historians, and let us avoid having too many heroes together on the stage, mindful of Horace's rule that a *Unus aut alter*[2] is sufficient.

    Pardon this hint from one whose zeal for the honor of our ancient race has often led him into indiscretions, whose soul is on fire when he sees that the heroes of his native country are in no respect inferior to those of Greece and Rome except in the want of a historian whose talents would not be inferior to the task of doing them the justice (without which they will be inglorious in the midst of laurels) and no more known than if they had never existed. . . .

    1. O'Conor of Kerry had proposed to write a history of Kerry and asked O'Conor's help. However Dr. Charles found no indication that O'Conor of Kerry ever fulfilled his promise.
    2. *Epistle* 2.1.74. One or the other.

7. To Denis O'Conor

OCD, 8.3 SE 028

6 January 1755

. . . I am here [caroused] by numbers on account of my little endeavors to serve a party. I am called to all their clubs and associations; but we break up without coming to any resolutions, while our enemies act in concert and bring their schemes to bear. Indeed, they have all the power as well as all the will to act as becomes a determined people. We propose and debate but do nothing. I could fill a sheet with the history of our perplexities. I proposed (and but once, for I act with much reserve); I say I proposed that *we should make a tender of our loyalty to the King; give him a Test of political orthodoxy and petition for the repeal of the penal and punitive laws.*[1] Should the King transmit [our petition] to the Parliament here and signify his [assent with] their concurrence, we would gain a most important point, whether the laws were repealed or not. This motion of mine was approved and objected to. I will press it once again as strongly as I can. More I cannot do.

    Charles is well. We dine today at Mr. Anthony Dermot's.[2] My duty to my mother and affection to the families of Baligloss and Bela. My affection to Brother. Tell him I shall write soon to Dan[3] on the purport of his letter. Let him send me up the £14 he promised immediately. Dan is severe in his letters and speeches, but they are the speeches of angry and unprovoked affection. In this shape his speeches should not be much nor long resented. You mention Dan Rourke.[4] I have done with him. His invectives are, I am sure, more useful than his friendship.

[Rest missing or unreadable.]

    1. This proposal of the Catholics' fealty to King George is O'Conor's first mention of a topic that split the Catholic party in two. O'Conor, John Curry, M.D., and Thomas Wyse allied with the merchants of Dublin on one side, the clergy and nobility on the other. The clergy and nobility believed that Catholics should keep quiet.

2. Anthony Dermot became secretary to the Catholic Association when it began regular meetings in 1756.

3. O'Conor's brother Daniel, who served in the French army. He received receipts from land rental which came as his portion of the estate after his father's death in 1750.

4. Capt. Dan ORourke, in Dillon's Regiment in 1761. John O'Hart, *The Irish and Anglo-Irish Landed Gentry* (Dublin: M. H. Gill, 1884; rpt. New York: Barnes and Noble, 1969), p. 557.

8. To Denis O'Conor

OCD, 8.3 SE 028

7 February 1756

Dear Denny,

I could not but laugh at the thoughts of your foolish neighbors about me. I was indeed during the late debates employed by both parties as far as a person of my little consequence might be employed for the good of both; Dr. Clayton, Bishop of Clogher,[1] sent for me, and I had a conversation for an hour with him in his closet. He gave me a commission which I have executed as well as I could, and I had yesterday the pleasure of acquitting myself of it in a letter to his Lordship. I reserved a copy for the inspection of my friends. If my sister's match goes on, Mr. Charles MacDermot,[2] you and other friends will conduct it for me. I give you full powers, and I shall in that case get an instrument drawn up here for my mother to sign what, if she executes, I shall then be enabled to live at home.[3] Depend upon it, I shall never live there again upon my former terms. I have been too long the dupe of my complying temper, and yet my good nature is as warm as ever, as I hope all my actions will ever attest.

I hope Cormick is conducting my affairs in concert with you with as much judgment as if I were on the spot. I need not, I believe, speak to that point. I had last week a letter from brother Dan. He presses warmly for the money due to him, and I request you will desire brother Hugh[4] to send it up, that I may remit it immediately. I am sorry to hear that Cousin Myles MacDermot's[5] affairs are not in so good a way as we expected. I hope Biddy[6] will conduct herself in the manner suitable to her circumstances and gain the affection of her husband's relations by her prudence as well as her good nature. May God pour down His graces on you, her, and us all. Charles is doing well here. I believe he converses with you every post. I am most affectionately yours.

P.S. Pray do not neglect improving yourself by some of the good books I left in my study. There you will find vast resources for your future happiness, which will depend upon a good mind improved by knowledge.

    1. Robert Clayton (1695–1758) was Dublin-born and educated at Trinity College, Dublin, and elected bishop of Clogher in 1745. His book, *Some Thoughts on Self Love, Occasioned by Reading Mr. Hume* (1751), and other writings caused him to be accused of Arianism (1752) and of heresy (1757).
    2. Charles MacDermot-Roe, a cousin who lived at Alderford (Camagh).
    3. O'Conor's mother died 22 December 1760. See O'Conor's letter to Ralph Owsley, 22 October 1789.
    4. O'Conor's youngest brother Hugh, who later sued Charles as a Protestant discoverer.
    5. O'Conor's son-in-law, married to Bridget.
    6. Brigid O'Conor, married to Myles MacDermot of Coolavin. The marriage was not a happy one.

9. To Daniel O'Conor[1]

Memoirs of the Late Charles O'Conor

3 March 1756

My Dear Brother,

    I write this from a wilderness which I converted into useful lawns where I spend one half the year reading, scribbling, and improving my grounds. The other half I spend in our capital city where I mix with men of all descriptions, accommodating myself to the manners of others, far from expecting they should accommodate their manners to mine. By this inculpable acquiescence, which indeed common prudence requires, I render myself not disagreeable to men whom the laws of this country, as well as their rank and fortune, have elevated far above me. This is the tenor of my life in its decline and very probably will be little altered until these eyes are closed. In every system there is imperfection, and no society is exempt from inconvenience; I doubt if the convents of France or Italy are more exempt from it than their armies. Men naturally fond of power and preeminence will study opportunities to gratify these passions; and every method whereby they can advance themselves, though it may not be as acceptable as the most honorable, will however be pursued. The ruling passion forever predominates in the human breast, and we must submit to what we can never remedy. In my opinion, those who temporize in some instances with wickedness are not as culpable as they are generally supposed to be; their object may be virtuous. The mariner does not always steer directly to the place of his destination; he steers as the wind permits him; I know that in many instances, and almost in all, the temporizer partakes of the guilt. But I say that there may be, and there are, instances in which even temporizing is justifiable. St. Paul says of himself that he was *omnibus omnia ut omnes lucrifaceret*.[2] Endeavor to follow his example and take men upon their own terms, or they will oblige you to take them upon none. Tell Durcan[3] I have done with him if he will not behave himself.

 1. O'Conor's brother Daniel voiced dissatisfaction with his position in an Irish regiment in the French service. O'Conor asks him to make up his mind and to stop "temporizing." *Memoirs*, p. 271.
 2. 1 Corinthians 10:33. Even as I please all men in all things not seeking mine own profit, but the profit of many, that they may be saved.
 3. Durcan is Daniel's batman or servant. In a letter to Charles, 26 March, Daniel accused Durcan of stealing his clothes and mathematical instruments.

10. To Denis O'Conor

OCD, 8.3 SE 028

13 March 1756

You write me to go home. I would want to know upon what terms? More of this in my next. I advise you and Cormick and others you confide in to set, let, and reform for me. I give you full power and the more as you are now no stranger to my affairs, though I am one myself. You send me no account of the little stock I left behind, whether alive or dead; be the amount good or bad, let me have it. I shall buy the seeds for my Cousin of Shrule[1] but to what purpose without some hand to bring them down in a reasonable time. Poor Biddy, she accepted rather than made a choice! But I hate retrospects of this kind. Let her behave as reason notes and religion dictates. Let her not be accessory to the support of a charge which may, though justly perhaps, be made to her conduct. Discretion goes a great way, prudence further, but virtue comprehends all. It is the sum total of the moral inventory, and it acquits us to God and to ourselves. I dined yesterday with Coll. French,[2] a worthy man, an amiable person struggling with physical evil. Whatever his opinions may be, his morals are good; his mind by the abstraction from matter is grown more clear. This day the Bishop of Clogher published his *Matters of Fact*, etc., which makes the *Case of the R*[oman] *C*[atholics] a kind of ground work for his main subject.[3] I shall give no judgment of it at present for several reasons. I wrote to you lately. It does not appear by your letter that I did so.

[Rest of letter taped over.]

1. Shrule in Co. Mayo was the home of Hugh MacDermot (d. 1707). Perhaps O'Conor's cousin is a MacDermot. O'Reilly, p. ccviii.

2. Perhaps Arthur French (1728–1799), M.P. for Co. Roscommon and Colonel of the French Park and Castlereigh Volunteers. *BP*, p. 705.

3. In 1757 O'Conor wrote an unsigned pamphlet entitled *Principles of the Roman Catholics* in reply to a pamphlet of Robert Clayton, Bishop of Clogher, *Matters of Fact*. In 1756 O'Conor had written the *Case of the Roman Catholics* which was printed by George Faulkner in Dublin. Gilbert, *Appendix*, p. 447.

11. To Dr. John Curry, Cow Lane, Dublin

OCD, 8.3 HS 023

Belanagare, 21 May 1756

Dear Sir,

I arrived here on the ninth instant, but would on the day before, if I was not on Saturday stopped after riding thirteen miles in the heaviest rain I ever felt. I was drenched all over and got a fit of the cholic the very night I came home, a disorder I was never before subject to. But you have not yet the worst of it. Soon afterward, stepping over a low stone ditch (of what I practiced with good jumps before I became a citizen) I slipped my footing and stripped my shin bone near two inches lengthways; this accident by my own unskillful management had like to cost me dear, nor is my danger yet over. To keep on my poultice I kept the small of my leg hard bound with a long silken ribbon for three days, and I made no sample of walking about. But my wound, it seems, highly resented this slight with which I treated it, and since that time it kept me day and night in constant wailing; neigh, it punished me with an inflammation down to the ankle and had I not stayed off it five days in bed and kept my leg in constant horizontal posture, I am very certain I should be thrown into a high fever. I have not been confined to bed these thirty years and am afraid my being so long in one position when my ability and constitution required motion will have no desirable consequences. This minute I quitted my grave of a bed, and in truth my pain alleviated by the employment I chose—that of conversing with an affectionate, sincere, and learned friend.

You are one of the first of these from whom I derive a great part of my happiness because you are, I know, one who will let me enjoy it while I have any right by that moral merit which alone can entitle me to it. I am now thinking with a feeling friendship of the several pleasing hours we sat together; they put me in mind a hundred circumstances which in my present condition both grieve and please me. But we will meet again, God willing. I owe a great deal to my Dublin friends and shall ever retain a grateful sense of their kindness. It is *there* in truth that I made my acquaintance, having but very little knowledge of the gentry of my own country, but by common fame; and it is *there* I can draw upon few friendships that a person of my inconsideration could store up for himself. This province with several other counties in the West is in a far worse condition than I expected—because two-thirds of the inhabitants are perishing for want of bread; *bread is come to 18p. a stone, and if the poor had money it would exceed* by (I believe) double the sum; every place is crowded with beggars who were all housekeepers a fortnight ago, and this is the condition of a country which boasts of its Constitution, its laws, and the wisdom of its legislature![1] Give my tenderest sentiments of affection to my dear *Doctor Clinch* and to Dr. Fitzsimons.[2]

When I am able to write to them, I will; my best affections also to Mr. Duany[3] and convince him that whatsoever I can offer him comes from my heart. I hope you had a revisal of your proof sheets of *The Principles, etc.*, for I gave Mr. Reilly and Lord[4] a strict charge on that head. That little trial wanted to be thrown out anew, to add, retrench, correct, etc. But I had not time; Adieu, dear sir, but present Mrs. Curry with my sincerest esteem and believe that I wish you every happiness.

    1. O'Conor remembered the famine of 1756 when in 1757 he wrote *The Protestant Interest Considered.* Gilbert quoted the following comment from O'Conor on the famine: "The years 1745 and 1756 exhibited such other scenes though in a degree less raging; and in this present year let the pale specters of town and country describe. Would to God we could efface all these frightful figures!" Gilbert, *Appendix,* p. 449.
    2. Dr. John Clinch and Dr. Patrick Fitzsimons were vicars to Archbishop Richard Lincoln of Dublin, who was co-adjutor to Dr. John Linegar, whom he succeeded, 21 June 1757. *Handbook of British Chronology,* eds. Sir F. Maurice Powicke and E. B. Fryde (London: Offices of the Royal Historical Society, 1961), p. 401.
    3. Francis Duany, a Dublin surgeon. *DJ,* 23–26 April 1757.
    4. Patrick Lord, the Dublin printer.

12. To Dr. John Curry, Cow Lane, Dublin

OCD, 8.3 HS 023

2 June 1756

I can not resist the pleasure of acknowledging your letter immediately because I know it was dictated by a real friendship and not by any of those civilities which usurp the nature and which in fact commences at first, only to detect the cheat and too often the reciprocal cheat at last. Our connections have been established upon different principles; nor can they be dissolved till you discover that I am not the person I profess to be, a discovery which by good assistance you shall not have the uneasiness of making, for indeed you love me too well not to feel a concern at any obliquity in my morals, what would put you under a necessity of convincing me. It is true I lost a correspondent of your profession who, in fact, treated me with great civility; but I never had his friendship; and he who caluminated me in private dared not join issue upon an explanation in the face of the public. I entered a civil protest against his crazy charge; there I dropped him and gave up my share in him to the common stock without reckoning myself any great loser by the bargain.[1] Let me only preserve the few, the very few, who are conscious of my good intentions and who, like Dr. Curry, have given me a share of their affections, and I shall be so far from complaining of the ill offices of others that I shall not even think of them: This is my real temper, till provocations of a public nature forbid all silence and license every honest reprisal that can be made. But this can seldom be the case of persons in the obscurity I am in and I needed not have mentioned it. I lately got the *Principles* from Mr. Reilly under covers. I told you before, they wanted a third draft and I now find it by a demonstration which gives no concern. When the mind is absorbed in the argumentative part, propriety of words is little attended to; inaccuracies follow, of course, and the strongest reasoning becomes in some sort ridiculous by the dirty apparel it appears in.—In page 24 there is an ugly and truly Hibernian blunder. In the antiphony line 19 and 20, "the cotter is secure because they practice the 'Farmer,'" it should be, "The cotter is secure because the true means of practice, the true doctrines of the Farmer. . . ." Why did you not advert to this blunder as you had the proof sheets before you? Other inaccuracies could be produced if it would be ever of any use.

I read over Harris's malicious *Dialogue*, and reprisals could be made to shame his patrons.[2] His interpolations of Ware's[3] works and of the *Annals of Donegal* are so frequent and so glaring that persons who make future researches must trust him in nothing but lie under the necessity of consulting the originals, which his voluminous works may render it difficult to come at in print or manuscript. Did you not observe how he has sacrificed common sense to his malice, even in his title-page? Were it worth the while, he ought to be gutted up and gibetted for the good of the public. I could wish, however, that you informed me whether the decisions which he charges on the University of Salamanca and Valladolid are genuine. I read Dr. Lesly's book[4] with pleasure. His theory of passive obedience I pass by. But his matters of fact opposed to the untruths of Dr. King[5] are excellent and may be of good use hereafter. Indeed were this work lost, we should entirely be strangers to several material historical facts. The want of such a work in regard to the decennial war of '41 gave party historians great advantages, as the want of common concert or common policy among the Catholics gives but a sorry chance for any good defense of their measures or principles. But certainly in proper time something ought to be attempted in this way for the instruction of the public. I am tiring you. My wound is skinned over, and I kept close to my confinement till all danger of my fever was over. I thank you and Mr. Duany most heartily for your kind concern, and may it be long before I am in any concern for telling you or him on the account of the loss of any health or spirits. I wish you every happiness and that it may have no interruption from physical evil; as to moral evil I know it will not come near you, and I shall guard against it even from the pleasure of being reckoned in the number of those you esteem.

P.S. Your objection to the concluding paragraph of designs for the *Principles* is just; and I thank you for hindering the publication. Could your leisure permit an equal attention to what *was* printed, my enemies could not have the advantage which ingenuous tempers are greatly qualified in finding out and which they never fail to improve.

    1. Reilly wrote O'Conor that Dr. John Fergus was impugning O'Conor's honesty by declaring that O'Conor had published Fergus's idea that Sir Isaac Newton's observations on the ancient Irish language were similar to those of the old Irish poets. Fergus never forgave O'Conor for this "plagiarism." Michael Reilly, Letter to Charles O'Conor, 10 March 1753, Ashburnham Collection, Stowe MS B11, Royal Irish Academy. Subsequent citations will be noted Stowe MS, RIA.
    2. Walter Harris (1686–1761) was an Irish historian, Vicar-General to the Protestant bishop of Meath, and editor and translator of Sir James Ware's *Works Concerning Ireland* (1739–1746). Harris attacked Curry's *A Brief Account from the Most Authentic Protestant Writers of the Causes, Motives, and Mischiefs of the Irish Rebellion on the 23rd Day of October 1641, Delivered in a Dialogue between a Dissenter and a Member of the Church of Ireland*, printed anonymously in 1747. Harris called his pamphlet *Fiction Unmasked or an Answer to a Dialogue lately Published by a Popish Physician*. . . . Gilbert, *Appendix*, p. 450; *Concise DNB*, 1:577.
    3. Sir James Ware (1594–1666), Irish historian. *Concise DNB*, 1:1367.
    4. Charles Leslie, non-juring Anglican-controversial writer, wrote among other pamphlets, *An Answer to a Book Entitled the State of the Protestants in Ireland under the Late King James's Government* (1692) in answer to Dr. William King's *State of the Protestants* . . . published in 1691. *Concise DNB*, 1:727, 767.
    5. William King (1650–1729), Protestant Archbishop of Dublin (1703–1729). *Concise DNB*, 1:727.

13. To Dr. John Curry

RIA, Stowe MS. Bi2a

Roscommon, 16 July 1756

Dear Sir,

... I shall write to Colonel O'Gara[1] in St. Sebastian, where he is quartered with his regiment, and reproach him with giving more of his confidence to a little, ignorant ecclesiastic than to me, his nearest relation in this kingdom, his father and mine being brother and sister's children. This expedient will, I hope, confirm the book to me.[2] In 1734 I got that work through the interest of Bishop O'Rorke, my uncle. I soon after put it into the hands of my friend, Dr. Fergus. It came in a wretched dress, but the Doctor put it into good apparel and, as he well expressed himself, gave it vigor enough to outlive another century. I would omit no circumstance when I might do justice to every merit in that gentleman. This is one, and he is entitled to much greater, notwithstanding his uncharitableness in saying *of* me what he was not previously generous enough to say *to* me. I parried his thrust in the face of the world; and had he appealed from his private judges to the same public tribunal, I would have little to fear from him as a *public* adversary, much less indeed than from those arrows which will sometimes hurt for no other reason in the nature of things but this one only, that they are thrown in the dark. What made me begin this account so well and end it so ill and so much in detail? I ask your pardon for it. In truth I wish the Dr. well and forgive him the weakness which no obligation of his towards me could impose any duty on me of not resenting, while the resentment itself was contained within the proper bounds of honor and self-defense. I thank you sincerely for the right you have established for me, as well as for yourself, over honest *Lesley*.[3] I am only sorry that you have established it to your cost, but I retract the expression since a work of charity is rather an obligation received than conferred. The certain people you mention I have long known; their nonsense is an impregnable fort, one which, if possibly I could make the least impression, yet I would not for many reasons. *Tuti sunt suis tenebris*[4] as poor *Erasmus* phrases it of their predecessors. There are some worthy men, however, among them, men more *of the party* than absolutely *for the party*. Believe me they have no records in their hands in this province worthy of your researches or mine. I am much obliged, though I know you are much put to expense of time by your searches for Harris's[5] reams. When you meet *Ross*,[6] I hope he will save you much of that trouble. Whoever foisted in the scandalous translation of Benedict XIV's excellent words into the *Principles* has manifestly injured the copy; and I am angry at myself for parting with that subject so lightly. Was it not necessary to place so extraordinary and indeed so seasonable a circumstance in the strongest light? The Spiritual Father of the Catholic World, pressing on his missionaries not only the duty of obedience to the *established Constitution,* but the obligation also of treating it (*cum honore*) with reverence— all this from the Pretender's best friend and even annexing *severe penalties* in case of contrary conduct! What act, what acts of Parliament could give a stronger or better security to this *Protestant* government? Indeed you have the merit of opening this wide field for us, but we cultivated it so wretchedly that one might be tempted to think we were either not in earnest or not in our wits when we quitted it so lightly. . . .

1. Colonel Oliver O'Gara commanded an Irish regiment in France. Edward MacLysaght, *Irish Families* (New York: Crown Publishers, 1972), p. 155.
2. *The Annals of the Kingdom of Ireland,* more popularly known as the Annals of the Four Masters, a name bestowed on them by John Colgan, O.F.M. The compilers were Michael O'Clery, Farfassa O'Mulchonry, Cúcoigriche O'Clery, and Cúcoigriche O'Duigenin. The annals were dedicated to Fergal O'Gara, Lord of Moy O'Gara and Coolavin. This dedication to an O'Gara would explain the possession of this copy by his descendant, Colonel O'Gara. O'Reilly, clxxxvi; Hyde, 573–582.
3. Charles Leslie, see note 4 in previous letter for 2 June 1756. Robert Ward, *Prince of Dublin Printers* (Lexington: University Press of Kentucky, 1972), p. 60n.
4. They are safe in their obscurity.
5. Walter Harris (1686–1761), historiographer, Vicar General of the Protestant Bishop of Meath (1753), and pamphleteer. *Concise DNB*, 1:727.
6. William Ross, bookseller and auctioneer. *DJ*, 10–13 May 1753.

14. To Dr. John Curry, Cow Lane, Dublin

OCD, 8.3 HS 023

28 July 1756

I begin with your postscript which indeed pleases while it reproaches me. My letter to you apologizing for blots, etc., looked too much like affectation; and it savored of those little delicacies which friendship disdains, but which what passes under that name exacts with great punctuality. I submit to your kind rebuke, and I deserve it because I benefit of it. If I have any one good quality to distinguish me, I think it is that of grasping at correction with a kind of avidity and of encountering abuse with a sort of phlegmatic moderation till I find it outrageous and until my moral character comes in question.

But let me rebuke you in turn. Why did you mention to me the want of punctuality in your correspondence? I aver it to you that I received more of your kind favors in this way since I left town than from all my friends there put together; and however I may be a loser by their silence, yet I would not have them break it often; as in that case I am the *only* loser and as their attention must be withdrawn from objects of more importance. If you should give interruption (as you certainly do to affairs of such consequence) on my account, I must charge it to the warmth of your friendship and to a conviction you have indulged that I am not unworthy of it. I shall labor to keep you as active as I can in this train of thinking, and yet without deceiving you in the least; for I think I know how to put the proper estimate on your friendship and that I really deserve it in that case, though I should not in any other, a p-x on these last periods: I began with a rebuke and slid into compliments, things unworthy of the connections between us! Your observations that *an honest man must be a man of sense* also I acquiesce in; but *cum grano salis*,[1] and I doubt not but the converse may be true likewise, i.e., *every man of true good sense must be an honest one*. I know one or two honest men, a sort of stupid necessary beings, so to speak, who are constitutionally in the right and who seem bereft of the choosing faculty. However it be, for I hate refinements, they have at best only sense enough to humor the ply which nature gave. They certainly cannot pretend to swell the bill of merit with a man of superior faculties, balancing like Hercules between the roads of ambition and pleasure on one hand and that of virtue on the other, which latter he chooses and pursues to the end of his journey. You do not deserve my thanks only: you merit the thanks of your country for the hint you formerly dropped to me of publishing in the papers the *Test* in the *Principles* at this critical time.[2] If I had not this minute my foot in the stirrup for the county of Sligo, I would sit down and endeavor at some preamble introductory of it. I am heartily sorry your citizens of Dublin did not invite all parties into their *association*.[3] The Catholics, however, should not take this pretermission or, if you please, this exclusion ill. It might be, I hope it is, an oversight. I once thought that an *association* might be formed on our side. I was mistaken, and reasons might be assigned for the difficulty which it would be indiscreet even to hint at in the *Principles*. There is pride, though no disaffection, at the bottom of this affair. He who would take the lead and who might be perhaps entitled to take it would at the same time be objected to for presumption, for insufficiency, etc. The want of good sense and of the honesty I spoke of above would certainly overturn such a scheme, and it were better never undertake it than let those who suspect us be spectators of a species of madness and nonsense which this very suspicious spirit of the times would construe into disaffection. Let me know whether you and I concur in this thought. Some refiners think we ought to be cautious in pressing officiously such a *test* as is proposed in our present state of bondage because that very state will render our sincerity suspicious and because people may be brought into such a condition as may render any revolution an object of indifference to them. I request I may have your sense on this head. They reason as if our Test and relief from Penal Laws should go hand in hand. Right. But should not some previous steps be taken? May not the suspension or repeal of those laws be brought to arise in some degree from a voluntary test even in our present condition. I say no more. I write in great haste and hope to give you my thoughts with less dissipation in my next.

    1. With a grain of salt.
    2. *Principles of the Roman Catholics, Exhibited* (Dublin: n.p., 1756) was O'Conor's pamphlet written and published anonymously.
    3. O'Conor's grandson Matthew wrote, "By Dr. Curry's great exertions, a committee for the management of Catholic affairs was formed in the city; but owing to the divisions and parties among the Catholics at that time it was confined to citizens merely. . . ." Matthew O'Conor, *History of the Irish Catholics from the Settlement in 1691 . . .* (Dublin: J. Stockdale, 1813), 249.

15. To Dr. John Curry, Cow Lane, Dublin

OCD, 8.3 HS 023

20 August 1756

Dear Doctor,
    I find it necessary to take a private as well as a public method of replying to letters which have more than the bare personalities of friendship for their object. This, therefore, I propose as a second answer to yours of the ninth instant. Were I base enough to put a severe construction on words which can bear a better, I think I could not be at a loss for objections to the cold reception your late proposal met with from certain persons. I would draw inferences without much regard to their own explicit and praiseworthy *conduct* in former times, and I would say their manner of rejecting the *letter* you showed them was but an improvable hint to you and your party that the *present time* was not the most proper for the consideration of the subject proposed to them. I would discern a scuffle of contrary principles in the breasts of such persons now dragging one way, now another, anon coming to

an awkward reconciliation, while *reason,* which would show that such principles can never be reconciled, is driven from the steerage. But my love and experience of those gentlemen will not admit me to explain away their intentions in a manner so injurious to them as well as to my own natural disposition. Let me suppose, let me convince myself that they saw further into the expediency or inexpediency of the step proposed than you or I did, and yet our end is the same, though our means may be different. Thus I explain for them, and yet to this conviction of the goodness of their intention, I would have joined the other conviction of the *reasonableness* of their judgment, if they really think that a thorough silence in the present conjuncture is the most eligible step we can make. To think thus they will say to themselves or, properly speaking, they will urge to us, "We have written, we have preached enough already. Our professions were deemed insincere, our conduct necessary, our obedience temporary. Shall we be better believed now, when the same causes of our complaints and of their incredulity subsist as forcible as ever, when those who persecute, and hate because they persecute, establish their disbelief of our sincerity on the principle established by nature that we must certainly hate bondage and consequently hate those who impose it." I allow this reasoning all its weight but no more, however, than it can bear. The present set of men either in the administration or in Parliament imposed no bondage on us, though their predecessors did. And this distinction ought to be made the more *as it implies a difference which is seldom attended to.* When those laws were passed, there was a recent change in the properties, as well as great rage in the minds of the people—a change which could no more be secured than obtained without violence. Violence had its day. Time gave *at last* the security which force gave *at first,* and what was once a lawless possession, as well as government, is by prescription become both valid and legal. The posterity of both parties is now in a different situation; and difference of situation will undoubtedly more or less beget a difference of principles and dispose consequently to a difference of conduct. With regard to the administration, I believe you will allow that none can be more indulgent than the present; and if those who sit in Parliament permit the operation of laws, which themselves would not pass, I think motives could be assigned for such circumstance distinct from those prejudices which have still a great share in it. A little experience would inform us of the difficulty of repealing laws which a party spirit dictates, and which, however unconstitutional, yet pass for constitutional by becoming habitual. Let the Septennial Law of Parliaments serve for an instance, to offer no other. Besides, Popery sounds ill, and many who feel at their hearts, because they suffer for it in their interests, the evil consequences of the Penal Laws on the prosperity of the kingdom and who are convinced that the Roman Catholics are *now* very improper objects of punishment, yet will choose to let those evils remain, rather than expose themselves to the odium of an unpopular motion, such as it might be in the power of their adversaries to defeat and such as those adversaries would improve to purposes and personal ends which party policy will never leave open to them and which therefore must yield till such a national party is formed as may overbear all opposition.—The case would be different if those laws were to be *now* brought on the carpet and fairly debated. In such a case, every member could and would be equally clamorous against the evil of Popery, nor would any give his brother the advantage over him in this instance, which he must give in the other. But the laws would never pass in the quantity or quality of the penalties now imposed. And let all this account for the continuance of party, not national laws, such as anger finds it much easier to establish than moderation to repeal. This deduction is longer than I proposed, and perhaps I refined too much in the process of it. I now come to another objection. "*Our professions of legal subjection (by principle) will be deemed insincere.*" Admit it for argument's sake. But will a repetition of those professions in this critical conjuncture, and that for *conscience's* not *interest's* sake, be productive of no good? Will the expression of our gratitude for the relaxation of many Penal Laws be of *no weight at court*? Will it offend the monarch on the throne to find his Popish subjects *at this time* joining in testimony to the equity of his administration, the lenity of his government? If all this does not acquit us to prejudice, yet is it of no consequence to acquit *to ourselves* and to the sounder judgment of several men in power?—"We are hated," not so much, I presume, as we were, nor do the motives exist; and an hatred one degree less is an earnest for another degree still the less in the *political* as well as in the *moral* world. But whatever this hatred be, is it the result of prudence to improve it by a sullen silence, by an unmeaning reservedness in time of danger, after some solemn professions of true subjection, when no danger but our own pressed us? Another objection is deemed strong and very apologetic for our silence, "*That our masters know we hate our bond and consequently must think that our allegiance is forced and unnatural.*" But those masters ought to be informed and some I hope may be persuaded that our religion requires of us in such cases to bear patiently what we hate. If they can be wrought into this persuasion, a persuasion not I hope impossible to time, they must see the injustice of their own inference, that allegiance is incompatible with persecution for conscience sake. All this may be needless because grounded on a mistaken application of it to the gentlemen mentioned above. I hope it is so. But I venture for once to open my mind fully to you on this important subject. And I must declare since it comes in my way that I do not like the hesitation of some in approving the doctrine *established in the letter, "That no act of the Roman Court, no Spiritual Power of the Roman see can Dispense with legal obligations to legal government."* Is this, sir, to be resolved and frittered away into matter of *opinion,* into a duplicity of doctrine wherein every subject is left free in the choice of the alternative? Is this the arcanum we are now to reveal to the public in our present situation? In plain truth I must own candidly *to you* that I am not free of very strong suspicions that personal ambition, foreign connections, subservient maxims, and future prospects prevail over the true interests of our party, and this in the breasts of men who surely should sacrifice very ill-purchased advantages of their own to the general good of poor people who support them and every other burden they lie under. By this key I fancy the whole mystery may be wound up, and I think all this will account for the conflict of certain principles hinted at above, pulling men backwards and forwards and leaving a back door open for *opinion* to enter in as a mediator to reconcile all differences. Enough is said, perhaps more than becomes me to say on so delicate a subject; but I write to my friend, from whom I can conceal nothing, to one who will tell me whether I am right or wrong when I observe further that it can be no breach of true Catholicity for the laity among us who have no bias of this sort hanging on them to look to themselves and avow principles not *opinions,* such principles as prevailed in the infancy of the Church and which, I conceive, cannot be now condemned in its maturer days.

16. To Dr. John Curry

OCD, 8.3 HS 023

7 September 1756

I received your last favor with Dr. C[linc]h's paper enclosed. The exceptions made to the Pope's instructions warmed me, and I wrote freely and fully my mind on this subject this night to the two vicars.[1] I indeed acquit them from the glaring partiality and open tergiversation made use of by your hyper-doctor.[2] The laity, however, had they an ounce of spirit but they have none, would not only properly and independently exert themselves in the present crisis but also oblige others to concur with them. I shall do what I can in reference to the paper you sent, but I am cramped and vexed. Whatever I do, it shall be sent diretly to Dr. Clinch, and I shall get out of the affair with as good a grace as I can. I am surprised that Mr. Duggan[3] has not sent you *Cambrensis*, etc. I shall immediately write to him about his neglect. Adieu, dear sir, till my next. I am fatigued all this day with haymaking and company, all this night with writing two long letters upon irksome subjects.

1. Dr. John Clinch and Dr. Patrick Fitzsimons, vicars to Archbishop Lincoln, were sympathetic to O'Conor's and Curry's efforts.
2. Archbishop Richard Lincoln, coadjutor to John Linegar, Archbishop of Dublin.
3. Michael Duggan of Bride's Alley, broker and auctioneer. *DJ*, 3–6 September 1768, obituary.

17. To John Clinch, Rosemary Lane, Dublin

OCD, 8.3 HS 023

Belanagare, 10 September 1756

Dear and Reverend Sir,

The liberty I have taken with the form of the paper sent me by Dr. Curry supposes that every person is to take the same liberty with mine. You will find the whole substance of the one transferred into the other, for the matter is so extremely well collected that in my opinion nothing can be added or retrenched in a work contracted within so narrow a plan, at least I could find nothing to add or alter, and yet Dr. Fitzsimons and you will find several things in the style I give to be amended. No one who writes in hurry can immediately see his own blemishes. Indeed I am afraid Faulkner[1] will refuse taking this paper in, as it is certainly conceived too much in detail for his crowded journal. Whatever is done, you have acquitted yourselves to your party in several excellent papers heretofore, nay exposed yourselves to some rubs on their account.

May we all be sufficiently grateful.

1. George Faulkner, publisher of the *DJ*.

18. To Dr. John Curry

OCD, 8.3 HS 023

22 September 1756

Dear Sir,

Yours of the 17th instant lies before me. I need not inform you of the pleasure I take in the perusal of every letter I receive from you and particularly this last, wherein you inform me that you will sit down to complete what another and I began and what you and I had much at heart in this critical conjuncture—I lately opened my mind to you but *intra penetralia Vestae*[1] in regard to a certain conversation wherein a reserve was made *for opinion* in matters which I laid down for doctrinal. I now renounce my jealousy; no person can be more satisfied than I am of the worth and probity of our two v[ica]rs. They might deviate from the line of prudence, so unhappily are our affairs constituted, without deviating in the least from the line of conscience; but surely it would be wrong in us to press them on to the *full* measure of the letter when we could not but know that malice would greedily seize on such a procedure to their disadvantage and expose them to those censures from which their party would, I am afraid, take no pains to protect them. The weight therefore of this affair lies properly on the shoulders of the R[oman] C[atholic] laity, on the persons acquainted well with the state of the case before us, and who have no foreign connections, nor any measures to keep with foreigners. I, after all, greatly applaud the courage of the worthy man you mention to me, who would set at defiance all enemies for the sake of our common cause. I could not read that period of yours without a tenderness and emotion towards him such as can be much easier felt than described.

Since I wrote the above I am returned home from Frenchpark fair, where I sat with our host, the Knight of the Shire,[2] and several foxhunters. You may judge that complacence made me trespass a little and therefore unfit for any subject except that of friendship wherein the heart is alone triumphant. Mine, my dear sir, is devoted to you; it is so to the last person I mentioned and more or less so to all mankind, professed villains excepted.

By professed villains I mean such as I would think it a reproach to be considered as honest men. I have known a few such, and you are happy if you have not! Poor wretches! They deal in extremes and therefore fail. They have not the wisdom of the enemy of our two v[icar]s,[3] for these last play their game tolerably not because they have more genius than the people above described but because they seldom let us look into their cards.

I hope you are changing your habitation for a better, I mean a cheaper, and I hope the church wardens will not make a double return on your account. I am in pain for the Hyper-doctor[4] on his own account. Our business can be done without his concurrence or assistance. May God bless you and your whole family.

P.S. This page of my letter comes not from the same head but certainly from the same heart which dictated the former. You will therefore make proper allowances.

    1. Within the shrine of Vesta or within the "poet's sanctum."
    2. *DJ*, 17–21 October 1761, listed William French as a member of Parliament and Knight of the Shire.
    3. The two vicars were Clinch and Fitzsimons.
    4. Archbishop Richard Lincoln.

19. To Dr. John Curry, Cow Lane, Dublin [1]

OCD, 8.3 HS 023

[13 January 1757]

Dear Sir,

When I received yours of the 8th instant I became a little uneasy lest Mr. Reilly should commit the paper you gave him to the press. Seriously I never liked it. I had another's thoughts to defer to and to incorporate with my own. It fell out that he disliked my manner, without adverting or considering that I wrote in leading strings; and besides this, the paternal fondness he had for his own production weighed very strongly with him. His judgment, however, was right in chalking out a middle between his method and mine, and you were appointed to strike the balance. You did so, and yet a little finesse frustrated your scheme also. Be it so, this proceeding left us happily both at liberty, and we have no measures now to keep but such as discretion prescribes to decency. Let us forget the treatment we met with, and let us persuade ourselves that our friends[2] were in the right. You and I know that they have published some good instructions to their people in regard to their civil conduct under this government. They did more than their predecessors ever did to soften our masters. This is their merit. If they declined the whole burden when not one of their function would lend a shoulder, can we blame them? May they not say with *Dolabella* to *Cicero, Satisfactum est a nobis partibus, satisfactum est et officio an non respiciendum denuo salute nostra?*[3] And may not the Hyper-doctor himself interpose with his authoritative gag and his foreign whip.[4]

What I send enclosed, I have extracted partly from the minutes I have been for some time drawing. I wrote it, you may conceive, in haste. You will therefore correct, add, retrench and improve as you think proper, and when that is done, let it be immediately committed by Mr. R[eilly] to the press in a fine bold type, and let it sell for a two-penny or three-penny touch, as the booksellers phrase it. Soon after, proper extracts from it may be published in all the newspapers, and from this method we shall derive a double advantage.[5]

I am concerned at the one disappointment you met from *Cambrensis Eversus,* but certainly, as you observe, the mistake was not willful. He wrote in haste and never, I believe, corrected a sheet of Gothic work. When the great and little mob of Irish were let loose to reprisals, after a bondage of forty years, no wonder if cruelty begot cruelty, or that such a mob knew as little how to prescribe bounds to their brutality, as the other *armed* party had to *theirs.* I never perused a better or more judicious account of those times than in the *Dialogue* now on my table.[6] The *Letter* will set those affairs in a clearer light, and I beg it may not be postponed from your desire of my previous perusal. As a manuscript is not to be trusted but to hands which you and I cannot often find, the delaying for such an opportunity may be injurious to the public. Besides I own that I wish to see the author of the book that should properly be entitled *Faction Unmasked*[7] punished before he went to the grave, which I am told is gaping for him. Have I not, my dear friend, given you a surfeit in earnest by this post? I did so, but I told you in bald Latin that I trust to your affection for me.

P.S. I marked the enclosed essay with sectional numbers; this manner I now think has a pedantic cast and the figures may be thrown out. *Nisi tu dissentis, doctissime Trebatti.*[8]

I would again recommend to Mr. Reilly a large and neat type, and I think it would be proper to change to some popular book seller.

13 January 1757
You must pardon the deficiencies in this essay after I assure you that I had no longer time than twenty-four hours to frame and end it.

1. This letter is added to a copy of O'Conor's *Maxims Relative to the Present State of Ireland.*
2. Dr. Clinch and Dr. Fitzsimons.
3. We have done enough for our part; we have done our duty; should we not now consider our own safety?
4. *HBC,* p. 401, lists Dr. Richard Lincoln as Catholic Archbishop of Dublin. Lincoln appears to be the "Hyper-doctor," who had differences with his own clergy concerning Church discipline. In 1761 he received an ordinance from Cardinal Spinelli allowing him to enforce certain regulations concerning the hearing of confessions. These powers are probably the "gag and whip" to which O'Conor refers. Curry sent O'Conor a copy of the Archbishop's directive to the clergy which was to be read before their congregations every day of the week. The directive discouraged Catholics from "any scurrilous libel or Grub Street paper which may seem to be written in the name or behalf of

the Roman Catholics. . . ." John Curry, Letter to Charles O'Conor, 29 October 1757, Stowe MS Bi1, RIA.

5. The paper about which O'Conor writes is his *Maxims Relative to the Present State of Ireland* written and published anonymously in Dublin in 1757. Gilbert, Appendix, p. 457.

6. O'Conor refers to the *Dialogue*, which was a subtitle for Curry's *Brief Account* . . . published in 1747. The *Letter* is a subtitle for Curry's *Historical Memoirs* . . . in *A Letter to Walter Harris,* . . . which appeared in 1758. Gilbert, Appendix, p. 450.

7. O'Conor is punning on the title of Harris's *Fiction Unmasked.*

8. Unless you disagree, most learned Trebatius.

20. To Dr. John Curry, Cow Lane, Dublin

RIA, Stowe MS Bi1

22 January 1757

Dear Sir,

I ask a thousand pardons for all the trouble I am giving you. Let me interpose your friendship and your known warmth in the cause you undertook; nay, let me throw a good part of the blame on yourself, who alone of all my town friends encouraged me to those intrusions on better employments of time. I know you approve of my endeavors and that you will make all proper allowances for the deficiencies in the execution. I sent you lately a paper in the shape of *Maxims*.[1] I did this to supersede a former attempt which you put into a friend's hands for publication. I thought it much wanting in force and that the materials were crowded to adapt them for a circulating newspaper. Much depends upon order and proper disposition, and without this the best arguments, like a picture placed in a bad light, make but an awkward appearance. I took but twenty-four hours to draw up the essay I sent you, and upon a review of my blotted paper I saw the effects of the precipitation. Next post I sent Mr. R[eilly] another copy somewhat enlarged. The whole is submitted to your censure and corrections, to be condemned in the whole or to be castrated and amended if you think any of the *parts* worth public attention at the present critical time. If such Maxims were strung together as they ought to be, I was thinking they might very properly be introduced by an *Advertisement* setting forth their use and propriety.—"That the following *Maxims* point out the causes of the prosperity and weaknesses, the advantages and defects of governments; that they are adapted to the principles and consequently to the *general utility* of all *free* states and seem *on that account* to be extremely seasonable in *our present situation;* that a *general dirth* is now spread over the face of the kingdom, and that the calamities of a *general famine* are threatened more than ever they were known to be *in any one period of time* since the Conquest, that the causes of all this is evident from the *neglect* of agriculture and from the necessity most of our farmers are under to follow a *life of pasturage.*"

That "the *insurrection* of misery differs but little from *that* of violence itself where the lower sort of people (who are vastly the majority) are *alone* concerned; that indeed the Constitution may be in no danger, but that the state will be thinned; that though the *government may be safe, yet that few will remain to be governed,*" etc.

To the "objection that things even in this situation are preferable to a landed property in the hands of men who profess a *hated religion;* who are enemies to the public by *principle.*" It may be answered that "granting, for argument's sake, that the charge against religion is well grounded, yet that the objection is built on a *great mistake. Because* the principle *itself,* being (a) *under a constant check* from the vigilance of the legislative powers can *seldom* (if at all) operate to any evil and *because* things *in the situation they are in at present* must operate *perpetually* to the ruin of the public and lastly *because* the representation made of the religion and principles of a great part of our people must be productive of much moral and political evil, of public weakness and private uncharitabliness, *if it be not true.*"

That "objecting the Rebellion of 1641 has as little weight in the present question as the *two* rebellions of the *preceding* year in *Scotland and England;* that they only prove what *Papists* and *Protestants* will often do amiss against the principles of that very religion and liberty which are the pretended causes of so much licentiousness; that we have *all* in our turn benefited of the ebreity and consequential sufferings of our ancestors by learning to be quiet and by drawing from *examples* that knowledge which the *severest precepts* seldom inculcate in this or any other instance."

"That since the Revolution the *most hated* among our religious dissenters have behaved so in *Ireland* as to invite the legislature to regrant them the *constitutional immunities left to them by King William,* and that the kingdom evidently suffered in its wealth and consequence by treating them for fifty-four years past like men who were giving constant alarm and repeated provocations to the government."

Spirit of Laws. Vol. 1. Dub. Edit. p. 31.

I throw out all these loose hints to save you some trouble and to subtract as little of your time as possible from other avocations. I am, my dear friend, killing you with these long letters, but you have the subject at heart and I shall make no apology.

P.S. In the paper I sent Mr. R[eilly] I entered some paragraphs to ease the minds of many in regard to the papal supremacy and showed from our own Irish history that the claims of Adrian IV (to which Henry II acquiesced) were treated here with indignation and contempt even in the twelfth century. I now think that the subject was dropped there too hastily. What would you think if the following Maxim was inserted immediately after?

"One pope only, supported by an *English* king, attempted this ridiculous invasion on the rights of an independent kingdom. This, however, can no more be a reflection on the *Roman* religion *in the one case* than on the *British Constitution in the other.* To speak in the least invidious terms, it was only the surprise of the *man* on the *bishop* and of the *tyrant* on the *monarch.* The one dropped his groundless temporal supremacy when he found the imposition too glaring even for that ignorant age; the other dropped for the present a design in which he succeeded a few years after."

In regard to all these things you will add and curtail as you like. If you think the design well laid, I request you will sit down to draw up the *Advertisement.*

1. On 19 February 1757, Reilly wrote to O'Conor that the *Maxims* were printed and that O'Conor's style had been recognized so it was idle for him to deny authorship. Stowe MS B11, RIA.

21. To Dr. John Curry

OCD, 8.3 HS 023

20 March 1757

Dear Sir,

I write this from Roscommon and upon a disagreeable subject. My brother-in-law, Mr. Roger O'Conor of this place, has long languished under a bad habit of body. He has been scorbutic from his earliest youth. In his more advanced years he suffered by a tertian fever. By joining with the healthy and robust he lived liberally before marriage; he lived so after marriage and behaved more intemperately than before. His evil habits, in consequence, increased. His constitution grew more and more crazy. His appetite decayed. He took to remedies, and all failed except the mineral waters which restored him much in the drinking seasons. Bitters, vomits, and other shop medicines seemed to be lost upon him. Exercise he could use but little in these two last years from the intemperature of our climate. He is therefore confined to his house five parts in six of the whole year. Every nourishment turns to phlegm, though confined to the lightest sago, broths, poached eggs, wine. Qualms begin, belchings succeed, and both increase his languor prodigiously. The smallest change, even that of uprising, produces tremblings, which he conceives to be the legacy of his former ague though probably it is only the consequences of the present evil condition of his stomach weakened to a degree of retaining very much what it could with sufficient strength throw off heretofore. He is greatly emaciated, and wasted as he is, yet his legs swell now and then as they were used to in his younger days. One of his legs was at all times subject to a return of eruptions, and in that state he found himself relieved from other complaints. In truth if some speedy course be not taken with him, he must proceed from bad to worse. I have him and his family greatly at heart, for he is one of the sincerest and best friends I ever had. Unfit as I am for such a task, I ventured to lay his case before you, fondly certain that your instructions will re-establish him. My friend presents his service to you and will take hold of the first opportunity from this town to make you recompense for the trouble I am giving you about him. Adieu, my dear sir, till my next, which you may expect soon. My heart is too full of my present subject to admit the competition of any other except what I will not detail you at present; my hearty affections to your family, my concern for your health, and my tenderest good wishes.

Your answer to this letter you'll please direct to Mr. Roger O'Conor in Roscommon—If you send a recipe for the apothecary, Mr. O'Conor requests it be in a paper apart from your instructions. He is in the 46th year of his life.

22. To Dr. John Curry, Cow Lane, Dublin

OCD, 8.3 HS 023

27 April 1757

Dear Sir,

I remained in Roscommon till your answer to my last arrived there. Your patient is thankful and will follow your directions religiously; he has a happy change for the better, and yet in truth I did not find or expect he could possibly drag life on to the first of June when I first wrote to you on his account. One paragraph in your last indeed gave me very sensible concern. The loss of our friend Duany![1] I think with melancholy regret on the happy hours we spent together, happy surely when nothing ever entered our conversations inconsistent with our moral duties and when nothing could interrupt such duties except those gaieties which take off from their austerity! May God be merciful to him and comfort his family. You have certainly a considerable loss in him as one of his turn could not but unbend your mind now and then from the severity of those reflections which good men can not avoid indulging when elbowed as you are every day in the crowd of base and treacherous mortals! I say no more as I am afraid the periods I wrote will provoke you to feel more than I desire you should. Indeed I am too full of this subject to go into any other with any taste. When we think of our mortality and immortality, all other considerations vanish or if they intrude, they do so only to raise our contempt. I sent you my last, and I think it will be my *last* performance on the subject of the Roman Catholics.

You will dislike, perhaps, to see so much said of King William, but truth warrants most of it and our little *astutia politica*² warrants the rest. We must take our adversaries in their own way and ply them as you must some of your weak patients, with such remedies as will lessen the evil when the constitution will not bear such as are more effectual or when obstinacy will not yield to them. I know you will be surprised to find a compliment paid to the Hyper-doctor, but it is *ad causam* not *ad hominem*. If this be not a good justification, strike out not only his name but any other paragraph or page you dislike. As the Roman Catholics of England are mentioned oftener than once, the piece is not merely local, and it may perhaps with a better grace come out in London, with some sort of address to the Lord Lieutenant there. What think you? This method, indeed, would absolutely require a laborious transcript from the fair hand of my cousin Reilly, and yet that I would not willingly impose upon him, as I know how his time is taken up in providing for a long family of young children. I declare it to you, my dear friend, that I am in great pain for him. It is to be in pain for virtue struggling with several wants and, therefore, to be in pain for ourselves when we cannot run to the succour of so much distress. The supplemental *Queries* from Bishop Berkeley are extremely apposite, and the work I send you may well be considered as a comment on them, though in truth I did not consult the *Queries* till I finished what I undertook. Such an agreement between our thoughts gave me great pleasure, and the insertion of so many arguments from so popular a writer must surely give some weight to mine. If you should think of a London edition, I would perhaps offer something more to be incorporated while the work is transcribing, but to do this I should have some hints from you as my own little stock is exhausted.

I have said too much on this subject and shall say no more till I have your thoughts on the whole. One thing I absolutely insist on is that you will treat everything you dislike without mercy. I write to you as thoughts come uppermost, all from the heart, which you possess with all the warmth and affection of a real friend. God preserve you and yours and comfort you under all the trials of the loss of dead or treachery of living associates.

P.S. Mr. Reilly in his last promised me a sight of the *Letter*[3] before it went to the press. Great as this gratification would be, I would decline it forever if I were not sure of the safety of the hand which would bring it down. There is no trusting a manuscript slightly, and I beg you will put him on his keeping in regard to an affair of this importance. I should tremble for myself if I had this work now in my hands, lest any misfortune of this nature should happen on my part.

1. According to Maurice Craig, *Dublin 1660–1800* (Dublin: Allen, Figgis, Co., Ltd., Riverrun Series, 1969), p. 136 n., the Catholic Duany brothers helped found the Charitable Infirmary in Cook Street in 1721. *DJ* in *Irish Newspapers in Dublin Libraries*, 2 (Ann Arbor, Michigan: University Microfilms, 1958), printed the following obituary of Dr. Francis Duany: 23–26 April 1757. "In Cow Lane, Francis Duany, Esq., an eminent surgeon" and 26–30 April 1757, a quatrain by O'Conor:

> He's gone, my lov'd companion, chosen friend!
> But self-lamenting strains I now forego:
> And, for my private loss, those tears suspend,
> Which rather for the public, ought to flow.

2. Political adroitness.
3. Curry's *Letter to Walter Harris* which appeared as the *Historical Memoirs*.

23. To George Faulkner

BM, Egerton 201, f-31

Belanagare, 4 May 1757

I heartily congratulate with you, dear sir, on your safe arrival in a country to which you have rendered more service than any other public or private writer for several years past. The hints you give and the truths you press are, I think, preferable to essays which fall but into few hands and become profitable in fewer. It was an observation of our patriot Dean (your particular friend) that plans of reformation from *without doors* were seldom considered *within*. The rule is, I believe, just, but several of his own works might be argued as an exception: yours must be excepted also, as well from the manner in which they are conveyed as from the very extensive circulation they meet with, above all others. It is the more incumbent on you to go on and goad a listless people into some feeling. Their present helpless condition must surely come to your aid.

But how shall I acknowledge your obligations on myself in particular? You before brought me acquainted with the Bishop of Clogher! You now bring Mr. Johnson and me together. In regard to the Prelate I willingly take an opportunity of professing before you the obligations I owe to him. He is possessed of great talents improved by great literary knowledge; but independent of both he is possessed of one endowment superior to any man I ever knew or read of, not excepting M. Bayle himself.[1] The nature of his works exposed him to opposition from friends and foes. But this he bore with an elevation of mind which neither the selfishness of erudition nor the peevishness of controversy could ever once ruffle. In his replications (which are but few) he shows a proper sensibility, but he shows it with dignity. Malignity and envy—self-tormenting as they are—derive, however, some pleasure from the vexation they but too often give: My Lord of Clogher deprived them even of this.

I say nothing of Mr. Johnson. His *Ramblers* and other works have set him (as Mr. Pope expresses it) *"at the top of the Sublime character."* As a communication with such men collects the most pleasing circumstances of private life, how much must I not owe to one who brought about such a communication in my own favor? I set this on the level with the greatest services ever done me.

I shall beg leave, dear sir, to trouble you soon with forwarding a letter from me to Mr. Johnson. I am this day too much taken up with the thoughts of my own good fortune not to communicate them to my Dublin friends; pride has a share in this, Mr. Faulkner's unmerited service a greater.

I have no news for you; it is none I believe to inform you that this and the northern province nearing on us are both undone. Here in particular we had great loss of sheep, and the frightful figures which surround us threaten a still greater loss of human creatures.[2] I think such an event to be inevitable. Meal is come to three shillings a stone, and probably it will not admit of a higher price, as the poor have nothing to give for it. Let it stand as an aggravation of our punishment that we have as good arable lands here as any in the three kingdoms. But the Roman Catholics live everywhere and have wasted all the lands they could lay hold on to carry on the useful business of pasturage, what alone enables them to pay their rents and what furnishes the landlords with the means of importing hither the wines of France.

But the occupation of pasturage has spread itself over all the provinces; and thus it is with us, after a profound state of reprise from the year 1691 to this day!

I hope your travels have contributed to your health. I am greatly interested in it, and I would request that you would release yourself from confinement often by taking the air in an open chair down to Clontarfe.[3]

1. Pierre Bayle (1647–1708), philosopher and encyclopedist.
2. The potato crops failed in 1756–57.
3. Clontarfe, suburb of Dublin, where one could see the Liffey River.

24. To George Faulkner

BM, Egerton 201, f-33

Belanagare, 10 May 1757

Dear Sir,

Enclosed I send you a letter to be forwarded to Mr. Johnson.[1] From these contents you must surely judge that I am myself in earnest turned *Rambler*; I request you will make my apology to him on this account; I would engage him in the cause of an innoxious people, punished by law for no other reason but because they are mistrusted by the lawmakers. Your engagements with the public brought you acquainted with the chief men of this party; and you cannot think so meanly of their honor and gratitude but that they are as willing as able to make Mr. J[ohnson] a suitable return, could he be prevailed upon to undertake the service of the public so far as it can be connected with their manumission from bondage. You who acquired so much popularity by weekly paragraphs in favor of the national interest and who have spread your influence by keeping clear of party reflexions, are the fittest man I know to negotiate this affair secretly with our people. Dr. Jennings[2] will assist you with his own interest among them, and I need not mention many more to you who certainly will be far from putting the least slight on a project which, if brought to bear (with your friend beyond the water),[3] is indisputably the best laid which could be thought on for restoring us all to that condition in which King William wisely left us. I shall dun and solicit my friends in the city on this subject as soon as you give me leave.

1. The next two letters concern O'Conor's plan to have Faulkner contact Samuel Johnson. O'Conor's letter for 10 May 1757 covers a letter from O'Conor to Johnson which Faulkner will forward. Unfortunately, both this letter from O'Conor to Johnson and Faulkner's containing the offer to Johnson are lost. From another source (Father

Charles O'Conor), one learns that Faulkner was authorized by the Catholic group headed by O'Conor and Dr. John Curry to offer Johnson fifty guineas if he would write pamphlets in the Irish Catholic interest.
   2. David Jennings, an English preacher and theologian. Author of *Jewish Antiquities*, 1766. *BMCPBCE*, 13:399.
   3. Samuel Johnson.

25. To George Faulkner

BM, Egerton 201, f-35

Belanagare, 25 May 1757

This letter is largely a repetition of O'Conor's last two letters to Faulkner (23 and 24). O'Conor also thanks Faulkner for books the publisher had sent him recently.

26. To Dr. John Curry

RIA, Stowe MS Bi1

17 August 1757

O'Conor is sending separately to Curry O'Conor's Preface to Curry's *Historical Memoirs* and a brief list of minor editorial changes. Curry is discouraged about his latest effort because his first history, *A Brief Account . . . of the Irish Rebellion . . .* , had been attacked by the Whig, Walter Harris. O'Conor calls Harris "a scribbler" and says that Curry has done his country a "service that no writer before you has done."

27. To Dr. John Curry

RIA, Stowe MS Bi1

29 August 1757

My neighbor, or properly a great man in my neighborhood, the B[isho]p of Elphin, is very inquisitive for some time past about the B[isho]p of Fern's *Iphigenia*.[1] I suppose he wants a little historical blunderbus to discharge at our heads in the next sessions and (to do the greater execution) borrow it out of our armory. This is the unfair method of handling an argument from which I find no party is free. I have not seen the book but I know enough of it out of Walsh's letters to understand the full scope of it.[2] You and I are of F[ather] *Walsh's* side of the question so far as to condemn heartily the proceedings of the Nuncio and his party [in] *Waterford, Jamestown,* and *Galway.* But we approve of the Association of the Confederate Catholics, and for my own part I can not (along with the *Bishop of Ferns*) but think their war a *just and necessary* one. I am sure a much smaller provocation than they received in the forty years preceding the year 1641 brought about the Revolution in 1688, so highly applauded and so strongly defended to this day by a deluge not only of ink but of blood. What made me say so much in consequence of our bishop's trifling curiosity is owing to its relation in some degree to the subject you have undertaken. You, in turn, have borrowed arms out of your adversaries' magazines, but you have not borrowed them (like most other disputants) from *opinions* [but] from *things,* not from *notions,* but from *facts.* This artillery you have turned effectively against them, and I heartily thank Mr. H[arri]s for the pains he took to receive it out of your hands. He only enabled you to point it better than you have done, or indeed, had occasion to do, before. I had a letter from our *common secretary*[3] (last post) expressing his panics in the modesty of a doubt whether the publication of the *Letter* in the present critical conjuncture might not bear some ill-construction. I shall [in] this place very freely give you and him my reasons why I believe such panics unreasonable, and yet I have no doubt but malice would be busy in any con[nection] to fix an ill-intention on the writer. What then? Is no such work to be undertaken [until] malice is fatigued? Was not the writer of *The Case of the R[oman] C[atholic]s* abused by *friends* and *enemies,* but had he not in a good degree the approbation of the honest and wise of both parties, and is not the case of the *Letter* and *Case* writer much the same?[4] Have not [each] on the *same principles* ventured to oppose prejudices supported by *public authority?* While they hold to *those principles* can they have much *or anything* to fear? Had a *Letter* indeed or *his Case* come out without an *Apologetic Advertisement,* the imputation of some sinister design might be fixed *on both* with some color of reason though not of justice. I would therefore advise such an advertisement to be prefixed *to the Letter* as would not only remove all malevolent objections and applications at this time but even justify the expediency of it in a conjuncture when R[oman] Catholics have nothing to trust to but the good impression of their legislative superiors and a purity of conduct which alone can produce such an impression in opposition to inveterate prejudices. You do not justify the *Insurrection* in '41, but surely no deference to old preoccupations can impose on you the task of justifying the *governors* who did what in them lay (and fatally succeeded too) to drive not only the *insurgents* but the nation also into a civil war? Is it not a justice due to all parties to show at this distance of time by *what* means and *by whose means* such evils were brought upon us as operate to this day and must operate much longer unless the endeavors of good men prevail to trace *effects* to *causes* or (what is still harder) to show the incongruity, the folly, and false grounds of *those causes* which hitherto are assigned *to the effects?* Little more need be said to calm *our friend's* fears in regard to the indiscretion of publishing the truth of *acts*, the scene of which was laid in a former age, marked by *actors* and circumstances very different from those now playing on our own stage. This, I say, is enough, and yet I candidly own I have some inferior motives (of my own) which have their degree of influence. I think that in your lifetime you ought to enjoy the satisfaction which every good man must have in finding himself the instrument of any public good. I also would have your adversary punished for his insolence and the illiberal manner in which he made his attack. With this view I threw in something into the Advertisement to harrow up his little soul (as Shakespeare expressed it with his usual force.)[5] But of the propriety of this, yourself must be the judge. Should not the varlet compound the matter and be content to lose on the side of honesty and fame what he has some equivalent for on the side of the pecuniary rewards of iniquity? Shall his loaves and fishes be seasoned to him by the consciousness of having defeated you? Is not this consciousness seemingly strong with him by advertising the book he wrote against you (the other day) in Williamson's paper? Is not this equal to a second edition and might not this be one motive (as far as it will go) to hasten and justify your defense of the dialogue? But I am prating too much and you must blame this hour of leisure for it. Write, however, more *addenda* to your book, as among the thorns you will surely hit upon a few more flowers. Let your *London* editor be consulted and prepared; and let the publication go on this winter. I write over *your letter,* and if I said anything *in this particularly* and to your liking it must be transfused from the matter underneath, which has warmed me so often and does so this minute. I have scarcely room for the enduring words, *vale et me ama.*[6]

    1. *The Bleeding Iphigenia* by Nicholas French, Roman Catholic bishop of Ferns, was published in Europe in 1674. It repudiated charges brought against Irish Catholics in connection with their activities during the reign of Charles I; Gilbert, *Appendix*, p. 464 n. O'Conor's neighbor is Edward Synge, the Protestant bishop of Elphin. "Blazon of the Coat Armour of the Irish Bishops," *Gentleman's Magazine*, 19 (1749), 504.

    2. Father Peter Walsh (1618–1688) encouraged the Catholic party to resist the proposals of the nuncio, Giovanni Battista Rinuccini, and to make peace with the Duke of Ormond (1646–1648). *Concise DNB*, 1:360.

    3. Anthony Dermot was secretary to the Dublin Catholic Association.

    4. Curry's *Historical Memoirs* . . . and O'Conor's pamphlet, *Case of the Roman Catholics.*

    5. *Hamlet*, 1.5.16.   6. Farewell and love me.

28. To Dr. John Curry, Cow Lane, Dublin

RIA, Stowe MS Bil

7 September 1757

Last Friday morning I sent you the *Letter* by Mr. Owen MacDermot's servant who drives cattle for him to Dublin Market. . . . But to my purpose I trust that you will receive the *Letter*[1] safe before you receive this. I shall not be pleased if the public shall any longer be deprived of what is so much its property. I threw some little addenda into a corner of the book to be approved or rejected by you when a transcript is made. I am in one respect pleased with your approbation of the *Advertisement*, as it will, when we are removed into another and I hope better life, be a testimony that we have been friends in this. This is the only conjunction which will admit of no separation even after death itself. If I thought you would like the *Advertisement*, it should be better executed to your intention and my own than it stands at present. The manner in which Lord Clarendon is described and dropped is unpardonable. It is a capital fault, and I wonder you did not object and censure. I have since endeavored to supply this defect in the manner here set forth. . . .[2]

    1. The *Letter* is O'Conor's allusion to *The Historical Memoirs . . . in a Letter to Walter Harris Esq. . . .*
    2. O'Conor comments in the "Advertisement" that Lord Clarendon shows his prejudices against the Irish: "But in representations wherein *spiritual hatred* comes in aid of *those prejudices* which were before *national, he no longer is master of himself or his subject*. He yields a *willing captive* to such informations as were correspondent to his prior *ideas* of the people he undertakes to describe. . . ." Lord Clarendon not only distorts the truth, but he also causes the historian Hume "to transfer the greatest outrages of the fatal year 1641 from the *original* and real authors to the unfortunate *Irish alone*, who for forty years before had suffered all the torture of a cruel bondage of mind and body. *A wound from such a hand is in great degree fatal.*"

29. To Dr. John Curry

OCD, 8.3 HS 023

5 October 1757

O'Conor excuses himself to Curry for having written nothing to him for the past six post days; his excuse is that he has had nothing to say. However, since he has just come from the Roscommon Assizes, he regales Curry with the anecdote of the book peddler who could not sell to anyone the books written by Curry's political hack antagonist, Walter Harris. O'Conor asked the hawker how profitable his sales of the Harris books were, and the hawker replied, "None at all, and may G-d D--m Harris and all his works." O'Conor asked the hawker about *Fiction Unmasked,* Harris's book in which he attacked Curry's thesis on the Irish Uprising of 1641.¹ The hawker bought two dozen of the pamphlets and could sell very few. Another man, a Mr. Irwin, read the pamphlet and asked O'Conor why he didn't answer the pamphlet, not knowing that O'Conor's friend Curry was writing a rebuttal. O'Conor inquires about the Catholic clergy and their activity in Dublin, since he has heard nothing from anyone. He asks Curry why O'Conor hasn't heard anything from members of the Catholic Committee.

1. Besides the party pamphlet, *Fiction Unmasked,* Harris had written *History of the Life and Reign of King William III, The History of the Bishops of Ireland, Antiquities and Writers of Ireland, The Ancient and Present State of the County of Down, Hibernica* (Sir James Ware's *Works Concerning Ireland*) advertised by George Faulkner in *DJ,* 31 October–4 November 1749.

30. To Dr. John Curry

RIA, Stowe MS Bi1

19 October 1757

Dear Sir,

From reflection and, I hope, from temper I am averse to censure where a good intention interposes to disarm it. I am, therefore, ready to upbraid myself with the freedom I took with the exhortation lately published because certainly the gentlemen who drew it up meant virtuously and [corrupt] to soften our rulers on the approach of a session.¹ Were they a little more explicit, more good would be done and the objection of keeping [double] measures would be removed. P[ri-ma]te Reilly's² pastoral letter is [liable] to this exception, but as the *manner* unluckily did not keep [up] with the matter, I am not sorry to hear of that performance being [   ]ed for the present. Mr. Reilly sent me enclosed last post a placard [of] the states of Holland for the regulation of the R[oman] C[atholic] clergy in the year 1750.³ This, I am assured, was published with the approbation of my Lord Clanbrassil. If so, we need not require a better key to his intentions in regard to the new-modeled Registry Bill, for which he moved last Wednesday [with such might].⁴ You have read the placard no doubt. It amounts to a full toleration with the proviso that the secular magis[trates] shall approve of the person presented by his ordinary whether bishop, metropolitan, or nuncio. An oath of fidelity (or a declaration [tant]amount) to the government is required; and if the Catholics of other [count]ries submitted to this ordinance, what should hinder a similar submission on our part? I could wish with all my heart that the clergy of our communion who live under Protestant governments hold a correspondence with one another, in which case their measures in regard to civil government would be concerted with more wisdom than can well be expected from men who are all apart and who may be more or less governed by notions with which the Catholic Church has nothing to do.

I am pleased with my Lord L[ieutenan]t's[5] speech on the opening of the session. I am strongly mistaken, or he comes over with excellent intentions towards us, however cautious his political prudence may be in making any explicit declarations. The Popery Acts we know have put a stop to tillage by throwing the majority of tenants into the occupation of pasturage. Till the cause is removed the effect must certainly remain. What then but the sense of this could produce the following paragraph in his Grace's speech after the passing of so many various and ineffective acts already in favor of tillage?—"It were to be wished that *some method* might be found out to prevent the calamities which are the *necessary* consequences of the want of corn in Ireland, to which this country has been too often exposed." May not the tract entitled *The Protestant Interest Considered,* which treats on this subject in full detail, be now a seasonable book?[6] I long to see those *Serious Thoughts* of which you give me so good an account.[7] I suppose they came from the same quarter with the *placard.*

> Quod divum promittere nemo auderet,
> Volvendo Dies en attulit ultro![8]

I know not how all this will end, but I must own that such beginnings flatter my expectations greatly. As the scene is opened and that you are on the spot, I beg you will steal a minute as often as you can to give me every information you can get. I shall see you and be happy with you as soon as my affairs can possibly admit. No man alive longs more for such an interview. My paper is out and the remainder of my letter you shall have by next post, God willing.

1. The public exhortation from Archbishop Lincoln directed the Catholics of Dublin to keep a low profile, to avoid riots, and to keep a modest demeanor by not cursing or blaspheming in public. He complimented those Catholics "who have given the strongest proofs of their abhorrence to those tenets by refusing to take oaths, which however conducive to their temporal interest, appeared to them entirely repugnant to the principles of their religion." *DJ,* 1–4 October 1757.

2. Primate Reilly was Michael O'Reilly, Archbishop of Armagh. He died the following summer, 1758. *HBC,* p. 383.

3. *DJ,* 18–22 October 1757. This placard was advertised in the *Dublin Journal* "by the Booksellers of Dublin, Price two pence, *A Placard of the States of Holland and West Friesland concerning Popish Priests."*

4. James Hamilton, Lord Limerick and later Lord Clanbrassil brought a Registry Bill in 1756 and again in 1757. Such a bill demanded that only one priest be allowed to a parish; that he be registered; that all bishops, friars, and Catholic dignitaries be deported; and that the grand jury of the county be the final authority on the nomination of a successor for a parish priest with the veto power over the nomination residing in the lord lieutenant and the Privy Council. The second bill passed both houses of the Irish Parliament and went to the lord Lieutenant and the English Privy Council. It was quashed by the Privy Council on 18 January 1758. Interest in the bill was so high that Oliver Nelson, a Dublin bookseller, offered for eightpence each copies of the *Heads of a Bill for a General Register of Popish Priests. DJ*, 25–29 October 1757.

5. The duke of Bedford became lord lieutenant in 1757.

6. *DJ*, 25–29 October 1757, advertised for sale *The Protestant Interest Considered relatively to the Operation of the Popery Acts in Ireland* by "the Booksellers."

7. *DJ*, 18–22 October 1757, advertised for sale *Serious Thoughts Concerning the True Interest and Exigencies of the State of Ireland. In a letter humbly addressed to his Grace the D--- of B-----d, L---d Lieut-nt of Ir----d.*

8. Behold, the day, returning, has brought forth of itself
The heavens which no one dared promise.

31. To Dr. John Curry

RIA, Stowe MS Bi1

2 November 1757

You have a right to hear from me and therefore you shall, especially at this time when the cause of our party is debated by a branch of our legislature. You and I have a right to give this affair a little attention, as no other two labored so much or perhaps suffered so much (of late) for the cause. We may, for ought I know, be considered as meddlers, but they who object would save us the trouble of being so had they been themselves as zealous and active as they ought to be. We would rejoice in silence at seeing the subject taken out of our hands by abler men. Since this has not been done, nay, since it has not been attempted in any tolerable compass, men of less capacity may be allowed the merit of a good intention and of discharging their conscience in giving the best idea they can of a subject in which the bondage of a million of persons is involved. The fault is theirs, not ours. But this is far from being the worst of the case. A pastoral letter has been lately drawn up and subjected to by five suffragans.[1] What a clamor, what an indiscreet clamor has not that piece raised? If the gentlemen who drew it up were in error, should not charity dictate to your metropolitan to draw them out of it by a private conference instead of posting them up at Rome as schismatic teachers? Has not this made a noise and was it not loud enough to reach the ears of those who with a nod can crush us all? Here is one of the propositions advanced by those gentlemen: "*It is not and never was a doctrine of the R[oman] C[atholic] Church that the Pope has any direct or indirect authority over the temporal jurisdiction of princes.*" Is this proposition Catholic? Not at all say the complainants, for it is a matter of fact that the Pope has at least an *indirect temporal* power wherever he confers a *temporal* benefit. Be it so. What is this to the proposition unless it can be proved that this power was obtained by the commission of our Saviour to the Prince of the Apostles and not by concordats with princes in those latter ages. If this cannot be proved, the proposition is safe in every country where no such concordats take place. We shall have no disputes with the court of Rome. But in Protestant countries the H[oly] See will not forbid us to take the Pope's supremacy in the idea it was conceived in during the first ages of the Church and no other. She can grant no less and we can desire no more. Is it not *here* therefore a true principle of Catholic doctrine: "*That the Pope has no power direct or indirect over the jurisdiction of George the Second?*" God forgive those who are an instrument of raising a schism among us in this day of trial and tribulation! What a ground of scandal, what a foundation of obloquies and ridicule to our adversaries! If the authors of this beginning schism should persist, they will, I am afraid, do so to their own sorrow and not fare as well as poor *French* of *Ferns* did in days of yore.[2] I hear you are carefully kept out of all their secrets; so am I. But were we taken into their councils, we would surely labor to stop their rash complaints to Rome and show a little more decency towards the metropolitan of the whole kingdom and too many other prelates to whom a deference ought to be shown so far as to endeavor to reclaim them previously from their

[Letter torn. The rest is missing.]

    1. A schism had developed in the Catholic ranks, and the Association broke into two groups, the middle class versus the bishops and nobility. O'Conor and Curry are commenting on the declaration of principles drawn up by James O'Keefe, Catholic bishop of Kildare and Leighlin. O'Keefe, speaking as head of the Catholic Association (without O'Conor's and Curry's knowledge or consent) "abjured in strongest terms the doctrine that any ecclesiastical power in the Church had the right of deposing sovereigns, absolving subjects from their oaths . . . or exercising any temporal power or jurisdiction in Ireland." Finally O'Keefe denied that Papal infallibility was an article of Catholic creed. He pledged that Catholics would do nothing "to disturb or weaken the existing establishments of either property, government or religion." Lecky, 2:203.
    2. Bishop French of Ferns (1604–1678) left Ireland under a cloud during Cromwell's conquest. His *Settlement and Sale of Ireland* (Louvain, 1668) further irritated the English. Brian Cleeve, *Dictionary of Irish Writers* (Cork: The Mercier Press, 1969; Mercier original, 1969), 2:50.

32. To Dr. John Curry

OCD, 8.3 HS 023

5 November 1757

My Dear Friend,

This letter, as it will not be doubly expensive, I shall venture sending; nay, it is my duty to send it as I know the honest thoughts of a friend, however undigested, will be acceptable to you. Mine at this minute are in the feeling strain, and judge how strong this sensibility must be from the loss of a friend to the public and to myself. I know not which took place most in my breast, affection or esteem for him. You knew him better than I did. I think he deserved the character given of him in our public papers, "*A man of true piety, sound judgment and consummate prudence,*" etc. Poor Clinch![1] I remember with a pleasing melancholy the night I had been instrumental in bringing him and you together. In the friendly éclaircissement between you, I was almost moved to tears. It happened that in the hurry of walking you had not noticed him one day in Fishamble Street at a time when that kind of coolness which separated *Paul* from *Timothy* kept you both asunder.[2] He apprehended that your not returning the civility was owing to that coolness. Can you forget his expression on the occasion to you in my presence? You felt it, so did I; but he felt more than both of us. The language of the heart is the first oratory. "*I was,*" said he, "*struck instantly. The man I loved turned away from me, the person in whose disesteem I counted myself a great loser made me a great sufferer, and I could not resist the tears which fell from me at that instant.*" Art is not equal to this panegyric which Nature gave while she added infinitely to the beauty by the unconsciousness of giving it. Were it graved in capitals on his tombstone, Europe could not furnish a finer. Let us (on your fine and feeling principle) "*entomb such friends in our breasts*" and open as often as we have an opportunity our sepulchral treasures to such living friends as may be edified by them! *Decet haec dare dona.*[3] Those are gifts indeed, and may we exhibit as good when nothing but the bare memory of us remains to do any service to those we leave behind! I now return to thoughts less useful; to mere temporary things, in which, however, we must take a share, because the condition of our nature requires it. The disease of the public *on our account* is brought to a crisis. Experience has shown not the inutility alone, but the great evil of penal laws *without their proper object.* If this experience is lost upon our L[egis-latu]re we cannot suffer more than we have done already, but take my word, others who are not so well inured to the pain will. Our numbers, in the natural course of generation, are increasing, and from our disability to do any good the national weakness must grow in proportion to our growth. Thus it is.—In fact there are only two methods for rendering Popery of any advantage to this country, either tolerate it or banish it. *Aut ornandum aut tolerandum* as Ceasar said of *Octavius*.[4] In the first place you convert its votaries into *useful subjects;* in the second you get rid of the *useless*. But the objections of the latter method are too strong to put us ever on the attempt of trying it, and objections to the former are refuted at once in this temporary suspension of those penalties which regard the exercise of religious worship. If the religion itself be tolerated, why should the votaries be treated as *intolerable?* Is it not the interest of our enemies on the continent that we should ever maintain such a policy? I am confident it is their wish, and should not that consideration alone open our eyes. I am sorry the writer of the *Protestant Interest Considered* did not give this argument a place in his reasonings on this subject. But I am tiring you on this threadbare argument. I read over with attention the *Serious Thoughts,* and thank the author for the strong and honest light in which he put our affair. I like him also as a free and bold writer, though I think as affairs now stand, many of his methods of reformation are better calculated for the *Polyteia* of Plato than the dregs of Romulus.[5] I request, as you are on the spot, you will inform me what is doing at this time in your busy metropolis. I know you cannot and ought not to be as prolix as I am. But you can dispatch a great deal in a narrow compass, especially to one who has leisure enough here to comment on hints and take information from the chewing of a finger, as is reported in Irish history of the celebrated hero and philosopher Finn MacCumhail. I purpose to see you in the holidays and be happy with you in conversations, wherein the dull compliments of the new year will have no share. A brother physician of yours reproached me formerly with publishing a few extracts from the *Leabhar Gabhala* and Newton, with owning that it was he who made those extracts first.[6] If such a quarrel became war with regard to works in which neither of us could pretend a share, what reproach will not you make to me now when I am already passing for the father of the genuine work of a friend of yours for whom you ought in this case to interpose much more warmly than *he* in the other. I had a letter last post on this subject which made me laugh. My friend tells me that your friend is ready to give the credit of his issue to the next that offers himself as a candidate for literary fame. But I who have been charged with petty larceny already am a suspected person; I must therefore request of the editor to provide himself with another father, and that I will turn sponsor for his right to it. Is this ending of my letter of a piece with the beginning. The query puts me in mind of my ill-timed puerility. May God preserve you in health and those advantages of family and friends.

> 1. George Faulkner wrote this obituary for Dr. Clinch, a Catholic priest:
> In Rosemary Lane, the Rev. Dr. John Clinch, many years parish priest of St. Michael's in this city, universally lamented for his great and good qualities both in private and public life. He was a man of sound judgment and consummate prudence, a true friend to the poor, the real Father of his flock, whom he was no less zealous to instruct by example than precept, and in his truly pathetic exhortations he never failed to enforce a peaceable and submissive behavior to the government. *DJ*, 1–5 November 1757.

2. O'Conor may have mistaken Timothy for Barnabus in the allusion of coolness between Paul and Timothy. Acts 15.36–41. There appears no coolness between Paul and Timothy in the Book of Acts or the two Epistles to Timothy.
3. It is proper to give these gifts.
4. He must be officially recognized or tolerated.
5. *Polyteia*, Plato's *Republic*.
6. The brother physician is Dr. John Fergus.

33. To Dr. John Curry

RIA, Stowe MS Bi1

18 November 1757

The more I consider your Registry Bill, the more I think I discover the latent intention in it, if I can call that latent which from head to foot is spread over with the thinnest gauze that ever was drawn out of a political loom. Men on the first consideration of things and whose objects are taken but in a half-light may mistake [and] may not be aware of consequences which might outweigh a real good intended. Such persons upon maturer consideration will give up or amend their scheme, but especially where they receive the conviction that one wheel in the machine counterworks the rest. In the latter case, the effects of mistake and surprise are all over. They will, therefore, certainly desist unless they design in fact that such a machine shall have this counter-operation and fancy to themselves some advantage in the foresight that in course of time one operation will yield to the force of the other. We are no longer at a loss in regard to the true design of the persons here supposed. Nothing can be better known than that our spiritual economy cannot be exercised a moment without the spiritual jurisdiction of bishops. This is not only virtually but effectually forbidden by the bill. What more do we want with regard to the true intent of it? No more is, in truth, necessary. Take away episcopal authority from among the Papists, and Popery in a few years is laid in its grave. This is the drift and scope of the indulgence intended, and the policy of precipitating it into a law, and that immediately, can escape no one. I am credibly informed that the free passing of it was negotiated previously not only with the leading men among the Commons here, but with the men in power beyond the water. If so, it wants only for forms and we may pronounce it canonized already. Be it so, but before the forms are given, I could wish that men in power deigned to listen a little to a [f]ew plain reasons against it and that the poor party concerned had spirit enough to offer them. But why should any of us *wish* what we can not *hope*. A great man in Tuam wondered that the R[oman] C[atholic]s have not formed some sort of association on such an occasion, and he wondered with good reason why at least they would not draw up such an instrument in these days of jealousy and suspicion as might acquit them to the public from maintaining any civil principles but such as the government could have no exception to. The reason of this is the stronger as the publication of such an instrument in the gazettes abroad (let the fate of it be ever so desperate at home) would certainly acquit the party to all Europe, not excepting even the Protestant states on the continent. But we have not even so much spirit or, rather, so much virtue among us.

Notwithstanding the querulous temper in which I write, yet I do not despair but that some good will be extracted from all this. The priests who mean well among us form certainly a very great majority. Upon this abolishment of the episcopacy they will think in earnest of seeking the countries where they may be safe in the full exercise of it and where they will be received with open arms and with full conviction that they will draw the laity after them. The acquisition of a laborious and useful body of subjects is power and consequently everything to an aspiring nation who has kingdoms unpeopled in their distant settlements. I wonder the framers of the bill would not avert a moment to this consequence which is so far from being a remote one that they might in a manner pronounce it instant. Should they not consider that the greatest enemy they have would wish that the bill had passed into a law! And should not that consideration alone have a great weight?

How shall I proceed on this melancholy subject which only affects me the more as for so many years past we have not afforded by principle or conduct the smallest provocation to the severity of depriving us of our religion after being deprived of almost everything else. You inform me that no more than 250 priests is intended to be allowed for the whole kingdom. This is not a priest to each barony in it. But what matters it how many or how few are allowed? Dr. Fitzsimons is a man of excellent sense. Let him call forth all the powers of it on this occasion! Let him have the popular and the conscious merit of laboring in the city, such an association of the chief clergy and laity as may represent the whole Catholic party of this poor Ireland; and let them, after a declaration of their principles, set forth their grievances at present in regard to their religion; and all this may be decently couched in petitionary remonstrances to the Lords and Commons now in session.

This may do good. The omission of it will do none at all, and all objections to it are not near as strong as the reasons for it. As I said before, it will acquit us to all Europe, and is not *that* a mighty point gained in our favor? If what I offer merits any attention, no time is to be lost while things are so evidently precipitated. Let us not flatter ourselves that our former method of getting over such danger is in the present case a sure one. In the supposal that the Bill is virtually agreed about already among the three estates, *no such expedient* (though no expedient ought to be left untried) can prevail.

I say no more and perhaps I have already said too much for so obscure a person in so obscure a corner. If I had not great confidence in you and had I not the certainty that you will acquit yourself of all you owe your country on this occasion, I should be far from giving you this trouble, though your indulgence to my scribbling made me give you often as much heretofore. On that indulgence next to your own zeal I depend.

34. To Dr. John Curry, Cow Lane, Dublin

RIA, Stowe MS Bi1

27 November 1757

Dear Sir,

Some time since I wrote to you my thoughts of the new modeled Registry Bill. I think I was not mistaken as to the true intent of it, *the destruction of Popery by Popery itself*. How could it be less? Here a *certain* number of priests are exonerated from all former legal penalties; and what price, what equivalent do they give a Protestant government for so much indulgence? It is this, to act without subordination to episcopal authority. Some will say that the intended toleration is not incompatible with this authority, which I absolutely deny. A registered priest supported by the civil magistrate may reject episcopal censures if he pleases. If he has virtue enough to submit to them, yet in that case must not the pastoral functions be suspended of the pastor? The bishop can turn in no other in his place, *till he is legally qualified;* or should he attempt it, will not the suspended person's friends fly to the next magistrate for redress and not only torment the new incumbent, but undertake for his expulsion also? The difference between Q[ueen] Anne's Registry Bill and the present consists in this: the former was too penal to execute itself, but [the one] yet now on the tapis is not so; the latter, therefore (no provision being made for episcopal authority) is by far the more dangerous bill of the two. This being so evidently the case, I wrote to you about the necessity on such an emergency of bringing so many Roman Catholics together (clergy and laity) in Dublin, as might form a representative sufficient to speak the sense of all their brethren, and from such a representation set forth the grievances and hint the consequences of such a bill, were it to pass into a law. It is your interest and it is the duty also of you gentlemen of the capital city to go into such an association. Your petition may indeed be rejected, but no color of reason will pronounce it bold or insolent.

To make a tender of the duty you owe the government is not insolence; to petition against the sacrifice of your religion after a previous sacrifice of almost all your civil rights is not insolence neither, but the assertion of a right, which as no government can possibly take away, so a government like ours will be very tender of meddling with it. Many well-meaning men in Parliament may not advert to this, and how will they be brought to think about it, while the persons concerned continue dumb and trust to an expedient, which however successful *formerly,* may fail *at present.* If you do not succeed in your petition, you acquit yourselves to the public as well-intentioned subjects and to all Europe as men aggrieved in the cause of religion; and may not this be of vast use to you all in the day of your exile? I could fill a sheet with reasons for this conduct, sufficient to anticipate and refute a ream of paper filled with reasons against it, but it is needless. It would be making very bad use of the attention you indulge so often to my thoughts to engage it on the subject of my wishes without the smallest hope that any will ever be complied with.

The news you sent me about a certain physician's negotiations in a certain place surprised me. He keeps no correspondence with me, but I am afraid that his exposing himself thus (whether with or without cause) to the resentment of a considerable body of people may prove hurtful to him as a public man more than the interposition of any Hyper-doctor can prove of advantage. The regular and his Catholic friend, whatever they may be guilty of in point of discretion, are, I am confident, safe enough in point of truth; and they have done well to sign no instrument of self-crimination where truth was on their side.

The load is left on the apothecary and there it is likely to rest, at least there (I think) it ought to rest, for should the affair be noised, the peer would think himself ill-used and perhaps bring his action of *scandalum magnatum*[1] home to a quarter where it would do mischief, not only in regard to the individuals concerned, but in regard to the whole party. As to the physician, I think it is impossible that he should have any instructions from his principals to give assurances of their being satisfied with the Bill in its present form. He might indeed declare their satisfaction as to the general tenor of it, but express their anguish at the part which struck at the fundamentals of our hierarchy, and that an alteration of the Bill on *that* head would render it palatable to the whole party. Such, I presume, was his commission; and it might be delivered in words, which at that instant might leave so good an impression on the peer's mind as might induce him to speak afterwards to the apothecary in a strain favorable to the R[oman] C[atholic]s and hence probably all the noise and clamor which arose from that incident. We know how things equally trivial produce mighty bustles among men.[2]

I part this minute for Sligo, which saves Cousin Reilly the trouble of a letter at this time. I received from him by a countryman of mine *Guiccardini's History*[3] and six other books from Mr. Lord,[4] for which I shall by the first opportunity remit the price. Your second Registry Bill was published with the blanks (I suppose) filled. I would be thankful for a copy from Mr. Reilly or for the chief contents by a letter.

    1. Great scandal.
    2. O'Conor's language is purposefully vague, but one can gain hints of surreptitious negotiations between some members of the Catholic party with the two most active men in the Ascendency party for such an act: the earl of Clanbrassil and Robert Clayton, bishop of Clogher.
    3. Francesco Guicciardini's *History of Italy* was first published in Latin in the 1560s. O'Conor must have seen the English translation similar to the London 1712 edition, *The History of the Papacy wrote by F. G. . . . which was fraudulently left out of the Fourth book of his history*. Translated from the Latin. Part I. London, 1712, folio. *BMCPBCE*, 11:241.
    4. Patrick Lord was a Catholic printer in Dublin (1750–1760). H. R. Plomer, *et al.*, *The Dictionary of the Printers and Booksellers Who Were at Work in England, Scotland, and Ireland from 1726 to 1775*. (Oxford: Bibliographical Society: rpt., 1968.)

35. To Dr. John Curry, Cow Lane, Dublin

RIA, Stowe MS Bi1

9 December 1757

[Six lines crossed out by another pen.] Things are not likely to mend on this legal annihilation of all episcopal authority which, I am afraid, is soon to take place in this kingdom. I can never think [about] it without alternate agitations of dejection and sorrow. Dejection from the consideration of the indolence of some and perhaps the approbation of others among ourselves; sorrow at the unrelenting spirit of our masters who, unsatisfied with resignation under all our temporal hardships, should after this long experience [corrupt] us now to resign our spiritual economy also! If we had not lost the spirit of men (not to say Christians) with the loss of our liberties, we would surely ma[ke] an humble remonstrance against this hardship and so far acquit ourselves to all Europe. We are timid. If we are so, it is because we want common sense. Our remonstrance some say might provoke to the execution of all the Penal Laws already in force against the exercise of our religion, as if all those laws put together could affect us half so much as this which (under the notion of an indulgence) qualifies our pastors to act as they please and shake off all episcopal government. In the former case, the spirit of religion would awake under all the stripes of persecution; we seem to want its consoling tears; if nothing less can wash out our stains, welcome the will of God. In the latter, tepidity will grow upon us, and where tepidity will end is easy to foresee. Catholicity will not long survive the loss of episcopacy, and when bishops are gone all good Catholics will follow them. Be the number great or small, the corn will be separated from the tares, and the government will acquire nothing in the event but subjects who can never be warm in their fidelity to men, while they are indifferent about their fidelity to God in the religion which they think most pleasing to Him. . . .

36. To Dr. John Curry, Cow Lane, Dublin

OCD, 8.3 HS 023

[late December 1757][1]

O'Conor flatters Curry about the contribution his *Memoirs* will make to enlighten the Protestant Ascendancy. O'Conor worries about Mr. Reilly's handling of the manuscript (i.e., Reilly is not making fast enough progress in obtaining a printer for the work) and tells Curry to take away the manuscript and give it to some more careful Catholic *factotum*. O'Conor says he will contribute six guineas to help pay printing costs since Reilly's attempt to have the book published by subscription was a failure.

[1] This letter is a fragment with no date.

37. To Dr. John Curry

OCD, 8.3 HS 023

23 December 1757

Dear Sir,

I am not sorry to find you for some time past silent to me, from the certainty that it has been much better employed in the relief of the sick in mind as well as body. I yesterday received by post a small pamphlet entitled, *An Appeal,* etc.[1] You'll be kind enough, I hope, to give the author my hearty thanks. He has indeed prescribed very properly for an ecclesiastical lunatic, as well as for his lay brother. It has been a long time my thought that in foiling such shameless writers no weapon is equal to ridicule, and you may be assured that I took very sensible pleasure in finding the author of the pamphlet so expert at it. It is excellent throughout, for the argumentative part is equally strong, and it is a pity that the narrow compass which the author prescribed to himself could not admit of his being more diffuse. I could indeed wish that the compliment of thanks in the second page for the opposition to the first Registry Bill was omitted; nothing is more certain than that the P[rima]te[2] opposed that bill on the principle of persecution, that he represented it not as an indulgence only but as a toleration of Popery by law, what he thought should never be admitted; and it is equally certain that the noblemen on the other side resented the thanks you mention and wondered, as they were known to repeat, how blindly we conducted ourselves in not having sense enough to distinguish better between our friends and enemies. I must confess that enemies on the first principle are preferable to friends on the tolerating principles of that Registry Bill. But still time and experience may correct the mistakes of the latter. The former can never be reformed, and therefore, in my opinion, are the last in the world to merit the thanks of any party. I fiddled myself last night with a captain of dragoons and one of the late bankers on Ormond Key; you will not be surprised to find some of the trimmer overshadowing these lines. I was set down with my family to drink the health and literary perseverance to *my honest free thinker.*[3] I shall try to be introduced to him. Would to God that the rest of the fraternity were like him. Adieu, my dear sir, with warmest affections to your whole family.

1. In a letter to Charles O'Conor, 23 May 1758, OCD 8.3 HL 016, Clonalis, Co. Roscommon, Ireland, Dr. Curry implies that he is the author of the pamphlet. The correct title was *An Appeal to the Lord Primate. In Vindication of the Political Principles of the Roman Catholics. The Second Appeal* appeared in 1758 and Curry admitted authorship. The *Third Appeal* appeared in 1760. *DJ,* 1–5 April 1760.

2. Stone, the Protestant archbishop of Armagh, opposed the first Registry Bill in 1756 but allowed the second Bill to pass in the House of Lords in 1757. Matthew O'Conor, *History of the Irish Catholics*, pp. 245, 251.

3. O'Conor's "Honest Free-Thinker" is Dr. Curry. This name was Curry's pseudonym for his *Appeal* pamphlets. *DJ*, 1–5 April 1760.

38. To Dr. John Curry

OCD, 8.3 HS 023

4 January 1758

Dear Sir,

I am provoked and indeed concerned at the account you give me that our party is divided into two factions and united it seems only in condemning and criticizing the well-meant efforts of the few who hazard a line in their favor. Those gentlemen have not good nature enough to allow, nor good sense enough to know that few first editions even of the ablest writers are free from inadvertencies and inaccuracies. The hurry of the mind, *currente calamo*,[1] cannot possibly attend to all, and this so true that I have not been displeased to find in a late celebrated critique on the writings of Mr. Pope that Mr. Addison was known not seldom to stop the publication of a *Spectator* after its being printed off, seeing that another might be impressed and published more to his taste. Our critics put me in mind of a pragmatical person who found fault with the cut of his coat. "Since I can't please you," said the workman, "here are the shears for yourself." Now what makes this poor joke the more apposite to our purpose is that the fault-finder was himself once the worst tailor in his country. It were to be wished that those gentlemen handled our shears for a while were it for no better use than barely complying with their duty and showing that their case is far from being that of the above fault-finder. Till this is done their criticisms come but with a very bad grace, through the channels of private whispers. I had a letter yesterday from our friend[2] wherein he makes a handsome and well-grounded apology for his not giving you some meetings of late. Most of his time is at the disposal of another; when he was at liberty, the boy at the bar of our coffee-house can aver that he made frequent inquiries for you, as he unluckily missed of meeting you. Your good nature will easily see the congruity of these reasons and therefore pardon what could not proceed from any negligence. He tells me that the title page to the *Letter* rendered his present undertaking suspicious to one party, and he therefore thinks that a more popular turn given to it might draw in more subscribers.

In this I think he is not mistaken. He would have it, *Historical Memoirs of the Irish Rebellion in 1641, extracted from Parliamentary Journals, State Acts, and the Most Eminent Protestant Historians in A Letter, etc.* For my part I have nothing to object, except the oddness of drawing out and printing new proposals on this plan. But where is the great harm? If a new and consistent title like this can forward the work, what have we but the same end brought about by seemingly different means; I ask pardon for delivering my opinion so freely. I hope to see you soon, to be your associate in pain, as formerly in sensible gratifications, when our minds were not so much disturbed by the loss of the dead and the perverseness of the living. You and I are too philosophical to correspond about any politics but such as regard the advantage of our own poor country. What think you of the present dance among princes? Will it be like that described by Sir William Temple in his own time, where, after a hundred twists and evolutions each performer finished by filling the place from whence he set out? Or may it not be compared to that, wherein you see most of them in the wrong corner, striking their heads against posts and making sport for us who are indifferent spectators? Whatever it be, they will in time sit down of themselves and put an end to *our* mirth, whatever end they may put to their own. See what efforts I am making to fill a blank which surely ought to be much larger than what I grant you from this to the bottom.

1. With fleeting pen.
2. Michael Reilly.

39. To Denis O'Conor, Belanagare

OCD, 8.3 SE 028

7 February 1758

O'Conor sends Denis a regimen for improving his health. Denis should eat mutton "and other white meats, generally boiled, but roasted at intervals if you be tired of boiled meats." He should drink wine mixed with water and sometimes pure wine for dinner. Buttermilk fresh from the churn taken with bread is the morning meal. Also Denis should ride in the morning. "You think much worse of yourself than the doctor does," admonishes O'Conor.

40. To Dr. John Curry

OCD, 8.3 HS 023

Good Friday, 1758

O'Conor has returned to Belanagare from Dublin and apologizes to Curry for not seeing him before O'Conor left town. O'Conor had a breakfast appointment with "The Hyper-doctor," Dr. Richard Lincoln, Catholic Archbishop of Dublin, concerning the archbishop's pastoral directive which instructed the diocesan clergy to discourage any attempt by the parishioners to form an association. (See letter 19 for a fuller explanation.) O'Conor comments on the deaths of the earl of Clanbrassil and the bishop of Clogher.[1] Finally O'Conor reports on the health of his older son Denis. Denis has followed the instructions given by Curry in the previous letter but "feverish infections appear on his face and legs; his lungs are, I am afraid, affected, for what he hawks up in the morning appears sometimes a little streaked with blood."

1. James Hamilton, earl of Clanbrassil, died in March 1758; Robert Clayton, Protestant bishop of Clogher, died in February 1758, Gilbert, *Appendix,* p. 460. Both men had been instrumental in bringing forth the Registry Bills of 1756, 1757.

41. To Dr. John Curry

RIA, Stowe MS Bil

22 April 1758

Dr. Curry has sent O'Conor a pamphlet[1] and asks O'Conor if he thinks such a pamphlet will help the Protestant Primate, Archbishop Stone, understand better the problems of the Roman Catholics. O'Conor replies, "You could not bestow a more welcome gift, and the author, whoever he be, has my thanks as he must have those of the honest public in a very eminent degree." Notwithstanding the good arguments in the pamphlet, O'Conor tells Curry that the men in power are "hardly tractable, and they hate all changes for the better, if not the better for them. I have, for this reason, no great matter to expect from *appeals* to them when enforced only by the *strength* of the argument...."

1. The pamphlet Curry sent O'Conor was *A Second Appeal to His Grace the Lord Primate of Ireland. In Vindication of the Political Principles of the Roman Catholics. By an Honest Free Thinker.* Dr. Curry is the "Honest Free Thinker." Altogether he wrote three *Appeals:* 1757, 1758, and 1760. The last Appeal was advertised in *DJ* 1–5 April 1760.

On 23 May Curry writes O'Conor about the *Second Appeal* and comments that some mistakes Curry has made in the pamphlet will mislead people into thinking he is not the author. Sheehan, p. 167.

42. To Dr. John Curry, Cow Lane, Dublin

OCD, 8.3 HS 023

[1758][1]

O'Conor mentions Denny's ill health and asks again for a new regimen for his son to follow. Denny's constitution is "scorbutic" and he perspires heavily. O'Conor also thinks that he should send Curry's *Memoirs* to Hume and Smollet to correct their mistakes about the Irish Uprising.

1. This letter is undated, but the editors think it was written in 1758 because of the mention of the *Memoirs* as well as the mentioning of Denis's continued ill health.

43. To Dr. John Curry

OCD, 8.3 HS 023

23 June 1758

A forty-six hour journey from Dublin brings O'Conor to his home at Belanagare. Notwithstanding being home, O'Conor misses Curry and the interests they have in common. O'Conor has nothing in common with his Catholic neighbors. He writes:

We are persons of different manners and principles, though not of different religious profession. Their creed recommends justice but they do not practice it, but I hope I do.

O'Conor continues his commentary on "justice" by stating his desire to stand by Curry as an "honest man" and to do "our nation or our party justice. . . ." This justice is to make known the truth about Catholic participation in Irish life.

To do this justice may never be in my power, and yet with health and books on my side, I may before I die attempt something. These, you see, are conditional things, and hard it is surely when after seventy years' silence none among our brethren and fellow-sufferers could be found to attempt this justice except a man of public and laborious profession on one side and a farmer on the other. Poor Rooth,[1] the author of the *Analecta Sacra*, now in my hands, said truly, that a silence in regard to the calumnies of our enemies was in some degree criminal and amounted to an acquiescence to the charge made. You and I, to the shame of our party, broke this silence and we both know what thanks we got for our officiousness, for so they call it. Let us forgive this nonsense and do our duty, for I hope we have call to it, fettered as one of us is and weak as the other is. . . .

Finally O'Conor comments on the health of his son-in-law, Myles MacDermot, and comments that the local Roscommon physician, Dr. Duigenan, and Curry agree in their regimens for "reestablishing" MacDermot.

    1. David Rothe was vicar general for Armagh and bishop of Ossory. *HBC*, pp. 405, 405n; see also Douglas Hyde, *Literary History of Ireland*, p. 164.

44. To Dr. John Curry, Cow Lane, Dublin

OCD, 8.3 HS 023

4 August 1758

    While Curry frets in Dublin about the publication of *The Memoirs*, O'Conor has been to Co. Sligo on business. O'Conor writes to Curry to tell him he has sent seven subscriptions for Curry's book to Michael Reilly in Dublin. O'Conor has scolded Reilly, he tells Dr. Curry, for not advertising the book and for not running off fifty sheets in galley proofs. Denis, O'Conor's son, is still "complaining of a sore breast, attended every morning with small expectorations, but the scorbutic infection renders him timid and desponding."

45. To Dr. John Curry

OCD, 8.3 HS 023

19 August 1758

    Three letters to Dr. Curry have become lost, while Dr. Curry's letters to O'Conor arrive on schedule. The letters related to "our religion in general and to our party in particular." O'Conor has had no reply from Reilly concerning the printing of Curry's book. O'Conor will furnish six guineas to help publish the book since Reilly seems to be in financial trouble. O'Conor's friend and guide in the collection of manuscripts, Dr. John Fergus, "has already made a charge that I have taken *from him* seven or eight extracts *from the works of others*. I denied, and this surely was a controversy in a reading and learned age. But whether he or I, or whether we both might hit on the same facts in the course of our reading has, it seems, been no important affair to the public, though it was greatly so to him, and in some degree so to me, as his charge leaned on my moral character. . . . If this were not my case, I should overlook in my former friend the poor and crazy conduct he held towards me on this occasion. . . ."

46. To Dr. John Curry

OCD, 8.3 HS 023

22 August 1758

Reilly, O'Conor's *factotum* in Dublin, has written O'Conor to tell him he has received O'Conor's three letters. However, O'Conor finds that Reilly is too slow and tells Curry to conceal the fact that O'Conor will donate six guineas toward publication of Curry's *Memoirs*. Also O'Conor has asked John Comerford, a Catholic merchant in Dublin, to expedite the printing of the book. Comerford is to help with the editorial work. O'Conor reads and harvests. He writes:

We have here a broken harvest, and when I cannot stand abroad, I sit down and read. I write nothing and am the most averse in the world to the task I have the impudence to impose on you, slaving in old fragments of history. The wild conduct of our old natives renders me splenetic; I close, I reject the page; and read Lord Bolingbroke, Rollin, Pluche,[1] and our modern reviews. Pluche in defense of Moses is an antidote to Lord B., and I take great pleasure in the truths I occasionally pick upon the contrast between these two philosophers, the one a most learned and rational believer, the other an enthusiast in theism, and that to various degrees of self-contradiction.

1. O'Conor's list of books are those published by George Faulkner and listed at the back of his *An Humble Address to the Nobility, Gentry, and Free Holders of the Kingdom of Ireland* (Dublin: Faulkner, 1751). They are Rollin's *Method of Teaching and Studying the Belles-Artes;* Bolingbrokes's *Dissertations on Parties, Political Tracts;* Oldcastle's *Remarks on the History of England,* and *Letters on the Spirit of Patriotism.* Gilbert, Appendix, p. 462; Charles Rollin was best known for his *Ancient History.* . . . Noel Antoine Pluche wrote *Histoire du Ciel.* A translated version appeared in London in 1741 as *The History of the Heavens considered according to the Notions of the Poets and Philosophers compared to the Doctrine of Moses.* BMCPBCE, 21:955.

47. To Dr. John Curry

OCD, 8.3 HS 023

3 September 1758

O'Conor tells an anecdote about Dr. Edward Synge,[1] Protestant bishop of Elphin, which describes the bishop's pride in considering himself a fine speaker and writer, better than some "little rhyming poet in England (one Pope) would be admired as much as a certain tall Bishop or Tillotson himself." Reilly is moved to Phrapper Lane and is near enough to consult with Dr.

Curry. Also Curry should persuade Reilly that he needs help from John Comerford.

    1. O'Conor is referring to Dr. Edward Synge, Protestant Bishop of Elphin. Gilbert, in "The Streets of Dublin," mentioned the bishop's nickname was "Proud Ned." O'Conor's irony fits perfectly.

48. To Dr. John Curry

OCD, 8.3 HS 023

23 September 1758

    O'Conor has been away in Sligo for a week. Reilly has become ill, which is another obstacle in the way of the preparation and publication of Curry's *Memoirs*. O'Conor advises Curry to keep a low profile when the book appears so that Curry will not be attacked as he was in 1747 when Curry's *Dialogue* appeared. A newspaper notice attacking two Catholic prelates has appeared. O'Conor's comments, often veiled, keep the reader wondering. For example he concludes this letter with: "Bonfires and an embargo on beef is all the news we have here in the West. In this philosophical way do we receive an event which it is computed will cost us in this province alone £30,000."

49. To Dr. John Curry

OCD, 8.3 HS 023

6 October 1758

    "An author is no sooner known than abused . . ." is O'Conor's caution to Curry. He advises Curry not to do much of his own revising and editing because of Reilly's illness, or Curry's writing style may be recognized by his political and religious antagonists. O'Conor asks that the type and paper be of good quality, "for who could abide to see a hero dressed in beggar's weeds?" Finally O'Conor gives news of his son and son-in-law. Denis is doing well and riding every day. The son-in-law is weakening. A neighbor, Mrs. MacDermot-Roe,[1] has been left in a desperate way through the death of her daughter's husband. He is MacDermot-Roe's son-in-law, Owen McDermot.

    "I do not think it was prudently advised by Dr. Duigenan to require you to write to old Mrs. MacDermot: She has not received any part of her daughter's fortune, nor can she, as I hear, pay what she has contracted for her in the country. You should surely write rather to her for Mr. Owen MacDermot, to whom the young lady's fortune fell."

    1. Mrs. MacDermot is the widow of Terence MacDermot-Roe, whose husband died and left her "in a desperate debt." Because he had no sons, Terence MacDermot-Roe's

fortune went to his son-in-law, Owen MacDermot. *DJ,* 20–24 December 1757. See O'Conor's letter to Curry, 7 September 1757.

50. To Dr. John Curry, Cow Lane, Dublin

OCD, 8.3 HS 023

23 October 1758[1]

"After reading the date of my letter I am put in mind of old Horace's sentiment—*Hic dies anno redeunte festus.*"[2] O'Conor's letter commemorates the date of the Irish uprising in 1641, and he asks musingly how many sermons will be preached in Protestant churches against the brutality of the Irish Catholics. Reilly is now printing Curry's book for which O'Conor gives thanks. Denis is ill again. Dr. Duigenan's prescription for oxymel of squills seems to worsen Denis's condition, giving him diarrhea.

1. Anniversary of the Irish uprising in 1641.
2. *Carmina,* 3.8.9: This day, an occasion for festivity upon its return each year.

51. To Dr. John Curry, Cow Lane, Dublin

OCD, 8.3 HS 023

27 January 1759

Dear Sir,

Your letter of the 20th instant found me in the desert upon a spot of four acres of land covered with stones and coppice and neglected by my family at all times. It cost me two hundred men for six days past to subdue this spot by stubbing and removing such a quantity of stones as enclosed it with a strong ditch. I am thus forty shillings a year richer now than when last you saw me, and I have one of the qualifications necessary for voting at our next parliamentary election, all acquired by my own industry. *O beatos nimium sua si bona norint agricolas!*[1] Without raillery, I have for nine years past reclaimed as much useless land as comes now to at least thirty pounds a year. I have ornamented and improved sixty acres of the creation, and I trust not only my friends but everyone, with my vanity in mentioning it. I am thinking Virgil was in earnest when he wrote the verse above quoted, but I must assure you that when I boast, I do it with discretion, and never admit my vanity to be impertinent, unless it be so at present. My answer in regard to our friend Mr. R[eilly] must be short. I never admitted him into the secret of my advancing the trifle you mention, and I had more reason than one for this discretion. I dreaded that a work of great and public use might be lost to the public, nor am I still free from apprehensions unless we put ourselves to some little expense in forwarding it. This should be done in so private a manner that no third person should ever be the wiser. I therefore request that you will not, out of any tenderness for me, spare a farthing for forwarding the work if our friend cannot proceed, but on the terms of advancing a small sum. It would be the worst economy in the world, and it would be depriving the public of what it has fairest right to for at least sixty years past. Are you not surprised that I have not troubled you for some time about *Denny?* His scorbutic spots still appear, but his crudities through a religious observance [of] what you prescribed are lessened. His indigestions in short are greatly abated; what he expectorated every morning is but little and what surprises me that what comes up, comes spontaneously without the least cough. His breast he still complains of, the old soreness remaining but somewhat lessened. He is the only phthisical patient I ever knew a desponder, and I really think he is giving ground now slowly. What you have been told of your other patient, my dear neighbor, is without the best foundation.[2] Last Thursday, Term Night, he has been arrested in his home by his father-in-law, Mr. Patrick French of Tyrone in County Galway, assisted by a band of armed men. I was sent for immediately. It was resolved to send him to Dublin where probably he is now arrived. I recommended to Mr. French to put him in the hands of his former physician where he was confined before for the same disorder, and I put him in mind of what was due to you for attendance on Mr. MacDermot's sister. He returned me so far a favorable answer as to assure that he would take the matter into consideration, and I request you will apply by letter to him at Tyrone, near Galway. I had a hearty affection for Mr. MacDermot *et doleo ejus vicem.*[3] Your letter was laid by carelessly in the post office; as I must conclude from my not receiving it but yesterday. The answer would cost you a groat and it is your own fault, who requested it by return of the post. I think that I have put you to double expense by the length of it, nor will I swell the amount by adding more except what is included in the assurance I give you that I am, dear friend, yours most affectionately.

1. O fortunate indeed the farmers if only they recognize their good fortune.
2. Owen MacDermot, who was mentally ill.
3. And I grieve at his vicissitudes.

52. To Dr. John Curry, Cow Lane, Dublin

OCD, 8.3 HS 023

17 February 1759

My Dear Sir,

On the next post day after I received yours of the 29th ultimo, I made a precise reply as you required. I am now mixing labor with study. I succeed in the first; in the second I am highly pleased, entertained and instructed. From the hands of Mr. Cusack I received 176 pages of a new work entitled *Historical Memoirs Concerning the Rebellion of 1641*. It is an admirable performance and the author (whoever he is) has thrown on that darkened and important period of our history such a light as with good reason I despaired of ever seeing. The author has done more. From this point of view he makes most judiciously a retrospect of the times preceding the Rebellion. He explains motives, develops incidents, opposes true facts to false, and by detecting the latter, strips them of all the advantages they received from the declamations and dishonest pathos of those popular writers who in their day carried all before them by the pen as well as the sword. We happily live in times wherein historical truths have a freer circulation, and it is hoped the public will be the better for them, notwithstanding the difficulty which many still have to resist the force of their earlier impressions. For this latter reason I would have our author's name concealed and the more if it be true (as I have heard said) that the gentleman is a man of profession. Men of some consequence, but of little minds, may take avantage in such a person's case, which they would not in mine. You, who live on the spot and who might have heard of this performance, may inform me about the true author. I request you will procure a copy of what I have seen and give me your opinion. I have ever been out of humor with the conduct of our clergy in Jamestown, a place within seven miles of my home and Galway. The writer before me[1] explained that affair admirable to my satisfaction, as he does every other fact relative to those miserable times, and Mr. Harris has my hearty thanks for being the instrument of all these truths. I long greatly to see the whole work finished, and I am really angry at the editor for his delay, unless he has prudently, as is probable, waited to make it more complete by his notes and appendix. I am charmed with the honesty of Carte[2] and highly pleased to find such frequent use made of his authority, as he is an enemy to the very people he has justified. I beg your pardon for taking up so much of your time on this subject. Read and peruse the work. You will in that case be obliged to me, as in your way you might have overlooked such a performance as little worthy your attention or curiosity. Were you not alert to yourself when you gave Mr. Cusack a receipt for the title I sent you lately as my physician? I have surely a right to rate you for this indiscretion as he saw and conversed with a certain person a hundred to one, but he showed him your receipt and you well know that of all men he would be the last I would let into such a secret, though I heartily love the man and I would hardly keep any other secret from being reported in his breast, where I know it would be safe and may say entombed. I had this month another new work published and written by the late Dr. Lawson.[3] I had a curiosity to know what an Irish professor would say on the subject of oratory. His style is elegant but I think in some periods stiff and affected. His critique on some lines in Pope and Swift is defective in point of propriety and [his] grammatical construction I think too minute. He indeed makes an apology, without hinting in the least to his reasons, that our language is not as yet fixed by any standard of rule and that such slips are in fact unavoidable. Though the whole work smells of the lamp, and in many respects it offers more instruction for the readers than fame for the author. I wish you may write to me as soon as you can because I long to hear from you. How is my near neighbor and friend now in your hands?[4] I hear he is very jealous of me as one of the conspirators who consented to his arrest. I pray be particular about him as I sincerely wish him well. Let your worthy uncle, my dear Mrs. Curry, Jack Comerford, Cousin Reilly, etc., be presented with my affections. I reserve the *last word* for my friend as it pithily is expressed in one of our Irish adages.

    1. O'Conor switches from the present publication of Curry's *Historical Memoirs* to an older history, Thomas Carte, *History of the Life of James, Duke of Ormonde* (London, 1736). See Matthew O'Conor, *History of the Irish Catholics* . . . , p. 78, who describes the Jamestown meeting of 6 August 1650:

> In this terrific Crisis several of the Irish Catholic bishops assembled at Jamestown to provide for the public safety. The emergency in some degree justifies this assumption of the management of public concerns ordinarily incompatible with the Christian sacerdotal office. . . . On the 12th of August . . . they published a declaration against the Lord Lieutenant charging him with improvidence and ill-conduct, of gross partiality to Protestants, of hostility to Catholics, cruelty to the clergy, of malicious misrepresentations and wicked councils to the King. This declaration was accompanied with an excommunication against all who should enlist with, assist or supply him or his troops. . . .

    2. Thomas Carte (1686–1754), historian. *Concise DNB*, 1:209.
    3. See Ward, *Prince of Dublin Printers*, p. 54n, 55. George Faulkner advertised in late October 1758 *Lectures Concerning Oratory* by John Lawson (1712–1759), Lecturer in Ora-

tory at Trinity College. No doubt Faulkner sent a copy to O'Conor as Faulkner mentions to the Irish poet Samuel Derrick that the earl of Chesterfield enjoyed his gift copy.
4. The neighbor is Owen MacDermot.

53. To Dr. John Curry, Cow Lane, Dublin

OCD, 8.3 HS 023

27 February 1759

I am alternately pleased and uneasy at the contents of yours of the 24th instant. Pleased to find your benevolence so animated for my friend and uneasy at your situation—among *false brethren*. These two sons of Aesculapius I have long known, and I no less than you am indebted to them for favors, which I could wish spared on their own account. This I can assure you that I love both much more than I fear them, notwithstanding the unequal combat on our stage between malignity and probity, between the versatility of a crooked heart and the integrity of a candid one. He of the city will gladly, I'm afraid, embrace this opportunity to gorge his revenge and punish an honest man for the crime which *I did not commit,* notwithstanding the inequality of the combat above referred to; I trust you will be able to disappoint him and entertain your friend here with highest sport he ever ambitioned to enjoy, that of seeing malignity baffled and returning into itself wounded and impotent. If he should prevail against you, his victory will surely be dear-bought. The Devil clapped his own seal on such friendships and, whether triumphant or discomfited, such spirits are real objects of a good man's pity, and they are really so of mine; for the pleasure I should take in their disappointment would not be against the man but against the crime, hard as it is (in such cases) to separate the agent from the agency. I have long lamented the situation of our friend, supporting decency, supporting a sickly wife, supporting six children on a poor salary. If you can rescue him, if you can succeed in lighting up a countenance gloomed from the inward agitation of so many calls upon its industry, *Thou shalt be my great Apollo* as well as physical hero.[1]

One method I would have you take with your brother here in this country (but he is not your brother, whatever relationship he may otherwise have to Apollo) one method I say you should take with him which I have known to have succeeded in my own case; to take him in his own way and treat him with less delicacy and ceremony than any other adversary; you must lay aside the knife for the handsaw and let it lie by to gather rust as a specific to cure, when you find it proper, the wounds you give by it. I had lately a letter from my brother in the Netherlands.² He there perused the first volume of Mr. Geoghegan's *History of Ireland* (just published) wherein the author gives very high commendations of Mr. Reilly's *Dissertations*.³ Surely he must be in raptures at seeing the *Memoirs*, wherein things much more interesting to the present times are put into the clearest light. I would wish you found some means for conveying all that has been printed to Mr. Hume in Scotland, that he may avail himself of the contents in his next edition of the *History of Great Britain*. This is not a thought which rushed in by chance; I have had it long resting upon my mind. I am this day to entertain company, Mr. French (your patient MacDermot's father-in-law); if I have leisure to add more I will; if not you will owe me an obligation which I did not intend to confer, that of sparing you the trouble of reading the trifles which may follow.

P.S. Are you not surprised that I do not write to you often or about Denny, my son? His horse physic, his shop physic, his care have had good effects in spite of his industry to deny much amendment. He guards against colds as much as possible and yet he is now and then caught! What would you think of a little venesection in such cases? What alternatives would you recommend in regard to change of air and regimen? He is not losing ground, but I think a little on the gain; and this in brief is all the light I can afford you at present.

Another P.S. Mr. French wrote to you by this day's post. He requested of me to press it upon you to observe the instructions of his letter to you religiously, to communicate his thoughts to Dr. Kelly⁴ and that nothing should be done in regard to Mr. MacDermot but by mutual consent. He is jealous of Dr. Duigenan, and take your hints from this, Mr. French is a gentleman of strict probity, and as such I think he will give you no reason to complain of not being considered properly for the labor you take in regard to his son-in-law's *tantrum*.

    1. Since Apollo was worshipped in Rome as a healer, the comparison with Dr. Curry is apt. *Oxford Classical Dictionary*, ed. M. Cary *et al.* (Oxford: Clarendon Press, 1964), p. 68.
    2. Daniel O'Conor.
    3. Abbé James MacGeoghegan (1702–1763) was an Irishman living in France and author of *L'Histoire de L'Irlande Ancienne et Moderne* . . . , which appeared in 1758. Volumes two and three appeared in 1762 and 1763 respectively. See O'Conor's letter to Faulkner, 8 August 1763.
    4. A Dublin physician. *The Public Register: or Freeman's Journal*, 8 (27–30 April 1771), 413. The University of Illinois has volumes 6–8 (1769–1771). Future citations will be made from *Irish Newspapers in Dublin Libraries*, 2, *FJ* (Ann Arbor, Michigan: University Microfilms, 1958).

54. To Dr. John Curry, Cow Lane, Dublin

OCD, 8.3 HS 023

31 March 1759

Dear Sir,

I am come from the assizes of Roscommon where I have lost my money and rest. I should have lost my patience also, had not long habits of apathy rendered me a resigned, if not indifferent, spectator of all the scenes wherein folly and perverseness present themselves. If evil examples have powerful influences, we must not expect better times or better manners; but let us make ourselves amends by a closer connection with the few good men among us, and let us, as far as the thing is possible, keep ourselves clear of the common taint. I come to you with new desires from such an interlude, which I take to be not the least of those advantages we derive from our encounters with moral evil itself. I echoed back your *Io triumphe*[1] to our friend without loss of time. Now that he is grown rich, he would take it ill of us not to treat him with this distinction due to the uncommon merit which our humble state can never pretend to. I have written to him by this post (as in duty bound) and forgot to ask him whether the supercilious air, the important strut, and the civil slight have anticipated his annual appointment. Indeed I should have but small hopes of his succeeding in those latter qualifications of great men, even in the most exalted state; and I partake warmly of his late good fortune as it will keep him from sinking under the load he lay under for several years past. You have known one Mr. Geoghegan in Paris. My brother in Ostend[2] tells me he published his first volume of the Irish History, wherein the *Dissertations* you have seen are mentioned with credit. My correspondent presses it on me to new model that essay and offered me a plan of method wherein he says our British compositions are generally deficient. I could wish he provided the materials as well as the method, and yet with both, what prospect have we of ever seeing here such a task executed from a very small number of readers and encouragers? I have compared Harris's *Bishops and Antiquities*[3] with the annals in my hands. Through the ignorance of our language, he has more mistakes than pages, many of which I marked in the margin from the original works I had before me. The ignorance of our language and the virulence of faction apart, he certainly had good talents for a compiler and I often wonder how well he has succeeded. Poor man! He was under the necessity (through poverty) of joining the hussar to the Swiss, of giving up his conscience to satiate the party lust of patrons who could not be gained but by such a sacrifice. When shall we see the *Memoirs?* The subscribers are ill-treated, nay the public is so, and I interrogated our friend this day on the subject. What think you now of my friend Mr. Owen MacDermot? I long to hear from him. I hope you correspond occasionally with Mr. French as I do, though he lives fifty miles from this house. Denny pursues punctually your regimen and is losing no ground. I expect in this solitude some news from you as soon as you can conveniently take up a pen. I go on with my rural occupations far from your dissipations and labors in the city. *Here contemplation prunes his muffled wings, and the free soul looks down to pity kings.* I have nothing more in contemplation than the happiness of my friends, and of my friend in Cow Lane particularly at the head of them.

> Tecum etenim longos memini consumere soles,
> Et tecum primas epulis discernere noctes:
> Unum opus et regimen poniter deponimus ambo,
> Atque verecunda laxamus seria mensa.[4]

These lines are from Persius, which struck me early in life. They surely contain all the sensibility of true friendship, and none can be more apposite to my conclusion.

1. (Shout of victory) Hail Victory.   2. Daniel O'Conor.
3. Walter Harris's *The History of the Bishops of Ireland and Writers of Ireland*, advertised for sale by George Faulkner, *DJ*, 31 October–4 November 1749.
4. I remember the long days I spent with you
   And the evenings set apart for dining with you:
   We both lay aside our work and responsibilities
   And relax with food and drink in moderation.

55. To Dr. John Curry

OCD, 8.3 HS 023

10 August 1759

My Dear Friend,

I longed to write to you, were it on another account but to pour out my complaints to you. Since November last I lost three brothers-in-law. Each died in low condition and the three widows fastened on me and hang still on a prop sinking under the impending weight.[1] Their affairs and my own under the burden [are] intolerable; my little liberty is destroyed, what I preferred to all other conditions of life, and I can neither read, write, nor think for myself. You have administered some consolations in your welcome letter of the fourth instant, and I hope I need not administer any to you on the loss of a worthy uncle, indeed, one of the worthiest of men; may Heaven grant that my sins may not hinder me of the share I had in his progress; may those who sought to take advantage of the Christian and primitive simplicity of his life repent and be like him.[2]

The want of such conduct as he held in fifty years of painful mission renders us what we are, a hated, suspected, and, in truth, an immoral lot of men. Wicked men have surely a stronger certainty of the torments of a future life than schismatics who mean well and are involuntarily wrong. When I consider the baseness and treachery of most of our own people, I find myself in little pain for all their sufferings; I would almost wish to see them weighty enough to open our eyes and derive from adversities those virtues which I am often apt to think nothing but adversity can produce. I am glad to find that our friend's historical task is at an end for the present. It is the most useful book that has hitherto appeared on the subject by vast odds, and as such must receive the stamp of public approbation, I mean the impartial public of all these western countries, as soon as it is sufficiently circulated. You did well not to trouble the gentleman you mention nor any of his subalterns with copies. They are as little able to *defend* as they are indifferent about *knowing* any part of the conduct of their predecessors. Let them account to themselves and to the public for their ignorance as well as they can, and I wish them that safety from censure which old Erasmus granted to some of his maligning enemies, *Tuti sunt suis tenebris*.[3] My cousin Reilly sent me down a pamphlet just published, entitled *Admonitions to the Papists of Ireland*. I threw it aside after one reading and shall never take it up a second time; *non tali auxilio nec defensoribus istis tempus eget*.[4] I think the writer too low for any animadversion. Your late patient Mr. MacDermot was with me here two days ago; he is still in his former condition and I despair of his re-establishment. You have surely been very ill-treated, and I must tell you that you deserve worse treatment if you do not exert yourself and take the proper notice of this. Without it, how can you acquit yourself to your family or even to me who have you and them so much at heart? Let me assure you that in this case I will not make the smallest allowance for indolence or delicacy, hurried and beleaguered as I have been this long time. No dissipations would hinder me from writing and answering your instructions about Denny but that in fact he is in a much better condition than I have known him to be when you first took him in hand. You have, I hope, re-established him, and I mention it to let you see what I owe to your instructions and friendship. If you should think of any new regimens for him, the sooner you write the better; but at any rate I would, as soon as your leisure permits, have a line from you including as much news about our party in town as one so remote from the city has some right to be informed of. I am thankful extremely for the recollection in regards to the *Annals of the Four Masters*. Why should we not honestly finesse the ignorant out of what they have no right to, but what is given by a silly unmeaning curiosity? I shall this day write to our friend if I can, and I should make an apology for being so long in arrears to him as well as to you. He mentioned a benefaction from an unknown hand to foreward the publication of his work and promised an equivalent in books. He seems to suspect me; but assure him that he has the real benefactor still to find out. My warmest affections to dear Mrs. Curry and your whole family.

1. Father Charles mentions that O'Conor had three sisters, but the names of two only appear, Maud and Molly. He does not name their husbands. Reverend Charles O'Conor, S.J., pp. 127, 139.
2. O'Conor must be referring to Father Archbold, Curry's Uncle. See Curry's letter to Charles O'Conor, 29 October 1757, Stowe MS B11, RIA.
3. They are safe in their own obscurity.
4. The time does not need such support or such defenders as these.

56. To Dr. John Curry

OCD, 8.3 HS 023

22 August 1759

Dear Sir,

I am just come in, having left my army of reapers under the direction of a subaltern. I was well employed, but now better, in a conversation with you, *O fortunatos nimium si sua bona norint agricolas!*[1] We agricolas, at least who can enjoy this mixed life, tempering its useful labors with the enjoyment of a true friend, though at eighty miles distance. It is to this sort of life, no doubt, that Cicero refers when he declared it to be his judgment that my occupation is next to that of a philosopher. "*Agricultura,*" says he, "*mihi videtur ad sapientis vitam proxime accedere.*"[2] I have this summer subdued nine acres of very unprofitable heath, and for nine years past I have been purchasing land *in the same manner very clandestinely*. I have acquired thirty pounds a year, which I do not think the less of that it was not left me by my family, for by a new creation I have converted a disagreeable waste of thorns into good arable land of my own. I commit this secret to you (my dear friend) but to no other, lest any acquisition should be liable to a discovery from the privation clauses in the Popery Acts. The government cannot be too watchful in regard to persons of my dangerous principles, especially when we thus audaciously elude the laws of the land by making that land the more useful by our labor and industry! The first line of my letter dragged so many others after it to this place. I now go into something else. What do the public say of our friend R[eilly]'s undertaking since its publication?[3] Who are vexed most? Those who envy the writer or those who want to suppress the truths he established? Of the two I would trust most to the latter as the more generous enemies and very probably the more equitable. You see your brother F———s[4] pretty often; what's his judgment? I hope that he can separate the work from the editor and that he has no relation to a certain Spanish inquisitor who forbade the reading of the most authentic edition of St. Cyprian because it came through a Protestant press. To be serious, I am uneasy and shall be so till I have some particulars from you relative to this new performance. I have lately met with the first volume of *The History of Poland,* written in a series of letters (by my namesake Doctor Connor) to the most eminent persons in England in King William's reign.[5] As he was physician to King John Sobieski and the first who gave a writer (I think) to our name, I would be thankful to you if you purchased the two volumes for me. It would be difficult to the search of any other person; but I never could find your industry in the pursuit of scarce books yet disappointed. I therefore presume to give you the trouble. Denny is in a better condition of health than you or I ever expected. If you can think of any new method to finish the work you have hitherto succeeded in, I know you will not delay in putting him into it.

When I am thus with you here, I have, I can assure you a disgust to return into the field where I have so many men armed with sickles and where I can command as arbitrarily as any general now in Europe without any dread about the event. But what right has such a rustic as I to detain a citizen as one of us detained Horace formerly in the *Sacred Way,* till he was ready to sink under the load of impertinances? Yet Horace, who makes no allowance for the poor man's affection, was not as good a man as you. You have ever taken my indiscretions in good part, nor shall I scruple now and then to divert you with them. Let them, as poor Delane[6] said (not the actor but his cousin German) *serve you as mustard to whet your appetite for some better entertainment.*

Give my warmest affections to Mrs. Comerford, Mr. John Comerford, your whole family.

P.S. By last post I got a letter from Cousin R[eilly]. I shall trouble him with one in return (and by hand) next week when I shall send one to bring me down seventeen or twenty copies of his undertaking for subscription. Please to give him my affection and best service.

    1. How fortunate the farmers if only they recognize their good fortune!
    2. Agriculture seems to me to come closest to the life of a wise man.
    3. Curry's *Historical Memoirs*.
    4. Dr. Fergus.
    5. Bernard Connor or O'Connor (1666?–1698) lectured at Oxford, London, and Cambridge and wrote an attack on miracles entitled *Evangelium Medici* (1697) and a *History of Poland* (1698). *Concise DNB*, 1:270.
    6. Dennis Delane (d. 1750) was the actor. *Concise DNB*, 1:331.

57. To Dr. John Curry

OCD, 8.3 HS 023

17 September 1759

Eighteen copies of Curry's *Memoirs* came by the mail to O'Conor for him to deliver to subscribers. Also Michael Reilly sent O'Conor fifteen lottery tickets, of which O'Conor has sold seven. O'Conor promises Curry that he will try to collect a doctor's bill from the father-in-law of Owen MacDermot. O'Conor wishes that the book had come out in London.[1] O'Conor sarcastically says that he would like to deliver a copy of Curry's book to "the great man at my door."[2]

    1. Unknown to O'Conor, a London edition of *The Memoirs* was published in 1758, 1765, and 1767. *BMCPBCE*, 13:24. Michael Reilly advertised an edition in *DJ*, 6 March 1760.
    2. Probably Dr. Synge, called "Proud Ned," *HBC*, 377.

58. To Hugh Stafford, Elfin

RIA, Stowe MS Bil

23 September 1759

Hugh Stafford, an apothecary in Elphin, is O'Conor's contact in the Protestant cathedral town of Elphin. O'Conor asks Stafford to give a copy of the book O'Conor calls *The Vindication of the Irish against the Calumnies of Sir John Temple . . .*[1] to the bishop of Elphin. O'Conor tells Stafford not to mention O'Conor's name when Stafford gives the book to the bishop of Elphin, but to say that Stafford received the book from someone in town.

1. While there appears to be no book listed by this name in the *BMCPBCE*, one assumes the book is actually Curry's *Memoirs* under a code name.

59. To Dr. John Curry, Cow Lane, Dublin

OCD, 8.3 HS 023

25 September 1759

I must write this letter and read it over afterwards before I can form a judgment whether it will be worth the while to forward it without a parliamentary privilege to pass gratis. Through the instrumentality of Mr. Stafford, my friend, an honest Papist, and my Elphin apothecary, I have yesterday slipped the *Memoirs* into the hands of my neighboring *Cardinal*.[1] He promised to read the work over with impartiality, and yet I have no great faith in these promises though *in verbo sacerdotis*.[2] I cautioned my friend to make no mention of my name and inform his Eminence that he had the book from a Dublin correspondent. Notwithstanding this caution, the *Cardinal* spoke of me and said he would be obliged to me could I procure him poor Bishop French's *Bleeding Iphigenia*. You are no stranger to that work. The author was a partisan to our wretched Nuncio Rinuccini and undertook the defense of our unhappy civil war in Charles the First's reign from principles no way popular in the present times and, I am afraid, no way well grounded in any. Be that as it will, the thoughts of a single person on that subject cannot affect those of many wiser men of his own religion in that ill-fated age, and I see no great hurt in gratifying the *Cardinal*. I therefore request of you to fall upon the search immediately, as of all men you have the happiest luck in detecting these literary fugitives. Duggan of Bride's Alley is a very good angler also; and I would wish that you employed him to labor along with you. It is a pleasure to me to find that the author of the *Memoirs* has not one quotation from him or the author of the *Cambrensis Eversus*. [Five or six unreadable lines follow.]

1. The Protestant bishop of Elphin, Dr. Edward Synge. "Blazon of the Coat Armour . . . ," p. 594.
2. In the words of a priest.

60. To Hugh Stafford

RIA, Stowe MS Bi1

Belanagare, 3 October 1759

Sir,

As soon as I received your last letter, I wrote immediately to a friend in Dublin, a very curious researcher into our history and one who is generally happy in discovering such historical fugitives as the author of the *Iphigenia*. He returned me an answer by the last post assuring me that after the closest pursuit of this writer for several years he never yet could drag him out of his lurking place. Would to God that all such works were equally inaccessible! The author was Titular Bishop of Ferns in the unfortunate reign of Charles I and rendered himself odious to the Confederate Catholics[1] through his close connection with the Nuncio Rinuccini,[2] whose conduct here was condemned by the Pope himself. The bishop, a man of poor abilities, undertook the defense of this nuncio's ruinous measures, as well as of the bigoted party who joined him, and at this day his memory would be lost with his book among mankind if the Marquis of Ormond and my Lord Clarendon had not preserved the memory of both by descending so low as to take notice of him. However, as the just offense taken by such great men at the writings of such a man may raise the curiosity of other great men in the present age, I shall not stop at my last disappointment but continue still on the hunt till this obscure writer is run down if possible. I should surely think myself happy could I in the least administer to the entertainment or curiosity of the Bishop of Elphin, undoubtedly a man of the first abilities in this nation, though fatally jealous of the principles of many who injure the public only by their inability to serve it, who through too many legal restraints lie a dead weight upon it. The book I lately sent you was well intended and would the Bishop spare an hour to look into it, I am confident his candor will overlook some faults to which, I think, controversial writings of all kinds are more or less subject. Let me have an account of my young cousins, your children. I am told one of them came lately by an accident which gave me trouble and renders me at present the more uneasy about them. I am with great integrity your very obedient and obliged servant.

1. When the Lords Justices, Borlase and Parsons, expelled the Roman Catholic party from the Dublin parliament, the party set up an executive council, which, in October 1642, formed the Catholic Confederacy of Kilkenny. The Confederacy had a su-

preme Council and an assembly of two houses. It was a Royalist body that sought to restore Catholic power by force. Curtis, pp. 245–247.

2. Papal Nuncio Rinuccini was in Ireland from October 1645 until February 1649. Although Rinuccini had been invited to Ireland by the Confederacy to help "restore public Catholicism and bring Ireland under the spiritual authority of the Pope," the Nuncio allied himself with the O'Neil faction of the Confederacy. When Charles I offered a peace treaty, O'Neil and the Nuncio opposed it. Catholics who favored peace were excommunicated and the peace was rejected. Cromwell and his forces landed in Dublin on August 15, 1649. Curtis, pp. 247–249.

61. To Dr. John Curry

RIA, Stowe MS Bi1

Belanagare, 3 October 1759

Dear Sir,

On my return two days since from Jamestown, I called in Elphin at Mr. Stafford's. He informed me that he put a book which lately came out on the fatal Rebellion in '41 into the Bishop's hands, who promised it an impartial reading. As you might probably have perused that work, you may be envious to know what *so great a man's* thoughts are relatively to it. They are indeed pretty much what I foresaw they would be. "The author," said he, "hath taken great pains to support his facts by authentic testimonies, but I cannot approve of the discretion of gentlemen who, in the present times, revive such facts." Mr. S[tafford] made no reply, nor could it escape his lips that such facts are revived incessantly in the anniversary sermons, pamphlets, and books of the most eminent men among us. But the charge of indiscretion is leveled particularly at any persons who should now have the audacity to controvert any matters set forth in these periodical writings. For my own part, I can not but approve entirely of the equity of this judgment; nor can I see the reason why a people who contended in open for civil justice in a former age should have any historical justice done them in this! Who does not foresee that under [un-]popular governments, unpopular contentions must sometimes arise and that every discomfited party (which party must be surely always in the wrong) owes at least one duty to the public, which is either to applaud the justice done them or leave the honor of the panegyric to others.

In the present case you see that nothing more than a respectful silence is required, and sorry I am that the author of the book I mention did not follow this example set him by his own party for seventy years past! Had he done so, nothing more than the *usual course* would be served up on the approaching anniversary of the 23rd instant. But now I am not without my apprehensions that the perusal of those *Memoirs* may swell the *Bill of Fare* and prove expensive to those for whom such feasts are annually prepared. [Eight lines crossed out.] Here I drop my melancholy subject, having only to add that his L[ordshi]p suspects strongly that the author of the book I mention lives this side of the Shanon. He will doubtless inform others of this idea.

I lay four nights ago in Jamestown nine miles off. It contains an area of four or five plantation acres in an oblong square surrounded with a strong wall of six feet thickness about twenty feet high, though two great gates are broken down. It stretches along the Shanon under a rising ground to the west, and no fortification was ever worse situated for defense. I give you this description of the place as it is almost as famous in history for its Council of Bishops in the Civil War as Trent is for another Council, which is equally the object of popular odium. I have tired you and myself. [Seven lines crossed out.] Adieu.

P.S. The great man set off for Dublin on Monday last. He thought that the not procuring him the *Iphigenia* was owing rather to a design in secreting the work, than to the real want of the book. I request you will do all you can to hunt down this historical fugitive and let him be delivered, *bound up* or even *loose* to one who is so eager to have him examined.

62. To Dr. John Curry

OCD, 8.3 HS 023

26 October 1759

[The first part of the letter is corrupt. O'Conor feels that Irish Catholics should not be silent but should write to counter the histories of Bishop Burnet and Harris.] My friend[1] may have right on his side in this argument; I satisfy myself with having prudence on mine. What of our poor fugitive *Iphigenia*? You shall be my Apollo if you promise me that work. Poor F[ather] Walsh in one of his letters to the Bishop of Ferns censured it much. What then? My friend, above mentioned, answers me that the errors of Protestant and Popish writers in those days of confusion and civil war can not hurt the truth whenever the equity of good government grants truth a fair hearing or patronizes it as in fact it is patronized by the present, notwithstanding the silly peevishness of some who would inspire our governors with different notions, had they but capacity and influence sufficient. [This section of the letter is corrupt. O'Conor returns to commenting on the closed minds of party writers.] My manner with so warm a friend is *quicquid in buccam venerit,*[2] as old Cicero phrased to one of his intimates. I have written by hand this day to our friend.[3] If you and he meet, I hope that you will put him in mind of the pamphlet I wrote for [corrupt] with him on the steady and determined disposition of Catholics to conciliate the government to themselves by that politic conduct which men in their peculiar situation ought at all times to hold; their duty lies within a narrow compass—obedience to a protecting government and gratitude to the mildest and most upright of monarchs.

1. Dr. Edward Synge.   2. Whatever comes to mind.
3. Michael Reilly? Or George Faulkner.

63. To Dr. John Curry, Cow Lane, Dublin

RIA, Stowe MS Bi1

[December 1759][1]

Last post I received enclosed in a letter the *libel* sent to the L[ord] Primate against the late printed *exhortation* of our friends.[2] It is truly a firebrand and my friend facetiously wished that somebody in town had thrown cold water upon it. I could indeed wish that somebody undertook it, conditionally that he had done so with the discretion and moderation which a party in our circumstances should always observe. Adieu, dear sir.

P.S. If you think proper to stir in the affair above represented, I request that my offering anything may be a secret buried in the breasts of Dr. F[itzsimons] and you. By the infatuated conduct of some among us I find that nothing can be kept a week from transpiring. Let the scandalous use made of the late *Pastoral Letter,* etc., witness this.[3] God forgive those who thus exposed us at this time of day to the imputation of a schism among the party on the terms of our civil duty. Surely any little differences on the occasion might be ended rather by secret and charitable conference than otherwise. I send this without a frank. But the importance of the subject and the ease I have in pouring out my heart to a friend must stand for an apology.
[fragment]

1. Undated. Internal evidence indicates this letter was written in late 1759.
2. The "exhortation" was the Address to the King that Anthony Dermot presented to the Speaker of the House, which was later published in the *Parliamentary Gazette*. See Matthew O'Conor, p. 257.
3. *DJ*, 1–5 September 1759, printed an exhortation from Archbishop Lincoln declaiming against Catholics entering into associations and taking oaths.

64. To Dr. John Curry, Cow Lane, Dublin

RIA, Stowe MS Bi1

8 December 1759

Though I did not for some time write *to* you, yet I am much wronged if you be not convinced that I did write *at* you; for I requested of our secretary¹ to communicate to you whatever I have written relatively to the present crisis;² I hated repetitions, I was disgusted with my subject, I feared for our unfortunate divided party, and my wishes were all over with me, as I found them always vain. I once wrote warmly to a citizen of the first rank among the R[oman] C[atholics]. It is to him I ought to write, not to you whose spirit I know too well to need any rousing; I sent a copy for your perusal and for your perusal only, as I desired my correspondent to conceal my activity in an affair wherein the citizens only ought to be active and wherein pressing them to be so would be affronting them; at least my delicacy presumed thus much in their favor, and the consciousness of my own inability taught me a better lesson than attempting to instruct men who either have decided already for their own conduct or who, having not done so, do think very justly that I have no call (except that of impertinence) to give them any instructions about it. These are good reasons for me at least to lie by; and after all, I cannot avoid being in pain (as I know you are) for these men. I am indeed very little surprised at the obstructions given to your political proceedings in Dublin, for you are the least resolute, the least thinking, and the least determined people I ever read of, not excepting the luxuriant example of the *dernière sottise*³ so frequently occurring in the history of our own island! I was not, I say, so little surprised at your divisions about obvious and plain points, as I was at your agreeing about any that might fill half a column in a gazette.

You have exerted yourself powerfully, more consistently indeed with your duty than your usual modesty. From your interposition I expect much good; but if your address be sent in creeping on the crutches of reserve or (it may be) of reservation, the Hyper-doctor was in the right to recommend (for I think he could not command silence).⁴ As that gentleman took it upon him to let you know what *you should not* profess in your civil creed, he ought surely to double the favor by letting you know what *you should,* and in doing this he would only do his duty. It would be following the example set by the Christian Church in all ages as to theological matters. It would be of use I say to know from him and his coadjutors which doctrines of state are orthodox and which are heretical in the present juncture and under the present government, for these civilians have a barometer of their own for the rise and fall of civil principles, it being but reasonable that since they are forbidden the use of such a gloss in ecclesiastical matters they should make themselves some reprisals by another and enable themselves to have our civil obedience as much under their direction as the religious; but our subject is too serious for all this trifling, though the expedient mentioned, ridiculous as it is, has prevailed too much in former ages and prevails to this day. Experience seems to be lost on mankind, and the philosopher who averred that they need not so much to be *informed* as to be *reminded* was certainly wrong if we should apply his rules to our political morals. Our duty to this or any government, one would think, requires but little speculation where the Gospel and reason speak so distinctly and so loudly. What then should create any doubt? Every such doubt could never be infused but by putting of fallacious cases, by perplexing, by disguising plain facts, and by torturing even the Sacred Text to embarrass and mislead. The gentleman above-mentioned threatened to anathematize the citizens who should aver, *that no authority can absolve us from our allegiance to the civil government we live under.* Is allegiance a civil duty commanded by *Him* who ordered the tribute for Tiberius, the abandoned and tyrannical Tiberius? If it be (by the Gospel) a religious as well as a civil duty, does that require any absolution? It were to be wished that the Hyper-doctor gave us his reasons for anathematizing in such a case, for the address supposed not, and indeed it could not suppose any other. In revolutions indeed where government is transferred from one to another and changed from this to that form, subjects in that case are from the nature of things absolved from their former allegiance and begin on the terms of a new compact; but where no such case exists I would gladly know where that authority resides which shall dispense with the duty of active obedience and absolve us also from what never yet was a sin! In the year 1727 the R[oman] C[atholics] here addressed the King on his ascension, and they made use of the very words here censured by the Hyper-doctor. I request you will look into Pue's *Occurrences* for that year to satisfy yourself and to convince you also how much a better sense of things the worthy

A[rch] B[ishop] of that time entertained. After all I am glad that the gentleman so often mentioned has been humored in his own way, as I would prefer any grievances to a schism among ourselves. Those who would make a merit of raising it and of raising themselves in that way when they could not by their talents or capacities do so *in any other* ought to be disappointed. But this is too much even in the querulous temper I am in. I go to the bottom to make room for the seal of this letter.

My son got lately a great cold attended with a lingering fever and a violent pain in the ear. Our physician ordered him to be blooded, and worse blood could not be seen. He fell into a slow sweat for two days and he seems to be much better this day. He has been well for several months before this attack. And I must inform you that the present cold did not yet fall on his lungs, though the discharges of bad stuff from his eructations is pretty considerable. I request you will write by the next post and send all the intelligence you can along with your instructions. Mr. F—'s[5] behavior to you is what I could not conceive he could be guilty of. I am sorry to find fact contradicting my good opinions of the man.

1. Anthony Dermot, secretary of the Catholic Association.
2. The present crisis is the division of the Roman Catholics over the question of addressing an oath of loyalty to the King. In response to a threatened attack of northern Ireland by the French, the Catholic merchants of Dublin presented an address of loyalty, written by O'Conor to Mr. Ponsonby, the Speaker of the House of Commons. The Catholic hierarchy and gentry opposed the address. The lower classes rioted. Commerce in Dublin was at a standstill. See Smollett, *The History of England*, 3, (Philadelphia: Thomas Davis, 1848), 793–795; Matthew O'Conor, *History of the Irish Catholics*, pp. 254–260; and Thomas Wyse, *History of the Late Catholic Association* (London: Henry Colburn, 1829), 1:60–70.
3. The ultimate folly.
4. *DJ*, 1–5 September 1759, printed an exhortation from Archbishop Lincoln which was read in all Catholic chapels in Dublin. He declared all oaths of allegiance "wicked and abominable," "commanded" all oath takers to withdraw from "associations." Offenders were to be "denounced" and "cut off from the Communion of the Faithful." O'Conor understates the Archbishop's opposition to the oath.
5. Probably Mr. French, from whom Dr. Curry is attempting to collect fees for treating Mr. French's son-in-law, Owen MacDermot.

65. To Dr. John Curry, Cow Lane, Dublin

RIA, Stowe MS Bi1

12 December 1759

Dear Sir,

I wrote a long letter to you by last post, and did my paper hold out it would be still longer to punish you for complaining of my long silence. I received a letter from our friend yesterday with the copy of the Hyper-doctor's pastoral letter[1] to the gentlemen who undertook to act for the fellow citizens[2] in addressing theologians in this critical conjuncture. His reasoning is a burlesque, and the wisest men can hardly afford better when they leave the road of wisdom and endeavor to turn others out of it. Such men having personal points to serve and such as they dare not avow must from the very nature of their undertaking fall into the absurd as well as ridiculous. "*You have no right to address.*" Why? "*Because*," says he, "*you are no people*, i.e., you are not subjects but slaves in the *eye of the law.*" Be it so. But if we be slaves, where is the hurt to obtain by every peaceable and every petitionary means in our power a mitigation of the slavery? This is not desired *in terminis;*[3] but, says the sage letter writer, "You ought to express your obedience *by a letter and not by an address like the poor, ignorant people from the remote parts of the kingdom who know nothing of our Constitution.*" By the way, this distinction between an address and an epistle puts me in mind of a dispute between two stupid fellows in the country I live in; one insisted on bargaining with the other for five groats, and the other absolutely denied that he was to pay but sixteen pence. Well, an epistle it should be, not an address and this should be subscribed by as few in number as *possible* that the government may have the fullest conviction *possible* that surely, *est private,*[4] [the] letter is the act of the whole body. This declaration of gratitude and obedience in a whisper is such a refinement in politics as has been reserved for the honor of our own age and country. Who would not wish to be the inventor of it? Did I choose ill-natured remarks, I could go much further; but I detest them in the present case, let them be ever so just. What I dread greatly is that our late pastoral communications and inhibitions will transpire and find their way to the ears of our masters. If so, the evil spirit we wanted to bury will only revive the redoubled jealousy, and the writer of the pastoral might spare himself the caution he gave us against *hypocrisy* and *dissimulation.* May all Catholics guilty in that respect repent and do us and our holy religion justice. I declare it over again that my fears are very strong in the melancholy case I am putting, for if the influence of some should prevail to render the majority of men of property (men of any consequence we are told they are not) from subscribing, you not only destroy the good effect of the address from the *poor remote* Catholics of the kingdom, but you revive the odium so long operating (till of late) against us in the three kingdoms. What equivalent the opposors of any address will or can make us, they best know. If they give it in stirring up persecution for our amendment, I wish we may all have virtue enough to face the fiery trial and derive from it *illam quam mundus dare non potest pacem.*[5] But surely we should not be exposed to such violent temptations in the weakness of our corrupt nature, and they cannot be true friends to religion who would in the least contribute to draw such an evil upon us. I say no more and this from so insignificant a person is, I am afraid, too much. But it is a consolation to a man in pain to pour out the effusions of an honest but querulous mind into the bosom of his friend. Write to me and tell me my fears are ill-grounded. You know I am too much a desponder, and you never fail giving me those comforts which I am unhappy enough never to have it in my power to return back to you in any shape unless you take comfort (as I am sure you do) in this penury of friendship.

P.S. [Crossed out. Reference to Denis's improved health.]

[In another hand: "The meeting above mentioned was adjourned to the twentieth of December following when the address was carried by a majority and signed by three hundred and seven persons. It was forwarded, etc.]

1. This pastoral letter is not the public exhortation referred to in O'Conor's previous letter.
2. The Catholic merchants of Dublin.
3. Unconditionally.   4. Between us.
5. John 14.27. That peace which the world cannot give.

66. To Dr. John Curry, Cow Lane, Dublin

RIA, Stowe MS B¡1

[15 December 1759]

Dear Sir,

By our friend's means¹ I have seen the Address of the R[oman] C[atholic]s of D[ublin]. I am informed that your friends are tearing you to pieces for putting your hand to it. The truth is, they should be sorry in earnest for withdrawing their own. What do the anti-addressers mean? The address is an excellent and spirited one, dictated by the necessity of the times, supported by common prudence, and, what is more, warranted by our common duty. What have they to boast of who pleasure themselves on their opposition to it? What mighty boon have they stored up for us in exchange for the favor which we are losing or which we have already lost through their wise and self-gratifying secession on this critical conjuncture? When Lord Chesterfield was in the government here, he informed the public by a speech in Parliament that our principles in regard to the civil government not only recommended but *justified* restraint. Are our anti-addressers afraid that such an impression made *then* on the public is in danger of being worn out by time, unless we renew it ourselves by an open refusal of contradicting the great authority I have mentioned? Is there a syllable in the address which our holy religion forbids them to avow? Suppose an act were passed to give up to the leading anti-addresser the possessions of his predecessors on the sole condition of subscribing to that address, would he in such a difficulty hesitate long? Does our religion tell us that we are to make no tender of our allegiance unless we *are paid* for it? Or what new casuistry is this, which started up of late among us, that in some cases a public declaration of civil principles is improper for men in our condition, but may however be cautiously preferred in a *private epistolary whisper?* Let such men answer for their casuistry to good sense, to our common cause, and the good of religion as well as they can. *Iliacos intro muros peccator et extra.*[2]. . .

    1. Anthony Dermot, letter to Charles O'Conor, 13 December 1759, Stowe MS. B11, RIA.
    2. There is a sinner within the walls of Troy and without.

67. To Dr. John Curry, Cow Lane, Dublin

OCD, 8.3 HS 023

In festo Nativitatis,
D. N. J. C., 1759

In a festive mood O'Conor asks Curry who was right and who was vindicated by sending an address to the king. O'Conor writes, "They always took our passive obedience to be only temporary and occasional, and your anti-addressers, it should seem, make it a point to confirm them in that opinion, as if disarming power and prejudice by a religious and open profession of our true duty were an evil by all means to be avoided. . . ."

We have shaken off with decent contempt the shackles they intended we should wear, and the extraordinary notice which the government took of our recognizance[1] will be delivered down in history to our credit as well as to the credit of those whom God has commanded us to obey. This event has struck opposition dumb, as it covered it with shame, and I am really angry at you for the pain you were in for some time on account of reproaches made to you as a subscriber by some friends who ought in earnest to reproach themselves for not following your example. After all, I must confess to you very candidly that I am still less in pain for the perverseness of those men than the nonsense of others who drew up the addresses of other cities. What right had those men, chained and fettered by law as they are, to use the style of freemen? This is the rock which you of Dublin avoided with much good sense; you on the contrary touched on the bondage you are under with great delicacy of sentiment; and to that very paragraph you owe your addresses, being so far distinguished from others as to merit being laid before the House of Commons, our Viceroy[2] recommending us by that procedure as objects of real political pity.

1. On 10 December 1759 the Lord Lieutenant replied through the Speaker of the House to Mr. Anthony Dermot and the addressers. The Lord Lieutenant assured the addressers "that the zeal and the attachment which they professed could never be more reasonably manifested than at the present conjuncture, and that so long as they conducted themselves with duty and affection, they could not fail to obtain his Majesty's protection." Matthew O'Conor, *History*, p. 257.

2. The duke of Bedford, John Russell (1710–1771).

68. To Hugh Stafford

RIA, Stowe MS Bi1

21 February 1760

Mr. Stafford had not heard of the activities of the Catholics in Dublin, and O'Conor summarizes the confusing events:

They are the most indetermined people alive, and to the common irresolution they have added indiscretion and folly. Those of Dublin, who doubtless should take the lead among us, are now divided into two parties, *addressers* and *anti-addressers*. The clergy are at the head of the latter, and the glad tidings of this wise *civil schism* have reached the Court. Since the days of Queen Elizabeth to this very year we had not so fair a prospect of standing well with our masters! Here a primate[1] preached before the L[ord] L[ieutenan]t[2] and House of Lords in our favor. The Speaker of the House of Commons[3] delivered the Dublin Address[4] to the Duke, and his Grace writes a letter with his own hand assuring the R[oman] Catholics of his Majesty's protection.[5] See what kind of soil these promising seeds fell upon. They have been blown away by the winds of nonsense, to speak in the most favorable terms; without fissure we are united in no wise measures regarding ourselves or the public, and it should seem that we labor to unite all parties against us. Thus it is in Dublin, and yet some have not dropped all hopes: Mr. Wyse of Waterford has employed an eminent lawyer and state casuist[6] to draw up our case and to show the ill effect of many of the Popery Laws relatively to the public interest. This work is soon to appear in weekly numbers. . . .[7]

1. Archbishop George Stone.
2. The duke of Bedford, John Russell (1710–1771).
3. Mr. John Ponsonby.
4. The Address to the King, written by O'Conor and signed by about 400 Dublin Catholic merchants. Presented to Mr. Ponsonby by Anthony Dermot and John Cromp, Matthew O'Conor, *History of the Irish Catholics*, p. 255.
5. On 10 December 1759, Mr. Ponsonby delivered the lord lieutenant's reply to the Address in the House of Commons. Matthew O'Conor, *History of the Irish Catholics*, p. 257.
6. Henry Brooke.　　　　　　　7. The Farmer's Letters.

69. To Dr. John Curry

RIA, Stowe MS Bi1

29 February 1760

Since I came home I have sent you through Mr. R[eilly] a tender of affection and acknowledgments. I have declared my surprise at the delay in publishing the third letter to the Primate,[1] when its appearance was so necessary to our common cause; I request you will give me a proper information on this head. I read last Tuesday's *Journal* yesterday and am pleased with the short exhortation delivered from our altars at this time of Thurot's attempt on our coast.[2] Mr. Reilly sent me the first of the modern *Farmer's Letters*.[3] I like it extremely. I only dread that our own people, by putting a slight on this first attempt, may discourage the author from proceeding in so useful an undertaking. I beg you will use your influence with your friends (who may use theirs with others) to keep this spirit alive by all possible encouragement till we can extract all the good out of it that it can bear in these times of prejudice and popular error. The author as a Protestant writer must write surely on Protestant principles and could not serve us so effectually had he written on any other.[4] . . .

1. Curry's *Third Appeal to His Grace, the Lord Primate*. The Lord Primate is Archbishop George Stone.
2. Archbishop Lincoln again exhorted his people to "avoid giving the least shadow of offense to the government, either by your behavior or conversation; and by this means to manifest in the most convincing manner in your power the grateful sense we all have of their favorable dispositions towards us." *DJ*, 19–22 February 1760. On 21 February 1760, M. de Thurot led three frigates from Dunkirk and attacked Carrickfergus; there was no rising of Irish Catholics. Instead a large group of volunteers marched from Belfast. After holding the town for five days, Thurot had to give it up and re-embark. Thurot was killed in combat fighting an English fleet which had overtaken him. Lecky, 1:470–471.

3. Reilly obtained an early copy for O'Conor. Patrick Lord advertised that *The Farmer's Case of the Roman Catholics of Ireland* would appear on March the second. *DJ*, 26 February–1 March 1760.

4. The Catholic Association hired Henry Brooke to write pamphlets favoring the Catholic cause. Their thinking was that these arguments would have more force coming from a Protestant. The arrangement did not prove satisfactory because Brooke constantly wanted more money. In 1763 he became editor of his anti-Catholic *FJ* and argued the Protestant cause.

70. To Dr. John Curry

RIA, Stowe MS Bi1

15 March 1760

O'Conor is telling his correspondent, probably Dr. John Curry, (Dr. Charles O'Conor, *Memoirs*, I, 402, ascribes the recipient as Dr. Curry) that he, Curry, was correct in returning the manuscript of the *Farmer's First Letter* to its author, Henry Brooke, without change. Henry Brooke wrote anti-Catholic pamphlets under the name of Farmer. Now he is writing pro-Catholic pamphlets from a Protestant point of view. O'Conor tells Curry that this method will catch the Protestants "in their own way" so that they will come to have a better opinion of Catholics. O'Conor defends Brooke's approach. O'Conor wonders if Brooke would have been read if he did not write from a Protestant position. O'Conor thinks that if Brooke had written from a Catholic point of view, he would still receive even more venomous retorts from Catholics and Protestants. Protestants have been conditioned all their lives to hate Catholic motives, O'Conor says. Consequently a writer, to gain the Protestant ear, must use "not only art but a little honest artifice also to reconcile men to measures which education, custom, and party rage" have conditioned them against.

71. To Dr. John Curry, Cow Lane, Dublin

OCD, 8.3 HS 023

13 May 1760

. . . I had yesterday a letter from poor Lord, our patriot bibliopolist,[1] distinguishable by being at present the greatest sufferer by Popery of any man in the kingdom, for he not only suffers in common with us all as a Papist, but he suffers by our party also. He expended more than eight guineas on the Farmer's scheme and received less than three pounds! Shame to us all that he should be such a sufferer! For my own part I would contribute to repair his expenditure on our account. You are a member of our representative committee, and I trust you have influence enough with your brethren to induce them to contrive ways and means for satisfying minute demands on our party. How shall we bring our great scheme to bear if we fail or even hesitate in little things? We Protestants and Papists are united on the principle of indolence, however we may be separated on every other. The *Farmer's* fourth letter is an excellent piece, and neither party gives it attention. . . .

1. In the *DJ*, 13–17 May 1760, O'Conor's "patriot bibliopolist," Patrick Lord, advertised Brooke's pamphlets: "This day is published and sold by P. Lord, Bookseller, at the Angel and Bible in Cook Street, price three pence each. The *Farmer's* First, Second, Third and Fourth *Letters of the Case of the Roman Catholics of Ireland*. In a Course of Letters from a Member of the Protestant Church in that Kingdom to a Friend in England. Wherein the Popery Laws are Considered and Arguments Drawn to show how They are Prejudicial to the Protestant Interest, in Particular, as well as that of the Public in General and that the Reasons and Motives which Give Rise to those Laws no longer subsists [sic]."

72. To Dr. John Curry, Cow Lane, Dublin

RIA, Stowe MS Bi1

24 May 1760

Lord Trimleston[1] has placed himself as the head of the Dublin Catholic Association. The members have contributed funds to the association, money which Trimleston has now refused to return to the members. O'Conor chastises Curry for being foolish enough to associate with Trimleston and to allow him to continue as the head of the association. Mr. Lord, the printer of the Farmer's letters by Henry Brooke, has complained that he is losing money on the sale of the Farmer's pamphlets. Lord mentions that a group of Catholics in Dublin would like to form a larger association which would encompass more Catholics than those living and working in Dublin.[2] Henry Brooke has written O'Conor and offers to be the secretary of a new association. Brooke argues that his connections in the government would help the Catholics.[3]

1. Nicholas Barnewall (1726–1782). *BP*, p. 2509. Lord Trimleston was entrusted by the Catholic Association with its funds collected from the merchants of Dublin to help lobby for the recision of the Penal Laws. When the Catholics broke into groups of Addressers and Anti-Addressers, Lord Trimleston refused to return the money. O'Conor and Curry contacted their friend, Viscount Nicholas Taaffe, to ask Trimleston to relent and give back the money. Lord Taaffe wrote to Trimleston on the 4th and 18th of April without success. Finally Anthony Dermot, with Trimleston's consent, relinquished the money to be used for other activities of the Association. Matthew O'Conor, *History of the Irish Catholics*, pp. 274–277. See also Wyse 1:82.
2. Wyse, 1:68, detailed the plan his father had for a more encompassing association with greater representation. Wyse set forth this plan at the Elephant Tavern, Essex Street, in April 1760.
3. Brooke wrote O'Conor about an association being formed to lobby on legislative measures before the Privy Council. Brooke wrote that his association was "already approved and entered into by several of the Privy Council and chiefs of this kingdom

whereby I am appointed secretary for register in all proposals that shall be deemed of national utility in order to have the same promoted by Parliament, and if I can push this association into proper effect, the next session, I trust, will be productive of all the advantages we desire." Consequently O'Conor wanted Curry to remind Thomas Wyse and other members of the Catholic Association to tolerate and use Brooke gently. Henry Brooke to Charles O'Conor, 20 May 1760. Stowe MS Bi1, RIA.

73. To Dr. John Curry, Cow Lane, Dublin

RIA, Stowe MS Bi1

18 June 1760

 Everything I hear from Dublin at this time displeases me. The trade of printing and publishing is, I believe, at the lowest ebb, but I can hardly persuade myself that curiosity and desire of information are so far laid asleep as the publisher of the *Third Appeal* pretends, for I have, even in this country of vandals, seen a couple of copies of it.[1] You should, therefore, be well informed about this affair before you submit to a tax which your public virtue imposed but which your experience will arrest, in this case, for the future. What signifies the public virtue of one, two, or six men where folly and perverseness struggle for superiority in the breasts of a whole people! Let us take up with employments less vain and less painful than that of an attempt to rouse or inform such a people. For my own part I have laid aside the bow without a thought of our taking it up again. I have shot my bolt, and though it be a fool's one, yet have I wisdom enough not to repeat the folly. I had a long letter yesterday from Mr. Lord and another from Mr. R[eilly]. The former sends me an account stated debtor and creditorwise relatively to the *Farmer's Letters,* and he brings in the public £5.11.1 indebted to him. Of the last of the four letters already published he could sell but seventy-nine copies, and he dares not, after this discouragement, venture upon the publication of the fifth letter. Notwithstanding the prudent resolution I took not to meddle with public affairs for the future, yet I am sorry that the *Farmer's* undertaking should stop till the *Farmer* himself laid aside the pen. Our masters, by having the whole performance complete before them, might be brought to come into some composition with their own prejudice, and were this the case they would *on their own account* give some relief to our unfortunate and insensible people. *Lord,* I think, deserves some consideration. I would drop half a guinea to indemnify him, and it is a sorrowful consideration that your city should (in their representative capacity of a Committee) see such a man complain a moment about the paltry sum of £5.11, even though they have no fund yet in their hands to supply any deficiencies or encourage any new undertaking. So much on that head.

I, last week, have written to our friend, and among other things I at last broke silence in regard to *the hospital*.² I had but a very melancholy account from him by yesterday's post; he is undone! From my heart I pity a breast corroded with the most mortifying circumstantials on this side of the grave, that of embezzling the little dependence on cripples, public orphans, and sickly derelicts! He knows not what turn to give himself, and so distracted is he with his present reflections that he requests I should not finger his sores by writing any more to him on that subject! It would not be the part of friendship surely to grant him such a request; I will endeavor to persuade him not to make his condition worse by dropping in a fit of coward-despondency those arms of defense which the highest adversity puts generally into our hands when we have resolution enough to use them. Whatever such arms bring (be it ever so little) it will lessen the sum of misery. May he not get some advance from Mr. Wall in the way of anticipation of his salary? May he not apply in this distress to Lord and Lady Kingsland?³ Purcell, his father-in-law, has an interest of about £40 a year in Ship Street. Could not a sum be borrowed on that annual interest? I have a scheme by which at least he will get ten guineas, the scheme of *Macaria*.⁴ These expedients wisely managed might possibly rescue him from that immediate ruin which an inactive conduct will render inevitable. I write to him this night feelingly on this subject, notwithstanding his interdict. It would be well for you that you never knew him or me. On our account you suffer present pains, but we are both honest men, yet I am afraid that he is not so cautious in regard to contingencies as I am. My sensibility would never admit me to embezzle money, which without your friendship I could never touch. I say no more. For God's sake find some expedient to make me copy about this unfortunate man, if that be possible, and write soon.

1. Dillon Chamberlaine of Smock Alley, Dublin, publisher of Curry's *Third Appeal*, advertised it for sale in the *DJ*, 1–5 April 1760.
2. O'Conor is referring to Michael Reilly, who has embezzled money from the Foundling Hospital. The *DJ* for the months of April and May contain several notices for the collection of money by both Protestants and Catholics for the Foundling Hospital. For example, in 10–13 May, the *Journal* asked for donations "for the support of foundling children . . . most of the foundlings being offspring of Roman Catholics." Another notice advertised the sale of a sermon by a Protestant, William Henry, D.D., entitled *The Cries of the Orphans*, "a sermon preached in the parish church of St. Michaels on Sunday, April 26, 1760, the day appointed for a general collection for the support of the orphans in the Foundling Hospital." *DJ*, 10–13 and 13–17 May 1760; 31 May–1 June 1760.
3. Lord Kingsland is Henry Barnwall, a Catholic.
4. *Macariae Excidium, Narratives Illustrative of the Contests in Ireland in 1641*. BMCPBCE, 18:1043.

74. To Dr. John Curry, Cow Lane, Dublin

OCD, 8.3 HS 023

20 August 1760

My dear Friend,

You must undoubtedly have a great loss by the miscarriage of my last to you, were you to rate it by the number of lines, for it cost me three long pages in large post paper. No matter, you will like this short script better for two reasons which I need not mention. Did I love revenge I had more than enough on the score of the miscarriage; but I really lament the fate of Mr. Birmingham, our Roscommon postmaster, a gentleman of £800 a year and a good neighbor so far as good negative qualities entitled him to that character. He has been for some considerable time hypochondriac and last Wednesday morning shot himself dead. I am grieved to hear of the apathy of our Roman Catholic friends in the city. On them we had our chief dependence. You alone have acted the part of a patriot, and from experience I am not so much surprised at the small acquisition you have made among our people as at your making any at all. I am, however, obliged to my friend Mr. Reynolds[1] and to the few others who adhere to you. I had last week a letter from Mr. Lord complaining still of his sufferings by the *Farmer's Letters*. As he suffered on *our* account it is surely *our cause*. I could wish his loss was repaired to him, and I would myself contribute. You and I (you particularly) have acquitted ourselves singularly to our party. We should not be tired still, were it of any use. I am thankful to my worthy friend, Dr. Reddy,[2] who would bring me back from the consideration of our present unfortunate times to the past from which I first started to the study of more ancient and better times within the limits of our own island. Any assistance I can afford in giving a clearer notion of those times than we have had hitherto is at his disposal. Alas! My assistance is next to nothing, not only because my studies relative to our ancient history have been long interrupted, but because materials at this distance from libraries are extremely few. The *Farmer* has already solicited me on this head and offered his own elegant pen to set off the matter. I answered with truth that my avocations and want of materials rendered me too feeble a crutch to be leaned upon, especially without those materials which lie at such a distance from me. But I repeat again what I said above, that the Doctor and Abbé shall want no assistance in my power.

I recall with pleasing melancholy the happy nights I had with the

Doctor, poor Duany and you. This pleasure recurs the oftener when I sit (as of necessity I must) with ignorance, selfish folly, and provoking impertinence here in my own western province. Your correspondence is a great relief to me; thus you bring Dr. Reddy and me again together. What would I not give to have you both within the attention of the *ear* as I have you so often by the *eye!* Were I not confined to a circle, and a narrow one, I should surely run and have you within intuitive enjoyment. Narrow as this circle is, I have yet ambition enough to look beyond it and resolution enough now and then to force my way through it, though not beyond the limits set by prudence. I am amazed at our friend's insensibility in regard to the hospital. I shall with your permission rouse him once more that I may not be deficient in the duty I owe him as his friend. Some men ought to be stimulated who without the spur will not come to the end of their journey on which alone their own personal safety depends. I have written to him by this post acquainting him with the good plan I have laid for bringing the *History of Macaria* to light. Lest this should miscarry like my last, I desired him make my compliments and explain my intentions to Dr. Reddy and you. I have a mind to be prating something to fill up the remainder of the scanty half sheet. It is the sort of paper we call *pro patria*,[3] and it is on such surely I ought to write when I write to you. . . .

When our millers made the page so scanty, it was probably from the reflection of the scantiness of our *pro patria* spirit. If this conjecture be right, it is, no doubt, the first satire that ever appeared upon blank paper.

1. James Reynolds is a colleague of O'Conor's and a member of the Ash Street, Dublin, family who were merchants in wool and silk. Wall, "The Rise of a Catholic Middle Class in Eighteenth Century Ireland," p. 111.
2. Probably Richard Reddy (b. c. 1718). *The Correspondence of Edmund Burke*, ed. Thomas W. Copeland (Chicago: The University of Chicago Press, 1958), 1:225n.
3. Patriotic.

75. To Dr. John Curry

OCD, 8.3 HS 023

16 September 1760

This letter is O'Conor's third attempt to reach Curry in Dublin, Curry's letters arrive, but Curry tells O'Conor that he is in arrears to O'Conor. O'Conor has little historical material available at Belanagare to help Curry's friend Dr. Reddy do any historical writing. O'Conor congratulates Curry on the publication of his *Memoirs* and cajoles him to keep writing "now that your hand is in" and to write another pamphlet on historical affairs.

76. To Dr. John Curry

OCD, 8.3 HS 023

3 October 1760

O'Conor commiserates with Curry concerning Lord's losses on the poor sale of Brooke's pro-Catholic *Farmer's Letters*, and Reilly's attempts to pay back embezzled money by promoting an edition of the *Macaria*. Shake Reilly up, O'Conor advises Curry, and tell him that O'Conor is trying to help. O'Conor's social news concerns his meeting with Chevalier Taylor:

On the day after his dining with the Bishop of Elphin I met here the famous oculist Taylor.[1] He is drunk with vanity, and of all men was the unfittest to sooth the vanity of another. In relation to the present state of Europe he contradicted the Cardinal in almost every particular. This incident gave me no pain. Taylor, whose manual dexterity brought him into the most conspicuous circles of mankind, has contracted from long habits an indifference to the smaller subordinations and to the value which the most limited set on themselves. He is called a forward and impudent man when, in fact, he estimates things by their real value not as a philosopher but as a traveler. You have a medical present to make to your country. Let it be worthy of you, for it is worthy of all your care and knowledge. Those who quarrel with truth in an historical process will, however, embrace it in a physical one. Though we have different interests (real or supposed) in civil affairs, we have none at all in what is common to all as material beings.

1. John Taylor (1703–1772), though a skilled oculist, a bombastic charlatan. *Concise DNB*, 1:1279.

77. To Dr. John Curry

OCD, 8.3 HS 023

15 October 1760

Curry has written O'Conor from Norris's Coffee House, and the thought of Dublin society and friends in a coffee house brightens O'Conor's day. However, this bright touch lasts only a moment, and O'Conor relates Denis's symptoms—a "complaint in the breast from which he has been thoroughly free since the vernal equinox, and yet he thinks he got no cold to account for so sudden a change." More bad news is the indecision of Henry Brooke to write a fifth *Farmer's Letter.* O'Conor tells Curry that playing cards for entertainment is boring compared with reading old Irish Annals. He congratulates Curry on the effects that Curry's pamphlets are having on members of the Ascendency:

Let me go back to the past from which I started, from the consideration of present times to those that are long since past. *Cogor iam cursus iterare relictos,*[1] as Horace phrases it. Several years since, I have written an historical account of our Irish Kings from the reception of Christianity to the dissolution of our monarchy; that book I burned. I am now sitting down to a second draft, and this, if finished, I may burn also. No matter. It will find employment for an idle hour, which I by no means will dedicate to cards while an old annal lies before me. Could I do anything to my own liking in such a work, vanity (which at my time of life no wise man would entertain) will have the smallest share in it. I propose something better, the bringing home to the heart by historical examples that wisdom which all our speculations have attempted to infuse in vain. This has been the well-judged plan of the three letters to the Lord Primate,[2] and we have certainly felt some good effects from them operating privately and in some degree (as you know) operating publicly also.

1. This is a paraphrase from Horace's *Carmina,* 1.34.3–5. I am constrained to embark again upon courses which I had abandoned.
2. Curry's *Appeals* to Archbishop George Stone.

78. To Dr. John Curry

OCD, 8.3 HS 023

24 November 1760

Writing from his room after entertaining prospective in-laws, O'Conor talks about marriage arrangements he is making for his elder son Denis. Since Denis's health is precarious, O'Conor tells Curry that the girl O'Conor has picked for Denis is one of a quiet nature, one who "affords the least likelihood of storms and tempests."[1] O'Conor comments on his frustrations as a historian:

Are you laboring at our medical work? Our Irish climate and Irish habits require instructions which are not yet given and which no foreign physician (however able) can give. You have laid the foundations, and you should not be lazy in rearing an edifice which your fame and (much more) your duty calls upon you to finish. Lazy as I am, I have been delineating something this winter, but my annals are no better than a file of newspapers, and I apprehend that such materials are to an historian what a barren invention is to a poet. The historical, like the poetical harvest will be poor indeed, and who can be found who will come to share in the repast we can afford?

1. Denis's approaching marriage to Catherine Browne, daughter of Martin Browne of Cloonfad.

79. To Dr. John Curry

RIA, Stowe MS Bi1

[Late 1760][1]

My Dear Sir,

I have written to you by hand four days since acknowledging my obligations to you. By the same hand you will receive five guineas which I owe you. I am ashamed and confused at your proposal to me in yours of last post. But I must forgive your bad treatment of me on the score of your partiality for me. It must be owing to you that I should be thought of in the affair of *an Address*[2] where so many men my superiors in every capacity must see nothing in an endeavor of mine but my arrogance or insufficiency. In my best and most vacant hour I could not do much, and what I should attempt would be only for a friend like you, who would doubtless throw a veil over my faults or correct them before they should be submitted to any other censure. I have been all this day upon the conclusions of [a] match for my son,[3] and this minute I conclude more vastly to the satisfaction of those I treated with than to my own. I am sick of mind and body from the action of the one on the other. See then how fit I am at this minute for any thing of what your partiality expects from me. I send you such *outlines* as now occur to me, and to you alone I send them that you may have a conviction of the deference I owe even to your most impracticable advices to me.

"THE ADDRESS ETC.

"We, your majesty's most dutiful and loyal subjects, the R[oman] C[atholic]s of Ireland, humbly beg leave to approach your Majesty with a *Tender of our* loyalty on your Majesty's happy accession to the Throne of these realms. (your ancestors)

"While we congratulate your M[ajesty] on the happy period put to jealousies, which generally divided, and to mistrusts, which too often weakened those kingdoms in former times; while all denominations of men are now laboring to be [forever] in the exertion of every duty and affection towards your Majesty [torn] and government; while every circumstance of affairs at home and abroad unite for [torn] happiness and future glory of your reign: permit us, Sir, to [torn] with your Majesty and pour out our sincere sorrow for the loss we have sustained by the death of a Monarch who has ever approved himself the common father of all his people: a loss the *more feeling* on our part as the repose we have so long enjoyed proceeded *entirely* from his Majesty's clemency and compassion.

"Ever since the accession of your Majesty's R[oyal] House to the throne of these kingdoms, we have in a particular manner experienced the paternal interposition of your Majesty's two R[oyal] Predecessors. We, *Sir*, most gracious sovereign, who are obnoxious to the operation of *such numberless Penal Laws* and so unfortunately distinguished from the rest of our loyal fellow subjects can not subsist a moment but by the royal protection of your Majesty's government.

"Sensible of the same hereditary compassion in your Majesty's breast, we beg leave to hope for that share in the happiness of your reign which our peculiar circumstances can admit. *We beg leave* to assure your Majesty *of our grateful return* of affection and loyalty, a loyalty *which no legal pressures can weaken* and which our religion enforces under the severest penalties.

"That your Majesty's reign over us may be long as it is happy is our constant prayer, and could we presume to add another it would be that every loyal subject in your Majesty's dominions may be free from every legal restraint which might be a bar to your majesty's clemency or the general prosperity of the public."

If you find but one line to spare in the above endeavor, I have my end. Now on reading it over I am thinking it is better than if I studied it beyond my strength.

1. Undated.   2. The *Address to George III.*
3. A marriage agreement between the eldest son Denis and Catherine Browne was made in 1760. Upon this marriage Charles O'Conor gave up to Denis the family residence in Belanagare and moved to the cottage he called his "Hermitage" which he had built on the estate. Charles Owen O'Conor, *The O'Conors of Connaught* (Dublin: Hodges, Figgis, and Co., 1891), pp. 296–297.

80. To Dr. John Curry, Cow Lane, Dublin

OCD, 8.3 HS 023

Coolavin, 29 December 1760

Dear Sir,

I send you this from Mr. MacDermot's[1] house in the County of Sligo. With him I now live in great festival, and I am happy in his family as far as my circumstances in life can permit. While you have been debating in Dublin about forms, etc., and while I have been in some suspense whether I should wait or not for your new regulations, behold a domestic event which absorbed all my thoughts and indeed all my affections: on the 21st instant my mother died: a good mother, a good neighbor, an honest woman, an excellent pentitent! She who tended my infant state with extreme tenderness, who was a comfort to me in my advanced age I have lost! This is a wound which I still feel at heart; but resignation is my duty in this as in all other contingencies, and when I think of this pious woman hereafter I shall make it my prayer to imitate her in her good actions and arrive at her worthy end. This event (I say) has put a temporary stop to my activity in the affair of the subscriptions.[2] I got some and I here send you their names, as the address is now at Belanagare and cannot be sent up till I go home. May God, my dear friend, grant you many a happy new year. May your family be a comfort to you, and may no disturbance arrive to interrupt it particularly by mortality till you, in a distant period, precede them by your own dissolution.

Subscribers who signed the address[3] before the 20th instant:

Edmund French of Bela., Esq.
John French of ditto
Robert Plunkett, Esq.
Charles Plunkett, gent.
Michael Plunkett of Ox-Hill, gent.
Michael Plunkett of Ardkeena, Esq.
Edmund Tiernan of Tulsk, mercht.
Robert Kelly, Esq.
James Tiernan of Strokestown, mercht.
Patrick Mahon, ditto, mercht.
Dominick Mahon of ditto, mercht.
Charles Mahon of ditto, mercht.
Martin Brown of Cloonfad, gent.

Roger Flynn, gent.
Michael Flynn, gent.
Edmond Corr of Roscommon, gent.
Michael MacDermot of ditto, gent.
James MacDermot, gent.
John Croughan of Roscommon, mercht.
John Purcell of Roscommon, mercht.
Pat Lynch of Roscommon, mercht.
Hugh Stafford of Elphin, apothecary
Andrew Comyn of ditto, gent.
Andrew Martin of ditto, gent.
O'Conner Don of Ballintubber
Dominick O'Conor of ditto
Charles O'Conor of ditto
Owen O'Conor of ditto
Roger O'Conor of ditto
Denis O'Conor of ditto
Dennis O'Conor of Belaghnadarn
T. O'Conor of ditto
Hugh O'Conor of Ballintubber

Four times this number could be gotten if the address could be sent into the several quarters of the country.

1. Myles MacDermot, O'Conor's son-in-law.
2. Dr. John Curry wrote O'Conor on 24 November 1760 that the previous day their committee had voted O'Conor to draft an address to George the Third. Stowe MS Bil, RIA.
3. The Dublin Committee adapted O'Conor's address and circulated copies in the provinces for signatures. In all 600 Catholics signed. Matthew O'Conor, *History*, p. 269.

81. To Dr. John Curry, Cow Lane, Dublin

OCD, 8.3 HS 023

Jamestown, 19 January 1761

Dear Sir,

I have been from home since I received your letter of the 9th instant and have this day repassed the Shannon from the Diocese of Armagh where I have been doing some business for a poor widowed sister of mine. Let these rambles account for my impunctuality as a correspondent. I am concerned but am not surprised at your unmeaning differences, difficulties, hypercriticisms, etc., relative to an address.[1] Thus it must be with people so peculiarly circumstanced as we are: we do not well know how to word what the Constitution seems to forbid us to speak. Self-sufficiency, timidity, and pride (contradictory as those passions are) throw in their weight, and from this combination of things I expect nothing or what is next to it. I could wish strongly that you kept the Farmer a-going, let his price be what it will. Till our enemies turn advocates for us, nothing can be done for us. For my part I have done with these affairs. My efforts have only gained me ill will from many of our own people. If ever I attempt anything for public instruction, it will for the future be in your way by historical lessons. I write confusedly here in a public house with the eyes of the company upon me. We have here the ruins of old fortifications and the noblest river in the three kingdoms before us. You cannot forget that the place is famous (like Trent) for the council held here in the days of Cromwell. I shall soon, God willing, be able to write to you something more consistently put together than what I now send. I would rather remit any scrawl than leave you any longer in suspense about the cause of my silence, where public and private duty require my breaking it.

P.S. I request that you will write as soon as you can.

1. *An Address to George III*. See Wyse, 1:71–74.

82. To Dr. John Curry, Cow Lane, Dublin

OCD 8.3 HS 023

6 February 1761

My Dear Sir,

Your very welcome letter of the 31st of last month I received by the last post. It arrived at a time when I looked on the affair undertaken by our people as utterly desperate, and I hinted as much in a scrawl I wrote to you from Jamestown. I received great pleasure from the share my worthy friend, Lord Taaffe, took in this affair, nor could we expect much from it if men of rank and others of the party known to the public (by their fortunes or professions) had not put their hands to it.[1] Several such I am afraid have neglected to subscribe. Despair, or pride, or indifference, or unmeaning motives have arrested their hands, and with these we must bear as with the other moral evils of life. Will it be overlooked that our ecclesiastics to a man have been entirely passive in the prosecution of this measure? The *only men* among us against whom the Popery Laws are not put in execution! The only *licensed* Roman Catholics in the Kingdom![2] We the laity indeed may see no end of our sorrows, but *our* address to the throne will certainly have a good effect with regard *to them*, and it must be one of those contradictions in life (of which life is full) to find them very little obliged to their benefactors. They may no doubt think themselves affronted that they have not on this occasion been called upon to prescribe in our civil as well as our religious duties, and had they sufficient knowledge in the former as well as in the latter case, we should be much to blame if we did not give them the weight they ought to have in deliberations which so much concern us both. But the leading men seem to want political knowledge more than their predecessors in former reigns, or they are foreclosed by some private reasons of their own, which if wisdom cannot *avow*, religion can never *approve*. Be this as it will, I have some hope that the government will consider them as associates in our address, and the more as they think we can do nothing without the advice or consent of this order of men. *Aliquis malo usus in illo*,[3] unless they deprive *us* of *this use* by declarations that they had no hand in our address, but it is to be presumed that they have more discretion. My concern on this head made me unawares enlarge too much on it.

I now return to the immediate object of your letter. The Primate,[4] as you observe, is doubtless a most worthy person, and were men of his temper at the head of the Protestant cause for two hundred years past, we should not have the history of Christendom disgraced by dissensions and those concomitant evils which can have no place where the spirit of Christianity prevails. Worthy as this prelate is from so happy a natural disposition, yet the public *appeals* to him, which I have seen, and some other papers on our affairs have, I am convinced, had a good effect on a man who wishes so well for the public and confesses how really it suffers by clapping bolts and manacles on two-thirds of the industrious and laboring part of our people. I am rejoiced to find that among so many essays the putting of the last hand to the address fell upon you, unwilling as you were to have either the envy or the honor of it. The peevish and self-sufficient will envy you; the good men who live now and the men who are not alive yet will honor you, for you will be known to posterity when those selfish gentlemen I hint at will not. I could wish ardently that our *Farmer* was kept in good humor; you told me he would, for your hopes are always stronger than mine. Let me be better assured that they are better grounded than my despondency. The retaining such a man in our service ought by no means to be neglected. I request that you will as soon as possible give me the history you promise of the dictatorial peer who put himself at the head of two counties when he failed in putting himself at the head of the whole party. As our ends are the same, his secession can do no hurt. I request you will pay Mr. George Faulkner, my particular friend, one guinea for me in discharge of what I owe him for his *Journal* during this last year. The post officer in Roscommon does not do me justice in the transmittal of that paper, and I think I ought to drop it. I shall by the next safe hand send you what you will pay him, and I have great occasions for your indulgence relative to the sums I take up so freely and many other troubles I give you from time to time. You have no alternative left but to discharge the friend you gave yourself or bear with the expense of him. I am growing old and would gladly have a license from a vigorous fast at one meal where fish is scarce. I suffered in the last Lent, and I fear for my constitution in this. Your patient here remits you his gratitude and best wishes. He appears no better than in any year for nine years past. I am thinking he is finished with it somewhat and that like *Sixtus* he rears up his head upon getting the keys of my house.[5] I shall write next to Cousin Reilly, for I am long in arrears to him. I am doing what I can to forward the affair of *Macaria;* and I do not (notwithstanding the delay attending it) despair of letting it agoing to his advantage. If you see him you'll please to tell him this. I am really in pain about him, though I would not one moment, could I, extricate him out of his troubles. Give my affection, my dear friend, to your worthy family; and when you see Lord Taaffe, put him in mind of the gratitude of my family to him, of my mother's death also.

1. Lord Taaffe supported the *Address,* but Trimleston opposed it. For a fuller treatment of their disagreement see Wyse, 1:73–81.
2. O'Conor drew up the *Address,* and the Association transmitted it to all parts of Ireland. Six hundred people signed it. However, the nobility and gentry of Meath and Kildare met at Trim and refused to sign. Instead they drew up their own address. Both addresses to the new King were accepted and printed in the London *Parliamentary Gazette*. Matthew O'Conor commented, "The clergy from motives of prudence and unwillingness to interfere in these disputes did not sign either of the Addresses." Matthew O'Conor, *History*, p. 269.
3. There is some use in that misfortune.
4. Archbishop George Stone.
5. Denis has taken over his father's house at Belanagare.

83. To Dr. John Curry, Cow Lane, Dublin

OCD, 8.3 HS 023

[13 March 1761]

I return you my warmest thanks for what I liked first and what you have written last in your letter of the tenth instant. I mean the very witty and very poignant verses on the arch-presbyter and his zealous co-operators with the Grand Jury of Dublin. Whoever the author is, I dare promise you *that he has a better ingredient in the composition of verses than indignation,* laudable as indignation must be on such an occasion given to it where the ravens are spared and the pigeons punished. The ridicule is indeed powerful and wrought up to the highest pitch that humor could raise it. I like this little piece too well, and I know its value too well not to preserve it from the mortality of the circulating modern manuscript, and I see no reason why it may not appear without offense in some of the public papers. By the way, I hope I think too favorable of our own clergy to suspect that any among them acted an underpart in the plot of Stephen's Street. One of the chaplains is my particular friend and countryman, Mr. Fitzgerald,[1] who had been my constant intimate in Mrs. Birmingham's house. Before the Oratory was opened in Stephen's Street he communicated his design to me. I requested of him by all means to have the Hyper-doctor's consent, and whether he followed my advice or not I know not, though I know what I suspect and what you will readily guess. God help us! What may we apprehend from enemies to whom we are literally captives when enmity and contention among ourselves league with those enemies to our undoing? Or is it any alleviation of the evil that the contempt of such enemies may help to blunt the edge of their hatred? We want good sense and common sense among us. I am afraid we want true zeal also. You who are endowed with these blessings, what have you not suffered by the want of them in others, nay what have you not suffered by the exertion of them? But I must recall the last line. The consciousness of doing your duty and of putting some life into our expiring cause will render what you suffered a mere feather counterpoised with that consciousness. Yet a feather which may be light may be sharp-pointed also. Its irritation will give some pain to so sensible a mind as yours; and I know that it had its effect with me to a degree which induced a strong resolution to leave party advocation for the future in the hands of more able and more resolute advocates than myself. Must I not be reduced to despondency by the account you give me of the nonsense of so many among ourselves who thought it more prudent to let the dirt thrown upon us in the *London Chronicle* stick, rather than throw it back on the head of him who raked it? Does not this incident offer us a decent and (may I say) a desirable opportunity of publishing to the world our true principles relative to civil government. What but the declaration of such principles and the frequent repetition of them (so as to make *at last* some impression on our *masters*) can entitle us to the repeal of any one penal law? When industry, the culture of our island, the public happiness, are all kept at a stand *on our account,* will not legislative wisdom one day or other apply some cure to the wound given to the public interest through our sides when this wisdom gets a conviction of its being safe in administering such a cure? But this is too much for you. I am glad that the refutation you mention has been sent off to appear in the very paper wherein the charge was made against us. It has been drawn up by a certain gentleman of my acquaintance. I have no doubt of its being effectual as far as prejudice (which is not over-fiery in the heads of our present ministry) will admit it to be efficacious. Could we since the first invasion of our island boast of such a secretary (I mean Mr. Pitt), such a viceroy, such a primate, as the present? Never had we surely a better security from prejudice, religious or national! In the refutation sent off, I would warmly wish that the motto from Lord Clarendon in the *Historical Memoirs* was advantageously thrown in. The authority of such an able, or rather such a popular, adversary must have great weight with minds too preoccupied against surer and better authority. Now that I mention the *Memoirs,* how came it that *Mr. Hume* of Edinburgh, was not served with a copy as I often requested? Surely this ought not to be omitted, as that gentleman will probably give another edition of his *History* and be obliged for any lights which render it still more valuable to the public.

You have been ill-treated with respect to the *Farmer,* and indeed in every other respect, but I request you will sacrifice your resentment on this fairest prospect we ever had. Write to Mr. Wyse that he may prompt and spur Dublin indolence. Do you prompt, shame, and spur also. Had the *Farmer's* undertaking been complete and brought into one pamphlet on the approach of next session, it would doubtless operate in our favor. The smallest alleviation of our misery would be a great point gained and prove the ernest of a still greater future alleviation. *Tu ne cede malis, sed contra audentior ito.*[2] I believe my last long letter to you has miscarried. It rolled chiefly on a just resentment of Lord Trimleston's treatment of our people in their representative committee.[3] When will your medical work be finished? Is it not a shame and a reproach that no able man of your profession has yet given those instructions relatively to our climate and its physical causes and effects which the ablest foreigner cannot possibly give? You, who in the long course of experience must know our constitutions, what most affect them, and what best can help them by preventatives and by remedies, should take the honor of this task while we have the profit. 'Tis a great honor surely to be useful, after your surrender of life, what every man must surrender. May yours be long and happy in friends and fortune. Mr. Faulkner has been mistaken in saying I did not owe him a guinea; I request you will pay him one on my account. You see how loosely and even solecistically I always write my prolix letters to you: *quicquid in buccam venerit*[4] is for our friends.

13 March 1761

    1. Mr. Fitzgerald became O'Conor's confessor at Belanagare. Perhaps this plan to become O'Conor's confessor is Fitzgerald's "design."
    2. Virgil, *Aeneid*, 6.95. "Do not yield to misfortune but oppose it with greater boldness."
    3. According to Wyse, 1:75–76, Trimleston refused to recognize the right of any group other than the aristocracy to participate in governmental matters. Thus his opposition to the *Address* which came largely from the commercial class of Catholics.
    4. Whatever comes to mind.

84. To Dr. John Curry, Cow Lane, Dublin

OCD, 8.3 HS 023

[12 May 1761]

    Could I come at a frank the last post, you should be troubled with as good, a better, or a worse letter than this I am now writing. In letters to a friend, I would indeed pay proper regard to the matter (did it lie in the way) but very little to the style. I would only guard against illiberal improprieties, the surest indications either of a want of respect or a want of common abilities; and yet you who seek only a friend's heart can overlook everything else. How else could you bear with my idle complaints and idler bagatelles for five years past? I call my complaints idle, when I see no remedy for the shameful conduct of our own people in whom you and a few others have been long endeavoring to infuse some spirit. You have labored surely in vain when in your representative capacity as a committee you bear with the dictatorial taunts of a single person[1] who has usurped the property of the public and who refuses to be accountable for it except in his own way, not in theirs. Do you not, gentlemen, deserve his treating you in this manner? They who can tamely bear such treatment deserve it most certainly. What service has that gentleman ever done you, except by a certain address penned by himself wherein the turgid style and puerile sentiments helped to set off that drawn up in your committee: that address, whose natural graces could not be better seen or recognized than by setting up the foil to it which we have seen. Were I one of your committee (what pity it is that I am not) I would humbly move that this gentleman should be exempted from all future trouble in regard to the application of our little public fund. I would with great deference also urge that in regard to the uses it should be applied to there is nothing so difficult or embarrassing as may not come within the extent of our own common penetration, without the dictatorship of any one person who might presume to exert a power over it. He lodged the money in an honest man's hands, but surely he did so under the control of the proprietors, and whether expressed or tacit is all alike. The committee as representatives of those proprietors have a right to ease him of the burden and fulfill to the best of their power the intention of their constituents, so little hitherto regarded. If the dictator should refuse to comply, another course should be taken with him under the limitation, however, of that discretion which I hope may prove effectual in punishing him without letting our adversaries into the secret. It is a shame, and a flaming one that you cannot or do not supply the *Farmer* and enable him to complete his argument. Were his papers all published here and republished in London (in one pamphlet), they must be effectual in opening the eyes of candor and good sense. To attempt opening any other is not in the nature of possible things; but every acquisition is gain to the poor, and acquisition in the light I mention must surely be great gain. I expect to hear soon from you on the *Farmer's* account but not with the disagreeable circumstances of your last letter. If Smollett should deign to correspond with me on points of history relating to this island, I shall point you out to him, after telling him who wrote the *Historical Memoirs*. I need not say much to him. In that case he will no longer be indebted to me for a correspondence with you. He is a man of very considerable historical abilities, and should he attempt writing our history, we should exert ourselves from all quarters to supply him with proper materials. His accounts and reflections would be of great use in curing old prejudices; and who would not drop a little of his domestic business to contribute to so desirable an event? I know not whether I informed you before, but the *Farmer* proposed it to me to assist him in writing a history of Ireland.[2] I answered as politely as I could and told him truly I could not (from avocations interesting to my family) go through the painful task of reading, selecting, transcribing, etc.; that all my own materials together were not sufficient, without visiting libraries to make up such a collection as would be necessary for him. This shall be my answer to the other gentleman, though what I have at present in my power I would refuse to neither. Nay, I would drop a part of my domestic affairs to be useful in some shape to my country. I expect a medical work from you, but yet under the control of your leisure and other businesses. I do not consult your fame alone in such undertaking. I am actuated from a higher principle, the good of my country. My paper is out.

12 May 1761

[cropped at top]

    1. Lord Trimleston held the subscription money collected by the Catholic Association and refused to release it to the group. Three letters from Lord Taaffe, written to Lord Trimleston in April 1761, were disregarded. Matthew O'Conor, *History*, 273–277.
    2. O'Conor was wary of Henry Brooke's invitation to co-author a history of Ireland. Richard Digby to Charles O'Conor, February 1744, Stowe MS Bi1, RIA. O'Conor's friend Richard Digby wrote O'Conor that Henry Brooke was going to separate material that O'Conor had loaned Digby for an edition of Ogygian Tales. Brooke had told Digby they would co-author the book. Proposals were printed. A copy of the title page is part of the Stowe manuscript. Brooke, unknown to Digby, had printed a proposal for a history of Ireland based on the same material. See *A Proposal for Printing by Subscription, the History of Ireland* . . . 1745, in the pamphlet collection of the Newberry Library, Chicago. See also *DJ*, 26–29 January 1744/45, which contains Brooke's advertisement.

85. To Dr. John Curry

RIA, Stowe MS Bi1

22 May 1761

Dear Friend,

    The enclosed lay some time in the post office through neglect, and I could not return it before this time nor acknowledge the honor done me by gentlemen for whom I have the highest esteem. I expect much from our Committee; the want of such a representative for sixty years past is a proof that all sensibility is lost among public societies as well as private men when confounded by a deadly stroke. We are now reviving from the trance and have acquired sense enough to mix wonder with complaint on receiving such a stroke from the hands which ought to be lifted up to protect us and which indeed promised us protection. Drunken men, men drunk with prejudices, strike at friend and foe. Such men must grow sober; these prejudices must wear away by the natural course of time and events, not that I think they may be wholly effaced, but that their characters must grow less and less legible.[1] Our Lords Justices are disposed to humane sentiments. They seem to prefer the prosperity of the nation to prejudices destructive of it. The laws have made Popery hurtful; they and such as they can alone make it useful to the public interest; and your *Remonstrance* could never be better timed than under such an administration.[2] They alone can prepare, that is, remind the Ministry in England, whose attention is at present turned to more striking objects; and they alone (if my idea of them be just) can prepare the minds of our leading men here in both Houses. Let your application have what success it will, I must repeat it again, that it could never be better timed. I have read it over and over and the oftener I considered it in every part the more was I struck with the force, propriety, and spirit of the whole. It is brief, as it ought to be, and I can not enough admire the art by which so much important matter has been condensed in so circumscribed a compass. It is an abstract of tragical events whose causes are developed and whose remedies are pointed out with becoming discretion. It is at the same time the epitome of an history little known with any sort of precision to the public; and you gentlemen, our representatives, have not only a call of interest, but a call of duty to make this history known where alone it can operate to public good and the particular advantage of your constituents. Put it in what light you will, such a *Remonstrance* can not operate to any hurt, a circumstance sufficient to animate the coldest and most misgiving tempers. Your proper business, therefore, is to go on with what has been so wisely begun and negotiate previously the acceptance of your petition with the Lords Justices, whose dispositions you have tried and tried with success in the transmission of your late, dutiful Address to the Throne. You want no encouragement in making a tender of your services. Do not want spirit in offering them. The present secretaries of State in England[3] are wise and able men; the increase of wealth, industry, and revenue of this island can not be an indifferent object to them; men supported by the public voice, unembarrassed by counter-schemes of fashion; the only men who since the Revolution could attend with safety to the fair play of reason and who could weed little private interests from public prosperity. Enough of this. As you have left a wide margin in the paper enclosed, I have with a trembling timerity put a few queries relatively to two or three paragraphs, and yet on a review I find them of little importance whether I am resolved negatively or affirmatively; I however let those queries stand as I can safely confide my weakness to my friends and as they will show how little I had to object to the matter of style of the *Petition.*

You are neglectful of the *Farmer,* who ought to be encouraged to complete what he began. Such a lamp should be fed with oil. I would have all his *Letters* incorporated into one pamphlet to which the letters in the *Chronicle,* Bishop Berkeley's *Queries,* relatively to us, [Page ends. Rest of letter missing.]

    1. O'Conor seems to refer here to Lord Trimleston and those like him, Catholic aristocrats, who oppose the actions of their fellow religionists.
    2. The *Remonstrance* is the *Address to King George III.* The original statement of grievances had been written by members of Curry's committee before the death of George the Second. It had not been presented at that time because the content of the Remonstrance (or *Address*) appeared to be too bold for the time. The Committee, when it did decide to present the Remonstrance, disagreed with Lord Trimleston on its content. Various charges such as communication with foreign powers and applications to Parliament for leave to purchase land under the Gavel Act were leveled at the Association. Such an application would have implied that Catholics recognized the legality of such an act. A split developed; the Catholic Association submitted one Remonstrance, and Lord Trimleston decided to submit one of his own. Wyse, 1:73–74.
    3. William Pitt and John, earl of Bute.

86. To Dr. John Curry, Cow Lane, Dublin

OCD, 8.3 HS 023

24 June 1761

Dear Sir,

I am really vexed at the perverseness of our people, and if you find the case desperate (incurable, I should say), I request you will give them up like your patients in another capacity. What patient can be preserved against himself, against one who rejects the most salutary remedies? Desponding as I am, I, however, hope you will be made amends in the spirit and fidelity of some for the falling away of others in whom you vainly reposed a confidence. Write to me soon and let me know whether I am only vainly flattering myself.

I last post received a letter from Mr. Warner in London, who is writing the general history of Ireland.[1] You have seen his letter to the nobility and gentry on this subject in *Faulkner's Journal.*[2] He solicits my assistance or rather contributions. He writes politely and puts some queries relative to several things advanced in the *Dissertations.* I shall write and in my answer fairly confess my own mistakes in one or two places to which he points. Those *Dissertations* lie under all the disadvantages of a first endeavor on a very difficult subject. They lay two years out of my hands before publication and are destitute of many corrections, additions, and chastisements which I could give them. After all, I will find it much easier to answer Mr. Warner's queries than his expectations. To serve him to any good purpose I should go through much painful drudgery, which my present avocations cannot permit. I hear of other able undertakers, Dr. Smollett, Mr. Nugent (the translator of Montesquieu, etc.).[3] I promise you they will be far from finding the road so smooth as imagination may conceive it, and I am afraid most of them will faint before they go half their journey. *Periculosae plenum opus aleae.*[4]

I ask your pardon for not acknowledging the letter of yours you mention. I shall make no apology for the judgment I formed of the *Remonstrance.* I have kept a copy of it and am able to vindicate all that I have advanced, though you, my learned *Trebatius,* should dissent, and yet I do not remember that I ever differed with you on any other point.[5]

Do not let our medical work lie over by sacrificing to laziness. Of all physicians in Europe, ours are most in debt to the public. When you appear *unus instar omnium*[6] your interest will be advanced while your credit will be undivided. Agriculture is my daily occupation. I am adorning *campum rudem et incultuan*[7] as Lord Chesterfield did his in the Phoenix Park, and my undertaking is vastly more extensive and profitable than his. You see that in one instance, I am, without boasting his superior. *Agricultura mihi videtur ad sapientis vitam proxime accedere.*[8] I quote that sentiment of Cicero in my own favor to give the citizen an idea of the importance of my present labors. What do I not owe to the inventor of these marks (made by a quill) and to one who brings me thus into conversation with my friend at the distance of eighty miles? Who brought me a visit from *Warner* in seven days from London? Who, by a miracle, brings sounds from the organs of light with more precision than through those of the ear? Whoever he was, I shall owe more to him when he brings me glad tidings in the next visit from you. Give my real and warm affections to Mrs. Curry, Miss Curry, your son, your whole family. Why do you not send the *Memoirs* to Mr. Hume of Edinburgh. You really deserve a *rating,* and I thank Dr. Smollett more than you for the information he gave *Hume* about that work in his *Review.* I am glad that my paper is out, lest I should run into more accusations. I believe this to be the only letter of mine which began and ended with them.

 1. Ferdinando Warner, L.L.D. (1703–1768), rector at Barnes, Surry, England. Warner had written a history of the Anglican Church and was about to begin a history of Ireland. *Concise DNB,* 1:1369.
 2. *DJ,* 6–9 June 1761.
 3. Thomas Nugent (1700–1772), a miscellaneous writer, L.L.D., wrote on his travels and translated Voltaire, Rousseau, and Montesquieu. *Concise DNB,* 1:958.

4. The task is full of dangerous risks.
5. O'Conor commends Curry's judgment and knowledge by comparing him to Trebatius Testa, a jurist, teacher, and the author of *De Religionibus* and *De Iuri Civili*.
6. One equal to them all.
7. The rough and uncultivated plain.
8. Agriculture seems to me to be nearest to the life of a wise man. Cicero, "The Joys of Farming," in *On Old Age*.

87. To Ferdinando Warner

RIA, Stowe MS Bi1

26 June 1761

. . . I return you most sincere thanks for the judicious exceptions you take to some parts of the *Dissertations*[1]; more than the common disadvantages to which a first publication is exposed glare through the whole, without insisting on little youthful flights which a riper judgment despises and which I am confident you have overlooked. That endeavor lay two years in other hands before publication and is destitute of several advantages which even I by castrations and additions could give it.

In some general accounts of primeval matters, I borrowed here and there a shred from various accounts in print and manuscript. In such a cento I omitted giving each particular line to its particular author; if, however, this little tract should be thought worthy of a second impression, that defect I shall supply and give the whole the rigorous chastisement it wants. In the omission of authorities you instance in the old Belgians, whose original I deduce from *South* Britain; I took this from Mr. O'Flaherty in *Ogyg. Insul.* p. 14, as he took the account chiefly from the *Book of Lecan* now in Paris.[2] The fact is as well attested as any of so ancient a standing can be.

What I said of Cimbaeth[3] was from extending a little the account of the Four Masters, who say that he established laws and good government after putting a period to the strange constitution of alternate governments between him, *Aodh roc* and *Dihorbes*. The words, "*gave History and the memoirs new life which ever after could not be extinguished,*" are my own and what is worse not true. The Attacolic Wars in some ages after put a temporary stop to good government and to the [unreadable] also in Ireland. Adieu. . . .

1. O'Conor's first edition of *Dissertations on a History of Ireland* appeared in Dublin in 1753, published by the Catholic printer James Hoey. The University of Illinois has a copy of this book.
2. *Ogygia seu rerum Hibernicarum Chronologia*, 1685.
3. A pre-Christian king of Ulster, who had his residence at Emania. O'Reilly, lxviii.

88. To Dr. John Curry

RIA, Stowe MS Bi1

6 July 1761

Lord Taaffe's taking the Remonstrance of the Catholic Committee to Primate Stone's Palace is the subject of much of the letter. O'Conor asks Curry why Lord Taaffe has not reported to them his conversation with Archbishop Stone:

He certainly transmitted a copy of our *Petitionary Remonstrance* to the proper place, and he was probably too delicate to negotiate its acceptance much; for the greatest and even boldest men must keep measures with prejudice, nay with the reigning ministerial temper whatever it be. This, I say, was our friend's manner of conducting this affair and sufficiently explains the meaning of his silence; when his dispatches on the subject of the *Remonstrance* arrive, we shall then be informed of its good or bad fortune, though care will be taken, no doubt, to conceal from us the manner of conducting which I have hinted; and it will be but common prudence in us to accept it in the light held out to us. Should we be told that the present time is improper for petitioning, yet the offer of our services, *if we should ever be called upon to serve,* will be applauded.

O'Conor mentions to Curry the visit of two unnamed bishops and a Protestant gentleman of Roscommon[1] to his house in Belanagare. If some noted historian like Tobias Smollet would come and do a history of Ireland, O'Conor asks, wouldn't it help the Catholic cause.

1. William Talbot, member of the Grand Jury of Roscommon. *DJ*, 1–3 November 1768.

89. To Dr. John Curry, Cow Lane, Dublin

PSPL, Gilbert MS 203

Belanagare, 3 August 1761

My Dear Sir,

I am returned hither after a ramble of ten days in the county of Sligo, and I no sooner arrived that I had the good fortune of meeting our dear Lord Taaffe, who alighted at this house early this afternoon. After dinner we walked out together, and I received his commands to acquaint you with the following particulars. He left Dublin on Saturday last and in his way stopped in to pay his compliments to his friend at Leixlip.[1] Though his Grace is an early riser, it was some time before he appeared; ceremonies discharged, the affair of our petition became the subject of conversation. "My L[ord]," said his Grace, "I can not at present resolve you in a decisive manner relatively to the petition of your people. The consideration of the matter contained therein naturally encounters difficulties and delays arising from the circumstance of tempers and times. Prudence must accomodate itself to such circumstances, nay, must be governed by them. I am not acquainted with our present Lord Lieutenant.[2] I should have a personal knowledge to know what his disposition of judgment may be in regard to your people; a perseverance in your good conduct must be acceptable to him and prove the only test of the sincerity of that loyalty which you have tendered in your several addresses. Though his Majesty's wisdom has far exceeded his years, yet a particular consideration of all the grievances which you in particular complain of must be the work of time, especially when so many affairs of greater importance must interfere; under these circumstances your L[ordshi]p will confess that the information I am giving is the only information you should expect." Lord Taaffe replied that "his grace was the proper judge in such a case; but that he apprehended no time was improper to let his Majesty know how much he was in possession of the good heart of this people who received such signal marks of indulgence from his royal ancestors; that the earlier the better such impressions were made upon the Royal Mind; but let this, like every other matter of our petition, be adjusted as your Grace and persons in your great station shall think convenient or useful; and that no consideration on earth could induce him to speak a little in favor of this people if he did not feel the goodness of their heart in regard to his Majesty and his government; that his Grace might safely depend upon it that the perseverance and patience of the people can not be worn out, let the consideration of their grievances be placed at ever so great a distance; for they flatter themselves that the enabling such people to be more useful to the public than they can be at present under numberless legal restraints will be one time or other the object of public and serious consideration." His Grace resumed by declaring his satisfaction in finding among our people so good a disposition, but at the same time he thought it proper of offer Lord T[aaffe] back the petition we submitted to his perusal. Lord T[aaffe] interrupted him by the following words, "Keep it, my Lord. It can not remain in better hands than your own. Let it remain in them as a testimonial of the uprightness of our intentions and of our deference to your Grace's judgment." On this genteel requisition, his Grace was good enough to put up the paper, and thus ended their conversation on the subject of our petition. All this requires little comment, though some persons may not observe in it the embarrassments of a good mind struggling with itself when under the necessity of declining public service when opposed to public opinion. For such a necessity there is, no doubt. I am glad however that his Grace kept that paper, and I can not sufficiently applaud Lord T[aaffe]'s sagacity in pressing him to keep it. It was, I think, putting confidence out to interest and Lord T[aaffe] could not lodge it in better hands. You know, my dear friend, that we must not only keep honest, but the most discreet measures with those whom God has required of us to obey. To deserve redress of grievances is entirely in our own power; to obtain any is in the power of others whose tempers must be consulted as their dictates must be obeyed.

As I have the honor to be Lord T[aaffee]'s secretary on the present occasion, I have nothing more to dread than a failure in making my report as faithfully as I ought. I think that no part of the substance of his commands has escaped me. He, however, regrets that the subject of my letter may be commanded only to yourself and Mr. Anthony Dermot. The generality of our people, though honest, yet want discretion. Let us not want it who mean to serve them. I request you will send me a copy of his Lordship's letter to Dr. Chevers.[3] Adieu, dear sir; I this week got a second letter from Dr. *Warner.* I shall communicate the contents another time, as I would not take off your contemplation at the present from a more important subject on which I pray to have your own sentiments as soon as possible. I request also that you will present my affections to Mr. Dermot and his family. I shall, if God grants it, pay you a visit next winter, though some misconceptions of a few among you would almost incline me to keep my distance.

    1. Archbishop George Stone.
    2. George Montagu Dunk (1716–1771), second earl of Halifax.
    3. Dr. Augustine Cheevers, O.E.S.A., was Bishop of Meath from 7 August 1756 to 18 August 1778. *HBC,* p. 391.

90. To Dr. John Curry

PSPL, Gilbert MS 203

27 August 1761

My Dear Friend,

My being from home these last twenty days will account for my not answering your important and very kind letter of the 8th instant till this day; before I do it, I can not resist the pleasure of informing you that this second voyage of mine by sea and land was extremely agreeable to me. It was not on business, but it was a relaxation from it, a suspension of cares, which however necessary for preserving a little independence in life, yet that very end of all our cares requires, I think, that we should not surfeit on the means. In the company of a friend we set ourselves down at the foot of Knock-na-Ree, which is washed by the western ocean. Here we established our headquarters as did Sir Edward King[1] and his lady some time before on the same errand of relaxation. Here are two great country houses. He occupied one, we the other; and I cannot express the civilities I received from our door neighbor, the baronet in his sweet retreat. We conversed, we enjoyed, we lived. Unsocial controversy, aggrieving distinction, embittering retrospects mingled not with our discourses on public and private happiness; by leaving those things to books, pulpits, and parliaments, benevolence taught us more wisdom than we could hitherto obtain from all three put together. The south and north islands here contain between three and four thousand acres at low water, a noble level which at a small distance appears to the eye like a fine carpet of brown velvet. The hill of Knock-na-Ree is not accessible on the east or west from the steepness of the acclivity on the one side and the vast cliffs on the other, but it is accessible on the north by taking the course to the top slantwise. I mounted it on foot, and from the bottom of the beach it measures near a mile and a half and can not measure less than 2,000 feet perpendicular height. On this natural and vast pyramid another has been raised by art. I have not measured the base, but you may have a good idea of it from its measuring thirty paces in conic height and twenty-six paces in diameter upon the level platform on the top. It is traditionally called Miosgan Meaibhe or the Carne of Meaba—daughter of Eochy Feylugh, King of Ireland, and the celebrated heroine, Queen of Conaght, who raised so much disturbance in this kingdom during the times of Tiberius, Caligula, Nero, and Claudius. From this platform on Meaba's Carn, I took a prospect on which I feasted for more than half an hour. The counties of Donegall, Derry, Fermanagh, Letrim, and Longford bounded my view to the north and east. That northward was terminated by the prodigious cliffs above *Killibeggs*, divided from the mountains of *Boylach* and *Barn'smor* stretching in a chain of pointed hills westward. Nearer were the cliffs of *Ben-Golban, Ben-Basgn, Ben-Boe,* and *Coloony*. Those spiny and ragged hills exhibit numberless, wild irregularities, and yet collect most of the water which falls from their sides into one noble basin which they surround. It is called Logh-Gilly and falls into the sea by a river of a mile in length; it covers 2,000 acres of land and throws out more water at Sligoetown than the Liffy at Essex Bridge. It is, thus considering the shortness of its course, perhaps one of the largest rivers in the world. Turning my eyes southward, my view extended beyond the Curlew Mountains and took in the great plain of Conaght (now called *Magheny*) which ran out of sight like the immense ocean to the west of me. The hill of Knock-na-Ree has at the top a platform of about thirty acres. It is covered with a black mold of ten or eleven inches in depth which the peasants cut into turf sods for firing where, if the surface is pared away, nothing appears but a baren gravel intermixed with stones as white as snow. On the next day after this view we went to sea, steered towards *Killala* and back towards the island of *Innis-Murry* in a great swell natural to the ocean here though the weather was very fine. The whole coast is intersected by capes and promontories in the Barony of Carbry; in that of Tireragh there are but few, but the coast is variegated by jagged rocks and high cliffs. Indeed the prospects from several parts of the Ocean were little inferior to that from *Knocknaree,* which by the way, signifies the *Mountains of the Moon,* very probably from the ancients celebrating their *Neomenia* on that remarkable hill. I have tired you with this description though I am sure a livelier imagination than mine would give you very pleasing sensations of the scene I have been enjoying. I now, after asking your pardon, return to the subject of your letter.

Your second thoughts on the last visit to Leixlip are entirely just. "Putting our suffering selves out of the case, what other answer could our friend[2] have received in the present conjuncture than what he got." Let us wait very patiently for a conjuncture more favorable, and if such never presents itself, we will with God's blessing bear the future better than our ancestors did the past as our sufferings are not as embittered as theirs were by any prior enjoyments. Resignation will work that effect on the few which insensibility will on the many. So evenly are things balanced here below in spite of efforts to render them————[The rest of the letter is missing.]

1. Sir Edward King was O'Conor's neighbor in Roscommon. He later became Viscount Kingsborough.
2. Lord Taaffe.

91. To Dr. John Curry, Cow Lane, Dublin

OCD, 8.3 HS 023

3 October 1761

My Dear Sir,

Tomorrow or next day I send up to Mr. Reilly by the conveyance of a country fellow *The Danger of Popery Examined*.[1] You are to get it from our friend and to pass sentence upon it. There may be some circumstances of time which may render the publication at present unseasonable, besides we must have a consideration for booksellers who lose by tracts on our subjects, for neither friends or foes will read them. I have addressed this little pamphlet to our new viceroy;[2] I had an artifice in this to gain attention. Could I gain one able convert to truth among our masters, it would be a conquest, and a conquest of triumph superior to any ever obtained by Roman arms. I had neither time nor patience to transcribe the essay I send you; you must therefore put on a pair of new spectacles to decipher interlineations and get over the sharp palisades thrown in your way by blots and counterblots, if you are in the temper of allowing the expression. If you find that putting the old argument in a new livery may be of any use, I believe you will agree with me that to obtain this end it would be necessary that an old acquaintance should not be suspected for the author. That suspicion would ruin all. You know of me (what I know of you) that I would prefer the smallest public advantage to my own credit, and yet, on the whole, what credit can be gained at present by a fugitive pamphlet on our subject which died like other creatures immediately after coming into the world? Yet I know that our creatures of the brain may revive hereafter, when present dissipations, present views, and present reigning caprice are over. I know that you have preserved pamphlets that had no good luck in their day, and others will no doubt hereafter imitate your example. 'Tis thus that many historical and important anecdotes are preserved. But this is no comfort of present consideration. I say no more. My bolt is shot, and I shall think, I assure you, no more about it hit or not hit. Tomorrow I high again for the county of Sligo. You shall hear of me after my return, God sparing life.

1. O'Conor is the author of *The Dangers of Popery Examined*. He cautioned Curry not to expose his "old acquaintance" as the author.
2. George Montagu Dunk (1716–1771), second earl of Halifax. Lord Lieutenant of Ireland 1761–1763. *Concise DNB*, 1:373.

92. To Dr. John Curry, Cow Lane, Dublin

OCD, 8.3 HS 023

Camagh, 29 October 1761

My Dear Friend,

I had a letter this week from Mr. Reilly informing me that you thought it proper I should enlarge on that part of the Lord Lieutenant's speech, wherein he proposes the encouragement of agriculture and the linen manufacture to our Parliament. I was so struck with your thought that I sat down immediately, though my foot was in the stirrup for this place, and sent up yesterday the crude and undigested page which you have (probably) seen before you can see this. Having the substance of it in my memory, I sat down here in the happy recess of a whole day to put that matter into some better form, and what I have done I send you enclosed in this letter. *Forsan et haec olim meminisse juvabit.*[1] I confess to you that I am intensely warmed with my Lord Lieutenant's speech, and in this warmth I flatter myself that the *Danger of Popery Examined* is a seasonable piece, however deficient in matter and argument, both which might be extended. I will see you in December; meantime I request you will write to me by the return of the post and inform me of what our people are doing, etc. Though I live now in the neighborhood of the county of Fermanagh, I shall be at home before your letter returns. The sheet I now send on agriculture and the linen trade is as full as it need be, and I hope will please you after you correct it. I have wrought into it a little on the precariousness of our judgment debts, but *oculo retorto.*[2]

1. Virgil, *Aeneid*, 1.203. Perhaps it will be pleasant to remember these hardships someday.
2. Looking back.

93. To Dr. John Curry

RIA, Stowe MS Bi1

10 November 1761

My Dear Sir,

I did not come home till last post night and had only barely time to write a billet to Mr. R[eilly] of my arrival and extremely glad I am that L[ord] T[aaffe] arrived so well in your capital. Please to present him my profoundest respects. The excellent little book he left me is translated by my second son.¹ He is now under my direction making the second draft, and you shall soon have it for your correction. Your scheme of a dedication without the privity of the patron is a happy thought. Indeed the omission of such an address would be doing great injustice to that worthy nobleman's zeal. I congratulate you on the progress you have made in our medical work; our country wants such a local performance, and it is a shame to us that we have no such here hitherto, while your brethren of Scotland are gaining credit in that way all over Europe.² *Macte bonis et dotibus animi.*³ While you are doing good every way to your country, your credit and fortune will be raised thereby in your own time, God granting you life, and your fame most certainly when you are no more. Have I not a considerable share in all this by goading you on, by spurring modesty and indolence? But I retract the word "indolence," for far from being indifferent to the good of your country, its unhappy fate in regard to prejudices and parties have given you great anxieties. You ventured to prescribe in so desperate a case and succeeded beyond your own expectations and mine. *Est quodam prodire tenus.*⁴ Others have caught a little of your fire soon after the *Dialogue* was written, and what has been done is doubtless primarily owing to you from your brother of Trim and others down to the writer of the *Case*.⁵

What is your C[ommitt]ee doing? Mr. Wyse, I am told, proposed a petition to Parliament and his motion (it is said) has been approved. You should negotiate a hearing for such a petition by previous conferences with some members of both Houses. Without this preliminary you do nothing. I saw *The Danger of Popery* advertised and thank you for your libation over the first printed sheet.⁶ I have last post received a letter from Doctor Warner and was astonished on his informing me he got the perusal of that little tract and that he knew the author by the handwriting. I thought Mr. R[eilly] would transcribe it for the press as well as to remove suspicion as to remove blots which must embarrass the letter setter. As the Doctor knew my hand, I knew it was in vain for me to conceal what he knew and only requested he would keep the secret to himself and if his leisure permitted to correct the inaccuracies of which he complained.⁷ But this was nothing. He objected strongly to my omission of anticipating the principal objection to our people, namely our *known,* our *necessary,* and our *unavoidable* attachment *to the Pretender.* I confess to you that such a charge warmed me all over, but after a little reflection [I rejected the answer, which my indignation was bursting to utter.]⁸ I replied calmly that I anticipated the objection he made by annexing a form of oath (in the appendix) which is a sufficient test to the present government of the fidelity of this people; that all parties among us have for several years past kept a remarkable silence in regard to the forgotten and friendless exile he mentioned; and that it would not become me to be the first to break that silence indiscreetly and officiously but let him sleep in his political grave. From this defense of myself I entered into closer combat and drew my weapon out of my never failing magazine, *The Third Appeal*, and I urged to him the account Sir W[illiam] Temple gives of the Dutch Catholics; and if, said I, the Dutch Catholics were such sound members of the civil constitution in thirty years after the great Revolution in the Low Countries, by what *fatality* or unavoidable necessity must it be that our Catholics must be attached to an infinitely less formidable Pretender than the K[ing] of Spain was to the Hollanders, and this not in thirty years after such a revolution but at the end of seventy years when all that we know of our own revolution must be from tradition or history. Such a *Fatal Attachment* has no precedent (res[pecte]d sir) in the history of any other country on earth and should it be peculiar to us, I request you will believe that I am not of the number, nay believe that very few are of it; for most of us, we thank God, understand the duty prescribed by religion which requires our obeying actively the *powers that be*, whether they punish or favor, etc. I request you will keep this a secret to yourself and say nothing of it till I see you, which will be as soon as possible; I am now chained to business and to that of others more than my own. I am doing what I can to get loose. I beg you will, as soon as you can, let me know what our people are doing. I trust that you corrected here and there my obscurities and improprieties in the tract now under the press. Adieu. (My dear friend)

1. Charles O'Conor (1736–1808).
2. O'Conor is alluding to John and William Hunter, the Scottish anatomists whose discoveries and procedures became classic medical history. O'Conor would like an Irishman like Curry to show the medical world that the Irish have medical talent also. There was no indication that Dr. Curry ever published this medical work. *Concise DNB*, 1:662ff.
3. Well done! May you continue to use the goodness of your heart and the talents of your mind to advantage.
4. It is possible to advance so far (up to a certain point).
5. O'Conor is the writer of the *Case of the Roman Catholics* (1755).
6. George Faulkner advertised in his *DJ*, 3–7 November 1761, that the pamphlet was "In the press and speedily will be published by the printer hereof, *The Dangers of Popery to the Present Government Examined.*"
7. Dr. Warner must have been in Dublin to see the holograph copy since the pamphlet was not advertised for sale in the *DJ* until 8 December.
8. Crossed out.

94. To Dr. John Curry, Cow Lane, Dublin

OCD, 8.3 HS 023

25 November 1761

Dear Sir,

I am angry at you for apologizing that you did not write to me since you received my last. You have a far better and more interesting employment, that of doing public as well as private good, and any minute you detach from that is a great loss even to me. Go on and rouse your own people, rouse their adversaries, and reconcile if you can, these to those. By no other means will you come at the *mollia tempora fandi*,[1] the halcyon days you mention. I never keep copies of any of my letters, and what I transmitted to you from my letter to *Dr. Warner* was barely from memory. The substance, not the identic words—, Peace to the political manes of the Pretender, our masters are silent about him, and to them let us leave his political resurrection. It would be indiscreet as well as officious in us to revive his memory. The writer of *The Danger* (I think) anticipated the objection relative to him in the form of the oath given in the appendix. This security is equal to the importance of the thing without going into abjurations, which were intended as they were made for legislators and placemen in church and state. We need not expose ourselves to fastening any such knot on ourselves by reviving any popular topics at present about *the person to be abjured*, at least I think so. When the Pretender is *publicly* objected to us, it will then be time enough to speak to that subject. Sure I am that King Wiliam required no such abjuration of a much more formidable pretender, the late King James. I like what you sent to me as a present from Mr. Henry, that little prattling pulpit orator.[2] His father, a Presbyterian parson, lived here, within eight miles of me, under the patronage of Sir Henry King. The son was made a convert to established forms because he lived at the distance of sixty miles from a conventicle. You and I are not men of the *Helvetic turn;* we work honestly, and we work gratis for the public; and should we flatter ourselves that a future historian might mention us as men who did some public service, we will fill a better niche than a Henry or a Brooke, who fight in the cause of their country because they are paid. Enough on this subject till you and I quaff together and con over the caprices, the inconsistencies, and the immoralities of the poor drama in which we are acting a part. A wretched drama it is, God knows. It puts me in mind of the complaint of poor Erasmus, in his preface to his edition of St. Ambrose, the last of his works—*poena nostra non meritis data sed furori—Quoties enim oppido capto saevitur propemodum atrocius in immerentes quam innocentes*, etc.[3] Things are not mended *much* since his time, not even in this country where they should mend most, but our dullness and folly have the effects here that faction and hatred have in other countries. If we cannot laugh, let us not be sad at those things.

 1. Gentle times of speaking.
 2. William Henry (d. 1768), dean of Killaloe. On 23 October 1761 he preached a sermon on "The Necessity of Unity," which was printed in Dublin the same year. Curry must have sent a copy to O'Conor. *BMCPBCE*, 11 : 1233.
 3. Our punishment was inflicted not because it was deserved, but out of passion. How often, when a town has been captured, the innocent are treated almost more cruelly than the guilty.

95. To [Archbishop Richard Lincoln][1]

RIA, Stowe MS Bi1

10 February 1762

My Lord,

As what is offered in the present application would be impertinent in four days hence, it is offered now to your Grace's consideration with great respect and humility. It relates to a very recent incident, the resolution of which is extremely important. This resolution is expected from your Grace as Metropolitan of this province, nay of the kingdom. To your Grace, therefore, the present application is extremely proper.

It regards an exhortation proposed to be read in all our chapels through the kingdom. In the preamble prefixed, *it is presumed* that the contents are conformable to the religious principles of the R[oman] Catholics; very sensibly on the part of those who framed it, they resolve the whole into a mere presumption. They rest it on ourselves to show how far that presumption is well or ill-grounded. They do not decide for us, like their unfair predecessors in former times. They leave us to decide for ourselves.

The exhortation consists of five members: 1. obedience and fidelity to the present government as a law of God. 2. gratitude to the present indulgence. 3. a memorial that the Penal Laws were not the acts of the present Royal Family, but the statutes of another race before their accession. 4. the observance of a general fast. 5. a prayer for spiritual and temporal blessings on his present Majesty, etc. We presume that what is recommended in the first instance is the doctrine of the Catholic Church. 2. The second is a moral duty. 3. The third includes an apology for the present R[oyal] Family as enemies to persecution. 4. The fourth recommendation, falling on one of our Fridays in Lent, requires nothing but what the Church commands already, fasting and prayer on that day, and the fifth recommends prayers for the King and his subordinate governors.

From the construction, matter, and form of this exhortation, nothing is more evident than that it has been the studied effort of much refinement and much caution also. All reservation relative to civil duty seems anticipated by the tenor of the construction. They leave us no middle way. If we declare for the civil orthodoxy of the exhortation, we may expect some civil good hereafter. If we determine otherwise, in that determination alone will they find a justification of all the Penal Laws against us and possibly load us with more, in which case, my Lord, at whose door will the blame lie?

Far are we, my Lord, from thinking but that your Grace will decide for us in this point as becomes a prelate of your great station and knowledge, not to mention that zeal which must prefer the peace and good of the Church to all inferior consideration on earth. We only fear for unseasonable opposition from some among ourselves, for some such we are assured have already appeared. They object, it is said, to the exhortation as coming from men who have no spiritual authority over us. But their authority is not the question, but whether what they recommend be admissible on our principles. If it be not, they should produce their reasons and in writing too for the greater precision, that we may have the better medium for the confessing *our* mistake or for demonstrating *theirs*. In the few days we have for deliberation this should be done to prevent such a schism among ourselves as proved equally fatal and scandalous to us in the reign of Charles II under the denominations of Remonstrants and Antiremonstrants.

We are informed that it is objected also that the Catholic powers may resent such an exhortation in time of war with them and exclude us from their colleges and seminaries. This surely is a strange objection. How does the like procedure affect the Catholic clergy in Brandenburg and Silesia, who pray for his Prussian Majesty's success? Will they be less acceptable hereafter in Austrian or Italian colleges?

But it is required of us to pray for the temporal happiness of our present governors. Yes, indeed, but as subordinate to their spiritual happiness which is prayed for first. This includes no equivocation, and those who framed the exhortation well know that when we pray for the happiness of persons out of the Church we mean thereby their embracing the True Faith and their living up to its dictates. The authors of the exhortation, therefore, mentioned temporal happiness in the second place and subordinate to the first petition for spiritual blessings. The one without the other is vanity and affliction of spirit, and for such things we can not be supposed to pray.

My Lord, it is worth the while to consider that since the defection of these kingdoms from the Catholic faith our masters never made any voluntary approach towards relenting in our case till the present time. In this good disposition we should go more than halfway to meet them, and in this affair of the exhortation particularly, no consideration should interpose but its repugnancy to our Catholic principles. It is in your Grace's power, we trust, to prevent the folly and misfortune of rejecting it on any other. The importance of the subject and the shortness of time for deliberation upon it will apologize for the trouble I give your Grace in this detail of fears and apprehensions which I wish may be groundless and which, if they be, your consideration for the goodness of the intention will be an ample apology for.

A Roman Catholic Layman[2]

P.S. My Lord

We shall count it a great misfortune if, by a refusal to read the paper in question, the R[oman] C[atholic] laity are put under any indispensable necessity of protesting publicly that they differ in opinion from some of their clergy as to the obligation of civil duty and allegiance to the present reigning family.[3]

1. O'Conor is in Dublin at this time working with Curry and the Catholic Committee. Both the Protestants and the Catholics are divided as a result of the recent Whiteboy uprisings in Munster. Lord Halifax and the Crown favor lenient action. The Undertakers argue that the uprisings are a sign of a deep and widespread opposition of Irish Catholics to the government. The Catholic Bishops of Dublin, Ossory, and Cloyne have issued exhortations instructing their people to be submissive to the government. The Bishop of Waterford kept the government informed about the plans of the insurgents. Apparently the Catholic Committee had framed a statement of allegiance which they feared Archbishop Lincoln might take objection to. Matthew O'Conor, *History*, pp. 289ff. *DJ*, 23–26 January 1762.
2. The signature is in another hand.
3. There is also an earlier draft of this letter.

96. To George Faulkner

BM, Egerton 201, f-37

15 February 1762

Dear Sir,

Since I had the pleasure of [corrupt] last of you, I had the ill luck of spraining my ankle on the stairs of Dick's Coffee House,[1] what confined me to my apartment all this time. I am now, I thank God, tolerably well and will be soon able to thank you in person for your many acts of friendship. As I have not an English frank, I request you will forward the enclosed to Dr. Warner.

> 1. "Like most of the other coffee houses in Dublin, Dick's was located on the drawing-room floor, one of the shops underneath being occupied by Thomas Cotter, bookseller and publisher, and another by the 'Hoop' eating house." Gilbert, "Streets of Dublin," p. 594.

97. To Denis O'Conor, Belanagare

OCD, 8.3 SE 028

2 March 1762

Dear Denis,

Last Saturday I sat the whole day in the company with the most considerable R[oman] C[atholic]s of the city and country [corrupt] consequences of a former [motion] the heads of a bill for securing [corrupt] to Papists were to be laid before the House. But the [corrupt] [about] resumed the chain that one [crossed out] and stood up to oppose the reading of the bill.[1] The real question was whether a [Papist] who lends a sum of money to a Protestant shall be entitled by law to recover it. Mr. [crossed out] would not [corrupt] the question decided because it would tend to lessen the Protestant interest and give an obstacle to the conversion of Papists. [Three lines corrupt.] that he was warmly against a bill of such a nature as that now spoken to because he was a warm Protestant.

All these weighty reasons were not sufficient to some members. They imagined that one man's being obliged to pay another the shilling he owes him would not nor could not affect the present [corrupt] either in its operations or consequences. That the anecdote (though admirable) related only to a particular case and ought by no means to affect those Papists who already lodged their money in the loan and who consulted priests of a different opinion. They did not conceive how a freer circulation of credit and cash could prove injurious to the Protestant interest, etc.[2] [corrupt] and urged that the bringing in such heads of a [corrupt] the end of a session was a step a little too precipited [corrupt] that ought to have time, considering the contents maturely; he therefore humbly moved that the heads of the bill should be printed and on this [corrupt] question of the day was put, and on a division the party who were against printing proved a great majority. The further consideration of the bill was put off till yesterday, and from yesterday to this day. (There being yesterday so much other business) before a committee of the whole House. [Three lines corrupt.] What the state of the bill will be this day no man can guess, but many are told and all hope it will not be clogged with any clause which would be deemed a punishment and not a favor.[3]

P.S. No Viceroy was ever more popular than the present, and none I believe ever deserved to be more so. His secretary is a young, lively man of great parts and he is considered as able an orator as any in these kingdoms.[4] Mr. Cumberland,[5] the other secretary, I am acquainted with. He too is a young man of fine talents and amiable manners. He distinguished himself by a fine interlude, entitled *The Banishment of Cicero.* Mr. Brooke favors me now and then with a visit. He has now a tragedy in rehearsal on Barry's stage.[6] He read to me a part of the first act. I think the dialogue highly supported and characteristic. His book in favor of the R[oman] C[atholic]s[7] is published and well-executed. [Corrupt.]

    1. The Elegit Bill, "a bill to enable Catholics to invest money in mortgages upon land." See Lecky, *History of Ireland in the Eighteenth Century,* 2:191.
    2. Lecky's observations echo O'Conor's. Lecky wrote:
Under these circumstances, the evil of the law which forbade Catholics from lending money on landed security was keenly felt. It added another to the many drains of wealth which exhausted the nation, for Catholics who had made fortunes in industrial life were naturally led to invest them in foreign securities. The law was part of a policy which the English government and the Irish Parliament had, with perfect harmony and undeviating perseverance, pursued ever since the Revolution, and which deserves to be regarded as one of the most signal instances of shortsightedness recorded in the history of legislation. 2:190–191.
    3. The state of the Elegit bill was hopeless. Matthew O'Conor wrote that "the bill was forwarded to the Lord Lieutenant for transmission. It was suppressed, however, in England by the advice of the Lord Chancellor Hardwick, who conceived that the Protestant interest and English connection would be endangered by the admission of Papists to even a temporary possession of any part of the soil." Matthew O'Conor, *History of the Irish Catholics,* pp. 290–292.

4. Gerard "Single Speech" Hamilton was Lord Halifax's Chief Secretary for Ireland (1761–1764), and Chancellor of the Irish Exchequer (1763–1784). *Concise DNB* 1 : 564.
5. Richard Cumberland (1732–1811). Dramatist and Ulster secretary, 1761. *Concise DNB*, 1 : 307.
6. *Antony and Cleopatra*. See O'Conor's letter to Curry, 21 July 1762.
7. *The Tryal of the Cause of the Roman Catholics*.

98. To George Faulkner

BM, Egerton 201, f-39

17 March 1762

This letter is a courtesy note to Faulkner informing him that O'Conor received a letter from Dr. Warner and that O'Conor in turn sends Faulkner a printed letter from Warner to Lord Lyttleton.[1] Warner had asked O'Conor to explain certain passages in O'Conor's *Dissertation on a History of Ireland*.

1. George Lyttleton (1709–1773), first Baron Lyttleton. His *History of the Life of Henry II and the Times He Lived In* was a lifetime work.

99. To Hugh Stafford, Elphin

OCD, 8.3 HS 029

8 May 1762

This letter is so corrupt that there is difficulty in deciphering O'Conor's message. He has found a manuscript which he mislaid several years earlier. Also, O'Conor tells Mr. Stafford that if there are any other manuscripts which Mr. Stafford has sent, they are safe, "though hid in a crowd." O'Conor comments on a bill which possibly must have related to Catholics' taking long tenures. However, the bill, it appears from O'Conor's tone, was defeated in the House of Commons. Political evil still abounds, O'Conor concludes.

100. To Dr. John Curry

OCD, 8.3 HS 023

14 May 1762

Since leaving Dublin and arriving home, O'Conor has been busy. He describes his journey from Dublin: "On the morning I left you I slept three hours, then entered a stage coach, arrived that evening at Mullingar and the next here at home, after crossing five counties. I am this day at rest at least for some hours, vacant for my friends, the sweetest of all vocations. I left you all in a gloomy state."

The failure of passage of the Elegit Bill and the continuous but ineffectual arguing among the members of the Catholic Committee frustrates O'Conor:

> Through the whole winter, meetings upon meetings, and not one resolution entered on your journals. Our last meeting constituted what we may call a *full house,* and the resolution entered into that night was the most important that could be framed, could it be but brought into execution. I moved that the preamble to it should be printed, as not liable to the blemishes of a transcriber, and that our several prelates and dignitaries should be served with copies, that a sum might (through their solicitation) be collected for the public utility.[1] You never will do anything to purpose without such a sum. Its intention is to conciliate government to an innoxious people, and by the reconciliation to render those people useful.

Finally, the affair of "The Roman Legion" is mentioned by O'Conor.[2] He hopes that a soldier named Colonel Brown might obtain commissions for Curry's and O'Conor's children.

1. See O'Conor's letters to Curry, 16 March 1763 and May 1763. O'Conor's idea for an all-Ireland collection was ultimately used by Daniel O'Connell's Catholic Association of Ireland.

2. Colonel William Brown, of the seventy-third regiment of Foot stationed in Ireland. O'Conor was hoping perhaps Colonel Brown would help in obtaining commissions for the young Currys and O'Conors. "Officers of his Majesty's Land Forces," *Gentleman's Magazine,* 31, (1761), 613. The "Roman Legion" was a project suggested to Parliament by the Catholic peers, Lords Kenmare and Kingsland. Seven regiments of Catholic Irish foot soldiers were to be recruited for service in Portugal against its enemy Spain. The opposition from Protestant gentry was so intense that the government laid the project aside. However, from this point on, instructions to recruiters to recruit no one but Protestants were dropped and Catholics were silently admitted into the services. Lecky, 2 : 186–188.

101. To Dr. John Curry

OCD, 8.3 HS 023

[Late May 1762][1]

O'Conor presses Curry to collect the debt that Owen MacDermot owes Curry for medical services. O'Conor alludes to his collection plan which he mentioned to Mr. Reilly and Dr. Kelly, a Dublin physician.

1. This letter is a fragment, but the internal evidence of the allusion to a collection plan places it in late 1762.

102. To Dr. John Curry, Cow Lane, Dublin

OCD, 8.3 HS 023

4 June 1762

I know not whether I acquainted you in my last that I had a long letter from Doctor Warner on Irish history, ancient and modern. He expressed great curiosity about your book and was led astray through want of precision in one of my letters, wherein I referred him to an account of the work in the *Review*. He examined the *Monthly Review* only. I set him now right by naming the *Critical Review* for February 1760.[1] He still has credulity enough to think the epic poem of *Fingal*, a translation. I endeavored to cure him of his prejudice by arguments that I think are unanswerable till the original is produced, what I am very sure cannot be produced. He purposes to give a critical and general account of the ancient and modern state of this island in his introduction, and what he has yet done in this method is now before the Earl of Halifax. He required of me to be particular with regard to what was intended for our people in the last session. I gratified him relatively to the Elegit Bill and the despondency into which the loss of that bill had thrown so many thousands of good and industrious subjects. In relation to the disorders of the poor in Munster, I assured him (Dr. Warner) that they proceeded from the throwing of that province, like Conaght and Leinster, into pasture enclosures that excluded those poor and reduced them to a state of desperation and into that rage which despair on such occasions will dictate. I told him that the whole proceeded from laws which leave the better sort of our people no occupation in the inland counties but pasturage alone, agriculture being virtually forbidden on account of the shortness of their tenures; that in such a state Papists worry Papists, the rich excluding the poorer sort to make room for flocks and herds which are easily converted into ready money and find a ready market. I told him that the exaggerated accounts in English newspapers were groundless upon any political principle but that which I have assigned and that the persons who called this a Popish insurrection and who meant to parallel it with the affair of 1641 were not true friends to Ireland etc. . . .

1. The reviewer concluded his article with the following comments:
We shall say nothing further, but that those who are desirous of surmounting illiberal prejudices, of having their eyes purged from the film of historical falsehood, and of seeing their fellow-subjects vindicated from the imputation of a crime, which

is indeed a reproach upon human nature, will find uncommon satisfaction in perusing these *Memoirs*, which in our opinion, are written with the accuracy of a scholar, the candor of a gentleman, and the moderation of a Christian."

"Review of the *Historical Memoirs* . . . ," *Critical Review*, 10 (February 1760), 122.

103. To Dr. John Curry

OCD, 8.3 HS 023

12 June 1762

I wrote a long letter to you relatively to one I received from Dr. Warner. I could wish he had a copy of your *Memoirs* as he intends to usher in his great work with an introduction setting forth the ancient and modern state of the island. He is anxious about your work and has a good right, if he means to be impartial. I told him he would get a good general account of the work in the *Critical Review,* and I labored to demonstrate to him the injury done to our nation by Mr. David Hume; and this I did by descending to facts such as you could not but omit as they did not enter into our subjects. Mr. Hume's general character of the old Irish before '41 is this: *that they were a degree below barbarians; they were savages.* I showed this not to be the fact by opposing to it the most stubborn evidence in the world, the manners and literary compositions of that people even in the worse stage in their history from the conquest to that fatal year he describes so pathetically and so unfairly. Of these literary and poetical compositions from the conquest to the year 1631, I have a quarto volume of 1,000 pages—many, as to sentiment and force, equal to the best of our times. I confessed that during those ages of bad government the Irish were barbarians, but not in a greater degree than the other nations of Europe during those periods. Savages they were not. I have perused Mr. Hume's history since I came home. On the whole it is an excellent and useful work. He leaves blanks in it here and there, which are only filled in his manuscript copy. He was, I supposed, advised to leave those parts untilled in the printed copy, lest some ears should tingle. That leaves me room to think that he resolves to serve the world with a more complete edition of his history; and, if so, we are the better qualified to urge him about some corrections and retractions relatively to Ireland. Had I known where to direct to him, I should trouble him with an expostulatory but civil letter on this subject. Jack Comerford[1] was remiss if he made no inquiries about his place of residence. Is Jack come back? How had he negotiated the publication of our medical work?

What news about our Roman Legion? In what manner will it be defeated, by the Spaniards or by ourselves? —I have the good and honor of my country at heart, but am I not anxious in vain? Should I not rather be resigned? You and I by an impulse have done some good because we have explained and developed some truths. You and I alone have broken that silence which our people have kept so uninterruptedly for near seventy years. Have we not acquainted ourselves and shall we not now stop? I have no objection to a relapse into our former silence, yet that rogue Hume is goading and indeed galling me. I would turn on him like another ass and ask Balaam what he meant by striking. But Balaam lies hid behind a bush, and I request you will discover him for me.

1. A Dublin merchant. O'Conor and Curry used Comerford to expedite some of their publications.

104. To Dr. John Curry

OCD, 8.3 HS 023

21 July 1762

I do not love you more for the goodness of your heart and the talents of your mind than I esteem you for your political inflexibility. Your laboring to fan the spirit you infused into our people and some part of the flame you must keep alive will make a part of the history you want from me, if ever it should be undertaken by me or some abler person. The truth is, our people, broken by long habits of general distress, give up all hope of relief. Fair weather once in sixty years was made for them, they came within cable's length of good anchoring, but a new storm arose; they put to sea again without rudder, without oars, without a compass. No wonder if, in a state of desperation, they should give themselves up for lost. This condition must increase the difficulty of rousing any spirit in the majority when you see it dying away in the least desponding men among us; for my part I am a desponder by nature, and but for you would throw up my game long ago. I, however, play still because you would have me. Let the consequence be what it will. I would by all means have you make one committee soon; Mr. Reynolds,[1] Mr. Egan,[2] or some two or three of the number will join you. In such a meeting you, no doubt, will be local chairman; and whatever your resolutions be, let them be entered in your journal. I had a letter of a sheet and a half last week from Dr. Warner. He plied me with queries, objections, etc. I answered as well as I could. I had a political end in doing so, for he is great now with the Earl of Halifax. *E re nata*,³ I threw in artfully some things relating to our late disappointments, our present dispositions, etc. He wants your *Memoirs* greatly since he perused the *Review*. I directed him to Mr. Purcell's in Ship Street. My son Charles is now in Dublin and will wait on you with my affections to your family. Grieved I was that I could not remit by him a copy of my long letter to Mr. Hume.⁴ I have been for fourteen days kept in the counties of Sligo and Mayo upon business which came to nothing; this prevented my finishing what I had in hand, and I was loth to send you anything in a ragged, mutilated condition. God willing, you shall have it next week. I got a letter along with yours yesterday from Mr. Reilly. He is now at his country house, and he tells me he will, through the hands of Mr. Cunningham of London, easily remit my letter to Mr. Hume. By the way, Dr. Warner tells me that *Hume*, like *Voltaire*, writes on dogmatically against positive evidence. "They are both," says he, "men of a diabolical turn." I confess to you that I laughed heartily at this description from the pen of a priest. More news! Mr. Reilly tells me (from Cunningham's information) that Dr. Smollett is coming over to Dublin to collect materials and encouragement for a history of Ireland (Warner having failed of any encouragement among us).⁵ If there be any truth in this, we cannot be long strangers to it. Mr. Brooke is struggling with want, but he is the worst computer I know. The pen is the worst tool for getting bread in Ireland, except it falls into the hands of lawyers and physicians, and but a few even of them. He, to my knowledge, flattered himself most sanguinely with removing distress by his tragedy of *Antony*. He had but one representative before a thin house. I thank you for not accepting of his fee. Our regimental dream (I find) is all over.⁶ Now that we are awake, I am thinking that we are happily disappointed. I could urge my reasons, but most of them will occur to yourself. I am not surprised at Lord T[rimleston]'s conduct toward you. He thinks and acts by others. He is in leading strings. My paper is out; my affection to you and yours will never be so. Write me as soon as you can.

    1. James Reynolds of Ash Street, wool and silk merchant. Reynolds, who was very wealthy, became a member of the Catholic Committee. See Wall, p. 111.
    2. Boethius Egan, born in Tuam 1739, became Bishop of Achonry in 1785 and Archbishop of Tuam in 1787. John S. Crone, *A Concise Dictionary of Irish Biography* (Dublin: Talbot Press, 1928), p. 68.
    3. Things being as they are.
    4. "A Letter to David Hume, Esq., on Some Misrepresentations in His *History of England*." O'Conor's letter, dated 30 March 1762, appeared in the April and May 1763 issue of *The Gentleman's Museum*. Yale University's Beinecke Library has a full set of the magazine. Professor Alan S. Bell, Assistant Keeper of Manuscripts, National Library of Scotland, graciously pointed them out to us.

5. Smollett never came to Ireland.
6. The Roman Legion proposition was set aside until later, but Catholics were recruited surreptitiously for the armed forces.

105. To Dr. John Curry

OCD, 8.3 HS 023

6 August 1762

My Dear Sir,

I have your kind letter of the 3rd instant before me. Plain it is from the intelligence you have received that Lord T[rimlesto]n is mediating some mighty matter for his constituents. I expect no good from him, but if he does any, I do not grudge him the sum left in Mr. D[ermo]t's hands. As for you gentlemen who take some of that money for the *Farmer,* etc. I am in no pain about the matter, as you can file a bill obtaining an injunction against all the proceedings till the merits of the cause are tried.[1] He will not, I am sure, join issue on such a scrutiny. He is a disease to our people, and I am confident they will never again subject any part of their property to his most arbitrary management. I have received by my son the third edition of *The Tryal,* and I thank the writer but little for the cold compliment tacked to the conscious untruth that the author is not known.[2] He shall, God willing, be soon known in capital letters. My letter to Hume is finished. It is stained here and there with inaccuracies, and transcribing will kill me, but there is no help for it. I think that such a work well-executed is much wanted. I saw your *Third Appeal* impudently advertised in my name by Chamberlaine.[3] He should be gazetted for such boldness, and I will write to him and tell him so. The letter to Hume will make a bulky sixpenny pamphlet. If he acknowledges the receipt to show my error or to confess his own, I think it ought not to be printed. But this must be submitted to your judgment. I wrote lately to my brother in Flanders[4] but enclosed it to my son in Dublin[5] who did not receive it to enter it in the post office there. If Mr. Peter Jordan[6] brings such a letter to you, I request you will forward it without loss of time as it is of consequence to his cause. The Roscommon post office played me many tricks lately, and I may defer sending you what your friendship is impatient for, but you'll get it by hand.

1. Although Lord Trimleston stubbornly refused to release the Committee's funds, the secretary, Anthony Dermot, "in whose hands the money lay, considering himself a trustee for the body, and not the agent of his lordship's caprice or passion, handed over some of the money to the committee, who applied it to discharge their debts to Brooke and to Lord. . . ." Matthew O'Conor, *History,* p. 294.

2. Brooke's *The Tryal of the Cause of the Roman Catholics* was a subscription venture published by Dillon Chamberlaine. The first printing of the pamphlet was advertised in the *DJ*, 9–13 February 1762. Only its quick sale would allow for two more printings for new subscribers.
3. Chamberlaine also published Curry's *Third Appeal* and obviously thought to make more money from Catholic buyers by using O'Conor of Belanagare's name as author.
4. Daniel O'Conor.   5. Charles O'Conor.
6. A tailor of Schoolhouse Lane.

106. To Dr. John Curry

OCD, 8.3 HS 026

[August 1762][1]

My Dear Sir,

After many interruptions I brought my letter to Mr. Hume to a close, and yet on reading it over and comparing several members of it I do not like it. Like other whimsical architects, I must pull down the building and begin anew. A critical reader will not and surely ought not to make any allowances for my *amor patriae*.[2] I must divest myself wholly of it and give up points which cannot be supported. There is no other method left for blunting points which our adversaries endeavor to support or for giving force to matter which *can* be supported. While I make the best use I can of the prejudices of others, I shall take care that they shall not avail themselves of mine. In the affair of '41 I shall have no difficulty through the assistance I have from your book; but I shall be brief on that head by referring my adversary to the satisfaction he must obtain from the book itself; for the force of it can not possibly be condensed in the narrow compass of the letter wherein so many other matters must be explained and developed. Hume (if the character I have of him be just) will not deign to answer my letter. In that case I have a thought of appealing to a more righteous tribunal by getting the letter printed in London. Where he talks of the miseries attending the Laws of Tanistry, I join issue with him and artfully yet humbly slide into the equally miserable effects of the parliamentary laws here since the revocation of the rights granted at Limerick to the R[oman] C[atholic]s by King William; and I extend this to the late disorders among the poor cottagers in Munster. I thought it a good opportunity for explaining that matter. I think you will not dislike such a digression, though it could be impertinent to my subject in any tract except a *letter* which admits of such licenses. I declare it to you on the word of an honest man, I would not sit down to take all this trouble if I did not think I would do some little good. I may be less mistaken as to that end. Be it so, the intention is never the worse! My time and labor were better bestowed in that employment than in the pleasures and follies of revels and horse racing. I wrote four several letters to my friends in Dublin, one of them to you. Sure I am they all miscarried, for I find no replies to any of them. The by-post from Ennis to Roscommon is the most negligent that can be. My best affection to your family, my friends on Usher's Quay,[3] Mr. John Begg,[4] etc. *Vale et me ama.*[5] You must by this time have some news; let me have it as soon as you can.

 1. This letter is undated, but internal evidence indicates that it was written before 21 August 1762.
 2. Love of country.
 3. Francis and Owen MacDermot, members of the Catholic Committee.
 4. John Begg of Bridge Street, Dublin, a merchant.
 5. Farewell and love me.

107. To Dr. John Curry

OCD, 8.3 HS 023

[21 August 1762]

 I have put what I must call the last hand to a letter for Mr. David Hume. After many amputations and prunings, more I know is wanted, and omissions should be supplied, but I have not patience for all this. You, I know, will make some corrections because you will see your friend exposed to ridicule or censure as little as possible. You shall see it, God willing, next week, for I am promised a messenger who goes to town soon upon his master's affairs. He is a servant of Mr. Owen Mac-Dermot's, your former patient. He is now in town, as is (they say) his father-in-law. So I wish you joy of your fee, which has been so long in a desperate way. If you can see Mr. Reilly, I request you will prepare him for drawing a fair copy of the letter to Mr. Hume to be forthwith remitted by packets to Mr. Cunningham in London, as it contains thirty-two pages in large and close-filled quarto. What would you think of corresponding with Mr. Hume from the printing press? Let it be as you like. In his declamation against the Tanistry Laws, I have contrasted them (*e-re-nata*)[1] with the Popery Laws since King William's demise and should think that the latter are more ruinous to the public interest than the former. This I hope will do no hurt. Grandison and Falkland[2] get their own share, but an opportunity is taken to felicitate with the public in our own bitter days under a Chesterfield and a Halifax. The Whiteboys are mentioned, and that affair is set in a proper light; Dr. Curry is mentioned also, and a parallel drawn between his candor and the unfair *astutia historica*³ of Dr. Robertson,⁴ Mr. Hume's countryman. A letter which is susceptible of digressions may profitably be interspersed with such matters, and indeed on their account a long letter may be well written, though other matter may be the ground of the whole. I long to hear of the reception of your few from the hands of men who have treated you so long in an indecent manner. I long to hear of the prosperity of your family still more. Let me be made easy in these particulars, *vale et te amo*.⁵

21 August 1762

    1. Things being as they are.
    2. John Villiers, earl of Grandison. Falkland, Lucius Cary, second Viscount Falkland (1610–1643). *Concise DNB*, 1:212.
    3. Historical tricks.
    4. William Robertson (1721–1793), historian, published *History of Scotland*, 1759. *Concise DNB*, 1:1116.
    5. Farewell and I love you.

108. To Dr. John Curry, Cow Lane, Dublin

OCD, 8.3 HS 023

4 September 1762

Dear Sir,

I have done with the letter to Mr. Hume, but you have not, as it will stand in need of your chastisements. Mr. R[eilly] [is] engaged to draw a fair copy, which he will forthwith remit to his friend Mr. Cunningham in London, who will forward it to Mr. H[ume] in print or manuscript. It is now in the hands of Mr. Dominic Mahon of Strokestown, who will lodge at Kitt Weldon's in your neighborhood and who, as soon as he arrives there, engages to leave the packet at your house.¹ He will set off for Dublin on Tuesday or Wednesday next. I need no more on this subject till I have your thoughts of my manner of treating it. I long to hear of *my Lord Dictator's* [Lord Trimleston's] negotiations in London.² If he procures any good for our people, we shall forgive the past; you cannot conceive what good a madman may bring about in a maddening age. You live in the center of intelligence, and I expect a communication of your acquisitions in that way. As to what is past, something ought to be digested for the next sessions, *here* I mean a review of what this nation suffered by penal laws since the Revolution; and this cannot be executed better than by a deduction of *matters of fact.* I want materials for the work. I think it should be a clubbed performance between two or three friends who have the good of their country at heart. We are in time for such a work, and you can improve this hint into a regular plan if you should not think the game a desperate one and drop your cards out of despair rather than out of lassitude from former disappointments. You were the first (after the Revolution trance) who raised, or rather roused, the spirit among us which set friends and enemies a thinking. You will not now, I think, throw water instead of fuel on the fire you kindled, though it is what I would be very much inclined to do after what I know, what I feel, and above all what I foresee. I wrote lately to you to know if you got your fees from Mr. D[ermot], who was then in town.[3] I thought that you and my countryman, young Dr. Kelly,[4] had a good opportunity of coming at your own, you in particular who long attended his sister without any consideration.

The public disappointments you met with proceeded from no fault of your own. I cannot say the same in regard to your private disappointments. In this particular you are too remiss. I should send off this letter by the last post, but I wanted a superscriptive license. Write me as soon as you give a reading to Mr. Hume's letter. Amend, improve, and curtail it where you think proper, and reserve the original in your hands. I have delayed it too long and could not help it. Mr. Reilly you should send for immediately to take a copy, that we may lose no more time. I would have it forwarded on the score of what is said relatively to the Popery Acts and the late Munster insurrection.[5] This is the invidious, but yet the most useful part, of the letter; and for that reason I omitted subscribing my name. The paper is out, and I hardly left room for expression of the affection with which I am yours unalterably.

    1. Dominic Mahon would be related to Thomas Mahon, one of the Parliamentary candidates from Roscommon. According to the *DJ*, 17–20 October 1761, the other candidates were John French and Fitzgerald Ayscough. The Mahons were landed gentry with some of the largest holdings in Roscommon.
    2. Lords Trimleston and Killeen were deputed by the Catholic gentry to try to negotiate in England a relaxation of the Penal Laws. They received a cold reception from Lord Halifax, who had returned there from Ireland. According to Matthew O'Conor, the Dublin Committee did not "concur in this deputation." *History*, pp. 295–297.
    3. Owen MacDermot, who had been committed to a hospital by his father-in-law, Patrick French.
    4. John Kelly, Dublin physician. *FJ*, 27–30 April 1771.
    5. Eviction of peasants from lands in Munster in 1760, 1761 caused the "Whiteboy" attacks on landlords. Lecky: 226, 226n.

109. To Dr. John Curry, Cow Lane, Dublin

OCD, 8.3 HS 023

23 September 1762

Dear Sir,

This day se'en night I wrote you a short scrip in which I enclosed another to a friend in Ostend.[1] For the sake of the last, I would wish you had received both, for it concerns a friend whose interest I have as much at heart as my own. He is indeed a brother who served in France but who lately quitted that service and wants through the favor of the government to reside in his native country. How this favor can be obtained is the great difficulty. I have written on the subject to Dr. Warner but received no answer. I request your friendly assistance on this occasion; you may open a good channel for me, and I apply with the greater confidence, as I never find you disappointed in any of your undertakings excepting that wherein we all fail as well as you; I mean our attacks on the indomitable spirit of party prejudice. But that I may not drop this subject too abruptly since it opened itself to me, I congratulate you on making a considerable progress even in this attempt, desperate as it is. *Est quodam prodire tenus.*[2] You opened the trenches and took the out-works; though your pioneers were not many on setting out, yet of late many have joined you, and (what promises a great deal) some of the first rank among our adversaries have deserted over to common sense and common interest.

The last extract of a letter from London, which you remitted to me, is an instance among many more which might be produced of this. What is Lord Trimleston doing? I expect some good from him if he has sufficient skill in guiding his strokes; for the pitching axe may pull down a tree where the razor would fail. I have been three hours this day, looking and searching for the magazine you want but did not succeed. It is one of the *Universal Magazines* published by Hinton in (I think) 1752. By looking into the index of the volume in a bookseller's shop you will find what you want relatively to the Powder Plot unless you are spared the trouble by my good luck in finding here at home the pamphlet you want. You are so happy in making discoveries that I expect to find from your hands the lights which could not yet be thrown on that dark period. You will, I hope, make it clear that the English ministry fomented that plot by practicing on the rage and enthusiasm of the most desperate among the English Catholics and that they could have stifled it in the cradle, had they not purposes to serve in throwing a stain on the whole party at the time. The guilt of men who permitted themselves to be seduced into so infernal an attempt cannot be extenuated but by their madness. On every other principle we must give them up. You speak so favorably in general terms of the *Letter to Hume* that I suspect you of prejudice. When you give me your judgment more in detail, you will, no doubt, detect some mistakes and, I think, some indiscretions. You can correct the former and expunge the latter. I had the matter of that letter too much in my head to attend to proper accuracy. Here also I crave your friendly corrections. I wrote to Mr. R[eilly], who I hope will soon transcribe the letter and send it to Mr. Cunningham. As it is of a public nature, I was thinking it might be conveyed to Mr. H[ume] through the printing press. Of this thought I leave you to judge the better than I have done. Mr. R[eilly] is the properest person for making the transcript as he certainly has more skill in giving the letter entire, without bulls and interpolations, than any other of our acquaintance. Your last words to me were *scribe cito*,[3] as if I had anything worthy of your attention from this obscure country. I have been traversing it through four counties for three weeks past, very little to my advantage. I say to you, who live in the center of all the intelligence we can glean up, *scribe cito*. I have really formed no plan of the work I would have prepared for the next session. But more of this in my next as my paper is written out.

1. O'Conor's brother Daniel, stationed in Belgium with the French army.
2. It is possible to advance up to a certain point.
3. Write soon.

110. To Dr. John Curry, Cow Lane, Dublin

OCD, 8.3 HS 023

5 October 1762

Why were you not more explicit with me in yours of the 28th past, where you make mention of our friend Thady?[1] You should be more particular that I might exert all the interest my brother has abroad in his service. My brother is now in London waiting for the royal remission, and while he is there he can write to his friends in favor of ours;[2] but to do this you must by the return of the post furnish me with the proper instructions. I wrote to Lord Taaffe by this post soliciting his interest with the Primate[3] for my brother, and I request it of you, my dear friend, to favor my suit by waiting on his Lordship and putting him in mind of this one merit in addition to every other he has with his countrymen.

Since you put me in mind of Lord Trimleston's interest, I would gladly obtain it through Mr. Anthony Dermot by a letter from him to his Lordship; as you know I have neither acquaintance nor influence myself with his Lordship. I request you will let me know by next post what I am to expect from Lord Taaffe's friendship, for living in London will be too expensive to my brother, and what is more, a state of uncertainty will be extremely grievous to him. He is absolutely resolved never to return without the royal grace. You see, therefore, how much I stand in need of friends on the present occasion. My utter separation from such a brother would embitter my future life, for he is one of the most virtuous and learned men that this country produced in these latter times. His future plan of life is *vacare litteris*.[4] Mr. R[eilly] lives at Prospect Point in Fingal (I think near Swords). Had you written a line to him he would come up to you to transcribe the letter of which you speak so partially. What I said of you in it is a compliment indeed to myself, for what I have written would avail nothing without your authority. How can such a letter as mine find attention in the present warfare of politics? I, however, would have it sent to Mr. Cunningham to dispose of as he thinks proper. This letter like that you sent to Ostend will be expensive to you. I must make amends as well as I can for my constant troubles to you. I might still write on to you for two or three posts till you put me out of my present anxiety.

1. Curry's oldest son.
2. Daniel O'Conor is in London to obtain permission to enter Ireland, a privilege he has forfeited by accepting a commission in the French army. O'Conor's main concern in this letter is strategies for obtaining favors for Daniel and Thady.
3. Archbishop George Stone.
4. To abstain from literature, to give up writing.

111. To Dr. John Curry, Cow Lane, Dublin

OCD, 8.3 HS 023

23 October 1762

My Dear Sir,

This day which cost so much trouble to statesmen, to historical divines,[1] to you in particular must be still troublesome to you, for it brings you a letter from me, and I wish it may bring you no greater trouble from the pulpit orator of the day. I hope that time and *you* have quieted them, if a sense of the anniversary iniquity of the thing itself has still no influence. I have written of late two several letters to my brother in London and in each have warmly pressed upon him to do all the good offices in his power for Mr. Curry by recommending him in the strongest terms to the friendship of Mr. Henessy,[2] who is the son of Widow Hennessy to whom I directed the letter you forwarded in the Dublin post office; this you may assure yourself will be done effectually. Meantime, I request you will tender my warmest gratitude to Lord Taaffe for his interposition in favor of my brother. I trust that his suit[3] with Lord Dillon in his case will succeed as it did already in the case of Major Taaffe.[4] Of all this I gave my brother an account and hope that Lord Taaffe's letter arrived in London time enough so that my brother's personal attendance on Lord Dillon may correspond with Lord Taaffe's letter in his favor. I shall be in a state of anxiety till I hear of the effect of this negotiation, for I am not free from fears (I confess to you) on the score of Lord Dillon's coldness. But this *tibi soli*,[5] you will see by the state of my mind, how necessary your friendship will be to me on the present occasion. When you wait on Lord Taaffe, you will probably hear of Lord Dillon's answer to his letter. If it should be favorable, my trouble will (I hope) be at an end. If otherwise, we must try other means through Dr. Warner (who communicates with the Lord Lieutenant) and through the Duchess of Wharton, whose father was a cousingerman to mine.[6] By all this you see how much I must be in pain till I hear from you.

I had a letter last post from Mr. R[eilly] and confess my obligations to him for the trouble he took in transcribing my letter to Mr. H[ume] and forwarding it to Mr. Cunningham, who will dispose of its fate. Mr. R[eilly]'s condition gives me sensible pain. His wife has lately added a tenth child to his family and in all likelihood will contribute several more. He left some papers in my hands when in town. In the hurry I was in I forgot enclosing them to him but left them in one of the drawers of Mr. Lord's desk, where by mistake I left some of my own. Mine are returned, but not Mr. R[eilly]'s; assure him that they are still with Mr. Lord, though he says the contrary because, doubtless, he did not make the proper search, having, I suppose, mislaid them in the hurry of removing his things when he quitted the house in Bridge Street. I would write by this post to Mr. R[eilly] to assure him of this, but that I grudged putting him to expense till I write by hand which will be soon.

I expect little from Lord T[rimleston]'s negotiations in London but wish most heartily I may be mistaken. His journey cost our poor people £250, with a good deal of abuse into the bargain on their representatives. The breach between him and those representatives is irreparable from the pride and selfishness of his temper. There is a fatality surely in all this, and the more as this nobleman has access to our masters! But after all, may not the Committee find access also in a way of their own? By exerting their good sense, by a proper spirit, by unanimity may they not draw advantage to their constituents, by acting on their own bottom as the representatives of the whole body? May not their *Remonstrances* have infinitely more weight than the engagement of any single person who, uncalled and uncommissioned, undertakes for the whole party? You who did so much by keeping the Committee alive may invigorate it also. You have a long time before you till the commencement of the next session. I do not suspect that you will throw your oar away, as other desponders dropped theirs, but ply the stronger, especially as the coast is in view. You will make more generous efforts for your credit with posterity, but much more for conscience sake, which requries the exertion of all your talents and zeal combined. I may make a *pars minima*[7] among you, for I design *An Address to the Committee, setting forth our obligation to you as our representative now, and how well you expressed our sense to the present government, the hopes we entertain from your unwearied endeavors to reconcile us to our superiors, what further good we expect from your consults, instruction for your conduct, etc.* I have but a distant view of this design, having not written a line yet on the subject. The whole is an ebmryo thought and must continue so, unless you should bring it to life by approving of such a scheme. In truth the whole committee should approve of it before any private person presumed to address them in such a public manner. I have tired you and put you to a double expense by so long a letter, yet my brother's situation is such that I cannot avoid importuning you now and then until I know his fate.

1. The anniversary of the Irish uprising of 1641.
2. Probably Richard Hennessy (1720–1800) an Irishman who settled in France. After his retirement from Dillon's regiment, he founded the famous Hennessy distillery. *Biographical Dictionary of Irishmen in France* (Dublin: M. H. Gill and Son, 1949), p. 121.
3. Daniel's suit.
4. Major Taaffe, who is related to Lord Taaffe, was able to procure permission to return to Ireland after having served in the Austrian army. O'Conor hoped Lord Taaffe would be able to acquire the same permission for his brother Daniel, who had served in Dillon's Regiment.
5. To you alone.
6. The duchess of Wharton was Maria Theresa O'Beirne, daughter of Colonel Henry O'Beirne in the service of Spain. She was the second wife of Philip, duke of Wharton. *BP*, p. 2637.
7. A very small part.

112. To Dr. John Curry, Cow Lane, Dublin

OCD, 8.3 HS 023

6 November 1762

Daniel O'Conor's desire to return to Ireland is one of the subjects of this letter. O'Conor thanks Curry for his help in investigating ways to allow Daniel to return. Curry's son Thady has returned to St. Omer (where many Irish were educated), and O'Conor asks Curry to advise his son to use his education for any profession other than military service. O'Conor alludes to Daniel's unfortunate situation. Also, O'Conor wonders whether his article in the form of a letter to David Hume has been forwarded to a magazine in England.[1] Curry's name as author of a true history of 1641 is spelled out by O'Conor in the introduction of the article. However, Curry changed the full name to J—— C——.

1. In O'Conor's "Letter to Hume" published in *The Gentleman's Museum* (April-May, 1763) 78, O'Conor recommends for Hume's perusal the *Historical Memoirs* of "J. C. A gentleman of eminent knowledge and equal candour." Apparently O'Conor let the initials stand as Curry wished.

113. To Dr. John Curry

OCD, 8.3 HS 023

13 November 1762

Daniel O'Conor's fate is a major subject of the letter which O'Conor writes to Curry. O'Conor tells Curry that an act of Parliament and the Attorney General's interpretation of it would involve a long and complicated court case. He writes, "These difficulties are not a little augmented by the present court revolution, as those who make resignations may be the persons willing to serve us without any reward but that of doing good for its own sake."[1] O'Conor makes a veiled reference to a member of their group, possibly Henry Brooke, who "has deserted us if we ever had him." Then O'Conor becomes cautious and says, "I cannot speak more fully to this point as letters are subject to a thousand casualties, too many for discretion to trust to."

Finally O'Conor explains his disillusionment with Dr. Warner. Warner had met Daniel O'Conor in England, but Warner would not or could not use any influence he had to obtain Daniel's re-entry into Ireland. O'Conor writes, "I little considered that this was a nail that would not drive."

1. Counselor David Murphy was Daniel's barrister. Murphy compared the case of Daniel O'Conor to that of Major Taaffe, another Irish officer in foreign service who wished to return to Ireland. Murphy said that Major Taaffe had talked to Lord Dillon and to Colonel Beirne concerning the procedures by which Taaffe could be admitted into England and Ireland after serving with England's enemies. Both men, Daniel

O'Conor and Major Taaffe, could be liable for arrest and prosecution in Ireland according to the present laws. Murphy wrote:

> I found he [Daniel] had quitted his former place of abode without formal leave and entered into this country [England] without passport or license; this was not Mr. Taaffe's case, and yet, Mr. Taaffe could obtain no other passport to enable him to go over into Ireland but an attestation barely of the fact from the Secretary's [of State] office, *viz.* that he came into Great Britain with his Majesty's license; the truth is, the last Irish Penal Law against French officers does not give the King a power to enable such officers to pass into Ireland though the English act made upon the same occasion and calculated for the same purpose gives that power (to come into Britain) to his Majesty by express words. Mr. Taaffe was therefore safe at all events here, but is by no means so in Ireland but subject to the penalty of the law though he may be pardoned by his Majesty, and if he was to remain in that country, I should think it highly impudent in him to put his life in the power of informer, judge, or jury who may, if they had any spleen to him, dispatch him before his friends could procure a pardon for him. You see, therefore, the risk he runs.

David Murphy to Charles O'Conor, 9 November 1762, Stowe MS Bi1a, RIA.

114. To Dr. John Curry

OCD, 8.3 HS 023

8 December 1762

The manner in which I sent you this letter, by my son, will save you a groat, the only groat I ever saved you, in lieu of the many you lost by your friendship to me. You are in pain that I have not been more explicit with you relatively to certain anecdotes lately imparted to me; I now relieve you. I had it from a historian of no ordinary connections in England[1] that the heads of *your Captain* and *his* Lieutenant are turned giddy by their elevation.[2] Whether they are so or not, they have exhibited the signals of it marked very strongly. Let Lord T[rimlesto]n pretend what he will, I have it from Major T[aaffe] that the Captain looked on Lord T[rimlesto]n and Lord K[enmar]e, at such a distance, that were it not for the goodness, I should say sharpness of his sight, he could not know them. You cannot forget that those two noblemen got a deputation from our people in April last, signed by the chiefs of the party, and that in consequence of such deputation, they followed the *Captain* in great confidence, as his *invitations,* nay his good offices here, were a sort of engagement for future favors on the other side of the water. He received them distantly and coldly. All this is very natural.

Dr. Curry's son Thady is going into the French army. Daniel, who served in the French army encampment at St. Omer,[3] has written letters of recommendation to his friends in Dillon's Regiment. O'Conor is waiting for the outcome of certain negotiations about Daniel that Dr. Warner finally transacted.

   1. Dr. Ferdinando Warner.
   2. "The Captain" was Lord Halifax and "his Lieutenant" was William Gerard Hamilton. Halifax became first lord of the admiralty and secretary of state in 1762 after leaving Ireland. From 1761–1764, Hamilton was chief secretary for Ireland. *Concise DNB*, 1:373, 564. Warner wrote O'Conor about writing to Lord Halifax and Secretary Hamilton concerning Daniel O'Conor's case. William Ponsonby, the former Postmaster General of Ireland, had visited Dr. Warner and had written to the speaker of the Irish House of Commons (John Ponsonby) at Warner's request. William Ponsonby gave a strong character recommendation for Daniel O'Conor and assured Warner that Daniel would be pardoned. However, without waiting for his pardon, Daniel left for Ireland. Dr. Ferdinando Warner to Charles O'Conor, 9 November 1762, Stowe MS Bi1, RIA.
   3. See Richard Hayes, *Biographical Dictionary of Irishmen in France* (1949), pp. 225, 226 for information about Daniel O'Conor, a captain in Lord Dillon's Irish Regiment, and about O'Conor's attitude about serving with the French. Also see note of previous letter.

115. To Dr. John Curry

RIA, Stowe MS Bi1

22 January 1763

This first draft letter has fifteen lines crossed out that concern O'Conor's brother Daniel visiting him and Daniel leaving a manuscript with Reilly in Dublin. Daniel is working on a philosophical treatise called "The Operation of the Mind." The major news that O'Conor imparts to Curry is the conforming of Lord Trimleston's son to the Established Church.[1] Sir Patrick Bellew has been a leader in the Catholic Committee, but he has been deposed.[2] Finally the Committee has voted an award to Mr. Gorges Edmond Howard[3] for his help.

   1. Curry informed O'Conor that Mr. Barnewall, the son of Lord Trimleston, has conformed to the Established Church under Dr. Mar at St. Andrew's Church, Dublin. Curry wrote, "The reason and motive for his having taken these steps is to hinder his Lordship from encumbering the estate." Five years later, a notice in the *DJ*, 30 January–2 February 1768, announced that "by Mr. Barnewall's and his brother's conformity to the Protestant religion, his father is but tenant for life" on his estate. Dr. John Curry to Charles O'Conor, 15 January 1763, Stowe MS Bi1, RIA.
   2. Sir Patrick Bellew of Barmeath in County Louth. Wall, p. 106.
   3. Gorges Edmond Howard (1715–1786) was a lawyer and writer of plays and essays. *Concise DNB*, 1:648.

116. To Dr. John Curry, Cow Lane, Dublin

OCD, 8.3 HS 023

16 March 1763

My Dear Sir,

I thank you greatly for the information you gave me in your last, that our superior clergy have agreed to a collection. My experience, however, of mankind gives me great diffidence, and I wish I may not be mistaken in my thought that those gentlemen should give such a test of their sincerity as would render suspicion ill-natured as well as uncharitable. My meaning is this: I would propose that on the approaching visitation through every diocese of the kingdom they should carry a printed paper along with them setting forth the expediency and necessity of the collection to be made.[1] Their warm recommendation of it to their clergy and laity would doubtless produce a considerable sum; and each subscriber's contribution should be placed after his name at the bottom or on the opposite page of the paper produced to prevent fraud or embezzlement. I have not time to find matter or words for such a printed instrument. Stinted, however, as I am, I venture to throw out a hint to be rejected or improved:

"The Penal Laws now in force, having thrown the principal Roman Catholics of this kingdom into the wasteful occupation of grazing, on account of the discoverable interest and the shortness of tenure, the poorer sort are thereby deprived of employment and driven into desperate courses. To remedy, therefore, so great an evil, it is expected that those R[oman] C[atholic]s who occupy great tracts of pasture lands and occasion great depopulation in this kingdom, will charitably agree to a voluntary contribution so as that some fund may be established for the relief, etc."

I leave the rest to be supplied if our betters think that such a hint is worth improving. I much approve of the scheme of putting together in apt words the resolutions in the committee book. I never liked the preamble though some of the matter is very proper and by no means to be omitted. Our future resolutions will, I hope, be more for our credit as to the expression, etc.

I lament for the sake of all our people the new insurrection in Munster. I think, however, that it must soon be over. It fatally prevents the necessity of an advertisement to the letter written last summer to Mr. Hume, as you will observe.

Mr. R[eilly] proposes a weekly paper, and I like the plan of it. I think it, however, impracticable, as the persons who would assist the undertaking are taken up with domestic concerns too much to carry on such a work with the proper spirit. Our committee cannot possibly choose a better secretary; he and his friends cannot be sufficiently grateful for your kind interposition for him. He has been unrewarded for the pains he took formerly, though you may remember that £10 were adjudged for him in one of our sessions. What have you relatively to Mr. MacDermot?² You have omitted giving any account in your last. This affair, dear sir, concerns your family, and you cannot wonder if I interested myself in it.

    1. O'Conor's idea paralleled the municipal tax paid by Catholics and other minorities for residence in communities. Although such a Protestant "quarterage" tax was unconstitutional, it was still collected. Ironically the government labeled such tax collections by the Catholic Association illegal. Yet O'Conor's collection was the precedent for the O'Connell all-Ireland Catholic collection in 1824. Wyse, 1:84. O'Conor's proposal was rejected by the Catholic bishops. As a result of the bishops' refusal, the Catholic Association shifted its focus from helping destitute Catholic farmers back to its original purpose of collecting money for lobbying purposes.
    2. Probably Owen MacDermot, who owes Curry money.

117. To Dr. John Curry, Cow Lane, Dublin

OCD 8.3 HS 023

25 March 1763

My Dear Sir,
    Your last letter gave me pleasure, and I wish it may give me more in the execution of the plan you mentioned, as consented to by the most impracticable of our own people, the ecclesiastical society. If they be sincere and active, the *collection* will undoubtedly succeed. A fund will be created for great and important purposes under the direction of our committee. I say under the direction, as they have much more knowledge, more prudence, and equal zeal at least, with former private undertakers. Volunteer, but at the same time *unaccountable*, representatives of whom no better can be said at present than that they effected nothing *positively* for us nor could give us any hope that aught ever *would be* effected, notwithstanding all that they have expended to give some satisfaction to their constituents. In my last I threw out some hasty thoughts before you relatively to a plan for making the collection consented to the more effectual. The committee will think of a better, and printed copies of it should be put into the hands of the chief ecclesiastics before they begin their visitation. Copies should be

given also to some of the principal lay Catholics in each county as cooperators with the prelates and as *trustees* accountable to the committee. I say no more on this head, as a hint is sufficient.

I had yesterday a letter from Dr. Warner in eight days from his house in Surrey. His first volume is printed all to the introduction, and indeed I took the liberty to tell him that you were his friend (as a subscriber) and that you informed me that Dr. Hughes was active in his service. He took this the kinder, as he was not known to either of you, and he wrote to Hughes to give him his thanks. He complains of disappointments from every quarter. The general fate of men of letters after a surfeit of literature during a whole century! By the way, who is Dr. Hughes?[1] But satisfy me first to a more important query. How is our friend Thady? From some late revolutions on the continent I am uneasy about his success. I request you will dissipate this uneasiness. My brother sends you his affections very warmly. The society he lived with for several years past is in a manner dissolved. He finds a satisfaction in excommunicating them before it came to their turn to excommunicate him.

I leave for last an affair personal to myself and what agitated my mind with some deep anxiety for some time. On Tuesday last—returning from a friend's house, my horse tumbled on his forehead, I on mine. The shock was so great that on getting up my eyes darted what resembled a multitude of little stars; I soon recovered my usual sight, but the next day I discovered that a cloud rested on the pupil of my right eye; it did not alarm me much then, as I felt no pain, but the case soon altered as I find that cloud hanging still over the pupil, and yet without any sensible pain. I was conceding that perhaps Nature laid a train there for some time past and that the accident of the fall set fire to it. Should I lose that eye and in consequence the other, I should be of all others the most miserable, as I have derived most of the comforts of life through the medium of those organs. I request you will by the return of the post give me your instructions and direct[ions] for me at the post office in Roscommon.

P.S. Some time ago our friend[2] sent me down the copy of a paper under the title of *Reconciler,* which he purposes should be continued weekly to prepare the public by knowledge and real facts for that moderation which is so necessary to open eyes prejudiced against not only the public interest, but even the private utility of every individual. The plan is good, yet I could not but inform him that I thought the execution would not be equal, as the gentlemen he depended upon could not from their several engagements of another nature give sufficient attention to such a work, that it were better not engage in such undertaking than carry it on languidly without the spirit which is necessary to recommend detached pieces. Has he consulted you on this head? Could he indeed engage others of ability to assist him, the plan would be an excellent one. In that case you and I might throw in an occasional essay.

    1. A Rev. Lambert Hughes subscribed to Faulkner's edition of *The Universal History*. *DJ*, 18–21 January 1746.
    2. Michael Reilly.

118. To Dr. John Curry, Cow Lane, Dublin

OCD, 8.3 HS 023

Roscommon, 31 March 1763

My Dear Sir,

    The kind letter you wrote to me 'ere yesterday lies now before me. I am here involved in various business at public assizes, God help me; it prevents my following your directions immediately. And yet I dread the ill consequences of postponing them, for my eye is still under a cloud, like the possessor of it since his birth. As soon as I am at home I shall religiously pursue your instructions; sooner is not possible. I will give you an account of the effects, for I know of none alive who has a stronger feeling for me—Dr. Dillon I knew. He thrived well by his profession in this country. He was a little singular in his manners and was charged with no small share of *astutia medica:*[1] on the whole he was a good man. I like the paper you sent me enclosed extremely. It has been drawn up and conceived with great judgment. I am convinced of the propriety and utility of printing it. You should have the session of a night at the Elephant and press it on the president of your committee.

    Numbers, my dear friend, are just come into the chamber.

    1. Medical cunning.

119. To Dr. John Curry

OCD, 8.3 HS 023

Belanagare, 19 April 1763

My Dear Friend,

After what happened [to] me, I know you will be surprised at my long silence: from the Assizes of Roscommon I did not return to this place but traversed several counties of this western province, though my circle was not large. I was bound by duty and friendship to other people. I acquitted myself at the hazard of my health and of an eye half-departed. I came home at last and to my advantage made use of your prescription. Sensible I am that I have lapsed much time. The good effect of the remedy proves that a little cloud, however, still rests on the eye, on the circle which surrounds the pupil. [Others] tell me a little spot or speck appears; hence the cloud I complain of. An apothecary who thinks himself learned viewed that point of spot and calls it a little collection of extravagant blood in the shock I received by my fall; I would (without learning) rather think it some shock given to the crystalline humor. I should doubtless, as you direct, wait on you in Dublin to be re-established thoroughly if possible after my long and, indeed, unavoidable neglect of any remedy; but, my dear friend, my condition as to domestic avocations is such as cannot admit of any deputation. I am involved in business which requires my own eye; (I have one still that I can call my own) with *that* I will see you next winter (God sparing life to such a loving pair). I will see you and I will feel you then. I think I do both this minute, the latter most certainly. I dwell too long on this. Let me change to a better subject. How are my dear Mrs. Curry—my dear Miss Curry, Martin,[1] etc.? Thank you for what you say of your friend, dear Thady. I request you will present my affections to Jack Comerford, Mr. Begg, Mr. Dermot, Mr. O'Brien,[2] etc.

I have but one frank and therefore will not put our friend Mr. R[eilly] to any expense this post. I also have a cup before me and here is your health. Mr. R[eilly] has laid the plan of a weekly paper for next winter; it is a good and proper one. To execute it with spirit, ten or twelve able stock numbers should be prepared, that the authors might not disappoint the public by unfinished or, in other words, hurried essays. It is doubtless easier to plan well than to execute. My brother[3] is more vacant than any of us, yet his speculations being employed on other subjects, I doubt he would make no good figure on ours. Your hands are full of a profession, mine full of rural occupation; I, therefore, despond of Mr. R[eilly]'s scheme, not indeed for want of materials, but of scaffolding and workmen. I declare to you on the word of a man of good heart to his party and to all parties that I would labor to my utmost in Mr. R[eilly]'s plan, were I not sunk in rural business, which must be attended to *chiefly* with the view of being *more vacant hereafter* for matters relative to our own people (as far as a poor capacity can extend). This I propose, however God may dispose of the proposer. I ought to rate you about the great delay of *our* medical work, unless you are extending it more and more for the benefit of the human race. In that case (and no other) we and posterity owe you great obligations while you are enlarging your stock of medical reputation and deriving at the same time advantage to your family. Be full with me on this head in your next. But previously take this advice; let the publication by all means be in London, and let not the copy be absolutely a present to a stranger, and the most ungrateful of all strangers, a London bookseller. This paper is out and if I scribble more, it must be on the franked cover. *Vale et me ama.*[4]

1. Curry's son.
2. Members of the Catholic Committee.
3. Daniel O'Conor.
4. Farewell and love me.

120. To Dr. John Curry

OCD, 8.3 HS 023

Roscommon, 7 May 1763

My Dear Friend,

My mind is so broken with my recent misfortune that I am unable to talk to you properly or consistently on any subject. My brother Mathew O'Conor, parish-priest of this place, died on Wednesday last of the current destructive fever. He fatally would not submit to take to his bed till the sixth day of his illness when he could sit up no longer. On Sunday last he lay down and died in two days after. This was his last and only disorder in the course of thirty-five years. He was a robust and very healthy man and died in the fiftieth year of his life. No man was evermore lamented by all his parisioners. None could have more merit as an honest and pious man or as a learned and zealous ecclesiastic. This gives me great consolation, though I am in more respects than one a great sufferer by his death. I am sick of this world, and I trust that my growing indifference is preparing me for a better;

I shall endeavor, however, to be as active in it as my duty requires, more seemingly than really fond of it. This is ill-expressed. But you know what my heart dictates.

States grow delirious like individuals. The scene exhibited and exhibiting still in the capital of these islands is the strongest instance I ever knew, in my own time, of state frenzy. To us neutrals it shows itself in the fullest light. Let it end as it will, we are far distant from the bolt and the thunder. It is your duty to go on with the work you began and keep some life in your own people by keeping life, if possible, in our committee. Who is *Northumberland?*[1] In this remote western corner we are strangers to most of those men who put this world in motion and who by their private characters make it what it is, more or less miserable. I long to hear from you, for I love you heartily, and I fear for you too, as you are as much exposed to the bitters of life as myself.

You are, no doubt, revising and extending your medical work, but you are delaying it perhaps too much. Had my brother read it, it might have preserved his life.

1. Sir Hugh Percy, the second earl of Northumberland, fourth baronet, became lord lieutenant of Ireland in 1763 and served until 1765. *Concise DNB*, 1 : 1029.

121. To Dr. John Curry, Cow Lane, Dublin

OCD, 8.3 HS 023

12 June 1763

My Dear Sir,

Through my journey to the county of Sligo and other avocations (the business of others not my own) I am long in arrears to you. I now discharge it to the best of my power. It, I confess, gives me pain that the Hyper-doctor's sickness has put a stop to our well-planned collection. It is, I am afraid, an ominous contingency, as I am certain neither he nor his brethren were ever fond of it; they yielded (such as did yield) reluctantly. The causes of such low, not strange, conduct could be assigned. You know them. When these gentlemen foresee that their own power is not to be re-established, they little care what becomes of their lay-brethren; nay they may entertain the silly, the nonsensical, and unconscionable idea that the more our people are discontented with unprovoked penalities, the better for them in their consequences. God grant that I may be mistaken. The conduct they held in former and more recent time gives but too much countenance to suspicions.

I am glad to hear that you keep some life in our committee. When the president is not among you, you should have a local chairman and enter the business of the night in your journal, be it what it will. I pity our friend R[eilly] for his peevish, unwitty witticisms. I shall not trouble him with any reproof on that head as I know it is now needless. It does not appear by your last that you have made up any traveling charges for the *Farmer*. To part with him with a good grace, I think it was right to give him some succor, if it was given.[1] I had a letter sometime since from Dr. Warner. His first volume is out and got a ready vent in London. Here, he complains of bad treatment from the whole nation. Your friend Dr. Hughes did not answer his letter, and Mr. Faulkner, in whom he reposed a particular confidence, neglected him. I have obtained nine subscriptions for him, and he confesses that next to the speakers of the House of Commons, I have done him more services than any lord or bishop of our island. He testifies sensible dissatisfaction through the whole. The few copies he sent hither are in the hands of Dr. Bowden of Stafford Street.[2] I could wish you gave me your judgment of the work, for my book is not come down nor can I say when it will from the neglect of those who send carriages to Conaght. By the way, I had a friendly letter this last week from Mr. Faulkner with a handsome present enclosed: a dissertation of Dr. Brown[3] on *The Rise, Union, and Power, etc., of Poetry and Music*. The subject is admirably handled. George [Faulkner] is very urgent with me to prepare a new edition of the *Dissertations* on our Irish history. Could I sit down to castrate and amend the work, I would indulge him. I would be better pleased to see those *Dissertations* dead and buried than to see them come out in a second edition under all the disadvantages of the first. Several things should be omitted and many supplied. If I can sit down to read old trash a second time, I will, and you may expect something in this way next winter if God spares me life to see you. I say you may expect this, for I am not certain that my other avocations will allow me sufficient leisure. I had lately a letter and a very polite one in French from Lady Lismore in Paris,[4] complaining of the injury done to Milesian families of Ireland, her own in particular, by the late Lord Marshal Thomond, representing all who had no patents of nobility before the late revolution as plebeians and imposters.[5] She requires of me to set this affair right from a presumption that the writer of the *Dissertations* would have weight in determining it. I made answer that as soon as her ladyship furnished me with the proper materials relative to her own family, I should willingly undertake the task and execute it to the best of my power in vindication of the surviving families of old inhabitants. I despair of the letter to Mr. Hume. I am certain it suffered shipwreck in its first voyage. Were it, as you think, worthy of a second voyage, I would wish you could get it transcribed and amended by your own hand. In that case, the delay would be no great matter, and the work would appear to more advantage.

1. Henry Brooke has obviously decided to end his association with the Dublin Committee. Subsequently he hired out to the other side, for he became the first editor of the violently anti-Catholic newspaper, *The Public Register or Freeman's Journal*, whose first issue appeared on 13 September 1763. However, Brooke did not remain long as editor because he was not satisfied with his pay. Richard Robert Madden, *The History of Irish Periodical Literature from the End of the Seventeenth to the Middle of the Nineteenth Century* (London: T. C. Newby, 1867; rpt. New York: Johnson Reprint Corporation, 1968), 2:389, 392.
2. John Bowden, D. D., Chaplain to the Lord Chancellor. *DJ*, 25–27 January 1776, obituary.
3. John Brown (1715–1766), Whig preacher, playwright, and essayist. *Concise DNB*, 1:153.
4. Maria Josepha O'Brien.
5. Charles O'Brien, sixth viscount Clare, and Marshal Thomond (1699–1761). *Concise DNB*, 1:960. See O'Conor's letter to Lady Lismore, 25 July 1763, 126.

122. To Gorges E. Howard[1]

RIA, Stowe MS Bi1

Belanagare, 4 July 1763

O'Conor has been to Tirawley in Co. Mayo. He replies to Howard's pleasantry that O'Conor's good opinion of him expressed to both Dr. Warner and Mr. Faulkner needs no reply. He comments that Ireland is "yet undistinguished in Europe by a good history. . . ." O'Conor flatters Howard by telling him that Howard, through his literary pursuits, has tried to give a clear picture of life in Ireland without prejudice to either side. O'Conor also describes the problems of Catholics, who had no civil rights and who were considered an "obnoxious race."

1. Gorges E. Howard, a wealthy Dublin attorney, wrote numerous poems and plays, all failures. His vanity made him a frequent subject of satire. Gilbert, *History of the City of Dublin* (Dublin: McGlushan, 1854–1859), 2:44–45. O'Conor is obviously playing to Howard's well-known ego.

123. To Dr. John Curry, Cow Lane, Dublin

OCD, 8.3 HS 023

4 July 1763

Postal service to rural Belanagare is improving. O'Conor writes to Curry that the latter's letter took only thirty-six hours to arrive from College Green to Belanagare. O'Conor asks Curry what can the Catholic Association accomplish with such a dictatorial person as Lord Trimleston as its head? O'Conor relates that he received a letter from Mr. Gorges Howard, who "doubtless intends us good." O'Conor comments on religious matters, the appointment of Dr. Fitzsimons and a visit from the two bishops previously mentioned anonymously:

You are the first who informed me of Dr. Fitz[simon]'s being made vicar-capitular.[1] I thank you warmly for an information so very agreeable to me. I wish and hope that this step may bring him into a chair which he is so worthy of filling. A man of his good sense would be extremely useful to us. He is already known and known to his advantage at the Castle. Every possible effort should be made by postulations, lay and clerical, to have him nominated for now the first see in the kingdom. The two bishops, Fallon and Kirwan, will be (I hear) at my house tomorrow.[2] I shall do what lies in me to procure all their interest. A stranger introduced to that see would not only be extremely disagreeable to all parties in Dublin, but even to all Catholics in the Kingdom. I need not press it on you to be active in an affair of so much importance to us. Every Catholic nobleman in the kingdom ought to be retained in our friend's cause or rather, indeed, our own . . .

1. Archbishop Richard Lincoln, with whom O'Conor had difficulty, died 21 June 1763. O'Conor was on much more friendly terms with his successor Archibishop Patrick Fitzsimons, who remained in office until 24 November 1769. *HBC*, pp. 401–402.
2. James O'Fallon was Roman Catholic bishop of Elphin, while Patrick Robert Kirwan was bishop of Achonry. *HBC*, pp. 407, 409.

124. To Dr. John Curry, Cow Lane, Dublin

OCD, 8.3 HL 024

23 July 1763

Nineteen days after he received Curry's letter of the fourth, O'Conor replies, "Some time since I sent you a letter. On this rainy, spleengiving Friday I wrote several: one to Lady Lismore in Paris,[1] another to Mr. G. Faulkner, one to Dr. Sullivan,[2] and one to Mr. Anthony Dermot. . . ." O'Conor complains that his writing his *Dissertations on a History of Ireland* influences people like Lady Lismore to refer to him as an expert on Irish genealogy. O'Conor tells Curry that he has suggested to Dr. Warner that Warner might ask the Dublin Society for a subvention to pay part of the cost of publishing and promoting an edition of *The Annals of the Four Masters*. O'Conor writes, "Hereby the old classical language of Ireland would be preserved also." Will Dr. Fitzsimons be picked as archbishop of Dublin to succeed the late Dr. Lincoln, O'Conor asks. Finally, O'Conor picks apart another flaw in Warner's history, the problem of conformity to Rome in the early Irish Church:

> In spite of all my arguments Dr. Warner has revived the exploded *Usserian* chimera, that the religion established here by Roman missionaries in the fifth century was that now established here by law. Such a groundless hypothesis hardly deserves a serious refutation. Ussher did not dare aver that the Roman missionaries did not preach the Roman doctrines, but he avers by the strongest implication that Rome herself in those days was truly orthodox to a scheme of worship established by Act of Parliament in thirteen hundred years after.[3]

1. O'Conor must have revised his letters to Lady Lismore and Dr. Sullivan, since the extant copies are dated 25 July 1763. No letter to Faulkner is available.
2. Francis Stoughton Sullivan (1719–1776) was a fellow of Trinity College and an author of a treatise on feudal law. *Concise DNB*, 1:1265.
3. James Ussher (1581–1656), Protestant archbishop of Armagh, historian and apologist. Ussher claimed that the Christianity of the early Irish was not in conformity to Rome because the Church was a national church not subject to the Pope, just as the Anglican Church is.

125. To Dr. Francis Sulivan

RIA, Stowe MS Bi2a
Doctor Sullivan

25 July 1763

Sir,

Irish history and literature, beginning at present to engage attention at home and abroad, a person so well-skilled in both as you are ought certainly to contribute to this branch of useful knowledge. It is a subject hardly yet attempted, and could I have the merit of prevailing with you to withdraw some hours from your severer studies and devote them to this, it would, I think, be the best service I could render the public.

To lay foundations for this knowledge, the *Annals of the Four Masters* together with other valuable fragments in your hands and mine ought to be printed accurately. Hereby the classical language of the ancient Scots would be preserved; many curious historical facts relative to the politics and manners of the nation would be preserved also; all would be lost if these manuscripts were burned or otherwise destroyed.

Such a work would probably be brought within the compass of three volumes in large quarto; and yet as the generality of our people have hitherto despised and yet despise all undertakings on this subject, plain it is that little could be obtained in the way of subscription to forward it. I see but one remedy for this evil, to engage the Dublin Society to lay by a part of their fund for promoting this branch of knowledge. Five hundred pounds would probably complete it, an expense which surely men of their spirit must deem a trifle when balanced with the honor it would derive to their country, not to mention the utility of such a work in bringing to light some important parts of literature which have hitherto lain in the shade.

If through your solicitation, such an expense were assented to, Malone or Percy should be employed to cast a handsome Irish type of which I could give a good cut, but I decline saying more when I know that the hint I have given is to you sufficient. I am so accustomed to think such an undertaking desperate and impracticable that my hopes lead me but a short way.

126. To Lady Lismore

RIA, Stowe MS Bi2a

25 July 1763

The honor your ladyship did me in your letter of the 6th of April last had been long since acknowledged had not my cousin MacDermot (who lives not a great distance from Paris) forgotten to favor me with your Ladyship's address. I know the value of such a correspondence too well not to improve by every effort the importance it gives me. In a case of this nature, self-interest is very strong; and however it may lessen the value of our gratitude, yet it removes any suspicion of our sincerity. Let me therefore assure your Ladyship that I am most warmly in the number of those faithful retainers to your person and family. The injury to your Ladyship in particular and to our nation in general from the late Maréschal Thomond gives me pain.[1] It would be easy (even for me) to refute the charge he brought against both, and I purpose to do so if God spares me life, to see a republication of the little *Dissertations* I wrote on the antiquities of our country. As to your Ladyship's complaint, I wait with impatience for the memoirs you promise to put into my hands to give you and the public every satisfaction in my power; and I am thinking that your affair is so connected with the calumny cast on our whole nation that there is no separating them without making your vindication more defective than it ought to be. However that be, I trust that your Ladyship would not take it ill if our few remaining ancient families received the benefit of your particular defense; but this is entirely submitted to your Ladyship's better judgment.

I enclose this to Cousin MacDermot[2] in hope that it may come to your Ladyship's hands; I return you the warmest gratitude for your regard which you express for my family and the services you have rendered some gentlemen of my name. Such services warm me the more, as they mark the extent to which the benevolence of some minds may be carried. On such tempers we can not presume too much. I, therefore, request you will add to the honor you have done me by introducing me to your children and prevailing with them to accept of my services.

1. Charles O'Brien, earl of Thomond. Viscount Clare, an O'Brien, and the earl of Lismore, from another branch of the family, both claimed the Thomond title, after the Marshal died. In 1762, after Lord Clare's death, his son was given the title earl of Thomond, which became extinct with Clare's death at Paris in 1774. So Lady Lismore lost the case. *BDIF,* pp. 215–216.

2. Captain Peter MacDermot served in the French Army (1741–1773). Dunleavy and Dunleavy, p. 31. OCD, 8.3 SH 051.

127. To George Faulkner

BM, Egerton 201, f-41

Belanagare, 8 August 1763

George Faulkner has sent O'Conor two books as gifts: *Sermons* by Dr. Herring[1] and the Duke of Leeds's *Thought on a Bill.* . . .[2] O'Conor writes, "I had, I confess strong prejudices against Dr. Herring from the character given of him in your edition of Swift's Works. . . ."[3] Dr. Warner wrote O'Conor complaining of the treatment he had received from the gentry and booksellers who did little to promote his book in Ireland. "Smollett (in the *Critical Review*[4])," O'Conor writes, "treated him with disingenuity. . . ." O'Conor thanks Faulkner for the books and for Faulkner's and Mr. Howard's good wishes. O'Conor concludes, "While two such men think well of my endeavors and studies, I take it that I have encouragement enough to proceed. To be useful to the public may not be in power, to labor to be so is doubly our duty."

1. Thomas Herring (1690–1757), archbishop of Canterbury, 1747–1757. Satirized by Swift when Herring was a court chaplain to George the Second.

2. Thomas Osborne was successively first earl of Danby, Marquis of Carmarthen, and Duke of Leeds (1631–1712). The production vaguely called by O'Conor "Thoughts" might possibly be a pamphlet which relates to the legality of the Irish House of Lords called, *A Letter from a Member of the House of Commons of Ireland to a Gentleman of the Long Robe in England:* Containing *An Answer to Some Objections Made against the Judicatory Power of the Parliament of Ireland.* To which is added *The Late Duke of Leed's Reasons for Protesting against a Vote made in the House of Lords in England Which Declared a Certain Tryal before the House of Lords in Ireland to Be Coram non Judice.*

3. Swift said in *The Intelligencer Papers,* No. 3: "But I should be very sorry that any of them should be so weak, as to imitate a *Court Chaplain* in England, who preached against the *Beggar's Opera;* which will probably do more Good than a thousand Sermons of so stupid, so injudicious, and so prostitute a Divine."

4. Smollett wrote in the May 1763 *Critical Review:* "Had this writer studied to increase the number of those who are but too apt to ridicule the Irish nation, he could not have done it more effectually than by telling us (as in fact he does) in his preface, that they employed the author of Warner's Ecclesiastical, to write their Civil History; that they invited him from London to Dublin for that purpose; and even paid him for his trouble."

128. To Dr. John Curry, Cow Lane, Dublin

OCD, 8.3 HS 023

Belanagare, 9 August 1763

O'Conor responds negatively to Curry's information that young Thady Curry has joined the French Army. O'Conor is disturbed because Lord Taaffe has placed much of his interest in Irish Catholic affairs in the hands of a young man. Lack of recognition as well as lack of experience with Irish Catholics will hurt the young man and will cause older, wiser members of the Association to leave, O'Conor writes. Also the army is commandeering horses to support their troops in dealing with farmers' unrest:

We are here almost everyday tormented with the march of troops into the neighboring province. They seize upon our horses for carrying their baggage from town to town, and we have all the apparatus of war without war. On the whole, the Puritans of the North will disperse their mobs, and we shall hear no more of them after a few days, for they are not friendless, a circumstance sufficient to render their enemies moderate, nay circumspect, in the exertion of power.[1]

1. O'Conor refers to the Protestant uprisings of the Oakboys and the Steelboys. Lecky, 2:45–51.

129. To Dr. John Curry

OCD, 8.3 HS 023

19 August 1763

O'Conor counsels the Catholic Association to hold on to the contact with Henry Brooke if it cannot use him as a writer. One reason Brooke was being unreasonable was that he felt he had not been provided with sources enough for his pro-Catholic pamphlet, *The Tryal of the Roman Catholics*. O'Conor becomes irritated by this news from Curry. O'Conor commiserates with Curry about an unauthorized edition of Curry's *Memoirs* being published in London. He and Curry share the joke that Brooke thought O'Conor had written the *Memoirs* and that this book had been the major source for Brooke's pamphlet, *The Tryal*. Also Dr. Warner still complains to O'Conor about the ill-treatment he has received from Smollett and the ex-viceroy:

He complains to me bitterly of the little notice taken of him by our nobility and gentry and of the treatment given him by Dr. Smollett in the *Literary Review* for May last.[1] Nay further, our late Viceroy[2] did nothing for him at court, and the usual gratification for a *dedication* has been hitherto withheld. I leave you to make your own reflections on all this. To me it is astonishing that a man of letters should be so treated by a great minister of whom so much is said to his advantage in the Doctor's preface. It is surely an anecdote which discovers *the man within.*

I am glad that we have so active an agent now in London as Jack Comerford. I am sorry, however, that he had not a commission from Mr. Reilly to get the two little tracts you mention out of Mr. Cunningham's hands. Otherwise, how can he come at them? The letter to Hume is not as well drawn up as I would wish, yet with all its faults I trust it has merit enough to be useful and truth abundant enough to show that Mr. Hume merited the rebuke he gets as a careless historian. . . .

1. Smollett wrote, "To do the Doctor justice, however, his narrative and apologies are sometimes not destitute of plausibility, though they always are of historical precision; and his style and manner are such as we may call historical romance. . . ." "Review of the History of Ireland," *Critical Review*, 15 (May 1763), 361–367.

2. Lord Halifax.

130. To Dr. John Curry

RIA, Stowe MS B i 1

[15 September 1763]

My [Dear] Sir,

[Ink faded and paper torn. The Catholic Association and its secretary Anthony Dermot are mentioned.] You should despair of any good from such men as we have to do with, or you should tell Mr. Dermot and Mr. Reynolds that you thought it in vain to [unreadable] them or the Association any longer with messages or meeting. I think as you do; you have acted your part honorably, warmly, and honestly and have nothing to do but to give up your political patients, as you do every other patient, when all the symptoms of dissolution are too strong to admit of any help from art or nature.[1] I am ill-natured enough to receive some gratification from this state of things. The scorners and censurers you mention do not deserve any revolution in their favor, and it is fit they should remain as they are, the objects of popular odium to their masters and of contempt to their abused friends. I am however (on the score of the few good and sensible among us) glad that some considerable members of the H[ouse] of C[ommons] have engaged to bring our Elegit Bill a second time on the carpet.[2] It may pass here; and if it be thrown under the table on the other side, we know to whom the disappointment will be chargeable.

I shall be in pain till you send me one of the *[London] Chronicles* of the 27 of September.[3] It is a very pleasing circumstance that the author is not known and that the staring graspers have attributed the work to such popular orators as you mention. The ridicule here reviles strongly against themselves. It is fit to foster them in this mistake for some time, that the awkwardness of their folly may glare upon them the more hereafter when they are brought to consider that what they extoll so much in a H[amilto]n or Burke they would readily censure in their best friend.

The "Letter to Hume" is, I am told by Mr. R[eilly], come out in some obscure London monthly collection, I suppose in broken and detached pieces. We must leave such orphans to their fate.

I would gladly know the *Freeman's* political plan. He and Dr. Lucas are associated in the execution of it.[4] We should return those gentlemen by the fairest [Top of letter corrupt. O'Conor is talking about publication as he mentions George Faulkner and the manuscript of the *Annals of The Four Masters*. He hoped to have its publication cost underwritten by the Dublin Society.] I was aware of the difficulty that stood in the way and gave him [Dr. Sullivan] my opinion that unless the Dublin Society favored the undertaking and negotiated with the House of Commons for a fund to bear the expense, nothing could be done. I received a polite answer from him; and he very readily not only adopted my plan, but assured me he had the matter in contemplation a long time. After all I am thinking on good grounds that the Dublin Society will not meddle with the matter, though certainly such a publication would do honor to the patrons of literature in Ireland if any such we have. It would preserve the classical language of the former inhabitants and many important facts also necessary to be known for discovering the manners, principles, and politics of that people. I shall write to the Doctor by this post or the next. He thinks I should go to town immediately that we might draw up such a plan relatively to this undertaking as would prejudice men of rank and spirit here in its favor. But my avocations at home prevent my going to town so soon as he requires. Without my assistance he is able and I believe willing to draw up such a scheme. Though publication of it will cost but little, I expect nothing from the success of it; though were there any hope of its being considered, I would in that case suspend the business which confines me at home. I apply to agriculture with the honest view of preserving my own independence. No literary engagements should draw me from an attention to this object, though I always endeavored to reconcile both. The pleasure of seeing you and conversing with you will certainly bring me to town this winter for some time if God spares one life. Write soon. Send me the *Chronicles*.

15 September 1763

1. Wyse, 1:89. wrote that the Association "rather gradually melted away than abruptly separated by a formal or direct act in 1763."
2. Monck Mason, Attorney General Tisdal, and Counselor Robert French spoke for the measure. Matthew O'Conor, *History*, pp. 394–310.
3. The correct date is 30 August 1763 and a copy is in the Ashburnham Collection, Stowe MS B11. O'Conor, like Swift, saw that the danger for revolution lay not with the Catholics but with the Presbyterians in Northern Ireland and the "Independents" of Scotland. His letter, like all his work, was written in the person of a moderate Protestant who had resided in Ireland.
4. Brooke and Lucas devised a strong anti-Catholic "political plan" for the *FJ*. According to Madden, 2:392, the paper was "rabidly Puritanical. The patriotism of this journal consisted in reviling the faction that was in power, abusing the Roman Catholic religion and denouncing the Roman Catholic people of Ireland." The first issue came out 13 September 1763.

131. To Dr. John Curry

OCD, 8.3 HS 023

30 September 1763

My Dear Friend,

Your last by some accident has lain in the office till yesterday. I am in pain to see the *London Chronicle*[1] of the day you mention but pleased to find that Exshaw took it in. It will occasion a controversy wherein I hope that much moderation will be opposed to much acrimony. This I confess to you is all I expect. The ministry of England is at present in such a tottering, such a reeling condition that spirited efforts cannot be expected. Their thought must be entirely taken up with preserving themselves in a state of defensive hostility. New revolutions are besides expected in Hibernian affairs, and if so our affairs will be forgotten, just as we farmers in collecting the harvest never mind what becomes of our stubble except the weather be fair. I wish I may not hear of your having written the political piece inserted in the *Chronicle,* and yet I am not without my fears that the indiscretion of your confidants will blab it out. I had more than a hint already on this subject. I am really concerned for Fergus. I found him a very civil and polite young man. I am not a little surprised that you have not been immediately called to his assistance. I told you that Dr. Sullivan and I were upon a scheme for printing a collection of our more valuable Irish manuscripts. It is, upon recollection, a chimerical idea, and our correspondence, I foresee, will be soon at an end. I will see you as soon as I can, and it is you alone I want to see. I utterly despair of the cooperation of our people with you, and, what is worse, I despair of our now timid masters. The times do not favor them nor us, and yet the superstition of prejudice is almost in as hot a fit as ever. You who are at the fountainhead of politics should sprinkle your friend here with part of the stream. You see I have nothing to communicate but my fears, and yet I must write soon again to you. I, therefore, request a letter from you, though it should be only one of three lines. What account of the fate of the Archepiscopal See? I am really in much pain about the succession to it. I request you will present your family with my warmest affections.

1. O'Conor had printed in the *London Chronicle,* 30 August 1763, an anonymous letter to the editor in which he warns that the Irish Catholics are not a real source of danger to the country but the non-Conformist Scots-Irish are.

132. To Dr. John Curry

OCD, 8.3 HS 023

10 October 1763

My Dear Sir,

Your letter of 'ere yesterday lies before me, and I need not inform you that I am extremely thankful for the contents. Of all our controversial pamphlets on Hibernian politics, not one has drawn more attention than the letter in the *London Chronicle* you were so kind to send me enclosed. The author lays the axe to a root which it was little thought would be ever disturbed in its shooting—hence the great notice taken of that letter, hence the asperity and acrimony in the animadversions upon it. The party concerned is a peevish patient. No wonder if the surgeon is exclaimed against. No matter, when I am sore, I take delight in making my adversary so, though it be all I get. The surgeon is an arch wight; he has pressed the peevish patient's friend into his own service. This may do good: when my neighbor is partial against me in every matter of arbitration, don't I gain a great point by giving him conviction, nay a conviction *ad hominem* that the fellow he favors is in reality more his enemy than I am? This conviction ought surely to bear some fruit. I hope it will. At worst I will be treated more favorably than I used to be, and this may prove an earnest of some future favor. A wise legislature can not perpetually remain inflexible in turning the public prejudice of the few against the public interest *of all!* Mr. R[eilly] was the person who informed me that a very particular friend of mine was the author of that letter in the *Chronicle*. I know not from whom he got his information. As I would not wish to have my friend suspected for meddling with a point in politics (of all others the most tender), I immediately acquainted you with my pain on that head. Perhaps Mr. R[eilly] was misinformed, but whether he was or not, the secret might safely be confided to him.[1] And yet if any of the confidants blabbed, he would be in danger of being suspected as every secretary in these cases will cast the blame from himself. We have, I am confident, an enemy in the *Freeman's Journal*.[2] He may abuse able men on our account, and those able men may be induced to serve us the more on the fine of that very abuse. There is nothing unnatural or inconsistent in resentments of this kind. I am astonished at Mr. H[owar]d's demand to Mr. D[ermo]t[3] for a sum toward the republication of his *Queries*. Since the shameful demand was made, he should improve his pamphlet by the superaddition of arguments, which in my thought have great weight. But (my dear friend) Mr. H[owar]d feels no pain. How, therefore, can he be anxious? I am totally taken up with rural and indeed expensive improvements. How could I quit this occupation for visionary schemes in favor of a people who will do nothing to cooperate with me, for a people who have been silent for half a century till you spoke for them and animated me to follow the example; how have we been thanked? But you have a thousand times more merit than I—you formed an association for honest and wise purposes. Have not the associates deserted you? Can any propsect, any hope, bear you out against the langour, the folly, the insensibility, and, let one say, the ingratitude of these people. —You have fairly acquitted yourself on your part. I have done so on mine. I am *cogor cursus iterare relictos*.[4] I read old Irish verse to amuse me or instruct me and return to my first studies as less irksome than those which I took up after the perusal of your dialogue. —I purpose to go up to town as early as I can this winter to enjoy my dear friend Mr. Curry when I can hardly say I enjoy any other of his and my own fellow-sufferers. Now that you are come thus far along with me, it will be a natural and obvious reflection, "What shift one makes sometimes to fill a letter where so little can be said." Indeed I would finish long since but that I have to converse with you and that you like to hear me even in my trifles.

1. O'Conor is obviously enjoying the furor caused by his anonymous letter.
2. Henry Brooke.
3. Anthony Dermot, secretary of the Dublin Committee.
4. Horace, *Carmina*, 1.34.5: I am constrained to take up again courses which I had abandoned.

133. To Dr. John Curry, Cow Lane, Dublin

OCD, 8.3 HS 023

1 November 1763

My Dear Sir,

You should hear from me 'ere now, but that I have been for a fortnight past rambling through the country of Sligo taking my leave till next spring of friends, the nearest connected to me by consanguinity. I should even from those parts scribble a line as I do now, were I not distant from any post-town and unpossessed of a parliamentary license which, indeed, is the case at present and which, I think, will deprive you of what I am now writing. How can I forward it when I have nothing worth a farthing to communicate? All the news is on your side though all the folly is not, for here people flatter themselves that the laws which forbid security for personal property to Papists will, in this session, be repealed; I say that those Papists are mistaken though a clause may be tacked to some bill or other (as in the last session) to indemnify them. Every security to a Popish pedlar or Popish rack-rent farmer (for a Papist can be nothing else) is so much deduction from the *Protestant Interest;* and thus the *Protestant Independents* will have it, notwithstanding the warning given of their intentions in a late *London Chronicle,* which you perhaps have seen. I am neither splenetic nor angry when I write all this; at least I ought not to be so, who am a philosopher, and take all evils, physical and political, as they pass over my head with the same apathy that I do the humming of the flies which pass around it.

Take you this recipe from me as a doctor of philosophical medicine, and you will certainly find the benefit; and yet, though I am at ease about the public, no man can be more interested as to the welfare of particular people. No news for several years pleased me so much as the elevation of our dear friend Dr. F[itzsimon]s. I confess that it was as little expected by me as any such event could be. But merit does wonders, even where it offends; I mean that unmixed merit which will very often gain esteem while it loses affection. The Doctor has added to merit by knowledge and good sense. Such a man was extremely wanted at the head of our clergy (for the primatial authority lies now virtually with the Archbishop of Dublin). Besides this, the government or the chief men here know him and know him so much to his advantage that the Catholics may expect indulgence even through him. I am only echoing back to you your own intelligence, for no man can be more barren than I as to modern facts. The *Freeman's Journal* I do not see, and those who do perhaps attend to it as little; and yet such a paper well-executed in the true spirit of patriotism would do some good. No such paper was ever yet published in Ireland. I study or pick up some ancient facts and some scraps of ancient, neglected literature. It is better than playing of cards. I have sent some old manuscripts lately to Dr. Sullivan and I think he will like them; but neither he nor I will ever be able to prevail with our modern gentry to preserve those works from the universal destruction to which Irish literature is doomed. God preserve you and your whole family. I wish you may write to me as soon as you can, for I long to hear of your welfare.

134. To Dr. John Curry

OCD, 8.3 HS 023

6 December 1763

My Dear Sir,

The bringing on the Elegit Bill, the acquiescence of the House to the first motion for introducing it, and the negotiation of this affair without the privity of the people concerned promises well. We are not, however, strangers to the difficulties which it must encounter before it passes into a law; and we *now* know by what weapons some of the thrusts against it may be parried.[1] I think *our* people will not neglect this affair as they have done before. To people who can enjoy no landed property, not even in wastes and mountains, it is a great consolation to enjoy any in the very produce of their industry. No more, it seems, are we to expect. There are still too many splinters in the broken bone, and I am really concerned very sensibly that the paper lately published in the *London Chronicle* should give offense to men in power against whom most certainly no offense was meant by the author of that piece. He had to do with the most peevish patients in the world who scream even at emollients. To me they seem incurable, and I form my judgment upon long experience. Our very Protestant advocates have deserted us (if ever they were our advocates, as you will observe). Be it so, and let our own wayward people improve on the experience they have gained by so many repeated trials of the superiority of prejudice to all considerations, nay to all sound reason!

Uno premente deo, fert deus alter opem.[2] They have the world open to them, and they will not part an *Eden*. The letter in the *Chronicle* produced reams of invective. It was well considered not to take up the argument, but let calumny enjoy its short triumph, though had the letter to *Hume* any chance of appearing, its appearance in that period of animosity might not be unseasonable. I am too long on this subject, so disagreeable to you and me. I am told Mr. Burke got £300 a year on our establishment, and I am extremely glad of it.[3] He is a gentleman of excellent and cultivated parts, and it is happy that the writer is not superior to the man. I am pleased to hear that our friend Lord T[aaffe] is well received by our new V[ice]r[oy].[4] The last had his coach wheels so smoothly shod that his approach gave a glimpse of new millenium. The dream ended as all dreams do; instead of an Elysium we no sooner opened our eyes than we found ourselves lying on the same hard bed. You are a physician, and I could wish you gave us a receipt for dreaming no more. I am most sensibly concerned for our unfortunate friend Mr. R[eilly]. I was strongly in hopes that the fright he was put into two years ago would have such an effect as must prevent his ever capsizing again. I am concerned for you, who in some degree became the guarantee of his good conduct in the affair of the charity of which he was the trustee. Were I a rich man I would for one extricate him, as I know that it was invincible poverty which cast him into his present great affliction. He has a house in Ship Street, and if he did not already dispose of his interest therein, I have some hope that he will still acquit himself to the Charitable Society. I request that in your next you will be more particular about him as I do not think it necessary to correspond with himself at this time since I can not relieve him. Who is the *great man* who took so much offense at the letter in the *Chronicle?* Whoever he be, could he not suppose it the work of a zealous Protestant alarmed by the insurrections of dissenters in the North?[5] Must the poor Papists of Ireland be acccountable for any such essay appearing in a London newspaper? This is truly a great hardship, but there are instances enough of it in history. My brother will be soon up with you and will in person give you and your family my affections. I will follow as soon as I can to act the same part and finish a little personal business. What other business can I employ myself in? Services to any man or body of men I can do none, and many among you who wish I had spared myself the trouble of former vain and fruitless attempts. I see and feel the weight of all this, and I should profit but little of all my experience if it were not a good lesson to me. I am passed the meridian of life and ought to prepare (were I wise) for a setting sun. I have known mankind too well not to drop into a Stoic indifference, which was heathen, or into resignation, which is Christian, philosophy. This is our case, and surely this is our duty—My head is discharged, though my heart is full. May God bless you and yours.

1. Matthew O'Conor outlines the debate on the Elegit Bill (pp. 304–310). It was defeated in February 1764 by a count of 138 against 53 for the bill.
2. When one god presses hard, the other offers [us] help.
3. Edmund Burke resigned the pension which Hamilton had gained for him in 1764. Burke remained in Ireland as Hamilton's secretary until the end of 1764 and then became the private secretary to the Marquis of Rockingham in July 1765. *Concise DNB*, 1 : 170.
4. The earl of Northumberland.
5. In the *London Chronicle*, 30 August 1763, O'Conor had written that 40,000 Independents had risen in Ulster not for redress of grievances, not to recover their right of "commonage," but to rise "with avowed and traitorous intent."

135. To Dr. John Curry

OCD, 8.3 HS 023

28 December 1763

My Dear Sir,

I should have acknowledged your last letter sooner but that I had not a frank and that my acknowledgment was not worth a groat, and yet I well know that you never grudge paying for a letter out of this desert when you find it in my handwriting. I almost give up your people when a bill should be brought into the House of Commons,[1] wherein a punishment is intended instead of a favor. Some of the Commons, I think, do not intend it because I think that there are not only men of good intentions among them, but men of good sense who feel for the common good, and men of an elevated turn who abhor any prejudice contrary to it. Thus I think and only wish that those men of good sense may prove the majority in an assembly where ignorance allied to prejudice promises so conspicuously a turn of the scale on the other side. You and I have dipped a little into the history of our own country and probably, very probably, you have discovered what I have to my sorrow discovered, that the O'Briens for near two hundred years past have proved a galling spur in the side of their Milesian countrymen. They were the first among us who renounced to the old religion of their ancestors, and with the spirit of all such converts they have proved of all enemies the most inflexible and rankled. See the prevalance of it in our modern Lucius![2] He has a bad Protestant name (very undeservedly indeed). He knows it and he wants to give a conviction of his being a good Protestant at the expense of common sense, common probity, and real patriotism. A fig for such Irish Protestants say the Whigs. A fig for such patriots, say all good men (whatever their number be); and a fig for all such enemies, says the poor Papist. So say I, who am a Papist and will die one. I do hardly think that this amphibious O'Brien will gain his point, not only because he is one but because the men of sense at Court and in Parliament not only scorn to receive him as an instructor, but mean to proceed to no more punishment wherein themselves would be equally and immediate sufferers with those on whom the first stroke would fall. In those cases, prejudice, even the strongest, must have some bounds. Nature is too prevalent and will keep some measures even in politics of the cast I intend here. I have known a strong man decline a stroke when he foresaw his hand would receive more detriment than the ear he aimed at. This is indeed our best security; and, whatever you do, I for my part expect no better after long experience. You and I must drop our curtain and open it on some other scene when we raise it again, but not till we vindicate ourselves against the charge brought against *your Memoirs*, but that does not relate much to present times. As to former times I am now revising what I wrote formerly on the subject. Faulkner wants a republication of the *Dissertations*. Whether he continues or not in the intention, I shall not repent of the time I devote to the corrections I am making or to the new matter I am preparing. But I think that he is wrong and that the work (should it appear) will have no sale equal to the expense. I pity Mr. R[eilly] and I would pay the £20 he owes had I the power equal to the will—I formerly, as you know, advanced six guineas in his favor. I would advance two more now were so small a sum of use. If you can protect him, my brother now is in town and is as much grieved for him as I am. He assures me that he has more due to him than he owes, and our Committee is a strange set of men if they do not advance the £10 formerly voted for him (by them) in my presence. Surely they can reimburse themselves out of the collection now making among us; you can move this when you meet. My paper is out and I will see you in fourteen days.

1. The Elegit Bill.
2. Sir Lucius Henry O'Brien, the M.P. for Ennis, "disapproved highly" of the Elegit Bill because it was "most dangerous to the Protestant interest." Matthew O'Conor, p. 306.

136. To Dr. John Curry, Cow Lane, Dublin

OCD, 8.3 HS 023

13 July 1764

My Dear Friend,

In two days after I parted you in Cow Lane I arrived here in Conaght in good health. The hurry and embarrassments one encounters on departing for distant places hindered my waiting on you at the coffee house in the eve before I set off. Where I now am I am overcrowded with business, and visits to relations who live remotely from me and from each other will engross more time than I can well spare from my several occupations. As to literary business, I must not think of it for a month to come at least. I have built a new house and am finishing its servant, another house.[1] All this creates considerable expense to me, but I do not grudge it as my family is the better for it.

After all, I doubt whether I shall pursue the business of housekeeping. I am sure I shall not if you forbid it. My two sons and only daughter are well provided for.² To live with any of them would in appearance be my most eligible method, but in fact such an option is attended with some disagreeable circumstances which I need not point out to you. I have acquitted myself fully to each of my family. Is not that enough for present? May I not hereafter by saving a little for the most worthy of them acquit myself still better to them? And how can I agreeably to my own inclinations do all this better than by living in my own way among my friends, particularly with you in a vacant hour. I conceal nothing from you, and let me have your advice upon paper. I have a profit rent owing to me of a hundred and twelve pounds a year; and as I did not rack the tenants, my payments will be constant to me. My house and demesne are chiefly worth sixty pounds a year. The aforesaid £112 and this demesne (if I let it to my second son) will bring me £170 a year, and I think that in Dublin I can well save half that sum and live more satisfactorily by following my own inclinations to study and vacating four months in the year for my family in Conaght. I may be the more welcome to them by living two-thirds of the year from them; and mixed life to one of my years and inclinations is best after all. I would do nothing rashly, but be in the judgment of my friends. Father Fitzgerald³ was the person who laid down the plan of life for me; and if you agree [with] it, I think I need no third person to consult with. See how I employ your time; I will make no apology, as I know you interest yourself in my future fate. You shall ever have every return that a grateful man ought to make to his benefactor. I request you will give my affections to dear Mrs. Curry, Miss Curry, Mrs. Gavin, and to every other of your and my connections as if I named them each apart. I trust that you have good accounts from your two sons abroad. And I hope that you are enabled to inform me of their success. I send this by hand, and I am resolved to cheat the post office as much as I can in this way.

P.S. Should you drop a note at Mr. Lord's (through Watt's hand), the bearer would convey it to me.

 1. The Hermitage, a small house O'Conor had built on the edge of the estate at Belanagare. He has given over the main house and management of the estate to his son Denis, who had two sons by this time: Owen, born 6 March 1763, and Charles, born 15 March 1764. Charles Owen O'Conor, *The O'Conors of Connaught*, pp. 319, 321. After O'Conor's death the Hermitage became the home of Denis's son Owen, heir to the Belanagare estate. Catherine Sheehan, unpublished biography of Charles O'Conor of Belanagare, RIA, p. 320.
 2. Denis, Charles, and Bridget, wife of Myles McDermot of Coolavin.
 3. O'Conor's confessor.

137. To Dr. John Curry, Cow Lane, Dublin

OCD, 8.3 HS 023

17 July 1764

My Dear Sir,

I wrote to you last week by a carman, and yet I cannot resist the present occasion of giving you my mind along with my perpetual gratitude on this bit of paper, the dearest half sheet in the world.

I find that my unfortunate brother's[1] sudden departure for Dunkirk was his owing to his license with men in power, what his mean subject did not require and what no subject should prompt him to because his charge was unjust.

He writes like a madman. "Life is a burden to him, but he will not part with it in the Roman way."—What his future fate will be, he knows not: "He is no prophet"—What impertinence, pride and folly! My heart grieves for this self-tormenting, honest man. He is a man of knowledge—, but he over-rates it; would to God he knew himself more intimately than he does and that he reflected that his father and grandfather lived with resignation under worse circumstances than his. —This is enough; it is too much on so very disagreeable a subject.

I write this from my new house, a small but decent one. After parting with my wife and children, I will be in your judgment whether I shall sit down in it and spend here the annuity I reserved for myself. I would do nothing rashly. My passions at present are, I think, directed to good purposes, namely to live near those whom I love and love me, my family excepted. My friends are not in Conaght. If I live here, housekeeping will not be more disgustful than expensive to me. May I not give up the house and demesne to my second son[2] for a consideration of sixty pounds a year? He will get a wife's dower[3] to have a place to bring her to. My plan is this; unless you object, I would live eight months of the year in Dublin and spend the other four (in summer and harvest) with my family in this province. By letting my house and demesne I shall have about £170 a year; may I not by quitting housekeeping save half that sum and have something to bequeath if God should spare me life for a few years? I like retirement and study as you know. I can be more vacant for both in a great city than here. This is a great motive with me to decline housekeeping in this decline of life. I say no more, but beg your advice, and give it like a father to his son. The relation between us is as indissoluable. Adieu. —When I intended to add more, two beggarly relations came in to take my half guinea from me. But I can not end before I make my request that you will present my hearty affections to dear Mrs. Curry, Miss Curry, Messrs. Gavin, Comerford, O'Brien, Biggers, etc. My affections to L[ord] and Lady Taaffe and to whom I shall now send my acknowledgments in a separate script.

1. Daniel O'Conor.
2. Charles O'Conor. O'Conor never did rent the house to Charles.
3. Charles married Mary Dillon.

138. To Dr. John Curry

OCD, 8.3 HS 023
Dr. John Curry

[23 August 1764]

Dear Friend,

What I had to impart since I received your last at our Assizes was not in any degree worthy your attention. I am here in Belanagare as busy as ever and my family are strangers to the resolution you know I have taken; I can hardly lay out an hour in twenty-four for the task I have in hand. This is my manner of life. My poor brother in France wants £40 to bring him to Paris, where imagination is doing great things for him. I must make a shift to indulge him, as probably experience will teach him at last the lessons I have been dinning into him at first. Mr. Lord has received three volumes in folio for me from France. It is a work I long mightily to see (Mr. Bullet's *Celtic Dictionary*)[1] and yet I am resolved not to bring it down but have it in your hands till I go up. I request you will get Matt to bring it to you and that you will give me some general account of the work. You will please also to give Lord, Lady Taaffe, Mrs. Curry, all our friends who care for me my affections. Mr. Jordan of Schoolhouse Lane[2] is the bearer of this and is in haste.

1. Jean Baptiste Bullet was a professor of theology at the University of Besançon. *Nouvelle Biographie Generale*, ed. M. Hoefer, *et al.* (Paris: Libraires de l'Institute de France, 1855), 7:767.
2. A Dublin tailor.

139. To Dr. John Curry

OCD, 8.3 HS 023

29 August 1764

My Dear Friend,

I write this from my new house (a neat and warm cabin) and have nothing to communicate, though a good deal to request. My first petition is that you will present my most grateful affections to worthy Lord and Lady Taaffe. I had a letter of great affection this week from his Lordship[1] and a short bill of complaint against Dr. Curry for his neglect or seeming neglect. You are acquainted with most of those who care for me, and I beg you will inform them that no man can have a deeper sense of their friendship than your correspondent of this day. I am revising some sheets of *Dissertations* in this choice retirement, and yet I am so busy with personal affairs that my literary progress is but poor. You are mining to good purpose when you can steal a minute from business; and you cannot conceive the pleasure I am even now taking in the thought that I will be present on your blowing up shortly all the ramparts of historical slander which party malice has been throwing up for 150 years past. When have you heard from our friend Burke?[2] He expects intelligence from you, and whatever you remit to him will be turned to good account. I am glad that you put the *Memoir* on the fifth of November affair in Mr. Reilly's hands.[3] It will wipe off much scandal or lay the odium of it on the proper persons. You will show by this and your other collections that the history of these kingdoms for 250 years past is not yet written and that the florid writers who have lately appeared on the subject have done nothing besides displaying their elocution and copying from one another. I rejoice very heartily with you on the good news from your sons abroad. So good a father (indeed the best I ever knew) must not be disappointed. May God bless you and them, and may your life be prolonged on their account and on account of the public which you serve in so many capacities. I wrote to you last by an honest man, Jordan the tailor in your beloved Schoolhouse Lane. I could write to you without expense as dear Lord Taaffe sent me three covers, all directed to John Curry, Esq., M.D. But, in truth, I have nothing to communicate but such common things as you have now before you—*vox et praeterea nihil*.[4] Even this *vox* I will repeat now and then for no other reason but you like a line from me, be it what it will. Here is a whole blank before me, and I am rummaging in vain for matter. You informed me of Dr. Brady lately come into the kingdom. Have you improved an acquaintance with him? My affections particularly to your family.

1. Lord Taaffe to O'Conor, 22 August 1764, from Dublin. Stowe MS Bi1, RIA.
2. Edmund Burke.
3. Curry's *An Essay towards a New History of the Gunpowder Plot* (Dublin: n.p., 1765).
4. A voice and nothing more.

140. To Dr. John Curry

OCD, 8.3 HS 023

15 September 1764

An invective against Catholics appearing in *The London Chronicle* has upset Dr. Curry, but O'Conor advises him not to think too deeply of the insult. O'Conor soothes Curry with flattery about Curry's upcoming pamphlet, *An Essay towards a New History of the Gunpowder Plot*. "You have already and will hereafter provide matter for new historians who will derive profit as well as pleasure from turning the florid histories of our own time into waste paper." Also O'Conor asks the rhetorical question why Catholics remain silent during a period when so much abuse is heaped upon them: "Is it not a strong symptom, my dear friend, of religious indifference?" O'Conor has heard of a Celtic dictionary compiled by a Frenchman, John Baptiste Bullet, and wishes that Bullet would write him about the dictionary.

141. To Dr. John Curry

OCD, 8.3 HS 023

28 September 1764

"I am just returned from a shirling journey through the counties of Mayo, Sligo, and Leitrim, where I for some days enjoyed the wonders of nature and the affection of a few connected with me by the ties of consanguinity," O'Conor writes Curry. He advises Curry to take the pamphlet material from Reilly, who is too slow. "Since he cannot execute what you confided to his care, you will find another to copy the work and Jemmy Berne[1] will print it faithfully under your own eye," O'Conor writes. Another letter from Faulkner awaited O'Conor when O'Conor returned home, he tells Curry. Faulkner wishes to print a revised version of O'Conor's *Dissertations on a History of Ireland*. Also Peter Wilson[2] has asked O'Conor to write a description of the county of Roscommon for a series of descriptive articles on Irish counties which Wilson will print in his magazine.

1. James Byrn, Dublin printer at the corner of Keysar's Lane in Cork Street. Plomer, p. 378.

2. Peter Wilson published the *Dublin Magazine* and printed the *Dublin Directory.* Plomer, p. 407.

142. To Denis O'Conor

OCD, 8.4 SE 148

1765[1]

Denis O'Conor, acting as head of the family, has written a letter to John Dillon stating that the marriage contract is unsatisfactory between young Charles and Mary Dillon, daughter of John Dillon.[2] Charles of Belanagare tells Denis he has done the correct thing, after consulting with O'Conor and Mr. Brown, Denis's father-in-law. O'Conor would like to talk to Denis about this contract later, perhaps in company with young Dr. MacDermot.[3]

1. Undated, probably 1765. A marriage agreement for O'Conor's second son Charles and Mary Dillon was recorded in 1765. Dunleavy and Dunleavy, OCD, 8.3 ES 045.
2. John Dillon, Mary's father, a Dublin merchant.
3. O'Conor's grandson.

143. To Denis O'Conor

OCD, 8.3 SE 028

[Shrove Tuesday, 19 February 1765]

This letter concerns family business as well as the business of recruitment of a Catholic neighbor for foreign service. Charles has received an amount of money for a neighbor, Luke Wallis, from Lord Taaffe. O'Conor will then send £8.19.3 to Denis for Wallis. Three guinea have been deducted for past loans—two guinea by O'Conor and one guinea by Lord Taaffe.[1] Furthermore, Denis should inform Wallis to prepare his elder son for a voyage to Germany. Charles's landlord, his uncle Daniel, has married the daughter of a Captain O'Neill in St. Omer's. O'Conor tells Denis not to expect him at Belanagare until "towards the end of spring." Also, O'Conor commands both Denis and Charles to "see justice done to me relatively to the house and little stock in Balaghkelew. You both know what ought to be done as well as I do, and it will be your fault if it is not done."

Genealogy and rank are very important for O'Conor and for many of his relatives who seek places on the continent:

I have lately drawn up the genealogy of my family from the old *Annals,* and Mr. Wm. Hanley, the Herald-at-arms, a fast friend of mine, is giving it all the forms of the heraldic office. Though this matter is not worth a rush to me, yet having the materials in my hands, I would think it a reproach to me not to give them a permanence and authenticity which may hereafter be necessary to my family should it be forced to exchange its native for a foreign country. The expense will, I believe, come to ten guineas, and to others it would cost twenty, to my own knowledge, as I have been lately several times in the herald's office in the Castle. It is every day crowded with suitors who are removing hence and establishing themselves on the continent.

... I had a letter here from your parish priest requesting a letter from me to the Bishop of Ossory that he should solicit with the Bishop of Elphin for obtaining the late Mr. Forrester's place.[2] I will write (as he requires) to Kilkenny this night and get Dr. Fallon sounded on the affair this morning. Mr. Teige[3] may assure himself that nothing will be done in the affair till after Easter when Mr. Forrester's superior will be appointed.

1. Lord Taaffe has received money from his son Francis, Count Taaffe in Vienna. Lord Taaffe has conveyed the money to O'Conor in Dublin, who is sending it to Denis in Belanagare. The funds are for Luke Wallis, a Belanagare neighbor. This is a circumvention of the penal laws. Francis, Count Taaffe, a bank order to Nicholas, Lord Taaffe, 6 January 1765, enclosed with letter from Colonel Patrick Wallis to Nicholas, Lord Taaffe, 30 January 1764, Stowe MS B11, RIA.
2. The bishop of Ossory was Thomas deBurgo, O.P., and the bishop of Elphin was James O'Fallon. *HBC*, pp. 405, 409.
3. The parish priest, Sheehan, p. 329.

144. To Denis O'Conor, Belanagare

OCD, 8.3 SE 028

5 March 1765

O'Conor asks that the marriage negotiations with Mr. Dillon for Charles be kept open; consequently, Charles should be preparing his house and negotiating for renting land to farm. Luke Wallis should provide Lord Taaffe's son "with some linen and keep him close to his studies till his Lordship procure a ship here to carry him to Hamburg from whence he will make his way to Prague and meet his uncle." O'Conor advises Denis to tell Charles to see Mr. Knox about renting land at Rafodagh.[1] Finally, if Dr. O'Halloran[2] sends any one to Belanagare for an "Irish Hippocrates," O'Conor tells Denis to be sure to give the book to him.

1. A Mr. Knox is mentioned in letters to O'Conor which deal with financial matters and young Charles's financial troubles. Dunleavy and Dunleavy, OCD, 8.3 ES 040. Also a Francis Knox was the High Sheriff of Sligo in 1766. *FJ*, 25–29 March 1766.
2. Sylvester O'Halloran (1728–1807) was a Limerick surgeon and antiquary. *Concise DNB*, 1:969.

145. To Edmund Burke[1]

SCL, W.W.M. Bk. 1-43

Dublin, 25 April 1765

Dear Sir,

I longed to thank you sincerely for the share you allowed me in your friendship, but (that my acknowledgments might not go alone) I waited all this time thinking I might be enabled to make you some little historical present such as might be acceptable from its rarity though it should have little other merit. Why I have failed was, perhaps, owing to my being a mere literary pioneer, digging in the rubbish of the ancients; I mean the ancients of our own island. Our friend Mr. Faulkner will let you see in a few months what I have, and what I have not been doing.[2] For the present let me pass from the ages of darkness and ignorance to our own enlightened days of good sense and sound policy. Some among us have of late discovered a keen appetite for detecting conspiracies in this country and of extracting (very obstetrically) the latent *treason* of the many from the *public* treason of the few; I mean of a few beggared cottagers in Munster who have declared war against their despotic landlords.[3] Though the inferences of these modern politicians be, no doubt, as just as they are judicious and though their zeal has more keys than one to wind it up, yet it is to be presumed they will think it no disappointment to find the materials they now work with too scanty for the fabric of merit they are weaving for themselves. Let me explain all this. You may remember that under Lord Halifax's government some of the laboring men in Munster have conspired against their landlords, first by nightly insurrections and soon after by assembling in open day to the great terror of several counties and to the great detriment of some.[4] Why these madmen are mad still will appear very strange on your side of the water, especially after the execution of so many to strike terror into the rest. But their desperate obstinacy must appear less wonderful when it is known that the fathers of these people lived with some comfort and that the sons who once tasted of it are, in their advanced years, reduced to the extreme where human misery must stop till a new creation of physical evil opens a wider circle for it. In the beginning of the present century and for many years after, the price of labor and the value of land held a reasonable proportion. The leasehold tenures of the former century were not yet expired; nor did the legislature then foresee that the confining Papists for the future to short tenures and frequent renewals would unavoidably turn a great part of the kingdom into pasture lands and render those very Papists the tyrants of the poor. So late as the year 1720, a cottager had a groat a day for his labor. He paid but twelve shillings for grazing a cow, and as much for an acre of soil annually. The stone of wool he could purchase for five shillings, leather and linen in like proportion. At present he is returned to the former wages while the price of necessaries is more than doubled; but that is not the worst of it. The annual rent of a cow is now raised to thirty shillings, the acre of soil to forty, and where the father paid but twenty-four shillings in cheap times, the son pays seventy in the dearest.[5] The cottager who has but a groat or at most five pence a day can not make good his covenant, and the landlord thinks himself a loser though he gets his laborer's whole property into his hands. Such an instance of oppression and cruelty can not be paralleled in the annals of mankind. The differences made by penal laws are in many instances counteracted by those of nature in trading countries particularly, which must flourish by industry and can not do it without the cooperation of all hands. Protestants are dragged into the common vortex of political evil. They grind the faces of their workmen, but the Papists exceed them, and here you have the source and foundation of the present treason of the poor. I would now ask whether this treason, this rebellion (as it is called) of the cottagers can fix any colors of treason or rebellion on their Popish landlords? It would be ridiculous to assert it. At no time since the change of religion in these kingdoms were the Roman Catholics more sensible of their civil duty than at present; at no time were they more united in the discharge of it. They owe their existence in this country to the sovereign not to the laws, and while religious duty quickens their allegiance (for their religion prescribes it) the royal protection excites their gratitude.[6] Any revolution would make the condition of the men of property among them worse than it is at present. This they know, and this knowledge alone would be a good security for their peaceable conduct. To charge such men therefore with treasonable intentions and practices is a game which I confess may be well played for the purposes of popular odium, but never for the advantage of the public or even of the players themselves till they are able to kindle fires without combustibles, what I think can not be done now so easily as in some former periods. I have tired you; indeed, I have tired myself heartily with this detail; I will only add that it were to be wished for the happiness of these nations that all believers in Christ came to some composition with one another. The example has been set in his Majesty's other dominions on the continent with great advantage to those countries; and after all our lights in politics and philosophy, it is a shame that the good sense of this conduct should hitherto be confined to Germany alone![7] As to the Irish cottagers, I here gladly dismiss them. Till legislative wisdom interposes for their relief, the law must take its severest course with those among them who are too impatient to die slowly or die with hunger. It is, however, a melancholy consolation that laws should lose their efficacy when their penalties are considered by undone men rather as means of relief than terror.[8]

P.S. Curry is laboring for the good of mankind and sends you his affections;[9] he longs to hear from you, and you owe him a line when you are at leisure to write it. Mr. O'Gorman,[10] who will deliver you this, is brother-in-law to the late French minister, the Chevalier D'Eon. He has been in his leisure hours making collections at home and abroad for the civil and ecclesiastical history of his native country, and I owe him great obligations on that account. He will tell you more minutely than I have done what is mostly in agitation here.

1. There is an earlier draft of this letter in the Royal Irish Academy. RIA, Stowe MS Bi1. O'Conor was aware that Burke would become the private secretary to Lord Rockingham when he became Prime Minister after July 1765, in a caretaker cabinet which lasted only a year. See W. E. Lunt, *History of England*, Third Edition (New York: Harper and Brothers, 1947), p. 546.
2. O'Conor has been revising his *Dissertations on the History of Ireland*. George Faulkner advertised the book for sale on 3 June 1766.
3. Richard Woodward, future Protestant Bishop of Cloyne, claimed in his book, *Present State of the Church in Ireland*, that the protest against heavy tithes on land in Munster was a Popish plot perpetrated by the Whiteboys, an association of disaffected Catholic tenants. Lecky, 2:19; see also Matthew O'Conor's *History of the Irish Catholics*, pp. 311–315.
4. Whiteboy attacks on farms and their threatening magistrates with death occurred sporadically from 1762 until 1785 in Kildare, Kilkenny, and Queen's Counties. Lecky, 2:20. *DJ*, 28–30 September 1769, reported an especially fearful attack of 120 Whiteboys, uniformed and on horseback, attacking a farm at Newtown, Kilkenny.
5. In 1776–1777, ten years later, rent for a cabin and garden averaged thirty-four shillings and ten pence. Rental for pasturage for two cows was thirty-two shillings and threepence. Although farm wages went up on an average of one and three-fourths pence in twenty years, many of the noble landlords doubled and even quadrupled their rent to the cotter in forty years. *Arthur Young's Tour in Ireland*, ed. Arthur Wollaston Hutton (London: George Bell and Sons, 1892), 2:36, 50, 237.
6. Burke must have been aware that O'Conor was active in advocating a pledge of allegiance for Catholics and had prepared or helped to prepare at least two addresses to George II.
7. Both O'Conor and Nicholas, Viscount Taaffe, consistently promoted this fact as well as the Government's leniency to French Catholics in Quebec by allowing them to retain religion and their own legal system.
8. A letter from Curry to O'Conor, 14 September 1765, indicates that O'Conor's letter to Burke produced its desired effect. According to Curry the Dublin Committee paid Burke for his services. Burke defended the cause of the Irish Catholics and was castigated for his action in the English press. Stowe MS Bi1, RIA.
9. Dr. Curry was writing his pamphlet on *A Candid Inquiry into the Causes and Motives of the Late Riots in Munster in Ireland*. It appeared anonymously in London in 1766.

10. Chevalier Thomas O'Gorman (c. 1732–1809), antiquarian, courtier, doctor of medicine, and vineyard owner, living in France. He asked O'Conor to help him find a translator and transcriber for many of the old Irish annals which he subsequently took back with him to France. O'Conor corresponded with him until O'Conor's death in 1791.

145. To Edmund Burke (earlier version)

RIA, Stowe MS Bi1

Dublin, 24 April 1765

Dear Sir,

I longed to thank you sincerely for the share you allowed me in your friendship. That my acknowledgments might not go alone, I waited till I thought I might be enabled to make you some little historical present. Why I failed was perhaps owing to my being a mere literary pioneer, digging in the rubbish of the ancients. I mean the ancients of our own island. Mr. Faulkner will let you see in a few months what I have and what I have not been doing. For the present let me pass from the ages of barbarism and ignorance to our own enlightened days of good sense and good policy. Some among us have of late shown a more than ordinary keen appetite for detecting conspiracies here and of extracting the *latent* treason of the many from the *public* treason of the few; I mean of a few beggared cottagers. Such deductions are no doubt very just; and though gentlemen who make them have more keys than one to wind up their zeal, yet we presume it will be no disappointment to find no materials for the fabric of merit they are now rearing up for themselves. They have indeed already gained one end, that of rendering themselves conspicuous. All this is a mystery to you, and I will explain it. You may remember that under Lord Halifax's government some of the laboring people in Munster have conspired against their landlords and have done great mischief, first in nightly insurrections and soon after in open day. Why these madmen are still mad will appear very strange on your side of the water, and especially after so many examples have been made among them to strike terror. It will not perhaps appear so wonderful when you are informed that at the beginning of the present century the predecessors of these laborers lived with some comfort and that the present race have been driven to that extreme of misery which can not be surpassed in the present state of things. The farmer, in my memory, paid twelve shillings a year for grazing a cow and as much for an acre of land to produce potatoes. They were allowed a groat a day for their labor; they could purchase a stone of wool for five shillings and other necessaries in the like proportion. At present the price of labor is the same as in those days, yet the annual rent of a cow has been raised to thirty shillings and the annual value of the acre of soil to more than forty shillings upon an average. Formerly there was some reasonable proportion between the rent and the wages; now a man can earn no more by laboring the year round than four pounds, and his rent for two cows and two acres of soil will amount to seven; that is, he will pay £4.12.0 more than his father paid and though the price of necessaries is doubled. An example of cruelty like this can not, I believe, be paralleled in the annals of mankind; and this relentless, this deliberate cruelty has been the sole foundation of the present treason of the poor. The landlord sucks the blood of the cottager, and the Popish landlord (for reasons needless to mention here) more than any. Can the treasonable practices (so we call them) of these laborers fix the crime or imputation of treason on their masters? It is impossible. It is even ridiculous to assert it. There is no lighting a fire without combustibles. At no time since the great Revolution in religious affairs were the Roman Catholics in Ireland more sensible of their civil duty than at present; at no time were they more united in the discharge of it. To royal indulgence alone they owe their existence in the land of their nativity; and while a sense of all this quickens their allegiance, it excites their gratitude also; for they are protected by the sovereign, not by the laws. To chrge such men therefore with treasonable intentions against the government is a game which I confess can be well played to increase the popular odium against them, but in no way whatever will it be played for the advantage of the players or that of the nation, which can not well bear the trouble or expense of any sham plots in its present state. Till legislative wisdom interposes for the relief of our cottagers, the law must, no doubt, take its course against such as are too impatient to die a slow death. It is, however, a melancholy consideration that laws should lose their efficacy when their penalties are considered by many desperate men rather as means of relief than of terror.

146. To Dr. John Curry

OCD, 8.3 HS 023

5 October 1765

I return my hearty thanks for your last kind letter and agree with you that Mr. Phillips's confidence is a little too bold in thinking nothing corrigible except typographical mistakes in his late performance.¹ My zeal in his case proceeded from that with which you long since have possessed me, the common good and common cause of our people. We should, if possible, act in concert with those who, like Mr. Phillips, labor for it. I knew not whether I told you that he cordially remits you his thanks and regrets that he is at too great a distance from the place where his recommendation of the fifth-of-November book might do some service. He promised to send me a tract intended for showing the hurt done in England by the disqualifying laws against the Roman Catholics. On that principle alone, would it not be proper to correspond with him? . . . A match has been proposed between him [O'Conor's son Charles] and Mr. John Dillon of Francis Street's daughter. Should it take place, his falling into the hands of a man of so much knowledge in business would have very favorable appearances for him. . . .

1. Thomas Phillips (1708–1774), an English priest, had written a biography of Cardinal Pole (1764) and was considering the possibility of a Dublin edition. Phillips to O'Conor, 14 June 1765, Stowe MS B11, RIA.

147. To Dr. John Curry, Cow Lane, Dublin

OCD, 8.3 HS 023

15 October 1765¹

My Dear Friend,

I wrote to you on the 8th or 9th instant a long miscellaneous letter and doubt it did not come to your hands. As I had no answer to the three several letters I sent off by the same post, I have nothing worth communicating but trifles, what you will dispense with from me at least as I have by this post a parliamentary privilege for remitting them. I expect (God willing) to see you soon. My son-in-law, MacDermot,² brings his family up this winter and I probably will lie over their heads, wherever they live. The *Dissertations*, I am told, are printing fast under the corrections of Mr. R[eilly]. I could not attend, and yet that will be no apology (though it ought) with the critical executioner. My unfortunate brother is now in London in the worst service in the world, that under a bookseller.³ It is not a service; it is a slavery and I pity the man who quitted the service of a monarch to enlist with such a master. I did not reply to Mr. Phillips because you deemed it unnecessary. I have finished a detached dissertation on the Scottish monarchy in North Britain, and this is a reply to the new scheme set up by the translator of *Fingal* and *Temora*. He pretends to show that we had no knowledge of letters in Ireland before the sixth century. It was proper (I think) to remove all his objections out of the way of the *Dissertations,* which assert the contrary. MacPherson resembles the cuttlefish, which endeavors to escape by involving itself in a flood of muddy liquor, not unlike ink. It cost me some labor to bring him into open light; I then found it easy to master him. What news in your town? Are the panics about a land tax over? Or does it give place to the terror of the late tremendous insurrections of the White Boys? Are there any bills preparing against the further growth of Popery? But enough of queries. I am pleased with the poverty of the nation because if it thrived, the Papists would thrive along with it. *Viva la bagtelle!* I have ten pioneers at work—from attention to the affairs of the public, I turn out to attend *them.* Is it not the proper employment of a philosophical agricolist (a word of my own) who is in this year securing the bread of the next, who takes care, in a word, that if the public should fall, he shall not fall along with it.

1. Gilbert, *Appendix,* p. 481, gives the date as 18 October.
2. Myles MacDermot of Coolavin.   3. Daniel O'Conor.

148. To Dr. John Curry, Cow Lane, Dublin

OCD, 8.3 HS 023

1 June 1766

Dear Sir,

The bearer is immediately to commence your neighbor, and I trust that both he and his wife will approve themselves worthy of your and your family's friendship.

I wrote to you this week in an enclosure franked to Mr. Reilly. The numbness in my left cheek continues and alarms me much. I should be happy had I been near you when I first felt this strange attack. I trust that I shall hear from you by tomorrow's post.

The Tipperary affair is, I find, become a very important one, not only to our people in general but to some *patriots* in particular.[1] Would to God that we had foresight enough to see the necessity of treasuring up all the facts relative to it from the source; we should in that case be enabled to let out the whole in so clear a light as to do ample justice to the innocent and the criminal. It would surely be rendering effectual service to our country. It may be said, and with truth, that those facts are recent and that the materials may be easily collected, but who would expose himself to popular prejudice or perhaps to what is worse by officiously collecting those materials. The collector could never act so secretly as not to run the risk of being detected by enemies or betrayed by friends. As affairs stand, there is something more than a probability, nay a certainty, that some persons will suffer and be more unhappy in their sufferings than any that have yet appeared on the stage. Their shame and sorrow will be perhaps a greater punishment than human laws can inflict. I hear nothing of the reception which the *Dissertations* got from the public.[2] I am only in pain for the generous publisher of that work. The author who expects no favor can the more easily put up with public censure.

Do you hear from *Dr. Warner?* I dread that he will receive no encouragement from Ireland and that he will be disgusted enough to drop his scheme. I have nothing new to offer you and nothing old but my affection to you and yours.

1. Nicholas Sheehy (1728–66) had been tried in Dublin, 10 February, for inciting to riot. Although he was acquitted, he was later tried and convicted in Clonmel Co., Tipperary, of inciting to murder a John Bridge. *FJ* states "that the immediate occasion of the murder of Bridge was that he had given information against the priest and some others and that he refused taking the Whiteboy oath. . . ." Matthew O'Conor noted that two juries in Dublin and one in Kilkenny had found the testimony of witnesses against Sheehy to be false. Two accomplices, Herbert and Bier, became witnesses for the government, incriminating two more men in the murder of Bridge. Consequently, these two men, James Buxton and James Farrell, along with Father Sheehy, were executed. Matthew O'Conor, pp. 313–316; Madden, 2:171; *FJ*, 18–22 March 1766.

2. George Faulkner advertised the second edition of the *Dissertations* in the *DJ*, 31 May–3 June 1766.

149. To Dr. John Curry, Cow Lane, Dublin

RIA, Stowe MS Bi1

5 June 1766

My Dear Friend,

After some compliments on the *Dissertations,* Dr. Delany subjoins, and I gladly take this occasion to assure you that no mortal has more cordial a good will to the nation or natives than I have; and I can give no "better a proof of it, than solemnly to declare that I wish them all as free from the *chains of Rome* as I am; and upon my conscience I know no other more beneficent wish either to them or *you in particular.*"[1] I could thank the Dean for the beneficience of his wish, but I could not do it without reminding him of equally beneficent wishes on my part, that all my friends were as free as I am from the chains of lay-synods, which are only binding till the same authority finds fault with its own work and forges new ones still alterable, *ad infinitum,* according to times and circumstances. I could tell him this and a great deal more; but I know it would offend him, and therefore I put up his letter, thinking no more of the matter till I wrote to you. My chains I rejoice in; they are the *jugum suave*[2] which I promised to wear at my baptism, and may I die as true a penitent as I am and ever will be a true Catholic.

Of all the periods you ever wrote to me, never did one enter more into my heart than your wish that I should march along with S[heeh]y, B[uxto]n and F[arrel]l to the fatal tree rather than enjoy the few remaining days under the guilt of infamy and apostasy![3] No man ever did or ever will give a stronger instance of affection than you have done in that declaration, and I shall not part with the impression it made on me till this heart ceases to beat. Whatever malefactions those men fell into, they have atoned for them by one glorious act. They preferred death to an infamous life, and this is the characteristic of the saints. *Pretiosa in conspectu Domini mors sanctorum Ejus*[4] [Three lines crossed out.] The Christian heroism of such men ever had and ever will have the most powerful effects, and many such examples would make us rejoice in the Penal Laws which are productive of them. You stirred up so much emotion in me that I could not forbear throwing out those thoughts.

May God preserve good Lord Taaffe and his whole family. Could he indeed be gratified in leaving one legacy of his zeal for the poor Catholics behind him, it would be so best. I have not sufficient health nor time for answering his intentions, and your public engagements have stopped a better and more zealous hand than mine.

You are, however, in a better situation for intelligence than I am, and I request you will preserve every memoir pro and con on our late transactions, so as to be compared and summed up hereafter. This burden is thrown on you and me, for no other of our people will put a finger to it. If it be a duty we owe to religion and to truth, the omission of it may be criminal.

My benumbed semi-face continues still benumbed, and I will follow your directions religiously to restore it to its former state. If you permit me to die at this time, my ghost will haunt you when this body can not. Meantime, I must haunt you with letters.

I ordered a copy of the *Dissertations* for Mr. R[eilly] to present to my landlord, Judge French. I had lately a letter from Mr. R[eilly], and he mentioned not a word about it. It would be a pain to me to hear that among my best friends the Judge should alone find himself slighted.

If Lord Chesterfield wrote to Mr. F[aulkner] about those *Dissertations*, I expect his censure and not his applause.[5] Mr. Slingsby has in a short acquaintance discovered some prejudices in my favor, and a grain of friendship is enough (generally) to blunt the edge of just criticism. If the writer said enough to excite the curiosity of abler men to study our ancient literature, he has his end.

I am here in my Hermitage surrounded with a forest in the form of an amphitheater and fine lawns upon a gentle hanging level between me and it. The hundred acres about me supply me with plenty of all kinds that the country can afford; but my enjoyments are now and then disturbed by visitors who are only unwelcome because their aversions and desires are not the same with mine. With you alone and such as you, I can live with true comfort; and as soon as this fine season is past, I shall, God sparing life, hive myself with the bees. I request you will present my best affections to Mrs. Curry, Miss Curry, Mrs. Gavin, Mr. Comerford, etc. Let me hear from Thady and Martin. God preserve them and you.

1. Jonathan Swift's friend Patrick Delany was still alive. As the senior Fellow and Tutor of Trinity College, Dublin, he was a legend from a bygone time. Notwithstanding his age, Delany's appreciation of the *Dissertations* must have pleased O'Conor, while Delany's patronizing tone concerning the Catholic Church must have angered him. *Concise DNB*, 1:331.

2. Easy yoke.

3. Sheehy, Buxton, and Farrell were the new Catholic martyrs executed in Co. Tipperary.

4. Psalm 116.15. Canon of the Mass for Martyrs. Precious in the sight of the Lord is the death of His saints.

5. Lord Chesterfield was bored with the book, but tried not to sound so when he wrote, "I thank you for the book you sent me in which there is great labor and great learning, but I confess it is a great deal above me, and I now am too old to learn Celtic." Lord Chesterfield to George Faulkner, 22 May 1766, Egerton MS 201, f-21, British Museum, London, henceforth cited as BM.

150. To Nicholas, Lord Taaffe, Dublin

OCD, 8.3 HS 023

[Belanagare, 14 June 1766]

My Lord,

At long run, that is as soon as health permitted, I have drawn up heads of a memorial such as your Lordship recommended.[1] I sent it this day by post to be revised first by Dr. Curry and to be amended afterwards by your Lordship.

Such a memorial, properly drawn up and presented in the proper place under the sanction of your Lordship's name, will have a better effect than a thousand pamphlets drawn up ever so well by private hands; for private adventurers on such a subject and in such times have not the smallest influence.

When such a memorial as I wish may be a proper one is published with Lord Taaffe's name at the bottom of it, it will be noticed by numbers who have power but who never before considered the subject. It may have effects that could not be expected even from our most sanguine expectations.

You were born, my Lord, to be useful in every country wherein Providence has placed you. In serving our poor people you only execute a trust and what your Lordship considers as a religious duty. No satisfaction on earth will be more warm than the consciousness of fulfilling such a trust.

My Lord, I prevailed on James O'Rourke[2] to execute a letter of attorney to your Lordship for putting yourself in possession of the late Count O'Rourke's papers and memoirs.[3] If your Lordship can procure such papers, your consigning them to Mr. Dillon of Francis Street[4] will bring them safe to my hands, and I will dispose of them according to your Lordship's orders.

Poor Luke Wallis,[5] My Lord, will be absolutely undone if some speedy succor be not remitted to him by his brothers. I have indeed advanced him a little to keep his family in these bad times from starving. But the rent now calls upon him, and his landlord cannot bear any longer with him.

May God preserve Lady Taaffe, your Lordship, and your whole family.

Belanagare, June 14, 1766

1. O'Conor, at Lord Taaffe's urging, drew up a memorial on the plight of the Roman Catholics in Ireland. Taaffe accepted the work and adapted it to his own style. It was published in 1767 as *Observations on Affairs in Ireland from the Settlement in 1691 to the Present Time* with Taaffe's name signed to it. Gilbert, *Appendix*, p. 452.
2. Unidentified.
3. Daniel O'Rourke. See Dunleavy and Dunleavy, OCD, 8.3 SO 015 and OCD, 8.3 SH 053 for the O'Rourke genealogy.
4. The son Charles' father-in-law, a Dublin merchant.
5. See letter to Denis, 19 February 1765.

151. To Dr. John Curry, Cow Lane, Dublin

OCD, 8.3 HS 023

Belanagare, 17 July 1766

My Dear Sir,

After my return from Coolavin in the c[ounty] of Sligo,[1] I found here your letter dated July 4 and postmarked July 10. It gives me pleasure that your *semper eadem*[2] includes your family. In every other respect I am pained, and the more as I expect no reformation in men's minds. The empire of error and self-delusion may one day or other be over-thrown; we cannot expect to see the day, and yet any man well-informed is accountable for the smallest neglect in communicating his knowledge of what passes under his eye, it being fit that posterity (as Grotius says) should be informed and the perpetrators of mischief among their ancestors known. About the disorders in the South I wrote to you sometime since and lamented that the several public accounts (good and bad) were not registered by some careful hand; and particularly it is much to be lamented that accurate notes were not taken at the trials of the late criminals. Their dying confessions, however, may in some degree supply the place of such notes, and materials enough can still be picked up to show that the Irish Catholics are no way accountable for the frenzy of a desperate rabble who had nothing to lose (but the lives of which they were tired) by any inconvenience they brought on the innocent public and themselves. That such wretches should suffer condign punishment is surely a good man's wish.[3]

This week I paid poor Wallis or rather to his order the sum Lord Taaffe was so charitable to advance for him; by that act his Lordship preserved a whole family from immediate ruin. You will be pleased to inform him of this and to present him and his lady with my affections.

I thank God that I have been rescued by your prescription from my late disorder. I would have told you so and thanked you most heartily, but that I could get no frank in this neighborhood. Even this note I remit to you under the cover of Mr. Thomas Le Hunte[4] to Mr. Reilly. Am I not, therefore, under an obligation to the squire? Is it not a great favor to an Irish Papist, and that under the self-conviction that every such person is an enemy to the peace and prosperity of this happy country? Give my affections to Mrs. and Miss Curry, who (I suppose) are now breathing the sweet country air of Summer Hill. Here we have hills enough, but no summer. God grant you health and may happiness and long life attend it.

1. Coolavin is the home of Bridget O'Conor MacDermot, Charles's daughter.
2. Always the same.
3. O'Conor is referring to the trial of Fr. Sheehy and others in Tipperary.
4. M. P. for Newtown, *DJ*, 23–25 February 1775, obituary.

152. To George Faulkner

BM, Egerton 201, f-43

Dublin, 25 September 1766[1]

While in Dublin O'Conor has had dinner with Faulkner's nephews at Faulkner's house in Parliament Street. Also he has dined with Dr. Thomas Leland at his home. O'Conor flatters Faulkner by praising his knowledge of the social and political world. He thanks Faulkner for introducing him to Leland. O'Conor writes that Leland "is one of the friends you gave me, one of the number who do honor to this country by their ability as well as rank: men of liberal and national endowments, who have thrown away the weeds of spiritual hatred, together with the jealousies and mistrusts which stick to the soil." O'Conor recounts to Faulkner much the same information he has written to Curry and others. Lord Taaffe asked a friend[2] "to digest the materials and throw them into present form" for a pamphlet, *Some Observations of Affairs in Ireland from 1691 to the Present Time*. Finally O'Conor lets Faulkner know that Burke of Wendover[3] paid him a visit at O'Conor's son's house in Anderson's Court.

1. O'Conor's letter to Faulkner finds Faulkner in London, possibly at the Bedford Coffee House.
2. The friend is O'Conor. O'Conor, at Taaffe's request, prepared a statement for him on the case of the Irish Catholics in Ireland.
3. Edmund Burke.

153. To Dr. John Curry, Cow Lane, Dublin

OCD, 8.3 HS 023

26 October 1766

This letter tells Curry that O'Conor stopped in Co. Kildare to see his friend James O'More and then returned home to Belanagare.

154. To George Faulkner

BM, Egerton 201, f-45

Belanagare, 28 October 1766

Since Faulkner has returned to Dublin from London, O'Conor writes him and thanks him again for the acquaintances that Faulkner has introduced him to: Lord Aran, Lord Moira, Judge Marshal, Dr. Leland, and the Dean of Down.[1] Dr. Leland's influence has gained O'Conor entry into the Trinity College Library:

Through Dr. Leland's friendship I can now have access to the college manuscripts, not withstanding the strictness of their university statutes. I amuse myself in the business of an Irish antiquarian; and I am pained at being alone in such an occupation: none to improve by, none to instruct me.

1. Lord Aran is Sir Arthur Gore, created earl of Arran in 1758; Lord Moira is Sir John Rawdon, first earl of Moira; Judge Marshall is Robert Marshall, judge in the Irish Court of Common Pleas; and the Dean of Down is Patrick Delany (1685–1768).

155. To Dr. John Curry

OCD, 8.3 HS 023

31 October 1766

I am much pleased to find that Lord Taaffe's *Observations*[1] have engaged the attention of the London public; but as they are so ill-calculated for the digestion of numbers who are habituated to other food, I doubt not but his Lordship's prescriptions will be thrown in his own face and bitterly decried as dangerous political medicines. If I be right in this conjecture, it will be shameful if some *English* gentleman does not take up the argument in defense of the Irish nobleman. Truth in common attire may be overlooked or not heeded. Coming forth out of the torture of debate, she puts on all her charms; she is owned by ingenious minds and welcomed as a stranger. I have mentioned ingenious minds, which surely every man should endeavor to have of his side; no other I know will own or welcome truth. If such minds be on the throne and about the throne (what we cannot doubt) is it not gaining a great point to *gain them*? If they cannot repeal Penal Laws, they may relax them in the executions; and as to the Penal Laws which execute themselves, I take it that the line which fastened many of them on our people is now between the shears. Land is come up to such an exhorbitant price that it has, as to tenures, put us all on the level. If a Protestant tenant does not give twenty shillings an acre for land, the Protestant landlord will not deal with him. The love of money will prefer the Papist who gives more; and whether it be farms in the country or houses in large towns, one and thirty years' lease is virtually as good as the times [Seven lines unreadable. Torn.]

You see how already I have broken my word with you and strayed from my subject into the bargain. I request earnestly that you will be on the watch and learn if ought has been published for or against Lord Taaffe's *Observations*. As to the tract, of which his Lordship has forbidden the publication,[2] I trust that he is mistaken as to his delicacy in entering into any minuteness relatively to the Munster insurgents. I am told that that tract is the work of a gentleman who to great judgment has added an equal degree of caution and candor. From the publication of such an inquiry, no danger whatever can be apprehended to the author or to the public whose cause he espouses. If you have read that work, I request you will transmit me your thoughts of it and send me a copy of it if you like it. I am not as yet determined whether I shall go up to town before or after the holy days. There or here I am fastened to you by such cords as will not only unite ourselves forever but take others in also with whom it will be a great part of our happiness to communicate. I, at least, flatter myself in this idea. When have you seen our friend Dr. Reddy? I am highly pleased with his candid and well-directed freedom in Lord C[lanricard]'s company,[3] and I trust you will tender him my affections. You are pained to outlive your good opinion of a certain much-esteemed friend; so am I, but though your resentment may be more quick than mine, I am afraid that mine is more lasting. [Top and side of page missing, corrupt.] I request you will write to him as often as you can with the contrition of a penitent laid open [portion missing]. Pour balm into them and do not quit him till, if possible, you make him confess and repent his greater mistakes. This I know is an extreme, delicate point and not to be attempted but by feeding his mind (as himself does the body) with milk. I know that I only recommend what you have anxiously yourself at heart and may God bless all your endeavors.[4] I am in great pain about my daughter-in-law in Anderson's Court, and my anxiety is no way lessened by hearing nothing from them by last post.[5] Should that girl depart from us, the young man married to her would be overset and undone, an event to be lamented by me especially as I am well satisfied with his upright intentions and the other quality of mind out of which I must derive much of my own happiness. My dear friend, I have tired you, but I shall never be tired of the affection I bear you and everyone of your family.

Write to me by the return of the post if it is possibly in your power, for I long to hear of the reception which Lord Taaffe met with at Court, etc.

[Upper left edge of this letter is torn. The first four lines are unreadable.]

> 1. *Observations on the Affairs of Ireland from the Settlement in 1691 to the Present Time*, written by O'Conor but signed by Taaffe, published in Dublin and London in 1766. BMCPBCE, 24:805.
> 2. Curry's *Candid Inquiry.*
> 3. Smyth Burke was earl of Clanrickarde. "List of the Peerage of Ireland," *Gentleman's Magazine*, 19 (1749), 507.
> 4. On 25 October 1766, Curry had written O'Conor that their friend, John Carpenter, had not received an appointment to the Dublin parish he desired, even though Dr. Fitzsimons had promised both Carpenter and Lord and Lady Taaffe to serve him. Stowe MS B11, RIA.
> 5. In the same letter Curry wrote that Mary Dillon O'Conor was suffering from a fever.

156. To Dr. John Curry, Cow Lane, Dublin

OCD, 8.3 HS 023

7 November 1766

Dr. Curry worries about his second son, Martin, who is studying at Louvain. O'Conor tells Curry not to worry about Martin's desire to go to Cologne. Faulkner had written to O'Conor that Judge Robinson[1] had praised Curry's pamphlet, *The Candid Inquiry into the Munster Disorders*, during a discussion of the work at one of Faulkner's dinner parties. O'Conor tells Curry that he is shocked to hear that George Faulkner reads O'Conor's letters to his dinner companions.[2] Curry had attended young Charles O'Conor's wife during her illness; and now that she is "reestablished," O'Conor thanks Curry for his help. O'Conor then returns to the subject of Faulkner's dinner party and comments on an account of the party that Curry had heard from Anthony Dermot, the merchant:

> Mr. Faulkner concealed from me the account your friend (Mr. Dermot,[3] I suppose) gave you. My letter to him was a mere commonplace on his being so beneficent a member of society and mixing together under his roof many persons of different persuasions whom he sent off pleased with one another and who never would meet if his hospitality did not bring them together. Now, as such familiar letters are never intended but for private communication, it is surely out of the way to expose them to public inspection.[4] I am, indeed, ready to think

that all this was done out of an ill-judged partiality in my favor, and on that account I omitted taking any notice of the matter to him in my letter of this night.

    1. Thomas Robinson, brother of the Primate of Ireland. Judge Robinson's opinion of the *Candid Inquiry* was complimentary compared to the opinion of an anonymous reviewer in London. The *Gentleman's Magazine,* 37 (January 1767), 32, saw the pamphlet as "a mere collection of different pieces, written with different views and published in the magazines in Ireland. The pretense of its being a letter to a noble lord is a stale trick to give it importance and excite curiosity."
    2. Curry wrote O'Conor on 4 November 1766 that at one of Faulkner's dinners Faulkner read to his guests, including Dr. Fitzsimons and Baron Mountney, a letter received from O'Conor.
    3. Anthony Dermot.
    4. Obviously Faulkner often read O'Conor's letters to his dinner guests. In Faulkner's letter mentioned by O'Conor, Faulkner had written that when he was in England and dining with Samuel Johnson, he read the contents of one of O'Conor's letters aloud to Johnson. Ward, *Prince of Dublin Printers,* p. 104.

157. To Dr. John Curry, Cow Lane, Dublin

OCD, 8.3 HS 023

2 December 1766

    I have been (my dear friend) many days on the ramble, and I write now from Elphin in answer to your letter of the 18th ultimo. I trust that by this time you have an account of Lord Taaffe's safe landing on the continent. His correspondence with you of late has been important, and I request you will religiously preserve his last five letters in your cabinet. The circulation and favorable reception of his pamphlet in England suprised me, as it must have you and every one like you who made our public prejudices any part of our private researches. I yet expect no great good from this present attention to his Lordship's speculations, and experience would be lost upon us if we had not foreseen that however some truths make a *transient impression* on the minds of men; yet in their aggregate body as legislators, they will think and act as they used to do. . . .

158. To Dr. John Curry, Cow Lane, Dublin

OCD, 8.3 HS 023

Belanagare, 29 December 1766

My Dear Friend,

Need I tell you that I wish you and yours many a happy New Year? I need not and will say no more about it. I wrote lately to you from Elphin. I want to hear from you that you and your Dublin family are well; I also would gladly know (all that you can inform me) of your family on the continent, for no friend of yours was ever more interested in your happiness than I am.

In Sligo I met with the *Freeman's Journal* against Lord Taaffe's *Observations,* and I hear more has appeared against them in the *London Chronicle.*[1] If the latter be no better than what I have seen, the writers hardly deserve any chastisement. They fly away from the argument and supply its place with railing, and yet (unfortunately) this does the business as well with the great as well as with the little vulgar. I said that Irish writers hardly deserve any rebuke, but by what I advanced in the last paragraph perhaps a little would be necessary, not from you and me *who are tired* but from some gentlemen in England who ought not to leave the whole weight of this affair on Ireland and (to our sorrow) on two only who dared to break silence amidst a million of distressed mutes and mutes for seventy years past!

I also saw in Faulkner's and other papers a contradiction to the last page in the *Candid Inquiry.* The contradiction, for ought I know, might be well-grounded. The *Inquiry* did not want that last page which (if false) is a hurt to a most excellent work. I request you will inform me on this head. The author of the work, whoever he be, appears to me to be a man of the greatest candor; now would he, I think, insert an extract of a letter in that last page unless he was certain that the writer of the letter was a man of cautious probity and wrote nothing but matter of fact.

I shall see you, God willing, in the month of February, for I want to see you. You alone are the possessor of my heart and mind. May God preserve you to our public many a year.

Our friend Dr. Reddy is, I am told, on a matchmaking in behalf of his son with my neighbor Mr. Mahon of Strokestown. It is said he will soon be on the move. If so, I purpose to wait on him as a friend. I purpose all the honors I can render him in this country in the memory of the many happy nights we passed together. Write soon to the *Man enclosed in the Hermitage.*

1. A correspondent to the *FJ*, 13–16 December 1766, described Taaffe's pamphlet as "the boldest and most bare-faced falsification of the principles and practices of the Church of Rome that have been published in our days." The correspondent attacked Taaffe's thesis that an Irish Catholic could accept the Pope's spiritual power to dissolve oaths sworn to heretical princes and still be a good citizen. The correspondent quoted Pope Clement XI's statement, printed 1724, that "All stipulations made in any case whatsoever by Catholics in favor of Protestants are utterly null and void." "How is this consistent with Pope Clement's declaration above?" the correspondent asked.

159. To Dr. John Curry, Cow Lane, Dublin

OCD, 8.3 HS 023

17 January 1767

We have an intense frost and deep snow in this province for ten days past, and it freezes still. As soon as the weather changes and that I can dispatch some business (of consequence to me) I will run up to town to meet you; for assuredly the few minutes you can spare to me from the public and from your family constitute a great part of my happiness. Last Thursday I completed fifty-seven years of my life.[1] My lot fell in with *evil days and evil times;* most of those I loved are gone whither I must soon follow. . . . From a long acquaintance with English journalists, I am not surprised at the illiberal abuse thrown against Lord Taaffe's pamphlet; but I am surprised that no English or Irish Catholic undertook a single line to vindicate or explain his Lordship's principles. I would be thankful to you if you kept by you some of the abusive *Chronicles* you mention. I would be diverted with their perusal, as I was with the invective in our own *Freeman's Journal.* . . .

1. O'Conor was writing on a Saturday; consequently he would have been born on 15 January 1710 according to the Gregorian calendar and 4 January according to the Julian calendar then in use in the British Isles.

160. To Dr. John Curry

OCD, 8.3 HS 023

28 January 1767

. . . I got here from a friend lately arrived from Paris, *Essai sur l'Histoire d'Irlande.* The last sixty pages are important as they contain some curious anecdotes relative to the time from the Reformation to the present time, particularly a memorial presented by a French agent for the Irish Catholics to the Duke of Orleans, late Regent of France. It was calculated to procure his Royal Highness' interposition with King George I relatively to the Castration Bill against our clergy.[1]. . .

O'Conor inquires if Curry has been able to place Curry's second son in a position in Europe. O'Conor says he hopes Lord Taaffe can find a place for Martin.[2]

1. Lecky, 1:163, 163n., stated that the *Essai sur l'Histoire de l'Irlande,* an anonymous book printed in the middle of the century, was "erroneous and exaggerated." Lecky wrote that a bill from the Irish Parliament in 1719 appeared before the Irish Privy Council. Instead of branding priests who returned to Ireland, the bill recommended castration. The English council felt this to be too harsh and returned the bill with the original penalty of branding restored. The bill, for other reasons, was rejected by the House of Lords and thrown out.
2. Curry's son Martin was in Vienna, and Lord Taaffe was trying to get him admitted to medical college there. Thady, another son, was in a regiment in the service of the Elector Palatine. Sheehan, p. 321.

161. To George Faulkner

BM, Egerton 201, f-47

Belanagare, 13 June 1767

. . . Dr. Leland's friendship I shall never forget, for it came recommended with an openness and candor which lays his heart bare and lets the person he gives it to see at once the value of the acquisition he makes. . . . Through his kindness I was made free of the College Library, and I am extremely thankful to Dr. Andrews[1] for his civility during the ten days that I have been perusing the Irish Annals through the reigns of the Plantagenets and Tudors. In fact, the history of our own country from the time of Henry II to the late revolution is to that of the present age the most important; an able man would instruct mankind by a recital of it, and materials are not wanting. It is a post of literature not yet (to our shame) occupied by any writer that deserves the name. Dr. Leland would fill such a post with dignity. He would, through his philosophical knowledge, render us wiser than we are, and no nation ever wanted the true knowledge of their proper interests more than ours. History in such hands would reform us much. Would to God he could be brought to think of this matter, this duty I should say, which he owes to his country. I should in such a case, though in the decline of life, sit down for months to translate the Irish Annals for him, and I think he would find some useful matter in the rubbish that I should throw out to him. But enough of this, till we hear of our friend's recovery. When he is well, you should urge him on this head and let him feel the reproach that if we do not exhibit a *Hume* or a *Robertson*² in our own island, it will be his fault. . . .

    1. Francis Andrews, D.D. (d. 1774), became Provost of Trinity College, Dublin, in 1758.
    2. William Robertson, D.D. (1721–1793), author of the *History of Scotland*, historiographer for Scotland (1763), and member of Johnson's Club. *Concise DNB*, 1:1116.

162. To Dr. John Curry, Cow Lane, Dublin

OCD, 8.3 HS 023

Belanagare, 13 June 1767

My Dear Sir,

After I parted you on the 8th of May, I arrived here, I thank God, in two days and have hitherto enjoyed good health. I spend my time in attending workmen and relaxing my cares by the perusal of better books than Irish Annals, and yet I confess I should be better gratified by reading and translating the latter, but that they are not at hand. If God spares life till I meet you again, I shall (I think) spend much of my time in collecting the flowers of those works, those especially which regard the times from the beginning of Queen Elizabeth's reign to the year of 1602 when those Annals end. It is one of the most active and important periods of our history, and my chief view in making the collection I intend is to be serviceable to you in your *opus magnum* from the Reformation downwards to the end of the treaty signed in Limerick in 1691.¹ You have materials enough or may easily come at such as you want. Your zeal calls upon you, nay it impels you to discharge this duty on this national trust to your unhappy country wherein ignorance of numberless facts, or rather the propogation of numberless untruths, has made wild havoc by souring the minds of men against men and rendering what should be the property of all our people a monopoly to one party only. Unfolding useful truths and showing what was wrong in our political conduct for one hundred years past is perhaps the best expedient for putting our monopolists *in the right* and showing them that their *own interest* is impaired not improved by excluding their fellow subjects from the common benefits due to every man who can approve himself a good subject under the present government. The whole scope of all your historical labors tends to this end, and I doubt not of your success anymore than of your zeal, if God spares you life and your present vigor.

A considerable part of your task is over already, and the other part you will find light enough by the application of your leisure hours from time to time. I say no more to you on this head, but I expect speedily an account of the progress you are making. Did Lord Taaffe answer my letter to him, or have you lately had any account of him or from him? What accounts from Martin, Thady, and Frank? I am uneasy about the latter, and I request you will give me the best information in your power. The turn of the human mind to particular occupations is a designation of Providence whose ends we cannot see and, therefore, should not attempt to control. In a faithful resignation our duty consists, and with that duty you have (I thank God) complied reluctantly indeed but still with religious submission. How is our worthy Mr. Carpenter? I could wish I had him here with me in the few weeks of good weather before us. His health would be improved by such an excursion, and I would be happy in contributing to his ease and quiet in this rural and tranquil place, I put into his hands (to be remitted to his friend in London) a *Vindication of Lord Taaffe's Political Principles*.[2] What was the fate of that short tract? My daughter is now with me and remits her heartiest affections as I do to dear Mrs. Curry, Miss Curry and to your whole family. With this truth I conclude my letter, for I never delivered any with greater sincerity.

1. Curry's *An Historical and Critical Review of the Civil Wars in Ireland from the Reign of Queen Elizabeth to the Settlement under King William*, published in 1774.
2. O'Conor's *A Vindication of Lord Taaffe's Civil Principles in a Letter to the Author of a Pamphlet Entitled "Lord Taaffe's Observations Upon the Affairs of Ireland Examined and Confuted."* Advertised by Faulkner, *DJ*, 22–26 December 1767.

163. To George Faulkner

BM, Egerton 201, f-49

Belanagare, 10 July 1767

After my return from the county of Sligo, I found your letter of the 23rd of June here before me. It gave me great pleasure to find you as inflexible as ever in the service of your country; and it gave me as great pain to find that iniquity of the Dublin pirates equally perseverant in robbing you.[1] Indeed they rob the public in spite of all your spirit, for how can you hold out under a discouragement which from its constancy is almost equal to a legal prohibition? And must not all this expose our people to the necessity of sending to England for well printed books? By the way, I am amazed at the supiness or inattention of the reputable gentlemen of your profession in not making an application to Parliament for a redress of a grievance which affects the whole public, as well as individuals. Would not a law to secure the property of publishers be more useful, would it not merit more attention than those statutes which have from time to time been enacted for preserving our grouse and partridges? I say that the inattention of fair publishers and of the manufacturers of paper and types to this point is amazing, and of none more than yourself, who have the friendship and interest of so many members in both houses for procuring a bill to remedy the evil. I am not apt to overrate the merit or spirit of my countrymen, and yet I think too well of them not to conclude they will resent the injury done you in pirating a book of which the noble author has made you sole proprietor in this kingdom. I thank you heartily for the honor you extended me in believing I could furnish some marginal notes relatively to that part of *Lord Lyttleton's History* which regards Ireland. A few such notes, I confess, could be supplied from the second volume of the *Annals of the Four Masters* now in the College library, and I think his Lordship would not be offended at the insertion; but, unluckily, I am not now in Dublin to select such particulars. If I was, no person in the kingdom would take greater pleasure in rendering you that small service than I; for I am so bound to you by interest that it can hardly give any display to my gratitude. If I could render you any service where I am, it would be by submitting to your consideration whether you should not issue a notice to the public through the channel of the *Journal* (a little bill of complaint) of injury done you, this the piracy of a work of which the noble author made you sole proprietor, etc. I am thinking that such a notice would produce the proper effect of leaving an ill printed and ill-corrected book on the hands of the pirate.

You gave me self-interested, and indeed, national pleasure in the account you give me of Dr. Leland's recovery. As a great scholar and, what is much better, as a philosopher, his country has a demand on his abilities, and however the history of a Greek King[2] who flourished in a remote antiquity has spread his fame, yet the history of his own country from the time of Henry II downward must (he must confess) be more useful to the public of our own kingdom, and I may even say, the public of all Europe. Such a man was born to moderate and repress the civil, the religious, and the shameful prejudices which poison us as individuals and weaken us as nations united under the same government. Providence bestows such abilities for the best of purposes, and if the possessors do not answer to the designation, they are accountable, and I am afraid culpable. — Had I not this affair greatly at heart, I would not be so presumptuous as to offer my own thoughts, even in a private letter, and under such an impulse (wherein I am acquitting myself of a duty). I am confident both the Doctor and you will pardon me.

   1. Faulkner in his *DJ*, 17–20 June 1767, made known to his readers his anger concerning the pirating of the second edition of *Universal History* in folio. The following advertisement could have been seen by O'Conor:
> To the Public.
> George Faulkner having for many years past, at great Expence and Trouble, printed and published several Books and Pamphlets for the Service of his Country, by promoting Knowledge, encouraging the manufactures of Printing Types, Paper, Copperplates, and many other branches of Trade, thereby saving large Sums from being sent out of the Kingdom for the above Articles: yet such hath been the Malignity, Hatred, Envy and Malice of some insidious People of his Profession, that they have not only pyrated Books and Pamphlets upon him, to the Diminution of his Fortune, but injury of his Copies, all which he obtained in the fairest Manner from different Authors and Proprietors in Great Britain and Ireland, at much Trouble and Expence, in his Journies to and fro: And whereas other Booksellers have lately had many Pyracies committed on them, they, in conjunction with each other, to save themselves and Families from inevitable Ruin, have been obliged to sell their Books and Pamphlets at less Expence than Paper and Print, to their very great Loss: And whereas Books of great Value, particularly one Work, the largest ever undertaken by any Bookseller in Ireland, and printed on better Paper, Type and Copperplates than were ever known in this Kingdom, have been pyrated on George Faulkner. . . . Many and just have been the Complaints of Books and Pamphlets not being well printed in this Nation: And how can it be otherwise, when the most elegant Editions have been pyrated to the irreparable damage of the Proprietors, by which Authors, Printers, Booksellers, Bookbinders, Paper makers, Letter-founders, and many other People whose Livelihood depend thereon, must inevitably perish or quit the Kingdom, unless these wicked Practices can be prevented?—Mr. Faulkner doth hereby call on all the Trade, to know if he ever offended one of them, or if he ever pyrated a Book, Play, Pamphlet or even a single Page or Line upon any of them. If he did not, why should they rob him?

   2. Gilbert, *Appendix*, 7:486, identifies this book as *The Life and Reign of Philip, King of Macedon*, 1758.

164. To Dr. John Curry, Cow Lane, Dublin

OCD, 8.3 HS 023

Belanagare, 17 July 1767

   For a fortnight past I have been on a ramble in the county of Sligo, what prevented my answering your last kind letter as early as I proposed. I like nothing in Lord Taaffe's letter to you but the account of his being well and his not succeeding in his suit at Rome.[1] . . . Since I received your last, I got *Exshaw's Magazine* for the month of May. Therein is a severe (and possibly not a groundless) attack upon *Lord*

Taaffe's Observations. The writer charges his amanuensis with misrepresentation relatively to the Imperial Queen's toleration[2] of her Protestant subjects, and he refers to public acts, edicts, and rescripts, published by her father and her against her Protestant subjects in *Hungary, Carinthia,* etc. If what he says on this head be true, his Lordship has forgotten or imposed upon the amanuensis, and in either case sacred truth is wounded. . . .

1. Taaffe was attempting to procure a dispensation for his son, Francis, Lord Taaffe, to marry his daughter-in-law, who had been recently widowed. Sheehan, p. 381.
2. Maria Theresa.

165. To Dr. John Curry, Dublin

OCD, 8.3 HS 023

Belanagare, 17 August 1767

Much of the letter concerns Lord Taaffe's pamphlet. Dr. Curry, O'Conor is relieved to hear, has not been infected with an "epidemic distemper" which "raged" in Dublin. O'Conor consoles Curry in the hope that nothing unforeseen will happen to Curry's three sons in Germany and Martin in Vienna. O'Conor vents his irritation with Lord Taaffe, who wants a secretary to travel with him but will not pay the man's fare:

I received civilities from the late Mr. Campbell. He was a worthy pastor, and I am sorry for our loss in such a man. I am equally sorry to lie under an apprehension or rather conviction that his place will not be filled by our friend who merits so well. He and the public will be equally injured. I wrote to Lord Taaffe to solicit for him; and I am amazed that instead of doing so he should only solicit for the poor post of an occasional secretary, a post which may be well filled by an inferior person who it seems *must be paid by ourselves.* You certainly must share in the disgust which such a conduct gives me.[1]

1. Dr. Curry wrote to O'Conor on 11 August about Father Carpenter. Curry mentioned a visit from Archbishop Fitzsimons who told Curry that Lord Taaffe wanted to have Father Carpenter sent to him as his secretary without any chance of preferment. Lord Taaffe's request implied that he would not be responsible for Carpenter's salary or travel expenses. Gilbert, *Appendix,* p. 485.

166. To Chevalier Thomas O'Gorman, Castle Street, Dublin

BM, Add. MS 21121

Belanagare, 1 September 1767

My dear O'Gorman,

Your letters of the first and 29th of this last month lie before me; assuredly the former gave me the most sensible pleasure as it informed me that you were well and safely arrived in your native country, and both gave me the satisfaction of being convinced that you persist in collecting materials for rendering this land of your birth better known at home and abroad. Poor O'Sulivan! You and I can not but lament the loss we both, nay the public, had in him. Let us repair such a loss as well as we can by augmenting the labor which he would have spared us. I could have lent a shoulder to your present undertaking had I been in Dublin, where by the care of Dr. Leland[1] we have undoubtedly the best collection of old Annals now in these islands. That learned and worthy gentleman made me free of the College Library, and my Conaght avocations have so unhappily superseded my passion to profit of the treasure there collected that hitherto I could do nothing for your advantage or my own. Your plan is the history of the County of Clare (on Smith's plan) and a good one.[2] Till the third century that country belonged to Conaght and was possessed by the Fir Bolgs.[3] In that period of time Leth Moyha and Leth-Quin (and not sooner) undertook the conquest of this western province and succeeded. The Hibernians seized upon the county now called Clare and added it to Tuamond; the Heremondans[4] seized upon the remainder of Conaght. Tuamond included the counties of Limeric, Clare, and some parts of County Tiperary, and that province (called North Munster) fell to the Rari of Cormac Cas, the great ancestor of the Rari of Dol-Cas, who after the tenth century was headed by the posterity of Brian Borevey, under the surname of Brian. But all this you know better than I can inform you, and I wonder why I said so much to you. What I should have told you is that relatively to the historical part of your work there are abundant materials in *The Annals of The Four Masters* from the tenth to the seventeenth century, and in my Conaght Annals there is a good account during the two hundred years before the Reformation. Those with your own collections will afford a vastly better historical narrative than any we ever yet had of any county of Ireland, and I reckon it a misfortune to myself that I can not be near you as a pioneer to throw up the materials which lay so long buried and which till very lately could not be discovered. In that way I could give you some assistance, though I could not pretend to give it in any other. Your being near me would give me some alacrity in the labor, for I would, as I am in the decline of life, want so good a prompter: but you are running away from me to London, to Paris, and God knows whither. I trust that it is to enable yourself the better to proceed in your undertaking and to return back to us speedily. Sorry I am indeed that you and Dr. O'Brien of Cloyne are so long asunder.[5] In your way he is a man of great knowledge, and I have it from a good hand who perused a good part of the work that he made a good progress in the ancient history of Munster. He is now in London, and it would be happy if some third person could be found to bring you and him together and lay the foundation of historical friendship between you. I have not the honor of being known to him. If I had, the poor *Dissertations*, of which you speak so partially, would come out under fewer disadvantages. By your education in the school of Hippocrates and Dioscorides, you are happily qualified for the natural history of the country you describe, and I rejoice with you in my prediction that your work will be the completest we ever had relatively to Ireland.[6] You have great strength and youth, and this first work I shall look upon only as the preliminary to many more on the same subject.

The political history of Ireland from Henry II to the late Revolution in '88 is to us the most important of any. Dr. Leland has abilities and philosophy equal to the task. I moved it to him indirectly by a letter to our worthy friend Mr. Faulkner; and it is a pity that a man who distinguished himself through Europe by writing the life of a monarch of a remote country and age should not bestow part of his abilities to adorn and (what is better) instruct and reform his own country. This I think is his duty as God enabled him to perform it; but it is a duty recommended by a person of little significance and therefore, I conceive, not attended to.

By the prolixity of my letter, you see what a desire I have to hold a conversation with you and how unwilling I am to part you or take the hint given by this paper that I should leave some part of it in the fair condition it was in a while ago. While you remain among us, I request I may have a letter from you every post. You will inform and improve me.

1. Dr. Thomas Leland (1722–85), librarian at Trinity College.
2. Charles Smith (1715?–1762) wrote histories of Down, Waterford, Cork, and Kerry, which were praised by T. B. Macaulay in the nineteenth century. *Concise DNB*, 1:1212.

3. According to the Irish tradition recorded in the *Book of Invasions,* Ireland was originally occupied by three races: the Tuatha Dé Danann, a semi-divine group specializing in magic and wizardry; the Firbolg, a short, dark, plebian race; and the Fomorians, sea giants. Curtis, p. 1.

4. The *Book of Invasions* records that the Gaelic Irish were descendents of the three sons of Mileadh of Spain: Heremon, Heber, and Ir. Curtis, p. 1.

5. John O'Brien became Roman Catholic Bishop of Cloyne and Ross. He was working on an Irish-English dictionary which appeared in 1768, a year after his death. His studies on Irish tanistry and gavelkind were published 1774–1775. *Concise DNB,* 1:961.

6. O'Conor's comparison of Chevalier O'Gorman to ancient physicians was a flowery compliment. O'Gorman was in the service of the French government, perhaps as an army physician. Dioscorides Pedanius (*c.* first century A.D.) was an army physician well versed in pharmacological literature. His *Materia Medica* is a classification and description of medicines. The editor described his work: "The observation is minute; the judgement sober and free from superstition." The *Oxford Classical Dictionary,* p. 290.

167. To George Faulkner

BM, Egerton 201, f-51

Belanagare, 4 September 1767

Dear Sir,

Your letter and packet of the first instant I received last night, and I return you infinite thanks for your frequent acts of friendship. I am a greater gainer by them, and they are enhanced greatly to me, as I receive them amidst so many avocations of yours, public and personal. The fifty-four pages you sent me of Lord Lyttleton's history I read last night and again this morning with great avidity, nor did he disappoint my expectations of him as a fine painter and a fair one also since that, as far as I can judge or know (from what I saw), he does not draw from prejudice or affectation, but each character sat for the picture and whether good or bad his coloring is excellent, without gaudiness or quaintness. I told you above I am a greater gainer by your friendship, for you gave me many friendships along with it, and all the return I can make you is not to put you under any pain for giving them; as I hope confidently that I have discretion and prudence enough to keep what I got, and, at worst, in the negative good quality of giving no offense. But I am, I know, a loser by not being oftener near you, and I am pained that I have not been lately so, as I should have seen Lord Clare, whose family and personal abilities I am well acquainted with. I am also a loser by not knowing Count Serant[1] personally. I am much pleased that O'Gorman made one in the circle lately about your table, and it gave me pleasure when he and I dined with you (on the Blind Quay) that he rendered himself so agreeable to Lords Moyra and Aran; we had indeed that night a long sitting but a very pleasing one. Mr. O'Gorman was bred a scholar and physician in the University of Paris and is better qualified to write the natural and civil history of the County of Clare (upon Smith's Plan) for which he has collected the best materials. He has a good mind, which is better than all the sciences without that quality. My worthy and beneficent friend (one of the friends you gave me) Dr. Leland is mounted too high on the steps of fame; does he not think it would be descending to write the history of his native country down from the time of Henry II? The history of freebooters on the one side and savages (what Mr. Hume calls them) on the other? But this is grounded on a mistake. We have not been much greater savages and freebooters than our neighbors during the Feudal Ages; and the history of man on every stage is worthy of being known, though doubtless one period of time rewards the pains of an able historian better than another; and yet is nothing due to the land of our birth? Shall this, and this island alone be a blank in the history of Europe? Dr. Leland will let it be so, and let him be answerable for it. He knows well that I have not abilities for the task I would wish he undertook. If I had, he knows that in the decline of life I could do but little and that little in the part of a pioneer to dig and throw up materials for him, or such as him. I am luckily saved that labor, and it may be happy for me as I am almost past my labor. I make my letter prolix because I love to be long in your company, and yet the desire has better grounds than mere selfishness upon such a principle. Alone I should be contemptible even in my own idea. I am employed by day in the business of agriculture and by night I converse with philosophers, and (by way of relaxation or contrast) with divines. In both I discern great weakness as well as great strength. If God grants life, I will next November change the scene, and hive myself (like the bees) during the bad season in your capital. Meantime, I request you will tender my affections to Miss Smith with whom I shall quarrel, if she does not change her name before I see her. My best services to my worthy young friend Mr. Todd[2] and Mr. Smith.[3]

1. Unidentified.
2. Thomas Todd, Faulkner's adopted son.
3. Samuel Smith, Faulkner's nephew.

168. To Dr. John Curry, Cow Lane, Dublin

OCD, 8.3 HS 023

11 September 1767

Dear Sir,
    Lord Taaffe, it is evident, resolves to proceed on the affair of the dispensation, notwithstanding all the repulses he received.[1] I loved the man from his own former worthy dispositions and from the less engaging esteem he derived from an old and worthy family. No good is likely to come of his present measure, and much evil is to be feared for his posterity at least. Sure I am that though he cannot lose relatively to our good wishes for him, he must suffer greatly in our esteem. So at least, I think, in my present temper, and I can assure you, my dear friend, that your last letter on the subject is the only one from your hand that ever pained me. It pained yourself, but we must submit on such occasions as on others to events we can neither prevent or even control. Dr. Fitzsimons (no doubt) did well to sign a characteristic memorial for his Lordship. It was his testimony to a truth for the bad use of which he is not accountable. There are two bishops in this country who will sign also, but I should have a copy of the form of such a memorial for them, as they might be strangers to the necessary form and as they would decline framing one of their own. When such a form is remitted to me, I will negotiate the affair though with a reluctant heart.
    I am rejoiced that Martin is well and that the disappointment he met with has given no interruption to his studies. All the pain I am in is that you have been put to extraordinary expense.
    This fortnight past I am reading Lord Lyttleton's *History of Henry II* sent to me in packets (franked by T. Le Hunte) from my friend Mr. Sheriff Faulkner.[2] I have yet received 270 pages. It is the work of an able, judicious, and criticial writer; and yet relatively to the ecclesiastical part of the history he fills the character rather of a good Protestant than of a disengaged philosopher. How few even of the greatest men have elevation of mind enough to assert their natural freedom on such occasions! They talk much of liberty and are themselves the slaves of opinion!
    How is our worthy friend Mr. Carpenter? His case goes much to my heart.[3] What do you hear from London? Or does the political controversy between the *Free Examiner* and their inquisitional adversaries go on still? I am here an absolute stranger to anything that passes in

the world and it may be good for me. Adieu, my dear friend, and let me hear as soon as possible from you.

1. The dispensation is a Papal dispensation for Count Francis Taaffe that he might marry Taaffe's daughter-in-law. Taaffe was hoping that Archbishop Fitzsimons and another prelate would sign a memorial attesting to the character of Count Taaffe. O'Conor felt this move to be a wrong one. Gilbert, *Appendix*, p. 484.
2. While he was in London promoting O'Conor's *Dissertations*, George Faulkner must have contracted with William Bowyer, Jr., and Lockyer Davis for the Irish rights to Lord Lyttleton's *History of the Life of Henry II and the Age in which He lived* . . . because Faulkner announced in his *DJ*, 13–16 June 1767, that the work was being printed. The *DJ*, 9–12 January 1768 advertised the first, second, and fourth volumes for sale. The third volume would deal with Henry's invasion of Ireland. Lord Lyttleton asked O'Conor to do the historical notes on Ireland. Robert Ward, "Friendship and an Eighteenth Century History of Ireland," *Éire-Ireland*, 7 (Autumn 1972), pp. 56–62.
3. Carpenter's desire for a better assignment.

169. To George Faulkner

BM Egerton 201, f-53

Belanagare, 15 September 1767

Dear Sir,

In one of the six packets I received from you last Thursday, I met with your most friendly letter, and you have my perpetual gratitude in return. When you ventured on remitting at once such a large cargo by one post, it was judicious in you to procure the pass of Mr. Le Hunte, lest the post officers should grow suspicious of so bulky a correspondence with a Papist. By the way, I am assured that Mr. Le Hunte is a humane and obliging landlord to his own popish tenants and that he can reconcile two (seemingly) strange extremes, hatred to the party and good will to the individuals. Lord Lyttleton's history will do good because it will make us wiser; and when we are a little wiser, we will, at worst, forbear and relent; if we do not reform. — This is gaining a great point at a time when gaining and (in Ireland particularly) was a happiness despaired of. — The reproach against us, that our historical productions were not equal to those of the continent, was, I believe, just. That reproach is now removed since Hume, Robertson, and Lyttleton appeared; and Mr. Hume in one particular perhaps excels all our ablest historians, as he is not fettered by principles, which though doubtless the best in themselves yet produce the worst effects when ill understood and, consequently, ill-applied. In truth, such principles, turned devious from their true intention, make no sort of difference between the Inquisitions of Spain and those of

England. The *matter* is the same, the *form* different, and we may thank our excellent political constitution that struggles with the disease and resists all its violence. It will be visited with greater force, nay it may be shaken off, if such men as Lord Lyttleton (men of authority and rank) continue to write: writers in a superior orb who do not permit religious zeal to extinguish the lights of philosophy. I shall owe a great deal to Dr. Leland's indulgence if [he] forgives me the warmth with which I would fain turn his talents to a more particular application, relatively to the interest and wants of his countrymen. He too is a philosopher as well as a Christian; he has youth and strength and will do good in whatever subjects he writes upon. I request that you will present him (the friend you gave me) with my affections and gratitude.

You have good and, I think, effectual interest with the leading men in both Houses of Parliament, and you will merit just reproach if you do not push that interest with them to obtain a legal remedy against the robbers of your and others' property relatively to the publication of good books. In other countries the press is restrained from doing good; in Ireland it is permitted to do acknowledged evil, even to the public as well as to individuals.

I wish I may hear soon from O'Gorman. You may sooner. If you do, be pleased to inform him that he is welcome to the use of my Ortelius, which I left with you for some time with a view to draw in subscriptions for his map of Ireland as it was inhabited in his time.

With the warmest gratitude I accept of your assistance in my occupation as a tiller of the earth, and if you send DuHamil's *Husbandry*[1] to my son's house in Anderson's Court, Cow Lane, it will be safely conveyed to me. I enjoy 800 acres still of the old family estate, the plank on which we came on shore (as I told Judge Marshal[2] at your table) after our great ship-wreck. You will enable me to reclaim the additional 300 acres, which are yet worth nothing. Meantime I thank you sincerely for putting me in mind of introducing my son to you. I will do so when I am [in] town. He will benefit of your friendship, for he is in the mercantile business.

You are too polite a man; for you pardon the prolixity of my letters. Indeed I should be still more impertinent in this way, only that my paper is a good monitor.

    1. Faulkner advertised in his *DJ*, 14–18 July 1767, "In a few days will be published by George Faulkner, printer hereof, in two volumes octavo, *The Elements of Agriculture*, by M. Duhamel DuMonceau of the Royal Academy of Science in France and Fellow of the Royal Society in London." It would appear that Faulkner did not advertise this book for sale until September. It was Faulkner's usual practice to send prepublication copies to his friends. (See *Orrery Papers*, 2:23.) Whenever Faulkner suggested that the book "is

soon to be published" rather than "in the press and soon to be published," he could be receiving the books unbound but already printed from London from the press of William Bowyer or Charles Reymer.

2. Robert Marshall, judge in the Irish Court of Common Pleas.

170. To George Faulkner

BM, Egerton 201, f-55

Belanagare, 25 September 1767

Dear Sir,

Last Monday I received your three packets of Lord Lyttleton's history (in continuation) wherein your kind letter of the 19th instant was enclosed. I thank you for both; and assuredly I compute the weight of obligation on myself by the weight of business which takes up your time and which must stand still while you are thus ministering to my improvement as well as entertainment. You are satisfied with my feelings and are one of the few who are so satisfied and give their friendship in return for the gratitude which themselves excite. What I received hitherto of Lord L[yttleton]'s history concludes with page 368 and leaves me in the midst of a very useful digression on the Crusade War: a most extraordinary suite of events, wherein the enthusiasm of some, the superstition of others, and the ignorance of all gave Rome a dominion over Europe superior to any it exerted in the days of its imperial greatness! It was a dominion over the human mind and the most melancholy proof of human weakness. But time broke the charm: mankind has acquired a little more knowledge, and but a little, since that time; for we still evidently wear some heavy chains and the few who shake them, or are shaking them off, bear no proportion to the many who are fond of them. I only wish that the work of great men like this you put into my hands may open men's eyes. I request that you will give my affections to my philosopher, to Dr. Leland. I shall owe much to his indulgence if he forgives me the liberty I took with him in my correspondence with you. It was a liberty excited by my well-grounded prejudices in his favor; and as you alone are privy to what I proposed to him, I can hardly repent of my indiscretion, and especially as you assure me that I am still in possession of his friendship. I thank you warmly for Du Hamill's *Agriculture*. Other books improve and entertain, but such as Du Hamill's qualify us for improvement because through their help we establish our independence, the greatest of human blessings.

From the first of July to the 19th instant our weather was broken and very unpromising; for eight days past we never had better. Our hay and corn are well saved, and we have plenty of both. It is pleasing to see our people so busy in this province. Men, women, children are grown industrious from the introduction of the linen manufacture among us. Some of the Penal Laws which have put restraints on the industry of Papists have been virtually repealed by the course of time, by the necessity imposed by nature that men cannot thrive without each other's co-operation, and by the prevailing genius of our civil constitution, which in spite of any by-laws permits not that labor and industry shall be quite unrewarded. I am encouraging the linen manufacture much in Belanagare, no land in the county being more commodious for raising and watering flax; and I am disposing of matters so as to render this fragment of the family estate much more valuable in a few years than it is at present. I have already subdued 200 acres of coarse land, and a district that never paid a shilling to the crown pays now four pounds a year in hearth money. You have the improvement of your native country at heart; and if you had not, I would not be so ostentatious before you relatively to the improvement of my part of it. To another this account would be both vain and impertinent. Adieu, my dear Sir, give my affections to your family and take care of that health in which your friends, nay the public, are so much interested.

171. To Dr. John Curry, Cow Lane, Dublin

OCD, 8.3 HS 023

From my Retreat, 7 October 1767

My Dear Sir,

On every fine day I fill my proper post, that which was laid out for our first fallen parent, tilling the earth. It contributes to my health and independence—those two enjoyments which baffle the physical and even political evils of life. In worse weather, of which we had a run for a week past, I sit down in this place and before this fire in the company of very sensible men who speak to me on paper and instruct me how to fence against those moral evils which health and independence rather entertain as friends than encounter as enemies. Even in such company I have discovered that one ought to be on his guard. On general hands of duty they are all united; on descending to particulars, hostility commences—ridiculous but fatal hostility wherein party interest is the combatant and fraud the weapon. It is ridiculous enough to find the managers of this warfare deriving no small share of complacency from the *only* point in which they are successful, the eternal exclusion of peace. We have nothing to do but establish our own internal peace in spite of men and hope for better times when more knowledge and more enlightened philosophy must render posterity happier than their grandsires! Pardon all this to me, my dear friend. I am so abstracted in this retreat and know so little of what is doing in the world that I must rush into mere commonplace topics, and what I accidentally have hit upon in the first line of my letter hurried me thus far before I was aware.

How is our worthy and neglected friend, Mr. Carpenter? I hope his bodily health is good; as to the health of the mind, he has happily secured *that* himself; and the want of any co-operation from others renders his merit the more conspicuous in yours, in mine, and in the eye of every discerning man.

What further intelligence from Lord Taaffe? I love him as a worthy and zealous nobleman and wish him success in every negotiation but one. What good his pamphlet did or whether it did any, I know not. I wish it may do no hurt from the evil construction put upon it or rather from the malevolence which it revived, and that *in amaritudine animarum*.[1] His Lordship has been pelted with abuse and, what is worse, charged with evil intentions and falsifications of facts for six or seven months successively; and yet, as if the cause he undertook was utterly indefensible, not a single line appeared in his vindication from any person in the three kingdoms. Perhaps it was prudent to drop the subject; and if so, it was surely very improper to revive it. I may be wrong, but I am wrong with my betters (in every light) in thinking that an honest explanation of our principles relative to civil government can never be offensive to our civil governors, unless it be an offense to undeceive, a circumstance which it would be really offensive to suppose and which infers that an acquiescence under the foulest *civil* charge that ever can be made must be acceptable to our rulers! This is what I cannot suppose. Let those who do show what *negative* good such acquiescence under a criminal accusation can do. A recommendation to favor it never can be but certainly a motive to *positive* evil. Here I drop the subject and leave these wise acquiescers (if you will allow the word) to their own rational refinements.

You wrote to me some time ago that Lord Taaffe wanted and obtained a certificate, etc., from the prelates on your side. I told you in answer that I could obtain the like from the prelates in my vicinity as soon as the form of the instrument to be subscribed was remitted to me. I suppose from your silence and further reflections that the numbers who have already signed their names will be sufficient for his Lordship's purpose.

You give me a good account of Martin, though he has not succeeded in his academical suite. It is what I feared from the beginning, but it is happy that the disappointment gave no worse effect than drawing all his supplies from you; the best out is that you have full value from the expense, however heavy. I think you must be well-informed by this time of Frank's situation, as well as of Thady's; I request you will communicate to me what you know, for assuredly I am interested greatly in their happiness, I mean their honor and morals, for as to wealth they have not chosen the best trade for acquiring it, though even in that they may live to be a comfort to you and gain credit for their family. My hearty affections to your worthy ladies. I cannot end my long letter better.

P.S. I write the enclosed to your neighbor in Anderson's Court,[2] and I request you will order Matt to drop it at his house. I know nothing of our Lord Lieutenant,[3] nor of any other matter now transacting. If you have leisure, I request you will send me a long letter.

    1. In bitterness of spirit.   2. O'Conor's son Charles.
    3. George Townshend (1724–1807), who was the first Lord Lieutenant to reside in Ireland.

172. To Dr. John Curry, Cow Lane, Dublin

OCD, 8.3 HS 023

From the Hermitage, 30 October 1767

... Your going through the drudgery of reading over *Strafford's Letters* was labor indeed but had its reward as you separated so much ore from the dross.[1] In spite of all you have said in one of your letters, it is not given you to resist the impulse to such researches. It is "direction which thou canst not see," as Mr. Pope phrases it.[2] The public has already felt and acknowledged the effects, and I predict will feel (and benefit by) more, though not so much immediately as we could wish. For *"there are still too many splinters in the broken bone,"* and the patient is too peevish. The *"passive slaves of prejudice,"* says that present Earl of Egmont, "prefer the implicitness of credulity to the *active* researches of their own reason and would rather continue ruinously mistaken than unpleasingly undecieved. To understandings of this stamp, truth would in vain and even dangerously hold out her torch, sure for her reward to have it dashed in her face." All this is, I think, finely expressed and may be considered as a good lesson to our people during the ensuing session.[3] . . .

    1. Thomas Wentworth (1593–1641) was the first Earl of Strafford. As Lord Lieutenant of Ireland, he managed to incur the hatred of both the Irish and the Old English. He was executed in 1641 on Tower Hill in London. The book to which O'Conor was referring was *The Earl of Strafford's Letters and Dispatches*. Two editions were currently available to O'Conor, William Bowyer's London edition in 1739, and a Dublin edition printed in 1740. *Concise DNB*, 1:1385; *BMCPBCE*, 26:991.
    2. O'Conor was quoting from "An Essay on Man," 1:289–290:
> All Nature is but Art, unknown to thee;
> All Chance, Direction which thou canst not see;

Alexander Pope, *The Poems of Alexander Pope*, ed. John Butt (New Haven, Connecticut: Yale University Press, 1963; Yale paperbound, 1966), p. 515.
    3. Lord Townshend has been sent to minimize the power of the Undertakers.

173. To George Faulkner

BM, Egerton 201, f-61

Belanagare, 24 November 1767[1]

. . . Our Popery Laws are so dispersed through our statute volumes that the seeking them out in that detached condition is a very irksome task. To draw them out under proper heads and proper arrangement would be a very useful undertaking, and my friend Counselor Ridge[2] told me that such a disposition was made and nearly executed. I shall inquire about this matter as soon as I arrive in town and will give you all the information I can get. . . .

O'Conor thanks Faulkner for the information about the new Viceroy and the men in his retinue and replies that with a group of wise as well as learned men on his staff, surely Lord Townshend's administration will be an enlightened one. Faulkner had sent O'Conor Lord Lyttleton's History of Henry II, and O'Conor has reached p. 400 in volume one.

    1. Faulkner in a letter to O'Conor dated 17 November described the visit of Lord Townshend to Faulkner's bookshop to ask him where he, Townshend, could get a copy of the penal laws against Catholics. George Faulkner to Charles O'Conor, 17 November 1767, Stowe MS B12, RIA.
    2. John Ridge, Irish barrister friend of O'Conor, Edmund Burke, and Oliver Goldsmith. For Goldsmith's comment on Ridge see Goldsmith's poem "Retaliation," in *Collected Works of Oliver Goldsmith*, ed. Arthur Friedman (Oxford: Clarendon Press, 1966), 4:153.

174. To Dr. John Curry, Cow Lane, Dublin

OCD, 8.3 HS 026

Belanagare, 9 December 1767

... I am pleased that you changed your mind relatively to a *Vindication of Lord Taaffe's Civil Principles*. I sent it off to you this day and *sine me liber ibit in urbem;*[1] but it will not be long in the city before me, for I shall set off (God willing) on Monday next. In case you like the plan[2] and the execution on the whole, I shall take the trouble of transcribing it in Dublin for the press and make such additions and corrections as you require.[3] The work is half reasoning, half history, the facts casting a light and giving strength to the argument. For the historical part I had all the materials I wanted, and for the other I am conscious it must suffer by falling into my hands. ...

Were our masters in earnest, a test oath would not be difficult. King *William* required of our people no more than a simple oath of allegiance; and did the wisest men now in the kingdom club heads to frame a test against perjury, duplicity, etc., they could not produce one more full to every point than *Dr. Nary's*, which is annexed to the *Vindication*, etc., Appendix No. 2.[4] ...

In passing a *Test* for our people (if any such should be in agitation) I apprehend that the practice in *Holland* and *Germany* will not influence much;[5] pride mixes here as in other things, men choosing rather in such cases to make than follow precedents. Assuredly they will throw in an abjuration of the exiled family. But my paper is out, and what remains will tell you what you know already.

   1. The book will go into the city without me.
   2. The plan or outline for *The Vindication*. . . .
   3. O'Conor must have copied his manuscript quickly because the *DJ*, 22–26 December, offered for sale *A Vindication of Lord Taaffe's Civil Principles in a Letter to the Author of a Pamphlet entitled Lord Taaffe's Observations upon the Affairs of Ireland, Examined and Confuted*.
   4. Cornelius Nary (1660–1738), an Irish Catholic priest, wrote *Case of the Roman Catholics* in 1724. It was reprinted in 1754 with Hugh Reily's *Impartial History of Ireland*. . . . BMCPBCE 21:351.
   5. Lord Taaffe had printed in the *DJ*, 9–11 June 1768, the oath of allegiance sworn by the clergy of Silesia to the King of Prussia. He suggested that Irish Catholics would be willing to take the same oath to George III.

175. To Dr. John Curry, Cow Lane, Dublin

OCD, 8.3 HS 026

From my Hermitage, 10 June 1768

This letter is a "keep-in-touch letter" in which O'Conor flatters Curry by telling him that no one is more worthy of the task of writing in favor of amelioration of the penal laws than Curry is.

176. To Dr. John Curry

OCD, 8.3 HS 026

From the Hermitage, 28 June 1768

Curry's sons have not written to him and he communicates his anxiety to O'Conor. O'Conor commiserates with the lonely Curry and replies that he has heard nothing from Lord Taaffe. O'Conor, when he is not directing his tenants in building drainage ditches (so he tells Curry), has skimmed the ten-volume *General History* . . . by Voltaire. O'Conor finds "several shameful mistakes of this great philosophic writer in matters of fact."

177. To Dr. John Curry

OCD, 8.3 HS 026

8 August 1768

I write this from the Hermitage, wherein I some time since received a letter from you and another from our worthy friend Mr. Carpenter. He flattered me with the expectation of seeing him in this retreat on a voyage of health in the situation of doing studying, reading what he pleased. He would be entirely at home with me. Either the weather or (I hope) some unforeseen avocation, not sickness, disappointed me of the happiness he intended me. . . .

Counselor Ridge on his circuit called upon me here the other day and ate a mutton chop with me, a worthy young gentleman and most heartily your friend. He is well acquainted with Dr. Smollett, one of the *Critical Reviewers*. It was in a sitting with him that he and Mr. Burke put the *Memoirs* into his hands, and from that event proceeded the judgment published in the *Critical Review*. . . .

178. To Dr. John Curry, Cow Lane, Dublin

OCD, 8.3 HS 026

From the Hermitage, 12 August 1768

After great longings, nay, after despairing of our dear friend Mr. Carpenter, he arrived here yesterday evening. This event (after desponding) has enhanced the pleasure I now enjoy in his company. We are here free to think, to converse, to read out of the reach of power and even of its worst effects, penal laws. It is a spot of ground created (so to speak) by myself, a sort of plantation, cleared of stones and underwood and now producing milk, animal food, and plenty of esculent vegetables. Penal Laws shall not pursue me into this retreat,[1] and I lament only that numbers who as little merit their stripes should be exposed to their severity. . . .

> 1. O'Conor's frequent allusions to Horace hint at the parallels he felt between his own position and Horace's. O'Conor, who alternated between political involvement in Dublin and retreats to his study and estate affairs in Belanagare, frequently quotes sections of Horace's first Epistle where the poet compares himself to the athlete Vejanus who retires "to bury himself in the country and never again / Pray for the 'thumbs up' from the crowd." Horace continues:
>
>> So I lay down my poems and other toys of my youth
>> To devote myself to one main subject: the truth.
>> What is right and honest? This I would like to know.
>> I am laying up stores, setting them all in a row,
>> Of the only thing that will keep on helping me grow.
>>
>> And who is the head of my house? With whose ideas
>> Am I most at home? I'm not obliged to swear
>> By the words of any one trainer. Wherever the storm
>> Drives me in, I take shelter. At times, I'm the Practical Man,
>> The heroic, Stoical Man, who takes Part in Life,
>> And Care of truth, and Charge of inflexible Virtue.
>> At times, I slip off unseen to the opposite side,
>> To fit the world to myself, not me to it.
>
> Horace *Satires and Epistles of Horace,* trans. Smith Palmer Bovie (Chicago: University of Chicago Press, 1959; Phoenix Books, 1963), p. 165ff.

179. To Dr. John Curry, Cow Lane, Dublin

OCD, 8.3 HS 026

From the Hermitage, 9 September 1768

. . . I had an account in this paper of poor Dugan's death[1] before I received your letter. I was, in truth, heartily concerned. I was the first, and he confessed it, who put him in the way of searching for pieces of history relative to our country, and I never knew a better angler; but he was, poor man, too selfish and on that principle, has shut the door of intelligence in my face, of which I could give you several instances. His collection is, I know, very valuable: and if the sale catalog be published soon (which I do not think will be the case till I go up) I shall trust to Mr. Carpenter and to you, who will mark out those books which we want. Mr. Carpenter will attend at the sale for us both, and I will previously send up nine or ten guineas as a stock for him. Some Irish manuscripts I know Dugan had, and possibly I will have but few to contend with me as the college is now sufficiently supplied with books in our native language. . . .

1. Michael Duggan was a broker and auctioneer in Brides-Alley. *DJ*, 3–6 September 1768.

180. To Archbishop John Carpenter

OCD, 8.3 HS 026

22 September 1768

My Dear Friend,

I long greatly to hear from, and I request that you will ease me of the pain I am in about you by the return of the post. I lately met our friend Fitzgerald[1] on the highway here, nor could I stop his flight a single hour. He is now, I am confident, some days settled in your capital; and no doubt, he has communicated to you that part of Mr. Charles Kelly's letter wherein I am remembered with distinguished friendship and wherein also (what pleases me as well) Dr. Curry and you have so great a share in his esteem. I earnestly entreat it of you to put us all in the way of turning Mr. Kelly's intentions (in our favor) to the best account by improving in particular his solicitations in behalf of a friend who has been laboring in the vineyard a long time without any consideration for the laborer.[2] It is your duty to do this, however meritorious your delicacy may be in declining it. It is your duty on a double account; for in the first place, you should endeavor that the aforesaid friend should be rendered more useful than in his present situation he possibly can be; and in the second, to prevent as far (as you are able) the forwardness, the astutia and (adulation of demerit) to occupy the post of zeal and knowledge. I say no more on the subject till I hear from you. I trust that you are more frequent in visits to

Anderson's Court than otherwise you would be as Charles is now confined to bed by a disorder of which I hear no particulars. Living or dying, spiritual comfort is the best remedy he can have; and as to physical applications I am in no pain as he is happy enough to have my best friend near him and administer for him.

Poor Dugan is no more! As Dr. Curry observes, he is a loss to the public, and we now forget the spirit of selfishness which in a good degree drove from him persons whose friendship he should cultivate. If his scarce books should be put up to auction, I request you will send me the catalog under covers that I may mark out such books as I want; and I must entreat it of you to attend the sale so that my absence may not prevent my possession of those tracts.[3] You will be supplied with money by my son if God should spare him life. I hear of a pamphlet printed in Dublin containing animadversions on the Bishop of Down's[4] (my acquaintance's) panegyrical sermon on the late Mr. Archbold, once a Jesuit.[5] If such a book be really out of the press, I request you will put it into Mr. Henigan's hands, Charles's clerk, to be forthwith forwarded to me. You will, I hope, soon after your receipt of this see Dr. Curry to tender my affections and tell him this letter is for him as well as for you. I write from your and my Hermitage. Denny and all friends of your acquaintance about me in the neighborhood think of you often, and be assured of being in possession of their most cordial esteem.

1. Fr. Fitzgerald, O'Conor's friend.
2. O'Conor wants Carpenter to enlist Fr. Charles Kelly, who is stationed at Rome, to use his influence in Carpenter's behalf.
3. Curry's letter of 17 September has not arrived. In it Curry told O'Conor that Duggan's books were not to be sold, since Duggan had willed them to Mr. Lodge and Mr. Beresford. Stowe MS. B12, RIA.
4. Dr. Traill.   5. Curry's cousin.

181. To Dr. John Curry, Cow Lane, Dublin

OCD, 8.3 HS 026

From the Hermitage, 23 September 1768

My Dear Sir,

Yours of the 17th instant I have not received until yesterday. I had another from Mr. Dillon[1] relatively to my unfortunate son. Among his other follies, his conduct with regard to you gives me cutting pain; neglecting your prescriptions was such a method of baffling your expectations and frustrating your intentions as I cannot forgive him on your account if I have no concern on his own. But on this infatuated conduct of his I shall be silent till I find him re-established if that be now possible. The truth is he has been doubly ill and concealed a disorder which medicine was hardly a match for. His poor feeling mind has been preying upon his crazy frame and all owing to his own flexibility. He engaged his credit in town for some worthless gentleman in this county who wanted money in April last and who neglected discharging his acceptances for them on the days of payment. Their bills are protested, I believe, by this time, and his credit is blasted. Thus affairs stand with him and though he has £100 of my money in his hands and his own capital to support him, I am afraid still that he will not easily get out of the scrape his folly brought him into. I cautioned him in particular against a gentleman of my own name and family, and yet he plunged into the snare that very person laid for him; on that man's account alone he is in for £240.2/6p. I am resolved to bear all this unforeseen misfortune with the firmness which prudence and religion require, and the more as it is in a case wherein my conscience is clear wherein no guilt on my part has any share.

Last post I wrote to our worthy friend Mr. Carpenter, and I hope before this time that he communicated to you the contents of a letter from Mr. Charles Kelly of Rome wherein he speaks of you and me in the kindest terms. That gentleman's activity is equal to his zeal in the service of every deserving countryman, and both ought to be improved by all the means on our side here at home for the advancement of good men who alone, in a land of frequent apostasies, can preserve the Catholic religion or what remains of it in our island. When once the place of merit is given up to intrigue, to favoritism, and a scramble for loaves and fishes, that religion which stood out every storm from power for two hundred years past among us will fall in the dead calm of a religious tepidity, allied to ignorance, its forerunner. I wrote to Mr. Carpenter also to attend at the sale of Dugan's collections, little dreaming of the silly disposition he made or sillier motive he had in making it. There was, no doubt, as you observe, a low astutia in the bequest he made; and when it became necessary to make a true discovery of his mind, his sincerity came out too late. Thus do we impose on the world to our last moments. I wrote also to Mr. Carpenter for the remarks on the Bishop of Down's sermon, lest you should not be at as much leisure as he to provide franks for covers, and that he might put them into the hands of Charles's clerk to leave them in the post office; I never longed for any work more, for I enjoy beyond measure their sufficiency by their rank and who, infinite of themselves, are humbled or rather brought to their proper level. Indeed, it gives me great pain that you have not seen Mr. Duane.² He would gain by your conversation, and good Dr. D.³ has hindered him of that advantage. View here the course of what is in general denominated friendship. See what return Mr. Duane had for *his* real friendship. You are also a loser by not knowing that gentleman personally, but that was no concern of your brother D———. Were Dr. D. a wise or even a prudent man, he should bring you both together; your countenance and friendship would be of use to him in Dublin.

I am sorry that your acquaintance with Macnamara⁴ was so very short; as a correspondent indeed he is a cold one and too laconic for information. As he is, however, a sensible man and in the acquaintance of men of worthy consequences, I am glad that your committee decreed him the genteel reward you mention. I trust that your next will be in the return of the post with good news from abroad as well as from home. May God preserve your health and every domestic comfort in the long course of it.

 1. The son Charles's father-in-law.
 2. Matthew Duane (1707–1785), coin collector, antiquarian, and conveyancer. *Concise DNB*, 1 : 366.
 3. Probably Dr. Duigenan.
 4. On 17 September Curry had written to O'Conor that he had paid Counselor McNamara for legal services and had retained him for further work for the Catholic Committee. Stowe MS. B12, RIA.

182. To Dr. John Curry, Cow Lane, Dublin

OCD, 8.3 HS 026

27 September 1768

Curry and O'Conor console each other about their children. Curry worries about whether or not the money he sent to the boys in Germany arrived. O'Conor bewails the debts that his son Charles is amassing:

> The account of my unfortunate son gave me the most anxious night ever had, and what you advance, that philosophy is nonsense on receiving such shocks, I can but too truly verify from my own experience. He went into acquaintances for £572, enough to ruin his credit; but I have satisfaction to inform you that I got £250 of that sum already and have hopes that the other £262 will not remain long uncharged. He has an annuity of £200 a year from this county, and I am

in possession of £200 more. Should I live, I trust I shall be able to reestablish him; and I thank you most heartily, my dearest friend, for advising me to write him an exhilarating letter, what I take the liberty of doing under your cover. His mind, no doubt, preys upon itself; and should by remedy overtake him, I trust it will have a good effect.

183. To Archbishop John Carpenter,[1] Liffey Street, Dublin

OCD, 8.3 HS 026

From the Hermitage, 25 October 1768

O'Conor speaks in general terms about the plight of the Irish Catholic. He thanks Carpenter for "the lock and other ornaments you bought for me to finish one of my bookcases." He asks Carpenter for more information about Duggan's historical collection.[2]

    1. Before Carpenter's elevation to the bishopric, O'Conor seldom put an address on the letter. This letter is interesting for its address: The Right Reverend Mr. John Carpenter, Liffey Street, Dublin.
    2. Carpenter had written O'Conor on 8 October that Duggan's bequest of his books to Mr. Lodge and Mr. Beresford was a mere courteous gesture and that since Duggan had tried to change his will before he died, the widow was contesting it. Sheehan, p. 402.

184. To Archbishop John Carpenter

OCD, 8.3 HS 026

From the Hermitage, 14 November 1768

. . . I thank you most heartily for the fine trimmings you sent me for a chest of drawers and bookcase. You may consider what a pleasure it gives me that so much a man as you should lay out his own money for a friend who is known to live on the Conaght side of the chasm. . . . I wrote this day to our friend the doctor. He will inform you of a strange commission I had the other day from a great man in England, indeed no less a man than Lord Lyttleton, to furnish him with some light relative to the Conquest of Ireland by Henry II. I will do what I can, though little to my own satisfaction, at this distance from the documents now in the Library of Trinity College.

What is to be done with Dugan's collections? He was possessed of some good documents relating to the period Lord Lyttleton is so curious about. Let me hear immediately from you. . . .

185. To Dr. John Curry

OCD, 8.3 HS 026

From the Hermitage, 15 November 1768

Curry's sons are the first topic of this letter. Frank, who is in military service in Austria, has been promoted; but Thady, also in military service, has been in jail. Martin is in medical school in Paris. O'Conor tells Curry to stop "murmuring" about his children and to thank God for his family. O'Conor then describes the correspondence and instructions for historical research that he is receiving from Mr. Vesey of Lucan[1] for Lord Lyttleton's history of Henry II.[2] O'Conor is trying to get a preferment for Mr. Carpenter.

    1. Agmondesham Vesey died 1785. He was Accountant General of Ireland. Boswell wrote of him, "When Mr. Vesey was proposed as a member of the Literary Club, Mr. Burke began by saying that he was a man of gentle manners. 'Sir,' (said Johnson) 'you need say no more. When you have said a man of gentle manners, you have said enough.'" Constantia Maxwell, *Dublin under the Georges* (London: George Harrap, 1936; rpt. London: Faber and Faber, 1956), p. 69n.; James Boswell, *Life of Johnson* (London: Oxford University Press, 1966, Oxford Standard Authors Edition), p. 1085.
    2. George, first baron Lyttleton, (1709–1773) was a patron to poets, privy councilor, and politician, serving as a lord of the Treasury and Chancellor of the Exchequer. *Concise DNB*, 1:805.

186. George, Lord Lyttleton

RIA, Stowe MS. Bi2

14 December 1768

I cannot at present give your Lordship a better proof of my gratitude for the honor of your letter of the 10th instant than by answering as precisely as I can your queries to me.[1] The short extracts conveyed to your Lordship through the hands of Mr. Vesey I took chiefly from the Four Masters. Those compilers were set to work by one Father Ward of Louvain in 1630. He dying, their undertaking was patronized by Mr. O'Gara of Coolavin, one of the representatives in Parliament for the County of Sligo in 1634. That gentleman laid a scheme for transcribing into several volumes all that escaped the gradual destruction of our archives in the Danish wars of the ninth and tenth centuries. To this end, those four compilers sat down in the convent house of Donegal and proceeded from time to time in their transcripts, as materials could be collected, till the fatal Rebellion of 1641 obliged them to desist and leave unfilled those many blanks we find in the work as it came out of their own hands. In their preface they make mention of the originals they made use of: Tigernach, who died in 1088, and his continuators in the same monastery of Clonmacnose; the Ulster Annals praised by Archbishop Ulster and whose author, the Dean of Clogher, died in 1498, etc. . . .

1. Lyttleton had written to O'Conor on 10 December and thanked O'Conor for the "extracts from Irish History," which O'Conor had sent him through Vesey. Lyttleton then asked O'Conor for further help. He wanted to know "whether the Extracts you have favour'd me with are from the Annals of the Four Masters, or from a Continuation of those Annals by a contemporary Writer; and whether you cannot add from that to some other Irish Chronicle of that age, which you believe to be authentick, the remaining transactions from the year 1173 . . . to the year 1189 . . . , whether the Counties of Tirone, Donegal, and Derry, which your Extracts call the North Hy-nial, with the independent Counties of Monaghan, Fermanagh, Ardmagh, Antrim, and Downe, were in the times of which I write a part of Meath or (as Camden has placed them) of Ulster." Lyttleton confused "Murchad O'Malachlin" with "Murtach O'Lochlyn." RIA, Stowe MS. B12.

187. To Dr. John Curry, Cow Lane, Dublin

OCD, 8.3 HS 026

10 January 1769

. . . You will be vexed when I tell you that I have to negotiate with our prelates here for our friend Mr. C[arpente]r (who deserved from them and all our people a good testimony *de vita et moribus*[1]) and that my negotiations ended in the strongest proof that I have neither influence nor interest with these gentlemen; they seek their own ease, they intrigue for it, they find it through the medium of intrigue, and they enjoy it! The unfortunate laity alone are persecuted; and if in the state of corrupt and fatigued nature, they combine what they *feel* with what they *see*, it is not to be admired if we should hear of many defections and apostasies. The fervor of zeal and simplicity of the gospel seem wanting to retain men in their duty; men become bound by servitude on the one hand and allured by rewards on the other. It is now that our spiritual guides should exert the spirit and exhibit the example of the apostolic times, and without both we are likely enough to be undone more from the danger arising from our own superiors than from all the dangers arising from our incapacitating laws. What a chain of grievous reflections in a country where the majority stood out all the strokes of power for two hundred years past and remained hitherto singular amidst all the northern nations of Europe! . . .

1. Concerning the life and character.

188. To Dr. Thomas Leland

RIA, Stowe MS. Bi2

[14 January 1769][1]

... From the accounts given by the enemies of the Irish during this period, one would conclude that their history might well be dispatched in two or three lines: "That they were a nation of cowardly brutes, indifferent to events and contingencies and to the last degree ignorant of the first principles of religion and civil government." In the highest form of barbarism this is a character ill suited to any of the northern nations, who at worst were animated with the spirit of liberty, even to a great and fatal degree of licentiousness. It was a spirit derived from causes (moral and physical) invincible to nothing but political slavery, a state confessedly unknown among them in those ages, and yet an historian, who must be guided by facts not by negative arguments, will (no doubt) take up with the accounts he meets with from the contemporary writers before him, unconfronted by any others of the same times. This, I am afraid, will be Lord Lyttleton's case, unless he is supplied with those Irish accounts which you saved from destruction. His Lordship, you see, has taken more than common pains to be well informed; and without pains on our side to inform him as far as our documents can enable us, he certainly must draw his picture on the outlines I have mentioned above, enlarged by his art as a writer and heightened by his coloring as a painter. No revolution of so great importance was ever less accurately described than that of Ireland in Henry II's time, and I trust that some good documents relatively to it may be found in Mr. Harris's collections and particularly in those of Mr. Lodge,[2] who is a very diligent, as well as able, antiquarian. . . .

---

1. Leland wrote to O'Conor on 5 January and expressed his appreciation for the extracts of the Annals which O'Conor had sent to Lord Lyttleton. Leland then asked for further help on Lyttleton's history:

> What am I to think of the rapid progress of the English adventurers of the victories they gained against Numbers so vastly superior? The Irish were disunited possibly, but were they cowards or ignorant savages? or are these accounts magnified or falsified? When Dermod was banished it seems there was another King, Chief, or Tanist or whatever you called it chosen in his stead. Who was he? . . . You give the most amiable character to your ancestor Roderic O'Conor. . . . How then came it to pass that when the Tyrant of Leinster with his handful of English had entrenched himself at Ferns and the whole confederate army of Ireland stood ready to attack them, that he chose to retreat? To attempt to Bribe an Invader was a manifest acknowledgement of fear and weakness. And to open a treaty with such a wretch as Dermot,

who he knew could be bound by no ties, was a conduct I cannot account for with honor to Roderic.

Leland asked further why Roderic did not stand and fight against Strongbow; and whether or not Roderic put his hostage, Dermot's son, to death; and why O'Conor's forces remained outside Dublin for two months without attacking and when attacked why they retreated. Leland continued, "These points you will be prepared to clear up for me without an impeachment of the valour of our Countrymen. At present I can discover but one man of Spirit among them. You call him Saint Laurence Toole." RIA, Stowe MS. B12.

2. Mr. John Lodge (d. 1774) archivist, compiled *The Peerage of Ireland*, 1754, and *Desiderata curiosa Hibernia*, 1772. This is the Mr. Lodge who O'Conor believed had inherited Duggan's books and manuscripts. *Concise DNB*, 1:789.

189. To Dr. Sylvester O'Halloran,[1] Limerick

RIA, Stowe MS. B11a

Cow Lane, Anderson's Court
25 January 1769

I came to this place last Saturday much harassed and sickened by the severity of the weather. I received your kind favor three days since and being now able to write, I sit down to return you my thanks and made the best reply I can to your queries relating to the Druid-worship of the ancient Irish. It will now be in vain to inquire after the particular of local rites of the first British Colonies (*Fir Bolg* and *Tuatha Dé Danann*) who planted Ireland; the Spanish colony who overpowered and succeeded them brought hither their own religious rites, little different possibly from those of their predecessors. Be that as it may, we are assured and all our traditions are concurrent that the Druids of the latter colony (*Cinedh Scuit* or *Clanna Miledh*) began very early to corrupt the original Celtic worship and that under the reign of *Tigernmas* the nation was punished by vengeance from heaven in the great annual festival at *Magh Sléacht* in *Breffny*. . . .

I have seen MacPherson's *Caledonian Dissertations*.[2] He resents greatly the treatment the Irish Dissertator gave to his friend James MacPherson, the translator of *Fingal* and *Temora*. However, as the former gentleman has not attempted to refute one single fact produced against the hypothetic reverie and palpable forgeries of the translator, the Irish Dissertator saved himself the trouble of making any reply. . . .

1. Sylvester O'Halloran (1728–1807) was a surgeon trained in Paris and Leyden. His *History of Ireland to the Close of the Twelfth Century* was published in 1774; Hyde, p. 364, gives the publication date as 1778.

2. Dr. John Macpherson (1710–1765) was a Scottish Presbyterian minister. His book, *Critical Dissertations on the Antient Caledonians*, was published posthumously by his son, also John Macpherson (c. 1745–1821).

190. To Dr. Sylvester O'Halloran, Limerick

RIA, Stowe MS. Bi2

[January 1769][1]

I entirely approve of the plan of study you have chalked out for yourself in your vacant hours. A knowledge of the principal religious doctrines of our Celtic ancestors would be the best clue to a knowledge of their politics and manners. The revolutions in the moral and civil system are influenced and governed by the revolutions in the religious system; and that scheme of heathen doctrines which came nearest the religion of nature gives us at once *the best* moral particles, as the reverse gives us the *worst* among nations as well as individuals. Corruptions indeed have entered into the best systems of natural religion....

1. This letter is undated. The editors assume a date from internal evidence.

191. To Lord Lyttleton

RIA, Stowe MS. Bi2

Dublin, 1 February 1769

... Your Lordship asks: "Whether after the expulsion of Donall O'Malachlin, Tirnan O'Ruark ws not king of that province in right of his marriage with Murchad O'Malachlin's daughter?"[1] He was not, nor was any such right claimed. It was an inviolable law among the old Irish that no prince of any one province should govern in the province of another, save only temporarily and in some extraordinary case as in this before us. ... The English historians of that age style O'Ruark King of Meath, though he was only an occasional administrator. Their mistake is excusable, but your Lordship will be convinced from this instance alone of the expediency of confronting the contemporary witnesses of one party with the witnesses on the other side who wrote in the same age.

Your Lordship doubts the credit of the Four Masters in their account of a convention between Roderic and Dermod in 1168. But perhaps the Annalist from whom they have transcribed may be reconciled with Cambrensis. "Dermod," says the latter, "lay concealed for some time in Ferns." This I believe to be the case. In that retreat he might negotiate secretly with his friends (for the most abandoned princes have friends) and dispose them to act offensively for him on the assurance of a support from a neighboring and powerful nation. On the landing of some auxiliaries from Wales, Dermod might venture to appear in public and put himself at the head of his domestic partisans. The Irish Annalist, a stranger to Dermod's lying concealed, might confound the time of that appearance with the landing of a few of his auxiliaries and mistake two events for one. Were *that* the case, the account of Cambrensis may be well reconciled with the report of the Irish Annalists, whose words literally translated run thus: "Meantime (after the states of the kingdom broke up and retired to their several countries) Dermod MacMurchad retired from Saxony (England) with foreign auxiliaries to establish himself in Hy-Kinsellagh. Roderic and Tiarnan O'Ruark marched against him as far as Killosna.[2] . . .

Your Lordship asks: "Was the stronghold in Waterford the same with Reginald's tower,[3] wherein Reginald himself and Malachlyn O'Faolan, Lord of the Decies, were taken?" It certainly was. This Ragnal, or Reginald, the Norman commandant, had the Irish surname of MacGillamurry. I need not inform your Lordship that the country of the Decies was a very considerable district of Munster, of which the O'Faolans were lords, subject to the King of South Munster. . . .

Your Lordship inquires: "Where was Ternan O'Ruark when Dermod carried off his wife?" He was in a sort of exile in the remotest part of his principality of Breffny, being stripped of the parts which lay bordering upon Meath. He was a very powerful and very factious man. In 1152 he had united against him Torlogh O'Conor, who bore the title of King of Ireland; O'Lachlyn, King of the North Hy-Niall; and Dermod MacMurchad, King of Leinster. In so unequal a contest Ternan fled into the fastness of Breffny. Dermod improved this opportunity to carry off his wife into Hy-Kinsellagh, being assisted in the base conspiracy by that princess's brother, Malachlyn O'Malachlyn. On that event Ternan negotiated himself into favor with Turlogh O'Conor, who in the year following made war on Dermod and after humbling that prince brought back Dervorgalla with all her effects and restored her to her friends in Meath.[4] . . .

Your Lordship inquires: "How came O'Ruark's father-in-law to join Turlogh O'Conor in stripping him of the district of Convacny?" This junction was in resentment of O'Ruark's conduct to that father-in-law in 1150. In that year Murchad O'Malachlyn, under a sentence of excommunication, was expelled from his provincial government. Ternan was so base as to become one of the triumvirs who administered in that province instead of assisting to mediate for his father-in-law. Murchad was restroed in 1152 and took his revenge of Ternan. . . .

1. Dervorgilla.
2. Now Kellistown, County Carlow. Roche, p. 54.
3. According to Roche, "The towers on the walls were the last posts to fall," p. 87.
4. After her return to Tiernan, Dervorgilla became a noted benefactress of the Church, in 1157 endowing the Cistercian Abbey at Mellifont, near Drogheda. Roche, pp. 33–34.

192. To Lord Lyttleton

RIA, Stowe MS. Bi2

7 February 1769

Oidhche Inide a nDuibhlinn[1]

We have seen (my Lord) how Roderic and the Irish chieftains thought but little of the petty war carried on by the English and Hy-Kinsellagh men in Ossory. As those adventurers had but a general license from Henry II to revenge the cause of Murogh,[2] they were considered as mere Free Booters, who like their Norman or Ostman predecessors pillaged particular districts and in reward of their services got establishments in Dublin, Waterford, Cork, and Limeric. In the year 1168 Roderic divided the provincial government of [Munster] between MacCarthy and O'Brian.[3] The latter complained of the partition as injurious to him who thought himself entitled to the government of the whole province in the manner it was enjoyed by Murkertach O'Brian, his deceased brother. — Though he was Roderic's maternal brother, yet he was the son-in-law of Dermod MacMurchad, and Roderic very justly dreaded their conjunction. He was taking measures to prevent the evil when intelligence arrived that Earl Richard[4] landed in Munster with a considerable army and took Waterford by assault. The English invasion became now (not before) a serious affair. . . .

1. Shrove Tuesday Evening in Dublin.
2. Ossory had been part of Dermot MacMurrough's territory in Leinster. When Dermot left Ferns after the winter of 1168, he and his Norman allies successfully waged war at Ossory.
3. Donal O'Brien, Dermot's son-in-law.
4. Strongbow landed at Passage on 23 August 1170.

193. To Dr. Sylvester O'Halloran, Limerick

RIA, Stowe MS. Bi2

Cow Lane, 10 February 1769

... The ancient Irish were the only exception to the general neglect of recording the actions of men among those Celtic nations, and you know that what we have left is come down in broken fragments of a great value at this distance of time. When I said that the old Celts did not leave even inscriptions on stones, metals, etc., I meant that assertion only of the times antecedent to Christianity. The discovery of Greek and Hebrew inscriptions at Clonmacnose proves only that those inscriptions have not an earlier date than our knowledge of the Greek, Hebrew, and Roman languages. The oldest of them could not possibly be more ancient than the fourth century. The Irish remained here in this western island, undisturbed by any foreign nation till the ninth century, and how through a series of many ages a lettered nation should leave no inscriptions in letters on stones or metals is amazing! Your investigation from the meanings of Celtic terms is useful as it is ingenious. But great caution is necessary lest one should be led astray, like [Grotius?], Becanus, Pezron, and Rowlands, who in such disquisitions lost themselves in the wilds of etymology and lessened the value of the *useful* by mixing it with too much of the *extravagant*.[1] It is a most reasonable hypothesis that Ireland was the metropolitical seat of Druidism, and I doubt not but that this hypothesis will come out a fact from your hands. I said something (not enough) on the subject in the *Dissertations;* and as you are employed about it, I need not recommend to your perusal Mr. Toland's *History of the Druids.*[2] ...

1. Martinus Becanus wrote in Latin an *Analogy between the Old and New Testaments;* Paul Yves Pezron in *Antiquité de la Nation et de la Langue de Celtes autrement Appelez Gualois* wrote on the Gaelic language; Henry Rowlands in 1703 (with a Dublin edition published in 1723) wrote a book on archeology, *Mons Antiqua Restaurata*, and put an appendix list of "primitive words and the derivatives of them in several of the tongues of Europe...." O'Conor's readings in language research appeared wide in scope. Apparently O'Conor wanted to impress Dr. O'Halloran. *BMCPBCE*, 2:697; 20:135; 22:59.

2. John Toland's *History of the Druids* (London, 1740?) was properly titled *A Critical History of the Celtic Religion and Learning Containing an Account of the Druids*. With the History of Abaris, the Hyperborean Priest of the Sun. *BMCPBCE*, 25:238.

194. To Dr. Sylvester O'Halloran, Limerick

RIA, Stowe MS. Bi2

Dublin, 28 March 1769

... I can not avoid thinking that the account given by our old annalists of the destruction of our Druidic writings by the missionaries of the fourth and fifth centuries is a real fact; and if so, the door of much useful information must be shut in our face forever. We must supply our wants, as well as we can, from the broken fragments of foreign writers and from those monuments over (and perhaps under) ground which still remain in every district of the kingdom as so many *Druidic* inscriptions (we may say) which are still legible to the critical eye. In your hands, such an inquiry will be rendered useful; for, I am confident, you will establish your reflections on facts and allow as little as possible to hypothesis or conjecture. It is many years since I perused Mr. Toland's *History of the Druids*. At that time I thought he wrote ingeniously on the subject. I think you would do well to give that work a diligent and critical examination ... I have now in my collection a poem of O'Malconary, senachy of Conaght in the fourteenth century, and recited before Felim O'Conor, elected king of the Irish Conaght in 1310.[1] Therein an account of his ancestors is given; and at the coronation of Alexander, the third king of Scots, you will find the highland senachy giving that prince's genealogy beginning with the words: "Failte dhuit, a Righ Alban,"[2] etc. I have not the book now before me, but you will find an account of the custom and the genealogy at full length in *Dissertatio Historica de patria et vita S. Ronald*. Lovain, Imp. A.D. 1662....

1. O'Reilly, p. xciv, stated that Torna O'Maolconaire recited this poem for Felim O'Conor on the Hill of Carn Fraoich, *c.* 1310.
2. "Welcome to you, o king of the Scots."

195. To Dr. John Curry, Cow Lane, Dublin

OCD, 8.3 HS 026

From the Hermitage, 21 June 1769

You have in great forwardness a work which the public wants and to which, therefore, the public has a right. Its appearance will make converts to truth greatly wanted because the ignorance of those truths fosters prejudices ruinous to our masters as well as to millions who are the immediate sufferers. As this will be a work of labor, London is the place where its impression must be negotiated, for in London alone will the author's pains be rewarded by a sale of the copy, and it should come out in a handsome quarto volume at a guinea price.[1]

1. Curry's *An Historical and Critical Review* . . . came out in London (n.p.) in 1774 and in Dublin (n.p.) in 1775. *BMCPBCE*, 13:24 and 6:745.

196. To Dr. John Curry, Dublin

OCD, 8.3 HS 026

From the Hermitage, 16 July 1769

. . . I yesterday sent you three volumes in folio, which may be of some use to your design, namely Morrison's *History of the Tyrone War*, the *Pacata Hibernia* by the Earl of Totness, and Walsh's *Irish Remonstrance*.[1] You will have those books before you have this letter in your possession. . . .

1. George Carew, Baron Carew, earl of Totness (1555–1629); lord justice of Ireland (1600–1603), wrote *Pacata Hibernia*. *BMCPBCE*, 4:1229. Peter Walsh's *Remonstrance*. Fynes Moryson (1566–1630), chief secretary to the lord lieutenant (1600), wrote a book of travel through Ireland, Scotland, England, and Europe and a history of Tyrone's rebellion. *Concise DNB*, 1:911.

197. To Dr. John Curry, Cow Lane, Dublin

OCD, 8.3 HS 026

[From the Hermitage, 15 August 1769]

. . . I should be sorry that Dr. B[re]tt[1] had not every material for his pamphlet that you and I could supply him with. I say you and I, for we are the only persons of our party who, in the course of seventy years, dared to break silence, and yet you cannot easily forget the reward we had from friends and enemies. By giving the question we have started every face and turn it can bear from Brooke, Brett, Howard, etc., etc.; the leaden hatchets of the Presbyterians may be blunted. It is gaining something. . . .

. . . You recommend Irish history from Henry II's time to me. I have done nothing yet in that matter though I have it in view. It will, I think, be of use to see what Lord Lyttleton and Leland will say on the subject. If God grants me health and life, I purpose to be one of their humble followers.

1. Dr. John Brett, an Anglican.

198. To Dr. John Curry, Cow Lane, Dublin

OCD 8.3 HS 026

From the Hermitage, 8 September 1769

Dear Sir,

In the course of the last month I wrote to you two letters by the post, one a long one on the business of *opus magnum,* the *Memoirs* and the correspondence with Mr. O'More of Ballina; I trust that all these things are now in the proper train and that the *Memoirs* are out of the printer's loom.[1] The circumstances of the present times and the unmerited popularity of a certain faction render the publication of such works necessary. The publication will be useful and consequently acceptable to a government attacked with fury and treated with equal indignity. It cannot but be acceptable that the Roman Catholics (ground as they are under penal laws) should appear now and do justice to the equity and lenity of his Majesty's administration. On this principle I think it would be proper to usher in the *Memoirs* with a short preface setting forth (by way of contrast) the equity of the present government compared with the arbitrary proceedings of the administration in the times described by the author of the *Memoirs,* and that the present publication is not only a tribute of gratitude on the part of the Papists but a fair admonition to subjects who enjoy all the advantages of our civil Constitution to put a proper estimate on their present happiness.

I had not a line from you for near two months past, and I am in pain for your health as I am sensible I should have a line from you on the subject of my two last letters if want of health or (what I hope) more pressing business had not made you postpone writing. In this obscurity a day of news does not enter except it be that of a fair day, which is news indeed to us in this province. How are your ladies? Are they come home from Winter Hill, (for so I have a right to call it if you have not fairer weather than we have)? How are the young gentlemen abroad? When is Lord T[aaffe] to arrive? The resolution of these queries is important to me, and indeed I long for a good account.

I have sent you the Earl of Totness's account of the Kinsale War,

Morrison's *History*, and Walsh's *Irish Remonstrance*. Have you received them or have you found them of any considerable use? The account of those times by the Four Masters would be useful, and I trust I will be able to furnish you with some anecdotes from those compilers. I long expected my dear friend Mr. Carpenter. I had not a line from him to account for his not making a voyage of health this season into the West. If he is well, it will make me the best amends for his absence from me, for his laziness in the vehicle of epistolary correspondence. In my last I bespoke your vote and interest in the choice of a clerk for the infirmary for Mr. Nicholas Dowdall, book-keeper to Mr. Anthony Dermot. You know him to be a deserving man, and I trust my recommendation of him was unnecessary. In this place I am in I read a good deal but write little, and yet I now and then commonplace some things; and if God grants me life, I propose to digest them for use hereafter. Write to your salutory friend soon as you can.

1. Curry's *Historical Memoirs of the Irish Rebellion* . . . appeared in an Irish edition in 1770 printed by the Catholic printer, James Hoey. Three previous editions appeared in London in 1758, 1765, 1767. BMCPBCE, 13:24.

199. To Dr. John Curry

OCD, 8.3 HS 026

29 September 1769

My Dear Friend,

Our by-post boy, or perhaps his principal in Roscommon, has thrown several of my letters aside. They could not otherwise miscarry. But as you are certainly no loser by the miscarriage, you are a gainer for you saved two groats. It is no great matter. I am indeed chiefly sorry for the miscarriage of a letter to Mr. Wagstaffe because it cost me some time and because (such is my malice) it was to make an adversary sore. Lord Taaffe's displeasure proceeds from the slight he thinks Martin put on his negotiation for him relatively to the Austrian Academy. His delicacy was wounded in such a procedure. But assuredly nothing is to be feared from the resentment of a good man, and no provocation, well or ill-founded, can ever preponderate the affection he bears you or the officiousness with which he would give proofs of that affection. Your son's miscarriage, and only miscraige in the Palatine service,[1] has been exaggerated to him; and it gives me great pleasure that the worst is over with Thady and that fair weather is finally made for him. As to Frank I am, I can assure you, in no dread about him. The rock on which his brother struck is full in his view; and though it should not, his own good sense must improve the instrument he has received and be in the place of the experience, which is the monitor, and too often the useless monitor, of others because generally its instructors come too late. You have given your family from the earliest time the principles of religion and virtue. Such seeds cannot but bear good fruit, and I congratulate you on the proofs you have that through a series of several years you have only one false step (and that produced by surprise) to complain of in your three sons. Instead, therefore, of being grieved, you have a real reason to be thankful. I now change to other matters; after my despair of Mr. Carpenter, he luckily (for unexpected pleasure is to me then most lucky) entered this house on Wednesday last and in good health after swimming rather than riding through our climate for two months past. I trust that better weather will bring him back to the capital and the stock of health he is laying up will more than counter-balance any better interest he might derive from the neglect of it. In truth, attention to his health is part of the duty he owes the public, as well as to himself; and should censure be busy about him on such an occupation, it would be busy in vain, and in its captious temper it would be busy relatively to any step he would take. I could wish warmly that you renewed your correspondence with Mr. O'More of Ballina, as you might know the utmost of Dr. Brett's frankness relatively to the subject on which he was so intent in May last.

Prejudice, as I observed formerly to you, may be compared to the elm tree; it is best cleft asunder by a wedge from its own side; and certainly if any good be intended our people, it must be produced more by the feelings of our adversaries than by our own best reasonings. I request you will not omit writing to Mr. O'More. I had (the other day) a letter from him on another less important subject than this before me, and he forgot mentioning a word about Brett's undertaking. Write to me when you have leisure, for you see by this letter that I want much useful information of which you must, by this time, be in possession. Give my affections to your ladies, who by this time are, I believe, come back to town.

1. Thad Curry, who was in the military service in Austria, had been imprisoned. Sheehan, p. 404.

200. To Dr. John Curry

OCD, 8.3 HS 026

27 October 1769

My Dear Sir,

I should long since have written to you but that I had nothing to write worthy of your attention, and I write now only to account for my silence and to assure you that I would omit no opportunity of breaking it could I do so with the smallest satisfaction to you. By satisfaction I mean furnishing you with any information useful to our common cause. God has blessed you with talents, knowledge, and zeal to serve your country. You have rendered it important services already: and if nature continues the health which seconded your zeal, you will still render it more important services. I am pleased much to hear that you picked some flowers out of the vast collection of thistles which I sent you. You are greatly a more patient reader of such collections than I am, and it is happy for the public that you are so. I am laying, not executing, schemes and drawing upon time which probably will not accept the draft. Mr. Carpenter has scolded me for my small advances; and however just his reproof might be, he does not well consider how many of the materials for such a fabric as he and you would expect lie absolutely out of my power in this desert from which I am writing. I find the decline of life for some time past coming on very sensibly. The gout has this last week seized upon my left hip and my feet begin to have gouty sensations, yet I live temperately and breathe good air. If I can shake off the upper pains and lower feelings, I purpose to be with you about the middle of next month. My little harvest is well made up; and by some improvements which I made lately in the agriculture, I am forty shillings a year richer than when I left you last summer. In another year I shall advance ten pounds more a year, and I mention all this to you because you will be pleased to hear that I am spreading the base of my independence and drawing from honest industry those advantages which the laws of my country have denied, or rather absolutely have forbidden me. This acquisition which I make from year to year gives me infinitely more pleasure than a pension from the government, and I am at my ease, and free too, in spite of the laws.

I have read the L[ord] L[ieutenant's] speech. It is in the usual commonplace ministerial style. His E[xcellenc]y observes, very justly, *"that the strength and riches of a country are in proportion to the number of its industrious inhabitants,"* and I would add (though not ministerially), *"that the depopulation and miseries of a country are in proportion to the numbers virtually forbid by law to be industrious.*"[1] The last proposition is equally just with the first, and both spring from the same principle. The force of the principle is felt and recognized by all men, and it will be improved in this island so far as party prejudice will permit and no further. But party is that monster which, as I have read in Irish fable, feeds upon its children without fattening them for the food: and, therefore, party can never make a good meal.

You have seen Mr. Carpenter. I long to hear from him and of him. I gave him the trouble of inquiry about my unfortunate men. Give him my service and remind him of my wish to hear from him as soon as possible. How is Dr. Fitzsimons? I wish him well, though by some fatality I have not for some time been in his good graces.[2] While we live we might take our lot with friends and foes, but we must for our own happiness carry about us the consciousness of giving no just cause of offense to either. Did you hear lately from your family in Germany? Is Martin in Paris? Frank will do well and be a credit to you. His elder brother will soon, I hope, re-establish, for he has not forfeited his right to the same character.

What do you hear from Lord Taaffe? His delicacy was wounded by the seeming slight put upon his officiousness to serve you, but he is an honest man, and his resentment can never be turned to the detriment of any deriving from you. Of this I believe you are well satisfied. I am glad to find that the *Memoirs* are almost ready for publication. I am really sorry for the late misfortunes of the first publisher. When have you corresponded last with Mr. O'More of Ballina? What is Dr. Brett doing? I would be glad to see his book published, whatever it be. Truth will come out best from those who are reluctantly struck with the force of it. The value of a victory is enhanced by the obstacles thrown in its way, and this is true of the victories we gain over ourselves in many instances.

After perusing what I wrote above, I am surprised how I found matter for so much of a quarto leaf; when I come back from potato diggers, I may find more words for the remaining blank. —I am now returned. What news from England? The next campaign at Westminster will be the warmest that was fought since the Revolution in '88. The contest will be between the representatives and their constituents; and in this, as in most cases, the artificial will get the better of the real power of the public. But what are state storms to us that have no goods on board? Be the event what it will, we on shore are to put to sea in fair weather or remain where we are while we are permitted. I just perused Hoey's[3] paper, and it informs me of another anniversary sermon by the Bishop of Down and Connor[4] on the Insurrection of October 23, 1641. I long to see that performance, and I long as much for your thoughts on it. I request you will write soon to me. You are on the stage of information—I, in an obscure corner where I am (foolishly) tired with quiet and its whole train of peaceful concomitants.

Give your worthy ladies my affection, and my good will to poor Watt. Take care of your health for their sakes, for your own sake, and for the sake of the public. It is good for you that the blank is all filled.

1. O'Conor changes Lord Townshend's meaning by changing the second clause. Lord Townshend had said "that the strength and riches of a country are in proportion to the number of its industrious inhabitants, and as a religious and virtuous education is the surest guide to industry and good morals, you will not be unmindful of that useful and charitable institution, the Protestant Charter Schools. . . ." *DJ*, 19–21, 1769.

2. O'Conor had once been close to Dr. Fitzsimons and had worked to have him named Archbishop of Dublin. Now as archbishop, Fitzsimons has ignored O'Conor's attempts to get his friend Carpenter promoted.

3. James Hoey, Faulkner's ex-partner at the *Dublin Journal*, became publisher of the Dublin *Mercury*, which was an organ of the Irish government of Townshend from 1766–1772. Gilbert, "The Streets of Dublin," 539.

4. Dr. Traill.

201. To Dr. John Curry, Cow Lane, Dublin

OCD, 8.3 HS 026

6 or 7 November 1769

My Dear Friend,

This last week you had a long, tiresome letter from me, and I will not repeat the subject I gave you in this. As I have no frank for my son Charles, I make bold to make use of your free wrapper to send him the enclosed by Watt that he may, after the perusal, transmit it to my brother[1] who at last opened a correspondence with me in favor of one Abbé Kelly of Mons,[2] who I find is writing the history of Ireland after Warner and Geoghegan. He gives him to me for a man of abilities and, if so, he shall want no assistance that he can reasonably expect from me. You see how things come about. You and I gave edge to his curosity relatively to Ireland so little known in modern history. Some good will come out sooner or later; and should God grant you and me some more years, we may show more light on the subject we first started. I find by an advertisement in the *Journal* that Dugan's auction is to come on the 22nd this instant. I will be up by that time if I can. If I cannot, I request you will supply Mr. Carpenter with money and request of him to take up for me such tracts as he knows are to my taste.

I shall punctually exchange my debt to you as soon as I stand under your roof which will be (God willing) before the end of the month. In the meantime you will give my affections to your whole family.

1. Daniel O'Conor.   2. Unidentified.

202. To [Brigadier Thomas O'Conor]¹

RIA, Stowe, MS. Bi1

[*c.* 1769]²

Sir,

After my return from Dublin six weeks ago, I thought I would have no delay in answering your kind letter in a manner satisfactory to you and pleasing to myself, but I have been disappointed, and when I last was sitting down to mix my complaint with my apology, Mr. Dowell at last came to my house and brought me some materials. I delayed not a moment but drew up your genealogy from the best lights, ancient and modern, that I could obtain. It is now in Mr. Dowell's hands; and when properly engraved and attested, he will no doubt remit it to you. Foreigners who prize these things now as much as our ancestors did formerly are, I know, extremely [cropped] in their forms. [Six lines crossed out] but I hope that what I have given in a summary way down from your ancestor, *Aodh Balbh mac Inreachtaigh* (who died King of Conaght in the ninth century) will be sufficient. The change in our fortunes and manners occasions a thorough slight of those things *now* in Ireland, and to this you may well attribute the listlessness of your relations here who delayed supplying me with the little I wanted. We lost indeed the pride, but we lost also the virtues and principles of our ancestors; from you and a few like you we expect the revival of the latter, and your good sense will undoubtedly guard you against the former. The styles, sentiment, and precision of your letters I admire, and I rejoice in the honor I derive from my relation to your family. Your great grandmother, Dorothy O'Conor, my father's aunt, was born in the house where I am now writing, and her sister was the mother of the late Colonel Oliver O'Gara, who died in St. Germaine en Laye. I only mention this from an apprehension that probably you are a stranger to your relation to the present Colonel, who I hear is in a very (languishing) state of health. I request you will present my profoundest respects to the Duchess of Wharton³ and your Lady.

1. Identification of Brigadier Thomas O'Conor is made first from internal evidence. In the letter O'Conor mentions that the correspondent's great grandmother was

Dorothy O'Conor. According to the genealogy in Charles Owen O'Conor's *The O'Conors of Connaught*, Appendix, Tables 3 and 4, Dorothy O'Conor was married to her cousin Dermot O'Conor (d. 1585). Their son was Sir Hugh O'Conor (d. 1632). His son was Daniel, who begot Andrew, who begot Thomas and Daniel, O'Conor Don of Clonalis. Thomas, then, would be Dorothy's great-great-grandson. A further reason to believe that this letter is to Thomas is that it refers to a matter mentioned in a letter which Thomas wrote to Charles from Rouen, France, on 20 November 1768. In this letter Thomas asked Charles to prepare a genealogy for him so that Thomas could have a coat of arms made for his wife who wanted "to convince her relations [in France] that her husband equals them at least by birth." Dunleavy and Dunleavy, p. 28, OCD 8.3 SO 031.

   2. This letter is undated.

   3. The duchess of Wharton was Maria Theresa O'Neill, daughter of Colonel Henry O'Beirne, second wife of Philip, duke of Wharton (d. 1731). O'Conor mentions to Curry that the Duchess's father was "cousin-german to mine." George Edward Cokayne, *The Complete Peerage of England, Scotland, Great Britain, and the United Kingdom, Extinct and Dormant*, Rev. Vicary Gobbs *et al.* (London: G. Bell and Sons, 1887–1898; Exeter: G. Pollard, 1910–1959), 12:613. Charles O'Conor to Dr. John Curry, 23 October 1762, OCD 8.3 HS 023.

203. To Dr. John Curry, Cow Lane, Dublin

OCD, 8.3 HS 026

From the Hermitage, 19 July 1770

... I must apologize for the conduct of our dear ecclesiastical governor towards you.[1] You are sensible that he had measures to keep with malevolence and envy, sentinels ever on the watch to oppress the intentions of men, and never more vigilant to blast a public character than in the first steps of its administration. I really think him orthodox enough in his political faith because his spiritual duty calls upon him to be so and that he knows his duty. If he declined encouraging a public Declaration of this Civil Faith by means of an address in the present time, let us partly ascribe it to the principle I have mentioned as well as to the delicacy of his situation on his first onset in his official dignity. I wish heartily I may make you a comment to my opinion on the present occasion; and yet as it is no more than an opinion, I perhaps should recall the wish. Sure I am that I must think the less of it if you should still think the present to be a proper time for an addressing. I have not yet written to Dr. C[arpenter]. When I do, I shall not mention a word to him of what passed between you and me on this subject.

We have at present a famine in this western province, and the other provinces are in the same situation. Half the people are preying on the other, but without violence. The Penal Laws, which were intended to prevent the growth of Popery, take their effect now in the exclusion of the Papists themselves. "Penal Laws," says the Baron Montesquieu, "are ever calculated to destroy." Assuredly no country on earth after a repose of eighty years of profound peace was in a more disrupted state than ours at present, and yet a single act of legislation would remedy the evil. . . .

1. Carpenter became archbishop of Dublin 3 June 1770. He died 29 October 1786. *HBC*, p. 402. Curry had proposed sending an address of allegiance to Lord Townshend, but O'Conor and the newly appointed Carpenter opposed the idea.

204. To Archbishop John Carpenter, George's Hill, Dublin

OCD, 8.3 HS 026

From the Hermitage, 10 September 1770

Rt. Reverend Sir,[1]

If I have postponed paying this tribute of gratitude, it was partly through discretion in not intruding on you under the weight of so much business as must have, of late, employed your whole attention; and it was partly through the conviction I had that your Grace knew me too well to put any other interpretation on my silence but this that I have urged. You are now returned from your second visitation, and I have strong hopes that your stock of health is increased and your constitution improved. These are things I have greatly at heart, for they are of great importance to your friends and, what is of much greater consequence, they are of great importance to the public. Providence has placed your Grace in the first ecclesiastical station in this poor kingdom at a time when a governor equally able and zealous was never more wanted. Religious indifference and apostasy, its concomitant, are making large and hasty strides among us, and this last period of our trial appears strangely marked with some of those corruptions which in general are the effects of prosperity and power. It needs no great refinement to discover the causes. Those Penal Laws which forbid any durable property to Catholics produce an intermitting temptation to renounce Catholicity. The still more severe laws against our clergy have been relaxed, nay suspended in the execution. The laity alone are persecuted and they alone, who *appear* free, must follow the example of their persecuted predecessors (in Queen Anne's time) or *lose* the respect due to them. The loss of that respect will be utter loss of religion among us. There can be but little respect for pastors who sleep on their posts or betray them when awake. They will have less of it if they exact on the poor, for excesses of that nature will scandalize more than their other virtues will edify. I am no stranger to the complaints made in my own province; some are groundless, no doubt; but to prevent their spreading, a reform should be made and such constitutions published as would remove every pretext to future complaints. You have this reform at heart and gave (God be praised) the earliest proofs of it. May your brethren assist you with equal zeal to spread it through every quarter of the island and may you joyfully succeed in giving a greater weight to the penalties of religion than corrupt nature gives to the rewards of parliamentary laws! This *Hoc tibi soli.*[2]

I have great esteem for worthy Mr. O'Brien, and I request you will put him, Dr. Curry, the Dean, Mr. Sherlock, etc., in mind of my affection. You will not forego your protection to my worthy friend, Doran, and he will not forfeit any part of it.[3] Father Provincial Netterville and Mr. Conor of Bridge-street honored me with a visit in this retirement, and I am greatly obliged to them. Mr. Fitzgerald parted me two days ago; towards the end of this month or beginning of the next, he will wait of your G[race] with my affections jointly with his own. A country circumstanced like this I am in can afford little particular news. In general, it is absolutely ruined from causes which operate and must operate every day still more from circumstances which I need not explain. The other provinces are but in much the like situation, and bankruptcies in the country must be soon followed by bankruptcies in the city from the necessary connections between both. I preserve myself by a little chain of economy in which, however, I must be content to see several links broken. I am (in aid of other calls) making some improvements, expensive indeed, but useful. I have surrounded my kitchen garden with a seven-foot high stone wall, well coped, and dashed with well-tempered mortar. I am also building a good barn, the old lying almost decayed on an inconvenient spot, etc. At my time of life the retirement I am in and the free air I breathe agree less with my constitution. In the city one is no sooner in the street but he is mixed with a crowd, and as he walks along, he must submit to several inconveniences and perhaps be hurried into unforeseen, as well as disgusting, engagements. As my best friends, however, live in the city, they turn the balance often in favor, and I resolve (God willing) to spend the winter among them at those times when they are at leisure to receive me. I am tiring you with trifles for want of better matter. But I am sure of your indulgence.

    1. O'Connor is writing Archbishop Carpenter to congratulate him on being appointed Archbishop of Dublin. See O'Conor's previous letter to Curry.

2. This [is] for you alone.
3. Carpenter is staying with O'Brien, probably Comerford's partner. Both were members of the Catholic Committee. Sherlock is a Catholic priest and so is Doran. Sheehan, p. 431.

205. To Dr. John Curry, Cow Lane, Dublin

OCD, 8.3 HS 026

From the Hermitage, 26 September 1770

... My brother's letter[1] addressed to you relative to his private concerns would not be quite impertinent were there any foundation for the charges he made (for a charge it is by the strongest implications) that I have entered into a conspiracy with my son in Dublin to rob him of the little annuity he has out of this country. The truth is, the man anticipated his little fortune. By such conduct he reduced himself to real, and I believe, grievous distress, and because his tenant here does not anticipate rent as he himself does, his support of £60 a year, *hinc illae lachrimae, hinc quoque calumniarum congeries.*[2] ...

Is the *Supplement* completed?[3] Is the author in a good state of health? These are questions of importance to me and to the public. Our poor deceived public! Who of all nations of Europe pay dearest for their prejudices; through our bad season and the failure of the harvest in the last year and in this, the bulk of the people are absolutely undone. Such are the consequences of legal discouragements to agriculture and of forbidding any durable property in land to the two-thirds of the people who should, by the strongest sanctions, be made interested in the cultivation of it. It is an evil without a remedy, and philosophy must teach us to bear with it as we must bear with an earthquake or a pestilence. ...

1. Daniel O'Connor rented out his portion of the O'Connor estate of Charles's son Charles, who sublet it. Daniel frequently wanted the rent prepaid and Charles would advance the money to Daniel before he himself had been paid. Daniel had written to Curry accusing his brother and his nephew of trying to cheat him. Sheehan, p. 432.
2. Horace, *Epistle*, 1.19.41. Hence those tears, hence also a mass of malicious charges.
3. The "Supplement" appears to be the additional material that Curry was adding to his Dublin edition of the *Memoirs*.

206. To Archbishop John Carpenter

OCD, 8.3 HS 026

From the Hermitage, 30 October 1770

R[ight] R[everend] Sir,

Your letter to the 20th instant (now before me) gave me a return of those feelings which form the greatest satisfactions of my life. It is well for me that my gratitude is rooted in its proper soil as words cannot come up to it; and as I write to one who does not want them, you require that I should stick to my old familiar style. I will obey, though I should ill-deserve such an indulgence if permitted it in the least to abate of the respect I owe, and every man owes, to the person who sits in Laurence Toole's chair. That prelate, though not the first Metropolitan of Leinster, was yet the first Archbishop of Dublin, was persecuted by a great prince and died a martyr on an ecclesiastical as well as civil account. May God preserve you for the good of this Church surrounded with greater perils in your own time than it was in his, invaded by temporal penalties and still more endangered by temporal rewards. The latter in our corrupt state seduce too many from their duty, indeed, more than are frightened by the former, for penalties confirm the good and in a great degree reclaim the tepid. It puts one in the mind of the poor countryman in the fable who the more the storm laid claim to his cloak, the more he kept a fast hold of it. Party animosity has rekindled the spirit of persecution against our people in the neighboring isle and that under the sanction of laws which have slept for some time and which should not coexist a moment as, in the *first* place, they have no object whatever relatively to the civil state or civil security and as, in the *second,* they only administer fuel to those very animosities which hazard both. An instance of this spirit is very recent in the case of our countryman Father James Dillon. He has been imprisoned, prosecuted, tried and only acquitted through the want of some legal proofs. His afflictions did not end there. His zeal has exposed him to new trials, and he must now quit all his connections in England by a local sacrifice of that zeal on the principle of *flying to another city when persecuted in that of his residence.* He is advised to return to his native country, and his zeal as well as his trials give him a right to the best reception his country can afford. His family I have known, and they have lived very reputably for some ages in this province, though some reduced to the condition of the rest of our Catholic families. I would, therefore, with the greatest deference recommend him to your Grace's protection, and I do this rather to inform than to recommend as it would be but a waste of words and, indeed, an impertinent display of them to solicit your protection when you can grant it to such suffering merit as Father Dillon exhibits in this day of his distress. I trust that you have some place open for him such as may give him some repose in this last state of life to one who acted so good a part on the *first*. I take great, indeed sensible, satisfaction in the promotion of my friend Doran and trust that he will acquit himself well in the post assigned him. I also enjoy the protection you granted honest Mulvy.[1] All your friends in this quarter remit you their most sincere affection, and among the rest my brother Roger (just arrived here) who remembers you daily in his prayers. I present my hearty affections to Mr. Sherlock and to Mr. O'Brien. Am I not now obeying you too literally, losing sight of the bishop while I am familiar with the friend? Whether, however, like it or not, I must return to my duty as well as affection.

1. A Catholic priest, Sheehan, p. 433.

207. To Dr. John Curry

OCD, 8.3 HS 026

From the Hermitage, 27 November 1770

My Dear Sir,

Your letter of the 24th instant was exceedingly welcome to me though it brought some disagreeable information. That relatively to your son Thady is not of the number. His marriage to the daughter of the governor with whom he was confined should not be entered into without consulting his friends and having your consent, but now that it is consumated it may turn out a fortunate event for his children and your posterity. In all events you will have the consolation of having acquitted yourself as a kind and generous father, and you have also the consolation of having in him a son who has by no means discredited you by any base action amidst all his youthful indiscretions. They were the indiscretions of inexperience. Corruption of the heart or mind has no share in them, and I have known many fathers who reckon themselves happy in having no greater complaints to make than you have of one out of so many with which God has blessed you. You will succor Thady still as soon as you find an opening for his promotion. He is a man of honor and probity. His early trial in the fire of adversity will new-edge his industry as it increased his knowledge. It will be the source of that future happiness, even in this world which the languid, uninterrupted quiet of another state could never arrive at. Were you, therefore, trusting to him alone, you could not be unhappy on his account. Reflect and rejoice (it is your duty) that of most men you have been one of the most happy in your family, living and dead. You owe great thanksgiving to the Almighty on this account, and I doubt not but you pay as well as owe, for I have been long a witness of your religious ground. You say nothing of Frank, and I request that you will not be forgetful of him in your next. You'll please also to present my affections to young Dr. Curry, whom I long to see and expect to see before the holy days are over. When he has any leisure, he will have an Augean stable to sweep in marshaling your library and fitting up a separate apartment for the ragged, though not less useful, authors furnished from the stalls abroad.

The several bankruptcies in your city are only signals hung out of that general national bankruptcy which is soon to follow infallibly; two millions in specie, (at least) have been drained from us this last year by absentees, by importation of foreign corn, and by importation of foreign luxuries. Our exports of all kinds hold no sort of proportion to such a drain and the consequences are inevitable. For some, life will no doubt remain, but it will be that of a body wasted and emaciated which may be recovered to some vigor by a parliamentary prescription of agriculture: a prescription which can never take place without taking in the body of the people to complete it. This I have hinted in a letter to Alderman Faulkner wherein I have congratulated him on his new dignity to bring agriculture into our three southernmost provinces. You must make the majority interested in the culture, or they will not cultivate; a stock of cattle not of men is the proper stock of tenants who have not a pecuniary, discoverable, limited interest in land. They will, therefore, for self-preservation keep our lands waste; the poor driven into the mountains will remain idle for want of employment and pounce down like birds of prey in summer to waste the provisions of the low countries. Papists will be the first sufferers, the Protestants second. In a word, Ireland, depending on another kingdom, is of all the countries on earth the worst circumstanced in holding out against a multiplicity of Penal Laws, things which (according to Montesquieu) are destructive in the happiest countries. But enough of this.

The listlessness and indifference which you say are growing upon you are become a habit with me. Whatever becomes of the public, I have enough to support me and economy enough not to outrun it. *Cum omnia sunt in incerto fave tibi*[1] was an old philosophic maxim, and the practice useful at all times is indispensible in the present. I must run into the fields to take a little exercise; when I come back I will write more. —I flushed a brace of woodcocks since I went out and would give a shilling [if] you had them at supper. I had not a single line from Dr. Leland since I left Dublin. I believe he preached on the Anniversary of the 23rd of October *ad captum vulgi*,[2] I mean the great vulgar. I suppose (in his favor) that he would not hazard the credit of his history on official calumnies, which honesty can hardly digest even on holy days set apart for pleasing untruths as well as for impunity if not reward to the preacher of them. I have read somewhere that since the late Revolution no able author dared to write the history of the times subsequent to it. I believe the observation just, for the fact is certain and the Revolution itself has closed up one avenue of liberty, though it threw many open. Thus it is, parties who bring about many good things by very unrighteous means will not permit their actions to be canvassed while they have the power of punishing the canvassers by various and effectual means or (what's perhaps as bad) of rewarding their silence. In a word, it is from you, or such as you who have no measures to keep with party iniquity but who are destined to inform and instruct, that truth can be expected; and the truths you unfold will one day or other obtain a hearing and produce good as soon as that attention is gained. I, therefore, trust that your *opus magnum* is completed; and if it be, prescriptions should be made in England for the publication of a work which cannot, without injustice, be much longer detained from the bulk of the people who have so good and so fair a right to information.

When you see Dr. Carpenter, I request you will present him with my respects and affection. Your whole family, I hope, know that they are many years in possession of those things, the effusions of a grateful heart. The alderman[3] will take his own time for publishing Lord Lyttleton's continuation and conclusion of Henry II's history. The present expectation of a war[4] has withdrawn the public attention from any other subject. You are as patient as you are indulgent if you attended me to this last line. I will, therefore, my dear sir, relieve you for the present and conclude.

1. When everything is uncertain, protect yourself.
2. For the comprehension of the masses.
3. George Faulkner.
4. The American Revolution.

208. To Dr. John Curry

OCD, 8.3 HS 026

18 January 1771

My Dear Sir,

This is the only way I have left of conversing with you. On the 2nd instant our province has been covered with snow, and it froze so ever since that our lakes and rivers may be crossed over with great safety by all passengers. This prevented my setting out for Dublin (ten days ago) where I should deliver you my heart and its sentiments with a warmth of affection which very few on this earth are entitled to. I have nothing to communicate to you at present; our common feelings indeed form a subject, a melancholy one which brings new pain by being opened. *Animus meminisse horret:*[1] like an incurable wound it never pains us more than when we strip off its covering and expose it to the air. Our Irish public are in a great degree undone; and nature, which supersedes several laws which she had no share in framing, mocks or punishes our deviations from her dictates. Experience has taught us (and I think, taught us in vain) that the Papist can not be absolutely ruined without involving the Protestant in his misery. Such is the nature of public credit; like an extended rope, strike it violently on one end and it will tremble to the utmost extremity; cut it across, and it will of each side fall to the ground. I am glad to find that our Parliament is to sit on the 20th of next month. There are some wise men of the country who know our disease well enough; but far from administering the remedy, they will not even propose or name it. More prudent than the gentlemen of your faculty, they will not offer a medicine which they well know the angry patient would dash in their own faces. They tell us that certain political wounds are of such a nature as not to admit of a cure, and nothing is more easy than to involve in such a general proposition, a case which by no means belongs to it. It is a common practice to do so, and society is extremely injured by it. Ireland can never be happy while one part of the people are excluded by the other from a participation of certain benefits which in political prudence ought to be common to all. By such an exclusion you oppose a private to a public interest; you make the Papist turn to a ruinous occupation for his self-preservation; you entitle him by law to work the land in which he can have no permanent property, and virtually you forbid his meddling with agriculture, the source of wealth and support of manufactures in all ages. The wound given to the public by such an economy is deep and is felt with a vengeance.

And will any man in the present state of things aver that this wound is in the number of incurables? If our legislature thinks that it is, we must acquiesce in their decision. It is one thing to submit to an unavoidable state of affairs but quite another to approve it. The first is our duty; the other would be in many instances a crime. You and I as philosophers of the world will think for the world when we can detach a moment from the care of the domestic business by which we preserve an independence that is true liberty in the midst of servitude. Though we do no good, yet we acquit ourselves to the part with which we are connected. *Forsan [et] haec olim meminisse juvabit.*[2] Perhaps we may do some good, and by flattering ourselves in that hope let us not like cowards quit the post we occupy, and let the *opus magnum* be compiled and published to inform the deceived and to reform the prejudiced. You give me no particulars relatively to the *Supplement.*

My dear friend, I beg a thousand pardons for troubling you lately with a letter to Judge French.[3] I trusted that Watt might have a spare hour for delivering it, and in that confidence I gave you the trouble of enclosing it to you.

I request that you will present your ladies Mrs. Hamill, Mr. Comerford, young Dr. Curry, etc., etc., with my affections. On Monday morning I purpose, God willing, to set off from here. And you will be soon relieved from persuing any more stained paper.

1. The mind shudders to remember.
2. Virgil, *Aeneid*, 1.203. Perhaps someday it will be pleasant to remember these hardships.
3. Robert French, M.P. for Jamestown, became judge in the Court of Common Pleas of Ireland, *BP*, p. 705.

209. To Denis O'Conor, Belanagare

OCD, 8.3 SE 028

Dublin, 23 March 1771

Dear Denis,

I thank you for the care you took in forwarding Mr. MacLagan's letter from Belfast.[1] He is a worthy gentlemen. I keep here and clear of dissipation as I can, but yet in spite of me, I trespass upon the time I choose to [corrupt] some useful occupation. I trespass upon health also, which at my time of life ought to be husbanded by grains and samples. In this case, and no other, it is allowable to be a miser. I spend no time more greedily than what I employ in the college library, where I am indeed well treated. I am much concerned about my daughter,[2] for I know the suspension, or perhaps end, of her son's cultivation goes to her heart. I wish heartily that she may bear with resignation every moral evil in which she does not herself participate. Such a resignation is but a discharge of our personal duty, and if we desert that duty we quit [corrupt] assigned to us by God and Nature. We are bad sentinels. Something will be done, though very little, for our people in this session. It is a service which our masters want, and they begin to feel the evil which the Penal Laws bring on themselves. The nation is undone, and they see the misfortune of breaking, like drunken men, the [taped over] on which they have so long rested all their . . . [Rest of manuscript taped over and unreadable]

1. Rev. James MacLagan, a Protestant clergyman interested in Celtic literature. Sheehan, p. 436.
2. Bridget MacDermot.

210. To Dr. John Curry, Cow Lane, Dublin

OCD, 8.3 HS 026

From the Hermitage, 9 August 1771

. . . In this province the majority of our farmers are undone, and I find that affairs are not in a better train through Leinster and Munster. Even the landlords by a failure of their rents will suffer distress, and distress the more intense as it was not foreseen nor prepared for. A repeal of certain Penal Laws would restore some life to the public; and were it possible to bring people to think of such a measure, the publication of some useful hints of the subject, a few days before the next session of Parliament would be the most proper time. I did not intend to trouble you with so many lines on this subject, but one idea superinduced another, and I request that what is said may remain buried in your breast. If ever I finish what I began, it is to come out as written by a moderate Protestant and conducted in a skeptical strain as will render the preference of one evil to another: rather a discovery of the reader's sagacity than a consequence of the writer's ability.[1] . . .

1. O'Conor is referring to his *Observations on the Popery Laws*. See O'Conor's letter to Curry, 26 November 1771. O'Conor's use of the Protestant persona is a device he picked up from Berkeley's *Querist*. See Catherine and Robert Ward, "The Catholic Pamphlets of Charles O'Conor," *Studies* 68.

211. To Dr. John Curry

OCD, 8.3 HS 026

13 September 1771

... I am now writing on the back of a pamphlet entitled *Some Thoughts on the Operation of the Popery Laws* in Ireland. But for the spur you clapped in my side, I should never think about it; our endeavors of this kind (in England and Ireland of late) having no little effect on eyes that will no more bear the light than their minds can bear useful information. It will be my last effort and such a gentle stroke at parting that I trust the ingenuous mind *you* apprehend will escape me. ...

The stress of this work is laid on a contrast between King William's political plan and that adopted from his immediate successor; and if I be not partial, I think all reasonable objections are anticipated and the argument made clear enough for all reasonable men to improve upon. The present miserable state of the nation is enlarged upon, and it is shown that this is not the time for political hesitation or cowardice, for concealing the conviction or renouncing the advantages of an important truth for no better reason but because it is odious or unpopular: that our relief must come from the legislature for taking such matters into consideration and that we have no alternative but a continuation of our disease or a spirited application of the easy remedy which now offers itself and which formerly operated with so much success from the hand of King William, etc. Through the whole the writer personates a moderate Protestant. ...

You will be pleased, I think, with the good use I make of Berkeley's *Queries* in the body of the work, as what goes before is a preparative for their appearance and as what follows is an illustration as far as I was able of the truths which run through them. ...

212. To Dr. John Curry, Cow Lane, Dublin

OCD, 8.3 HS 026

8 October 1771

Dear Friend,

I write to you on this scrip of paper through want of a frank. With all my stoic apathy I find that my natural constitution of mind is like your own, a feeling one. Let us not feel to our reproach and detriment. It is only the extreme that is bad. God keeps us both in the Golden Mean. I wrote to you some time ago a huge, long letter; if you were not stinted in time, I should get a short one in return, were it only to hint to me that I should not be so prolix, and yet such is your partiality to the man you love that you are pleased with the long letter that I can send you. I have here at my leisure yet in disagreeable situations written *Observations on the Popery Laws.* You shall have them by the first safe hand. They are written in the character of a moderate patriot Protestant. If you should think them of use, I would be better pleased that they came forth from Mr. *Ewing* at Capel Street's press than from *Hoey's* for many reasons. — If, I say, you like what I have done, I would wish you to get somebody to negotiate the matter with Ewing; for in that case somebody less suspicious than I am might be supposed to be the writer, and this would be some point gained. In truth if I am going to the public as the writer, the whole silence will come to nothing or next to nothing. As the session of Parliament is begun, no time should be lost as to publication. If anything on the subject can be of use, and I thought a hundred times that nothing will, though you differ from me, and it is in deference to *your* thought that I have written anything at present on the subject. I say no more till you see what I have written. When you do, perhaps you will think as I do. I'll write more on your way of thinking as you peruse what is to be laid before you. God bless you and yours.

213. To Dr. John Curry, Cow Lane, Dublin

OCD, 8.3 HS 026

From the Hermitage, 12 October 1771

Dear Sir,

Some three weeks ago I wrote you a long letter and then last week a short one enclosed under cover to another person. Lest you should not see either, I write the present under some dissatisfaction because it will be expensive to you. In the character of a moderate Protestant I have written *Observations on the Popery Laws.* Under such a character they may have some chance to come before the persons for whom they are chiefly intended. Were the works suspected to be yours or mine, it would be reported at once and without a reading from friends and adversaries. The secret is between you and me—and we will have prudence enough to keep it even from the most intimate confidants, one or two excepted. On this principle I would wish that the publication should be rather from Mr. Ewing of Capel Street than from Hoey. The former is the most sensible bookseller I know; Mr. Morris, a Roman Catholic, is his compositor. Morris and Mr. John Fagen are intimates, and through *both* the printing and publishing might be negotiated with Ewing, under the sanction, however, of absolute secrecy from the negotiators. I think you may safely repose confidence in Mr. Fagen should you think it proper to open the affair to him. You alone are the best judge of this. You shall have the work by the first safe hand that goes from hence to Dublin. It cost me some pains, and I know you will like some of the arguments I have made up of. The whole consists in a contrast between the different schemes of King William and Queen Anne for the good of this kingdom; and you will observe that it is a comment throughout on Bishop Berkeley's *Queries,* of which I inserted those that answered my purpose in the body of the pamphlet. I took the operation and the effects of the Popery Laws in bulk without entering into the details of prohibitions, restrictions, penalties, etc., such things being obvious to the legislature should my general and, indeed, unanswerable argument gain the attention of the great leaders in the assembly. You will find, however, that I have not confined myself so much to generalities as not to point out, with all the strength I was master of, the principal causes of our present exhausted state, after a repose of eighty years, to put us into the most prosperous state that our civil constitution and national advantages entitled us to. —But too much of this, nor do I mention it to anticipate your judgment but to inform you what you are to expect on a review of the work. You who are on this spot, may hear of some things at present in agitation among our chiefs in politics. I request you will write to me speedily of all you know as it may enable me to reform or add something in my *Observations;* but should the pamphlet come into your hands before I receive your instructions, you will yourself, I trust, be at leisure to make the proper amendments or alterations either in the body of the work or in a postscript. In truth I am uneasy about you as I have not heard from you this long time. I hope, however, that you are well and happy with your family for whom I retain the warmest affection.

214. To Dr. John Curry, Cow Lane, Dublin

OCD, 8.3 HS 026

From the Hermitage, 16 October 1771

My Dear Sir,

At your solicitation I have put the last hand to *Observations on the Popery Laws*. It is the last work of this kind that I shall ever have a hand in. There is no opening of eyes which people willfully shut against the light; and yet I find a disposition in some to reform old errors if they dared. Can anything tend (*sed oculo retorto*)[1] to such an end more than the sense of government in the following lines which you have read? I must recommend "to your consideration such laws as may be salutary for the benefit of the lower orders of the community, for these have ever been found the most effective means of binding their affections to their country and securing their allegiance to one common parent"— Nothing can more plainly show the good intentions of the executive power. I have made no comment on the words in the pamphlet I send you that I might give no handle to malice, to stop for a stone to throw at the present administration. I know not how you will like what I have done *on the whole*. Some parts I know will please you, and you have it in your power to rescind what you find remiss or impertinent, for doubtless things will occur to you that escaped me and such you may throw into a postscript or insert *e re nata*[2] in the body of the work. The sooner it comes out the better that men of sense and patriots may have time to comprehend the argument and digest it for their own use if the matter should have any chance for being brought into debate. I could wish that it came out from Mr. Ewing's press; Mr. Morris, his compositor, might open the affair to him; and, should he choose not to undertake it, it must at worst be left to Mr. Hoey. It will be absolutely necessary that neither you nor I should be suspected to have any hand in it, and on this principle it was that the pamphlet is written as coming from the hand of a moderate Protestant. There may be some disturbance at this time from mobs, and I trust our clergy will strenuously exert themselves and from their actions keep our people from joining in riots of any kind. Such conduct in a critical time will recommend us to that protection from government which the laws refuse us. I have enclosed along with this a letter to Mr. Morris to be forwarded to him or disposed as you like. I shall take up no more of your time as the enclosed pamphlet will engross too much of it. Nay, I will, I am afraid, give you a surfeit. I am sensible your family does not doubt of my affections; I therefore will make no useless professions to such dear friends.

1. But looking back.
2. Arising from the present circumstances, according to the exigencies of the case.

215. To Dr. John Curry, Cow Lane, Dublin

OCD, 8.3 HS 026

22 October 1771

Dear Sir,

Yours by last post lies before me. I sent you the *Observations* by (I hope) a safe hand. I know you will be pleased with some parts but not the whole, for though I supressed several pages in the last draft, it was far (upon a review) from pleasing myself. If it had the merit the subject required, its publication would at this time be opportune beyond anything yet published on the subject. For who would suspect that in our age such paragraphs should come out as you have sent me? I have a glass before me, and here is long life and prosperity to the King and the present administration. I'll drink your own health by and by. Oh, let the secret be kept that we have no act or part in the *Observations*. I should write a letter of thanks to Mr. Fagan this night, but I must, I think, postpone it to the next post day. Some notes are wanting to the *Observations* under the page wherein Mr. Hume is quoted; the following note should be, if you think proper, inserted at the bottom:

"The following declaration of ecclesiastical power was published by the clergy of France in March 1682: 'Kings and princes are not by any command of God subject in temporals to any ecclesiastical power; neither can they be deposed directly or indirectly by the Papal authority, nor can their subjects be exempted from their allegiance, or obedience, or oath of fidelity sworn.'"

You will know that this is one of the four famous Gallican Propositions published in 1682. This I have quoted is enough for the proposal of the pamphlet I sent you. Again under the page wherein notice is taken of the small number of Protestants converted from Popery since 1702, perhaps the following note may be inserted:

"On a return made of the number of souls in Ireland in 1731, the number of papists amount to 1,309,768. Through the great famine in 1741 and several other visitations of the same kind since that time, not to mention emigrants, the number must be greatly less at present."

I request you will with all the severity not partiality of friendship give me your judgment of the little tract I sent you. I do not purpose going to Dublin this winter from a disgust the occasion of what you are no stranger to; I lost better then £200 lately by my residence in your neighborhood, and I foresee the loss of £100 more at least. I am utterly exhausted and must remain at home an hermit when I cannot fill the rank of gentleman elsewhere. After all, my temper of mind is as usual unruffled and equable. Do you follow my example in this instance and tread anxiety under your feet.

216. To Dr. John Curry, Cow Lane, Dublin

OCD, 8.3 HS 026

Tuam, 12 November 1771

My Dear Sir,
    The death of a brother-in-law who died lately in this metropolis brought me hither and I purpose to quit it soon. It grieves that I can not accept your invitation. How can I? Your unfortunate neighbor drained me off to the dregs. When I left town, he owed me more than £200; and since I parted you, I was obliged to pay £105 more for him, and after all I foresee that before the ensuing holy days I must provide £110 more to discharge my Dublin engagements for him. Must I not have good stamina to be able to make up a sum of more than £400 in eighteen months? And the expenditure would not grieve me much but what it was in favor of his sharpers, without a farthing in favor of his poor wife and children.[1] What you laid out for Thady, Martin, Frank was not thrown away, and in that reflection you are happy. You had your trials no doubt. But your sensibility was tempered with consolations of which I am not permitted to taste. God's will be done. Believe it from me that I keep anxiety from my losses at as great a distance from me as you would wish; religion requires it and I yield to its dictates. Even philosophical fortitude, the shield of the heathen, covers me from most of the arrows which fortune has discharged against me hitherto. After all (that I may not excite too much your feelings for me) I must inform you that, God granting life, I have still strength enough to recruit and appear once more among my friends. I have an annuity of £200 a year on which I have yet made no encroachment except £100 which I borrowed this winter and which, as you see, I will be able to discharge the next year. I shall then be able to see you again and live sometime with my dear Dublin friends. I take great satisfac-

tion in having thus a bosom friend before whom I can discharge all my anxieties with all their remedies, moral and physical, and yet I should have more discretion than to pour out my heart to you in this manner. If I had not those remedies and this fortitude of mind to relieve you from all pain about me. *Tecum etenim memini longos consumere soles,*[2] etc. My mind is relieved by those few lines of Persius to his friend. I shall, God willing, spend some *soles*[3] and *noctes*[4] with you still.

I am glad that the *Observations* are come out in so seasonable time, but I am sorry that I had not time to give them more force with readers who will read anything in favor of our people with disgust.[5] I hope that you have made some alterations and castrated such expressions as you might justly think indiscreet or too bold. We political physicians should touch the sores of our patients with a delicate hand or we do nothing, or rather we do great harm instead of good. You have not informed me who the publisher is, and you have omitted to inform me (what is of much greater consequence) whether our secret be kept. I confess to you that I am under great apprehensions that Morris will blab it out and expose both you and me to the censure of our friends as well as our adversaries. We shall share the fate (I dread) of sticklers in a quarrel and take sound blows from the combatants on both sides for our well-intentioned interposition. Whatever our fate be, I request you will not at this time be sparing of your pen but let me know how the town has received these *Observations,* whether there was a demand for them and what progress is made in the bills you mentioned as lately introduced in the H[ouse] of C[ommons], etc. You should take pity on an old friend sequestered from the world as I am, and yet perhaps, you could not extend that pity better than in advising me to think no more of what is doing or what may be doing among us. Experience is teaching me not to meddle with subjects which, however handled, may offend and which on my part must be only so much waste of time. You may, therefore, believe me when I assure you that I am at the end of my political warfare, and you well enough know that but for your solicitation, I would not attempt to scour my rusty old armor and fight this last campaign. I have other things to communicate, and you may be thankful to the company that just came into the room, or you should have the trouble of reading still down to the bottom of the page. God preserve you and yours. You are satisfied with the cordiality of this prayer. And I say no more.

1. At this point Charles O'Conor had little hope that his son Charles of Mount Allen would ever succeed in life. Ironically, Charles of Mount Allen's grandson, Charles O'Conor of New York, a famous trial lawyer, defended Jefferson Davis in his trial for treason after the Civil War and also became the first Catholic presidential candidate in 1872. *Dictionary of American Biography* (New York: Scribner's, 1934).

2. For I remember that I spent long days with you.
3. Days. 4. Nights.
5. Both Charles O'Conor and John Curry were listed as the authors of *Observations on the Popery Laws*, Dublin, 1771. Another printing occurred in 1772. BMCPBCE, 6:745.

217. To Dr. John Curry, Cow Lane, Dublin

OCD, 8.3 HS 026

From the Hermitage, 26 November 1771

My Dear Friend,

I am just returned from Tuam where I dated my last to you and on alighting here I found your reply of the 18th instant before me. My loss of £300 by your neighbor has racked me off to such a degree as to tear me away from you personally for some time. I must, like an exhausted bankrupt, take time to recruit some strength and appear again in public to enjoy a few friends who care for me because we have the same aversions and desires and that our studies lead us to benevolent efforts. The last effort I made was entirely owing to your injunctions (commands, I may call them) in my last. So that the poor bantling was not left at your door or mine, I cared not who should be suspected for the father, and yet you see I am detected by one chance which had a thousand against it that I never be discovered by a private letter. This must be explained. My good friend Major Vallancey[1] sent me some time since Mr. MacPherson's book against the pretensions of the Irish to any early knowledge of letters. I was engaged by my obligation as well as friendship to acknowledge his civility. In doing so I was naturally led to make him a compliment on his book relating to our proposed inland navigation. *E re nata*[2] I gave him my sentiment that so great and national an undertaking could hardly survive without engaging the body of the people to interest themselves in it, etc. By this *et cetera* you will easily conceive that I made use of some of those arguments which are come out in the *Observations* published by Ewing. How could I suspect that Vallancey would be so simple as to expose my private letter to a bookseller? Was it not a thousand to one he would not? Along with yours came a letter to me from Major Vallancey himself informing me of the tract as if it were a mere matter of indifference (not of importance) to me or to the success of the subject I wrote upon. All this is odd enough, and it is equally strange, surely, that Ewing should be guilty of the folly of pointing me out when the success of the sale of the pamphlet depended on leaving the public to its own conjectures especially when those conjectures laid hold on a man of eminence not on an obscure man, obnoxious on the score of his religious principles: *quo ad me valeant omnia haec; quo ad populum valeant quantum valere possunt.*[3] Ewing's indiscretion, no doubt, hurts himself, and it hurts the argument much more. There is no help for all this; and in truth it is my belief that were it handled much better and by the ablest of men in either House, it would in the urgent disposition of men's minds have no effect. It is, therefore, no great matter who the real or suspected author is, and after all, the whole discovery depending only on similitude of handwriting, cannot amount to a positive proof. Mr. Vallancey has also informed me that he has, "occasionally shown my letter to many of our legislators who are at this very time engaged on the very subject," and he "has great hopes that some laws will be passed this session which will preface those of another considering us all as one people whose properties shall be equally valid, consequently all equally alert to stand forth in the defense of it whenever invaded by foreigners of whatsoever nation or principles." All this is well enough from a private gentleman, and I doubt not that he speaks the sense of some of the legislators he converses with. I think it will come to nothing. I have shot my last bolt at your instance, nor do I mean to return to our local political warfare. If God spare me life, I purpose to draw up another volume of the *Dissertations* and correct the first as far as I am able to correct them. Major Vallancey sent me in packets about a hundred of Mr. O'Halloran's *Introduction to The History and Antiquities of Ireland* against the MacPherson, etc., *periculosum et plenum opus aleae.*[4] This work is magnificently printed; when you see it, you will find that were he to defend a bad cause, he would be no formidable adversary. In the defense of a good one you would wish that he and I had better abilities and a better knowledge of our subject. In this busy time I request you will inform me regularly of all you know as it will give a suspension to the disagreeable reflections which you know intrude upon me in spite of all my endeavors to keep them at a distance.

I have indeed derived comfort from the account you give me of Dr. Carpenter's recovery, and I will next post congratulate with him on it. I request that you will prescribe a regimen for him to preserve a man dear to us. You are sensible he has measures to keep; and you will, therefore, overlook his reserves and cautions, for I am sensible his heart and wishes are at bottom what they ought to be. I was informed of my friend Denny's promotion by the public papers. His living in my neighborhood will bring him £200 a year, and that in the county of Kildare will probably bring him in more. I am truly very glad of it. We are told that the White Boys are again up in some parts of Munster. If they be, it is the fault of the neighboring magistrates, for it would be easy for them to find means of seizing and hanging those reprobates. Something on this subject, if the account be true, should be published by a friend in Hoey's *Mercury*. But I am tiring you beyond all patience.

    1. Charles Vallancey (1721–1812) was the son of a French Protestant. He became Engineer-in-Ordinary to Ireland in 1762. As an antiquarian and a founding member of the Royal Irish Academy, he became interested in the Gaelic language and its similarity to the Punic language. *Concise DNB*, 1:1330.
    2. Things being as they are.
    3. To whatever degree all these things influence me; to whatever extent they affect the people, just so far can they succeed.
    4. Horace, *Carmina*, 2.1.6. A task (which is) dangerous and full of risk.

218. To Colonel Charles Vallancey

RIA, Stowe MS. Bi2

Belanagare, 29 November 1771

... I had a letter from a friend in town informing me of the publication of the pamphlet you mention, *Observations on the Popery Laws*. I have not yet seen it and I am amazed, if what I am told be true, that Mr. Ewing has pointed me out as the author from the ambiguous similitude of handwriting in that tract and my late letter to you. He could not, surely, devise more effectual means for hindering the sale of such a work than fathering it on one, obnoxious from his religious principles. It is true that to enlightened men truth is acceptable from whatever hand it comes. But the majority of men have never been thus disposed; in all public distempers they must properly be attended by their own physicians, not by a suspected and intruding prescriber. It is, therefore, to you and such as you that I should communicate my thoughts on the present ruinous state of this country. I believe it owing in a great degree to the exclusion of half our people from the benefits of our excellent Constitution. Were there but few Papists in Ireland, all our Penal Laws against them could not be hurtful because a few only would be punished. But those laws have from time to time been multiplied for the very reason why they should not be so, because a multitude is affected and because it is the worst policy in the world to tie up the hands of industry and cooperation. I am very glad to hear from you that some of our ablest members of the legislature think in this manner.

Here in Conaught I have seen several old astronomical manuscripts in our ancient language. They are all conformable to the Ptolemaic system and have been written, no doubt, before that of Copernicus or Tycho was known. When those works were composed I could not learn. I am exceedingly thankful to you for the offer you make me of the book on the *Remains of Japhet*. I have not seen it and inquired for it in vain in some of the shops. . . .

219. To Dr. John Curry, Cow Lane, Dublin

OCD, 8.3 HS 026

From the Hermitage, 4 December 1771

My Dear Friend,

Now that I have a frank I must scribble to you as a postscript to my last. I have answered Major Vallancey's letter expressing my concern at Mr. Ewing's indiscretion as well as my wonder at his blindness to his own interest relatively to the sale of his pamphlet. There is no help for all this, for I find by a letter from my worthy friend Counselor Ridge that I am now suspected to be the author of the *Observations*, etc. He tells me that the pamphlet is considered as a work of merit, that he has sent for it to Mr. Ewing's and had not time to peruse it, having only received it just at the time he was writing to me. If any merit it has, it must be owing to the leading ideas which run through the Bishop of Cloyne's *Queries*. On those ideas I could enlarge more than I have done but that I considered that an unpopular argument ought to be drawn within as narrow compass as possible. My mind was also telling me all along that I was laboring in a barren soil, productive of nothing, and I certainly would throw aside the pen only that you differed in opinion with me. When those who can recoup a known, a public calamity, spend their time in altercations and *in* trials of each other's strength, when men think of themselves and for themselves, what good can be expected? In truth he must be an unthinking person who expects any, and on this certainty it is really a matter of little concern who did or who did not write the *Observations*. When I say of *little concern*, I mean as to the public, for it is of some to me. As I fear, the censure of our own people will be the heavier as they have the writer in the wind, and it is on this principle that I have not yet written to my dear friend Dr. Carpenter to congratulate with him on his re-establishment. I wait, therefore, for a line from you to know how I stand with my jealous friends before I renew my correspondence with them.

If they forgive this last effort, they shall never hear more of me on any local subject; and, in truth, it is time I should return to lick into some form what I have essayed on another and what I have to superadd, should God grant me life and spirit to do it. I am thinking that I shall have some information from Vallancey and Ridge about the thoughts of some of their intimates on the subject they so freely opened to me. If I have, you shall be put in possession of what they communicate. Meantime, I request you will inform me of what transpires as you stand in the center of intelligence. It will be a consolation to a mind unsettled as mine has been of late with family misfortunes. I take consolation this moment from writing to you, for it lightens my burden.

220. To Archbishop John Carpenter

OCD, 8.3 HS 026

From the Hermitage, 13 December 1771

R[igh]t Reverend Sir,

 Since I parted you in May last, I have omitted no opportunity of inquiring about you from friends whose time is more at their own disposal than yours can be, and of late Dr. Curry informed me of your escape from a dangerous cholerical fit. That worthy man shared no part of his pain (on your account) with me, but he took care of making me a partaker of his joy on your recovery. You owe yourself a great deal, and you owe more to the public not to be religiously observant of the regimen prescribed for you to keep off so terrible an enemy as that which has lately made its attack on you. I shall here account for my not troubling yourself directly now and then with a line. I could not do it without giving you some uneasiness as I know you would expect to hear something about myself. I forebore that subject, and I go into it now with reluctance, though you will be pleased to hear that I *reflect* and make my *natural sensibility* yield to my duty in bearing the past and preparing for the future. I was laying in, I thought, a stock of repose for my old days. Incidents little foreseen overturned my whole scheme. It may be so best. Some evil, moral or natural, is perhaps prevented and some good will offer itself if it be improved. Within eighteen months past, I lost by your neighbor in Anderson's Court better than £300, and as I lost so much rather to his sharpers than to him, I cannot but feel painfully for his poor wife and children. These feelings cannot be thoroughly subdued, but I had some success cheating them by attending workmen at every fair day and by my reading or writing at nights *pro solaciis negotia qu[a]erens*[1] as Tacitus happily expresses himself describing an old Roman who suffered great family afflictions. On this occasion I make good use of the task you set me, that of giving some form to the chaos in which the ancient history of this island is involved. The government, language, literature, and manners of former ages as well as the revolutions in the religion of politics of modern times, *periculosum et plenum opus aleae.*[2] Dangerous as such work is, I will, at your instance, attempt it; and (if God grants life) I will spin the thread down to our own days. The employ will lighten the weight of the melancholy hours which pass over me; and if my friends consent to the publication, a monument will remain such as I can erect that the writer has labored not to discredit the partiality of Dr. Carpenter, his best friend and patron.

In a late letter to Major Vallancey thanking him for the present of books on Irish antiquities, he very innocently shared my letter to Mr. Ewing, the bookseller; and the latter, thinking he found some resemblance in my handwriting with a manuscript he was printing, very indiscreetly pointed me out as the writer of *Observations on the Popery Laws*. For his own sake he should forbear publishing his suspicion and the more as it might fall on a moderate Protestant who under the common shelter of anonymous writers might take the unpopular side of the question without any danger of personal abuse. The writer of the *Observations* contrived the matter so as to make the quarter it came from doubtful; but now that the pamphlet is given as the effort of an obnoxious party, no good can come of it. Such is the temper of the present times, resembling exactly what I have in my youth been an eye and an ear witness to. Poor Carolan,[3] once requested by his son to avoid relapsing into fits of intemperance, the old man replied harshly: "By the Bible of God, Sirrah, I would not take the most salutary advice on earth on the score of your giving it." This is ridiculous and childish, but it is a puerility which runs through grave councils and senates. I think it now vain for a Roman Catholic to write a syllable on our Penal Laws; sure I am I never will. We must rest, satisfied to bear those things as we do the storms which blow down our houses. We should, God knows, be infinitely more anxious about our own moral evils, the true causes of all our apostasies. Several of our clergy have aposticized of late in these parts and we shall be undone, I dread, before the end of this century if our watchmen, the prelates, do not double their diligence in providing good pastors. I request you will present my affections to my dear friend Mr. Sherlock. Mr. Fitzgerald tells me he has been lately on a disagreeable errand at Castledermot. I hope that by this time he is safe in Francis Street. You will please to tender my affections to Mr. O'Brien, Mrs. Troy, and my other friends and your acquaintances. I am grown prolix and will therefore conclude here.

1. Seeking employment as a source of consolation.
2. Horace, *Epistle*, 1.1.19. A task (which is) dangerous and full of risk.
3. Torlogh O'Carolan (1670–1738), the blind Irish bard. *Concise DNB*, 1:962. Carolan visited O'Conor frequently and taught him to play the harp. Carolan's harp is on display at Clonalis House.

221. To Dr. John Curry

OCD, 8.3 HS 026

From the Hermitage, 21 December 1771

My Dear Sir,

As I did not hear from you a long time, I am greatly in pain lest you should be unwell, nor shall I be at ease till my apprehensions are removed. To hear that you are in no danger would allay my other mortifications from the quarter of Dublin whence I lately had accumulated accounts very distressing to me. I bear up against such things with more fortitude than I thought myself master of, and I give you this account because you had apprehensions that my sensitivity was an overmatch for my strongest resolutions. This post I had a very kind letter from Mr. Vallancey requiring some satisfaction about the antiquity of our Irish literature; and as he made wonderful progress in the knowledge of our old language, I suspect that he purposes to write on the subject. I shall satisfy him as well as I can, though perhaps not so soon as he would wish as my leisure and temper at present are ill-adapted for studies which concern but very few, mere holiday readers and writers, who have much curiosity to gratify and perhaps a name to establish by new discoveries in the wilds of ancient time. He seems to be in pain for Mr. Ewing's indiscretion and adds that, "He hopes that matter in the *Observations* will have some weight with our Commons to pass a bill Sir Charles Bingham[1] has presented to the House for permitting Papists to take leases for building in towns corporate," but at this time, he says, "to give you my own sentiments, I fear this step is rather precipitated. The gangrene is not yet quite eaten away." I really believe him in these sentiments, and I gave you my fears on this subject as soon as I discovered some ill-omens in the silence of both Houses in their addresses on the commencement of the session, nor am I now sorry that in spite of our endeavors the *Observations* should be considered as the effort of an obnoxious party because that very idea will acquit them, nay declare them, unfit objects of any destructive penal laws since their putting themselves thus (as it were) on their trial, throws all blame on the men who decline receiving any test of their fidelity. There are times wherein the language of nature is not to be borne, and that it never should [be] is the interest of the natural enemies of these kingdoms; for doubtless the less cooperation and confidence we have among us the better for them. It is odd enough that we are obstinate in doing here what our greatest enemies on the continent would have us do. —Let us laugh at those contradictions; it is better to do so than grieve, for we may as reasonably grieve at those innundations which in this very week threw down most of the cabins in the neighborhood. I wrote last week to our dear friend Dr. Carpenter and pressed it upon him to pursue the regimen you prescribed against a relapse of his late terrible disorder. How's Dr. Martin? How are his brothers abroad? I request you will present them with the warmest affections.

1. Sir Charles Bingham, 7th baronet (1735–99), later (1776) first baron and (1795) first earl of Lucan. *Burke*, ed. Lucy S. Sutherland, 2:470n.

222. To Dr. John Curry

OCD, 8.3 HS 026

[January 1772][1]

I wrote you a long letter last week which the bearer to the by-post lost on the road, and you would be as little gainer by perusing it as the man who picked it up. Nothing, I thank God, ever passed between us that might be posted on a market cross without any impeachment on our probity as men or as citizens, however we might be uneasy at the publication of our bagatelles or those personal incidents which strangers have no right to know. I have been furnished with the heads of a bill brought into the H[ouse] of C[ommons] to qualify Papists to take long leases in corporate towns, and I have seen severe animadversions on that measure in the *Hibernian Journal* not hinting but asserting in explicit terms that a scheme for easing Papists of some of their burdens has been a ministerial device from the commencement of the D[uke] of Bedford's administration to the present time.[2] No proofs besides negative arguments are brought to support this charge; and however the ministry might be minded to give no opposition to such a measure, they will, I apprehend, take no step toward proposing it. In this case wherein they have the smallest concern, they will undoubtedly leave the patient to the physician to die or revive in the hands that have been prescribing to it for seventy years past. The new dose (called Bingham's Bill) will not, I think, be approved in the first place because it is deemed injurious to the Protestant interest, and in the second because its operation must have no efficacy if compounded with other ingredients which must render it absolutely nauseous. To drop this figure, for which I should ask your pardon, no man will take a long tenure under a law which tells him that when he does, *it must be at his own peril;* that is, if you purchase such a property, it must be for the use of a Protestant son who of your whole family may be the greatest reprobate! In such a case the greater temptation will, like Moses's serpent, swallow up the leper; and a tepid Catholic will sooner take the full plunge, which qualifies for every constitutional benefit and renders him his own master, than purchase under a law which ties up his hands and leaves his younger family at the mercy of a man who, in poisoning the very fountain of religious obligation by hypocrisy and perjury, is not to be trusted even in a small act of natural justice,[3] *non tali auxilio tempus eget.*[4] In *The Votes of the H[ouse] of C[ommons]* (p. 113) I have perused a petition of The Dublin Society in behalf of the tillers and corn farmers setting forth that the great drain of cash for two years past out of this kingdom through the importation of foreign corn has been a great cause of the high exchange, the many bankruptcies, and the scarcity of money so severely felt among us; and they urge that a premium upon the exportation of corn would remedy the evil and keep plenty at home at a cheaper price than at present very well; but will Great Britain grant us such an indulgence in prejudice to its own market? Or supposing that such a law passed; might not our neighbors have a redundance of corn as well as ourselves and consequently defeat the purpose of our premiums by leaving our corn on our own hands? In truth, as affairs now go, there is little to be dreaded from a redundance and were there any, our manufacturers would thrive the better. In its nature of things, the price of corn (upon an average) must bear a price proportionate to the price of lands. These gentlemen seem afraid to touch a principal sore, that of *forbidding a participation of the public welfare to the majority of our people.* Again they urge that we have great wastes in this island capable of being improved to tillage, and to remedy this evil they purpose an exemption from certain taxes.⁵ This is a right measure undoubtedly, conditionally that *you do not exclude the body of people from having an interest in it*. As a partial undertaking it can produce but very little advantage. Protestants have too much good land to improve independently of those wastes, and Papists alone are fit for so desperate an undertaking; but why do I write so much on this subject? It is useless. Let us be thankful for the lenity of the executive government, nay, let us be thankful to the legislature as we have much greater privileges than the poor Negroes imported from Guinea, though it is a little odd in such a distinction that we should owe more to our white complexion than to our innocence with regard to government.

You'll please to inform the gentleman who inquires about our antiquities that Keating's work⁶ is an ill-disguised farrago wherein some important truths are disgraced by silly fables. It was never printed in the original, and the pretended translation by one O'Conor is but a heap of shameful interpolations and impositions. You'll please to inform him also that *O'Mulloy's Irish Grammar* was printed in Rome about one hundred years ago. I have a copy of it, and several can, I believe, be found in private hands as well as in our public libraries in Dublin. Dr. Leland will no doubt give us a well-told story without going into minute detail. I expect, however, that he will give us a large appendix of the state tracts and records which it would be otherwise difficult to come at; I mean only papers which you have not seen. As soon as his volumes come I expect to see them succeeded by the excellent work *I have seen* and that without loss of time from one of the London presses. The author will draw fame and advancement from so speedy a publication, and the right to the public to useful information is indisputable, as mankind appear now so well prepared for receiving it.

I am amusing myself with correcting and improving the former volume of *Dissertations* and collecting materials for a second. It is *pro solaciis negotia qu[a]erens*.⁷ The occupation will cheat the time and keep me from attending the very sorrowful reflections. The *Observations on the Popery Laws* have interrupted me much in this inquiry into the ancient state of our country, for half what I [have] written is not in the printed copy. I have thrown out many arguments (which you would certainly oblige me to retain) from an impulse of mind that I was laboring to no purpose. I request that you will let me know if the work I mentioned *above* is well transcribed and prepared for the press. If it be not, I must reproach the writer with the advice given by the poor dying man to the preacher, "Reverend Father, be careful not to neglect yourself the good advice *you give me*." I make my letters long to bring myself as near as I can to our old *tête à tête* enjoyments. Torn away from you as I am, I follow (as well as I can) the rule old Horace prescribed to himself, *non mihi res, sed me rebus submittere conor.*[8]

I am growing indifferent to everything except my friends. You know most of them.

1. This letter is undated. It is a response to Curry's letter of 23 December 1771. Stowe MS. B12, RIA.
2. The *Hibernian Journal* was not the only periodical complaining about Papists wanting long leases in corporate towns. A letter from Cork signed "Protestant" in the *FJ*, 15–18 February, warned of the growing boldness of Catholics in Cork. The correspondent wrote:

> Three new chapels have been built at vast expense, and added to five others here. With these may be numbered many private places of worship where friaries are held; besides swarms of Jesuits daily imported, we have had nuns brought from France to preside at and conduct a nunnery lately built here; in this seminary they mean to receive children of Protestants for tuition, and you may judge of the principles they are likely to imbibe from their teachers who will lose no pains to seduce and make converts of the young and weak minds committed to their care. . . .

The writer concluded, "I take up the pen to request you will warn the friends of our country and religion of the evil that must follow if the intended act takes place to admit Papists to take long leases. . . ."

3. *DJ*, 30 January–2 February 1768, showed the unfortunate case of Lord Trimleston. After his two sons "conformed" to the Established Church, they advertised that their father had no legal power to contract since he was "but a tenant for life."
4. The times do not need such help.
5. Catholics were enabled to take leases of sixty-one years for fifty acres of bog with half an acre of arable land adjoining for a house. The bog land upon reclamation was exempted from taxes and tithes for seven years. Government officials clogged the Bogland Law with clauses which specified that the bog be at least four feet deep, that half of it be reclaimed within twenty-one years, and that the bog not lie within a mile of any market or town. Consequently, O'Conor could proceed to drain his bogs without fear of prosecution. Lecky, 2 : 192.
6. Geoffrey Keating (Seathrún Céitinn, 1570?–1644?) wrote *Foras Feasa ar Éirinn* (Foundations of Knowledge of Ireland), a history of Ireland to the English invasion.
7. Seeking employment as a source of comfort.
8. "I try to subordinate myself to (circumstances) not circumstances to myself." *Epistle*, 1.1.19.

223. To Archbishop John Carpenter

OCD, 8.3 HS 026

[10 January 1772]

R[igh]t Reverend Sir,

Your letter of the 28th of December gave me the highest satisfaction because it brought me information that you are well and yet, as every human enjoyment is attended with some painful feelings, mine has received abatement from reflecting how little I can do justice to your partiality for me relatively to the task I have in hand. My materials are scanty; such as they are, I shall exert my whole strength (such as it is) to make the most of them; and I expect to fill some chasms out of Dr. Leland's and our friend Curry's appendices of state acts and records. The volume of printed *Dissertations* I am chastising and amending. The second will be of much greater value as it will include the times from Henry II to the present. We are interested in this latter period of history more than in any other, and it will require the greater labor to give a just idea of the civil and ecclesiastical revolutions which fell with it. This second volume is yet (for the reasons I gave) in *disjectis membris*,[1] and it were better it never should appear than be destitute of some important facts not yet come to hand. I must now give you information (but to your Grace solely) that our worthy friend has an excellent work in his hands collected from a multitude of writers down from the first dawning of Protestants under Henry VIII to our own times.[2] He very justly keeps it a secret, and it will come out in London in two quarto volumes. I expect great assistance from his collections should God grant me life to finish what I began.

The bearer hereof is a very honest young man as any I know. He is a good Catholic, and for discretion and modesty he can not be excelled. He is by profession a printer of the first class, and on these accounts I presume to recommend him to your Grace's protection. He purposes to introduce himself to the public by printing by subscription a spiritual work such as will be deemed most useful for present and general edification. How practicable such a scheme may be at the present time I know not. Formerly, I well remember that some of our publishers were losers by it. It was to this young man I trusted those unfortunate *Observations* which came out, and he kept the secret inviolably, though it transpired by the chance of a million to a single unit. Indeed as such publications can do no good, it is no great matter who is pointed out as the writer. I have thrown my last javelin at popular prejudices, for as old Swift observed, "A needle can have no effect against a stone wall," or as our own bard MacDavy has expressed it with equal success, [*sgrimsedh na hairm don charmaic*][3] I leave that rock to other marksmen. Sure I am that no ink, not even Hannibal's vinegar can dissolve it.

I am greatly pleased with my dear friend Sherlock's success in Castledermot;[4] I never doubted his prudence in any undertaking, but I admire his courage in the last. I request it of your G[race] to present him with my affections. Would you believe it that an Irish *dám*[5] was patronized in the age we live in, and yet poor Gorman got five guineas for his poetical bagatelle from Sir George MacCartney.⁶ But the Secretary is our brother Milesian, and he mingled his benefaction with an act of charity. I am improving about this Hermitage every day. Between such an employment and study I am cheating all anxieties, keeping them at a distance by Horace's rules: *Non mihi res, sed me rebus submittere conor*. In whatever situation I am in, I shall never forget the obligation I am under to your G[race] and my other friends.

10 January 1772

1. Horace, *Satires*, 1.4.62. "In scattered parts."
2. Curry's, *An Historical and Critical Review*. . . .
3. Tadhg Mac Dáire Meic Bruaideadha (Teige MacDaire MacBrody) (1570–1652), *Iomarbhágh na bhFileadh* or *Contention of the Bards* (ed. Lambert McKenna, 1918). O'Conor had copied the poem as a boy. Professor John Armstrong gives the translation as follows: The Gaelic is corrupt for *sg(e)innid na hairm don charraig*, "the weapons glance off the rock" occurring in one of MacDaire's poems (XVIII.5d) in the *Contention*.
4. The pastor of Castledermot had conformed to the Established Church. See letter 225.
5. Bardic poem.
6. On 14 December 1771, Vallancey had written to O'Conor that he had presented Gorman's verses to George MacCartney, the Chief Secretary for Ireland, who gave Gorman five guineas. Stowe MS. B12, RIA. Sheehan identifies Gorman as a scribe, p. 451.

224. To Dr. John Curry

OCD, 8.3 HS 026

From the Hermitage, 28 January 1772

. . . I am reforming the *Dissertations* and find that my implicit confidence in Mr. O'Flaherty's¹ accuracy plunged me into some mistakes. Should God grant me life, I purpose to rectify the mistakes I have committed and add a second volume of *Dissertations*, more interesting as coming more home to our own affairs than that about antiquities in which we have now little or no concern. . . . I had this week a letter from Vallancey telling me that Lord Lyttleton has made very flattering mention of me in the last volume of his history, and I had another letter from Mr. Faulkner with one from Lord Lyttleton enclosed, praying the Alderman to send me a copy of his last volume as soon as they come out in Dublin. I can not but be gratified by his Lordship's kindness as, in fact, I have rendered him no service except the transmitting him some extracts from our Irish annals of the twelfth century. . . .

1. Roderic O'Flaherty (1619–1718) was the author of *Ogygia,* a history of Ireland in Latin.

225. To Dr. John Curry

OCD, 8.3 HS 026

Hermitage, 12 February 1772

I heartily condole with you on our public loss in the death of so worthy a man as Mr. Usher.[1] I have not known him personally, but there was a kindred between us which drew us vastly closer to one another than ties of consanguinity, which I shall ever renounce when attended with vice or unworthiness. I have, however (as you must have) some consolation even in the decease of such a man because it has clapped a seal to virtues now out of the power of corruption and because the example he has set, the difficulties he overcame, and the labors he went through will be a spur to the virtues of others who stood out hitherto and will to the last stand out against the rewards which Usher threw up and against the punishments which he faced. Men like him we lost would not only keep Catholicity alive in these islands but be instrumental in producing the best Catholics, persons refined by the fires of persecution and displaying merits to which the Catholics of Paris or Rome can have no claim. Of late we have many apostasies among our clergy, and I am told that Mr. Burne, pastor of Castledermot, has newly conformed to the Established Religion. The best on't is that such men have no influence in bringing any of their flocks along with them and that the rewards offered for occasional conformity can reach but very few among us. . . .

1. A Catholic priest. Sheehan, p. 454.

226. To Dr. John Curry

OCD, 8.3 HS 026

From my Cell, 11 March 1772

My Dear Sir,

I am just returned from the county of Galway where I have sojourned for ten days past, and that absence from this place will account to you for my silence relatively to the contents of your letter of the 27th of last month. Is it not pleasing enough that your Lord-

Mayor, the chiefs of the city, and the majority of the Commons without intending to prove the best friends to our people in the late questions about giving them long tenures in corporate towns? Perhaps the superabundant zeal of Mr. LeHunte[1] has contributed not a little to our good fortune on the fate of that question; and I think the poor Papists will have good sense enough to toast his health in those corporations which, like the waters of Lethe, extinguish the feelings of all their misfortunes; they may forget those misfortunes the sooner when they answer that in the nature of things they cannot be undone without *sociis doloris*[2] through every quarter of the kingdom. In a northern country wherein every comfort of life is obtained chiefly from the hand of industry, there can be no prosperity independently of the majority of the people, and the legislative power must take its alternative either in general poverty or in general encouragement for its prevention. Our alternative has been taken long since and three or four severe seasons coming in aid of our Penal Laws are bringing about and will complete the consequences of Penal Laws without their proper object. We must sink in the same proportion that other nations (of a different policy) rise and this circumstance of general distress may hereafter force men in power to reflect and listen to the call of those who cry aloud, and I have cried long *in the desert*. They may think that a cultivated country is preferable to such a desert and that it is absurd to punish men for crimes which such men renounce both in principle and in practice. If such reflections do not take place, we have no more to do but to live on quietly in our own way without giving or taking offense, rejoicing in those sufferings which prepare us for our future state, and preparing our young for their flight into regions wherein they may enjoy in some security the fruits of their labor. *Sic sic juvat ire sub umbras*.[3]

I had this week a considerable part of Lord Lyttleton's history sent under covers from my worthy friend, Alderman Faulkner, and you will be not a little surprised at the honor done me by his Lordship in page 300 of the volume which, I believe, will be published next week. I must retain the most grateful memory of so honorable a testimony as it must be a spur to my industry in my present researches into our ancient history. His account of our Irish affairs in Henry II's time is by far the best I have hitherto seen, though his Lordship (as may be expected) gives but little credit to our antiquities. The subject, in truth, has not been yet sufficiently handled for the eye of criticism from the discouragements thrown on the subject and the general prejudice against it. By the way, have you seen Moran's letter on this subject in the *Freeman's Journal* of the 7th instant?[4] It is well written, and this writer promises more on the subject. It relates to the shameful neglect of our ancient history, but, *tibi soli*,⁵ I am suspecting that it was written by my friend Vallancey. I request that I may hear from you, if possible, before Easter in Corn Lane or at our own house on Summer Hill. My hearty affections to dear Mrs. Curry, Mrs. Gaven, Mrs. Hamill, Dr. Martin.

    1. On 27 February Curry wrote to O'Conor that Tom LeHunte had cast the deciding vote in the defeat of the bill which provided for long leases in corporate towns but which had a gavel-kind clause attached to it. Stowe MS. B12, RIA.
    2. Companions in sorrow.
    3. "It is pleasant to go thus under the shadows" (to withdraw to a quiet place).
    4. The correspondent argues that "the present State and Constitution of Ireland can only be comprehended by returning to the more remote Periods of our History—nay, that thro' *Ignorance of it, many eminent Patriots have fallen into Mistakes!*" *FJ*, 5–7 March 1772.
    5. Between us.

227. To Dr. John Curry

OCD, 8.3 HS 026

Hermitage, 25 March 1772

Young Charles O'Conor has gone into debt and has depleted his father's resources. O'Conor recounts this unfortunate experience, "A loss of £400 in the last eighteen or nineteen months has run out my finances, and nothing but economy can re-establish them, *non mihi res, sed me rebus submittere conor*.¹ That is my philosophy, and prudence is a sentinel to it." O'Conor comments on the Irish Parliament and on his antiquarian interests:

This day I received under a franked cover Mr. Langrishe's excellent speech in the House of Commons.² I am extremely glad that he consented to its publication as in that shape it will make a more lasting impression than in the utterance of fugitive words spoken between four walls. . . .

Perhaps I told you already; if not, I will inform you now that I have met in the hands of one Mr. Morris in Galway, a manuscript entitled the *Ogygia Vindicated,* etc., by the late Mr. O'Flaherty. It is a refutation of the objections of Sir George Mackenzie to that book. It is well written and throws some useful lights on our antiquities. The present proprietor offered to make over the work to me but for the sum of money too gross for me to pay as I might rather be a loser by the publication. It wants an illustration by notes which would take up more time than I can well spare; and should I consent to be the editor, it would be chiefly from the view of an appendix to the work in refutation of the two MacPhersons. Thus we should have the latter as well as the former historical hypotheses of the north British writing demolished in one book and under the same cover. I wrote to my friend Dr. Leland on the subject.[3] He says (perhaps inconsiderately) that I must publish that manuscript.

1. "I try to subordinate myself to circumstances, not circumstances to myself." Horace, *Epistle I*.
2. Sir Hercules Langrishe (1731–1811) was a classmate of Edmund Burke's at Trinity College. He was M.P. for Knocktopher in the Irish Parliament from 1760 to 1801. Langrishe introduced the third Catholic Relief Bill in 1792. See also Edmund Burke, "A Letter to Sir Hercules Langrishe, M.P.," in *The Works of Edmund Burke* (London: G. Bell and Sons, 1916), 3:298. *Concise DNB*, 1:747.
3. Leland must have contacted both Major Vallancey and the publisher George Faulkner. George Faulkner wrote O'Conor on 2 April 1772 alluding to the *Ogygia Vindicated* manuscript: "I should be proud of the honor of being the printer and publisher." O'Conor felt that the manuscript should be published, but he did not have the money to buy it. At this point Dr. Leland and Major Vallancey came to O'Conor's aid. They proposed to a new Select Committee on Antiquities of the Dublin Society that the Society buy the *Ogygia* manuscript and elect Charles O'Conor as editor of the project. Faulkner wrote to O'Conor on 16 November, "I am very glad that O'Flaherty's *Ogygia* has been approved of by the Committee of Antiquarians. . . ." Faulkner published *Ogygia* in April 1775. George Faulkner to Charles O'Conor, 16 November 1772, Stowe MS. B12; Gilbert, "Streets of Dublin," *Irish Quarterly Review*, 3 (March 1853) 37n.

228. To Dr. John Curry

OCD, 8.3 HS 026

To my dear friend Dr. Curry
on this tenth day of April 1772

. . . My last to you was a long and very rambling letter wherein I have given you an account of *Dr. Leland's* friendly sentiments towards you together with a pleasing quotation from his letter relatively to the chronology of the massacre in the peninsula of Magee.[1] Here is more historical news for you. I had a letter yesterday from the Abbé O'Kelly dated from *Mons* in Hainault, 10 December 1771. Through the carelessness of the gentleman to whom it was entrusted, it has been four months on the road, and I must reckon myself a loser by this privation of correspondence with a gentleman who (as I am told) is a man of excellent natural talents improved by knowledge. He writes in French and his inquiries are the inquiries of one who knows what he is about. Being born abroad, he understands English as a dead language, my own case relative to his language. I must, therefore, reply to him in English and will sit down tomorrow to give him all the satisfaction I can. He goes on a very judicious plan, that of Père d'Orleans and Abbé Vertot[2] and his title is *L'Histoire des Revolutions d'Irlande*. . . .

1. On 8 January 1642 Scottish colonists killed about sixty men, women, and children of the native Irish population on the Island of Magee, east of Carrickfergus, which was a promontory and not really an island: Peter Berresford Ellis, *Hell or Connaught* (New York: St. Martin's Press, 1975), p. 71.

2. Although Abbé O'Kelly of Mons is unknown, his exemplars are not. Père Pierre Joseph d'Orleans was a Catholic priest and historian noted for his *History of the Revolutions in England under the Family of the Stuarts from 1603–1690*, and his *History of the Revolutions of Spain;* Abbé Vertot (Aubert Vertot d'Aubeuf) followed a similar pattern in his *History of the Revolutions of Sweden.* One assumes that the Abbé O'Kelly planned to study the history of Ireland, using the revolutions and invasions in Ireland as his focal point as did the two previously mentioned writers.

229. To Dr. John Curry

OCD, 8.3 HS 026

7 May 1772

. . . Major Vallancey is engaged on a philosophical work relating to our ancient language. He has been long in this study, and is now collating our Irish Celtic with the *Punic* speech in the *Poenulus* of Platus. He has sent me a specimen which amazed me. Some sentences in that Carthaginian speech (not withstanding the corruptions of ignorant transcribers) can be plainly understood by a tolerable Irish scholar; I have been urgent with that gentleman to proceed in his collation; and if he has the success to hit off but a few more sentences, he will have the merit of making one of the noblest discoveries in the annals of ancient literature. It will, beyond contradiction, show the early use of letters in Ireland. It will account for the name of Phenii or Phoenicians, which our ancient inhabitants retained in all ages; and it will show that our ancestors, while living on the continent of Spain, had a continued intercourse, nay were mixed, with the Phoenicians who possessed the maritime provinces of that country. . . .

230. To Dr. John Curry

OCD, 8.3 HS 026

26 May 1772

. . . I think with you (that in his last volume) Lord Lyttleton is a little prolix and digressive in some parts, but this is not the worst of the matter; I am concerned when I find a work intended for the instruction of future time and labored for that end, sprinkled here and there with facts disgraceful to our nation and yet not authentic. I once, and but once, presumed to caution his Lordship against the malicious accounts of Giraldus Cambrensis, who attended King John into Ireland and who met no doubt with some personal treatment here which incensed him against the nation. He was such a man as Burnet,[1] who made history subservient to his passions and set down what they dictated with little regard to truth. Yet this disclaimer (for he was a wit also) who by Lord Lyttleton's own confession merits no faith relatively to his invectives against Henry II is his Lordship's principal voucher with regard to the state of character of this nation in the twelfth century. Take on instance, *instar ominum*,[2] of Giraldus's indifference as to the facts. He gives us a letter from Dermot,[3] King of Leinster, to Roderick[4] in the following terms, "I will not," says he, "lay down my iron till I conquer Conaght and acquire for myself the monarchy of Ireland, which I claim from my grandfather, Murrogh O'Brian." It is impossible that Dermot would write such ridiculous stuff, for in the first place he had no such grandfather as Murrogh O'Brian, nor did any king of that name of Murrogh ever reign in Ireland. In the second, Dermot was not of the Thomond family, but of the Hy-Kinsellagh line, who governed the province of Leinster uninterruptedly for six hundred years before the time in question. Lord Lyttleton, however, adopts the account as a matter of fact (Vol. III, 62, 63, 71). . . .

1. Gilbert Burnet, Protestant Bishop of Salisbury, wrote *History of His Own Times*. *Concise DNB*, 1:173.
2. Typical of them all.   3. Dermot MacMurrough.
4. Roderick or Rory O'Conor (1116–1198), King of Connaught.

231. To Archbishop John Carpenter, at Mr. O'Brien's, George's Hill, Dublin

OCD, 8.3 HL 027

[early June 1772][1]

R[ight] R[everend] Sir,

Some time since I informed our worthy friend Dr. C[urry] that I purposed to trouble you with a letter, and I had the indiscretion to tell him at the same time that it would be a long one. I am not certain but that I now will be guilty of the greater indiscretion, that of making the habit of these trials daily since your labors have been increased, and I know how readily you can pardon the officiousness of those friends whose intentions you approve and whose weaknesses you can readily overlook. I would not trouble you with matters merely personal because I would not make you a partaker of some events which I know would be disagreeable to you. I will only inform you that I bear up against the strokes of ill fortune with fortitude and that I endeavor to make them subservient to the end which every honest man should chiefly have in view. Instead, I say, of troubling you with such matters, I proposed to amuse you with the substance of a correspondence opened between me and a select committee from the Dublin Society relatively to the ancient polity and literature of this country. They have not yet acquitted their plan as far as I can learn, but I lately had a letter from Major Vallancey (one of the principals of the Committee) with a pamphlet enclosed written by himself on the origin and antiquity of our Irish language. He labors to prove that it is a compound of the ancient Celtic and Punic, but he presses some arguments into his service that I think will desert him, though our old senachies have left us documents to show that he is right in the main. . . . These traditions[2] have been constantly and invariably retained by our senachies; they inform us further that those Phoeni and Gadelians were transplanted from Africa into Spain and from thence into Ireland. Now if these traditions relating to our original and early use of letters can be proved from an affinity between the ancient language of the Phoenicians and that spoken in Ireland, a light will be thrown on our antiquities that will not only convince but surprise the learned of Europe. Vallancey will have the credit of the first discovery, and his successors in this literary voyage will have that of adding to what he has done as well as of correcting his mistakes. I may probably (if I can spare the time) make some remarks on this work of Vallancey's, and should they be thought of any weight, they might properly come out in the *London Chronicle*.[3]

Those things may be thought, and probably enough they are, matters rather of curiosity than use. Your health is a thousand times of greater consequence to me and the public. I trust you take care of it, and I wish I may have a good account of it under your own hand. Dr. C[urry] throws me into a state of anguish by his repeated accounts of his declining fast, and I draw some consolation from a fond hope that he exaggerates. I request that you will give my affections to my worthy friend, Mr. O'Brien, Mr. Troy, Mr. Lee, and Mr. Sherlock. My brother[4] and others of his brethren are gone this week to town to assist at the election of a superior for their provincial circuit. Mr. Petit of Elphin, a very worthy person, is gone up also, and were he elected it would be reputable to Conaght and good for the whole Society. Could Mr. Sherlock speak in his favor to the gentlemen of *Adam and Eve*,[5] it would in truth be a good act, and it is from the knowledge that it would that I presume in this manner to speak out of my own sphere. I humbly beg your Grace's and his pardon for saying so much on the subject. If I am wrong, all that I have said is retracted with the greatest deference and submission. While I have life you will find me in this temper, and while it continues I shall labor to give you proofs of the affection and respect with which I am your Grace's most affectionate, obliged and obedient servant.

P.S. My good pastor who is now with me presents you with his respects.

    1. Undated.
    2. The traditions are that ancient Gaelic was a language composed of mixed dialects, one of which was Phoenician.
    3. Vallancey's *Essay on the Antiquity of the Irish Language* appeared in 1772. O'Conor then wrote *Remarks on An Essay on the Antiquity of the Irish Language* and sent it to the *London Chronicle*. Both pieces were combined into a book and reprinted. By 1818, these two pieces were in their third edition. BMCPBCE, 25:1049.
    4. Matthew, parish priest of Roscommon-town.
    5. Adam and Eve's was a Franciscan chapel. Entrance to the chapel was gained by going through a pub which bore the sign of Adam and Eve. Craig, p. 114.

232. To Colonel Charles Vallancey

RIA, Stowe MS. Bi2

Belanagare, 7 June 1772

I have delayed too long giving you my thoughts on your comparison of our Iberno-Celtic with the Punic Plautus.[1] Through my ignorance of the oriental tongues, I could be only a judge by halves; that is a very imcompetent one of so important a subject. I should at least have a tolerable idea of the genius, phraseology, and terms of the oriental dialects before I ventured to pronounce anything decisively as to the absolute identity, though I saw enough to convince me of a real affinity of our Irish with the Punic speech in Plautus. And I expect still that the identity as well as affinity will be proved to the requisite extent: I say to the requisite extent because true criticism will make ready allowances for the corruptions in Plautus's text and for some casual changes in our own language in the course of so many ages. To mark out such words in the Irish as are not of Celtic origin will hereafter be a matter of very curious inquiry. Some are Scythian, some Teutonic, but I dare say most will be found Phoenician and that the Celtic and Phoenician are the chief ingredients of the *berla teibidhe*[2] or properly the *berla fene*[3] of this country....

When I read the names of the noblemen and gentlemen who are at the head of this association, I expect a great deal from it.[4] The want of it has been long a reproach to our country, and I request that you will tender my respects to Sir Lucius O'Brien and assure him and the Committee of my readiness at all times to render them every service in my power. Under their patronage I expect that some useful discoveries will (*at last*) be made relatively to the ancient state of this country. Your grammar, as it will prove a new accession to European literature, will be a spur also to inquiry; and I would not be sorry if you kept the manuscript a few months longer under your eye, that it might come out as complete as possible. I promised you some lines out of a very poetical romance in my hands and you shall see them in Irish and English.

I am making additions and corrections to O'Brien's Dictionary and giving examples all along the margin of the meanings of words from our old poets. If I can finish this work, so far as I am able to do it, I trust that it may be hereafter of service: *facile est inventis addere*.[5] I can claim but little merit in this walk, but he that opened it and brought it to a conclusion was entitled to a great deal.

Your papers on Plautus I thought to send you by a safe hand going up from here to town. But as you require them by the post, I send you as many by this post as my franks can convey. . . .

1. Aodh de Blácam, *Gaelic Literature Surveyed* (Dublin, 1929; rpt. New York: Barnes and Noble, 1974), p. 369, mentioned Vallancey's *An Essay on the Antiquity of the Irish Language* being published in 1772. De Blácam wrote, "his extravagant theories had at least the good effect of rousing curiosity." O'Reilly, p. ccxxvii, pointed out that Vallancey was unaware of previous work done in the same field. Teige O'Neaghtan, or Norton (Tadhg ÓNeachtain), a Dublin schoolmaster, had done a collation of the Punic speech in Plautus with the Irish. The collation was done on 12 August 1742. Aodh Buidhe MacCruitin (1680–1755) and many others well into the nineteenth century propounded this Phoenician theory.

2. "The extracted language," a name for the Irish language reflecting the medieval doctrine, put forth above all in *Auraiccept na nÉces, The Poets' Primer,* ed. George Calder, that a certain Fenius Farsaid "extracted" the Irish language from the seventy-two languages that arose with the destruction of the Tower of Babel. Professor John Armstrong, Harvard University, Department of Celtic Languages and Literatures. The editors are indebted to Professor Armstrong for notes in this letter as well as for the Gaelic transcriptions.

3. "The language of the Feni," reflecting the same doctrine as *bérla teibidhe, Féni:* being a name for the Irish, taken as derived from *Fénius Farsaid.*

4. On 14 May 1772, a standing committee on antiquities was appointed by members of the Dublin Society. Besides the chairman, Sir Lucius O'Brien, the committee members were Lord Charlemont, Lord Moira, the Protestant Bishop of Cloyne, Vallancey, Dr. Leland, the Protestant Bishop of Derry, and the Speaker of the Irish House of Commons. See Gilbert, "The Streets of Dublin," p. 36.

5. It is easy to add to what has been discovered.

233. To Dr. John Curry

OCD, 8.3 HS 026

[7 June 1772]

I lately had a letter from Major Vallancey informing me that after repeated struggles and solicitations he prevailed at last with the Dublin Society to appoint a select committee from their own body to make researches into the polity, manners, and literature of the ancient inhabitants of this country.[1] Soon after, I had another letter from Dr. Leland (a member of the Committee) telling me that they were to sit weekly and hoped that I would cooperate and correspond with them. After this I received a very civil letter from the President of the Committee (Sir Lucius O'Brien) to the same purpose.[2] I replied to each testifying on my part the estimate I put upon the honor they did me and that I was ready at all times to render them any service on a subject so grateful to every Irishman, to me in particular who have been a considerable time endeavoring to gain some knowledge of it.

They are inviting the public to cooperate by discovering to the Committee any valuable old manuscripts in private hands. I advised them also that it would be proper to open a correspondence with the Keepers of Public Libraries in England and France....

I have perused the *weighty* reasons of several members of our own House of Commons against passing the Mortgage Bill.[3] ...

1. O'Conor had written Vallancey about the price asked for the manuscript of *Ogygia Vindicated*. Vallancey replied that the new antiquary committee could raise the amount needed to buy the manuscript. Colonel Charles Vallancey to Charles O'Conor, 25 April 1772, Stowe MS. Bi2, RIA. See also *DJ*, 21–23 May 1772.

2. Sir Lucius congratulated O'Conor on his service to the history and antiquities of Ireland. He asked O'Conor on behalf of the Antiquarian Committee of the Dublin Society if O'Conor would be correspondent to the Committee. Sir Lucius O'Brien to Charles O'Conor, 26 May 1772, Stowe MS. Bi2, RIA.

3. Monck Mason introduced a Mortgage Bill in the Irish Parliament in 1772. The bill carried in the Irish Parliament and in the Irish Privy Council, but was quashed in England. Lord Townshend opposed the bill, writing on 10 April 1772 that it "tended to revive an influence which it had been the study of the legislature to destroy." Lecky, 2:192–193.

234. To Dr. John Curry

OCD, 8.3 HS 026

[12 June 1772]

... I really think that no service was intended our people by the bills brought into Parliament to give them security for lent money and a liberty of taking long leases in corporate towns. The sickly state of public credit and indeed the improbability that one part of the nation can thrive without the assistance of the other has produced those bills. But prejudice yielded to interest very unwillingly in framing them, and, therefore, such clauses were tacked as rendered them dangerous to our best principle. The most unalterable in their ill-will to us have on this occasion proved our best friends, and they will doubtless on the next trial serve us in the same manner, though at their own expense and at the expense of the nation. Oaths of allegiance to the Establishment our people have already and repeatedly offered whenever they are called upon to give such a test, but no oaths will do; the Pope can dispense with all oaths; to what purpose then should we offer ourselves, uncalled upon, to give a test in which they say we are insincere.

235. To Dr. John Curry

OCD, 8.3 HS 026

From the Hermitage, 21 August 1772

... I lately had a letter from Major Vallancey with his pamphlet on the origin and antiquity of the Irish language enclosed therein. He has thrown out a hard crust for the reviewers, and if they do mange softly, the tooth of criticism will, I think, run some hazards. The writer was much warmed with the discoveries which he has made or thinks he made. In my thought, he has succeeded happily in some. I told him my mind candidly. Like Columbus he will tempt many to follow him in his literary voyage; and probably I shall spend some thoughts on the subject (that I may clap a spur on some new adventure) to the publisher of the *London Chronicle*. For some days past I have done wonders as haymaker. ...

236. To Dr. John Curry, Cow Lane, Dublin

OCD, 8.3 HS 026

31 October 1772

My Dear Sir,

I return you much warm thanks for the part of the new history you sent me from pp. 88 to 137.¹ There is a chasm of 29 pages, the rest to p. 192 is complete as to the succession of pages, though not as to the succession of facts, for some are omitted that are undoubtedly of importance. In his account of De Courcy's² invasion of Conaght in 1186, his neglect of several particulars is a proof of his writing in too much haste. The operations on both sides ought to be more fully described. The characters of Donall O'Brian³ and of Conor Monmoy (Roderick's son) ought to be marked with some historical attention due to their rank and the abilities of marches, countermarches, and encampments of the contenders. Some short account should be given, but the whole is hurried in a too short and too general account; nor is it sufficient to say in justification of the author that such particulars are of no consequence at this distance of time, for though it be true in general that minute details of those times of anarchy are now disgustful, yet some particular transactions that lead to the forwarding or retarding revolutions in the civil state of a nation ought never to be run over in a careless manner. On the contrary, they should be marked with great attention that the reader may be interested in the event and that his disgust in viewing a perpetual change of the actors without any change in the scene may be removed. I could give over instances of the historian's hurry, and indeed of his inaccuracies, but that the matter I have pointed at will be sufficient to *you*. As is to the latter part of the work wherein the writer finds himself under a party and even personal obligation to gratify the passions of men in power we have no more to say but that he resigns his literary merit and all credit with impartial men in favor of present advantages either within his grasp or within his expectations. Such a man's injury to himself will last as long as his book; his injury to truth will be of short duration. Don't you believe now that you had an impulse in some measure unaccountable to yourself when some years since you turned your attention to the more important part of our national history? Can anything fall out more opportunely for the present and future time than your being prepared and armed at all points to foil every modern adversary to the historical justice due to your native country? *Macte tua vir-*

tute.⁴ But your virtue cannot be fully enjoyed by yourself nor in any degree by your countrymen unless you publish the services you have rendered them. Let it be done immediately and as fair a page (by all means) as the adversary specimen you sent me. Let a particular attention be given to the unfair apology for the massacre in the peninsula of Magee, and let the *astutia historica* of Mr. Hume and of our more late historians be detected. You have no measures to keep but with truth alone; you can pour a flood of daylight upon it, and you hazard nothing but your health, which you know how to preserve by a proper intermission in labors which are almost at an end. I have been frequently urgent with you on this head, nor am I now sorry, but greatly pleased that your researches have not been put to press till you were in possession of the spirit and tendency of the new history even before its publication. It gives you a double advantage as it will render your investigations more complete and clap a spur to your side while you are making them so. Let me solicit you no longer on the subject of your *opus magnum*. The secret of it is only known to me and one or two other friends. Why do you not impart it to Dr. Carpenter, who loves you most sincerely? He would oblige you to part with a work to which the public has, at present, a better right than yourself, and he would recommend it also to negotiate the publication in London with some popular bookseller for your own advantage. Sure I am that were I not bound hand and foot, I would venture to communicate this matter to our dear friend, but since I must be mute, I request you will immediately open it to him yourself, and surely the respect due to his judgment as well as character demands it. To his most friendly incitements are owing what I have been doing for some time (by snatches, indeed) in historical researches. My materials, like my abilities, are scanty, but I will not cease doing as much as I can through the course of interruptions to which you are in a good degree no stranger. By the way, I have lately written some observations on Vallancey's essay on the origin and antiquity of the Irish language; far from being as they should be, yet I have ventured them out of my hands in the present form, and you may smile in finding this essay come out (anonymously) in one of the *London Chronicles*, but all this *tibi soli*.⁵

You may seem displeased that I have communicated some anecdotes to the author of the new history. I should set you right as to that particular. He neither required nor wanted any documents relatively to times from the accession of James I, but he wanted to know what the Irish annalists have recorded in the reign of Queen Elizabeth and some antecedent reigns. I have translated some of the more important facts preserved by the Four Masters in the sixteenth and in some prior centuries; what use he made of those documents I know not. I am afraid very little, and if I am right in this conjecture, he is certainly under no great obligation to me.

I shall be impatient to hear of the success of my importunities with you relatively to your book; write to me, therefore, as soon as you can. Meantime, give my affections to your family and to our dear Dr. Carpenter. That this scroll may cost you nothing but the trouble of reading it, I sent it by my friend Mr. Luke Ferral,[6] attorney in William Street. I need not tell you I love and shall ever love you. I will, therefore, conclude in my usual manner.

1. Leland's *History of Ireland from the Reign of Henry the Second*. . . . Dr. John Curry to Charles O'Conor, 30 September and 10 October 1772, Stowe MS. B12, RIA.
2. John de Courcy became justiciar of Ireland in 1185; his territory was carved out in Ulster. Leland appears to be at fault in his date 1186 for de Courcy's invasion. A modern historian writes, "The following year 1188 saw continuing disturbance in Donegal, and de Courcy's Ultonian host marched across Armagh towards Dungannon but was worsted by Donal MacLoughlin. De Courcy himself hosted into Connacht and turned north to Ballysadare with the intention of falling on Donegal. When, however, it became clear that it would be no walkover, he again changed front but while traversing the Curlew Mountains was attacked by the Connacht army and only extricated himself with difficulty and after suffering heavy losses." Michael Dolley, *Anglo-Norman Ireland* (Dublin: Gill and Macmillan, 1972), p. 93.
3. Donal Mór O'Brien was king of Munster and a notable warrior. He died in 1194. In 1189 Conor O'Conor was murdered by members of his household. Dolley, pp. 97, 94, respectively.
4. Well done!   5. To you alone.
6. Luke Ferral was the attorney who handled O'Conor's defense against Hugh O'Conor's Discovery Suit in 1777.

237. To Archbishop John Carpenter

OCD, 8.3 HS 026

[From the Hermitage, 9 December 1772]

Right Reverend Sir,

As your station has subjected you to various and frequent correspondence, it has in consequence increased your labors. This I well know, and discretion has often arrested my hand from filling the crowd when I reflected how much you had to do and how little I had to say unless I gave you impertinent information of my affections or a needless profession of respect I owed you. . . . Though even a stranger to me should sit in his chair. Since I mention that holy man (the first who received the pall for Dublin),[1] I cannot forbear comparing the resemblance between your situation and his. He received very little out of the temporalities of his see, and what he did was employed for the good of a people rent by factions and debased by immoralities. He had some rebellious clergy to govern, and he endeavored to win rather than force them to their duty. He had sweetness to relax, but occasionally he had courage to enforce what time and circumstances demanded in the exertion of his authority. As he was persecuted by the jealousy of the English monarch to whose government he submitted, so are you by the jealousy of the present laws. He labored and so do you for the peaceable conduct of the people God has entrusted to your care; though he was not rewarded by men in power, yet he was respected by them, and that to my knowledge is precisely your case. He lived poor, but not in want as a man of his character could have hardly any wants; the same may certainly be said of you. He had not a groat to dispose of on the day of his death, a circumstance in which I would be far from wishing the resemblence complete in you, who want more than he did a subsidium for age and accidents. I have in this retirement seen an *Address* from our people to the late Lord Lieutenant.[2] It was perhaps proper; however some discontented with the administration may dislike it. It conveys a prescription and surely a strong one that he who did not bear hard on a people obnoxious to their laws could not be less favorable (on every account) to those who had the laws on their side. Praised be to God, through instructions and those of your brethren our people know and practice the duties they owe to the government God has set over them, whether it enforces or withdraws the penalties of law. Punishment without a crime bears hard, no doubt, on our human nature, yet what consolation must it be that conscience pronounces us innocent and that our reward will be more than a counterbalance to our sufferings! But enough of this.

    I usually conveyed my affections to you through the hands of our dear, most valuable friend. Since his late trial (the account of which I had from the newspapers) I had no courage to write to him. I should mix only my own tear with his or throw out untimely commonplace topics of duty which no man knows better than himself. To you he will listen as to a father on the occasion; and you will, I trust in God, restore him to his fireside. He will not reject the consolation which religion offers, and next to that he should partake even of the means which natural wisdom suggested even to heathens. Tacitus makes mention of a great Roman who on such a sop returned to public occasions that he might cheat the anguish of his mind in the discharging of his office, *pro solaciis negotia quaerens*.[3] He should, as far as his health can admit (and by his health may be the better), go about and visit his friends and patients more than ever. I request you will acquaint him with my thoughts as well as feelings. . . .

From the Hermitage, 9 December 1772

1. St. Laurence O'Toole.
2. *DJ*, 12–14 November 1772:

Yesterday the following Address of the Roman Catholics of the Kingdom of Ireland was presented to his Excellency, the Lord Lieutenant General, and General Governor of Ireland.

"May it please your Excellency:

"We, his Majesty's most dutiful and faithful subjects, the Roman Catholics of his kingdom of Ireland do with the greatest respect approach your Excellency, the illustrative representative of the best of kings, with our sincerest acknowledgement of the LENITY extended to us during your Excellency's administration, and we consider it a duty incumbent on us to make you this tender of our general thanks before your departure from this kingdom. We most earnestly beseech your Excellency on your return to the Royal Presence to represent us to his Majesty of our most firm and steady resolutions to preserve in the same loyal disposition, and that every act of ours shall always tend to the tranquility of this kingdom, and the support of his Majesty's person and government.

"We humbly hope, my Lord, that our conduct for near a hundred years may be admitted as a proof of the sincerity of our present declarations and obtain for us some relaxation of those restrictions which have hitherto disabled us from cooperating with the rest of our fellow subjects to the improvement of this our common country.

"That eminent honors may ever grace your Excellency's distinguished merit, is the ardent wish of your Excellency's most dutiful and devoted servants.

"Signed by order,
"Owen Hogan
"Agent."

George Faulkner made the following corrections after the Address: "The following address, we are assured, was not drawn up by an attorney, nor was the meeting on Sunday, but on Monday, nor were there any disputes among the gentlemen on that occasion, everything being very decent and polite."

3. Seeking comfort in keeping busy.

238. To Dr. John Curry

OCD, 8.3 HS 026

[26 December 1772]

This letter is an exhortation to Curry to finish the book he is writing:

You love your religion and the public; you have made all your studies sufficient to the good of both. I hope, therefore, that you now have returned to your former occupation or rather duty, and the more from the efforts made and making to lead the public astray. You can, if you persist in finishing what is almost completed, level all the entrenchments thrown up by prejudice and error. Let it be done immediately and let me end with an advice to you from a very able man: *Tu ne cede malis, sed contra audentior ito.*[1]

1. Virgil, *Aeneid*, 6.95. "Do not yield to evils, but go against them more boldly."

239. To Dr. John Curry

OCD, 8.3 HS 026

1 January 1773

My Dear Friend,

In a letter dated the 26th ultimo I received a circumstantial detail of the proceedings previous to the measure of presenting our new Viceroy[1] with an "Address from the Roman Catholics of Ireland." I request you will present my warmest affections to Mr. C[omerfor]d for the satisfaction as arises chiefly from the accuracy, precision, and even elegance of his account. In other respects much of the narrative gave me disgust, and I still wonder at the happy event, how the good sense of a few overrode all the embarrassments which nonsense heaped on so just a measure.[2] I liked the address presented to the late Viceroy, nor need I repeat here what I have already communicated on the subject to our most reverend friend.[3] Much has been claimed on the impropriety of not concerting that address with our landed gentry; but if it contained *their* sense, the offense was not great. Had they taken the lead in such a measure, the citizens would go more than halfway to meet them. Why did they not? Would that and the latter address ever appear if those citizens were equally indifferent and inactive as their brethren? I am afraid not. It is fortunate, however, that our differences have arisen entirely from the *manner,* not from the *matter* in which our civil principles should be conveyed, and I trust that what has passed so ridiculously on this subject will never transpire but be buried in eternal silence. Were our adversaries in possession of the details now before me, you may easily conceive how welcome the account would be and what use they would have made of it. The late Address came from a masterly hand. It is declarative of the eagerness of our people to give a satisfactory *test* of their loyalty if ever called upon to do so. It insinuates in the strongest terms that a religion imposing *civil* duty is useful, not detrimental *to civil* government; that to tolerate such a religion is an act of wisdom and to tie up the hands of all its votaries a perfect solecism in politics. In a word, this excellent Address insinuates that however prejudice may make exceptions to the religious conscience of those people; yet that instead of making any to their political conscience, this [unreadable] prejudice must extol and appove it. I mean only the prejudice of sensible men, not the rancor of men destitute of sense and knowledge. I would wish that the latter formed the minority among us. Like the preachers on certain anniversaries, they will fasten on our religion the mistakes of some enthusiasts and overlook the multitude who had no concern in the overt acts of such men except that of censuring them, but *magna est veritas*.[4] Truth will, one time or other, prevail; and if it does not prevail in ours, let us turn our punishment to account and offer it along with active efforts of contrition as an expiation for our many sins.

People here as well as with you in the city make the administration of the late viceroy a topic of conversation. In a mixed society some time since, one gentleman advanced that the Lord Lieutenant was attended to the waterside with acclamations of the people; "Yes," said a certain dignified parson, "he was huzzaed by the Papists." "Pray, sir," said another gentleman, "what particular service has Lord Townshend rendered the Papists, or were there none to wish him a prosperous voyage but such as never shared of his bounties?" The reverend dignitary made no reply for a good reason, no doubt, and it will not pose you, I believe, to find it out.

Packets of weekly printed libels poured down upon us thrice a week in the provinces have stirred up discontents in the minds of many. Those libels, like some of your medicines, may lose their effect by frequent repetition; or if they should operate still, is it not a great fortune that one half of our people, at least, will be quite clear of all contagion? The discontented *must* remain quiet. Administrations can never be opposed or distressed under such circumstances, and I ventured to advance all this to one of my Protestant correspondents.

I request you will present my most cordial affection to our dear reverend friend, to your whole family, to Mr. C[omerford] and his brother, no less to Jenny Reynolds, etc. May this new year be a happy one to each of them. Some ten days ago I wrote a long letter upon an affair important to you, to me, to the public; I will not repeat here what I have urged so strongly already.

1. Lord Harcourt became lord lieutenant 29 October 1772. *HBC*, p. 991.
2. On 26 December 1772, John Comerford wrote O'Conor that Curry and James Reynolds had prepared an address to Lord Townshend, who was "worried by a set of men who are our sworn enemies." Although the address was not supported by the

Catholic Committee, it was well received. Consequently the two men are now framing an address to the new Viceroy. Sheehan, p. 478.
3. Archbishop Carpenter.
4. 3 Esdras, 4:41. "Truth is mighty and will prevail."

240. To Dr. John Curry

OCD, 8.3 HS 026

[9 February 1773]

My Dear Sir,

What can a man remit from such a solitude as I live in? Can the idleness of setting on paper, *quicquid in buccam venerit*,[1] be any entertainment for a citizen who has employment for every hour that passes over him? No, it will hardly afford you even amusement. I have written this day a long letter to Dr. Carpenter to account, not to apologize for my silence for a month past since the apology to be made should be for staining paper with professions of affection which my friend did not want and which indeed are impertinent when unattended with anything else. However, I have searched every recess of my mind to get rid of my barrenness. I hinted that the good done or rather the evil avoided by the late and seasonable conduct of our people that have seen storms which our former prudence helped to dissipate and that the present fair weather made for us should be improved also by our clergy and gentry, as to give an insurance of its continuous or perhaps a prospect of some emancipation from grievances which it is not in the power of administrations to remove. I also informed him of the information I had from Vallancey that the *Select Committee* expressed a wish that he should do them the honor of being one of their corresponding members and that my reply included that I believed the labor of his other occupations would not admit of all the attention necessary for such a correspondence, but that I doubted not but he would supply them with historical documents if any such worthy of notice fell in his way. I also informed him that the Committee have perused and approved Mr. O'Flaherty's *Ogygia Vindicated,* that they recommended the publication to me and that I should write such notes on the work as might explain the obscure or correct the fabulous which should be found in it.[2] Had I thought the work could answer the expense, I wanted to undertake it, and I see no other method of safety but proposing the publication by subscription and returning the money if this subscription did not fill so as to save the editor.

I would, I own, be the fonder of engaging in this affair, as I could with great propriety find room for a work of my own against the *two MacPhersons* who have declared war and committed all the hostility they could against me. You will very reasonably think that *our* public will have no relish for a controversial debate of old times which no way concerns the present. In most things the public taste must quiet us, and I shall on that account be the more careful not to engage in any business hurtful to my health or family. Write if you can by the next post.

I am pleased much that you have established a new committee of our people; and, please God, before it be a fortnight about I shall be among you.³ It should be comprised chiefly of men of industry who bear the *pondus diei aestus*,⁴ who have more Catholicity and better sense than those who live by *no industry* but greatly at their ease. I once spoke to a gentleman of zeal and parts of the lukewarmness of those gentry. "Be not surprised," said he. "*A man of £2,000 a year in fee simple is no Papist at all; the Penal Laws against Catholics don't affect him, and he is exempt from many expensive occupations to which Protestants are exposed.*" What we are to do is to keep such gentry in the best temper we can, give them more weight than they really deserve, and interest in our cause by every incitement such among them as have merit. God bless and preserve you and your worthy family at home and abroad. You forgot to give me any account of Thady and Frank, and that I know it was forgetfullness you should have run a bill of complaint against you. My paper is out; *et tant mieux peut-être pour vous.*⁵

1. Whatever comes to mind.
2. Vallancey wrote O'Conor on 23 January and informed him that the Select Committee had received the manuscript of O'Flaherty's *Ogygia Vindicated* that O'Conor had obtained and that the Committee had decided to sponsor its publication. Vallancey asked O'Conor to prepare an appendix, Stowe MS. B12, RIA.
3. A second general Committee was formed 20 January 1772 under the auspices of Lord Kenmare. Its minute book from 1773 to 1792 is printed in *Archivium Hibernicum*, 9 (1942), 1–172. "The first three leaves (and four others in the body of the Ms. and two at the end) are now missing and a new book would appear to have been acquired soon after August 1772. . . ." "Introduction," p. 1.
4. "The burden of the heat of the day."
5. And so much the better perhaps for you.

241. To Archbishop John Carpenter, at Mr. O'Brien's, George's Hill, Dublin

OCD, 8.3 HS 026

[From the Hermitage, 9 February 1773]

Most Reverend Sir,

I would have acknowledged your Grace's most kind letter of the first ultimo earlier had I not hopes I should have something to communicate within the month better than a repetition of obligations I owed or of the feelings they produced. Entitled as I really am to the merit of a grateful friend, I should not be pleading it too often before real friends who never disputed my claim. I would gladly interpose some other matter to cover the seeming affection of acknowledging debts and of lamenting the want of less equivocal proofs than bare words in the discharge of them. It is, indeed, by the former proofs I would wish to be tried, nor should I be concerned in being told that I am greatly interested in standing such a trial wherein my heart would league with my friends in acquiting me. It is my highest interest to have and deserve the good will of good men, nor shall I ever forfeit my right to the possessions I took of a few, however gratuitously they have yielded it to me hitherto. I covet greatly to have it known (after these eyes are closed) that I have been noticed by men eminent from the dignity of their stations and still more so from the virtues with which they fitted them. I have been many years in possession of Dr. Curry's friendship; I enjoy beforehand the credit which such a friendship will spread over my grave, and I prefer it to every other inscription which the partiality of the surviving kinsman might devise. Posterity will speak of that gentleman as a champion for Catholicity and for the means of preserving it here in lukewarm and apostatizing times. He will be revered as a man of virtue and learning which employed his talents in the service of his country. I love him now, if possible, more than ever on the score of his Christian fortitude after his late severe trial: *Idem velle, idem nolle, idem sentire de republica*[1] has grafted him upon you, and am I not happy in standing by his side before you as one of those you selected for your friendship and confidence? Your rank in the Church has exposed you to great labors; praised be God, you embrace them for his glory with all the perils attending them, and your wisdom in conducting them has already engaged the attention of all parties and particularly of many of your episcopal brethren whose union with you for the good of the Church must produce consequences that could not be expected in less placable times than the present. A little sunshine from men in power is opening upon us. I remember storms from the same quarter; we improved the latter to our own great credit, and government retorted. It will require prudence and discretion to improve the former also, nor will anything (in my thought) contribute more to our quiet than the character you bear abroad and at home.

I will descend to matter of a more private nature from a confidence of your readiness to pardon my impertinence. It goes to my heart that you are made weary by the apostasy of some of your children. Nothing else can make you so, for no man alive, I believe, can overlook with more charity small failings; I mean such as may take good men by surprise. Mr. Morris, your intimate for several years, was, I am told, surprised in this manner. I wish with all my soul (for I wish him well) that he may be restored to your good graces. I have the greater satisfaction in being his advocate upon this occasion as he is quite a stranger to my interposition and never expected any from me.

In a late letter from Major Vallancy I am informed that the *Select Committee of Antiquarians* expressed a desire of your doing them the honor of being a corresponding member.[2] I replied that I believed the urgency of your affairs would hardly admit of your attention to any other, but that I doubted not of your readiness to communicate to the Society any documents relating to our ancient civil and ecclesiastical history if any such fell in your way.

They had before them for some time a manuscript entitled the *Ogygia Vindicated,* a work of the late Mr. O'Flaherty against Sir George MacKenzie. They have approved of the work and, I am told, recommended the publication of the work (with notes) to me. Their recommendation would, I own, be an inducement to me to undertake it; and, what is more, as I would annex a work of my own against this new historical hypothesis (if it be not a bull we call it historical) of the two MacPhersons. The public, I think, have not taste for our historical controversies, and for that reason [page torn] would make a trial by subscription and restore the first [page torn] subscription money if a sufficient number did not appear [torn] to answer the expense. Mr. Fitzgerald is still in this neighborhood but purposes to depart in a few days. I shall, God willing, travel up to town in his company to kiss your hand and enjoy my friends for some short time. Meantime I suggest you will present my affections to Mr. Sherlock, Mr. O'Brien, Mr. Troy, Mr. Lee, etc.

From the Hermitage, 9 February 1773

1. "To wish the same thing, to oppose the same thing, to feel the same thing about the state."
2. Also asked to be members of the Antiquities Committee were Archbishop Carpenter and Dr. Sylvester O'Halloran. The committee completed its work on 24 September 1774. Gilbert, "The Streets of Dublin," p. 37n.

242. To Dr. John Curry

OCD, 8.4 HS 141

[1772/1773][1]

... By the way, I am now writing observations on Vallancy's essay on the origin and antiquity of our old Irish language. I put them in the form of a letter to the publisher of the *London Chronicle*. Vallancey shall see them, and should he dislike them, they shall be ferreted as I have no call upon me to make any remarks on his book without his own permission.

The sheets you are reviewing give an unfavorable construction (you say) of the tender of loyalty made by the Catholics of Ireland in 1639.[2] In this instance there is no room left for *historical fraud*, a fraud which Lord Castlehaven endeavored to anticipate in the preamble to his book,[3] though Catholic members in Wentworth's Parliament[4] (I may call it such) were mostly of the old English race, of different political principles from their old Irish brethren. There was a mistrust between both (the consequences of old animosities) which no quantity of religious principles could remove. To tax the former with insincerity because the Irish, dispossessed of six counties by James I, were not so thoroughly attached to the son of their destroyer is confounding things which ought to be kept separate and making a poor but foul use of the equivocation in the word *Catholic*. ... Sir Phelim O'Neill[5] and others endeavored in one desperate plunge to shake off the oppression and the oppressors they so long groaned under. The general defection in 1642, that is the necessity which all the Catholics found themselves under to take part with the old Irish they disliked, was entirely owing to the wicked administration of Borlase and Parsons[6] and to the edicts of destruction published by the English Commons. This you have proved and will still prove more fully in the work now in your closet. ...

1. Although the editors had thought this letter to be "1773," they now believe it to be 1772. However, in order not to disturb the chronology the editors have left it in its present position. The following reasons for believing that the letter was written a year earlier than was previously thought are these: 1. "Remarks on an *Essay on the Antiquity of*

the Irish Language . . . addressed to the Printer of the *London Chronicle* . . ." appeared in 1772 and was reprinted with Vallancey's *Essay* in 1818, *BMCPBCE*, 25:1049; the historian about whom O'Conor is speaking is Dr. Leland, and the pamphlet is Curry's *Occasional Remarks on Certain Passages in Dr. Leland's History Relating to the Irish Rebellion in 1641.*

2. In the following two paragraphs O'Conor is discussing the events which preceded the Rebellion of 1641. Hugh Oge O'Conor's participation in this revolution resulted in the confiscation of the O'Conor lands. When the war against the Scots began in 1639, Parliament was summoned and the Irish vowed their complete loyalty to England and voted subsidies of £200,000 over three years. For a fuller account of these years see Curtis, pp. 240–245; Matthew O'Conor, *History of the Irish Catholics* . . . p. 28ff; and Charles Owen O'Conor, *The O'Conors of Connaught,* pp. 242ff.

3. James Touchet, third earl of Castlehaven (1617?–1684), published his *Memoirs* in 1680. *Concise DNB,* 1:1307. O'Conor edited these *Memoirs* in 1753.

4. The Wentworth Parliament met from 1633 to 1635.

5. Sir Phelim O'Neill (1604?–1653) of Kinard or Caledon in Armagh led the Rebellion of 1641. Curtis, pp. 231, 243–4. *Concise DNB,* 1:976.

6. Sir John Borlase (1576–1648) and Sir William Parsons (1570?–1650), both appointed Lords Justice in 1640. According to Curtis, "Their rule was destined to be most disastrous and to drive Irish Roman Catholics, even of the most loyal type, into rebellion," p. 243. *Concise DNB,* 1:124,1009.

243. To Denis O'Conor

OCD, 8.3 SE 028

From Anderson's Court, 9 March 1773

. . . I lately sat with the Committee of Antiquarians and introduced Dr. Carpenter to them. He was received with great respect: a revolution in our moral and civil affairs the more extraordinary, as in my own days such a man would only be spoken to through the medium of a warrant and constable. I am well, too well perhaps, treated here by the *literati* especially, and this day I am to dine with Dr. Leland. . . .

244. To Denis O'Conor

OCD, 8.3 SE 028

16 March 1773

. . . Dr. Carpenter and I being elected to the Select Committee, we sat there for the first time last week, the Earl of Moyra in the chair. I was greatly pleased on my presenting the Archbishop that great respect was shown to him. The Society have entered into resolutions too long to be inserted here and are to meet again the 4th of April. I have lately dined at the tables of several of those gentlemen and am much obliged to them on the score of civilities. I have paid 5 s.5 for *Ellis on Sheep,* etc. It is an excellent work which you should study with assiduity. . . .

245. To Denis O'Conor

OCD, 8.3 SE 028

Anderson's Court, 20 April 1773

Here alone yesterday I received yours and Hugh's letter with the sad tidings of my sister's death. I started up and wept; indeed I am now weeping, but it is only an overpouring of nature and will soon be over. She was a plain woman, but one of the best I ever knew. Her death must quicken my pace to Conaght.[1] . . .

1. Although O'Conor does not mention the name of his deceased sister her name was either "Molly" or Maud, two of the three sisters of Charles mentioned in Charles O'Conor, S.J. "Charles O'Conor of Belanagare, An Irish Scholar's Education," *Studies,* 23 (March 1934), p. 139.

246. To Dr. John Curry, Cow Lane, Dublin

OCD, 8.3 HS 026

From the Hermitage, 3 June 1773

My Dear Sir,

I was here but two nights after I parted you when affairs of my late sister's orphans hurried me into the county of Galway. When I returned (three days since), I found your letter and one enclosed from Dr. B before me.[1] At first perusal I was equally incensed with you at the contents. The next reading produced melancholy reflections in my mind. Here we have the remains of an ancient people who forfeited all power and property in their native country for their adherence to the Catholic religion. The bondage, the repeated calamities of two hundred years' persecution could not shake them in the best of their principles. Their obedience to the government which punished them made men in power relent at last towards them, and some signs of a relaxation of the Penal Laws began to appear. You and other zealous Catholics labored to show that nothing in the religion or principles of this ill-fated people could hinder the operation of such good intentions. What was the consequence?—A divine,[2] eminent from his rank in the Church, took the alarm and leagued with our most hardened enemies to prevent any relaxation whatever of those legal severities which, by fatiguing our people, have already produced so many apostasies among us. Doctrines unknown in the first millenium of God's Church and reprobated, I may say, among all modern Catholic nations are trumped up in this poor country and fastened upon us as our true principles! Has the abettor of such doctrines any reason to apprehend any danger from our inveterate enemies? No, truly, but thus he is entitled to and he will obtain their warmest thanks for furnishing them with barbed arrows to fasten in our sides. He will be quoted as the *honest man* who published the *real* principles of the Irish Papists without disguise, and I know not what our friends in both houses of Parliament (if any we have) could have to oppose to such popular misrepresentations from friends and foes united. Ghillini (my correspondent, tells me) is only the organ of the College of *Propaganda Fide,* and he adds that Dr. Hervey knew well that the test he proposed to some of our people here was but a mockery as he previously knew that it would be censured in the *Vatican,* but all this stuff includes a poor fallacy: there indeed might be some exception taken to the *manner* but not the *matter* of the *Test* then proposed. If any word seemingly disrespectful to the Holy See transpired, it should certainly be rescinded, but the substance of the oath was Catholic in the mean; and if it was, no excommunication would lie. Very possibly we will not be soon called upon in any country to give *any test* of fidelity to our Protestant government, and it may be so best for some time at least to avoid scandal; but in fact, were such a test called for, I would say in the words of old Chrisostom, "*Melius est ut scandalum oriatur, quam ut veritas relinquatur.*"[3] The measures of obedience to the Holy See are not irreconcilable with those due to secular princes; they are too well known in the present age to be overturned or confounded by the Ghillinis of Rome or Ireland. This knowledge may, I confess, produce no effects on determining adversaries here at home. But let us acquit ourselves. The rest must be left to Providence.

My Lord of Ossory tells me there are more provoking sentences to Protestants in our catechisms than any in Ghillini's letter, and he strangely instances in our pronouncing a sentence of damnation against heretics. Was ever any position more impertinent? Has such a *sentence* one title in common with the affairs of civil government? Have not the Protestants themselves adopted that *damnatory* sentence by taking the *Athanasian Creed* into their liturgy? Have they not ratified it by an act of Parliament? Do they not profess solemnly that the disbelievers of that creed will be damned eternally?

"We ought," he says, "to banish out of our minds all thoughts of applications and religious tests." I apprehend, on the contrary, that it is our duty to declare to the world what our true principles are and to renounce those frightful principles which our adversaries fasten upon us. This was the constant practice in the first ages of the Church, and truth (though after the current of some ages) triumphed at last. Is it not strange that a Catholic divine should recommend silence to us under a load of such calumnies as are everyday issued against us from the pulpit and from the press? I conclude from your short letter that you have expostulated a little with his Lordship on the subject before us. If you have, I doubt not but you have done it with temper. There is an art, though no artifice, in such a conduct toward an adversary; the form of argument will fall the heavier upon him by finding all passion weeded from it.

If Dr. Carpenter be returned from his visitation, I request you will present him with my warmest affections. Let me return the same to your whole family. Has Mr. O'Brien published his tract entrusted to his care? I long to see it as well as hear of your judgment of Dr. Leland's history, now no doubt perused by you. I must conclude that the *opus magnum* is now finished, and that it is to meet with no further delays or obstacles. In the appendix or preface it will be necessary to insert the true civil principles of British Catholics with a view *oculo retorto*[4] to Nuncio Ghillini's exploded revived doctrine.

1. Doctor "B" is Thomas deBurgo, O.P., Catholic Bishop of Ossory. In 1762 de Burgo in his book *Hibernia Dominicana* strongly opposed a similar oath. He felt Catholics should remain silent and accept what they had gained under the present government. *HBC* p. 405; Lecky, 2 : 196. See letters 249 and 250.
2. The Protestant Bishop of Derry, Frederick Augustus Hervey, while in Rome proposed to the Catholic Church an oath of allegiance for Irish Catholics. Tommaso Ghillini (1718–1787), Papal Nuncio to Brussels and later Cardinal (1778), apparently rejected Hervey's proposal. See *Enciclopedia Italiana di Scienze, Lettere ed Arti* (Roma: Istituto della Enciclopedia Italiana, 1949), 16:916, for fuller treatment of the Ghillini family.
3. "It is better that a scandal should arise, than that truth should be neglected."
4. Looking back.

247. To Dr. John Curry

OCD, 8.3 HS 026

Amidst many rubs of life your letters bring me great consolation. Your last has done so indeed. It came accompanied by another from

Dr. Leland. Lord Lyttleton, Mr. Burke,[1] Dr. Johnson, he tells me, have pronounced a flattering sentence on his history. It is a counterbalance to Hibernian censure which he expected and consequently was prepared for it. . . . You make me happy in assuring me that you have put the last hand to the *opus magnum*, but I must be so only by halves if you do not send me assurances (and speedily) that the work is negotiated for in London and put to the press.[2] . . .

P.S. Instead of obtaining the Prebend of Rathmichael and Rectory of Bray (worth £500 per annum) Dr. Leland is obliged to sit down with the curacy of St. Anne's, Dublin, worth little more than £100 a year. He calls it such an exchange as Glaucus made with Diomed (in the 6th *Iliad*),[3] and it is in truth a proof that literary merit *alone* stands a man in little stead in the present times. Dr. Domville has obtained the prebend and rectory above mentioned, for he can throw weight by his family connections into the political side. . . . Meantime, I request you will send me a copy of the *Remarks* as soon as the 250 copies you mention arrive;[4] they will certainly be remarked upon; and therefore, you ought to prepare a defense. . . .

1. On 9 November 1771 Burke expressed his confidence in Leland's ability to write an Irish history free of bias. Later (letter to his son Richard, 20 March 1792) Burke expressed his disappointment in Leland's history. Burke wrote, " . . . when he began to write history, he thought only of himself and his bookseller. . . ." *Burke*, 2:285.

2. The medical work on which Curry had been working for several years was now ready. *BMCPBCE* 6:745 lists it as *Some Thoughts on the Natures of Fevers; on the Causes of Their Becoming . . . Mortal, and on the Means to Prevent it*. (London: J. Johnson, 1774).

3. Glaucus exchanged armor with Diomedes as a sign of friendship, but Glaucus got the worst of the bargain because his sword was gold and that of Diomedes was bronze. *Iliad*, 6:234–6. *The Oxford Classical Dictionary*, p. 388.

4. Faulkner printed the three volumes of Leland's *History of Ireland from the Reign of Henry the Second* . . . for R. Moncrief. Curry read the material and became dissatisfied with Leland's interpretation. Consequently, he contracted in London to publish a pamphlet entitled *Occasional Remarks on Certain Passages in Dr. Leland's History of Ireland Relative to the Irish Rebellion of 1641*. It was published in London in late 1773. The University of Illinois Library has a copy of the book. *DJ*, 25–27 May 1773.

248. To Colonel Charles Vallancey

RIA, Stowe MS Bi2

[25 September 1773]

. . . I shall with pleasure look over the new treasures brought you by Mr. Gardiner.[1] It is, I find, a miscellaneous work containing, I believe, many old documents in my own possession. The *tegusc flatha* of

Corbmhac ua Cuind is indeed an invaluable acquisition to Irish literature;[2] if it be the genuine work of that monarch, the evidences of originality on the face of it will not escape you; should it, however, bear the marks of a modern composition and imposition, it must be laid aside.

I have told you long since that your *Essay* would engage the attention of the Celtic literati of foreign countries;[3] and, as they are by no means in possession of your knowledge, I do not wonder at their mistakes. You will certainly set Bullet right in numberless places and tempt him to a new edition of his Dictionary, especially if you should previously publish an Irish dictionary for which you have collected excellent materials. . . .

I am sorry to find your learned friend Governor Pownall[4] is running into an indefensible extreme also, relatively to the writings of Moses. Nor he, nor Voltaire, nor Hume himself will depreciate a work on which our Divine Master has clapped his seal on many occasions and in one extraordinary instance particularly: *Dar ndóich (a chara) ataoi níos mó na sáith bídh & dighe agad do gach aoidhidh taoi ҫho húaigneach ris an tShaxanach & ris an bfhrancach ar a labhrann tú.*[5]

I have put the last hand, or what I must call such, to the *Memoir*[6] which you will soon see. I subdivide it into five sections addressed to the President. . . .

1. On 14 September 1773, Vallancey wrote to O'Conor that "Charles Gardiner has lately brought me an invaluable ms. from the North." *RIA*, Stowe MS. B12.
2. Dr. O'Conor listed the manuscripts that his grandfather had collected. He described this manuscript thus: "An abstract of the Teagusg Flatha attributed to Cormac O'Cuinn, King of Ireland, and transcribed in 1396. Mr. O'Conor collated it with an ancient copy in Colonel Vallancey's possession, the cast of the phraseology shows that it is very ancient." Reverend Charles O'Conor, D.D., *Memoirs of the Late Charles O'Conor*, p. 258.
3. Vallancey had previously published an *Essay on the Antiquity of the Irish Language*. *DJ*, 13–15 May 1773, advertised for sale in quarto, his *Irish-English Grammar*. . . . Vallancey wrote to O'Conor, 14 September, that the "Celtic authors of France have caught the flame" from his essay, and that both Bullet and "my friend Pownall" had disagreed with Vallancey's observations, hence the "Englishman" and the "Frenchman" O'Conor mentions in his Gaelic quote (note 5).
4. Thomas Pownall, called "Governor" Pownall (1722–1805) because of his service as governor of the Massachusetts and South Carolina colonies. He was author of twenty-five books on various subjects. *Concise DNB*, 1:1065.
5. "Of course, my friend, you have more than enough food and drink for every guest who is as distinguished as the Englishman and the Frenchman of whom you speak."
6. O'Conor's "A Short View of the Ancient State of Ireland from the Earliest Times to the Establishment of the Tuathalian Constitution."

249. To Dr. John Curry

OCD, 8.3 HS 026
Doctor Curry

2 October 1773

My Dear Sir,

I wish you great joy on the return of Frank to his native country in health. His remaining with you for some time must surely be a great comfort to you, but you omitted giving me any account of his rank in the society he is in, and you omitted further giving me any information of his brother. As I am interested much in their happiness, I must not quit my claim to information about them. I am indeed much obliged to you for the other matter you communicated, particularly the sensible and honest observations of worthy Dr. Keefe on his brother O[ssory]'s[1] conduct, principles, and publications. It is not indeed likely that our masters here will soon call upon us for a civil test of allegiance, as admitted by our religious principles. If they do not, it is, I think, better for our own quiet to be silent about the Doctor and his book than begin a fruitless schism among ourselves to make sport for our enemies.[2] If our masters were sincere in thinking we might be safely admitted into their civil commission, we might in that case give them a conviction of their being right in that idea; and should any of our own religion take pains to prevent our doing it, then St. Chrisostom's Rule might surely be a good one to be practiced: *melius est ut scandalum oriatur, quam ut veritas relinquatur.*[3] Persecution indeed may be good for us, but is it wantonly to be provoked by the publication of doctrines which plainly set the civil power at defiance? Had common prudence, common discretion, common charity any share in this late publication? But, says he, our masters are long already in possession of Ghillini's doctrines. If so, where was the occasion to take so much pains to confirm them in it, and if some doubted, as many have, among their writers, what advantage could be reaped from removing their doubts? Experience has taught us that of late these matters concern themselves but little about the real or supposed civil principles of Catholics, and the public suffers by their inattention. I dare, therefore, to be prophetical without the gift of prophecy that the inattention I mentioned will have now the only good effect that can ever be derived from it; I mean their taking no notice of the Doctor or his book. It indeed came out sixty years too late, and it is happy for our people that it did not appear from an Irish press in the days of pious Queen Anne, but so much of this.

It might indeed be of some service to you or rather to the common cause that I were near you to stop your hand from the overscrupulous corrections of your *opus magnum*,[4] especially as I am sure it wants none. As to the fruits, after so many revisions that your hands have given it, I have this day written to Dr. Carpenter requesting of him to lay his commands on you to negotiate your work immediately for your own benefit with some London bookseller. Your corrections of *minutiae* make, no doubt, many blots on your copy, and on that account I request you will employ a good clerk to copy your work fair for the press as you can not attend to all the compositor's business at so great a distance as five hundred miles. The expense will not exceed six guineas or seven at most. No man in Dublin (if he undertook it) would consider your purpose better than Mr. Martin Gavin. He might transcribe this work in his parlor ready at a call for any business in his shop. By the way, who should pay me a visit here in the Hermitage but Mr. Michael Reilly. I have employed him to copy out Mr. O'Flaherty's *Ogygia Vindicated*, etc., and half the work is now over with him. I doubt he cannot return to Dublin till he negotiates (with his creditors) the liberty of so doing. I will, God willing, see you about the end of this month, and I want to see you much as I find considerable inquiries made of late of my health.

I am in arrears to Dr. Leland and cannot expect any information from him till I discharge it. How he relishes the *Remarks* you may easily grasp.[5] My word for it, he will make no reply. How can he? I approve of your thought of writing a friend by letter to Dr. Keefe as a hero for truth. His words, quoted in your letter, are the sort that would be described by any man, and he deserves the most grateful thanks from you, me, and every Catholic, but in the present temper and constitution of legislative minds, I think all that we offer on the subject of the Doctor's book should be only whispered among ourselves. Adieu, my dear friend. Give my hearty affections to your family.

1. De Burgo, Bishop of Ossory from 1759 to 1776; James O'Keefe, Bishop of Kildare and Leighlin from 1752 to 1787. *HBC*, pp. 404, 405.
2. Bishop De Burgo in 1762 wrote *Hibernia Dominicana* in which he declared that any oath was unlawful which declared the Pope not to have temporal or civil jurisdiction within Ireland. On the other hand, O'Keefe had stated in 1757 that Irish Catholics "abjured in strongest terms the doctrine that any ecclesiastical power in the Church had the right of deposing sovereigns, absolving subjects from their oaths, making war upon heretics as such. . . ." Lecky, 1:416; 2:196, 202.
3. "It is better than a scandal should arise than that the truth should be neglected."
4. Curry's *Historical and Critical Review*. . . .

5. Curry was unhappy about Dr. Leland's treatment of the Irish revolt in 1641 in Leland's *History*. Consequently, he wrote *Occasional Remarks on Certain Passages in Dr. Leland's History of Ireland Relative to the Irish Rebellion of 1641*. It was published in London in 1773. The University of Illinois Library has a copy of the book.

250. To Archbishop John Carpenter

OCD, 8.3 HS 026

[From the Hermitage, 2 October 1773]

Most Reverend Sir,

Before the present time I thought to have the honor of waiting on your Grace in person or to have informed you why I have not done so. Indeed, I should have complied with this duty sooner than I do it now, had not our friend informed me you have considerable time where, I trust, your spiritual labors have been attended with the best of temporalities, the enjoyment of health. I derive much satisfaction from the hope that you have laid in a good stock of it to resist all the attacks of a winter in a smoky town. I intend to be there shortly to face the same danger but with the resolution of being more careful than I used to be in my younger days of guarding against it. Since I parted you, I had a letter from L[or]d O[ssor]y. He has unfolded his mind to me in the most explicit manner. "Let us," says his Lordship, "be grateful to a lenient government for the suspension of some legal severities we are exposed to, but let us at the same time suspend our own idleness in expecting any further favor. Our masters know well and have known long that the positions contained in G[hillin]i's letter are those of the Church, and this knowledge is sufficient for them to guard against any occasional profession of a different doctrine censurable in any season and useful in none." If his Lordship has not convinced me that all this is right, yet he certainly has silenced me. We have no call, nor is it likely we soon will have any from the higher powers of any test of our civil tenets as admitted by our religious principles. Let us, therefore, act as his Lordship requires till time requires our acting otherwise if such a time should ever offer.—In such a case, perhaps St. Chrisostom's rule might be a proper one, "*melius est ut scandalum oriatur, quam ut veritas relinquatur.*"[1] An important squabble on this matter at present would have no other consequence than a bad one, the making sport for our enemies, *Multa sunt toleranda propter bonum pacis speciatim in his temporibus ubi sentire proprie vales quae dicere ullo modo non licet.*[2]

I lately had the great satisfaction of remaining a whole day with our worthy Metropolitan, Dr. Skerrett.³ You are truly in possession of his warmest friendship and good wishes, and I have reason to be thankful to him. In this retreat I have drawn up a memoir divided into five sections on the ancient state of Ireland to be laid before the Committee of Antiquarians. It must be previously put into your G[race]'s hands and after perusal, I would wish you to hand it over to Vallancey and Leland that they might prepare it for its trial and add their own corrections to yours. I am in arrears to Dr. Leland for a letter and purpose now to discharge it. I have not yet seen his history but have been much pleased with the *Observations* upon an important part of it published in London. The author of the *Observations*⁴ had certainly no grievance to keep with prejudice. He and the writers of his side are the only historians who literally and in fact are free, and it is odd enough to see men otherwise possessed of every constitutional advantage gagged and bound whenever they meddle with incidents played on our stage for two hundred years past. It must be indeed a mortifying consideration for men of unique abilities to have a certainty that they do not write for posterity, and present [advantages] must be great deal to counterbalance the mortification. I received a most kind letter from our worthy friend, Dr. Curry, wherein he informs me of some reading relatively to G[hillini]'s letter and of your predecessor's prudence to a secret what is now public to the whole world; but enough on this unpleasing subject.

After his late trials, the Doctor has the consolation of seeing his son Frank, who lately arrived in Dublin to pay his parents a visit. Our friend is delaying his *opus magnum* too long and perhaps doing hurt to it by overscrupulous corrections. I would wish that he not only enjoyed the credit but also the emolument due to his labors in his lifetime. I request you will by your commands (for your recommendations are such on him) to negotiate his work immediately with some London bookseller for his own and the public benefit. You have preferred Mr. Morris, and I trust he deserves being preferred. I am vastly pleased at it as the promotion makes so amiable a feature in the history of your administration. I request you will present my affections to Mr. O'Brien, Mr. Sherlock, worthy Mrs. Troy, Mr. Lee, and other common friends.

From the Hermitage, 2 October 1773

1. "It is better that a scandal should arise than that the truth should be neglected."
2. Many things must be endured for the sake of peace especially in these times when you can feel privately things which you are not permitted to say.

3. Michael Skerrett was archbishop of Tuam from 1749 to 1785. *HBC*, p. 406.
4. Curry and O'Conor wrote *Observations on the Popery Laws* in 1771.

251. To Archbishop John Carpenter

OCD, 8.3 HS 026

From the Hermitage, 20 October 1773

Most Reverend Sir,

I send you by the bearer *the Memoir* I drew up for the censure of the Society of Antiquarians. I really had not time to annex the proper notes and authorities; that must be done as soon as I arrive (with God's good will) in town. After you peruse it, I request you will send it to Major Vallancey, who I hope will put it into Dr. Leland's hands; I would gladly have your Grace's judgment as well as theirs (nay, your several corrections also) before it is presented to the Committee. You will find the whole to be but more than anything drawn on an extensive canvas. If there be any true likeness, others may sit down to the coloring part. I met with several interruptions in the writing of this essay, and it must receive corrections still from the hand that drew it up if you all agree that it is worthy of publication. I say no more of it. I trust that this paper will find you and our friends in good health. Dr. Curry is in arrears to me. May God preserve him to finish and enjoy the work he has been so long about for the instruction of the public. I request you will present my affections to Mr. O'Brien, Mr. Troy, Mr. Lee, and our other friends.

P.S. Some time since I have written to your Grace on a subject which was far from being agreeable, and I remembered to enclose under cover a script to Dr. Curry.

252. To Colonel Charles Vallancey

RIA, Stowe MS. Bi2

[Belanagare, 22 October 1773]

Dear Sir,

On Wednesday last I have remitted by a safe hand to Dr. Carpenter the *Memoir* I have drawn up for the consideration of the Committee of Antiquarians. It consists of six short sections and is entitled, *A Short*

View of the Ancient State of Ireland from the Earliest Times to the Establishment of the Tuathalian Constitution in the Second Century. Loath to lose the opportunity of a messenger I might depend upon, I made the last section too short by two or three pages, but the deficiency can be easily supplied, and yet enough is inserted in case the preceding five sections do not meet with approbation. I should have given a section on our old laws and jurisprudence, but it would be a very lame one from me who never studied our law language nor met with any glossary that could give me the smallest assistance. This is a task denied to any hand but yours who have already made so good a progress in the Phenian dialect. You have before you some fragments from *Forchern, Néidhe,* and *Athairne* of Ben-Hedar, all writers and lawyers of the first century; any tolerable explanation of their judgments *Breithe Nemhe* would give the highest idea of the early rise of legislation and cultivation of knowledge in this island. Had a good explanation of such writings been digested and published in the sixteenth century when the Egans of Tipperary[1] and other expressors of our laws flourished, some modern controversies, no better than negative arguments, had never appeared and the world would be enriched with a branch of very curious knowledge, the recovery of which is become in a great degree desperate. But the times do not admit of any patronage of that sort of local learning because, in fact, the people who professed it were despised.

I requested of Dr. Carpenter to send you the *Memoir* as soon as he perused it. I would have it some time in your and Dr. Leland's hands that it might have his and your corrections before it was presented; should it meet with any success (such success I mean as would entitle it to publication) I should then annex my authorities and some explanatory notes in the margins. I say no more on the subject until I am [in] possession of your thoughts on my new manner of handling it. I only request that you will put the *Memoir* into Dr. Leland's hands when you have done with it, for I shall benefit by his instructions as well as corrections. He will not deny this good office to a friend who bears him the highest affection and respect.

Our middling and laboring poor are almost undone in this western province, a case which possibly could not happen without some defect in our laws or some extraordinary revolution in our climate. In 1763 this nation was happy in a flourishing condition. It has been for ten years past on the decline; the peace abroad no doubt affected our manufacturers at home, but that incident will by no means account for our present low state. Some lurking evil pervades the whole mass, and it should be explored. The northern contagion of emigration has made large strides toward us, and some among us are forming associations and preparing like birds of passage for a flight into North America.² I have seen invitations from correspondents in that part of the world to their friends in this and (what you will think odd enough) the flattering accounts published lately by Mr. Guthrie, the geographer, are no small incentives to their taking wing.³ When we are ill-at-ease (said old Swift) on one side, we turn on the other though it should be for the worse.

Adieu, my dear sir, I hope to hear from you if you can spare leisure for a line to one who lives in the Hermitage. I expect to have the pleasure of seeing you in three weeks at farthest.

Belanagare, 22 October 1773

1. The MacEgans kept a famous law school at Bally MacEgan in Tipperary. Sheehan, p. 491.
2. O'Conor must have seen the news item in *DJ*, 10–13 April 1773, which stated that nearly 400,000 people had emigrated from Ireland in the last forty years. Faulkner wrote, "There are now fourteen ships at Belfast taking in passengers for America most of whom are manufacturers and husbandmen as also many of different professions...."
3. William Guthrie of Brechin (1708–1770) wrote for the *Gentleman's Magazine;* he was best known for his *Geographical, Historical and Commercial Grammar and the Present State of several Kingdoms of the World*, published in 1771. *Concise DNB*, 1:547.

253. To Archbishop John Carpenter

OCD, 8.3 HS 026

[c. November 1773]

Most Reverend Sir,

The account you give of our dear friend¹ gives me the most sensible concern, and it doubles my pain that I can not immediately fly up to town to see him because he expresses so warm a wish to have me with him. I never enjoyed a more affectionate friend. Our affections and aversions were the same, and I was bound to him by every tie; his heart, his studies were devoted to the good of the Catholic cause; he in his writings and conversations planned out the conduct which Catholics ought to pursue under a lenient government which permits their existence in a land where the laws forbid it. He brought the wisest among us into his sentiments; he did more; he brought them to cooperate with him, and you may remember that to his solicitations were owing my own poor efforts in the cause he undertook and indeed undertook alone for some time. He overlooked the censure of some who reproached him for officiousness in undertaking that cause uncalled and uncommissioned. With the testimony of a good conscience of his side, he went on and opposed zeal to tepidity; the consequences have surely proved that he was right. His words were well received; they have been even applauded by the more moderate of his adversaries. May he live to see and enjoy the publication of his *opus magnum,* a work the best I have seen for opening the eyes of the public! I trust in God that in the next account I receive from your Grace I will be assured of his recovery for the sake of the public rather than his own, as I have no doubt of his happier lot in another state of existence. Whatever his fate be, the *opus magnum* must not lie by in a corner. The public have an indisputable right to it; and as he urged me to preface that work to the world, I will use all my efforts to fulfill his requisition and introduce him with that justice to his writings and character which his own too great modesty would decline. It will give him some satisfaction to be assured of my obedience to his commands, and for that reason I request that your Grace will inform him of my forward readiness to execute them to my utmost. My heart is so full of him that I shall enjoy no ease till I hear from him, and I trust that your G[ra]ce will be enabled by the return of the post to remove my pain.

Some hours since I had the honor to write to your Grace and presumed to enclose a letter to our friend. I ventured to remark a little on the indiscreet publication of Ghillini's letter to your predecessor. But happily the matter was lost and certainly will be overlooked in the present disposition of things.

By one Mr. Browne I sent you a *Memoir* I drew up for the censure or consideration of the *Society of Antiquarians.* It was disposed of in six sections on the *Ancient State of Ireland* and inscribed to the President. I request that after perusal you would send it to Major Vallancey, the secretary. Possibly it was not delivered to your Grace, as you make no mention of it.

1. Dr. Curry was ill.

254. To Colonel Charles Vallancey

RIA, Stowe MS. Bi2

From my Hermitage, 4 December 1773

Dear Sir,

Your memory of a solitary friend in the hurry of a parliamentary campaign is such a proof of your friendship as can not easily be forgotten by one of a feeling and grateful temper, such as you will ever find me to be. I now and then peruse the heads of some of your senatorial harangues setting forth the wretched state of our country and people. The disease is known; it might be prevented also, but those who offer a remedy in the present crisis put me in mind of the Irishman (a Milesian Irishman) who diligently fell to repairing the bad fence about his field after his crop was eaten up by his neighbor's herds as well as his own. Old Bishop Berkeley and old Swift offered remedies long since when remedies were available, and the latter said humorously and bitterly also that he instructed our people from the closet to as little purpose as if he had preached to them out of the pulpit. In truth the inefficiency of such instructions is as certain among us, the gentiles, as those of the prophets among the children of Israel. In both cases, we took our knowledge from the completion of the prediction. Our great landlords take their feelings from the fall of their rents and the insolvency of Popish graziers who have turned their tenures into wastes and are amazingly licensed by law to do so. Our manufactures have been demonstrably for some time past on the decline, and from the great rise on provisions our manufacturers are on the wing and inviting our laborers to follow them; but there is an extreme in political diseases which cannot be exceeded, and whenever we touch that boundary there must be a natural retrograde progression to political health. The Irishman I have mentioned above built his strong fence after his corn was demolished, but it preserved the next year's crop, and one year's hunger taught him to be a provident husbandman during his whole life. From this view of Ireland in its modern condition I return to what you know I have been long studying, its state in ancient time when natural wealth supplied the want of commerce and when the ignorance of many vices made room for the operation of some virtues which dignify barbarism itself. I have touched on these topics in the *Memoir* you gave Dr. Leland. In the last section (which was chronological) I have hurried over the subject too hastily; for, however dry it may be, it is important and I have a good deal to say on that subject. We have little certainty on our accounts till the building of Eamania; the succession of kings and genealogical descents prior to that era are evidently artificial; and your synchronism from the Book of Lecan, like several others I have seen, is technical and conjectural. When Concovar MacNessa reformed the fileas in the beginning of the Christian era, we may well suppose that he published the best accounts he could obtain of his own family, and his senachies have given but fifteen or sixteen generations back from that time to the Milesian expedition from Spain; by counting these at thirty years to each generation, that expedition will fall at 480 or 450 years before Christ.

You should lay no stress on the accounts given of the regal succession of the Tuatha Dé Dannan. If such kings have reigned in fact, they could not, as being elective and advanced in years, reign above twelve or thirteen years apiece, as the experience of history in such governments testifies through all ages. But the nine kings of the Tuatha Dé Danann are made to reign one with another twenty-two years apiece, which circumstance never happens, except in lineal hereditary successions, as Sir Isaac Newton has sufficiently proved. In the forty-four reigns of our Christian monarchs from Laeghaire to Maoleachlainn Mór, who died A.D. 1022, we find that those princes reigned one with another little above thirteen years apiece, and their chronology we know is indisputable. How little the forgers of the Tuatha Dé Danann succession were masters of their trade you may easily see from their absurdity in making seven of the nine Danann Kings die an unnatural death and yet giving them the reigns of hereditary princes in a well-regulated constitution.

I am sorry to find the learned Mr. Whitaker[1] so dilatory in his correspondence with you. His heart is set on discoveries in our British antiquities, such as have escaped Camden and others. He has undoubtedly sufficiently expressed and confuted the hypothesis of the MacPhersons; pity it is that he is laboring to establish one of his own on its ruins with no better crutch than Monk Richard[2] to lean upon. I suppose your quotations from Hieronymo are distressing him and that he is at work to set aside their authority. I purpose to make use of your *Discoveries* in notes to strengthen what I have advanced in the *Memoir,* so that the Committee of Antiquarians think it worthy of publication. I could wish, by the way, that you requested of Dr. Leland to put the *Memoir* into the hands of Sir Lucius O'Brien that he might have the perusal of it before it is laid before your Committee. Our controversies on British antiquities will ultimately have a good effect in making us stop at the line which marks the boundary between truth and falsehood, *ut ex conflictu et collisione opinionum elucescat et eruatur veritas.*[3] Some truths useful to society, civil and moral, may come out, and the fables which envelope them will be stripped off. Adieu, my dear sir. I shall, God willing, see you or rather you will hear from me in town next week, for in your present hurry you must be invisible to all idlers.

1. John Whitaker (1735–1808), antiquarian and historian of Manchester. *Concise DNB,* 1:1395.
2. Richard of Cirencester (d. 1401?), a monk of St. Peter's Westminister, and compiler of *Speculum Historiale* (447–1066 A.D.). *Concise DNB,* 1:241.
3. That from conflict and difference of opinion the truth may emerge and shine forth brightly.

255. To Denis O'Conor

OCD, 8.3 SE 028

19 January 1774

... I lament the fate of poor Nancy. Till I go down I think it would be well if she retired to her sister MacDermotroe's house, where she will create no expense as I shall be accountable for her diet.[1] But she must not think of removing her children from the care of those who ruined her and who are bound on a double account to provide for them....

    1. "Poor Nancy" is a reference to O'Conor's daughter Anne. Her marriage to James Dermott (c. 1760–1776) appears to have disappointed O'Conor because he never mentioned her name in any of his letters but this one. Charles Owen O'Conor *The O'Conors of Connaught*, p. 293; Dunleavy and Dunleavy, pp. 24, 56.

256. To The Bishop of Derry[1]

RIA, Stowe MS. Bi2

[5 March 1774]

My Lord,

    With great gratitude I acknowledge the honor your Lordship has done me in committing to my care your thoughts of an oath of allegiance to his present Majesty from the Irish Roman Catholics to which an explicit declaration of their civil principles (as dictated by their religion) should be annexed. I have conferred on that subject with some of the principal persons of that denomination here, and your Lordship's confidential letter received by me on Monday last gave sufficient weight to my application. With grateful cheerfulness they embraced an opportunity of conveying through your Lordship's hands a test of their fidelity to the present government and of conveying information at the same time which the public has long wanted. On Thursday last the assembly (deputed by Dublin and the other great towns to speak the sense of that body of subjects) came together for drawing up a Formulary of their loyalty and civil obedience. Delicacy in mentioning the Pope by name stuck with some as it seems to imply a personal charge; as some truths also, however well-known, should not be laid too close to a character respectable to *them;* and as the rigorous execution of the laws at home against their worship, their disrespect might be remembered abroad to their detriment, if obliged to fly out of their native country. This cautionary delicacy, however, was overruled from the present call of duty for satisfying a jealous legislature. They have mentioned the Pope by name in their Test and have renounced his claims to temporal power in the most express terms. I cannot sufficiently acknowledge the honor your Lordship has done me in committing to my care your thoughts of an oath of allegiance to his present Majesty together with a Test from Roman Catholics of their hearty reconciliation to our present civil constitution. I lost no time in discharging a duty which your Lordship's countenance alone could give me a right to undertake; and as soon as I could bring together the gentlemen who drew up the Formulary lately laid before your Lordship, they have cheerfully taken into consideration the additions and personalities deemed necessary for the satisfaction of such protestants as do not believe that occasional license for committing it is tolerated by our religion. These gentlemen thankfully acknowledge the goodness of your Lordship's intentions toward them, but at the same time they could not without injustice to themselves overlook for a moment the conditions on which they have any right to your Lordship's interposition for them in these times of distrust and misapprehension. They find themselves, therefore, the more bound to give your Lordship and the world, the strongest proof of their obedience to the civil government. Happily, their religion requires their ready compliance with so necessary a duty, and they can only prefer a wish that the belief of their sincerity may not be postponed to a time when the conviction may come too late for taking its proper effect on our public prosperity.

Relatively to renouncing the late Pretender's son *by name*, they can have no difficulty; and knowing well that a regal title has been denied to him in all countries, even in Rome itself, they cannot swear *positively* that he has *assumed* such a title. They rather suppose that, in prudence, he has declined it. Whether he has or not cannot affect their renunciation of him. They, therefore, think it proper to suit their oath to what they know, not to what is doubtful and depose: "That the person who formerly assumed the title of Prince of Wales and who since his father's decease *is said to have* assumed the title of King of England, or Great Britain, etc., by this name of Charles III has not by the Laws and Constitution established in these realms any right or title to the crown of Great Britain, Ireland, or any dominions thereto belonging, and that they renounce any allegiance or obedience to him."

Relatively to the present Pope, they still think that a decent reserve is necessary towards him, and they are no strangers to the instructions of some of his predecessors on the temporal rights of princes and states; one in particular has in a bull, well-known, claimed an indefeasible right to all islands of the ocean and by virtue of that claim has made a donative of the crown of Ireland to Henry II of England.[2] Such a pope, or any pope following the example, is not to be exculpated. But the present, not avowing by any act whatever such odious claims, has a right to respect from all in communion with him; here in particular they think it improper to point him out by name as hostile to our civil government. They think it improper to charge by implication and indeed by anticipation against him in their Formulary. In a rescript I have seen, Benedict XIV[3] required strict obedience from English Catholics to our present government. He preferred the good of Christianity to any temporalities whatever, and may we not suppose the present pontiff equally well-intentioned till the contrary appears. Besides, my Lord, the rigorous execution of the laws against the Popish worship in this country would annihilate the ministers of it in a few weeks. Royal compassion, and I may say Royal experience alone, has hitherto sheathed the sword of law; but should it be drawn, should the ministers fly and their flocks follow them, what would a personal charge by direct implication on the present Pope produce. It would, my Lord, render their condition abroad as well as at home equally desperate. They, therefore, think it wise in them to leave one door open for them in case of any expulsion from home; and let us put it to heart of the severest Protestant, if after examining it on this point, he can find anything reprehensible in such a caution.

Most undoubtedly your Lordship does not intend that those gentlemen or the party for whose sentiments they undertake should involve themselves in any odious personality. They only find it necessary to guard against any *odius construction* that might put abroad on an act intended for assuring them obedience to the civil power at home; nor indeed does it seem to be the business of a Test to exculpate or criminate the Pope by name but to vindicate the doctrine of the Church, which they are obliged to believe and which it would be happy for states and invididuals that they should religiously practice.

Whether a pope has claimed to himself the power of deposing princes or not is not at present the question, but whether we disavow such a power; and surely, my Lord, we make no use of vague terms when we assert that no bishop or ecclesiastical person or council or assembly of ecclesiastical persons or any power on earth can absolve or dispense with the obligation or any part of the obligation contracted in our Formulary, we say enough; for it cannot be said that the Pope is excluded out of number; and we say enough for the conviction of any who believe that we hold oaths to be obligatory and that we have no absolutions prepared for occasional perjury.

We hold the doctrine of "No faith to be kept with heretics" as unchristian and impious, and so we depose expressly in our Test. But relatively to your Lordship's quotation from the nineteenth session of the Council of Constance[4] asserting that doctrine, I am commissioned to say that Protestants and Catholics understand the canon there referred to very differently. For the latter can see no such doctrine in the words of that canon and deny that it has been practiced by the Council.

1. Frederick Augustus Hervey, Protestant bishop of Derry suggested to the Catholics that they present an oath of allegiance to the English king and abjure the temporal power of the Pope. In February 1774, he invited Charles O'Conor to confer with him on this subject. Stowe MS. Bi2, RIA. According to Lecky, 2 : 211, it was Hervey who first suggested to the Irish Parliament the test oath passed in the winter of 1774.
2. Pope Adrian IV in his *Laudabiliter* claimed that all islands "belonged" to the Catholic Church. He based this claim on the "Donation of Constantine," a forged document addressed by the Emperor Constantine to Pope Sylvester (314–35) in which Constantine conferred territories on the Pope and his successors. Roche, pp. 42–43.
3. Benedict XIV was pope from 17 August 1740 to 3 May 1758.
4. The Council of Constance, which met in forty-five sessions from 5 November 1414 to 22 April 1418, ended the schism resulting from the Avignon Papacy. It also rejected the writings of John Wyclif and John Huss as heretical.

257. To Mr. Daniel McNamara[1]

RIA, Stowe MS. Bi2

Dublin, 20 March 1774

... In February last the Bishop of Derry applied to some R[oman] Catholics here (to myself in particular) recommending the propriety of our giving a Test of our Allegiance to his Majesty, urging at the same time that a declaration of our being united with our fellow subjects in the same summary of *civil faith* might entitle us to some relaxation of those Penal Laws, which tie up the hands of industry among a million of people in this ill-fated country. We have already in an Address of the Lord Lieutenant declared our readiness to comply with such a duty and, therefore, embraced with cheerfulness an opportunity to do so, which the Bishop seemed to open to us. In an Association of the Dublin Catholics (having a power of acting from the other great towns of Ireland) we drew up the Formulary of Allegiance and Abjuration, which I herein enclose to you (in print); immediately after our agreeing to it I sent a manuscript copy of it to the B[ishop] of D[erry], and we heard no more of it or very little more of it till the 7th instant, when a gentleman who attended that day in the gallery of the H[ouse] of C[ommons] brought us information that Mr. French, one of the members, presented heads of a bill that day to the House for enabling R[oman] C[atholic]s to testify their allegiance to his Majesty. We fondly entertained a hope that our *own* Formulary was the one brought in. But in that, as in every other hope, we have been disappointed. From some expressions, however, it appeared that ours served as a groundwork for the formulary printed in the votes of the House, but interpolated with new matter. Before the subject of it came under debate, we had the precaution to put printed copies of our *own* test into the hands of several leading members, and some have been just enough to confess nothing stronger or more express could be required from men of our principles. But the majority (in a thin House) judged otherwise, and the interpolations I have mentioned took place. It was contended for by one sensible member that if our *own* Formulary was inadmissible, it should be rejected without any alteration, as it must be from our own Test, not from one made for us, that the legislature could best judge of the degree of favor or penalty which should be measured out to us; that however the House had a right to declare the security both in kind and degree necessary for our civil Constitution yet that it was but just to leave others free in declaring the security they can give without putting any violence on their conscience. This reasoning had no weight. After our engagement to maintain the succession in his Majesty's family and abjuring his enemies, we declare, "*that no foreign prince or prelate hath any civil jurisdiction or power within the realm.*" The framers of the *new* Test made it to run thus, "and we declare that *no foreign prince or prelate hath, or ought to have, any civil jurisdication,* etc." . . . It appears that the words *ought not* (in the place inserted) do not come properly or constitutionally out of the mouth of a Papist, a mere passive being in the community, who though legally permitted to recognize the persons who have jurisdiction have certainly by the Constitution no right to declare *who ought not to have it,* as that right is solely vested in the body of constitutional freemen, who occasionally *give* or *dissolve* power as it is well or ill-administered; to them therefore, it belongs to declare who *ought not* to be vested with political power and to them alone. The interpolated words in the formulary are *suited* and *suitable.* . . .[2]

    1. Daniel MacNamara of London (1720–1800), a lawyer and agent for the Catholic Committee, Sheehan, P-500. This letter and a second letter, dated 24 March 1774, appear to be preliminary drafts because they are filled with words crossed out and others added.
    2. An amended version of the Parliamentary Test which "moderate Catholics" might sign was printed in *DJ,* 22–24 March 1774. The passage of the Parliamentary Test of 1774 indicated an important change of attitude toward Irish Catholics both in England and in Ireland. According to Maurice O'Connell, "The oath conferred no ex-

plicit benefit, but it did give the Catholics a certain legal status valuable for the future."
Irish Politics and Social Conflict in the Age of the American Revolution (Philadelphia: University of Pennsylvania Press, 1965), p. 107.

258. To Denis O'Conor

OCD, 8.3 SE 028

[Dublin, 4 May 1774]

. . . I [am] now a little better supplied with matter from my conversation this morning with Messieurs Luke Ferral and John Dillon. The former issued out a writ of outlawry against Kelly of Springfield (if that be the name). As to the issuing execution of Kelly's bond in your favor, judgments must be previously revived, expense will be incurred, and probably nothing good will accrue, as Kelly is (they say) of such desperate fortune as to admit of no useful hold of him by law. . . .

259. To Dr. John Curry, Summerhill, Dublin

OCD, 8.3 HS 026

From the Hermitage, 8 July 1774

My Dear Sir,

I should 'ere now have informed you of my safe arrival in Conaght but that I wanted a frank for conveying intelligence of that nature. I am uneasy about your health and truly about your family at home and abroad. Your *great work* is, I trust, by this time negotiated with some London publisher.[1] It is wanted much because it brings along with it those informations which will make men reflect and which will make them the wiser by reflection. I am certain, for obvious reasons, that you will be far from obtaining the consideration for your copy which it deserves, and the more as Dr. Leland's history of Ireland has so much come short of the expectations of the booksellers, but you have one consolation, that your intention from beginning was not to enrich the writer but the reader. Nothing would flatter my ambition more than to have the satisfaction of *introducing* your work, as it would be a lasting monument of our friendship and of my own happiness in being connected with one of the worthiest men (pardon my saying so to yourself) I ever knew. The introduction of the *Memoirs mutatis mutandis*[2] would do, but still with the addition of some new matter (*e re nata*)[3] as you have formerly observed to me. Prefaces and introductions are the last things printed in any work, and I shall I hope be in time for that business, though your book should at this day be under the press. Let me know what you have done and how far you have proceeded relatively to it since we parted. I trust that I shall be able to see you in September at farthest.

The Herveyan Test is passed into law,[4] but the framers have never been suspected of ability; and had they any and were serious, they would not tack a controverted and controvertible proposition on the back of a true one; and had they not wanted to horse an insult on the backs of both, they would not require our swearing that we have no previous absolutions for future occasional perjury when it is obvious that no law or oath on earth can bind any man who makes occasional perjury a principle of his religion. It is an insult linked to an absurdity, and both should be given back to the true owners. Sure I am that if our people have a grain of spirit, they will act this part and renounce to another proposition in the Test: *"that no power whatsoever can dispense with this oath,"* though certainly the people of Great Britain can upon great emergency do it, as they have done recently in the code of the late King James. The price has undoubtedly been overcharged, and it must surely recoil on the persons who wanted the skill of charging it properly.

I request that along with the worthy gentlewomen under your roof you will give my affections to Mr. Comerford, Mr. Gaven, and my other friends of your connection.

From the Hermitage, 8 July 1774

1. *An Historical and Critical Review.*
2. Changing those things that must be changed.
3. After what has happened, arising from the present circumstances.
4. This law enabling Catholics to swear allegiance to the king went into effect on 1 June 1774. It still contained the phrase "I do declare that I do not believe that the Pope of Rome or any other foreign prince, prelate, state or potentate hath or ought to have preeminence directly or indirectly in this realm. . . ." Consequently O'Conor did not sign the oath.

260. [To a Member of the Irish House of Commons]

RIA, Stowe MS. Bi2[1]

Vigil na Féile Parhaloin aniú,[2] 1774

I entirely agree with you in your judgment on the late Act of Parliament enabling subjects of all persuasions to testify their allegiance to his majesty. . . .

1. This letter appears to be the first draft of another (263). Note that the two letters come from a different collection—an example of how disastrous was the breaking up of the letter and manuscript collection after O'Conor's death.
2. Vigil of the feast of St. Bartholomew today. The feast day is 24 August.

261. To Dr. John Curry,[1] Summerhill, Dublin

OCD, 8.3 HS 026

From my Hermitage, 27 August 1774

... No religion on earth can afford, as you well know, a stronger test of security to civil governments than that of Catholics, but the framers of such a test ought to spare anything irritating and much more, anything injurious or captious to conscience therein. It is irritating to oblige men to swear that they have no previous papal dispensations for preconcerted treason or occasional perjury when the test could be made stronger by deposing that no pope *has or ought to have* any such power from any law evangelical, political, or natural. It is an insult on me to offer me an oath wherein I am to declare that no foreigner has or ought to have temporal dominion in these kingdoms without letting me at the same time declare upon what grounds I rest, not indeed, my belief alone but my conviction. It is not only captious to conscience but insulting to require my swearing to an *implication* and to require also in the next paragraph an abjuration of all mental reserve! I would rather drag my chain to the end of life as my father did in resignation and patience than adopt of such a test. At worst, my recusancy will afford a proof that *I do not believe* that the Pope can dispense with any lawful oath that I am ready to take or may take for the security of the government I live under. The penalties of law on men guiltless of any civil crime are grievous, but those of the Almighty on apostates are much more tremendous. Good Catholics who fear the latter will have no difficulty in facing the other. May they not find repose in Canada.[2] ...

1. There is an abstract of this letter in O'Conor's hand in Stowe MS. Bi2, RIA.
2. The Quebec Act, passed in 1774, allowed Canadians freedom of religion.

262. To Dr. John Curry

PSPL, Gilbert MS. 203

[September 1774][1]

... I trust that before this time you and he[2] met, and I take it for granted that if he can prevail with the *Usserian* Society to negotiate the publication of the *Review, that* performance to which the public has the chief right shall not long remain a private property. . . .

I have written (as you will see) "Remarks upon The New Test of Last Session" and I applaud the intention of those who framed it. I only point out a few omissions which may be rectified in a future session, and through the whole I personate a constitutional and well-meaning subject. To one of my objections (to the present form, not to the matter) I know you will agree. You will say that my second objection is an evasion. If it be, it is an evasion in favor of the Constitution, and as the Test is to be sworn to, all pretense for an evasion (how disagreeable soever to the framers of the Test) ought to be explained, and be being so, the evasion (if it be one) may be removed. . . . No Test will ever be profitable in our case but such as will take in our clergy as well as laity; and had it been framed on my constitutional principles, the clergy, who stand now at a distance, would most certainly come in, as not a tittle contrary to Catholic doctrine would lie in the way to keep them back—; you are sensible of the delicacy of their situation and that our little human prudence forbids the double risks of losing all favor abroad and at home. . . .

1. The editors date this letter from internal evidence. Curry was working on his book, *An Historical and Critical Review of the Civil Wars in Ireland*, . . . which appeared in Dublin the next year; also the act for taking the Oath of Allegiance was passed in 1774.

2. Dr. Carpenter. O'Conor has urged Curry to meet with Archbishop Carpenter and ask him for his help in getting the *Review* published.

263. To a Member of The Irish House of Commons

OCD, 8.3 HS 026

13 September 1774

Sir,

I entirely concur with you in your judgment of the late Act of our Parliament enabling Irishmen of all persuasions to testify their allegiance to his Majesty. It is a noble effort of legislative wisdom to bring a people unhappily divided on the doctrinal points of religion to the profession of one general summary of civil faith, loyalty to the same king, submission to the same laws, deference to the same civil Constitution. The happy effects of such an union on the prosperity of several Protestant states on the continent have been long experienced, and to account for the causes which retarded the adoption of so salutary a measure in my own islands would be a matter of disagreeable rather than difficult inquiry. The trial, however, is at last made, and we must be fortunate indeed should it fail of being awarded with the success at home which attended in every step of experiment elsewhere. At worst, it will be productive of one good effect which may lead to a better; it will discover infallibly the true seat of a distemper which has long preyed on the vitals of the public; and that being once known, the proper remedies can no longer be mistaken.

With pleasure I have submitted to the injunction you have laid upon me to sound the Roman Catholics on the subject of this *late* law and the test of fidelity inserted therein. I now sit down to give you the best information I could collect from my several conversations with persons of *their* persuasions in city and country; and previously I can assure you that far from discovering the shadow of a division among them on the duty of allegiance to his present Majesty I could not find even the slightest hestitation (among the majority) on the propriety of annexing to the declaration of such an allegiance an absolute renunciation of the Pope *in temporis rebus*[1] and of every other foreign pretender whatsoever.

They have indeed, expressed a concern that tests of allegiance which have been found effectual in other Protestant states should not be deemed sufficient in our own; but undoubtedly (as you have oftener than once observed to me) the case of our *native* Papists requires to be distinguished from that of our brethren on the continent. The *latter* enjoy the privileges of citizens, and security on the side of the subject disarms jealousy on the side of the government; but the *former*, existing in our own country on bare sufferance and precarious property, stronger sanctions are necessary *for binding them;* it being natural to suppose they are but little attached to a constitution from whose principal benefits they are legally excluded and that from their feelings on this account they may be tempted to prefer the gratification of a passion to the discharge of a duty.

From the consideration of this wide difference in their case, the Irish Roman Catholics must find themselves under more pressing obligation of giving every additional security that natural jealousy may demand to labor that public prosperity should suffer as little as possible on *their* account and that the odium they lie under may be abated by proofs that their principles relatively to our government are as sound as their practices have been found to be in the course of the present century. To all this reasoning on *my* side, they have agreed on *theirs,* declaring that our government is not the less to be obeyed; that they do not find their own proper station, or what they consider as such under it; that let the legislative power of any country be lodged where it will, government should be served on its own terms; and that resistance (were Papists able to resist) cannot on these principles be employed against the present civil constitution but against any invader of it spiritual or temporal.

In the whole of this declaration they appeared to me to be in earnest; and one should think that on the principles they laid down, the framing of a good test of loyalty could not be difficult. In reality nothing would be less so if care be taken that no words explanatory of the complex propositions such a test may include are omitted. For certain it is that the omission of a monosyllable may in some paragraphs raise scruples in the minds of plain men who, sensible of the sacred nature of an oath, would leave nothing dubious or defective in the terms *of it*. On this tender principle it is that many of *every persuasion* forbear subscribing to the New Test in this late statute, though nothing can be more evident than that the sole view of the framers was to give security to government on *one side* and to conscience on the other, but oversights in all new experiments are natural and may be easily supplied in a second revision. Meantime, it will not be improper to recite here the reasons offered for *non-subscription* because they seem to be *constitutional* and may afford some useful lights on reconsidering this important matter before the next session.

In the close of this new formulary of allegiance, it is required of the jurors to depose "that no authority whatsoever *can dispense with or annul* the whole of it or any part thereof." In this paragraph the framers of the Test meant most certainly no foreign authority whatsoever, as they well knew that in desperate cases the nation of *Great Britain* may in a future, as they have in a former period of time, *dispense with and annul* some parts of any test and frame another according to events and exigencies of time; yet in the present test no reservation is made for such a possible, however remote, case. The formulary, therefore, is in this instance defective, and there is an inattention, not uncommon in questions that admit of little debate; the omission of the adjective *foreign* passed the three estates unnoticed.

In another paragraph of this new Test, it is required of the juror to depose on his belief, "that no foreign prince or prelate *has or ought to have* any temporal jurisdiction, dominion, etc., directly in these realms." Each of these negative propositions is undoubtedly true. The *first* by its own evidence, the *second* by a fact ratified as it is ascertained by *law;* but the framers of the test forgot to insert a recognition of the legal obligation, though doubtless, they intended it should be declared in express terms and that the paragraph should run thus, "that no foreign prince or prelate has or by law ought to have any jurisdiction or dominion in these realms." This, I say, was their intention, because that antecedently to legislative decision, ignorance of the truth contained in this *second negative* could not be criminal and because it is not with some political maxims, mutable by local exigencies and events, as it is with moral maxims, mutable by no event whatever. In such cases, the law points out to the subject the line of legal obedience. All doubt is removed, and the juror's belief being under legislative direction, an additional sanction and consequently an additional security is given, which surely would not be the case if the deponent omitted declaring expressly the *ground on which he rests his belief.*

Thus, sir, have many of different persuasions, Papists and Presbyterians, reasoned on an omission in this as in the former paragraph, and I have endeavored to remove their scruple as to the *latter* by arguing to them that the supplemental words they want (by law or by the present constitution) are unnecessary since they are sufficiently implied in the context of the paragraph itself; but they are answered and not improperly, I confess, that an implication in a complex proposition, be it everso strong, yet refers to *something latent,* and that *anything latent* in so solemn an engagement can not without the guilt of perjury be sworn to by men who abjure all *mental reservation.*

I now come to the part of the formulary which bears a direct relation to the Roman Catholics alone. By its terms, it seems to be admitted that this people, like their brethren in his Majesty's German dominions and in Holland, may be bound by their religion to their civil duty; and a prospect is opened to them that the degree of *legal punishment* may hereafter be proportional to the degree of their *civil guilt.* When such a ray of confidence appears to beam on them, they can not without very sensible grief see a mist of jealous interposing by a requisition (in this enlightened age) to abjure principles which Christians of *all persuasions must abhor and which no human law can prevent anti-Christians from secretly professing.*

They are sensibly grieved indeed when they are called upon to depose that they have no previous dispensation from the Pope for *preconcerted treason or occasional perjury.* Such an abjuration includes an odious charge, indecent in them to admit and the more, as it must help to confirm the idea many Protestants entertain that the charge has some foundation. They would, therefore, humbly petition for a change in the form of the Test, but yet *not without strengthening the matter of it* and to show how remote they are from making treason and perjury a principle of their religion they are ready to depose, "that no Pope has, nor Pope and council united *have,* or by any law or constitution, divine or human ought to have, power of dispensing directly or indirectly with such un-Christian iniquity."

Thus, sir, have I laid before you in the briefest manner I could, the sentiments of many persons of *all persuasions* on the subject of this recent statute and the Formulary inserted therein. In this, as in other laws of experiment, omission might be made which a future act of explanation may supply; and as the matter is important, the whole appears worthy of a further parliamentary revision.

13 September 1774

1. In temporal matters.

264. To Colonel Charles Vallancey, Cumberland Street, Dublin

RIA, Stowe MS B1 1a

[Belanagare, 16 September 1774]

... Whenever the world is enriched with your dictionary, we will be in possession of a key for unlocking the hidden treasure of the Celtic tongue. I am greatly pleased with the information of your French correspondent who discovered a kindred between the Celtic and the Sclavonian. Such discoveries must assist better in tracing nations to their true originals than the most ancient inscriptions on stone or brass.

Our countrymen differ vastly from yours; we give no encouragement to inquiry into the ancient state of Ireland, though unconquered (as to its language) till near our own time. You have been destined to restore our Irish Celtic to its primitive vigor, as well as trace it to its true roots. You will also, in spite of discouragements, restore our antiquities as you have now so noble a collection of ancient annals for that purpose....

265. To Dr. John Curry, Summerhill, Dublin

OCD, 8.3 HS 026

30 September or 1 October 1774

My Dear Sir,

I believe you are the first writer in historical controversy who has been charged with pecuniary payment for the publication of remarks on any new work. On the side of the bookseller (who had the sole profit of sale) it was the most shameful, barefaced fraud or the most inexcusable condescension on the side of your agent. In either case the injustice to you is manifest, and I am glad for the ease of your own mind that you made short work with this moral evil as you judiciously do with some of the physical evils of life. It is, doubtless, often the best remedy in both cases. From your *Remarks*[1] you got reputation; your adversary got none from his book. You got no money, but he got money and you lost. Who is the gainer? Were I to be left the alternative, I should not a moment hestitate on the choice. You are wrong surely in thinking he had his revenge of you, and since *that* as well as all the reputation is with you, or properly will be with you as soon as the *Review* is made public, I have written on the subject of its publication to a friend[2] who really loves you. He and you have, I hope, come together before this time, and if the path I opened be practical to *him*, he assuredly will cheerfully employ all his influence to bring forward a work to which the right of the community is indisputable; but alas, this right (of all others) is the most delayed and the causes which concur to it are most shameful. I have (I am afraid) surfeited you lately with a prolix letter wherein the writer addresses a member of Parliament on the subject of the late *Test Law*. If it be deemed expedient to publish anything about it (in some London paper), it will be proper to insert some useful matter which did not occur to the writer and expunge the weak arguments which possibly he has employed for suspending our subscription till the Test itself is made *more constitutional* in a future revision of the statute. A paper of such importance should come from the united strength of the most sensible men among us, not from the efforts of any single person. Among the laity we have abilities sufficient for the discharge of this office, nor need we (I think) call upon our clergy for assistance. *They are coy,* and some of the best have reason *to be so* till affairs come to a crisis. If the work is once done (done well I mean) without them, they will certainly at last embrace the measures which prudence requires us as well as justice requires *at home* and which undoubtedly authority *abroad* will not censure; Rome, as we all know, does not previously approve the *doctrine libero et tolerato*,³ but ulteriorly she *acquiesces,* and her acquiescences will be enough for our clergy. I am apt to think, or I am rather convinced, that this ecclesiastical policy is necessary and that it may be useful as on some occasions it proved hurtful. It is hurtful only when the Ghillinis, the ignorant, dogmatic Ghillinis, are in possession of the chief ecclesiastical authority, a case not likely to happen soon as well in this more enlightened age as in this declining state of secular power in the clergy. To you, who anticipate all I can say on this subject, I have rather said too much. You will, God willing, see me about the middle of the month. Meantime, give my affections to your family and all friends.

    1. Curry's *Remarks* . . . is a criticism of Dr. Leland's *History of Ireland relative to the Irish Rebellion of 1641*. Dr. Curry's publication cost him seven pounds.
    2. Probably Dr. Carpenter. See end of letter 262.
    3. I absolve and tolerate.

266. To Dr. John Curry, Summerhill, Dublin

OCD, 8.3 HS 026

25 October 1774

Dear Sir,
    Yours of the 21st instant lies before me and gives me great satisfaction from the information you give me that your medical work¹ is out and from the certainty I have that it will gain you exceptional credit from the truly learned in your own profession. I receive equal pleasure from the cordiality of friendship between you and the clerical gentleman² you mention. The interchanges of it were only interrupted, but it never could be broken from the conviction I had that the *idem velle* and the *idem nolle*³ was so identic among you that no little difference in non-essentials could have any effect but such a temporary one as I mentioned. The *Historical Review* is put into the best channels we (I think) could hit upon, but more of this when we meet, which must (I trust) be soon as I quit this Hermitage tomorrow morning and set off for your capital. I am pleased that you like my scheme of "Reasons for Forbearing our Subscription to The New Parliamentary Test," till it undergoes a future revision. Is it not happy that the framers of it can not on *their own principles* press the obligation of subscribing? For they inadvertently have inserted that "no authority

whatsoever" (instead of "no foreign authority whatsoever") can dispense with a single iota of the formulary. I hope that you have not forgotten the mention of this omission to Sir Pat Bellew; a happy omission surely it is, as it at once apologizes for the *forbearance* of our subscription. But what have I said? It surely *justifies* our absolute rejection of it and that upon *constitutional* principles. The purport of the Test was to divide us from each other, nor was that intention concealed from myself as I (I think) told you heretofore. If ever we divide, it will produce nothing but scandal to ourselves and contempt from our enemies, for a difference on Ghillinian principles could not properly be called a division as the minority on that side will hold no proportion to the great body of loyal Roman Catholic clergy and laity. The gentlemen who have objected to the publication of "Reasons for Forebearance, etc." are very probably right in their judgment. I only thought it might be expedient at present lest some among us might be giddy enough to run Assizes and Quarter Sessions and subscribe before they took every caution to consult with their principals. I request you will give every one of our common friends my affections.

    1. *Some Thoughts on the Natures of Fevers* . . . (London: J. Johnson, 1774).
    2. Archbishop Carpenter.
    3. Sallust, *Catiline*, 20. *Idem velle et idem nolle.* . . . "To wish the same things and to reject the same things that indeed is true friendship."

267. To Denis O'Conor

OCD, 8.4 SE 148

18 March 1775

Dear Denis,

It was not so much forgetfulness as the despondency of my mind which occasioned my not advertising you sooner of Mr. John Dillon's agreeing to your drawing upon him for the sum you require in favor of your brother. You may do it when you will, but you should be certain of being safe in doing so. As to your brother, I think no act of yours or mine can render him any service; he has beggared me without the smallest advantage to his innocent and helpless family. I received your draft (through Charles Mahone's hands) on Mr. Talbot. Luke Ferral will take out a writ of outlawry against Kelly of Springfield, and I see no benefit in such a proceeding. Mr. Ferral told me he wanted no money at present and declined taking from me the two guineas you ordered for him. You will see him at Roscommon Assizes.

I lately had the pleasure of dining with Mr. Martin Browne and his son Pat. They have not succeeded in their treaty with Mr. Caddell.[1] The work you mention (on Irish affairs) has been written by Dr. Curry and is now in the press. Give my affections to your family. I wonder I see no car man from Belanagare, that I might remit the books and papers I intend for the children.

1. A landlord of O'Conor's brother, probably Hugh.

268. To Denis O'Conor, Belanagare

RIA, Stowe MS Bi2

11 April 1775

Dear Denis,

The bearer will deliver you a box containing books which will entertain and improve you greatly; others relating to our times will afford you some useful knowledge, particularly Dr. Johnson's tour into the highlands, Dr. Shebbeare's *Parallel between K[ing] W[illiam] and George III*,[1] Hawkesworth's *Voyages*, MacKenzie on Health, etc., etc., etc. You'll please to give the children from me Mair's *Sallust*, Dauphin's *Virgil*, and Hubner's *Geography*, I send these books in the best order and hope that Owen will be careful to keep them so, as well as his diligent perusal of them can permit; I had no time to send you a catalog, but you may take one and keep these other books by you till I go down. I send Art a coat and waistcoat little worn. I request you will oversee him and my other servants in every part of what I gave them in charge and supply by your own instructions all that I omitted. I shall be vexed much if I do not find things in and about the Hermitage in as good order as they can bear. I send the paper bought by Pat Brown here for the children. I request you will speak to Jack Fagan and oblige him to send his uncle (in the Four Courts Marshalsea) a satisfactory account of his negotiations for him in the county of Sligo.[2] I have revised sixty-four pages of Dr. Curry's book now printing in 4° very elegantly.[3] The historical matter of his work is good, but it is a mere compilation without any ornament of style. All along he produces proofs of the civil injuries done the Irish Catholics, and while he justifies the conduct of the latter in various instances, he makes no mention of their follies or imprudence in any. This is not history, which like every true picture should consist of shade and coloring, but it is a mere justification on one side and a disguised invective on the other. He, however, supports what he advances from good authorities, and his merit must terminate in that of good pioneers and quarry men who throw up materials for master workmen. He is a very worthy man, and I must at his request introduce his book by a preliminary advertisement. I now go out to buy the seeds Art wants; I therefore, take my leave of you for the moment. I have written lately to my daughter; give her and your whole family my affections.

P.S. If the land taken by my brother from Mr. Caddell be not worth the stipulated rent of the last year, he should have an abatement or throw it up before it ruins him. I hope his own prudence will anticipate this advice.

1. John Shebbeare, M.D. (1709–1788) was a political writer who defended George III's American policy against the attacks by Burke and his party. *Concise DNB*, 1 : 1189.
2. Both Brown and Fagan would appear to be in-laws. Charles O'Conor married a Catherine Fagan; Denis married the daughter of Martin Browne.
3. O'Conor was reading the proofs of the Dublin edition of Curry's *Historical and Critical Review* published in 1775.

269. To Dr. John Curry, Summerhill, Dublin

OCD, 8.4 HS 141

24 June 1775

Dear Sir,

On Monday morning I quitted Dublin and arrived here in Belanagare on Wednesday, leaving some parts of my disorder behind me in the several provinces and counties I passed through. I am, thank God, recruiting a little every day and hope that I will, after some time, be re-established. It gives me pleasure that your son is at last returned to you from the continent with a young family that you will soon naturalize by your care as well as affections. Thady is actually at present in the case of a stranger, entirely unacquainted with the arts of industry fitting for our climate and soil. The details necessary to be well understood in the business of agriculture and pasturage are so many and complicated that he should not hastily undertake them. It would be like running into a wide ocean without understanding the use of the compass or the sails and tackles. He should be previously well instructed; and until he is so, you may put him to some business in town which requires no great time in learning and wherein little hazard is run. I beg your pardon for all this, and I have only presumed to offer it from the interest I take in everything that concerns you. I trust that your excellent work will be soon out of the press;[1] and as I have seen several blots and interlineations in the *preliminary discourse,* I request you will press Mr. Morris to more than ordinary care, that blunders may be avoided. You are next Tuesday to have a meeting of R[oman] Catholics in Fishamble Street to appoint a day for subscribing to the Parliamentary Test in the King's Bench Court.[2] I wish they may not precipitate this affair. They should have patience till in the approaching session a few words may be petitioned for to render the Test the more clear and acceptable to all; and as the prayer of our petition will be constitutional, there can be no doubt of its being granted. Should the gentlemen at the meeting reject this prudential conduct, they will, by dividing a people who should be counted, make sport for those who wish we were divided. They may (and even that is doubtful) obtain a relaxation of some penalties in corporate towns and mountainous tracts, and should they be allowed leases for 99 years tacked with a gavel clause, they would have only the merit of being the instruments of a new law against the growth of Popery![3] In such a case I would ask who would be best off, the juror or nonjuror? By no means will I swear that "*no authority whatsoever can absolve me from the obligation imposed in the new Test,*" but I will swear that no *foreign* authority can absolve me. I will leave a reservation in my oath for the nation of Great Britain on whom we depend; that nation occasionally and in great emergencies can dispense with oaths of allegiances. They have done so in the days of our fathers and have the right of doing so again in a future emergency. To give them, therefore, the exclusion (in a new oath) is neither safe nor constitutional, and the gentlemen ready now to give such an exclusion ought to reflect seriously before they do it. I have troubled you too much, my dear friend, on this melancholy subject. I return to a better, to your own family who are long in possession of my warmest affections; to make particular professions to yourself would be impertinent.

P.S. I request you will write soon to me that I may know the particulars of the proceedings at the Music Hall on Tuesday next.

    1. A Dublin edition of Curry's *An Historical and Critical Review.* . . . O'Conor refers to the same work in letters 267, 268, 271, and 272.
    2. The Catholics met on Monday instead of Tuesday. Many decided to go. "A very numerous and respectable body of Roman Catholic gentlemen" led by Lord Trimleston went to the Court of King's Bench to sign the oath of Allegiance on 28 June 1775. *DJ,* 4–6 July 1775. Obviously the group had not followed O'Conor's advice.
    3. Heads of a bill for the Better Encouragement for Papists to Become Protestants were brought in on 11 February 1774. It provided that a Catholic might take leases for

any number of years in any city or town in Ireland after taking the oath of allegiance. However, when he died, his land would still be gaveled (divided) and the wife or child who conformed would receive the larger portion of the divided estate. This bill never passed beyond the earliest presentation. *DJ*, 12–15 February 1774; Lecky, 2 : 193.

270. To Dr. John Curry, Summerhill, Dublin

OCD, 8.4 HS 141

[From my Hermitage, 5 August 1775]

My Dear Sir,

I well know that you never would withdraw your friendship from me except by my own fault, and that I shall take care not to commit. I do not want gratitude; and if I were not bound (as I truly am) by it, yet the low principle of self interest would not permit my losing possession of the hold I have of you. I am truly bound to you by every tie; you led the way in breaking the chain of public prejudice against our poor people. I followed you in the same laudable and, indeed, desperate task; and I think that we both had the merit of forcing (so to speak) men in power to take a review of laws which have done great mischief to the public and brought no advantages to counterbalance it. We probably contributed, though indirectly, to the late Parliamentary Test offered us, and though you and I differ a little about it, yet it is between us as it was with old Horace and his philosophic adversaries: *incolumi semper amicitia.*[1] I am truly in pain that our poor people united for seventy years past should be now divided into jurors and non-jurors to pass from the contempt to the mockery of those who hate us. Some of our divines, you say, approve of the Test.[2] They will, I presume, show their sincerity by subscribing to it themselves; for my own part, I shall not subscribe to the paragraph: "*that no authority whatsoever can dispense with the oath now tendered, or any part thereof,*" for in swearing so I would depose what is *not true.* Judge Blackstone says that the British nation have occasionally an authority to absolve oaths of allegiance, and without that judge's assistance I know that the people of this country in my father's time have been absolved from their oath to the late King James and have been obliged to swear a new one to his successors, William and Mary. The truth is our legislature have overlooked the matter and undoubtedly meant "*no foreign authority,*" and it were better to wait till the next session for the insertion of the adjective *foreign* than swear precipitately to the proposition as it now stands and defend their Act by advancing that the word "*foreign*" is *implied*. What will our enemies say of men who *swear to implications* in a test wherein they abjure all mental reservation? Our jurors, as I have heard from a member of Parliament, will have a bill brought in their favor for allowing long leases in corporate towns and reclaimable wastes subject to a gavel. Should this be the case, the jurors will be made the instruments of a new law against the growth of Popery and will be worse off than the non-jurors, or else they will become firmer men than I expect in abstaining from taking any benefit from such an intended law. God help us, as you often pray.

You omitted saying a word to me on my friend Thady's scheme of life in his native country; I have ventured giving you my thoughts on the subject I wrote you on my arrival here. Whether I was right or wrong, I would not omit giving you a proof that I am interested in every thing that concerns you. I request you will tender him and your whole family my warmest affections.

From my Hermitage, 5 August 1775

    1. With friendship always unimpaired. O'Conor is disturbed that Curry's decision to sign the oath and his own decision to abstain may endanger their friendship and even divide the Catholic leadership.
    2. Archbishop John Carpenter to Charles O'Conor, 12 August 1775, Stowe MS. B12, RIA. Carpenter wrote to O'Conor the following strong statement concerning the oath: "From the very first moment that the form appeared, I gave my opinion vigorously, according to the dictates of my conscience, and which I thought perfectly conformable to the commands of God and the precepts of Holy Church: and you are sensible that I took care to make my sentiments on the affair known very early to many of my brethren to prevent a division from taking place among us. But if some of them choose to differ in opinion from me, and to oppose what I condemn, I have only to lament the misfortune of our disagreement in this point, my having done my duty, and that my behavior on this occasion is certainly the most irreproachable and least exposed to error."
    Archbishop Carpenter was justifying his position for not signing the Oath. He concluded his letter with the knowledge that many of the Munster bishops had signed the form.

271. To Dr. John Curry, Summerhill, Dublin

OCD, 8.4 HS 141

From my Hermitage, 27 September 1775

My Dear Sir,

I really longed for a letter from you; and yet considering our avocations from profession and from family concerns, you place me too highly in your debt and rather give me too much of your time. The debt I will discharge, my dear sir, not in the common epistolary gratitude, but in real feelings of the heart. In the new work with which you enrich the public, you have placed me next to yourself by a little introductory discourse; and I surely (in that instance) owe you more than ever I shall be able to repay. We shall now walk down together to posterity, and by a most pleasing anticipation I enjoy the truth that in your lifetime you singled me out among the first of your friends. Let me press it upon you to fish for as much useful matter as possible for your appendix, for it should be a magazine to level every battery that a Hume or less popular writer can raise for overthrowing historical truth; and yet I demur against delays of publication because your town is filling and the session approaching when the critical time of information is come when evidently some of our legislature are not adverse to truth and begin to think that they have sacrificed too much to their prejudices; I do not mean those prejudices by which interest may be served, but those by which it is daily wounded. Literary publications like all other wares brought to market have their proper seasons and fall in their price as soon as the demand when postponed too long. I am concerned to find that, notwithstanding all your care, there are some typographical mistakes; there is no remedy but by a good table of *errata*.[1] Last post I had a copy of the *Introduction* enclosed to me by Mr. Morris; there are two or three capital blunders, and it is well that there are no more, as I had not time or health for giving the composition a fair copy. I requested of Morris to correct those blunders in the *errata*.

Relatively to the new Parliamentary Test, I find that you have a majority of the Divines on your side in the approbation you gave it, its being subscribed to by our people. It will have the good effect of acquitting them to all Europe as to the soundness of their political principles and of showing to demonstration that our Penal Laws must for the future derive their sole justification from civil and spiritual malevolence. There is great good in this, and no other can be expected in the present temper of the majority of our lawmakers. The Court indeed might give no obstruction to a relaxation, but it will hazard nothing by requiring it. One member assured myself we should have a relaxation; that is, we would be allowed to take long leases in corporate towns and limited districts of mountainous lands, subject, however, to a gavel tack. I observed to him that such would be only *a new law against the growth of Popery;* he replied that it was so intended, and he hoped it would be more effectual than any other. Should this be the relief granted, I would ask who should be the best off in the upshot, the juror or non-juror? But *jacta est alea*,[2] the jurors, as I said above, will have the satisfaction of leaving the Penal Laws, injustifiable *as to them,* and I trust they will have the merit also of taking no advantage from any other new law against the perpetuity of their spiritual duty. I confess to you, *sub sigillo*,[3] that I am not concerned that our friend in Ash Street[4] has been supplanted by others, so that they are possessed of the knowledge and discretion necessary in intercourses with great men; and yet I have not and never had any opinion of the knowledge or discretion of one man who has taken the lead among you. For my part I had (as you know) no exception to the new Test, but that it was defective in two or three words to render it constitutional; you have said and said truly that those words are implied, yet it is not hard to swear to *implications* in a formulary where all mental reservation is abjured? Perhaps my scruples are groundless as some implications may be so connected with the matter sworn to us as to leave all reserve of the mind inoperative or needless; thus when I say with great truth that the sun gives us light *by day* is implied, but the mental reservation of those two monosyllables is undoubtedly inoperative and needless. There are, however, implications that cannot so safely be left without explanation, for instance that paragraph in the late Parliamentary Test which sets forth that: "no authority whatsoever, can dispense with the oath taken or any part thereof." Evidently the legislature meant no *foreign* authority, and it would be so given if we voted for it by a petition to the House of Commons in the next session, but I have tired you with my wretched, prolix letter. I beg that I may hear (as soon as you possibly can) from you about those particulars hinted in your last.

1. List of errors.
2. Suetonius, *Lives of Twelve Caesars, J. Caesar*, 32 "The die is cast."
3. Under seal (confidentially).
4. Thomas Reynolds of Ash Street, Dublin, a member of the Catholic Committee. See Wall, p. 111.

272. To Dr. John Curry

OCD, 8.4 HS 141

26 October 1775

My Dear Sir,

After my return from a County Sligo excursion, I found your letter of the 17th instant before me in this Hermitage. It pains me that relatively to your *opus magnum* you have met with a disappointment for which you could not be prepared had it been foreseen. I know better than any man that the end you proposed in that labored work was to make your countrymen better and wiser men than they are by removing the misinformations which rendered them malevolent and consequently unjust in the dispensation of power; and yet, after making so many presents to the public heretofore, it would be hard indeed if in this last publication the bookseller alone should receive the whole advantage without any consideration to the author, but this cannot be the case while all the copies are still in our own power. Let me, however, obtain one request from you, namely, that you will not persist in your resolution of standing to the whole expense of paper and print rather than submit to the expense of £20 or 30 in giving two hundred copies to your subscribers bound. This request I would never prefer to you had I not foreseen you would be a loser by the resolution you are taking; most of our Irish readers appreciate books more by the weight of the paper than of the matter; and, little as they may think of expending 13s in a tavern, they will think that sum too much for a book of five hundred pages in boards. On this knowledge I have of our people, I take it for granted that the bookseller will (sooner or later within twelve months) give the work bound for 13s, and if so, it would be hard that your subscribers should be worse served than the shop purchaser, nay, that in fact they should be losers. The *Hibernia Dominicana*,[1] a larger book than yours and printed closely on small Elziver type, was given bound to the subscribers at half a guinea. Five hundred copies of your book (if quick in the sale) would come £375, and from this state of the case there would be a profit (a poor one indeed) of more than £100 after all expense of paper, printing, and binding, etc., was discharged; but from the knowledge I mentioned of the temper of our people, I apprehend that the sale will not be as quick as I wish for the good and honor of the public it may be. You see, my dear friend, how freely I throw out my mind to you on this subject, and I shall surely owe much to your indulgence if you pardon the liberty I take. Indeed, I never before made so free with any friend in any affair that required delicacy in delivering my judgment, but let what I throw out on this occasion be *inter penetralia Vestae*.[2] Let the whole be buried with ourselves if you think me wrong; I will this evening write to Mr. Reynolds feelingly as you require, and after he puruses my letter, you and he may come to such an understanding as will leave no impression on his mind that his requisition of binding will not make such an impression on yours as to make void all obligation to him. To the shame of all your friends of weight, he was the only man who solicited encouragers to your undertaking and had success in his solicitations.

I had not a line from Dr. O'Gorman[3] since he left the kingdom. As he is a man of honor, I take it that he will, sooner or later, remit me an account of his success in disposing of the proposals I have put into his hands at his own request. I am well-pleased with my friend Mr. Keon's[4] activity; I have in this place drawn up a few lines in the form of a Letter to one Secretary B. acquainting him with the temper of our civil united gentry of Conaght in the present crisis, and I am told he procured many subscribers to that Letter at our great fair of Balinasloe. Government, by obtaining a good and merited impression of us, has at last relented towards us, and yet it can be easily foreseen that the executive power will be very cautious to encounter the general prejudice of proposing anything directly in our favor. The Legislature feel the effect of tying up the hands of labor and industry by penal laws which now have no object moral or political to justify their continuation, but the members of that body hate Popery because its votaries had once contended for power and property with the Reformers. They would impose on themselves that the old (and indeed real) danger is still present; and in this situation of things little can be expected from their deliberations. Like men beginning to be free from groundless ideas, they will possibly make attempts in this or a future session to give us something like a deviation that will be no deviation from the Penal Laws. They will tack a gavel to any landed property and perhaps give some security to a monied property. This will be far from being any cure for our national health, and we will be forced to emigrate into Canada, as you physicians send patients to Lanquedoc for the benefit of the air.[5] Be it so! Emigration may turn out as well for patients in one case as in the other, and I am glad that the hint was dropped in the introduction to your book. Adieu, my dear friend, and let me hear soon from you. How does Thady employ his time? How is Frank?

1. *Hibernia Dominicana* was de Burgo, Bishop of Ossory's history of the Irish Dominicans, published in 1762.
2. Within the shrine of Vesta, confidential.
3. Thomas O'Gorman, M.D. (1732–1809). Born 16 September at Castletown, Co. Clare. Educated at Irish College, Paris. Married the daughter of Count d'Eon and received as her dowry a number of vineyards in Burgundy. A member of the Irish Brigade created a chevalier by Louis XV. Henry Boylan, *A Dictionary of Irish Biography* (New York: Barnes and Noble, 1978), p. 266.
4. Ambrose and Francis Keon were wool merchants in Bridge Street, Dublin. *DJ*, 2–4 May 1769. Members of the Catholic Committee.
5. The political air of Canada was purer. The Quebec Act passed by the British Parliament in 1774 guaranteed French Catholics religious freedom and their own French law courts. Lunt, p. 658. See also the comments of young Lord Lyttleton on the Act. *DJ*, 2–4 June 1774.

273. To Denis O'Conor, Belanagare, Roscommon

OCD, 8.4 SE 148

Pill Lane, 3 December 1775

Dear Denis,

I have delivered the substance of your letter to Mr. Bennet. Without hesitation, he informed me that he agreed to your request of respiting the payment of £60 (a part of the sum you engaged to him) till the next wool fair of Dunlo. He added that the personal esteem he has for yourself would not permit him to do anything by you but what might bear the best construction in your own mind. Bennet is a good man, and I have experienced proofs of his kindness. I am unfortunate in my family. A niece here laid seige to me and, weak as I am, I was obliged to give her half a guinea to bring her down to the country. A milliner has begotten me with complaints that my daughter owes her £3.16 for millinery trifles and that she cannot obtain an answer to her letters. I gave Charles, a few days before my arrival here, 12 guineas, for which I request you will press him, for you know even within this twelvemonth he has distressed me by the discharge of his rents. He remained here but one night, and I think Mr. Knox will not now make good his promise to him, as probably he [is] jealous of him on the score of his tardiness in payments. The unfortunate man in St. Omer's,[1] like the rest, gives daily instances of his imprudence, and I need not describe the conduct of his weak brother at home.[2] I request you will strain every nerve to make the former the remittance he expects. I could wish you made inquiry about the MacCormick of whom he speaks; I am unfit for such an inquiry and will tell him so when I write to him. I wish your sister-in-law great joy on the late revolution in her life. Give my love to Cathy.

P.S. Mr. Bennet requests you will take care to remit him the £100 you speak of as soon as it becomes payable. I request you will superintend my little affairs and press Nicholson to go on with the stone wall I marked out for him; should it be completed I should have a very useful little park, which in the state of Nature I remember to be worth nothing or indeed very little. Let nothing be done for me without your own previous direction.

1. Daniel O'Conor.
2. Hugh O'Conor, who two years later filed the discovery suit against Charles.

274. To Dr. Charles Kelly[1]

RIA, Stowe MS Bi2

Dublin, 4 April 1776

Reverend and Dear Sir,

Since the promotion of your worthy and unalterable friend, Dr. Carpenter, I had no opportunity open to me for informing you of any affairs of material importance in your native country; and I thought it would not be just to let a bare expression of my grateful affection come alone before you without remitting some intelligence more worthy of your notice. Some late events have proved extremely disagreeable to us, and I shall sum them up in as few words as I can. Our people had hitherto the merit of distinguishing themselves among all the northern nations by a steadiness to our best principle. The majority for more than two hundred years have rejected the rewards and born the punishments of parliamentary power, and the legislature redoubled their blows from time to time till blows were found to be vain or till the hand which inflicted them was fatigued. This cruel policy has of late been somewhat remitted. Severity, which seemed to relent, only changed the manner of its attack. Finding that the former manner had no better success than putting the Catholics in the case of the traveler in the storm (who the more the wind laid claim to his cloak, the faster he held it) they have hit upon a new scheme of dividing them among themselves; and unhappily the scheme had but too much success. To effect this end they have formed a Test of Civil Allegiance for the Roman Catholics and published it in a late Act of Parliament, but so embarrassed with matters open to casuistical doubt and so exposed to implications in a Formulary wherein all mental reservation is abjured, that the intention of framing it to answer the purpose of dividing and perplexing is but too evident. Thus it fell out. The Metropolitan of Cashel[2] and a few other prelates have subscribed to the Test in its present form, and they are resolved to abide by their act, notwithstanding the disapprobation of the Holy See. For the first time, our people are divided into subscribers and nonjurors and yet the former had as little regard paid to them as to the latter through a long session of Parliament which is now ended. We stand still on the same level; and such among us as are ready to give government a complicated Test of Allegiance but such, however, as is sufficient for the ends of civil security will be more esteemed by all wise men among our adversaries than the subscribers who swear to points, of which few are judges and which the most learned casuists may be divided upon. You have had, I doubt not, some information from other hands on this disagreeable subject, and I here dismiss it for a better and one more comfortable to the duties of the holy week in which I am writing.

Dr. Francis Kirwan, our worthy Bishop of Achonry,[3] died a few days ago, and I am certain you will have many applications from several quarters for your interest in the promotion of a successor. It is a duty I impose on myself to apply in favor of a worthy pastor of the diocese of Tuam, Dr. Boethius Egan.[4] I have known him several years, equally distinguished by his labors, learning, and piety. But my knowledge is anticipated by testimonials of his sufficiency from the Bishop of Bordeaux, in whose diocese he completed his studies. He has the most authentic testimonials also from Dr. Skerrett, his own metropolitan; from Dr. Fallon, the Bishop of Elphin; and from Dr. Philips, Bishop of Killala; and copies of their evidences may be sent you from hence signed by a Notary Apostolic. Though your worthy friend Dr. Carpenter has established it as an invariable rule to himself not to meddle in extraprovincial matters; without [ink blot—unreadable] from the Holy See; he would not, however, hesitate in doing justice to the character of Dr. Egan had any mandate come to him from Rome to inquire into his sufficiency, and undoubtedly the Archbishop of Dublin's testimony superadded to the testimonies of the three other prelates would have great weight in deciding upon so weighty a matter as the provision of a proper superior for the government of our clergy. You, who never have anything more in view than the good of God's Church, receive a part of your reward in this world by the deference paid to your judgment and the justice done to your zeal at the fountainhead of spiritual authority. In my suit for your interest in behalf of Dr. Egan I should be impertinent if I added more to what I have written. You will, I believe, have fuller information about him from undoubted judges of his merit.

I have been lately at Clonalis, and I was happy for several nights with the owners of the house. O'Conor is a man of different understanding from his late unfortunate father. In a word, he is an honest and worthy man, and your neice is one of the most valuable women in every respect I have ever known. I am happy in remitting you any good news from this wretched country. Were I to mention myself, I would inform you that I am happy in obtaining and retaining friendship of men you esteem; Dr. Carpenter, Dr. Burke, Mr. Fitzgerald, etc. This situation is to me an equivalent for many rubs of life I meet with.

1. Dr. Charles Kelly is the uncle of Catherine O'Kelly O'Conor, wife of the O'Conor Don, Dominic of Castlerea, Charles' cousin. He is a member of the faculty at the Irish College of Rome.
2. Archbishop James Butler II. *HBC*, p. 393.
3. According to *HBC*, p. 407, the bishop's name was Patrick Robert Kirwan.
4. On 19 March 1776, O'Conor received a letter from John and Sam Egan, asking O'Conor to help their brother Boethius obtain appointment as bishop of Achonry. On 30 March 1776, Boethius repeated the same request in a letter to O'Conor. Stowe MS. B12, RIA. O'Conor's letter did not help Egan, who did not become bishop of Achonry until 1785, and archbishop of Tuam in 1787. Instead Philip Philips, bishop of Killala, was translated to Achonry. *HBC*, p. 407.

275. To Denis O'Conor, Belanagare

OCD, 8.4 SE 148

30 May 1776

... For ten days past I have lived in the county of Kildare among worthy families with Dr. Carpenter. In one of those days I have dined with O'More at Ballina, and I shall be hard set for an apology if I pass him by on my quitting this town for good. Indeed it may be there that art will take me up. We had not a day of rain for three weeks or rather a month, but moisture begins this day. ...

Now would be the time for opening a passage from the river at "Sranta Karata" to the bridge opposite to your house. The earth and gravel of the extended canal spread on both sides would double the value of the land. Such an object is not to be overlooked, and I would contribute as well as I can to the expense. So favorable a season at the present for such a work should, I think, be improved. The line may take in a hundred perches, and I trust that seven or eight shillings per perch would complete the work.

P.S. Through Dr. Fallon's[1] favor, I have had transmitted to me this week his recommendation on Denis MacDermot [unreadable] to one of the best colleges in Europe (Salamanca) where he will be no charge on his friends. Let him prepare himself and pick up the best viaticum he can among his kindred that he may lose no time in preparing for his voyage. Let him also take his baptismal certificate, well-authenticated. Dr. Carpenter will consolidate Dr. Fallon's recommendations with his own and confirm Denis here if he be not confirmed already. I take pleasure in the success of my negotiations on this. ...

1. Dr. Fallon is James O'Fallon, bishop of Elphin.

276. To Hugh MacDermot[1]

OCD, 8.4 HS 141

12 June 1776

I derive very sensible satisfaction, my dear Hugh, from the account I receive of the progress you make in your studies. It is in Paris that they can be conducted to the best advantage, and I need not remind you how much it imports you to persevere in a course so happily begun; your discoveries in the sciences may be intensive and ought to be so, but they should all converge to one point to a single and capital science from the possession of which you will be enabled to establish an independence for your future days and enjoy the most pleasing of all reflections, that of drawing the advantages of life from your own studies without drawing any from contingencies which may come encumbered within disgusting circumstances. Now is the time for setting such a distance between Fortune and yourself; there has to be but little in her power hereafter, but this distance is marked and must be filled by personal endowments. Nature may have dealt her gifts to you with no illiberal hand, yet this Nature can do no more than to lay foundations. Well-cultivated, she marks out the lines between virtue and vice with tolerable precision, but she furnishes not the means for pursuing one or avoiding the other, or she does it very imperfectly. A sense of this will give your reflections a new spring and discover to you the true means of conducting life to its proper end. Religion alone furnishes those means. Nature, as far as she goes, leads surely, but her line is short and terminates in a labyrinth. There she drops us. . . .

1. O'Conor's grandson, who is studying medicine in Paris.

277. To Archbishop John Carpenter

OCD, 8.4 HS 141

From the Hermitage, 1 September 1776

Most Reverend Sir,

The emotions which feeling minds suffer on parting with those they affect most were very strong on me when I wished your Grace a happy time of it on setting off for your several visitations through the districts of Dublin and Glendalough. The like impressions recurred very forcibly a few days after on setting out for the place I now live in. With Mr. and Mrs. Lee I became one of the family, and the gratitude I owe them partakes so much of instinct or is attended with so much pleasure as to cease in some degree of being a duty. I parted them with pain; wherever I am, I must still consider myself as one of their family. The memory of my enjoyments at the worthy Mr. Luby's cannot be worn away, and the kindness of my other friends in Dublin must be ever present to me. In a particular manner I request of your Grace to tender my affections to Mr. Troy and Dr. Sherlock. We expect you in Conaght in the next summer. The good of the Church demands you. The fame of your wisdom in ecclesiastical government has smoothed the way for you, and all parties here are prepared to pay you the respect due to the Metropolitan of Leinster. When I said that the good of the Church demands you, I need not explain myself. Since our last provincial constitutions, made (I think) in 1672, many circumstances in the times call for new regulations very pressingly, and foundations must be laid by the Metropolitans to bring their suffrogans to finish the edifice in concert with them. In the present calm (a calm indeed not to be paralleled in this or the preceding century), such a great work (under the conduct of prudence) can be effected without any hazard. I beg pardon for saying so much out of my own line. What follows comes more within my department. A young lady here, Miss Mary Welsh (connected with my family and the daughter of a reputable merchant formerly of Fisher's Lane), has taken the resolution to enter into a religious order. Mrs. Welsh, her mother, does not oppose it but wants that her daughter should postpone taking the veil and remain with herself till she pays the last duties to an old, sickly mother who has not many years to live. The daughter would assist in that pious office to a grandmother if she did not conceive that another duty is superior to it, and she scruples the not putting her resolution into immediate execution. It is the struggle between one virtue and another, nor would our reasoning to persuade her that both may be fulfilled (by suspending the latter for some time) avail till she had the sentence of the Archbishop of Dublin on the point. It is a distress arising from the best principles; and as it is an act of charity to relieve her, I need say no more in this address to your Grace. My son Denis, my whole family present you with their affections. I am still affected with rheumatic pains.

278[1]

OCD, 8.4 SH 152

13 December 1776

On this day of a general politico-religious feast. It is not out of the way to consider that two-thirds of the people know nothing about it. The majority of the nation, finding themselves legally excluded from the benefits of our civil cause, can draw no great benefit from its preservation. Surely the existence of such a case must force a reflection upon us that there is something very defective in our legislative policy. It would seem that our laws should be so framed as to render the people fearful of a revolution instead of putting them into a situation as to expect no relief from civil misery but through revolution. It must be confessed that penal laws against Roman Catholics were a necessary, though hurtful, expedient in an age when that people were stripped of power, when their passions were warm to reinstate themselves, when resentment became revenge, and when worldly interest pressed religious maxims into its service to regain what was lost.

1. Fragment.

279. To Dr. John Curry, Summerhill, Dublin

OCD, 8.4 HS 141

30 December 1776

My silence to you has indeed been as you observe, long and unusual. I should have informed you that I have arrived in safety in the Hermitage because it was a fact you would be glad to know, and yet I was loath to give you that information unless I could remit it free of the post tax, and this I could not easily accomplish as my neighboring friend, Mr. French, lost his election in Roscommon.[1] To put you to expense on such a topic as myself or any commonplace topic would be too much, though your good nature would induce you to think otherwise; and as to matter worthy of your attention, this western province is as barren of it as Siberia. We are beginning a new year, but no new life relatively to our endearments and good wishes. It is more than twenty years since I have obtained your friendship and that upon the most generous terms that friendship was ever bestowed, for you gratuitously put me in possession; that possession I can not lose but by my own fault, and such a fault I can not commit.[2] Even the lowest of our principles would forbid it and the best render it impossible. You were the most sincere and most learned friend I ever had; you were the most affectionate also. . . . The division among ourselves into *subscribers* and *nonsubscribers* has produced a little coolness among men who loved and still love one another; and let me inform you, for I can do it from knowledge, that you are esteemed and will ever be esteemed by certain persons who, since the time subscribing, have not lived with you in their former familiarity. . . .

1. Arthur French was defeated for his Roscommon seat in the Irish Parliament by Edward Crofton. Thomas Mahon was returned. *DJ,* 11–13 June 1776.
2. O'Conor is still deeply concerned that Curry's swearing to the Parliamentary Test of 1774 and his own nonswearing will damage their friendship.

280. To Mr. Thomas Lee[1]

OCD, 8.4 HS 141

Belanagare, 5 February 1777

. . . I have perused your *Catholics' Address to Lord Harcourt*[2] with pleasure. It sets out with giving us importance in the State, though our masters have taken incipient care we should have none: "We are no inconsiderable part of his Majesty's subjects," say the *addressers.* Had they said: "We are no inconsiderable number," they would assert the known truth, and their address would by no means be less acceptable. Their gratitude for obtaining the late Test is burlesque, it being an indirect censure on the Holy See and of the civil Constitution also, as it denies to the people their often exercised power of dispensing with oaths of allegiance. Will not such thrusts conveyed in a poor, heavy period make our adversaries laugh?

They advance that the late tumultuous risings were from every denomination of religion among us. If they added "Quaker and Methodist excepted," the humor would keep pace with the thrust of the paragraph. Indeed, the whole paragraph is most impertinent and, therefore, unwise in such an address, as no religion is chargeable with the conduct of its *miscreants.* . . .

1. O'Conor frequently lodged with Mr. Thomas Lee of Pill Lane in Dublin.
2. Lord Harcourt resigned as Viceroy and was replaced in November 1776 by John Hobart, the earl of Buckinghamshire. Lecky 2:168. In September 1775 Catholic lead-

ers presented an address of loyalty which was "prompted by the outbreak of the American Revolution. The opportunity provided by Britain's growing difficulties in America was too good to be missed, and Irish Catholics began to press tactfully for some redress of their grievances." O'Connell, p. 107. See also pp. 32–35 and Lecky, 2:165.

281. To Dr. John Curry, Dublin

OCD, 8.4 HS 142

[25 February 1777]

My Dear Sir,

Your letter of the 17th instant was a relief and a great one to me in these pangs I suffer of late, and yet I feel new pain from the account you give me of your son Frank. Mr. Slingsby is in many instances a worthy man, but the degree of precipitance and austerity which mixes with his better qualities is highly injurious to friendship by preventing many of its good effects. His jealous temper leads him into misconstructions because he has not coolness or, in other words, strength enough to view a question but on one side; and if by chance the fairest side is first exposed to him, the proper impression is made, and that it is so you must thank your own good fortune rather than your friend's judgment. Had I (and perhaps I have) a friend of this stamp, I would not dismiss him from my affections, but he should have no great share in my esteem. Your temper and mine, God be thanked, have been cast in a different mold, and I ever thought that a suspicious man must have something wrong within himself and copies his notions of his species from a very bad original. In a word we both would give a fairer trial to an avowed adversary than Mr. Slingsby does to an old and intimate friend. But let me not condemn his present conduct too much. I am not well reconciled to Frank's long silence, and God grant that the indiscretion of youth has not in his fatal intercourses with O'Kelly[1] betrayed him into some deviations which may justify or partially justify Mr. Slingsby's present estrangement from him, though nothing can justify any estrangement from you, as he knows that you sincerely love him. Your sympathy in my afflictions summons up all my feelings relatively to yours; and I shall be in pain till I hear further from you on this subject of your son. I combat my afflictions with fortitude, and you have set me the example through the severest trials that man can undergo. You will not, I know you will not, stop short in any encounter with future rubs of life but approve yourself with the *semper idem*[2] which religion and even your own manly sense of things have hitherto made you. What we suffer and what we may yet suffer will be for our good, if it be not our own fault. After the many shipwrecks which for ages have ruined my family and after the last of all which left us but a bare plank to come to shore upon, I am now on the score of my religion called upon to deliver it up to a younger brother by a right of primogeniture in Protestancy (being the first of the family who has got his birth in it).[3] But happily for me (I hope) my father gave up or was forced to give up the fee of Belanagare in 1720 to John French, Esq., who foreclosed or paid off an old mortgage on that land in 1699. On the agreement then made, Mr. French admitted my father to possess this land, subject however to rent charge of £80 per annum. By this agreement my father held his estate by (what they call) a *base tenure* and therefore not open to the operation of the Gavel Act, as my lawyers assure me. My brother, however, has filed a bill against me, suing for a Gavel; but lest that should not succeed he has armed himself with another bill against me, suing for the whole property of Belanagare as a Protestant Discoverer, pretending that my father's agreement with Mr. French was in the nature of a lease wherein a Papist can have no perpetuity nor a tenure beyond thirty-one years. If lawyers do not give me flattering hopes for my money, the agreement of my father with Mr. French has no intercommunity with the Lease Law and that in either case my adversary will be defeated. If they should prove mistaken and I must give up this property to a discoverer, there is no remedy nor can I pay too much for a religion which among its other duties towards God and man requires of me to be as faithful a subject to the present government as the civil constitution itself with all its sanctions demands. In such a case surely, my punishment will hold no proportion with my crime; I, however with reverence approach the altar and offer myself a willing victim, should such a sacrifice be necessary. But enough on this subject.

In the public papers I have perused the Address of the Roman Catholics to our late Viceroy. I think it wants spirit both in the matter and composition. A good meaning ill-expressed may, from the probity of the intention, be overlooked to an individual, but in a public act it is shameful and conveys an idea that the inferiority of our condition extends to an inferiority of ability in the expression of feelings which render poverty itself eloquent. The address begins with asserting that, *"We are no inconsiderable part of his Majesty's loyal subjects."* It would surely be better to say, *"We are no inconsiderable number and since as a part or a party we are* (and our enemies rejoice at it) *inconsiderable indeed."* The last paragraph exhibits imporant matter, but in my opinion it is ill-digested and expressed clumsily. In the *Hiberian Journal* I have seen most illiberal and malevolent remarks made on this address, and I have received information here that those invectives have not sprung from the dissenters, but from some among ourselves who have on this occasion assumed the puritanical garb.[4] If so, the finesse is equally shameful and wicked. I say no more on this head, reserving my indignation at present till I find better authority for the information I received. I rejoice with you, my dear friend, on the justice done you by the reviewers in their collection for December last; foreign lands recognize the value of your historical labors and know how to appreciate the merit that envy or ill-will endeavor to oppress at home. It is one of the comforts of my life that you handed me down to posterity as your fast friend by incorporating a billet from me with your late publication. *Simul ibimus ambo*[5] is the motto I delight in, and may it extend happily to the next world as well as the present. God bless you and spare a moment from your better avocations and employ it in writing to me on the present state of things, either personally regarding yourself or generally on our public concerns. You know I live in a hermitage, from whence nothing can transpire but my affections for my friends and chiefly those connected with you: Mrs. Curry, the young couple, Mrs. Bigger, Mrs. Hamill, Jack Comerford, Martin Gaven, etc.

25 February 1777

P.S. This week I received two volumes of the epistolary correspondence of the late Pope *Clement XIV*.[6] How do you like those books? In my opinion no writing of this age will do more good by opening the eyes of Protestants relatively to impressions made on them (from their infancy to manhood) by their preachers supported by some of our own Doctors in their apocryphal writings. In this collection we find the Pontiff himself disclaiming all jurisdiction over the temporal rights of princes, censuring some opinions of the Schoolmen and condemning the intemperate zeal of those Doctors who instead of quenching error by the waters of charity set fire to the house of God by stimulating the Faithful to inquisitions and persecutions. Edifying as such apostolical doctrine must be, yet it will vex and vex sorely the *Blackstones* of the present age to find a pope renouncing the only doctrines on which they justify the Penal Laws against British Catholics. From sad experience we know that some men are made worse by disarming them of a favorite error, particularly any error wherein they have a real or imaginary interest. Even their pride is wounded by the discovery of a truth they always combated. It is a consolation, however, that such men will aim at the good of the country and may sooner or later have the power of establishing it on the broad bottom of all parties. Adieu.

    1. Comte John James O'Kelly (1749–1800), French Minister at Mainz.
    2. Always the same.
    3. Why did this discovery case lie dormant so long? Why did not O'Conor mention that his brother Hugh was suing him before? These questions cast doubt on the statements made by Charles Owen O'Conor and Gareth and Janet Dunleavy that the discovery case began in 1756 and continued until 1784.

    The editors contend that there was more than one discovery suit against Charles and Denis O'Conor (See letter 314), but that the major case of Hugh O'Conor vs. Charles was not instituted until 1777. All internal evidence in the letters supports this conclusion. In "Corrigenda," *Éire-Ireland*, 14 (Winter 1979), 154–155, the editors presented the following argument:

> The Dunleaveys list a letter written by Charles to an unknown correspondent as 8.3 SE O33, n.d. 1756. Actually this letter was written in 1777. In it Charles speaks about the suit recently brought against him by his brother and closes with a reference to the American Revolutionary War and the hardships it is causing in Ireland. O'Conor makes first mention of the suit in his frequent letters to Curry and to Archbishop Carpenter, only after 1777, and it comes up repeatedly thereafter in his correspondence with them until 1784. It is his chief concern in his letters to his son Denis from 1777 on. He gives Denis almost a weekly account of the progress of the suit while Charles is in Dublin negotiating with lawyers. In fact O'Conor's main defense against Hugh is that the Statute of Limitations had run out before he filed. O'Conor claimed that his brother should have made his case known when his father's estate was settled after his death in 1750.
>
> Finally, O'Conor's letters also make clear that he had not taken the oath of allegiance of 1774 at the time the suit was filed. O'Conor, in his letters to Curry and Carpenter, objected strongly and repeatedly to the wording of the oath in which jurors swore their allegiance to King George III and denied the pope "has or ought to have any temporal or civil power." O'Conor felt that the oath was an invidious attempt to divide Irish Catholics into jurors and non-jurors. This it did in fact do. When Curry signed immediately, and O'Conor and Carpenter delayed, a strain appears in O'Conor's letters to his friend. Also, at this time he pleads with Curry not to resent Carpenter's action in the affair of the oath. Eventually Denis signs, followed by Carpenter and finally O'Conor, who holds out the longest, until 1779. Charles takes the oath only after he had been held under house arrest for a month because his lawyer had failed to make a response to the court in regard to the Discovery Suit. No doubt the timing of the suit and the humiliations of the house arrest pressured O'Conor to sign in spite of his objection.

    4. See *HJ*, 4 September, 29 September, 3 October, 10 November 1775. O'Connell, p. 36.
    5. We shall both go together.
    6. R. Moncrieffe advertised a four-volume set of the *Letters of Pope Clement XIV*, translated from the French. *DJ*, 19–22 July 1777.

282. To Dr. John Curry, Dublin

OCD, 8.4 HS 142

From the Hermitage, 15 March 1777

... In the *Freeman's Journal* of the 11th instant, which I found in a neighbor's house, I find the late Address of the Roman Catholics to the present Viceroy, with his Excellency's answer. I thought that these public acts would not be printed, and I suspect that our enemies are the publishers from the worst intentions and with the view of falling foul upon us on this ground. ... I am really concerned at the account you give me of the approbation given in a certain society to *Calvin's* libel, for it can answer no end but a bad one to approve of a political schism among despised people whose deliverance (if practicable) must be the consequence of a thorough union in political orthodoxy, in active obedience, I mean, to a government which God commands us to obey. Whether the writer was a real or simulated Calvin, he is equally a libeler who should be despised by all parties and approved by none. I would wish with all my soul that his libel was traced to the true source because, should it prove a real puritanical work, an aspersion on our people would thereby be wiped away and nothing would be censurable but the imprudence of the approvers. On the other hand, if one of ourselves should be detected as the author, we should know how to deal with a man who, to wound us the deeper, has employed the weapon of a capital enemy. I am sorry at the attack in *Freeman's Journal* on the person you mention. I have not seen that paper, and its not being displeasing to many among us is really a grievous consideration. ...

283. To Archbishop John Carpenter

OCD, 8.4 HS 142

Belanagare, 2 April 1777

Most Rev[eren]d Sir,

I have of late been thrown into a state of anxiety; and as it fell unforeseen, I was but ill-prepared for it. Suffering may indeed be best for me, and on that principle I should get the better of this last surprise upon me and center my future destiny as I ought in resignation. Yet I cannot, I confess, so easily shake off my feelings for a son and ten innocent grandchildren who must share my fate, whatever it may be. Even in this trial, submission to what heaven permits is our duty. Wise providence permits what it does not will and turns the deviations of one man or set of men into straight paths for others, however rugged the way may appear. All this trouble to me came from the youngest of my father's sons, who, having dissipated his own fortune, has turned Protestant with a view to seize upon mine by a Bill of Discovery on the Popery Acts. But my case, being a singular one, will not, I trust, come within the operation of those laws, as my property is subject to a perpetual rent charge and to the eventual operation of old mortgages long since forclosed. By what I could hitherto learn, such a tenure is not forbidden by any of our Penal Laws, and to decide that it does come within their interdict at this distance of time and after a peaceful possession of twenty-seven years since my father's decease would surely be a violent ingraftment on an old stock which has already yielded all the fruit it was expected to bear. I am not yet destitute of some hope that the severest civil punishment cannot fall on a person who is as guiltless of a civil crime as any other of his Majesty's good subjects without exception. If, however, I am left nothing to inherit but the religion and misfortunes of my ancestors, the victim and victims are prepared, nor will they (I trust God) be the less resigned that they will be led bound and corded to the altar. Better things, however, are to be expected from the lenient temper of the present interpreters of our Penal Laws. I would gladly put my case into the hands of your worthy neighbor Councilor Dwire Lyster, one of the ablest lawyers in the kingdom. My son Denis has already furnished him lately in Roscommon with such a brief of my case as I could draw, and I have given Mr. Ferral, my law agent, orders to put a copy of my family deeds into his hands for his opinion. He has received my son kindly and promised he would give our case a friendly attention. Should you see him, it might fall in your way to recommend your friend to him as a client who knows how to put the proper estimate on his labor. You see with what freedom I pour out my heart to you, but this is to the friend, not to the metropolitan. In the latter character I beg a thousand pardons for this trouble and all this impertinence also. No man alive can be more sensible of the respect due to your Grace than I am. I shall ever pay it, and you will find I will; yet as I began in the familiar style, I shall be bold to end in a request that my gratitude and services may be presented to my warm friends Mr. Thomas Lee and Mrs. Lee, Mrs. Troy and my fast friend Dr. Sherlock.

284. To Denis O'Conor, Belanagare

OCD, 8.4 HS 108

Pill Lane, 24 April 1777

... A case very parallel to mine is now canvassed here in a court of law, and Mr. Lyster thinks that the decision upon it will throw new light on this novel question which has dragged me into Chancery. It is thought that this new matter, now so warmly debated in the King's Bench, will be determined this term; and where the letter of the law is not explicit, people do not doubt of a favorable interpretation. My case is indeed very complicated. That of my adversary is very simple. A penal law is his fort. He grounds *his hope* of success upon the *lucky* circumstance that the Papist he attacks is not as good a mark for *legal prey* as the law requires. I trust that his fear is not groundless, and it may be that the misfortunes of my family are in one respect my best answer.

285. To Denis O'Conor, Belanagare

OCD, 8.4 SE 148

[17 May 1777]

... Indeed, my affair wears a good complexion from the temper of the times, so well prepared for giving a liberal construction to hitherto untried cases; and yet it will surprise you to hear that the question whether the statute of limitations be extendible to Papists has been debated with great warmth for several days in the King's Bench; and so reserved have the judges been on the point that they have postponed pronouncing decisively on it till the next term. As I am assured that I shall not be compelled to put in my answer to my adversary's Bill till next November, nor so soon, I think I should return to my own home, but I will remain here during the short vacation that I may have my lawyers more at leisure for considering my case and hear from their own mouths the hopes I am to entertain and the conduct I am to hold. As mine is a maiden case, all my friends are anxious for the consequences. . . . How these things will end cannot be foreseen, but it flatters my expectation that I have so many friends without ever soliciting any. The late wound from the death of the dearest friend I could ever have or enjoy makes me almost forget every other. . . .[1]

1. O'Conor's daughter, Bridget MacDermot, died 10 May. Sheehan, p. 547.

286. To Denis O'Conor, Belanagare

OCD, 8.4 SE 148

Pill Lane, 10 June 1777

... The judges have not yet come to a decision on the late statutes of limitation, nor probably will they pronounce upon it till next November term. I find no steps yet taken by my adversaries to compel me to put in my answer. I shall keep this matter at all the distance from me that the law allows to persons who have many materials to collect before they can answer fully. . . . My worthy friend Councilor Rice departed from me this moment. We held a conversation on my affair for half an hour. He tells me that an affair of the limitations is to be debated in the King's Bench on Friday next and that should the judge decide that the Law of Limitations does not extend to Papists, an appeal to the King's Bench in England would be extremely proper, and he believes the matter will not rest here. . . .

287. To Denis O'Conor

OCD, 8.4 SE 148

From Pill Lane, 21 June 1777

... My counsel are very clear that the Bill of Discovery against me will be immediately dismissed on the hearing. As to the *limitations* matter (which has been long debated here) it ended oddly enough on Wednesday last, for the judges divided upon it, the Chief Justice holding one opinion and his two assessors another. This very division wears a good complexion, and as no doubt is entertained, but that when this matter is brought before another tribunal, it will meet with a construction equally liberal and equitable. And yet, as my affair is less complicated than that of Copinger against Copinger, it is hoped and believed it will receive its proper interpretation here, without putting me to the expense of removing it over the water by a Writ of Error. This next week I shall wait on Mr. Kelly and Mr. Lyster to receive the instructions necessary for my conduct in the long vacation before me. . . .

. . . The late Count O'Gara[1] has, unknown to me, borne me real affection. He was high, and as he found I had some reputation abroad through a book entitled *Dissertations,* he claimed his kindred to me in the most effectual manner; for yesterday morning I received a letter dated June 6 from Monsieur Deusin (Secretary to the Household of her Serene Highess the Archduchess of the Netherlands) informing me that the Count appointed him one of his executors and left me a legacy of *ten thousand livres French,* to be paid to me before the end of the current year, and he requested my order for that sum. . . .

1. MacLysaght, p. 155, states that Count Charles O'Gara of Brussels was a millionaire.

288. [Addressee not named]

OCD, 8.3 SE 033

[Summer 1777][1]

. . . In every line of your conduct let probity be your guide, for without it you will infallibly be corrupted by some companions you must unavoidably mix with and, like them, end with misery and remorse what began with dissipation and folly. My unhappy brother Hugh has run out of his whole fortune through [corrupt]ness and want of industry. He conformed to the religion established here and filed a Bill of Discovery (as a Protestant) against me to wrest from me the poor plank that brought my father to shore after the great wreck of the family fortune in 1688. This affair is not yet come to trial before our Lord Chancellor and I must abide by the event. I have no crime to answer for but professing the religion of my ancestors; and as this circumstance included no civil delinquency, it is hard I should, in so innoxious a state, be exposed, to civil punishment. Indeed the case is so hard, to say not worse, that our Parliament here have lately repealed our Laws of Discovery and Disqualification, but those only regard the future; have no retrospect to the past. The other branches of my family have not departed from the rules of moral conduct and are well; but most are in a state of distress, a state which it seems we are tied down to by a prescriptive and hereditary right. . . .

1. In dating this letter the editors have used internal evidence: mentions of early stages of the Discovery Suit and a reference to "the American war," which "has reduced us" to a distressed economic condition. This letter is misdated "1756" in OCD, 8.3 SE 033. Dunleavy and Dunleavy, p. 28.

289. To Denis O'Conor, Belanagare

OCD, 8.4 SE 148

3 July 1777

... My affairs here wear the best complexion they can bear. I dined yesterday with Counselor John O'Conor, a lawyer of repute here; he thinks that my adversary will be foiled easily, and he assured me that he will plead gratis for me when the occasion affords. My pamphlet[1] underwent the revision of Mr. Caddell.[2] He struck out a few lines which he thought impertinent and other periods which he thought indiscreet. He approved of the rest, and I have now modeled the piece to his liking. ...

1. O'Conor's *Reflexions on our Present Critical Situation*. ...
2. Thomas Caddell (1742–1802), bookseller and publisher in the Strand. *Burke*, ed. Holden Furber with P. J. Marshall, 5:164–165.

290. To Denis O'Conor, Belanagare

OCD, 8.4 SE 148

Dublin, 8 July 1777

... Numbers like my pamphlet, and if my lawyers permit, it will soon come out under the care of a worthy friend[1] who will see it correctly published after my departure hence. From what I have said, you see [torn] nothing stands in my way but the Gavel Act, Lord [unreadable], thinking the Limitations Act a bar to adversaries like mine, will have more influence on the other side than his assessors who differ with him. Nay, as Mr. Kelly says, every incident of these latter times tends to a liberal construction of every Penal Law wherein there is the smallest open for it. I need no more at present on this subject as we have the long vacation before us to prepare for every necessary defense. I will probably (next post) write to you for horses to receive me at Mulingar. ...

1. Pat Wogan.

291. To Charles Ryan,[1] Church Street, Dublin

RIA, Stowe MS Bi2

Belanagare, 10 September 1777

... If on the whole you all think this little piece[2] can be of service to our common cause (on opening of the session of Parliament) I request you will get to Pat Wogan[3] to give it good paper and good type as it may fall in the way of men of consequence and rank who reject anything presented in ballad paper and ballad printing. If (I repeat it again) you think the thing worthy of publication, I would have five or six copies covered with Dutch gilt paper, put into hands of Captain Jephson,[4] that he might disperse them at Court a day or two before publication. . . .

    1. A member of the Catholic Committee. Apothecary in Church Street, Dublin.
    2. O'Connor's *Reflexions on our Present Critical Situation in a Letter from a Landed Proprietor*, published by Pat Wogan, a Catholic printer in Dublin in 1777, reprinted in London in the same year. Charles Ryan to Charles O'Conor, 4 October 1777, Stowe MS. Bi2, RIA; *BMCPBCE*, 21:299.
    3. After the death of James Hoey, Sr., in 1775, Pat Wogan became the principal Catholic bookseller and publisher in Dublin. He was in business at 23 Bridge Street from 1771 to 1795 or perhaps later. Plomer, p. 408.
    4. Robert Jephson (1736–1803), playwright and poet, was Master of Horse to the lord lieutenant. O'Conor's acquaintance with him dates from the publication of *The Speech Delivered by R. Jephson . . . in the Debate on the Committing of the Heads of a Bill for the Better Encouragement of Persons Professing the Popish Religion to Become Protestants* (Dublin: n.p., 1774). Obviously, O'Conor must have felt that he could count on Jephson to pass the pamphlets to M.P.s friendly to the Catholics. *Concise DNB*, 1:689, *BMCPBCE*, 18:976.

292. To Dr. John Curry

OCD, 8.4 HS 141

From the Hermitage, 1 October 1777

My Dear Sir,

I am glad to hear that things promise well for us on this as well as the other side of the water. The executive part of the government are well convinced through long experience of our good intentions, and they are convinced from recent experience that their enemies are among protestants, but I think that they must touch upon our affairs with a very delicate hand, as the subject itself is so unpopular. In both Houses numbers and, I believe, a majority will stoop for the old stones and throw them at us incessantly. The foresight of this calls upon us at this critical time to stand upon our defense, and the little piece you mislaid and found was intended as a foundation for it. The *Sketch* you mention would be a better had the London booksellers printed it. At all events, it should be brought back and published at home. I thought that an *Association* should be now formed (but of a select few) under your eye for the refutation of invectives and for the publication of our grievances; such a scheme, supported with spirit and conducted with discretion instead of being deemed offensive, would be well received. It might also prevent what, if possible, should be prevented, the intrusion of indiscreet and injudicious volunteers who always do hurt but never serve any cause they undertake. Am I chimerical in this proposal of an *association?* You may say with Horace, *vires deficiunt animique*,[1] and indeed we want strength, but should we not exert the little we have and that in concert? Mr. *O'Leary*[2] of Cork might be called into our society and *Poplicola* of the *London Packet* (could we discover him) might also be brought to enlist with us and transmit essays from London. Mr. Martin Gaven and Charles Ryan might be also associated with us and would be very serviceable by attending to the impression of all our essays, and they both gave proofs of spirit in some essays of their own. I need say no more on this head till I hear from you. You think I should be more particular relatively to my own grievance in the little tract I send you, and so I would indeed, but my lawyers have forbidden it. In the preliminary discourse to the *Historical Review*, I have four or five corrections to make, which I will send you as soon as the printer wants them, and I trust you will find a chasm for the insertion of a little morsel I gave you lately, if you like it now as well as you did on the first reading. Some things relatively to our affairs ought by no means to be communicated by the post, and you have been quite right in forbearing to inform me of those matters till we meet, which will, I fear, be soon as the term is now near at hand and as I may be under the necessity of attending it. I wonder Frank does not write to you, and yet I know that when young men receive a remittance of money, they are more tardy in writing than otherwise they would be. I bless God that he has been honorably acquitted of the late foolish as well as malicious charge against him. These rubs in life every man is exposed to, and I hope this that he got over will be a good lesson to him hereafter and instruct him how cautious he should be in disposing of his confidences. I am sorry to hear of the sudden end of Doctor Charles Ferral. He had one of the Council Books (thrown formerly out into the street when the Castle of Dublin took fire). It contains some valuable documents, and I would wish that it had not fallen into secreting or improper hands.

So many sudden deaths of late form an alarming circumstance. You inform me of our late Attorney-general's death.³ He was the friend to our people, and he was the principal person concerned for my adversary. Write to me when you can and form an association if you can. Adieu, my dear and best friend.

1. Strength and spirits fail.
2. Reverend Arthur O'Leary (1729–1802), Irish priest, writer and politician, returned to Cork in 1771 after having lived in France for many years. He spent the years 1756–1762 as chaplain to war prisoners. He wrote pamphlets exhorting Catholics to remain faithful to British rule. *Concise DNB*, 1:972. See also O'Leary's debate with John Wesley in the *FJ*, 11–14, 14–16, 16–18, 18–21, and 21–23 March 1780.
3. Philip Tisdal (1703–1777), Attorney-general (1760–1777) and principal Secretary of State and manager of the House of Commons, 1763. *Concise DNB*, 1:1302.

293. To Charles Ryan

RIA, Stowe MS Bi2

Belanagare, 1 October 1777

... I have in my last two letters to you made some corrections, perhaps for the better, but of this you must be the judge. Should you think the printing of that little tract useful as a foundation for succeeding publications, I think Mr. Bean will have spirit enough to give it good paper and a good type should he and Mr. Wogan undertake the publication. I request that Mr. Gaven and you will pare away any indiscretion I might fall into; for, as I told you before, we have to do with tender patients who, if curable at all, must be so by gentle applications. Others we well know will accept of no remedies. They are powerful, they are numerous, and they are already embodied against us. ...

294. To Myles MacDermot, Coolavin

RIA, Bi2

8 October 1777

Dear Cousin,¹

I send the bearer with the hope that he will return to me with a good account of your re-establishment after the late accident which has been so alarming from the circumstances attending it.

I have viewed your cousin's genealogical memoir carefully and find it authentic except in two places where, without authority I presume, he gives the honor of knighthood to William O'Malley of Aughtertire, as well as to his son-in-law, Charles O'Conor of Belanagare. I made a correction by giving them the rank of esquires, which they really had. He gives the title of princes to Charles MacDermot and John O'Gara, chieftains of Moyburg and Culavinne in the reign of Charles I. We had no Irish princes of that age anywhere. They were but dynasts and that title (as their right) I have given them. To call them princes would be ridiculous, and to testify by subscription that they were princes would have no better effect than exposing the subscribers to disgrace as well as discredit.

Instead of my transcribing this memoir, as our cousin requires, it is surely enough to transcribe it from his own copy by a clerk who can write a fair hand. It should be done on a sheet of good paper that room may be left for the seals and signatures. Let a copy be previously drawn out for the perusal of Dr. Philips that he may make the corrections he thinks necessary in the form before the fair copy is laid before him for his signature. When he and other prelates or dignitaries sign, I shall sign very cheerfully as your cousin requires.[2] Could I render him a more solid service (for this is nothing) I certainly would. I request you will give my affections to Kitty and your whole family.

1. Myles MacDermot is O'Conor's son-in-law. O'Conor uses the term "cousin" loosely.
2. It was customary to have genealogies signed by prelates, members of parliament, or other prominent figures who attested to their authenticity.

295. To Charles Ryan

RIA, Stowe MS Bi2

[1777, after 8 October][1]

My dear Friend,

I had lately a letter from our worthy friend Mr. Braughall,[2] who speaks tenderly of you and enjoys with me and your other friends your recovery from your late illness. He has seen the *Reflexions,* and like other friends, forbore rebuking me for what was written or what was omitted. I think I told you that these *Reflexions* were intended as outlines for our abler artists to work upon, and though some capital lines are omitted, it would be too much to insert them without the concurrence of an *Association,* who alone would be indebted to pronounce on the utility or prudence of inserting them in the present conjuncture. I had one matter much at heart, but discretion arrested my hand. Take it in a letter where it may sleep safely.

When the Roman Catholics of these islands were persecuted without respite or compassion in Charles II's time, Sir Christopher Calvert, Lord Baltimore, obtained from that prince a patent for removing those obnoxious people into Maryland, a waste province in North America; of that province they were put in possession, and the worthy nobleman I mentioned brought thither a number of emigrants from England and Ireland. The colony prospered for a time, and yet James II, the successor Charles, was advised to question the terms of their charter; the poor people were alarmed, and the poor people at home who were preparing for following them have been discouraged from proceeding on their intended emigration. The Revolution soon followed, and what was begun by James' infatuation was completed by King William's politics. Our province was seized upon by Protestant Puritans. The posterity of that race are now in rebellion and their grandsires were usurpers. They, therefore, merit confiscation on a double account and would not this be the proper time for petitioning the King for reinstating us in our right? A right never forfeited by sedition or disaffection? Would not the Ministry see by simple intuition the propriety of making men *useful* abroad, who at home are *useless* or indeed rather hurtful to the improvement of this island by their Tarter occupations of a pastoral life, occupations imposed by law and ever injurious to a trading nation? Would not the *repossessing* Maryland with Catholics be a bridle hereafter on the Republican provinces north and south of them? And can it be possible but the Ministry must be struck with the expediency of such a scheme? Assuredly a regrant of their former province to the Roman Catholics would be more effectual in bringing our masters here to a sense of the hurt of our Penal Laws then all the reasoning that ever was or ever can be employed on this subject. But the Ministry should be previously sounded relatively to the scheme before us, and our ablest as well as discreetest men should be employed in negotiating it. It might be done through the credit and influence of Councilor MacNamara[3] and others. After all, you may think all this chimerical, a maggot biting an idle brain; but think again of it and read Mr. Burke's book on the subject written before the present troubles commenced.[4] Read particularly his account of *Maryland*. The work in two volumes has been reprinted and published in Dublin by Wilson. Write to me immediately if you can. I think I must be in town ten days at farthest, and I would wish to be prepared for ruminating on some domestic matters before I set off from hence. Adieu, dear Charles.

P.S. I have by the last post written on the subject above to Dr. Curry. How it affected him I know not. Some plausible objections can be made (no doubt) and what political scheme was ever free from any? Wise men will lose nothing by a little labor in weighing matters of this nature, and wisdom will discover the preponderating scale. My mind goes too fast for my hand, and let this apologize for blots and inaccuracies.

1. Undated.
2. Thomas Braughall (c. 1730–1803) was a merchant in Bridge Street, Dublin, and a leading member of the Catholic Committee. See the references to Braughall in *Burke*, 4 and 10.
3. Daniel MacNamara, a London lawyer and agent for the Catholic Committee. See O'Conor to MacNamara, 20 March 1774.
4. Burke's *History of America*, 1777.

296. To Charles Ryan

RIA, Stowe MS Bi2

15 October 1777

My dear Sir,

Nothing but the dislike I took to putting you to any unnecessary expense in the article of postage prevented my not replying immediately to your kind letter of the 4th instant; and yet had the subject required it, I would not scruple putting you to a much greater expense as I know well the little estimate you would put upon it in a cause truly national and *apparently* friendless. I do not recall the expression and have I not a right to pronounce our cause *really* friendless when so few among us at present can be brought to *associate* for putting it in its true light? I have but one apology to make for our friends; they think our cause too desperate and shelter themselves under the experience that what we have advanced for it in the course of twenty years past has been labor thrown away. But this is not a sufficient justification, and perhaps they who think it so are mistaken. Some knowledge may silently glide into the minds of our masters, however ill-prepared for admitting it; and we have good reason to think that from the efforts made some favorable impression has followed. Be it as it may, can despondency over-rule the duty of publishing our justifications and grievances in the present critical period, the like of which has not presented itself for eighty years past? The *Reflexions* were intended only as a preparatory outline for such an undertaking. The details should follow from our ablest hands, and should no notice be taken of the voice of truth and nature, yet would no good follow from the very disappointment? Some would certainly; it would instruct men who are not permitted to cultivate the earth they stand upon to quit it and the unfavorable climate which hangs over them. No law ties up the hands of the King from providing for them in waste countries where they must certainly be useful to him instead of remaining in a land where they can render him but very little service except as a counter-balance to our Republicans. I am really concerned at Dr. Curry's and Mr. Caddell's delicacy in making our corrections in the *Reflexions* and still more in making no supplemental additions, but I gratefully thank Mr. Gaven and yourself for the corrections you made, though I am afraid you have not made as many as you should. Your observation is just that few of our members of Parliament can bring themselves to purchase, much less read, any work on the subject of our Popery Laws. Yet the few who will both purchase and read are some of the ablest; and as real friends to their country, they will be pleased to have arguments prepared to their hands which might otherwise escape them should any debate on our subject be opened within the doors of the great house in College Green. The attention of the public should be excited as much as possible, and a better expedient cannot be used than yours of selecting the more striking parts of every publication and retailing them in *Walker's Magazine*. I have omitted inscribing the *Reflexions* to the two Houses because the doing so did not occur to me, nor is the omission of any consequence. I am afraid that Mr. Wogan, a young man I long wished well to, has exceeded in stamping off five hundred copies. I should be extremely sorry that he should be a sufferer on my account. I would have him (and at my expense) present *Captain Jephson* with three copies, handsomely made up with Dutch embroidered covers and gilt edges. The Captain will, I think, lay one of them before the Lord Lieutenant. If the Committee would bear the expense, a dozen or more of the leading members should be served with copies gratis. I entirely approve of your thoughts relatively to the distribution of party justice and the infliction of party punishment; whichever party prevails, "It is the same rope at different ends they twist." No people have written better than the English of these islands on the iniquity of persecution; and few nations have excelled them in the practice of what they so vehemently condemn. No impudence can come up to this, but these men have power; and it is for that reason, for the knowledge I mean we have to this readiness to persecute and stoop for more stones to throw at us, that I would remind them in as gentle terms as possible of their injury. Be the terms ever so gentle, many will be vexed, nor have you trespassed against propriety in what you have written because you have generalized your charge and only protested against making any one party criminal in a case wherein all parties are so when malevolence, not knowledge, gives the law to the helpless part of the community. I despair of an Association among you; and yet if two or three joined heartily as watchmen in the present crisis, much good would insure from their zeal and labor. Have you the *Free Examination,* published first in London. There has been a second impression of that work in Dublin, published by Dillon Chamberlain, under the care of the Rev. Mr. Field of Rosemary Lane. You'll find it prefaced in a few lines from me, and it concludes with an appendix from me also. In the course of the session some excellent matter may be selected from the *Free Examination,* and some other matter may be selected also from some of our domestic tracts. Such republications would lessen the labor of our watchmen.

I congratulate with you on having Dr. Sherlock for your pastor. He is one of the worthiest of men; and he shall, while I live, be in full possession of my affection. I request you will present my hearty good wishes to Mrs. Ryan, to worthy Pat O'Brien, and our common friends. Though I hate prolixity, my letter is spun to too great length; and yet I have forgotten some things, you can never be forgotten by, dear sir, your most faithful friend and servant.

15 October 1777

To fill this blank I must observe to you that the potato and corn crops have beyond example (to take in the last ten years) failed from this severe and rainy season. I question much whether we have nine months' provision in this kingdom, and the tragical effect must fall (as in all countries) on the majority of the nation and here on the poor, who are all R[oman] Catholics. This is an object of legislative contemplation as the prosperity of the public must be derived from the number of hands which can be employed in agriculture and manufactures. This circumstance can furnish one of the most interesting arguments in the world for giving the majority of our people an interest in the cultivation of land instead of the fugacious interest derived from pasturage. To give men a durable property in land is not solely an invitation to agriculture. It effectuates the thing and attaches the cultivator to the government which secures the duration; to forbid such a property by law to any considerable body of men is the highest solecism in politics; it is the necessary consequence of that famine which is already staring us in the face and is unavoidable, as the people who are to be sufferors have not money to purchase the corn of foreign lands. I have put these loose thoughts together as hints for an essay from you on this important subject. Adieu.

297. To Dr. John Curry

OCD, 8.4 HS 143

[28] October 1777

... We may have a law for taking long leases; who can grant them in a country where almost all the lands are bound to short leases by family settlements? Where such family settlements are in force, to talk of a law as useful where the law can not operate is nugatory. It is the great grievance for a long time past of industrious Protestant tenants themselves who are by those settlements tied down to a lease of three lives only and consequently are restrained from building, planting, or improving except in the measure that such temporary tenures render prudent. You may qualify Papists to take leases of lands for sixty-one or even ninety-nine years; yet of what use can such a qualification be unless the landlords be qualified also to grant such terms? Doubtless no landlord bound by settlement can grant them; and lest a qualification of this nature should be considered as a favor, an essay setting forth the true state of the case should be published in the *Freeman's Journal*. A law for long leases to Catholics would, I know, be useful in your great city and other corporate towns, but what is this to the whole body of our people, who are the laboring and more numerous part of the nation? Were the Catholics allowed to purchase the waste (improvable) parts of the island, the revenue of the crown and wealth of the nation would be vastly improved in a few years, and I defy any of our politicians to afford a good reason why a law to this end should not be enacted if no better (that is King William's) terms can be obtained....

... When *Sir Christopher Calvert, Lord Baltimore,* obtained a patent for the province *of Maryland* (from Charles II) for the Roman Catholics of these islands, we were put in the way of possessing forever in the fullest freedom one of the finest provinces on the globe, but the Revolution of '88 overturned that scheme. Should our army now prevail in North America, may we not with confidence and even success petition the Crown for a re-establishment of our patent? Most probably our Majesty would rather upset all Queen Anne's laws relatively to us than admit a general emigration into that part of the world where so much would be lost to this nation and so much would be gained to the Crown by making subjects *useful* in one part of the empire instead of having them almost *useless* in the other part. Our friend *Ned Burke* has given an excellent account of North America (before the present contests began). The work was reprinted in Dublin (by Wilson) and I would wish you perused his account of *Maryland* and *Pennsylvania* particularly. Had we in the present crisis formed an *association* for the publication of our grievances blended with our justification, many things would occur by our acting in concert that must escape us as private volunteers. . . .

298. To Charles Ryan

RIA, Stowe MS Bi2

[11 November 1777]

. . . One argument for our silence in the present conjuncture does not escape me, and it is the best that can be produced. It is feared that writing on the subject of our grievances may betray us into indiscretions; but surely under the government of a president and a few select members, indiscretions could be avoided, whereas without such a control they cannot, as many self-sufficient and ignorant volunteers will thrust themselves into our service to our shame and (what is worse) to our detriment. If some publications under the control of prudence do no good at home, may they not have the chance of making a strong impression elsewhere and perhaps to our advantage? R[oman] Catholics are in a great degree *useless* subjects in this island; may not the King find means for rendering them *useful* where he is constrained by no laws from it? Would not such a conduct increase his revenue and the power of doing good along with it? Even at home I trust that some things but barely hinted at in the *Reflexions* might be enlarged upon without any impeachment of our discretion. After this profound repose of ninety years, a fifth of the improvable part of our island lies a perfect waste, utterly unproductive. Could this happen without either a want of inhabitants or a defect in our laws? Should the Constitution given us at Limerick be refused to us, would not a liberty of purchasing those wastes by Roman Catholics be a profitable measure? And would not the property acquired through the cultivation of those wastes be a good hostage for the good conduct of the cultivators? Would not long leases and a power of purchasing lots in corporate towns have the same effect? . . .

299. To Denis O'Conor, Belanagare

OCD, 8.4 SE 148

Pill Lane, 25 November 1777

If you be not absolutely disabled, I think that, notwithstanding what I have urged in my letter of Saturday last, you must come up and obey the order of the Committee of Elections here. Mr. Crofton,[1] it is true, engaged to Mr. James Ferral that he would not call upon you without absolute necessity; but this indefinite engagement gives no security. You may probably, however, forbear coming up till you hear further from me by the next post. You are to be allowed four pence a mile for your journey; [torn] a day, while you are kept here. . . .

1. Edward Crofton is M.P. for Roscommon. Apparently Crofton and a Parliamentary committee wish both O'Conors to appear in relation to their law suit with Hugh O'Conor. For example, the *DJ*, 8–10 February 1774, describes the sitting of a Parliamentary committee for the Courts of Justice in which the committee examined a Mr. Noble concerning his failure to submit a bill for a *custodian* cost. The Committee also ordered that a Cornelius O'Callaghan, under house arrest, be discharged by the Sergeant-at-Arms without fees. Apparently Denis and Charles must appear before a similar committee.

300. To James O'More

RIA, Stowe MS Bi2

Pill Lane, 30 November 1777[1]

. . . I have been with Mr. Whitten[2] on the commission you gave me;[3] the poor man is laid up by the gout and I think him sincere in the declaration he makes of his readiness to serve, as well as oblige you. Your observation is just, that the sudden change made in the fortune of our Northern Irish families in 1607 involved ignorance of many matters along with it. In so mighty a shock the consequence of it was natural enough. Our exiled gentry, regardless of English heraldry and indeed the futile learning attending it, found their error in foreign lands which put an equal estimate on such knowledge. They, therefore, finding it necessary to conform to its devices, took up with arbitrary armorial ensigns, such as they received. Irish informers, who were ignorant of the true; by the true I do not mean the simple bearings used on their standard by the old Irish, but those they took from English monarchs on their submission to English government. Thus it was with Rory, first Earl of Tir-Conall.[4] He might have overlooked the arms as he forsook the patent granted him by James I; or if he retained the former, yet the seal which he bore them, he might have lost before he landed in Spain, or he might for some reasons unknown to us lay those arms aside....

1. There is an earlier draft of this letter, Stowe MS. Bi2, RIA.
2. Edward Whitten, the herald.
3. James O'More had written O'Conor on 23 November. O'More's grandson, acting as secretary to General O'Donnell, who was in Spain, had requested aid in establishing the correctness of the O'Donnell arms. General O'Donnell wanted to obtain documentation of the family's former importance in Ireland. James O'More to Charles O'Conor, 23 November, Stowe MS Bi2, RIA.
4. Ruairí Ó Domhaill (O'Donnell) (1578–1608) of the Flight of the Earls.

301. To Denis O'Conor

OCD, 8.4 SE 148

[Pill Lane, 25 April 1778]

I sit down to reply to your letter of the 22nd instant. Last week Dr. Carpenter has written to Dr. Skerrett in the most friendly and warm terms recommending your son Charles[1] to him as a proper subject to fill the place which in this year or the next will be open to a student for Conaght in Propaganda Fide.... As to Denis MacDermot,[2] I am very far from despairing of a proper place for him; nay, I am almost sure of it through Dr. Carpenter's attention to his interest. He has shown me copies of his letter to the K[ing] of Spain; and to the King's Minister begging a charitable foundation for our Irish youth devoted to the Irish Mission. Success may be hoped for from the King's zeal and the worthiness of the Minister. Dr. Carpenter is also soliciting the same graces at the Court of Portugal. By the information I give you, you see that we have a good prospect before us for my nephew and grandson. As to your son Owen,[3] he is now master of the elements of erudition; I quit school at the age of fifteen, and let him do as I did; that is, let him pack up the rest by his own industry from books, which well attended to are our best masters....

I do not think as indifferently as you do of the turn of mind in the English Parliament relatively to a manumission of Catholics after this long trial of their principles. The political excommunication of those men has by experience been found hurtful to the national interest, and the retaining them perpetually to the temptation of disaffection is considered dangerous. Reason begins to take its proper station, and the example of England may bring about its natural, that is its proper, exertions here.⁴ Our Parliament will meet on the fourth of May, and I have good information that before it breaks up, our Penal Laws will be brought under a serious examination.⁵ . . .

    1. Denis's second son.
    2. Charles O'Conor's nephew.   3. Denis's eldest son.
    4. On April 7 Thomas Townshend argued in favor of relief of the Irish Catholics before the British Commons. Lord North, Charles James Fox, and Edmund Burke supported him. By early June two relief measures were passed by the British Parliament and approved by the king: a relief measure for English Catholics and a repeal of laws prohibiting Catholics from buying forfeited Irish estates. O'Connell, pp. 100–109.
    5. Edmund Sexton Pery, Speaker of the Irish Commons, arrived in Dublin from London on 30 April 1778 and informed the viceroy that the king wished that the Irish Parliament in current session would make some "reasonable concessions" to the Catholics. O'Connell, p. 109.

302. To Denis O'Conor, Belanagare, Roscommon

OCD, 8.4 SE 148

[Pill Lane, 9 May 1778]

You may be assured that my pleas and answer to my adversary's bill will be filed in the present term, and I think I do not purchase delay at a higher price than it is worth.¹ The delay of my legacy gives me greatest pain, but we must submit to the legal forms which create the delay; and, as in the former case, it is worth more than it will cost us. This week I had a polite letter from Dr. Skerrett, but he has given the answer to my request which indeed I expected. He assures me that the place I required for my grandson has been more than a year disposed of. On this disappointment I was advised by Dr. Carpenter to write immediately to Mr. Charles Kelly to negotiate with our protector *Marafoschi* a place for my grandson in the Ludovician College at Rome; I have done so, and I have no doubt of success in this suit from the experience of the activity and friendship of the person I employed. As to my nephew Denis, I have strong hopes of a proper place for him in Spain or Lisbon through the solicitations of Dr. Carpenter in both kingdoms. Let Denis,² now in the interim, keep school for your children to cultivate himself and them together. I cannot think you can do better, conditionally that you keep a watchful eye yourself over their conduct and progress.

You can manage my affairs better than I can myself, and I expect that you will see justice done to me, and to do it effectually you should be present and give directions in the most minute matters. Are the young firs and other plantations of the last year preserved and thriving? What progress has been made in the stone wall buildings? Is the shepherd's house built? And have you removed Mulvihily and Teig's boy from their old cabins, which were a nuisance where they stood? As to the disposal of Denis Mulvihily's former holding, I submit it to your best judgment. May it not be best to take the plot into my own hands and let the house and cabbage garden to their poor boy who possessed both last year? I never think of my old nurse but with feeling gratitude; and though I lost her when I was not full eight years old, her memory is and ever shall be dear to me. But I have very little regard for her grandchildren (Nicholson excepted), and I believe them to be very worthless fellows.

Whatever is put into the hands of your unhappy brother may be compared to the god of Thulouse, which, if history may be credited, was annihilated in the hand that received it. After the loss of near £200, which Mr. Dillon suffered by the house in Anderson's Court, yet his son-in-law had the confidence to draw upon him for the sum of £80 some months ago. The drawer minded not the draft, and the acceptor was obliged to pay the contents. I am shocked at this rental, and I forbear mentioning to you or myself more on this subject, though a great deal could be added.

From the number of bankruptcies in this town, public credit is reduced to the lowest ebb, and the whole kingdom is become a scene of distress.[3] Affairs abroad wear the darkest complexion,[4] and men in power here, finding the Penal Laws feelingly penal to themselves, are thinking of a relaxation. What their scheme is we know not, but I dare predict it will be such a partial one as will defeat its own purposes. Our uncertainty on this head will be soon over, as the matter will be debated in a few days before a full House. A book has been this week published here entitled *A Philosophical Survey of the South of Ireland*. It is very well-written and on the most liberal principles; I bought it, and on the perusal I was amazed to find my case particularly mentioned in it as a great hardship flowing from laws which punish without having a criminal for their object. Where the Protestant and English gentleman received his information I know not. I am under the greatest obligation to this learned stranger as in other parts of his work he pronounces a very favorable judgment of my *Dissertations*.

Make an effort to satisfy speedily the unfortunate man in St. Omer;[5] for, however defective he may be as to conduct, he is not so in principle. Give my affections to your family.

Pill Lane, 9 May 1778

1. O'Conor's main tactic in the discovery case was delay in hopes of passage of relief measures.
2. O'Conor's nephew, Denis MacDermot.
3. The American Revolution and an increase in the Pension List caused a severe depression in 1777 and 1778. See Lecky 2:168–171.
4. France entered the war in March 1778.
5. O'Conor's brother Daniel.

303. To Denis O'Conor

OCD, 8.4 SE 148

Pill Lane, 16 May 1778

... Public credit has never been at a lower ebb here [than] at present, and on account of the American War our manufactures are in no demand. We expect relaxation of the Popery Laws in England and hope that the example will be followed here. A few days will inform us if those expectations are [corrupt] by experience that our Penal Laws have not prevented the growth of Popery, [corrupt] the growth of prosperity in this country. It is felt that the distress of two-thirds of the inhabitants operates only to the weakness of all and occasionally, as at present, throws the whole body politic into fainting fits. Certain it is that many who dreaded, or pretended to dread, the growth of Irish Popery, now in reality dread its extinction through emigration of its votaries to a country which invites them by the offer of freedom and property on the broad bottom of universal toleration. ...

304. To [Colonel Charles Vallancey][1]

OCD, 8.4 ES 156

From No. 58, Pill Lane, 16 May 1778

... A gentleman who attends the Navigation Board came to me this minute, requesting me to wait on you with their respects and to give you information that in opening the course from the town of Carrick-on-Shannon to Lough Allen, the source of that river, they mistrust the abilities of their present engineer; that, in consequence, they ardently wish that you, Sir, could spare a few days from your present important employments and by taking a view of the line, give your instructions for the proper way of conducting the work and make an estimate of the expense. Could you gratify those gentlemen (and your love of the improvement of Ireland obliges them to think you will) it will be far from being expensive to you. I will tell you more on this head when I have your commands for meeting you which, on account of the shortness of the time, my informer requests should be this day or tomorrow at any hour you appoint. . . .

    1. The editors assume that this letter is to Charles Vallancey for two reasons: (1) Vallancey was Engineer-in-Ordinary for Ireland and an officer in the Royal Engineers; (2) he was the author of *A Treatise on Inland Navigation* published in Dublin in 1763. *Concise DNB,* 1 : 1330; *BMCPBCE,* 25 : 1049.

305. To Denis O'Conor

OCD, 8.4 SE 148

Pill Lane, 30 May 1778

    Through the negotiation of my worthy friend Mr. Thomas Braughall, I yesterday received bills of exchange from Brussels to the amount of £453 sterling. They are drawn upon different bankers in London at four days' sight and will this day be remitted to that city for acceptance; which, when done, I will obtain bills at Mr. LaTouche's[1] here for payment of the whole sum. This will occasion a delay of ten or twenty days. Is it not a most seasonable succor while I am involved [in an] expensive suit of law: And yet £109 of this sum must be paid immediately to Mr. Pat Dease to discharge my old engagement for your unfortunate brother.

    Last Wednesday I dined (by engagement) with Mr. Arthur French at Philipsbourg; Mr. French of Frenchpark dined there also.[2] I spent the day comfortably with your two landlords, and it concerns me that one of them is greatly on the decline. My suit is now [corrupt] in a quiescent state, and I suppose my adversaries will renew their attack on the next term; when they do renew it, you shall be acquainted with their maneuvers. Great debates on the Popery Laws are expected to come on next Monday; and now it is that our writings on that subject are called for. We expect some good from the issues of the debate and especially as the example has been set in England on liberal [corrupt]. All this gives our affairs a good complexion even here.

[Rest of letter taped over.]

    1. The bank of David LaTouche and Sons was the most prominent one in Dublin. In 1778 when the Irish treasury was exhausted, the Lord Lieutenant asked for a loan of

£20,000. When he found that more money was needed to move British troops in Ireland, the Lord Lieutenant asked for the loan of a second £20,000; he was refused. Gilbert, "The Streets of Dublin," p. 315.

2. O'Conor is referring to two Arthur Frenches, father and son (the elder, d. 1799; the younger, d. 1820). O'Conor had obviously been discussing the suit with his landlords.

306. To Denis O'Conor, Belanagare, Roscommon

OCD, 8.4 SE 148

[23 May 1778][1]

Mr. Robert Dillon is requested to direct this letter under a franked cover.

Your letter of the 16th instant has been written in a querulous temper and I do not wonder at it. Your unfortunate brother got a better temporary property to begin life with than you have obtained; it is, however, a consolation to me that yours has been turned to a good account; his has been thrown away. You have lived with credit and have added to your stock; he lived without any credit and yet dissipated a very considerable fortune without account. Next to the loss of my best friend, my dear daughter, her brother's conduct brings me the greatest affliction. But I derive comfort from his being one who hitherto has brought no shame to me, nor infamy to himself by any moral turpitude. He has been here nine days and left me last Wednesday. He will tell of what he has been about and will inform you also that I have at last done everything relatively to our law suit which my counsel deemed most proper. My plea will not probably be received by the Lord Chancellor till next November, and my adversaries will be so embarrassed by my answer to their bill that it will put them to the necessity of filing a new bill to discover my title and inform themselves of the ground they may go upon when they renew the attack. This will take them up some time. If the plea should not be admitted here, I will remove it to another tribunal, and that I will have success beyond the water I have reason to hope. About ten days ago a motion had been in the British House of Commons to repeal most of the Penal Laws which affect the Catholics of England, and the motion has been agreed to without a single dissenting voice.[2] The example has been followed here. Yesterday Mr. Gardner moved for leave to bring in the heads of a bill for the adoption of the legal penalty on the Irish Roman Catholics.[3] He has been supported by the Attorney General,[4] by our friend Yelverton[5] and other able commoners; some opposition is given, but it was overruled; and next Monday the heads of the bill will be brought in and debated. In anxious agitation, I hope and fear our people wait for the fate of this question, and as information comes in, you shall be made acquainted with the minutes of it. Your letter to the unfortunate man abroad is a proper one, but it is a shame that you are careless of orthography.

[Rest of letter faded.]

    1. Undated. Mr. Gardiner moved to bring in the Heads of a Bill for Catholic Relief on Friday, 22 May. O'Conor writes "yesterday" in his letter to Denis, thus clearly identifying the date of the letter. *DJ*, 21–23 May 1778.
    2. The second reading of the English Bill for the Relief of Catholics was read in the British House of Commons on 13 May. It passed on 21 May. *DJ*, 23–26, and 26–28 May 1778. See note 4, letter 301.
    3. Gardiner's Relief Act of 1778. It provided that Catholics could take leases of indefinite tenure but not freeholds if they took an oath of allegiance. They were allowed to inherit land on the same terms as Protestants and Gavelkind was repealed. In order to qualify a Catholic had to take the oath of allegiance to the English king by 1 January 1779, but he was not liable to discovery after 1 November 1778. Lecky, 2:213–217; *Irish Historical Documents, 1172–1922*, eds. Edmund Curtis and R. B. McDowell (London: Methuen and Co., Ltd., 1943), 194ff. See also O'Connell, Chapter V.
    4. John Scott (1739–1798); Attorney-general and Privy Counciler (1778–1782); dismissed from office for denying the right of England to bind Ireland by acts of Parliament. *Concise DNB*, 1:1168.
    5. Barry Yelverton (1736–1805), later (1795) first Baron Avonmore. *Burke*, eds. Barbara Lowe, P. J. Marshall, and John A. Woods, 10:505.

307. To Denis O'Conor

OCD, 8.4 SE 148

                                      Pill Lane, 2 June 1778

It is the practice of our courts of law that pleas to bills in Chancery shall be entered for a certain day; mine has been entered for Thursday the 4th instant. The Lord Chancellor[1] may give it a hearing on that day or postpone it for some future time. All my briefs are prepared and will be put into my lawyers' hands immediately; but my agent will consult this day with Mr. Lyster to have his opinion whether if the Chancellor should consent to give the plea a hearing on Thursday, we should rather join issue without further delay or pray the court for leave to postpone it to next term. In either case nothing will come on us by surprise. I have perused the briefs carefully and think them fully to the purpose. Poor Hugh is now here, and he and his agent have been this week examining the courts of records to pick up matter for their next attack, as they found so little to their purpose in my answer to their bill. Should the Chancellor admit the justness of my plea, the suit will be decisively ended for me in his court. If otherwise, we will appeal from his sentence, and my adversary will be left no resource then but in common law should the Lords of England confirm the Chancellor's decree here. But of this there is no likelihood, and I will give you hereafter strong reasons for this idea if they do not occur to yourself already. It is certain that we can put off the hearing to the plea till next term if we choose it, but I see no reason that we should, conditionally that the Chancellor consents to receive it immediately, but in this circumstance I will be led as I ought by the judgment of my lawyers. . . .

1. James Hewitt, Lord Lifford, was lord chancellor of Ireland from 1768 to 1789. Previously he had been king's sergeant in 1760, and judge of the king's bench in Ireland, 1766–1767. His decisions as chancellor were published in 1839. *Concise DNB*, 1:615.

308. To Denis O'Conor

OCD, 8.4 SE 148

Pill Lane, 6 June 1778

My plea is still in its dormant state and lies over till the next term. Possibly it may not come on even then, and the delay of a hearing till November term will do no hurt, so that the delay be admitted; if not, we are prepared, for any day the Chancellor will appoint for hearing short causes in the ensuing term. I shall give you notice of the time (when appointed) that you may come up yourself to attend to the debates and gratify the unpleasing curiosity which comes mounted on the back of anxiety. The temper of the times is for us, and the galling part of the Penal Laws against Catholics has been repealed in England; Heads of a Bill to the same purpose were brought into our H[ouse] of Commons yesterday and are *committed* for the 15th instant.[1] How the Committee will dispose of those *Heads* we know not; but our hopes and fears are in the political scales, and the latter seem to cast the balance, as the prejudices of party are higher in this than in any other country.

My worthy friend Braughall came into this room yesterday and brought me the sum of £459.2.6 as my legacy from the late Count O'Gara: *viz.*, £9 in cash and £450 in a draft on LaTouche's bank. . . .

1. Gardiner's Relief Act of 1778.

309. To Mr. Sherlock[1]

OCD, 8.4 HS 141

[Belanagare, 2 October 1778]

Dear and Reverend Sir,

The information I have received of the disrespectful treatment of the A[rch] B[ishop][2] (soon after I parted from him and you) gave me very sensible pain, and the more as it came from our own party. From history we know that some of his predecessors have been so treated and none more severely than Holy Lorcan,[3] whose sufferings have contributed to cast a luster over his virtues and whose example is a lesson of fortitude to any of his successors under similar trials. Under the present circumstances our differences are the more unhappy as they supply matter of gratification to the malevolence of many who grudge us any favor from government. May these differences be soon composed to the disappointment of those men and the edification of better. For obtaining that end, nothing could come out more seasonably than the late excellent instructions of his Grace relatively to our civil duty now that we are put on the footing of subjects instead of being proscribed as aliens in the land of our birth, as we long have been. Those instructions point out the principles of the instructor and virtually contain all that is required of Catholics by the late Parliamentary Test;[4] and yet as no man take the benefit of the late relaxation without subscribing to that Formulary, I apprehend that most of our laity and even a great number of the clergy will accept it, and the more as the example has been set by the majority of Catholics in England. On Tuesday last there has been a meeting of our prelates in the county of Galway on the subject of the Test, but nothing of what they have done has as yet transpired, and I doubt much of unanimity among them. On my own part (and it is the case of many others) I have long hesitated on the paragraph:[5] "*That no power whatsoever can dispense with the obligation of the allegiance sworn to,*" though certainly the sense of the legislature refers to nothing more or less than the allegiance which is due to the executive power while *it can afford* that protection, or *withdraws not* that protection which the Constitution requires for the security of the public. In any other sense the oath would be absurd; and if this case be as I state it, the only question to be solved is whether an act of the mind which refers solely to the security of the civil Constitution can be deemed that criminal *mental reservation* which (and no other) is supposed in the whole scheme of the Test or whether a reserve of the mind that is not criminal, and cannot be so, has any relation to what is intended by abjuring the mental reservation in the Test in question? In the commerce of life and ordinary course of conveying our thoughts, there are many mental reservations, to express which in words would be ridiculous as well as unnecessary, but to consider which, as things to be abjured, would certainly prevent the taking the simplest oath of allegiance that can be framed. Thus when we swear to bear true allegiance to a constitutional king, we certainly have a mental reservation to the words, "while he reigns," but I believe that most men would not hestiate in subscribing to such a simple oath of allegiance, though it might be required in it that they had no mental reservation in their subscription. The question merits description for the satisfaction of scrupulous consciences, and the proper judgment upon it is the more necessary at present as nonjurors will be exposed to all their former sufferings, and as others (your friend in particular) will soon be brought to their trial in the courts of law and as their adversaries would gain an advantage by fixing an impression of disaffection to the government upon them. If God spares me life and health, I shall towards the close of this month or commencement of the next have the pleasure of seeing you, and before the time I would wish to hear from you. Meantime, I require you will present my affection to the A[rch] B[ishop].

Belanagare, 2 October 1778

    1. Mr. Sherlock is identified as a parish priest in Dublin in a letter, Charles Ryan to Charles O'Conor, 4 October 1777, Stowe MS. B12, RIA.
    2. Archbishop John Carpenter. Carpenter and many prelates had not yet taken and subscribed to the oath of allegiance. For example, Dr. John Troy, Bishop of Ossory and Carpenter's successor in Dublin did not take the oath of allegiance until 27 March 1779. Perhaps this refusal to take the oath was the cause of Carpenter's "disrespectful treatment." *DJ*, 1–3 April 1779. Also in order to qualify for the Catholic Relief Act, that is to take long leases and to inherit lands on the same terms as the Protestants, Catholics had to sign the Parliamentary Test of 1774. Carpenter's not signing was a stumbling block for some Catholics. However, by October, he had signed. See letter 311.
    3. St. Laurence O'Toole, archbishop of Dublin, incurred the displeasure of Henry II. O'Toole followed Henry II from England to France to plead his and Ireland's cause, took sick and died in France on 14 November 1180. He was canonized in 1226. Roche, p. 125.
    4. Apparently Carpenter had implied permission for Catholics to sign the Test.
    5. O'Conor did not sign until late 1779.

310. To Dr. John Curry, Summerhill, Dublin

OCD, 8.3 HS 141

[From the Hermitage on this instant, 23 October 1778]

My Dear Sir,

In three days after I parted you on my arrival here in the West, we have obtained that relaxation law for which you have labored without intermission in the course of thirty years. With pleasure you must join me in reflecting on the event and on the consequences. After a dead trance of more than forty years, you had the courage to break silence in 1747 and expose the wounds given to a nation through the sides of a small and innoxious party. Your example roused others here and in England to abandon their despondency; you excited opposition also, and the good sense of the public decided ultimately (though silently) for its true interests and for you who demonstrably showed in what that interest consisted. I never imagined that you could obtain this sweep against prejudice, and I have reason now to think more favorably of party than I have been accustomed to. Without a previous revolution in our habits of thinking and judging, we certainly could not experience this great revolution in our politics. May you live to enjoy some of the fruits of your labor, as you at present enjoy the gratitude of every good Catholic. In poor Reynolds[1] you had a zealous and indeed useful assistant, and I join you in your feelings for the loss of that worthy man, a loss, I think, the greater as he fatally neglected making a will for the disposal of his effects till it was too late. I must now run up to your law courts to be tried as a party delinquent and for no other crime than a profession which, I thank God, is no longer a crime. If I am stripped of the little property I possess, I must submit to a misfortune which has, for the ages, been invariably hereditary in my family. I rejoice in the account I have received that the Archbishop has finally agreed to subscribe to the Test of Allegiance, which is the only qualification required for receiving our people into the number of his Majesty's subjects, instead of being proscribed as aliens, which has been our fate for seventy-five years past.[2] We are subject to mistake and to mistake honestly too, but surely it is edifying to yield to the right instead of sticking to the wrong because we once were inflexible in it and making it a point of honor not to recede because a charge of inconsistency might be made unjustly against us. A delicacy of this kind, I doubt not, has been one of great importance to a relaxation of our Penal Laws.

I believe I need not inform you that all our vendibles: yarn, wool, oxen, sheep, etc., have upon an average fallen more than 40%. Should this state of things continue, lands and landholders will fall, and the landlords will have only the consolation (if that be any) to be the last undone. Misery in the extreme has fortunately a retrograde which may, nay must, sooner or later touch upon prosperity, and I wish our misery may not continue to verify the fact. I have no member of Parliament in this neighborhood to frank letters for me; I, therefore, spare my friends the trouble of reading trifles, as a hermit can remit nothing else. You should otherwise be addressed to more than any other of my correspondents and be assured that it pains me that you should pay a groat for saying things well-known to you, and of all that you know, no fact can become more certain to you than the affection I bear and ever will bear you. I extend it, my dear sir, to your lady, to the captain and his lady, in a word to all your connections.

From the Hermitage on this instant, 23 October 1778.

1. James Reynolds, appointed treasurer of the Catholic Committee, March 1778.
2. Denis, Charles's son, took the oath of allegiance on 9 November 1778 at the Court of King's Bench, Dublin. Perhaps Charles O'Conor's house arrest in 1779 had some relationship to his refusing to take the oath. Dunleavy and Dunleavy, p. 67, OCD, 8.4. SH 230.

311. To Charles Ryan, Dublin

RIA, Stowe MS Bi2

Belanagare, 28 October 1778

... I am highly satisfied with the account I received that our worthy Archbishop has finally, upon mature examination, reconciled himself to the new parliamentary Test, and I wish you may forbear subscribing to it, till you and I do it together. The account I have given you of the misery in the country is literally true, nor is there any appearance of better times till our affairs become still worse than they are, that is till landlords feel and are forced to let lands at their value. . . .

312. To Denis O'Conor

OCD, 8.4 HS 205

[Pill Lane, 23 January 1779]

... I have attentively perused Cocking's Bill of Discovery and have very easily picked up the spirit of it.[1] He makes Hugh O'Conor as well as my other brothers confederates with the view to establish a gavelable interest, alleging at the same time that my father had only a leasehold interest from John or Robert French in the lands of Belanagare, Corvally, Gortnaggan, Knockroe, Cashel, etc., an interest to which Denis O'Conor or his heir Charles were no way entitled as Papists. He prays the Chancellor to call into his court all the deeds which passed on or before the year 1723 between John or Robert French and Denis O'Conor, as well as to Arthur French (pretended to be in combination with me) to declare an oath the nature of his title to the lands aforesaid, to compel me and my brothers to declare also, on oath, the title by which I hold as heir and they claim as gavelers. From this short sketch you will easily perceive that the conspirators (and their tool who is still here), diffident of their Gavel scheme, have strong hopes that their new scheme will have a better chance for success by proving that the late Colonel John French (by foreclosing mortgages, etc.) vested the fee simple of those lands in himself and consequently that Denis O'Conor as a Papist could by no deed (between him or Robert French) hold any perpetuity of interest in said lands or any interest whatever beyond a term of thirty-one years, nor even that without a reservation of two-thirds of yearly value to the landlord. By all this, you can easily discern this last art of the conspirators and their artifice also in making Hugh O'Conor a sort of defendant in this cause. I have deferred putting in my answer this term, though our friend Counselor O'Conor sees no reason why I should postpone it or incur an expense (by postponing) which could be avoided.[2] ...

    1. Dunleavy and Dunleavy, p. 64, 8.4 ES 214 A, list records of petitions filed, including Cocking v. O'Conor and O'Conor's answers to the complaint.

    2. Charles O'Conor's law agent's delay in answering Hugh's charges led to O'Conor's house arrest in April. See Letters 318ff.

313. To Denis O'Conor

OCD, 8.4 SE 148

[Pill Lane, 6 February 1779]

The delay in putting in an answer to the last Bill of Discovery against me is, no doubt, attended with expense but yet with no injury to our cause.[1] Be assured that my answer will be prepared and filed in the approaching vacation, prefaced with a plea for dismissing the Bill as calculated to harass me with expense and vexation, there being one before filed against me on the same principle and to serve the same cause.[2] I am told that Mr. French of Frenchpark has not yet put in an answer to the bill filed against *him*. I wonder at this, but whenever he does, it must be grounded on the same materials with ours, and the proofs will be fully that my father came in as an inheritor not as a lessee to the lands of Belanagare. The poor machine played against me is still here, still in expectation that he will share in the spoils of my family with those who have set him to work. They still flatter themselves that my answer to their *last* bill will give them a fine marrow bone to pick; and I have some satisfaction in a delay which keeps them in the disagreeable situation created by anxiety and suspense. I say no more at present to this subject because more would convey no useful information.

I was not much surprised at the apostasy of my sister's daughter. I renounce her, for where there is no kindred of principle or morals a kindred by blood is, of course, dissolved. Though my nephew is in a fair way for reception in the Ludovician College, yet as the course of lectures there will not be opened till the next harvest, I am advised to write to my friend Charles Kelly at Rome to inform *him* of the steps taken by our bishop to recommend my nephew and to request of him to inform *me* whether such recommendation be sufficient or whether exposed to any hazard. This previous step is, I think, a prudent one, and the more as we are in time for taking it. It will be time enough for Denis MacDermotroe to set off in May next; MacDermotroe and I think my grandson Charles may study profitably where he is until May also.

It is not clear to me that you received my last letter, which was a long, rambling one. Therein I informed you of my receiving a letter from the man of St. Omer's,[3] and I quoted a part of it, wherein the acrimony against his litigant brother is repeated. I was lately summoned to attend the Catholic Select-Committee (Lord Kenmare in the chair).⁴ We entered into one resolution to which the Catholic prelates have made exceptions, and I think justly. I frankly informed his Lordship and others of the Committee of my sentiments, and I proposed to them the propriety of another meeting to reconsider and to reform our last resolutions. I am confident that my application will be attended with success, and I am under obligations to Lord Kenmare for remitting me (occasionally) the letters he lately received from the Munster prelates on this subject. In truth I am well-received by the whole society, and I have been appointed along with Dr. Curry to draw up the circular letter which they resolved should speedily be addressed to the bishops. Mr. Caddell and I are on a very friendly footing in the Committee and out of it, for he paid me several visits where I now write, and I expect him here again on Monday next.

I forgot to tell you that my adversary has not yet filed his exceptions to my answer, but you may conceive that they are indirectly made in the matter exposed in his last Bill of Discovery, the intent of which is to pick out the title by which I hold the lands he sues for as a discoverer.

You gave me no account of the state of my little affairs or whether any progress is made in the task of sanding and walling, which I left in charge with Nicholson, etc. If I wrote more now, it would be mere bagatelle. You may remember that young MacMahon when here was believed to be in suit for the fair Miss [Laffan]. Dr. Carpenter has married her last Monday to Mr. Owen Dermot. Adieu. My affection and blessing to your whole family.

1. O'Conor is wrong. The delay leads to his house arrest in April.
2. O'Conor is distinguishing between the first bill of 1777 and the Cocking vs. O'Conor bill of 1779.
3. O'Conor's brother Daniel.
4. O'Conor's invitation to attend the meeting at the Elephant in Essex Street on 26 January on "business of the greatest importance" is in Stowe MS., B12, RIA. At this meeting it was resolved that Dr. Curry, Dr. J. M. Daly, Robert Caddell, and O'Conor prepare a letter to be sent to the Catholic bishops in Ireland "to promote a voluntary annual" collection by parish priests. At an earlier meeting, 11 November 1778, it had been agreed that £450 be sent to Daniel McNamara, in addition to the £1050 already sent to him; that "a compliment" of 500 guineas be sent to Edmund Burke, and that Daniel MacNamara continue as the London agent for the Catholics of Ireland. "Catholic Committee Minute Book, 1773–92," pp. 32–39.

314. To Denis O'Conor, Belanagare, Roscommon

OCD, 8.4 HS 205

[February 1779][1]

This morning (at breakfast) Mr. James Ferral informed me of the receipt of a letter you directed to him by the last post. He desired me to inform you that he will immediately employ Counselor French to draw up an answer (for Mr. French of Frenchpark and for me) to my adversary's last bill of discovery and that it shall be filed in the present vacation. This is putting the matter into the best train. We will prove by authentic deeds and documents that my father was not a lessee but an heir-at-law to the lands I inherited after his decease. The misfortune is that this proof (in the high Court) will be attended with vexatious expense; but it will, however, be a proof still more vexatious to my enemies, and let this stand for some alleviation of the misfortune I mentioned. You are under some anxiety on the vague report that my adversary has made affidavits of his applying often to me for a division of the lands he now sues for as a discoverer. Were the report true, it would only throw ridicule upon his agent and advisor as my oath will (at least) counterbalance his, and I am not vain in thinking that it will even cast the scale against him in or out of any court of justice. To avail himself of any affidavit in this cause, he must make it by others whom he employed to make frequent applications to me for the dividend he claims. If such an affidavit be made, it must be (as you well know) through the guilt of the most flagrant perjury; and I dread but little from the consequences of such an affidavit as none but one already notorious for an iniquity of character will make it; in truth I think no such affidavit will be made, though I am far from thinking that the declining it will be owing to any principle of morality. . . .

1. Undated. O'Conor mentions the upcoming meeting of the Catholic Committee for 26 February 1779.

315. To Denis O'Conor, Belanagare, Roscommon

OCD, 8.4 SE 148

[Pill Lane, 27 February 1779]

. . . Through Colonel Vallancey's kindness I have been introduced here to a most amiable gentleman Colonel Burton, a privy Councilor and Teller of the Exchequer.¹ In a society of learned antiquarians I have dined at his fine house in Harcourt Place near Merrion Square on Wednesday last. I could not have a happier day, and our conversation rolled chiefly on Irish antiquities. A plan has been laid for rescuing them from their present obscurity; and could Colonel Burton infuse his own spirit into others, the plan would succeed. He doubtless will meet with obstacles and, I am afraid, with disappointment. He made me a present of some scarce books, and it was in vain that I declined taking his post chaise to bring me home. He forced me to accept of it, attended by two of his servants. Last night I sat with some lords and gentlemen in our Catholic Committee. My letter to the prelates was therein read and approved, and so was another paper drawn up by the hand of Mr. Caddell, intended to be printed for a further explanation of the purpose of my letter.² The scheme is for a general collection through all the parishes of the Kingdom, for maintaining a resident agent in England on the behalf of the Catholics and for other uses which, when known, will give our legislature a further good impression of our people and pave the way for a relaxation of some severe Penal Laws which still hang over them. . . .

1. Colonel Burton was an antiquarian. O'Conor's discovery suit has not interfered with his social acceptability. Cf. Gilbert, *IRQ*, 3 (March 1853) 36ff.
2. Both O'Conor's letter and Caddell's printed explanation of it are published in the "Catholic Committee Minute Book, 1773–92," pp. 35–39.

316. To [Colonel Charles Vallancey]¹

RIA, Stowe MS B1 1a

[Pill Lane, 12 March 1779]

Dear Sir,

I send you the enclosed, as it will convey to you some idea of the state of things in Ireland antecedently to the introduction of Christianity.

It is an abstract of the *Teagusg Flatha of Cormac O'Cuinn*, king of Ireland at the close of the third century.

That monarch was a *filea* (a philosopher) and professed himself a pious theist in opposition to the pantheism and superstition of the Druids, whose order he attempted to reform, not to abolish.

The copy you gave me I have compared with one now before me, transcribed in the year 1396. In both I find some variations and transpositions, all owing to ignorant transcribers, and the difficulties thrown in our way by bad copies are not greater than those occasioned by the complex terms and the mixed modes used in the third century. We want a glossary for explaining these obsolete terms; and yet as far as I proceeded I believe that my translation will be found just. The more obscure parts I would not attempt till better instructed than I am at present.

This piece should not be considered as the composition of King Cormack but as the epitome of some writer of an ulterior age. The cast of the phraseology shows that the work is very ancient. You will discern force, but no ostentation in the style, and on the whole, this composition lets in some characteristic light on the Irish of the third age. They were not barbarians in the common acceptation of that word, but a people who, secluded from the rest of the world, endeavored to cultivate themselves. They struck out a local civilization of their own, but we do not know enough of it, though a good part of it may be still dug out of the ruins of our antiquities.[2]

In a savage state the conversion of the heathen Irish to Christianity would be very difficult, but the quick progress of the Gospel among them demonstrates that they were long and well prepared for its reception through intellectual researches.

Pill Lane, 12 March 1779

1. The statement "The copy you gave me ..." leads the editors to believe that O'Conor is writing to Colonel Vallancey. For example, Dr. Charles O'Conor, *Memoirs*, p. 258, describes a manuscript in the O'Conor collection that matches the one described in the letter.
2. O'Conor is again presenting his case that the pre-Christian Irish were literate and civilized.

317. To Denis O'Conor, Belanagare, Roscommon

OCD, 8.4 SE 148

[13 March 1779]

The persons who two years ago started me as game[1] to be easily hunted down begin, I believe, to be tired of the chase.[2] I discover a wish among them to bring me to a party, as several gentlemen have of late interposed as mediators and recommended a composition between me and my hunters. To the most pressing of those *goers-between* I replied that his interposition would be viewed in a very friendly light on my side if the suit instituted against me were at common law and rolled merely on controverted property; but that this was not the case;

that herein lay his mistake; and that I would set him right by informing him that the challenge to me was grounded entirely upon a *penal law* on the score of my religion; and that I needed not inform him that such a penal law can not be compounded, as our legislature have been careful to arm it on all sides against a composition of any kind. This distinction was a stroke which the mediator could not parry; it took him wholly unprepared for a reply, and we both easily took up another subject. I have mentioned all this, that I may have your own reflections on these applications during an interval wherein our law-suit is laid asleep.

I have perused Dr. Philips's[3] letter recommending the speedy departure of Denis MacDermotroe for Rome. Be it so, though I thought it proper to wait for Mr. Charles Kelly's answer to my letter on Denis's account. It may not be so necessary as I have been told; I will, therefore, immediately consult about the most convenient passage for him, and I doubt that we have at present no ship in our river bound for Leghorn. You shall have (by next post) all the intelligence I can obtain on this head. Let Denis, therefore, be prepared for his journey hither, paying in the meantime a visit to Dr. Philips as he requires. Your unfortunate brother arrived here yesterday with the view of obtaining an abatement of rent and a long lease from Mr. Knox. He waits for the presence of young Mr. Knox (soon expected in town) before he sees the father. What success he may have can not at present be foreseen, but it is easy to foresee that, whatever it be or however favorable, his family will not be benefited. More of this in my next. You have received the person mentioned in the close of your letter as a poor orphan into your family. Lose no part of the merit of that conduct; and whatever cause of resentment you have with regard to her or her brother, I would have you dissemble it for some time, that you may acquit yourself the better, in a case where they have acquitted themselves so ill. In every debate, (said old Swift) be careful to put your adversary as much in the wrong as you can, as such a conduct will render your justification complete. I request that you will improve this fine season by attention to improvements on my course lands. The beggars of my colony have no other means of paying me. May God bless you and yours.

13 March 1779

1. This supports the editors' contention that Hugh's lawsuit was filed in the winter of 1777.
2. O'Conor is over confident.
3. Philip Philips, bishop of Achonry. *HBC*, p. 407.

318. To Denis O'Conor, Belanagare, Roscommon

OCD, 8.4 SE 148

[April 1779][1]

[Letter cropped—no date]

I have been sadly served by the law agent you provided for me. You may remember that I told you how Mr. O'Conor advised me to put in my answer to Cocking's bill in the last term.[2] I informed my agent[3] of this advice and pressed him to prepare my answer immediately. He said that he had time enough before him and would make a motion in Court to obtain further time for putting in my answer. But this intended motion was neglected: a process of Contempt was made out against me and in consequence, I was yesterday attached by a warrant from the Court of Chancery, was obliged to pay down £2.16.10 1/2 as the caption fee, and am now to remain (God knows how long) in the custody of a sergeant-at-arms, at the expense of fifteen shillings a day until my answer is put on the file.[4] I remain in a sort of honorable captivity with the liberty only of lying in my own room and walking about the streets when my occasions call me out. My enemies will triumph on this incident, to me equally expensive and mortifying; and they will proclaim it about that it was through diffidence of my cause that I declined to answer their last Bill of Discovery. But their triumph will be short. However this event may and must affect my pocket as well as mind, it will by no means affect my cause, nor can it otherwise serve my enemies than through the satisfaction my captivity will give them. Mr. James Ferral, to whom I owe my misfortune, is still in the country, so is Mr. French, who is to draw up my answer. The former will soon be here to repair, as well as he can, the injury he did me; and the latter you'll see at Roscommon Assizes. You'll inform him of my sufferings and your conversation with him on the subject will, I hope, hasten his return to this city. The agitation of my mind after a restless night begins to subside; nay, I am now almost composed, and I request that this intelligence will give you no more uneasiness than its merits. It is but a temporary evil, and let us thank God that it is nothing more; to make it as short as possible shall be my daily labor, and in my next letter I shall be able to inform you of the steps I shall take and of the success I may expect from them. Adieu and may God bless you and yours.

P.S. There is no ship in our river bound for any part of Italy.

1. This undated letter appears to be one written in early April since in the March letter, O'Conor was elated about a possible settlement of his case. The next letter after this one, dated 10 April, continued O'Conor's complaint about his house arrest.
  2. See O'Conor's summary of this advice in letter 312.
  3. James Ferral.
  4. O'Conor's general tactic has been delay. Hugh may feel that time is running out because repeal of the penal laws is imminent.

319. To Denis O'Conor, Belanagare, Roscommon

OCD, 8.4 SE 148

10 April 1779

Dear Denis,

Since my last I have (by advice) lodged an affidavit in Chancery setting forth that I never meant to give any delay to putting an answer to the ill-grounded Bill of Discovery filed against me and intended only as a measure to harass me by my adversary in the name of one lacking a perukemaker; that I have urged my law agent to prepare my answer by putting the proper materials for the same into the hands of my counsel, that far from incurring a process for contempt of this court against me, I have repeated[ly] pressed dispatch on my attorney; and that why my answer was not put in was owing entirely to his neglect.

After lodging this affidavit, I have entered a petition to the Lord Chancellor setting forth my case and praying for a relief from the great expense attending my custody with a sergeant-at-arms till my counsel and agent return from circuit to put in my answer as speedily as possible next term. This petition is put into the hands of the officers with whom you have dined along with Mr. James and Luke Ferral. He has put it into the Chancellor's hands, and how he will decide upon it I shall know by Monday next. What has Counselor French communicated to you on this subject? I bear with this misfortune as I would with a broken leg and lie under the disease till time brings the cure. It is not a mortal disease, and that is a great consolation.

Partick Parlan[1] is now here, and I send you by him Skinner's *Survey*, a work you will like undoubtedly.

  1. Patrick Parlan was a tenant of O'Conor's. Parlan had leased lands at Ballintubber from O'Conor since 1748. Dunleavy and Dunleavy, p. 21.

320. To Denis O'Conor, Belanagare, Roscommon

OCD, 8.4 SE 148

[13 April 1779]

My present state of captivity would be avoided if my instructions to my law agent made the proper imposition. I complained to Mr. Braughall, who told me a year ago that he was afraid Mr. Ferral might injure me by an indolence constitutional to him, but he told me then, as he does now, that he is a man of the best intentions towards a client. I find this to be his character among those who know him well; I believe them, and I request you will be sparing of casting any other censure upon him but that of neglect in the particular I now suffer by. How the Chancellor has disposed of my petition to him, I am yet to learn. Luke Ferral will, I believe, let me know by tomorrow; but all will be set right (though with expense) as soon as Counselor French comes to town. I have made up my mind on this transient evil, yielding to it as I would to a fever which, including no bad symptom, insures a speedy cure. Who knows but my mischance may have the effect of such a fever and end in giving my affair a better complexion through more spirited efforts of my physicians than they otherwise might use. It is fitter I should flatter myself with this reasonable expectation than indulge myself in useless complaints and vain discontent.

I lament the death of the worthy young man Mr. Mahon, and none but one who is himself a father can feel for another who finds himself in his old days stripped of a good son and only son. May God comfort every such father.

I request you will go to my cabin, see that everything is forwarded and forwarded judiciously for me. Curraghnahivry could never be better improved upon than in this fine season. If the hillocks be all cut down, they must soon dry for burning. I can not press you more, being in such a hurry, as you have been when you wrote your last from Roscommon. May God bless you and yours.

13 April 1779

321. To Denis O'Conor, Belanagare, Roscommon

OCD, 8.4 SE 148

[Pill Lane, 21 April 1779]

My affidavit and petition to the Chancellor had better success than I expected from either, and you and I have been mistaken as to the advice of Luke Ferral. Here follows the Chancellor's order: "On reading the affidavit made by Charles O'Conor I was ordered by the Chancellor that the [deep] Day fees be suspended until further order: and it is further ordered that the process of contempt to a sergeant-at-arms entered against the petitioner be set aside unless, in six days after a service of this order, good cause be shown to the contrary, and it is further ordered that the said defendant have time to answer, plead, or demur to the first day of Trinity term next." A more favorable order than this could not be expected, and depend upon it that we will be prepared by counsel to argue against the defendant should he endeavor, at or before the sixth day recited to their camp, to show cause why the process of contempt against me should be revived. As soon as James Ferral arrives, Jack Dillon and I will attend him to expostulate with him on the injury past and to spur him on to repair it by active diligence for the time to come. You shall be informed of our proceedings as they occur, and you have no manner of occasion to come up hither till after the present term. I compassionate the case of poor Duiginan. He and I had been schoolfellows, and the friendship between us was constant for thirty years. I did not through the whole period suspect him of insincerity, and I overlooked his failings as

[Rest of letter taped over.]

322. To Denis O'Conor

OCD, 8.4 SE 148

[Pill Lane, 4 May 1779]

... It was only this morning that I have seen James Ferral, and it was only yesterday that he arrived from the County of Galway, where he met with an ugly accident (a blow on the leg) which confined him there several days and which confines him still to his chamber. I have dissembled my resentment of his neglect, and he interposed the best apology he could for what has passed. Depend upon it; he is faithful to us. His fault is a constitutional indolence of which many complain and from which he has experienced bad consequences to himself in the way of business. He seems to feel for the past, and I have no doubt but that feeling will be a spur to his future activity in our cause....

323. To Denis O'Conor

OCD, 8.4 SE 148

[Pill Lane, 11 May 1779]

... My adversary is still here. Of late he has swelled the inventory of his calumnies against me, charging on me a sacrilegious robbery of the Church by getting into my hand sums of money belonging to the poor Community of Elphin and never accounting for the same to the fraternity.[1] He likewise affirms that I have set a poor, old brother adrift, refusing him either a room or bed in my house and leaving him on the common to shift for old age and infirmity as well as he could.[2] These charges may have weight with those who do not know me; but, I thank God, they are such as can not stick to me, and I pray to God for the conversion of the unhappy man who made them. I had like to forget in informing you that we have a ship here bound for Cadiz. What you think of sending your son and uncle[3] by that conveyance in case the Leghorn ship sailed off [torn] Monday next and your son could not be here by that day? From Cadiz [he?] would every day find a ship bound for some port in Italy....

    1. Apparently O'Conor was a conduit for money sent by Franciscan friars from a religious house in Paris to one in Elphin. Dunleavy and Dunleavy, p. 28, OCD, 8.3 SE 032, list a receipt for £166.5 signed by Charles O'Conor. O'Conor received the money from Anthony Dermot, a Dublin merchant, and Reverend Morris of Paris. O'Conor's brother Roger, a Franciscan priest, was also involved in these transactions.
    2. Daniel.
    3. Father Roger and his grandnephew, Charles.

324. To John Fallon[1]

OCD, 8.4 HS 149

24 August 1779

At a time when his Majesty's Protestant subjects of Ireland are arming themselves for the security of the government even without waiting on the usual commissions,[2] the Roman Catholics are virtually called upon to take some active part in the service of their country; such a cooperation, however, as the law permits, not such as it forbids to men in their circumstances.[3] A national measure upon this ground has already been adopted by the Roman Catholics of Limerick, and it is to be wished the Roman Catholics of the county of Roscommon should not be the last in following the example. Several gentlemen with whom I held a conversation on this subject have expressed the same desire. They think it expedient that a few of the principal Catholics of the county should meet speedily at Roscommon to concert such measures of conduct for themselves and their brethren as may be most proper and practicable in the present alarming crisis of public affairs. Those gentlemen have requested of me to make this application to you as to one who has the most influence among us in recommending their scheme. If approved of, various private occasions may be more pressing at present than those others. They would not appoint a day of meeting lest it should be inconvenient to you. . . .

 1. John Fallon is the nephew of Joseph or James O'Fallon, bishop of Elphin. See letter 328 for the results of this meeting of the Catholics at Roscommon.
 2. The French entry into the American Revolutionary War in 1778 and Spain's alliance with France in June 1779 saw increased support for the English even by Irish Presbyterians who had opposed the war and by the Catholics. See O'Connell, Chapter IV, "War with France and the Formation of the Volunteers."
 3. On 15 July 1779 the select committee sent an address of loyalty to King George III in which they deplored "the insidious and base attempts of the French and Spanish courts of disturbing the peace . . . of your majesty's dominions." They sent a separate address to the viceroy, Buckinghamshire, in which they expressed their gratitude "for the recent benefits conferred on us by the legislature." This address was sent in the name of the Roman Catholics of Ireland and signed by Lord Gormanston. O'Conor is attempting to produce a similar address from the Catholics of Roscommon in an attempt to legalize Catholics' entry into the military and their subsequent right to bear arms. "Catholic Committee Minute Book, 1773–92," pp. 40–41.

325. To Charles Kelly

OCD, 8.4 SH 150

20 September 1779

The safe arrival of my brother and grandson in Rome, and the reception of the latter under your protection is one of the few events which fortune, as if she relented, has admitted as a counterbalance to her persecutions of me in the course of a life which is now near its period. . . .

326. To Denis O'Conor

OCD, 8.4 SH 150

[27 September 1779]

The bearer, Father Kelly, is the gentleman who is to receive the cash advanced by Father Kelly in Rome for my grandson. I send you a bank note of £15 on a double account, first that you may remit it to Mr. Dillon of Francis Street that the cash may be got immediately as my old acquaintance, Mr. Pat Lawless (one of the principal bankers) is dead. . . .

327. To Charles O'Conor[1]

RIA, Stowe MS Bi2

Belanagare, 5 October 1779

. . . I request that you will every day of your life read a chapter or two in the little book entitled *The Imitation of Christ*. There you will find united the sublime and the affecting in Christian philosophy, recommended by the noble simplicity which adorns every species of good composition. In that summary of Christian piety, you will everywhere meet with truths which lead to the most lucrative reflections and which warm the heart while they improve the head. Of your school courses, I say nothing; they are now under the best regulations and particularly in Rome. As you have so many years before you, I would wish that you understood Moses and the prophets in their own language, as through the perusal of Kennicott's *Collations*[2] of the various readings of the Hebrew text you will be enabled to form a just judgment of the commentators who succeeded best in explaining that text and consequently in unfolding the true scheme of the Old Testament as an introduction and as a proof to Christianity. . . . As to Latin it will not be enough for you to understand it well, but you should write it well also. By writing it well I do not mean writing it grammatically, but classically, as Bembo, Sadolet, and other Italians have done soon after the restoration of letters under the patronage of the House of Medici. To learn the sense of *words*, their arrangement and construction in several languages is undoubtedly painful (when in our short period of life the study of *things* alone would give us sufficient employment). But there is no remedy for this evil if it be one; and we must submit to a task which is imposed upon us in the constitution of things and which ultimately is attended with advantages which become the reward of our labors. The polyglot book I have put into your hands in Dublin will be of use to you in learning the modern tongues of Italian, French, and English; and these tongues have a connection (in arrangement and phraseology) which will make their acquisition very easy to you....

    1. O'Conor's grandson, The Reverend Charles O'Conor, D.D.
    2. Reverend Benjamin Kennicott, D.D., *The Ten Annual Accounts of the Collation of Hebrew Manuscripts of the Old Testament Begun in 1760 and Compleated in 1769* (Oxford: n.p., 1770). BMCPBCE 13:1154.

328. To Dr. John Curry, Summerhill, Dublin

OCD, 8.4 HS 141

Belanagare, 13 October 1779

My Dear Sir,

It was but yesterday that I have received your most welcome letter of the 4th instant. I thought my former letter to you had miscarried and the more since one of mine to Mr. Ryan appeared to have the same fate, as I received no answer to either. Now I discover that some people have had you and me in the wind for some time and that curiosity at least, if not a worse principle, had peeped into our correspondence and in some degree prevented its renewal but on such cautionary terms as would render it disgustful to us both. How I had the luck of receiving the letter before me I know not, but the former I have never received any more than the letter you tell me Mr. Ryan forwarded to me. This day I shall write down my complaint on this subject to Mr. Guy, Postmaster of Roscommon, and yet I expect but little satisfaction from him or his clerk.

I am not much surprised that our great friend Mr. B[urke] has refused the offer made him,[1] and perhaps the manner in which it has been made was indelicate. Indeed delicacy is not the forte of our people, and there are good reasons for our failure in that prospect. Mr. B[urke] foresees some difficulties in our way relatively to the completion of what has been done for us in the last session. He does not explain himself on this head to you. But I think you can, from what you have lately seen, discover the true cause and spring of this matter. Was ever any conduct more improper and indiscreet than incorporating ourselves with Protestant militant associates, with the laws of our country so express and so penal against us for meddling with arms?[2] Was this a measure dictated by prudence or is this the proper mode of gratitude to our gracious Sovereign, the first Protestant prince that ever granted us the smallest legal favor? If this be not *giving hostility for benefits received,* it surely bears a construction leading to such an idea, and the idea should be promptly removed if we be not infatuated into the neglect of it.

On the 9th of September last through the scheme laid by my son and through the approbation of it by our Bishop,[3] the R[oman] C[atholics] of our country had a meeting in Roscommon, and it was both respectable and numerous. The following address to the Viceroy was prepared and assented to with the ratification of 140 subscribers:

"To His Excellency, etc.

"May it please your Excellency, at a time when these kingdoms are threatened with invasion from foreign and hostile powers, we the R[oman] Catholics of the county of Roscommon beg leave to approach your Excellency with assurances of our being firmly united with his Majesty's loyal subjects of all denominations in *every exertion within our power* for the defense of his Majesty's person and government and the disappointment of all his enemies.

"Fidelity to government (may it please your Excellency) is a duty exacted by our religion at all times. It is a duty we have inviolably adhered to for near a century past, and it is a duty also strengthened of late by the participation of constitutional privileges with us through the beneficence of our most gracious Sovereign and the wisdom of an enlightened legislature. With grateful hearts we join with our brethren of this kingdom in the recognition of that indulgence, and we are more happy in the consciousness of having deserved it as our conduct under it will certainly bring a conviction to the guardian of our liberties that we are the faithful subjects they always wished we should be. It is by our conduct we deserve to be tried, and we recollect with pleasure that the lightening of our burdens and the earnest now given of growing strength to our civil establishment has fallen on a period which in a peculiar manner signalizes your Excellency's government in the annals of our country. A happy period certainly, wherein the ablest men of our nation have concurred in the great truth that an active union of sound civil principles among all religious parties is sufficient for the internal security of every civil government.

"We earnestly beseech your Excellency to add to the obligations we owe you in common with our fellow subjects by assuring our gracious Sovereign of our inviolable attachment to Him, and of our promptness to hasten the proofs by a faithful discharge of every service that we can be employed in at the present or any future time."[4]

On the ratification of the above instrument of loyalty, one of our society (Mr. Fallon, a worthy gentleman and the Bishop's nephew) undertook to negotiate the acceptance of it at Court through the interest of the first peer of the kingdom; his Grace has most benevolently consented to deliver it to the L[ord] Lieutenant. He has done so, as you will see by the following copy of his letter to Mr. Fallon:

"Carton, 4 October 1779

"I waited on his Excellency, the Lord Lieutenant with the Address of the Principal R[oman] Catholics of the County Roscommon, which you transmitted to me. I have the pleasure to inform you that his Excellency will take the earliest opportunity of laying the zeal and loyalty of those gentlemen before his Majesty, who might at this important crisis receive great satisfaction in such declarations of loyalty and regard for his person, crown, and dignity. I cannot conclude without requesting you, once more, to lay my most sincere thanks before those gentlemen for the high honor they have done me in fixing on me to be the person to present that address, at the same time requesting you will assure them of my sincere regards and affections and shall at all times be happy to show by acts and not by words how sincerely I am, sir, theirs and yours, etc.,

"Leinster"[5]

By the perusal of the above you will see that this was his Grace's second meeting on Monday next to frame some account for expressing our gratitude to his Grace for the honor he did us. You'll show this letter to our friend, but I think that no copy should be taken lest it might fall into the hands of indiscreet men who might get it printed in the public paper. My affections most heartily to your whole family; as soon as you read this, write to me.

1. On 11 November 1778 the Catholic Committee voted to present Burke with 500 guineas. O'Conor's letter to Denis 27 February 1779 indicates that a general collection was taken up. Curry wrote to Burke on 6 August asking Burke to accept a payment of 300 guineas to be delivered by Anthony Dermot, treasurer of the Catholic Committee. Burke declined the money and later suggested that it be used to educate Irish Catholic youths, who were barred from Irish schools—Dermot sent the 300 guineas before being aware of Burke's refusal. Burke returned the bill of exchange. *Burke,* ed., John A. Woods, 4:117–121.
2. Although it was illegal for Catholics to bear arms, a number had joined the Volunteers.
3. John Fallon of Elphin.

4. The Roscommon Catholics appear to be offering their services to join the military; however, O'Conor wants such service to be legal.

5. William Robert Fitzgerald, second duke of Leinster (1749–1804), Colonel of the Dublin regiment of Volunteers. *Concise DNB*, 1:439.

329. To James O'More

RIA, Stowe MS Bi2

1779

My dear O'More,

I heartily thank you for the concern you express at the attack made upon me for no other offense than my preferring (in spirituals) an obedience to the law of conscience rather than to that of the land wherein I was born. The perpetuity of *civil pumishment* where no *civil crime* exists is one of those political dispensations which distinguishes the wisdom of this enlightened age and country, a dispensation however which accords but little with that providence which never annexes rewards of dissimulation nor pronounces sincerity criminal. Let us accept these severities from our legislature as a punishment due to our sins and as a trial wherein the little virtue we have may be exercised. After the storm of '88 my poor father was thrown on shore on a broken plank. His family for three hundred years has been gradually on the decline and now as the catastrophe to the last act an effort is made to leave me nothing to inherit but the religion and misfortune of my ancestors. I am doing what I can to evade the blow, and I hope that I am prepared for the heaviest that can fall upon me.

I have been with Mr. Whitten on the commission you gave me, and I can easily show that the genealogy made out for O'Donnell is as authentic as any that can be produced from the most accurate annals. You observe very justly that on the sudden change made in the fortune of the family and their consequent exile they might, in a foreign land, take up with arbitrary armorial ensigns taken from some ignorant informer rather than take pains to procure the true arms, which were mislaid or neglected by them at the time of their flight.

[fragment]

330. To Colonel Charles Vallancey

RIA, Stowe MS Bi2
Colonel Charles Vallancey, Dublin

[7 January 1780]

Dear Sir,

... I trust that before I return you (next week) the last that I shall be able to acquit myself to your satisfaction relatively to an Irish translation of the *Formula* remitted to you from Petersburg and now lying before me. I owe you this, my dear sir, and a great deal more. My present task is indeed light, nor shall I consider it as the discharge of a debt, but as an addition from your kindness in conferring a new obligation upon me. The translation of the *Formula* from p. 25 to p. 29 in French and Latin you shall have (God willing) next week, and as a specimen of what I am doing I send you here the form in p. 32 which is entirely in French:

> Que chacun soit soumis au
> magistrat qui est ètabli sur lui
>
> Car il n'y a point de magistrat
> que ne soit ètabli par Dieu.
>
> Et quand il y a un magistrat,
> il est placé par Dieu.
>
> Bíodh gach aon cennsaidh don fhollomhan
> taoi dechtaidh fair
>
> Óir ní fhil follamhan (nó úachtarán) ar
> bith acht ó Dhía
>
> Agus mar a mbíonn follamhan, as ó Dhía
> thig a fhollamhnacht

In our vulgar dialect it runs thus:

"*Bíodh gach aon urramach don úachtarán [t]aoi curtha os a chionn, óir níl úachtarán ar bith acht re ordúghadh Dé, & an t-ionadh a mbíonn úachtarán, as e Dia bheir ionadh dhó.*"[1] ...

---

1. "Let everyone be obedient to the chief who has been placed over him, for there is no chief at all except by the order of God, and where there is a chief it is God who appoints him (lit. gives him place)."

331. To Archbishop John Carpenter

OCD, 8.4 HS 141

From the Hermitage, 14 January 1780

Most Rev[eren]d Sir,

Your Grace's letter of the 5th instant brought me great satisfaction, and I shall lock it up in the little treasury of my correspondence that my posterity may know that I once enjoyed the communicative friendship of some men equally distinguished by their talents and virtues. At my time of life this is not vanity, for I have reflected a little and yesterday I have completed my seventieth year. But I would wish to excite a laudable ambition in my descendents to fill up a better station in society than fortune can bestow and that they might find a spur in the perusal of a correspondence which seldom falls to the lot of an obscure person. Denis and I are very thankful to your Grace for the account you give me of my grandson in Rome. His first appearance on that stage has flattered my parental hopes as the Cardinal to whom he was introduced was pleased that a youth ignorant of French and Italian could hold a conversation with his Eminence in the language of the *Scipios* and *Gracchi*. It pains me indeed that our other fine youth, O'Conor Luby,[1] is at present in a decling state, but as he is kept under the most skillful regimen, we have a fair prospect open for his re-establishment.

I am really giving all the attention that my personal avocations can permit to the task you have long since laid out for me. I have made some progress but little, I confess, to my own satisfaction. The times antecedent to Christianity offer some matter which ought not to be overlooked, for man in every state of society is an object of attention. To make a proper arrangement of the materials we have left and strip history of the poetical veils thrown over it by the fileas has indeed cost me some labor and still will cost me more. The latter periods are to us by far the most important and luckily the easiest in the execution as in this we see our way clearer, and yet the state of our insular Church before Paparo's time is so singular that it will require a laborious investigation which, when undertaken by an able hand, will be rewarded with some knowledge of which hitherto we have only a glimpse.

I am glad that you sent Mr. Butler's notes of the *Life of St. Lawrence*, the first palled A[rch] B[ishop] of Dublin, as you give me an opportunity of correcting his mistakes, which are not few.[2] I request to your Grace to present my affections to Mrs. Troy, to Miss Taylor if in town, to my fast friend Mr. Lee, his Lady and family, and to my worthy friends the Vicars.

P.S. I am just returned from French Park (pretty late) where a commission was sped on my unfortunate law suit. I have not, therefore, time to fill up this night the blank before me with the notes I prepared for Mr. Butler's work, and the bearer must set off early tomorrow morning with the law packet intrusted to him. I trust that I will be in time for remitting those notes next week, and it concerns me much that I have not a frank to enclose them in.

1. O'Conor Luby is a cousin of the archbishop's. See Charles O'Kelly to Charles O'Conor, 14 April 1779, Stowe MS Bi2, RIA.
2. Alban Butler (1711–1773) compiled *The Lives of the . . . Principal Saints* 1756–1759. He was educated at Douay in France and was president of the English College at St. Omer.

332. To Colonel Charles Vallancey

RIA, Stowe MS Bi2

Belanagare, 22 January 1780

. . . We do not so much want information as to turn that information to a good account by teaching us the most profitable lesson of preferring a practical good to an ideal state, which if obtained would prove a womb of mistrusts and jealousies and of no better a progeny. A free trade for our natural productions has been granted to us, and Britain could not grant a greater.[1] I hope that the wisdom of Parliament will be content with this, and I wish from my soul that our H[ouse] of C[ommons] will overlook the public complaints about Poyning's Law.[2] It has been a useful law in its time, calculated for a certain period. It is now an eyesore and indeed little else in our Constitution. Debates about it after what we have obtained would be invidious, and as money bills originate in our own lower house, is not Poyning's Law virtually repealed thereby? But I beg pardon for a sketch in policy, which I intended should be very short, and is to you impertinent. *Ionntaidh don taobh aile don duilleoig.*[3] . . .

1. See Lecky 2:242–243 for an evaluation of the free trade measures passed at the close of 1779 and the beginning of 1780. See also O'Connell, VI, "The Free Trade Movement."
2. On April 26 Yelverton introduced heads of a bill for the repeal of sections of Poyning's Law. However, the motion was defeated 130 to 105. See O'Connell, pp. 233–234, for a fuller treatment.

3. "Turn to the other side of the leaf." This script appears at the bottom of the first page of the letter.

333. To Myles MacDermot, Coolavin

OCD, 8.4 SO 114

[From my Hermitage, 2 February 1780]

... I lately received a letter from my grandson in Paris, and the proof I find therein of his erudition and good taste brought my sensible satisfaction. His time is chiefly employed on the science to which he has devoted himself, and as I have no doubt of his progress you have the satisfaction that the expense you are at in his account is not thrown away. ...

334. To Denis O'Conor

OCD, 8.4 SE 148

Dublin, 1 April 1780

Owen is well in the Academy. I have for some days past been employed by Dr. C[arpenter] to write notes on the parts of the *History of the Holy Fathers and Martyrs* which regard Ireland. This occupation confines me much at home and I can vacate to it with the greatest liberty as every active proceeding in our law suit is suspended till the commencement of Easter Term.... I will certainly be ill served. I would have you (as an act of your own) to settle for the ensuing year with the tenants of Balinatown. Let them remain at the former rent, but after Michaelmas day stipulate for me that they are to give me up the acre of small tract of ground I pointed out to you when I opened to you my intention of drawing a straight stone wall though *Gort a Cran* (my meadow for the next season) down to the red bog. The poor wretches of Dereenatinny pay no rent; and it will, therefore, be the more necessary to hold them tightly to graveling and draining the ground they occupy, and you must press them *in terrorem*[1] as they must infallibly be turned out, unless they make some reasonable reparation for their insolvency. I have [taken a review yesterday] of my dear friend's (Dr. Curry's) posthumous[2] works. He left [the care of them so] far as a few corrections (may be proper) to me. They are to be printed [corrupt] for the use of his family, which he did not leave in affluence, as I have been assured that his whole property did not exceed more than £4,000 in value. . . .

1. As a warning.
2. John Curry, M.D., died at age seventy-eight at Summerhill, Dublin, on 21 March. *DJ*, 21–23 March 1780.

335. To Denis O'Conor, Belanagare, Roscommon

OCD, 8.4 SE 148

[Pill Lane, 25 April 1780]

. . . Mary's death,[1] aggravating the memory of that of my dear Biddy leaves me this moment in a state of mind which unfits me for writing or thinking properly on any subject. I am the more depressed by being the father of a man who brought disappointment from the beginning and grief in the end to the family. . . .

. . . Your brother . . . is now, I suppose, unfit for housekeeping as he has exhausted the last shilling of his property, and were he willing he would not be able to bring a new family into his house or support the overgrown children of another, when he can not afford a bit of bread for his own orphans. Away with such a silly and impractical scheme, etc. I request that you will hit upon some other scheme for those orphans whom you are to consider now as fatherless, as well as motherless.

1. The wife of O'Conor's son Charles, Mary Dillon O'Conor, died and left four children.

336. To Denis O'Conor

OCD, 8.4 SE 148

Pill Lane, 1 May 1780

. . . I had a letter from your brother where in he gives me an account of his last misfortune. I pity him, and I pray you will form some scheme for preserving what is left of his fortune, so that his little family will benefit by it. He is himself fit for no business, and that he is not you know well from accumulated proofs through a course of fifteen years. His failing invariably in every undertaking I attribute very justly I think to a defect in his understanding, a defect more fatal as it was [unreadable] imposing appearances of a sound mind. Let his two little boys be brought to my lodge and kept at the neighboring best school.[1] I am glad that Cathy takes one of his daughters under her care. Jack Dillon is already proposed to the eldest girl, and the youngest child of all may be left with my sister (the widow) till we think of a better place for her. What I now write to you will serve for an answer to your brother's letter to me. His farm from Knox would, in the hands of very moderate industry, be worth £50 a year. In his, it will produce nothing but an ejectment. I would wish you could get a good fer-tenant for that land who would afford some annual profit to the present. . . .

1. Thomas and Denis.

337. To Archbishop John Carpenter

OCD, 8.4 HS 141

From the Hermitage, 14 September 1780

Mr. Arthur McManus, a gentleman of my acquaintance, called upon me this day requesting I should give your Grace (what indeed he deserves) a good character of him. The reason of this application I shall here explain. A gentleman of Cordova in Spain named Joseph Solis (one of the canons of that city) is the son of James Jolli, a French gentleman who on his removal to Spain took the surname of Solis. By his last will the said James left a considerable legacy to Bridget Solis, his sister still living. She received an account of this bequest eight or nine years ago but pursued her right too negligently hitherto. . . . [1]

1. Apparently Arthur McManus has asked O'Conor to write a recommendation for him and to send it to Carpenter. McManus is the son of Bridget Solis and is making a legal claim based on the genealogy O'Conor has prepared for him. The letter itself is very corrupt and difficult to decipher in detail. It is significant because it shows the kind of service O'Conor regularly supplied for Irish Catholics in exile and because Carpenter, as archbishop, served as a conduit for this type of affidavit.

338. To Archbishop John Carpenter

OCD, 8.4 HS 141

[From the Hermitage, 22 November 1780]

Most Rev[eren]d Sir,

I should have acknowledged the honor of your Grace's letter on the affair of Mr. McManus, but that the latter has hitherto neglected following the steps you traced out to him as preparatory to your interposition for him. His tardiness justified my not giving your Grace any further trouble on this subject.

I am extremely obliged to your Grace for the postscript to Mr. Morris's letter of Saturday last to me. I will execute as well as I can the dedicatory epistle he requires. It should (as your Grace observes) be short and simple, yet even in that form it will require a little art to recommend it to the noble patron mentioned to me. But that art I never studied, nor am I sorry for my deficit in it. By the next post I shall remit you the effort of a new beginner, and I well know it will not only want your corrections but your amputations also, short as it may be.

In my idea, a dedication prefixed to the *Lives of the Martyrs* is not so much wanted as a postscript (from the editor) to the last volume setting forth the superior value of the Irish edition and the acknowledgments due to the prelate who, with great labor, revised the whole and made a judicious arrangement of the manuscript amendments left by the pious author before his decease, etc. Surely they would be the best recommendation of the work, and omission of it would be an act of injustice. Would it not be preferable to a dedication to one nobleman which might excite a jealousy in others of his rank equally zealous?

I had a letter from Denis acknowledging your Grace's kindness to him; he informed me also of your invitation to Court and your reception there. This new practice in Irish history pleased me much. It is phenomenon in our long clouded political sky which announces fair weather.

I am, *alternis vicibus*,[1] laboring at the work your Grace has been long recommending to me;[2] and though I am conscious enough of my want of ability, yet I flatter myself with some hope that I will have better success than my predecessors in exciting a writer of talents to give us the history of Ireland. Our antiquities, through the want of documents long lost, are shrouded in much obscurity. But I should by no means omit putting such disjointed documents as we have left into some good light, and the more as much labor has been taken of late to put them into the worst, particularly by our own Doctor O'Brien of Cloyne, by Mr. Innes of the Scotch College in Paris, and by Mr. Whitaker of Manchester, three able writers.[3] In the text I *indirectly* demolish their objections by well-authenticated facts, and when I mention their names, it is chiefly in the margin when I show that instead of giving us history, they only entertain us with hypothoses, each choosing such a ground for his own as his opportunities and his studies led him to. The difficulty does not consist in overturning their structures, but in erecting something solid on better foundations than these gentlemen have chosen. From being stinted in maturity, your Grace will easily see that my building must be a small one; I shall, God willing, soon give it the last hand and take up our history from periods more important to us than the more ancient times.

I enclose this to my fast friend Mr. Lee. I request you will present him, Mrs. Lee, and his whole family with my affections, Mrs. Troy also, the Dean, the Archdeacon, and one another friends that you often see. I shall ever remain your Grace's most affectionate grateful servant.

From the Hermitage, 22 November 1780

> 1. In one vicissitude after another.
> 2. A history of Ireland that O'Conor never finished.
> 3. John O'Brien, Catholic bishop of Cloyne, d. 1767. His work on gavelkind and tanistry in Ireland was published, 1774–5. Thomas Innes (1662–1744) wrote a *Critical Essay on the Ancient Inhabitants of the Northern Parts of Britain*, 1729. John Whitaker (1735–1808), rector of Ruan-Lanyhorn, Cornwall, 1777–1808. He wrote *History of Manchester*, 1771–5 (two volumes). *Concise DNB*, 1: 961, 673, 1395.

339. To Archbishop John Carpenter

OCD, 8.4 HL 144

From the Hermitage, 25 November 1780

Most Rev[eren]d Sir,

In obedience to your Grace's requisition (which to me shall ever stand in the place of a command) I have drawn up the annexed outlines of a *dedication* for Mr. Morris's publication of the *Lives of the Martyrs*. I give them for outlines only; some to be cut off, and some to be amended.

To the Rt. Honorable Arthur James
Earl of Fingall, Lord Killeen, etc.[1]

From many circumstances in your Lordship's life and conduct, the publisher of the following volumes is amply justified in laying a claim to your patronage of a work which on its first appearance has found so good a reception at home and abroad.

It is, my Lord, a body of ecclesiastical biography deduced from the earliest ages of Christianity. In the *Lives of the Martyrs* the pious and learned author instructs by example, next to divine Grace the most powerful incitement to virtue. Acts which appear extraordinary are here explained in their motives and sanctified in their consequences. An infallible rule is discovered whereby we may discern the difference between the true and the spurious in moral actions, really or pretendedly founded on the Gospel.

Men, my Lord, who consult their own feelings under the government on sober reflection can not be divided on the judgment they ought to form on the sufferings of Christian martyrs whose lives have been written by authors of unquestionable credit, not by legendary writers who with great credulity and no critical discernment have made collections that can by no means be depended on. Such collections are now laid aside. The authentic documents remain and are the sole foundation of the following work, on the perusal of which the reader may easily make the necessary distinction between the obstinacy of suffering error stripped of benevolence and the perseverance of suffering virtue clothed with charity.

The learned author of the present work, my Lord, did not confine his views of doing good to one body of Christians solely; for from so partial a motive he has calculated it for the edification of all. It is a noble effort for superseding the malignity but too discernable in many modern controversies. This circumstance alone calls for the attention of all parties to the labors of so learned a man and so acute a critic as the late Mr. Butler.

A dedication, my Lord, wherein so much is said of the work and so little of the patron is uncommon, but we think it will not be the less acceptable to your Lordship on that account. We meddle not with the honors heaped upon your Lordship's family through a succession of four hundred years by English Kings. They were the rewards of virtues for the enumeration of which we refer to royal patents.

1. Arthur James Plunkett (1759–1836), a relative of the Irish martyr, St. Oliver Plunkett; the only Catholic peer in Ireland qualified to take a seat if eligibility is granted. *Burke,* eds. Barbara Lowe, P. J. Marshall, and John A. Woods, 10: 436.

340. To John Dillon[1]

OCD, 8.4 SO 168

1781

Your benefaction to my grandsons has arrived safe.[2] On that event you should have my grateful reply immediately, but that I waited for a frank. In this I have been disappointed. In writing to my friends I would wish that my correspondence would cost them nothing but the trouble of reading. I never reflected on the great disappointment you have met with by alliance with my family without very sensible sorrow. Among the many misfortunes which depressed my life, I reckon this as one of the heaviest. . . .

    1. Father of Mary Dillon, recently deceased wife of O'Conor's son, Charles of Mt. Allen.
    2. In another hand, "from my father to Mr. John Dillon on his sending two suits of clothes to his two grandchildren, Tom and Denis O'Conor." Eventually these two sons emigrated to America with their father. Thomas became the father of Charles O'Conor of New York, the famous American lawyer.

341. To Chevalier Thomas O'Gorman,[1] Dublin

BM, Add. MS 21121

Belanagare, 17 January 1781

You are welcome, my dear Chevalier, to your native country and surely you are thrice welcome to me: I am obliged to you for paying your first visits to Colonel Burton[2] and Colonel Vallancey. I am indeed under great obligations to both, upon a personal as well as public account. I should [have] sat down closely to the investigation of our insular antiquities if early in life I met with such a patron as Colonel Burton; but my best days are gone, and even the few before me must, for the greater number, be employed in providing (as Dr. Johnson expresses it) for the day which passes over me. I will however inform you that in every vacation from that employment I am busy in learning as much as I can of the language, literature, and politics of the old inhabitants of Ireland, and that I purpose giving an idea of their history down to the time of the first monarch of the *Stuart* line when, in a great degree, they ceased to be a nation. The outlines of the work are drawn; to fill them up and give the picture the best coloring I can afford must depend on time; and time (I am afraid) will not answer my drafts upon it.[3] It gives me great pleasure to find that you are not to quit us till the end of March, for about the middle of that month I shall, God sparing my life, meet you to receive your instructions on the plan of our antiquity researches and to deliver you up the books and manuscripts you committed to my charge. I shall also put into your hands a *summary* (chronological and genealogical) of the principal families who flourished for more than a thousand years in Ulster, Conaght, and Meath. . . .

1. Thomas O'Gorman (1732–1809), born in Clare, educated at the Irish College in Paris. A physician, he married the daughter of Count d'Eon, a member of the Irish brigade, wealthy wine grower and wine merchant. He compiled pedigrees for expatriate Irish in France and Spain and collected Irish manuscripts; through his initiative the Book of Lecan was transferred from the Irish College at Paris to the RIA. *A Dictionary of Irish Biography*, p. 266.
2. Burton-Conyngham, an Englishman living in Dublin, one of the founding members of the RIA. Colonel Burton assumed the name of his uncle, the earl of Conyngham, when the uncle died and left his large estate to Col. Burton and his brother. Sheehan, p. 618.
3. O'Conor never finished this history of Ireland; at least it was never published during his lifetime.

342. To Archbishop John Carpenter, Usher's Island, Dublin

OCD, 8.4 HS 141

From the Hermitage, 20 February 1781

Most Rev[eren]d Sir,

I have so strong a proof of your Grace's great kindness to me and my family in your letter of Saturday last that the gratification we have received on that account can be exceeded only by our gratitude. When the family we derive from began to be (what the world terms) unhappy, the then Archbishop of Dublin proved their best friend. Through his interposition at Rome and England, he prevented their fall from being rapid. It was only by degrees that they lost all consequence and though reduced to that state, and for them (very likely) the best state, yet a reflection rushed upon me that fortune has relented in regard to myself in giving me an equal in O'Toole's[1] present successor. With God's assistance, I shall keep possession of what I have gratuitously obtained and will exert myself to my utmost in the business you recommended to me.[2] My age (as I am well) is not the greatest obstacle in my way. I meet with frequent interruptions not only from my domestic associations, but from correspondences which cannot be dismissed without incurring a charge which in prudence as well as decency I should prevent. Governor Pownall,[3] who quitted his seat in Parliament for a philosophical retreat at Richmond, has written to me on the subject of our Celtic antiquities. I made him the best reply I could, and probably I'll hear again from him. This correspondence between us is owing to Colonel Vallancey. I had other letters from friends on the continent on a work of labor and barrenness, that of the genealogies of some of our principal Irish families. As this is, however, a subject of importance to our gentry abroad, I thought it a duty to comply as well as I could with their demands, and I am now at work on the families of Leinster, Ulster, and Conaght. The Chevalier O'Gorman has undertaken for the Munster families; and the whole, when completed and properly prefaced, is to be published in France. I do not like the employment, and I think your Grace would wish it in other hands rather than in mine.

Denis and his family thank your Grace exceedingly for the account you give of our boy in Rome.[4] I also lately had a letter from him that pained me exceedingly; our clear and worthy friend Father O'Kelly is not well-treated, and how grating it must be to find unedifying factions in the bosom of orthodoxy! He likewise informed me of a fact which should never be published, the brutality of the last prince of the Stuart line[5] at an entertainment given by him to some of the nobility of Florence on the 30th of November last. When grown intoxicated, he abused his company but particularly the Princess his Consort in an afflicting manner. She retired to a convent and from there was soon obliged to depart, as her husband threatened to take her away by violence from that retreat. She implored the Pope's protection and obtained it. *Sic sic juvat ire sub umbras!*[6] I am pleased that young Mr. Luby O'Conor and my grandson study together in the same place. It will lay the foundation of an intimacy which will be lasting as it will be centered in piety. I expect warmly that they will derive credit to their country when we shall no longer exist in it. I thank your Grace most heartily for your recommendation of Dr. Boethius Egan.[7] He is a worthy man and will undoubtedly answer your description of him in whatever station of dignity he is placed. I request you will present my affection to worthy Dean Sherlock and to Dr. Morris also. I had a very friendly letter (and I never received any but one in that style) from my friend Mr. Thomas Lee. I intend sometime in March to pay him and Mrs. Lee a visit. They have excellent children and I love 'em all. I will put an end to my prolixity by assuring your Grace that I am and shall ever remain your most affectionate and most grateful servant.

1. St. Laurence O'Toole, following the defeat of Roderic O'Conor by Strongow in 1171, went as ambassador from Roderic to King Henry II at Windsor in 1175. In 1179 Laurence attended the Third Lateran Council in Rome and presumably interposed again for Roderic. O'Toole returned to England in 1180, where he attempted again to make peace between Roderic and the King. *A Dictionary of Irish Biography*, pp. 288–289.

2. O'Conor's unfinished history of Ireland.

3. Thomas Pownall (1722–1805), lieutenant-governor of New Jersey, *c.* 1753; governor of Massachusetts, 1757; transferred to South Carolina, 1759. *Concise DNB*, 1:1065.

4. Dr. Charles O'Conor, grandson, who had gone to study at the Irish College in Rome in 1779.

5. Charles Stuart (1720–1788), the Young Pretender; born and bred at Rome; married Louisa von Stolberg, 1772. *Concise DNB*, 1:228.
6. Thus it is pleasant to withdraw to the shadows (quiet and leisure).
7. Boethius Egan became bishop of Achonry 1785 and archbishop of Tuam 1787.

343. To Chevalier Thomas O'Gorman

BM, Add. MS 21121

[From my Hermitage, 14 March 1781]

After the re-establishment of your health you are welcome back, my dear Chevalier, to our capital city. Your return thither will hasten me in my intended journey to see you; God willing I shall join you before the end of the present month and bring you up a transcript of the first volume of *The Four Masters*. I have long since sketched out the outlines of the genealogical task you recommended to my care, yet on a revisal I have met with some defects, particularly in the pedigrees which relate to Meath, as the great families there have been stripped of power and property long before any other in the kingdom. For the other and western families I had good documents, but it required still to digest and methodize the accounts I give under certain periods, political and chronological. But these accounts are brief, as bare genealogies do not admit of much historical detail. I say no more of them till you see what I have done and have the pleasure of your farther instructions. For many years I have been collecting materials for a general history of this island down to the forfeiture of the six counties of Ulster in 1608. But these materials, deranged as they are, present a resemblance of ancient chaos; they frighten me, and I despair in my old days of reducing them to any proper form.

The boy I have instructed in Irish is far from being sufficiently instructed. He is yet but barely fit for a *facsimile*, for transcribing what is laid before him without understanding it. This he does well and no more. The parts therefore of the Annals which relate to the Hymbairce family must be selected by myself when I have an opportunity of doing it. I shall look upon it as a pleasing relaxation.

Worthy Colonel Vallancey was kind enough last week to enclose in packets his last *Collectanea* for my perusal.[1] I evidently see therein the hand of the late Dr. O'Brien,[2] who indulged too much to fancy in his researches both philological and historical. I found some capital mistakes in those *Collectanea*, as well as some good observations, but I thought it not polite to point out those mistakes to the Colonel except in one or two instances, which I trust gave him no offense.

I lie under great obligations to Colonel Burton, and I never have been treated with more satisfaction than under his roof, where I enjoyed a select society of gentlemen, all engaged to learn as much as possible of the ancient state of this country. His Frenchman, *Beranger*,[3] and his Italian, *Beccari*, have been with me here in my Hermitage, and I attended them to Roscommon, where they took plans and elevations of the abbey built by my own family and of the castle built by Ufford,[4] the Lord Deputy, to bridle that family as they richly deserved by their contumacy in keeping possession a long time of the lands they were born to.

I am hastening to see and enjoy you. Meantime I request you will present my affection to Mr. Browne and my other friends of your acquaintance.

From my Hermitage, March 14, 1781

1. On February 23 Colonel Vallancey sent O'Conor the fifth number, Vol. 2, of the *Collectanea*. Sheehan, p. 613.
2. John O'Brien (d. 1767), Catholic Bishop of Cork, Cloyne, and Ross; compiled an Irish-English dictionary, published in 1768. *Concise DNB*, 1:961.
3. Gabriel Beranger, a Huguenot antiquarian who kept a print shop in Dublin. Maxwell observes, "His main pleasure in life seems to have been in making archeological tours, on which he produces such admirable sketches and plans of ruins . . . it is said that no one could draw an old castle . . . or a Round Tower better than he." *Dublin under the Georges*, p. 217.
4. Roscommon Castle was erected in 1269 by Robert de Ufford. Charles Owen O'Conor, *O'Conors of Connaught*, p. 171.

344. To Denis O'Conor, Belanagare, Roscommon

OCD, 8.4 SE 148

Pill Lane, 6 April 1781

. . . Charles MacDermotroe[1] is still here and probably will remain here a considerable time before he can find a neutral ship bound for the Austrian Netherlands to bring him off. I yesterday received a letter from your brother requiring me to lay out four guineas for that young man's clothes. . . .

. . . I trained up a little boy, one Martin Hughes, to transcribe Irish annals for Chevalier O'Gorman on being certain that the latter would give some consideration for the task. I advanced that boy a guinea, which the Chevalier advanced me cheerfully together with two guineas in addition, which I shall remit by Paddy Hart or some other safe hand. It will be a relief to that boy's poor parents. . . .

1. The MacDermot Roes were cousins of O'Conor, from Alderford (Camagh). Carolan died at the MacDermot-roe house and is buried at Kilronan. *A Dictionary of Irish Biography*, p. 51.

345. To Denis O'Conor, Belanagare, Roscommon

OCD, 8.4 SE 148

Pill Lane, 12 May 1781

Dear Denis,

Our affair wears a good complexion, and it should be desperate [torn], degree before we should consent to come to any composition [torn]. I was before hand with all my friends here in rejecting such a pressure. Yesterday Luke Ferral and I waited on Counselor Lyster with the Bill of Exceptions lately filed against me, together with the briefs of my former several answers [answering?] the Exceptions (contained within a few lines). He declared I need be under no apprehension as to the issue. I left him those papers for his perusal at leisure and on Monday morning I shall wait on him to receive his instructions, relatively to the steps I should take at present in our affair. He returned me back the two guineas I laid before him, but I insisted on his accepting them, and I had some difficulty in prevailing, and I am well-pleased at my victory in so generous a struggle. I wish you may find it convenient to come up yourself, as it may have a good effect in blunting the keen edge of your anxiety; for undoubtedly the mind may prey on the body; in their reaction Nature holds the scales, and her purposes are defeated when the balance inclines too much on one side. I am to dine tomorrow at Lord Fingall's, and within the present hour I had a visit from Lord Killeen. [Manuscript corrupt.] [A referenc to a lawsuit of Lord Killeen's.] I am subpoenaed to that trial for proving the handwriting of the late Counselor John Plunkett.[1] Your enclosed observations on our affair, I showed to Mr. Dillon,[2] and we thought it advisable to let them lie by for a time till we have Mr. Lyster's instructions previously. . . .

1. Fingall is the earl of Fingall, and Lord Killeen is the title given to the elder son of the earl. The family name is Plunkett and they are Catholics. Obviously O'Conor must be helping the Plunketts settle the estate of the late Counselor John Plunkett. *Peerage Chart for 1821* (London: Shackel and Arrowsmith, 1821).
2. John Dillon, father-in-law of O'Conor's son Charles.

346. To Archbishop John Carpenter

OCD, 8.4 HS 141

Pill Lane, 12 May 1781

Most Rev[eren]d,

I am most sensibly pained that I cannot at present wait on your Grace and on my worthy friend Mr. Lube. Not to mention my own engagements among lawyers and attorneys, I am subpoened to appear in the King's Bench on Monday next to prove a handwriting in the cause between my Lord Fingall and his adversaries. It is to be a trial by a county of Meath jury, and I wish his Lordship (with whom I am engaged to dine tomorrow) good success. This among my misfortunes (I repeat it again) that I cannot wait on your Grace at the present time and in the place where I should be happy with you; even my health would be the better for it. Your silence relatively to your own bears a good interpretation, and the whole family here conclude with me that you are fully re-established. We are interested, the public are interested in the event. Your Grace will ever find me your very grateful, very affectionate and truly faithful servant.

P.S. I remit my warmest affections to Mr. Lube and his whole family.

347. To O'Dwyer Lyster[1]

OCD, 8.4 SE 148

[Pill Lane, 17 May 1781]

My Dear Sir,

Enclosed I send you a copy of the order you required, and tomorrow morning I shall wait on you to receive your instructions. To your labor I owe the good complexion which my cause has hitherto worn, and from your labor I expect a happy decision of it. To the learning of the advocate, you have annexed the feelings of a friend.

Pill Lane, 17 May 1781

"O'Conor vs. O'Conor

"A transcript of the copy mentioned
above—26 November 1778—
A further hearing.

"My attorney for the defense says the prayer of the bill is to be decreed to a share in the lands in question as a Gaveler and that the plaintiffs might be decreed to the whole of the lands as a Protestant-discoverer upon the Popery Acts; and there is no provision for a very numerous family but the interest of the lands: Says, the plaintiff's title, if any, he has accrued in the year 1750: Says there is no other brother desires to be decreed to any share of the lands and the defendant has pleaded the Statute of Limitations to such part of the bill as desires to be decreed under the gavelkind clause, and to the account of the defendant being in the sole and quiet possession without any demand by any person for above twenty years; and also pleads the statute against any discovery of the lease and has answered the bill in all other respects: Therefore and, as the plea is a substantial one, hopes it will be allowed; says the defendant in his answer, denies all fraud, instance the case of Coppinger and Coppinger in this kingdom, and by the statute of the Second of Queen Anne, they are not to be considered as partners or tenants in common: instances to show the entry of one partner on the rest, they not being strangers—Brooke title co-partners Philo 8—FitzHerbert's *Natura Brevium,* 197 et Salkeld, 243, 421, so that twenty-one years possession is a like possession; but the question is here what length of possession; what will bar, and the persons before the court are neither gavelers, tenants-in-common, or co-partners, and they must be gavelers of the whole or not at all; hopes, therefore, that the plea will be allowed.

"The court reserves the benefit of the plea to the hearing with liberty of exception to such parts of the answer as are not covered by the plea save only as to any account of the rents and profits to this hearing with respect to which the court will give such directions as shall be necessary."

1. This letter also supports the conclusion that Hugh filed his suit in 1777 rather than in 1756, as Charles Owen O'Conor has stated.

348. To Denis O'Conor

OCD, 8.4 SE 148

[Pill Lane, 22 May 1781]

... It was only yesterday in the hall of The Four Courts that Mr. Lyster returned back to me the above copy with the other materials I put into his hands. The Exceptions filed against me being short, requires but a short yet precise answer. "Let it be done," said he, "and as soon as it is, let it be laid before me that it may receive emendations and corrections such as I shall judge most effectual." Under this instruction I have employed Luke Ferral this morning to draw up an answer to my adversary's Exceptions, and he engages that it shall be ready for Mr. Lyster's corrections tomorrow. You will probably object to this step and say I should rather get my answer drawn up by Counselor French. But as my answer will be short and as Mr. Ferral has all the materials before him and particularly as Mr. Lyster is to amend and correct the whole, there is surely no hurt in postponing an application to Mr. French at this time. We are not pressed for an immediate answer, and now at the close of term that Mr. Lyster is returned to Clontarf he will be the more vacant for a closer attention to my affair. Mr. James Ferral is entirely indolent about my affair, and for the present I am obliged to act in my own person. . . .

349. To Chevalier Thomas O'Gorman

BM, Add. MS 21121

[From my Hermitage, 28 June 1781]

. . . Above you have the testimonies of the Bishops (of Tuam, Dublin, Elfin and Kildare) to the authenticity of O'Clery's Collections,[1] called *The Annals of The Four Masters*. I remit you also a copy of the approbation of Flan MacEgan of the County of Tipperary and of Conor Mac Bruodin[2] of Killkeedy in the County of Clare (the son of Moyleen Og Mac Bruodin). Their language though classical is plain, and Gorman,[3] after translating their testimonies in his bad English, will enable yourself to dress them up in better. I am really so employed this day in writing post letters that I cannot sit down myself to save you that trouble. I shall ever claim the strongest sense of Sir Lucius O'Brien's[4] great kindness to me. However ill-entitled I am to his partiality, yet on that very account, the obligation is the greater, and it imposes the greater degree of gratitude on me. . . .

1. Michael O'Clery's manuscript is accompanied by testimonials from the Franciscan superiors of the convent of Donegal stating who the compilers of the *Annals of the Kingdom of Ireland* were, how long they had worked, and what old books they had used. The four testimonies are all included in the beginning of vol. 1 of O'Donovan's edition of the *Annals*. See also Walsh, *Gleanings from Irish Manuscripts*, 69–85.
2. Conor Mac Bruodin: The signature of the approbation is actually in English, Conor Mac Brody, with the Irish form of the surname added after it. For the latter O'Donovan's text reads (*Annals* I.lxix) Mac Bruadan, corresponding to O'Conor's Mac Bruodin; but Walsh's, which is better, reads (*Gleanings*, p. 78) Mac Bruaideadha, corresponding directly to the English form preceding it.
3. Maurice Gorman, the scribe.

4. Sir Lucius Henry O'Brien, third baronet (d. 1795), M. P. Clare, 1768–76; Ennis, 1776–83; Tuam 1783–90; Ennis, 1790–95. Privy Councillor 1787. *Concise DNB,* 1:961.

350. To Chevalier Thomas O'Gorman

BM Add. MS 21121

From my Hermitage, 4 July 1781

Dear Sir,

I am pleased that you have received the packet I directed to you lately because it was acceptable to you. To copy a few attestations was no labor, but it proves by the estimate you put upon trifles how much you are entitled to more effective service. The letter which accompanied those attestations[1] included a mistake on my side. There is no signature of the Archbishop of Ardmagh to *The Annals of The Four Masters,* but there is one from the Archbishop of Dublin with the title *Hibernia Primas;* and, the word dwelling on my mind, I mistakenly told you that the Archbishop of Ardmagh was one of the approvers of the work. Relatively to your query, I take *Frater Rochus Kildariensis* to be *Father Roche, Bishop of Kildare*. By inspecting the *Register of the Catholic Bishops* of that diocese (to be found I suppose in Dublin) you will obtain the satisfaction you want on that head: the *sc,* about which you hesitated, is only a contraction for *silicet,* and I will observe to you that the old prelate was not accurate when he Latinized the name of *Flann MacEgan* by *Florentius Kegan;* yet I gave you the whole as I found it in my original, having, perhaps wrongfully, thought that I had no right to correct the inaccuracy. My poor labors on Irish antiquities and Irish history I have mentioned, under a doubt that my remaining days and avocations will hardly admit of my finishing the work in which I have made some progess. This is the idea I would wish to propogate as I would have the hopes of my friends to keep pace with my own fears. I am extremely thankful to Sir Lucius O'Brien for his Milesian partiality in my favor. I had so many O'Brien mothers in the course of descents (paternal and maternal) that I make myself (and that on the surest side) one of the family. O'Rourke's wife, my great grandmother, built and endowed the Abbey of Observants of Carrick-Patric near Dromahare, and I possess one of the chalices sent to her from Rome with this inscription, *Margarét inghen, Uí Bhriain,* A.D. 1508,[2] and that Margaret was the daughter of *Conchabhar na Sróna* celebrated in *The Annals of The Four Masters.*[3]

I thank you for remitting me the remarks made on MacPherson's

Ossian in the *St. James's Chronicle,* and I would be much obliged to you if you remitted me by some safe conveyance *The Enquiry into the Authenticity of the Poems Ascribed to Ossian,* together with *Remarks on Dr. Johnson's Tour into the Hebrides.* I was often amazed at the credulity of Dr. Blair and Mr. Whitaker, who took the works under the name of Ossian as compositions of a remote antiquity and for the following obvious reasons:

1. The reputed author, who lived in the third century, is said by Mr. MacPherson to be an illiterate bard who consequently could commit nothing to writing and who lived among a people represented as illiterate as himself.

2. The language of Ossian must differ greatly from the Erse used in Scotland in the twelve hundred years after his death.

3. A language learned by the ear since the time of *Kineth Mac Alpin* in the ninth century must change more or less in every age and accumulate corruptions in its progress; nothing being, among the Highlanders, committed to writing, as Dr. Johnson has discovered.

4. The dialect now used in the Highlands of Scotland can no more be deemed the language of the third century, spoken undoubtedly by Ossian, than the jargon of a modern *Grecian* can be considered as the language of *old Homer.*

5. No schools being kept in Scotland for the preservation of its ancient languages for 900 years past, the translator had surely a hard undertaking on his hands to explain compositions of the third century, unless he found them in modern Erse? and should they be found in the latter dialect, they could not be Ossian's work, but chiefly Mr. MacPherson's own.

6. The poems ascribed to *Ossian* have, according to Mr. MacPherson, been preserved by oral tradition till he has rendered them into English after a period of near 1,500 years that they lay concealed from the notice of the Scottish antiquarians, nay of Buchanan himself, born among the Highlanders, and undoubtedly as good a judge of poetical composition as any of his age.

On the whole, the works fathered upon *Ossian* are undoubtedly grounded on fables still recited among the common people in Ireland and Scotland; they refer chiefly to the exploits of *Fin macCumhal* and the heroes who acted under him in the third century. Some of those tales *Mr. MacPherson* has set off with his own embellishments and, having succeeded to his wish, it may for the future pass for what it really is, an ingenious forgery, which as it proved entertaining to many, can be injurious to none, except to those who believe it useful in their researches concerning British antiquities.[4]

You cannot but perceive that I have written the above observations in a hurry. I would wish however that had you approved of them in their loose dress, you would get them inserted in the *St. James's* or *London Chronicle* on your arrival in England. They should in any form be published anonymously.

    1. See reference under previous letter.
    2. Margaret, daughter of O'Brien. See *Annals* A.D. 1508, where her founding of the monastery is recorded.
    3. Conor of the Nose.
    4. A good summary of the Ossianic controversy may be found in Edward Snyder's *The Celtic Revival in English Literature 1760–1800* (Cambridge, Mass.: Harvard University Press, 1923; rpt., Gloucester, Mass.: Peter Smith, 1965). See especially pp. 81–82 in which O'Conor and Dr. Warner are cited as doubters of Ossian's authenticity, while Dr. Hugh Blair and John Whitaker are described as Ossian's champions.

351. To Chevalier Thomas O'Gorman

BM, Add. MS 21121

[Belanagare, 13 July 1781]

My Dear Sir,

By the account you give, in general terms, of the peaceful meeting at Bellewstown you have quieted my apprehensions and those of my family greatly. It is upon no slight grounds that Catholics in this country are fearful of evil constructions on their conduct.[1] They have joined some corps of Volunteers by invitation, and they prided in the circumstance of being trusted in active service at a time of threatened invasion. I say they joined by invitation, nor could they decline the service without disobliging their Protestant landlords. Between those who trusted and those who detested any communication with them, they had no alternative that was not attended with difficulty, and I was thinking that to remove all jealousy, they should return to their proper post. I mean to that *passive* state prescribed to them by the laws of their country; yet upon revolving the matter further in my mind, I am apt to believe that under the present uncommon circumstances, wherein the people uncalled and uncommissioned, armed themselves, government will take no alarm at the junction of Catholics; sure I am, it should take none. In any division of parties their weight would preponderate to a degree which would leave the opposite scale so light that the most desperate *partisans of resistance* would remain quiet. The Roman Catholics to a man would be true to their oaths and range themselves immediately on the King's side, their protector and the guardian of our excellent Constitution. It is perhaps from a conviction of this circumstance that *some* are so averse to their cooperation;

though the aversion of *others* arises from an opinion which accumulated lights, so to speak, are every day proving to be a mistaken one. I am so full of this subject that I am afraid I have spun it to too great length. I now go back from the modern to the ancient state of this island on the study of which I have been long employed. I was pleased to find that in all the treaties between the Irish and the Normans of the ninth century (on their settlement in Dublin, Cork, Limerick, etc.) there was no stipulation that the latter should change their religion, nor was any penalty annexed to the continuance of their heathen worship. In some time after, these Normans embraced Christianity from conviction, and the state gained good subjects, instead of hypocrites who are forced to be bad ones. I knew well that the late Dr. Sullivan[2] was unable to translate many parts, and those the best, of our ancient Annals. None but men learned in our old classic phraseology can undertake such a work, and it is a difficulty that attends the language of The Four Masters from the second to the sixteenth century. Indeed, I expect but very little from your present county of Clare translator. The topography you mention, particularly that of the second century, is one of the most curious remains of Irish antiquities. In your *Book of Balymote*[3] it has been copied from the compilations of the monks of *Glendalogh,* and it corresponds exactly with my copy from the MacFirbis collections.[4] When I am at leisure to give this topography to the public, it should, or it shall be, illustrated with a map. In the third and fourth centuries the several districts of Ireland have been mostly changed from the old to new names, and those should properly be inscribed on a new chart to come up to your idea relatively to *Triallom timcheall na Fodhla*.[5] I thank you for the information in your last letter concerning the detection of Mr. MacPherson's literary forgery. It was a pleasing imposition on the public, and the author must be rejoiced to find all the panegyrics on *Ossian* revert back to himself. Had he indeed published those poems in his own name, those exaggerated praises of the work would undoubtedly never appear; and on the whole, critical sagacity was never more egregiously duped. I am pleased to find that Dr. Campbell's history of the Tyrone war is soon to make its appearance.[6] Had his materials been proportioned to his abilities, it would be an instructive work. I request you will present my affections to Mr. Brown, Mrs. Brown, Miss Brown, and Mr. Thomas Brown.[7] I am under obligations to all for receiving me into the number of their friends. On your arrival in London I wish you may not forget remitting me the new pamphlets relating to *Ossian*.

Belanagare, July 13, 1781

1. In the summer of 1781 the Volunteers, instead of having one-day reviews, began to hold large-scale maneuvers, one of which was held at Bellewstown. Drunkenness and other disorders accompanied these maneuvers. The newspapers were full of accounts and warnings of disorderly conduct. O'Connell, pp. 92–95. See *FJ*, 15–18 September 1781, for a list of the Volunteer groups.

2. Francis Stoughton Sullivan (1719–1776), Professor of Feudal and English law at Trinity College, Dublin. *Concise DNB*, 1:1265. See O'Conor's letter to O'Gorman, 1 September 1767, where he relates Sullivan's refusal to collaborate with O'Conor on an edition of the *Annals of the Four Masters*.

3. O'Gorman had in his possession a copy of the *Book of Ballymote*, which O'Conor heavily annotated while it was in his possession for three years. An interesting account of the disappearance of this manuscript in 1720 and its later reappearance is in Fr. Charles O'Conor's "Charles O'Conor of Belanagare, an Irish Scholar's Education," *Studies*, 23 (Sept. 1934), pp. 466–468.

4. Duald MacFirbis (1585–1670), Irish historian, secretary to Sir James Ware, for whom he translated manuscripts. Gilbert, "The Streets of Dublin." *Irish Quarterly Review*, 2 (June 1852), pp. 290–291. See *Ogygia Vindicated* (1775), Preface, pp. viii–x, the genealogical collection, dated 1650, of AntDubhaltach Mac Firbhisigh, or Duald Mac Firbis, of which the long introduction (only) has been edited by T. Ó Raithbheartaigh, *Genealogical Tracts I* (1932). The "topography" of the *Book of Ballymote* must then be the extensive genealogical compilation of that manuscript, or some part of it. See note to letter 382.

5. Let us make a journey around Fódla (Ireland), a long poem by Sean Mór ÓDubhagáin (+1372), ed. O'Donovan, *Topographical Poems*, 1862; J. Carney, 1943.

6. Reverend Thomas Campbell (1733–1795), Chancellor of St. Macartin's, Clogher, was interested in Irish history. He was the author of a *Philosophical Survey of the South of Ireland*. *Concise DNB*, 1: 197; Maxwell, p. 138.

7. The Chevalier lodged with the Browns. Mr. Brown was a register of the Court of the Exchequer. Letter to Daniel O'Conor, December 1781.

352. To Chevalier Thomas O'Gorman

BM, Add. MS 21121

From my Hermitage, 25 July 1781

My dear Chevalier,

I return you a thousand thanks for your last, which I received yesterday: Among the other good information it brought me, I am gratified with the happy consequences of the Bellewstown meeting; and yet I am really concerned that a few men of rank and fortune in the county of Meath should, under their subscriptions to a public declaration, declare themselves enlightened in the present philosophical sunshine. Hamden, in the paper you sent me,[1] has chastised them soundly, and whether he has reformed them or not is indeed of little consequence; they have the majority of the nation against them, and their act, instead of doing hurt, is really useful because it spreads a knowledge which otherwise would not be so clear. I now return to our antiquities. The topography[2] you mention and particularly the earlier part so full of names and tribes now unknown will be useful.³ The other, belonging to a much later period, will have use also. At my leisure I shall sit down to both, and yet it will be a mere task which any man may execute, and which I would wish was undertaken by a person of more industry (in such a work) than myself. I say this by recollecting that drudgery I underwent in improving *Ortelius's* map, and yet what I have done is far from being complete. Nothing is more wanted than a reasonable account of our ancient manners and government and laws which these manners produced. The revolutions which made changes in each should be marked with precision, as far as it can be done, nor will any provincial rights [calculated] for a single period of time serve for anterior or subsequent periods. I am glad to find that the great change lately made in Colonel Conyngham's fortune serves only to sharpen the spur he put on for the investigation of our antiquities. But I would wish he kept *Seabright's* collections⁴ for some time in his own hands before they are laid up or rather interred in the manuscript library of our college. I am much obliged to you for the promise you make me that you will remit me from London the pamphlets on the *Ossian* controversy.

   1. O'Gorman wrote O'Conor on 19 July and enclosed an article from the *Dublin Evening Post,* 17 July, concerning the Trim Resolution.
   2. See preceding letter.
   3. O'Conor is preparing a topography of the second and eleventh centuries. Sheehan, p. 621.
   4. Colonel Burton, now Conyngham, has returned from England. Sheehan, p. 622. Sir John Seabright has decided to give his collection of Irish manuscripts to the College of Dublin. A full account of the details of the transfer of these manuscripts is found in *Burke,* 5. O'Conor had studied the manuscripts in 1769 when they were in Leland's hands. *Burke,* 5:292.

353. To Daniel O'Conor¹

HS, STO 888

[December 1781]²

... I am now beginning the fifth year of my defense against conspirators who hoped through my religion to seize on my property or to enjoy the alternative of making it of little or no value to my family in case they failed. On that principle they confine me in the courts of law from term to term and from year to year, subjecting me to an expense which would be intolerable, but that the legacy of my cousin Count O'Gara came opportunely to my relief and eased me of a great part of my burden. In the next or in Easter term I purpose (if advised by counsel) to petition our Chancellor to dismiss their suit as I have fully answered all their bills and as I think that they have no materials for any new Bill of exceptions. But the evasions and tricks of law agents in this country are almost inexhaustible, and I may probably be kept at expense and in suspense another year. . . . I say this under great limitation, as I have now completed seventy-two years of my life and that I have hardly any time to draw upon at such a period. Mr. O'Gorman I have known for seventeen years past; he has been long collecting materials for Irish history and through my means he got our best Annals transcribed. He carried them to France in five quarto volumes, yet he wants a knowledge of our maternal language to make the proper use of them; and I strangely suspect that he will find no man in France capable of explaining the phraseology of the sixth and seventh centuries. . . .

1. Wrongly ascribed to Matthew O'Conor in CfmH.
2. Although this letter is not dated, it was probably written in late December 1781 in answer to a letter from Daniel O'Conor of 6 December 1781.

354. To Dr. Charles O'Conor

RIA, Stowe MS Bi2

Belanagare, 6 February 1782

. . . If mistakes in some instances have mixed with the administration of well-intentioned pontiffs, yet the spirit of Christianity still prevailed, and its true principle which secures its perpetuity could not be affected. Protestantism varied, varying, and variable has no principle but such as it is restrained to by the civil power; and some lovers of virtue among the several sects fatigued with the different interpretations of the Divine Text, have taken their uneasy repose in Deism. This is what they call philosophy, and it is gaining ground among them every day; a consequence derived from uncertainty and which, according to Berkeley, one of the ablest Protestant bishops, will sooner or later produce a return to the religion he denominates Popery. . . . In this study you, fortunately, have the best materials collected to your hand; and I would not only recommend to your perusal *Baronius, Tillemont, Fleury, Calmet, Orsi,*[1] etc., but also the works of Protestants on the same subject and *Mosheim*[2] in particular. You will find it necessary also to compare the Greek with the Latin ecclesiastical historians from the time of Photius to the present time. . . . At this very time they are framing a bill in Parliament for the relief of the R[oman] Catholics;

what success it may have we know not. If it meet with any, you'll hear of it in the public papers.³

1. Caesar Baronius was the author of *Annals Ecclesiastici* considered by some to be the official historian of the Catholic Church. For a fuller description of the importance of Baronius see Eric Cochrane, "Caesar Baronius and the Counter-Reformation," *The Catholic Historical Review*, 66 (January 1980) 53–58, and Cyriac Pullapilly, *Caesar Baronius, Counter Reformation Historian* (South Bend, Indiana: University of Notre Dame Press, 1975); Claude Fleury, French theologian; Louis Sebastian de Tillemont, *Histoire des Empereurs . . . durant les Six Premiers Siecles de l'Eglise* (1700–1738), *BMCPBCE* 15:23; Augustin Calmet, *Dictionary of the Holy Bible* (1732), *BMCPBCE*, 4: 996; Guiseppe Orsi wrote *Della Istoria Ecclesiastica*, 21 vols., 1746–1762, *BMCPBCE*, 18: 1197.

2. Johann Lorenz von Mosheim wrote German and Latin commentaries on the Gospel of St. John (1777). *BMCPBCE*, 17:1129.

3. On 31 January, the Honorable Luke Gardiner gave notice to the Irish House that he would bring in Heads of a Bill for further relief of Catholics. The members of the Ascendency were agreed on two points: (1) complete religious toleration for Roman Catholics, and (2) full and unrestricted ownership of land. However, main arguments developed over whether Catholics could bear arms, have the vote, and intermarry with Protestants. There were letters to the editors, as well as coverage of the debates in *FJ* from 2 February to 2 March. Mr. Gardiner divided his bill into three parts since the House felt it was too complex. Two of the measures for the religious freedom and unlimited holding of land passed, but the measure for intermarriage failed. *FJ*, 2–5 February; 28 February–2 March; 9–12 March 1782; Lecky 2: 279, 313. See also Curtis and MacDowell, pp. 196–198.

355. To Denis O'Conor

OCD, 8.4 HS 039

Pill Lane, 20 August 1782

Dear Denis,

Nothing has occurred here since you left me worthy of being mentioned. My adversaries served me hitherto with no notice relatively to their commission for the examination of witnesses. Luke Ferral is returned back from the County of Roscommon to return thither in a few days. The Catholics (mixed with a few Protestants) have formed themselves into an Irish brigade, and last Sunday presented a splendid appearance in scarlet uniforms.¹ Last Friday here we had a most terrible rain which laid all the corn in the contiguous counties prostrate. I wish you may have it in your power to inform me that our province escaped the calamity. I trust that you are careful to oversee my little affairs and that you will discharge my ungrateful orphan servant if you discover that she misbehaved. I laid out a line for the cutting of a drain in Kaldrugh. I request you will view the line and give directions about it if all are undertaken. You'll also view my sheep and see if any be fit for the market here. I have some yearling bullocks which surely now are fit for sale. If you want such take them, and I shall be satisfied with the price you put upon them. All our newspapers are silent about your *Loughrea Review.*[2]

I see Martin everyday and he is well. Give my affections to Cathy, Kitty, and your whole family. I am uneasy about your brother, not knowing what he is doing and hearing nothing about him.

P.S. I send you a newspaper wherein you'll find my friend Gorges Howard ungenerously mangled.

    1. Until 1780 the Volunteers were largely Protestants. After 1780, though Catholics were "admitted more readily, . . . the force remained essentially Protestant." O'Connell, *Irish Politics and Social Conflict in the Age of the American Revolution*, p. 80. A Dublin parade of a Catholic brigade is significant of the changing times.
    2. Presumably O'Conor is referring to a review by a Volunteer group in Galway.

356. To Denis O'Conor

OCD, 8.4 SE 148

Dublin, 21 September 1782

. . . Mr. Browne[1] and I waited also several times on his and my kinsman the Count O'Rourke,[2] who yesterday paid his court to our new Viceroy[3] and was really or apparently well-received. I am of use to him in the business he came about, and I ought to be so. I have diverted him from his intended journey [to] Conaght, and this was rendering him a service. His brother Con in Russia is married to General Lacey's niece[4] by whom he got a considerable fortune and is besides a Colonel of Horse. The Count thinks much of your son Martin and would (in the Russian Service) take care to see him preferred. . . .

    1. Denis's father-in-law, Martin Brown of Cloonfad.
    2. Count John O'Rourke, born at Leitrim, served in the Royal Scotch regiment of the French army until 1758, became a major in the Czar's regiment of bodyguards, fought in the Russian forces against Prussia, returned to France where he was appointed colonel of cavalry and was created a count. He died in Russia in 1786. Richard Hayes, *Biographical Dictionary of Irishmen in France*, p. 257. Stowe MS., RIA, contains a number of letters from O'Rourke to O'Conor.
    3. George Nugent-Temple Grenville (1753–1813), later (1779) third earl Temple and (1784) first marquis of Buckingham. Viceroy 1782–83 and 1787–89. *Burke*, 10:337.
    4. Con O'Rourke married Dorothy O'Conor, daughter of Bryan O'Conor of Sligo. Hayes p. 256.

357. To Hugh McDermot,[1] Coolavin, Boyle

OCD, 8.4 SH 060

[Pill Lane, 28 September 1782]

Though I share in your anxiety, yet by no means can I bring myself to think that it is well-founded. What can your father have more at heart than the good of his family? It would surely be doing him the greatest injustice to suspect that any stipulations of paper and wax could bind him more to his children than parental affection! When I was married to your worthy grandmother, no other provision was made for her issue except only £600 for her daughter in case she left no other child. On the contingency of a more numerous family, the provision for them was left to the fees imposed upon us by Nature and to what my industry and fortune could throw in *my* way should I outlive my wife. I, therefore, take it for granted that as soon as you bring your father and uncle to confer together on the best means they can devise for the settlement of your family, nothing will be omitted that should be done in a case where the calls of natural affection are so strong, as in a great degree to supersede even those of common justice. . . .

1. O'Conor's grandson, son of Myles MacDermot of Coolavin. Dunleavy and Dunleavy, p. 36, record a letter from Myles MacDermot to Charles's son Denis in which Myles complains that Hugh "has ruined himself and his family by the imprudence of his conduct." Myles had sent money to Hugh, who he thought was studying in Edinburgh. Instead he was squandering funds in Paris and London. OCD, 8.4 SE 022.

358. To Denis O'Conor

OCD, 8.4 SE 148

Dublin, 28 September 1782

. . . This morning I breakfasted with our Cousin the Count.[1] He pressed me to urge Mr. Browne to send me an account of his mother and grandmother, etc., that his kindred to the Count should be inserted in the genealogy now to be registered in the Herald's office here and to be signed by the Lord Lieutenant. Such a registry may do good should Mr. Browne's youngest son go into the service wherein the Count's brother Con is a Colonel of Carabineers; and in my circumstance such a registry can do no hurt. I request you will not delay in writing to Mr. Browne on this subject and let me have the account by return post. I shall insert my own family and as a descendant of the

O'Rourkes in the same genealogy because it cannot in the least do us any hurt, though we should never appeal to such genealogy for our kindred. Some booksellers here have published proposals for Sheridan's *English Dictionary,* and they prevailed on me to draw up a dedication of the work to the *Volunteers of Ireland.*[2] I have yielded to their request, and enclosed I send you a copy of those proposals with the dedication annexed. . . .

<small>1. Count John O'Rourke. O'Rourke wants Browne to establish a genealogy which will show Browne's kinship with the O'Rourkes, whose genealogy O'Conor had written thirty years earlier. Con O'Rourke is at the Russian Court, so the hope is that Browne's son will get a Russian commission.

2. O'Conor signed the dedication as "the Editor." The editors have in their possession a photocopy of the dedication, "To the Lords and Gentlemen of the Volunteer Associations of Ireland," in Thomas Sheridan's *A General Dictionary of the English Language* (Dublin: Pat Wogan, 1784). The University of Illinois has a copy of this edition of the dictionary.</small>

359. To Denis O'Conor

OCD, 8.4 SE 148

Crampton Court, 9 November 1782

. . . Whether it be due to my age, to my fortitude, to the temper of the times, or to these united, I do not feel your anxiety relatively to the exertions (for I doubt not the frigidity) of our adversaries at the present hour. I have been subpoenaed to a commission for the examination of witnesses, but I had no notice of time or place for their examination. Should you think their maneuver to be but an artifice and that it was to throw dust in our eye to steal a march upon us; I am assured it will not take effect. I this day waited on our attorney, but he is not yet arrived, and he has so little to do in his profession I do not wonder at it, but I profess his clerk Walker to watch our affair, and Luke Ferral promises that he will also be attentive to the conduct of our adversaries. . . .

360. To Denis O'Conor

OCD, 8.4 SE 148

[16 November 1782]

I sit down to answer yours of the 10th instant—on the receipt of it. I instantly stepped to Mr. John Dillon's,[1] that I might prevent its being put into Mr. French's hands; but Mr. Dillon was out at the Four Courts at the time. I followed him thither; and meeting Mr. French in the hall of the Courts, he informed me of the receipt of your letter from Mr. Dillon who (he said) just parted him. I informed him that the accomodation proposed to you was far from being fairly intended and that you discovered it to be only a trick to bring you into some concession which the plaintiff might hereafter derive some advantage from. We sat down together on one of the benches in the hall; and after dismissing the subject of your letter, he told me that our adversaries could do nothing to injure our cause during this term, as they served us with no notice relative to their intended Commission . . .

1. Father-in-law of O'Conor's son Charles.

361. To Denis O'Conor

OCD, 8.4 SE 148

Dublin, 26 November 1782

. . . A tract of mine on the *Heathen History of Ireland* came out lately in one of Colonel Vallancey's *Collectanea* wherein I detected some of the mistakes of Messieurs Ledwich and Beauford, who published tracts formerly on the same subject and in the same *Collectanea*.[1] Mine has been approved by critics in this walk of literature, and yesterday the Colonel entertained Mr. Ledwich, Dr. Carpenter, several other antiquarians, and myself at dinner. Mr. Ledwich was complaisant enough to say that I was just in my remarks on his mistakes, and we parted well satisfied with one another. . . .

1. "Reflections on the History of Ireland during the times of heathenism with observations on Some Late Publications on that Subject," III *Collectanea de Rebus Hibernicis*, ed. Charles Vallancey (Dublin: n.p., 1782). Rev. Edward Ledwich (1738–1823), antiquarian. *Concise DNB*, 1: 758. William Beauford of Athy. Ledwich, Beauford, O'Halloran, and O'Conor contributed to Joseph Cooper Walker's *Historical Memoirs of the Irish Bards*, 1786.

362. To Denis O'Conor, Belanagare, Roscommon

OCD, 8.4 SE 148

30 November 1782

. . . A near friend of yours and mine was lately in conversation with a gentleman here who informed him that our adversaries would come to a settlement of all differences with us through the mediation of two judicious gentlemen. I replied that on dropping and expunging the bill against us, we long since offered to submit to the arbitration of such referees whether I have not made a provision for my youngest brother more than adequate to the circumstances of my fortune and that if such referees adjudged that I could bear more, I would abide by their adjudication. I told our friend that this offer of ours was rejected; and that I suspected that the offer now made was calculated for no good end but would have the same fate with the former offer on our side; that I judged it was a maneuver to throw us off our guard, etc. In fact they begin to feel and dread the consequences of joining issue on the commission they proposed by their late subpoenea. They will not come forward during the present term, and you need [not] be anxious at present on this unfortunate subject. . . .

363. To Denis O'Conor, Belanagare, Roscommon

OCD, 8.4 SE 148

[17 December 1782]

With the dormant state of our lawsuit during the last term you are sufficiently acquainted, and so you may make up your mind on that subject as it will keep on till the next term. . . .

364. To Denis O'Conor

OCD, 8.4 SE 148

[Pill Lane, 18 January 1783]

The central part of the letter is missing; however, O'Conor tells Denis that Hugh O'Conor, "my unhappy adversary" has tried a new means of wresting the land from his older brother. Hugh has asked both a Mr. Reilly and Mr. French of Frenchpark "to interpose" (to bring influence) for him with the Court of Chancery when he couldn't get any satisfaction from the Court of Equity. O'Conor says, "He [Hugh] hopes to derive some advantage from appealing to another tribunal. . . . Through the means of misrepresentations and calumny he may obtain from the pity of others what he could not obtain from their justice by a true statement of our case." O'Conor continues that he believes Mr. French will not take Hugh's part in a case "already lying six years before a Court of Chancery." O'Conor needs more money to pay court costs, so he asks Denis to collect the farm rents and bring them to Dublin. If the tenants do not pay, O'Conor threatens to remove them and place a new tenant on the land. He instructs Denis to negotiate with the tenant John who was injured in the "first-of-May riot." His rent was eight pounds, and O'Conor asks Denis to "stipulate for as many gads and scallops." He further asks Denis to "cast an eye over their conduct and keep them to their duty. They will be more afraid of you than of me."

365. To Count John O'Rourke

OCD, 8.4 HS 159

Pill Lane, 4 February 1783

... In the discharge of this obligation I wanted to express my concern at a paragraph in one of your newspapers (the *Evening Post* of Saturday last) wherein I apprehend that you have been ill-treated. For though the attention paid to your merit by the German Emperor is acknowledged, yet the manner of introducing it in regard to *you* was impertinent and in regard to *me*, what is inserted is false; for I am represented as one employed to collect the proofs of the hereditary right you have to distinction from your ancestors.[1] Though you undoubtedly have the justest claim to such a right, yet you would not wish to have it hawked about in a newspaper; and from the whole tenor of your conduct, I am certain that you would rather reflect luster back on your family than receive any from it....

I rejoice with you on the certainty that we have now no obstacle to the prosperity of your country from Britain, and it must be our own fault if we retain any at home. With Mr. Gardiner[2] and the other able senators with whom you are connected, you have done a great deal and indeed a great deal more than was thought practicable for our emancipation in the last session of Parliament. More than two-thirds of the people who, under severe penalties from conscience, are obligated to be obedient to our government are *so far* orthodox, and it is the interest of the government to reward not punish those who hold that principle in practice as well as belief. With difficulty you and your fellow laborers could impress this truth; and as ye have found a majority for it, it is hoped that what remains to be done will be completed in the next session. Papists, who, as I have said, are orthodox enough for the *civil duties* of life should have a participation of the inferior offices in the law and army and have votes at elections and freedom in corporations as they had in King William's reign....

1. Although Count O'Rourke led troops that stormed Berlin during the war with Russia, Frederick the Great later received O'Rourke at the Prussian Court and presented him with a diamond-studded sword. Hayes, p. 257. See also "Account of the

Genealogy of Count O'Rourke," *Hibernian Magazine* (March 1782), 144–148. O'Conor prepared this genealogy for his cousin in response to a request from O'Rourke. 14 July 1781. Stowe MS. B12, RIA.

2. Gardiner's second bill for Catholic Relief, which passed in 1782, "allowed Catholics to teach, provided they held a license from the local Protestant bishop, and then could teach only Catholic students; but no Catholic university, college, or school could receive endowments. An important family safeguard was that Catholics could . . . be guardians to Catholic children." O'Connell, p. 356.

366. To Denis O'Conor

OCD, 8.4 SE 148

15 March 1783

By the last post I remitted you two letters, lest one should miscarry. It was to inform you that our adversaries at last served your agent with notice for joining issue on a commission for hearing evidence on interrogatories. He was served on Sunday the 9th instant without naming any precise time or place for holding the commission. I really think it is the last struggle of an expiring cause. However, let me have a list of your commissions and your other instructions that nothing may be omitted on our side which ought to be done. I need say no more on this subject at present. . . .

367. To Denis O'Conor, Roscommon

OCD, 8.4 SE 148

29 April 1783

I am certain that the complaint of my detaining a lease from my adversary is only trumped up to render me odious. I found the enclosed paper this day, which will show you that lease was made to my brother Matthew and that the latter never attained or challenged possession of Knockroe, etc., from my father or me; but as soon as I discovered that bad use was intended to be made of that writing, I took measures to prevent it, and my brother Matthew, sensible of his mistake, returned me back and canceled with his own hands said lease, as you will see by the enclosed. . . .

368. To Mr. Gorges E. Howard[1]

OCD, 8.4 ES 160

Belanagare, 5 May 1783

... In 1750 I succeeded to my father's estate, a small remnant of old family possessions. As well as my real and personal fortune could bear, I provided for younger brothers and two sisters. To qualify my youngest brother to marry his present wife, I handed him over a property exceeding 800 pounds in value. But having wasted that and his wife's portion, he, by conforming to the established Church, sought to repair his broken fortune either by the Gavel Act or a Bill of Discovery. For the latter he had no discoverable matter to proceed upon, and for the former he had an unimpeached possession of twenty-seven years of my side against him. My right to the benefit of the Act of Limitation was ably argued by the Attorney General Scot[2] and Mr. Yelverton;[3] and the counsel of my adversary, foreseeing that the Chancellor would decide accordingly, have never attempted in this course of more than four years to bring the cause to be re-heard before the Chancellor but harassed me, as you will see, by law stratagems from term to term hoping to discover some new matter for obtaining their end. Their proceedings are set forth in the paper my son will lay before you, but I must add that my attorney is an indolent man and, I am afraid, not anxious to bring my affair to a speedy end. I should think that a simple question like this of the Act of Limitation should take up but little time instead of several years to decide upon it. It is, my dear sir, on this principle that I apply to you for your best instructions to the bearer of this letter. ...

1. Gorges Edmund Howard (1715–86), Dublin solicitor, poet, essayist, playwright. The Catholic Committee had subsidized the publication of one of Howard's essays. *Concise DNB*, p. 648.

2. John Scott (1739–1798), earl of Clonmell; attorney general and privy councilor 1777; dismissed from office for denying the right of England to bind Ireland by acts of parliament, 1784. *Concise DNB*, 1:1168.

3. Barry Yelverton (1736–1805), first Viscount Avonmore; attorney-general, 1782. *Concise DNB*, 1:1450. Both Scott and Yelverton had defended James Nagle in the treason trial following the Whiteboy riots in 1767. *Burke*, ed. Thomas W. Copeland, 1:276n.

369. To Denis O'Conor

OCD, 8.4 SE 148

16 May 1783

I can hardly think that a suit in equity calling on a simple question (whether we are or are not open to the penalties of a lately repealed law) can hold out a seventh year. It does not afford matter for too long a litigation, though it may for delays interposed by men who live with inequity because they are allowed to do so with impunity. . . .

370. To Chevalier Thomas O'Gorman

BM, Add. MS 21121

From my Hermitage, 31 May 1783

. . . I ventured to write two tracts on our antiquities, one published in the tenth and the other is now in manuscript with Colonel Vallancey, who promised its insertion in the twelfth number of the *Collectanea*.[1] I think that this second tract will come out in the ensuing month of June, and both were drawn from me to refute very injurious as well as false representations published in the ninth number of the same *Collectanea* by Mr. Ledwich, minister of Achabo, and Mr. Beauford, a schoolmaster in Athy. Little moved by anything I have written against these gentlemen, the latter published his "Topography of Ireland" in the eleventh number, the most flagrant imposition that I believe ever appeared in our own or in any age. This impelled me to resume the subject of our antiquities and add the topography of Ireland as divided into districts and tribes in the second century, a most curious record preserved in the Lecan and Glendalogh collections, as well as in your Book of Balimote. I have shown that Beauford, a stranger to our language, had but very slight materials from our ancient topography and distorted such as he had to a degree which has no parallel except perhaps in the dreams of a sick man in a frenzy. I shall say no more on this, my last tract, till you see it in print. I have been so battered by a fit of the gout that I now write nothing, and it is with great pain that I write these lines with a numbed hand. I fear I never will be re-established as I am now in the seventy-fourth year of my age, and should my fear be verified I will burn all that I have in manuscript on our history unless I am enabled to put the last hand to it. I approve greatly of your intention to get our *Annals of The Four Masters*,[2] etc., translated. But if not undertaken by a man who has a critical knowledge of the phraseology with the changes made therein from the sixth to the tenth century, the sense will be frequently mistaken, and a bad translation in such a case will be worse than none at all. Even a publication of the Irish text would require the collation of the several manuscripts for restoring the original reading and correcting the blunders of ignorant transcribers. . . .

    1. "Reflections on the History of Ireland . . . with Observations on Some Late Publications on that Subject" and "On the Heathen State and Ancient Topography of Ireland," *Collectanea* . . . , vols. 3 and 4.
    2. O'Gorman had a complete set of the Annals. O'Reilly, clxxxix.

371. To Archbishop John Carpenter

OCD, 8.4 HS 141

23 June 1783

Your letter of the 11th instant with one from my grandson in Rome I received here near the colliery of Munterkeney at my son Charles's house. I have made my way to our western ocean to take the benefit of the salt bath as well as of air and exercise. The gouty-matter has pervaded my right side, and I can hardly write with a numbed hand. . . . I received great satisfaction from my grandson's letter, and to your Grace I doubley owe the reception he got where he is; you'll probably hear soon from me from Balishanon or Sligo. . . .

372. To Denis O'Conor, Dublin

RIA, Stowe MS B1 1a

From the Hermitage, 8 July 1783

. . . I never received through my whole life more comfortable satisfaction than from a letter lately received from Rome by Dr. Fallon and written by Father Charles O'Kelly describing the fame obtained by your son on his examination through his course of philosophy. Our worthy bishop, enraptured with the success of his spiritual son, published everywhere the account he received and immediately sent a copy of it to your house. Here then is a counterbalance to all your adversities. You have a virtuous son in the capital of Christendom, who at the age of nineteen has done honor to his country and at that period of life has outstripped his coequals in erudition and the knowledge of languages....

373. To Chevalier Thomas O'Gorman

BM, Add. MS 21121

From my Hermitage, 9 July 1783

I am just returned from my northern rambles through the counties of Leitrim, Fermanagh, Dunegall, and Sligo. With great pleasure I took an ocular survey of places greatly celebrated in our old annals; the districts of Moyling, the western Breffny, Tuai-ratha, Dunagall, Carbry, and Conn, the countries of the Mac Dermots, O'Roarks, O'Flanegans, O'Donalls, O'Conors, and Mac Donoghs; districts now in others' possession but still almost in the state of nature through the interdicts of penal laws equally active and ruinous. Yet that nature has dispensed her gifts here with a bountiful hand. The countries of Tuai-raha and Donegal are intersected by the noble river Erne, whose winding and several cataracts exhibit the most romantic prospects; and, indeed, the whole scenery of land and water along the western ocean from Killibegs to Sligo form an admirable picture of lights and shades.... In my absence my worthy friend Colonel Vallancey sent me, by post, the twelfth number of his *Collectanea*. If it was published before the present time, you will find therein a second tract of mine on the heathen state of Ireland....

374. To Chevalier Thomas O'Gorman, Dublin

BM, Add. MS 21121

23 July 1783

I return you my warmest thanks for your most friendly letter of the 19th instant, and I confess that I have derived much satisfaction from your thinking that in my two last essays in the *Collectanea* I have thrown some light on the antiquities of this kingdom during the times of heathenism. I only wish that your judgment was no way biased by your partiality to the subject and to the writer. The able writer Mr. *Whitaker*, jealous of any attempt to demolish the foundation and superstructure of any part of his *History of Manchester*,[1] will differ from you and may probably publish his dissatisfaction; but as to the writer of *Ossian,* we have nothing to fear from him relative to leading facts, and as to those fabricated by himself they are already sufficiently detected, and it is amazing that so eminent a judge as Mr. Gibbon should be imposed upon by his declarations, for they are nothing better. I have the labors of my worthy friend Colonel Vallancey in high estimation. Three volumes of his *Collectanea*[2] are now published, and yet, to omit a better principle, so low is the curiosity of our countrymen with regard to any part of our history, saving only what relates to their own times, that these volumes have hardly any sale. . . .

1. John Whitaker wrote his *History of Manchester,* 1771–1775. Only two volumes were published. *Concise DNB,* 1:1395.
2. 1770, 1782, and 1783. *BMCPBCE,* 25:1049.

375. To Chevalier Thomas O'Gorman, Dublin

BM, Add. MS 21121

From my Hermitage, 6 August 1783

. . . Has not my worthy friend Colonel Vallancey done wonders through the collation of our own ancient language with the languages of the orientals, which formed the ground of the ancient Punic? He has demonstrated from that collation the truth of our old and perpetual tradition, that a colony from Spain had in an early age been established in Ireland and introduced the rudiments of arts, taught in Spain by the Carthaginians, to its rude Celtic inhabitants on the former getting a footing in that country. . . .

376. To Denis O'Conor

OCD, 8.4 SE 148

[30 August 1783]

. . . As to your condition in life you are better off than thousands who would [missing] themselves happy with a tenth part of the fortune you enjoy. They assuredly put a better estimate on things than you do, and should there be a decline in your affairs, it will never arrive to the low condition that they would compound for. . . .

377. To Chevalier Thomas O'Gorman, at Mr. Browne's, Kennedy's Lane, Dublin

BM, Add. MS 21121

From my Hermitage, 14 September 1783

You are welcome, my dear Chevalier, from Thomond[1] to our capital city, and I don't wonder that you have quitted your native country in disgust. Spiritless and ungrateful Thomond, which on the present prospect has thrown a damp upon it by preferring ignorance to knowledge, doubtful to real patriotism, and one we may call a stranger to an O'Brien in the representation of the County of Clare in our next parliament![2] Is this, sir, a good omen on the commencement of our first *Constitutional* parliament? I say constitutional, for I shall not pronounce it a *free* parliament till we have proofs of its senatorial virtue in its first session.[3] Let us flatter ourselves, however, that the want of spirit discovered in one of our counties will be confined to it and that to its disgrace Sir Lucius O'Brien will be returned to Parliament by wiser constituents than those who deserted him.[4] Should things fall out otherwise, men of Sir Lucius's principles must sensibly feel the want of him in their patriotic exertions. Our inland navigation, our agriculture, our woolen manufactures, our sea-coast fisheries, still infants in the cradle, will suffer without a majority in Parliament to nurse them till rendered able in a future state of maturity to provide for themselves. In or out of Parliament Sir Lucius will be an active member in the service of his country and in every department of life must be profitably so. *For his fame he is not indebted to the race of Brian Borovey, but returns back to it, the lustre he derives from it.* My dear friend, you speak too partially of my labors to throw some light on the ancient state of this island. I have indeed collected many good documents on the subject; I have endeavored to select the useful in what I have read, and if I live, shall serve myself with the same critical caution in selecting from the notes I have taken. At present I have neither health, nor spirits, nor indeed leisure for reducing the chaos before me into any order. If I am ever re-established I shall religiously follow the instructions you give me relative to our ancient families. Without attention to them, through a course of ages we should write nothing worthy of perusal. Indeed we should have no history at all without a specification of the men who adorned or disgraced it by the good or ill use they made of the power they received from their families in an hereditary succession. It pains me that at the present time your affairs did not permit my seeing you at my hermitage that we might talk over on a subject very little regarded by my countrymen. We would drown their contempt in some glasses of your own nectar. By the next safe hand I meet with, I shall send you the Conaght Annals. Your little servant will by care make a good *facsimile;* but the worst out is, I doubt that you have a man in France or Ireland who can decipher the contractions; in my province of Conaght I know of none, I am sure there is not one, myself excepted, who can read those Annals or explain many of the terms, though he could read them. In the margins of those Annals you'll find several notes of mine, and I would caution you against their being transcribed, lest they should be mistaken for any part of the original. I lately wrote to my worthy and learned friend, Colonel Vallancey. Through his great knowledge of the oriental languages and his collation of many oriental terms with those found in our own Irish language, he has confirmed the truth of our own tradition that a colony from the continent had in an early period arrived in Ireland and held the government of it for many ages. By his researches the Colonel will every day throw more and more light on this subject. On the perusal of an excellent letter written to him by Mr. Edmund Burke, I could not but acquiesce thoroughly in the judgment of the latter, that some of our best documents should be printed in two volumes, one of the original text and the other in a literal translation as exact as possible. *"Until something of the kind,"* he advances, *"is done, the ancient period of our history which precedes official records cannot be said to stand on any proper authority."*[5] This judgment is certainly just, but it is equally certain that the gentry of this kingdom will never patronize such a work, small as the expense of it would be when divided among them; *"et sic* (as Virgil said on another occasion) *juvat ire sub umbras."*[6] Your friend, Counselor Owen, was kind enough to call upon me here and rest a night with me on his way from Roscommon to Sligo. It pained me to see him going our circuit with hired horses. I request that you will present my warm affections to Mr. Brown, Mrs. Brown and his whole worthy family. I can hardly say that I am gaining any ground over my distemper.

    1. Medieval Irish name of Co. Clare. Ruth Dudley Edwards, *An Atlas of Irish History* (London: Methuen and Co., 1973), p. 84, Map 23.

    2. Sir Lucius O'Brien, M.P., Co. Clare, 1768–76; Ennis, 1776–83, who had advocated removal of trade restrictions between England and Ireland and establishment of Irish legislative independence.

    3. Parliamentary independence was conceded by the British Parliament in April–May 1782. Curtis, p. 321, describes the situation:

> Although Ireland had apparently secured a 'Free Constitution' and seemed to be a sister kingdom of England's, in fact the new order presented not only many faults

and defects but positive dangers for its own continuance. Parliament had no rival parties as in England, its corruption was far greater, and above all it had no regular and ordinary control over the Ministry. Although Bills now began and went through the two Houses as in England and were then sent direct to the King, The English Cabinet could still advise him to veto them. The Lord Lieutenant, with his secretary, usually an Englishman, stood to Ireland what the King had formerly been to England, but he again obeyed the instructions of the Home Secretary in England and he again was controlled by the Prime Minister. From the Irish Privy Council, the Lord Lieutenant selected the Ministers of State who formed the actual government. They could not be removed by a vote of the House of Commons, they did not think it necessary to resign either as a group or an individual on the defeat of a measure. . . .

4. O'Brien was elected M.P. for Tuam, 1783–90, and later Ennis, 1790–95.
5. Burke to Vallancey, 15 August 1783. *Burke* 5:108–110. In this letter Burke called O'Conor a "judicious antiquary" who had recommended twenty years before that the ancient Irish annals should be published "with literal translations into Latin or English."
6. "And it is pleasant to go thus under shadows (to withdraw or to repose)."

378. To Chevalier Thomas O'Gorman, at Mr. Browne's, Kennedy's Lane, Dublin

BM, Add. MS 21121

From my Hermitage, 8 October 1783

My Dear Sir,

I knew not of my son's servant's setting off for Dublin till some time after his return, and I confess to you I should be unwilling to entrust him with the carriage of the Conaght Annals, as he had the care of oxen for the Smithfield Market. It pains me indeed that your little servant should be at this time unemployed, and I wish you may discover some tract fit to be copied by him till you receive my book. I am assured now of a very safe conveyance by one of my own people, who he tells me will set off for Dublin in ten days. I will then remit you the work directly, and you shall have it sooner if I can find an equally safe hand. I thank my dear friend for the concern you take in my present crazy state. I trust I am hardly gaining any ground, and yet on this very day I have ventured to write a long letter to Colonel Vallancey on the subject of some late discovery he made relative to our antiquities. He is kind enough to grant a place for a third letter from me in the *Collectanea*. I am preparing one, but I dread I shall not have spirits enough to finish what I have begun.

Our next session of Parliament is likely to be a busy one.[1] I wish it may show itself to be a constitutional one, in which case it will want no spur from the National Association which is to meet at Cork-hill.[2] Very lately we became a free and independent people, and that description alone comprises the happiest revolution we had here for 700 years past. We have obtained that change without the loss of a single drop of blood. We are united in a single creed of politics. May we make a wise use of the prospect before us and of the real power we gained. I finish my prayer for the public, and I pour out my next for your happiness and that of all my friends. Mr. and Mrs. Browne are of the number, and I request you will present them with my best respects.

    1. See O'Connell, Chapter XIV, "Class Conflict and Parliamentary Reform."
    2. On 10 November the Volunteers held a national convention in Dublin to consider parliamentary reform. O'Connell, p. 375ff.

379. To Chevalier Thomas O'Gorman, at Mr. Browne's, Kennedy's Lane, Dublin

BM, Add. MS 21121

[Belanagare, 8 November 1783]

Dear Sir,

At last I found a messenger that could be trusted with conveying the Conaght Annals safe into your hands. In this province I know of none but myself who can read or explain them, and this difficulty being likely to increase every day, it will be the more necessary for your copyist to transcribe them exactly as he finds them. Let his transcript be what we call a *facsimile,* for otherwise corruptions will creep into the text and consequently your copy, far from being of use, will only have the effect of multiplying mistakes. In trust, as our originals will be soon lost, I dread that our copies, falling into unskillful hands, will have this effect. Our originals therefore, as our great countryman Mr. Burke recommends, should be printed under the eye of a learned editor with a literal translation in English or Latin.[1] If this be omitted, as I foresee it will, the treasures still preserved in our language will be as certainly lost as those that have long since perished. In the annals I send you, the marginal notes are all my own. Let them not be transcribed lest they should be considered as a part of the text. My health is still, I thank God, in a very crazy state and doubtless my dissolution is at hand. When I can command a vacant moment, I labor on a third letter to Colonel Vallancey on the former subject of the heathen state of Ireland.² It will come out in the thirteenth number of the *Collectanea* now under the press, and I am doing what I can to prevent any delay to the Colonel's work on my account.

I request that you'll present my affections to Mr. Browne and his whole family. Denis, who will pay you all his respects soon in Kennedy's Lane, will perform a like office for me.

Belanagare, November 8, 1783

1. In a letter to Vallancey, 15 August 1783, Burke made this suggestion. *Burke,* 5:108–110.
2. O'Conor's third essay appeared 10 December 1783. Sheehan, p. 614.

380. To Archbishop John Carpenter, Dublin

OCD, 8.4 HS 141

Belanagare, 17 December 1783

I congratulate with the public on your Grace's recovery from a dangerous fever. Alarming as such maladies are, yet on amendment they are attended with good consequences. The constitution is reestablished, nay it is improved after such trials, and yours under your own care must be invigorated, unless you should impair it by the labors of government, labors which certainly your wisdom must lessen; and your burden will in a great measure be lessened by having young, able, and worthy gentlemen to put their shoulders to it—a happy circumstance and I congratulate with you upon it. . . . This week I received a packet of letters from Rome, and I had one enclosed addressed to your Grace by my grandson with a postscript from Mr. Luby O'Conor for whose father's death I suffered sensible concern, for he was a worthy man, a good husband, and a good father. I must caution my grandson against his affectation of style and particularly against his freedom in describing the present administration of ecclesiastical matters in a place where he is too young to judge and where, were he even competent, he should be reserved and in many instances silent. A line on this subject from your Grace to him would undoubtedly have its proper effect, for indeed the youth is docile. I beg your Grace's pardon for what I am now going to offer—a worthy and very decent young clergyman by name *Francis Xavier Blake* requested of me to crave your Grace's protection for him in one of the chapels of Dublin and that on your granting it, he will bring you the necessary testimonials from his own metropolitan, for he belongs to the diocese of Tuam, where no provision can be made for him. . . .

381. To Dr. Charles O'Conor

HL, STO 887

From Belanagare, 27 December 1783

. . . In drawing characters, you paint well, and your colorings are strong for a writer of your time of life. I therefore request that you will cultivate this talent and draw up a commentary of what passes in Rome during your continuance in it. *Haec olim meminisse juvabit,*[1] but be careful to keep such a work to yourself and not express it to any person except one you can confide in from his judgments as well as secrecy. Such a man, if he can be found, will correct your mistakes and prevent your falling into improprieties. A more important work should engage the attention and labor of young students; I mean the history of the Church during the four ages which succeeded the time of the Apostles. . . . There [England] Protestantism fatigued by systems is taking a sort of repose in Deism, and Deists without their knowing it serve the Catholic cause by bringing division to such an extreme as must necessarily bring about a return to truths first controverted by men who styled themselves reformers, who in the second place varied from one another in their several local reformations. The Deists took advantage of their contradictions: "The builders of our political reforms," said one of the Deists, "resembled those on the plains of Sennar. Not one of the workmen understood the language of the other; dispossession and confusion was the consequence; and that consequence involved the mischief we lament and feel." The missionaries of discordant doctrines are the worst of guides. They preach discord, they promote malevolence, etc. "During the fury and contention of such men, let us," said Hume, "happily make our escape into the calm through obscure regions of philosophy." But this was surely an *unhappy* escape into confessedly an obscure recess. . . . To the credit of our own country, the *insula fidei tenacissima,*[2] as Baronius[3] calls it, we had theologians who never departed in an iota from the Catholic faith. . . .

1. Virgil, *Aeneid,* 1:203. "Someday it will be pleasant to remember these things."
2. "Island most steadfast in the faith."
3. Caesar Baronius. See letter 354.

382. To Chevalier Thomas O'Gorman

BM, Add. MS 21121

Belanagare, 2 March 1784

I thank you most warmly, my dear Chevalier, for your kind inquiry about me.[1] For several months past I have been tormented with rheumatic pains and weaknesses which succeeded to a fit of the gout. They announce that I shall never be reestablished. It is a warning and a merciful one if I make the proper use of it. In a great measure this state has put a stop to the undertaking recommended to me by yourself and others, and excepting a third letter to Colonel Vallancey, very incorrectly printed, I have been disabled from laboring at the design of giving an idea of the revolutions within our own island from the second to the seventeenth century. . . . As far as it is conducted, the attack upon Colonel Vallancey is feeble indeed.[2] In the collation of our Irish Scytho-Celtic with an oriental, the Phoenician, language still more ancient, the Colonel has produced a number of terms in ours that have been borrowed from the latter: a demonstrable proof of our own unvaried tradition that a colony from Spain, a country colonized by the Phoenicians, arrived in Ireland in an early period of time and introduced the elements of arts and literature among the indigenous inhabitants. . . . *Saeghal & slainte dhuit. Mise do charaid shiorraidhe.* . . .[3]

1. O'Gorman wrote to O'Conor on 28 February inquiring about his health. O'Gorman said that he was copying the Connaght annals as fast as he could and the boy O'Conor had trained, Michael Hughes, was copying the Munster annals. Gorman said that he expected "better deeds" from the new Viceroy, the Duke of Rutland, than Ireland had received from his predecessors. He spoke of the anarchy of the British Senate and predicted that Pitt would maintain his position. HL, Stowe Coll., O'Conor Ms.

2. Vallancey's attempt to link the Irish civilization with the Phoenician and other ancient oriental cultures was under attack. His opponents rejected his philological evidence and maintained that ancient Ireland had been populated by Viking barbarians. *Burke*, 5:108–109. See also W. D. Love, "Edmund Burke and an Irish Historiographical Controversy," *History and Theory*, 2 (1962), 180–198.

3. (Long) life and health to you. Your eternal friend.

383. To Chevalier Thomas O'Gorman

BM, Add. MS 21121

2 April 1784

My Dear Chevalier,

I delayed replying to your letter of the thirteenth of March[1] in the hope that some of my County of Mayo acquaintance might supply me with some satisfactory information relative to the O'Dowda family since the annihilation of the order of men called *Ollamhain le Senchus*[2] among our ancient chieftains. The dissolution took place at the close of Charles the First's reign when our celebrated antiquary Duald MacFirbis,[3] the hereditary *Senchaidhe*[4] of the O'Dowda race, drew up the genealogies of all our Irish families in 1650 and ended each line with the chieftain existing at that time. His book is now in the hands of the Earl of Roden,[5] and it is complete through my means, having restored to his Lordship a truncated part of the work which luckily fell into my hands forty years since; and the whole is the more authentic, as every line of it is in MacFirbis's own handwriting. For 130 years past you are sensible that we have no documents relating to our ancient gentry but such as can be picked up from tradition or family settlements, which indeed are mostly lost through the neglect of registering them in our public offices. Thus it is, and from this statement you will not wonder if I hitherto failed in obtaining any satisfactory accounts of the branches which grew on the stock preserved by MacFirbis in 1650. This, however, I well know that Dominick O'Dowda, the head of the family, lived in my own time possessed of a fragment of the ancient vast estate of the Hy-Fiacra race of Tirawly and Tir-fiacra. [Last three words are faded.] He was married to a daughter of Dillon of Belgard and Bracklin. His elder son, David O'Dowda, was married to the daughter of Mr. Brown of Kellty-Colla in the county of Mayo. How nearly the gentleman for whom you are concerned is related to this stock I know not, and it would import you to make inquiries that cannot be made by me in my present infirm state. The Reverend Mr. Edmund Fitzgerald of the chapel in Steven's Street will give you some good information and put you in the way of obtaining a more minute account. You have the merit of making a better collection for the ancient and modern history of this kingdom than any gentleman I know, and the longer you remain among us the better. The copy I had from Colonel Vallancey of the Tigernach Annals is very defective; some interpolations I have discovered, and a part has been cut away.[6] The copy in Oxford[7] must be more complete, and I take it that the whole is but a chronological index to a larger work which I dread is lost. The unfortunate War of 1641 stopped the hands of our Four Masters; the blanks they left for additional matter are numberless and can only be supplied at present by scraps from the compilations of Lecan and Baltimote, etc. My domestic avocations have cut out so much employment for me in my younger days that I have not made the progress relative to our politics and manners which a mind more at ease could make. Should I be re-established what I begin to despair of, I shall labor to lick into some form an understanding which some of my friends have been long pressing on me.

1. O'Gorman wrote to O'Conor for help in establishing a genealogy for O'Dowd, "a worthy countryman abroad," CFmH, Stowe Coll., O'Conor MS.
2. "Professors of History." The quotations around the Gaelic translation indicate a conventional but somewhat free translation.
3. Duald MacFirbis (1585–1670) was the last of the tribal historians and a consultant to Sir James Ware, the historian; MacFirbis composed a treatise on genealogy. See William M. Hennessy, ed. *Chronicum Scotorum* (1866), "Introduction," and Paul Walsh, *Irish Men of Learning* (1947), Ch. VII, "The Learned Family of MacFirbhisigh."
4. "Historian."
5. Robert Jocelyn, first earl of Roden (1731–97), Auditor General of Ireland (1750–97), *Concise DNB*, 1:692.
6. Concerning the late copies of these annals see Eugene O'Curry, *Lectures on the Manuscript Materials of Ancient Irish* (1861), pp. 62–67.
7. Bodleian Rawlinson B 488, ed. Rev. Charles O'Conor, *Rerum Hibernicarum Scriptores*, Tom. II (1825) and Whitley Stokes "The Annals of Tigernach," *Revue Celtique*, 16–18 (1895–97), Fragments II, III, IV, Continuation.

384. To Chevalier Thomas O'Gorman, at Mr. Browne's, Kennedy's Lane, Dublin

BM, Add. MS 21121

Belanagare, 14 April 1784

My Dear Sir,

I am much pleased to find that you are now in the way of obtaining as much knowledge as can well be found on the O'Dowda family in this eclipse of our Milesian affairs for more than a century past. David, whom you have seen, is head of his family, a family which gave formerly several kings to Conaght and possessed the territories of Tirawly and Tirfiacra for near a thousand years. The MacFirbises were their hereditary antiquarians, and to the latter the O'Dowdas gave the large district of *Lecan*, wherein those antiquarians completed the compilation which at present is deposited in Paris. The bearer, the

Reverend Mr. Brett, a very worthy clergyman, will take care of the Conaght Annals[1] I sent you, and I am glad to find that the copy you took has been transcribed so speedily. The copy I had from Colonel Vallancey of the Inisfallen Annals[2] is shamefully mangled and interpolated. Even on the first setting out the interpolator omits any mention of Cork *Mac Luighdheach* the first king of Munster who established the provincial seat of the kings of Munster in Cashel and was certainly one of the most celebrated princes of his time. I omit the other omissions, and I give you this information that you may consult the genuine copy in Oxford. I am glad that you are not to quit us till the end of May, and I surely would wait on you in person before that time but that I am so bound by rheumatic pains that I could not venture on holding a bridle for half a mile. Indeed fettered as I am, I fear much that I shall never be able to reduce to any decent order the work you have recommended to me. The cares of a family and the domestic anxieties prevented my exertions in the days of my health; I thank God that my judgments and the little vigor of mind that nature gave me are not yet impaired, and should I be any way re-established, I shall vacate for the task I long laid out for myself; whatever becomes of it, I shall at worst leave some monument of the obligations I am under to yourself and other friends who thought I could cast some light on a subject that still remains in much darkness. I request you will tender my service to Mr. Browne and his whole family.

P.S. I thank you for the newspaper you enclosed to me. I find that our people are in a ferment and highly displeased with their representatives in Parliament.

    1. Perhaps the original manuscript, which passed through O'Conor's hands, RIA, Stowe Coll., iii 1, ed. Martin Freeman, *Annals of Connacht* (1944).
    2. Bodleian Rawlinson B 503, ed. Sean Mac Airt, *The Annals of Inisfallen* (1951).

385. To Chevalier Thomas O'Gorman

BM, Add. MS 21121

Belanagare, 1 June 1784

My dear Chevalier,

    You have given a new edge to the strong passion I had for several years past to visit the southern and northern provinces of this kingdom.[1] Last summer I ventured on a journey into Ulster and made but a small progress through two counties only when I was obliged from the crazy state of my health to return to this place where ever since I have been going from bad to worse. Rheumatic complaints have doubled upon me, and to the pains of nature are added afflictions of the mind when I reflect how great a loser I am by my inability to attend you at this time to the Lake of Killarney and other parts of the South. Assuredly, few disappointments I ever met with, and I met with many, have affected more than the present. The opportunity is lost, and from my feeble state in this advanced time of life I foresee that it will never offer itself again.

I thank you warmly for remitting me a copy of Mr. O'Flanegan's[2] letter to Colonel Vallancey. To show that we have heathen inscriptions still preserved in Ireland would render other arguments to prove that literature was cultivated by our pagan ancestors in a great degree unnecessary. Of one funeral inscription in *ogam* characters, I found an account in your book of Balimote and communicated it to Colonel Vallancey, as you will see in the *Collectanea*. It is to be observed that the *Ogam* of the Irish had several forms, and that which Mr. O'Flanegan met with should doubtless be explained by the peculiar rules adapted to it so as that he might not mistake nor we doubt. The next visit to the Tumulus [?] by a critical inspector assisted by Mr. O'Flanegan will, I hope, throw a full light on the discovery. A stronger principle than curiosity would be hereby gratified. The authenticity of the inscription would not only increase our stock of knowledge relative to ancient times, but enhance the value by being reputable to our ancestors.

Let me observe here cursorily that an inscription which through the course of more than 1,400 years, has withstood the depredations of time must be very deeply cut in very strong lines. Small strokes certainly would not hold out two centuries, as can be proved by experience.

The periods most important in the Milesian pagan history of Ireland commence with *Conchabhar mac Nesa* and end with *Dathi*.[3] The times of *Conn Cédchathach, Art, Corbmac, Olioll Oloim, Mac Con, Fionn,* etc., are filled with memorable actions and able actors; but our authentic documents relating to those periods are too scanty, and the endeavors to supply deficiencies by works of imagination had the fate such works generally meet with, for though the credulous believe, the critics will detect and despise; of those spurious performances I have a number in my possession, and let me mention the *Cath Mhaighe Léna*.[4] This farrago has obtained credit with MacDary, O'Clery[5] and O'Flaherty,[6] relatively to Goll mac Mórna, and their credulity has imposed on your friend in his letter to Colonel Vallancey; not adverting to the moral impossibility that *Fionn Mac Cumhaill* and *Goll Mac Morna,* who lived in the time of *Cairbre Lifeachair* should be distinguished warriors in the days of the prince's great grandfather.[7] The fabricator of this account, probably the spurious *Torna Éges,* could not render it even plausible. Thus if *Fionn* and *Goll* fought in Moylena, A.D. 192, even at the youthful age of twenty-five, they must in the beginning of Carbry Liffacar's reign be 112 years old. Was Goll at that time of life fit for the command of an army? Could he, as Mr. O'Flanegan advances, lay a claim to the government of the *Fianna Erenn* after Fin Mac Cumhal's death? By the way Mr. O'Flanegan is induced to believe that *Conan mac Mórna* was the great grandson of *Goll.* All the documents I ever perused are invariable in the fact that he was *Goll*'s own brother. The *Clanna Baoisgne* had their country in Leinster, and their celebrated general had his residence in *Almhuinn* in the present county of Kildare on the borders of *Ui Fáilge.* They had no territory on the west of the Shannon, as the whole country on this side of it belonged in Fin's time to the Belgians. *Corca Bascinn* had its name from *Baisgenn,* who possessed that territory before the Christian era. I mention this fact, as Mr. O'Flanegan advances that the *Clanna Baoisccne* possessed *Corca Baisginn.* To advance this on account of some similarity in the names is giving too long and too slender a line to conjecture. I should, my dear Chevalier, say a great deal more on this subject, but that I am confident I have already tired you out.

1. O'Gorman was trying to persuade O'Conor to tour southern Ireland with him. O'Gorman to O'Conor, 15 June 1784, HL, Stowe Coll., O'Conor MS.
2. Theophilus O'Flanegan and the Mt. Callan ogham hoax has been treated most recently by Siobhán de hÓir, "The Mount Callan Ogham Stone and Its Context," *North Munster Antiquarian Journal: Irisleabhar Seandáluíochta Tuadh-Mhumhan,* XXV (1983), 43–57. See letter 387 where O'Conor shows himself already suspicious of O'Flanegan's discovery, as he had been from the first of Macpherson's Ossian, because it did not pass his historical litmus test—chronology. Nonetheless, letter 402 shows him still correct with O'Flanegan and in reference to him with O'Gorman, who first brought O'Flanegan's discovery to O'Conor's attention.
3. About from the birth of Christ to the coming of St. Patrick.
4. "The Battle of Magh Léana or Moylena," a relatively late tale concerning the struggles of Eógan Mór (representing the Southern Half of Ireland) against Conn Cétchathach (representing the Northern Half); ed. Eugene O'Curry, *Cath Mhuighe Léana* (1855), later ed. Kenneth Jackson, *Cath Maige Léna* (1934).
5. Tadhg Mac Daire and Lughaidh Ó Cléirigh, the contestants in the first debate of the *Contention of Bards,* which commences with the citation of two poems by the legendary Torna Éigeas, whom O'Conor mentions just below.
6. The author of *Ogygia;* see Eugene O'Curry, *On the Manners and Customs of the Ancient Irish* (1873), Vol. 2, pp. 63–68.
7. Conn Cétchathach.

386. To Denis O'Conor, in care of John Dillon, Francis Street, Dublin

OCD, 8.4 SE 148

8 June 1784

... I expect as little from the friendship as from the probity of our law agent,[1] who from the beginning gave daily proofs of his indifference to our interest. I know not how to account for his omission hitherto in not presenting us with his bill of costs, as men of his profession are of all others the most active in laying demands of that kind close to their employees.... By neglect of our affairs Mr. James Ferral suffered my being put under arrest by law bailiffs and retarded for several terms putting materials for my answer (to my opponent's bill) into the hands of counsel. He must surely be accountable to us for this expense because it was flagrant and bore the worst appearance relative to himself and no fair one even in regard to me. God give us a good deliverance....

... As we are subscribers to Sheridan's *Dictionary*, I would have you take up our copies from my friend Pat Wogan's, who received the first subscription money.[2] Bring me also the *Parliamentary History*[3] in the new and correct edition lately published by my friend Mr. Pat Byrne[4] of College Green, who also published some political letters said to be the work of our celebrated Burke.[5] These I would have you bring along with you or any new pamphlet now thought worthy of being preserved....

1. James Ferral.
2. O'Conor's dedication, "To the Lords and Gentlemen of the Volunteer Associations of Ireland," appeared in this dictionary.
3. *History of the Last Session of Parliament,* published in Dublin in 1784, contained the debates on the Volunteer Reform Bill which had been sent by the all-Ireland Volunteer Convention—a rival parliament. See Lecky 2:372–379.
4. A Dublin Catholic printer.
5. Perhaps *A Letter to a Peer of Ireland,* which Burke sent to Lord Kenmare, president of the Catholic Committee, on the subject of Gardiner's Catholic Relief Bill of 1782. This letter was published in 1783, *Burke,* 4:405–418.

387. To Chevalier Thomas O'Gorman

BM, Add. MS 21121

19 June 1784

... I am obliged to you for remitting me an enclosed paper from your friend O'Flanegan, who hesitates on the justness of my remarks relative to the *Fiana Erenn*[1] and the Chronology of Princes who have been celebrated in Ireland through the third and fourth centuries.[2] I advanced that *Mac Daire* and *Ó Cléirigh* were bad critics in allowing that the *Dáil Chatha,* etc., was a poem of the fifth century, and I should add a more learned man than either the Archbishop Conery,[3] who agrees with them in believing that poem to be the genuine production of *Tórna Éges.* In that piece it is advanced (for the translation at foot of this letter)

> Do rad goll cenn na gcoradh
> a cholg i gcenn Rígh Múmhan
> gur bladhadh leis cnámha a chinn
> 's gur liadh an lár dá inchinn[4]

Now, sir, could a grown man at the head of the Conaght troops in Con's reign be a candidate for the command of the whole Irish *Fían*[5] in the regin of Con's great grandson? Must not this Goll (according to O'Flaherty's anachronism) be at least at that time 116 years of age....

Again: Fin MacCumhaill, far from being contemporary with *Mogh Nuadhad* in 192, was certainly not born till thirty years, at least, after that prince's death. Were Fin born (as the romance sets forth) in the year of Mogh-nuadhat's exile, i.e., A.D. 183, how could he be the son-in-law of Cormac King of Ireland, who very hardly could have a marriageable daughter before the year 266. Would not Fin in that case be eighty-three years old when the Irish King gave him his daughter *Gráinne.* I suppose that Fin was born about the year 220, and on that supposition he was certainly somewhat older than his father-in-law, as could be easily proved. He might have given his daughter in marriage to *Córbmhac Cas* about the year 267 and hardly sooner. According to the Lecan Records and the Four Masters, Fin died a year before Carbry Liffacar fell in the Battle of *Gabhra* in 296. Fin, therefore, must be killed in the year 295, not in 283....

1. "The Warrior Bands of Ireland" such as those under the command of Fionn Mac Cumhaill.

2. O'Conor's many references to early kings of Ireland, along with their principal allies and opponents, are best understood in terms of the sources of the type with which he was familiar. The main ones, all with translations, are:

The *Réim Rígraide* or "Roll of Kings" appended to the various medieval versions of the *Lebar Gabála* or "Book of Invasions," ed. R. A. S. Macalister (1933–1956), Vol. V, pp. 152–352 (kings before the Faith, i.e., the coming of St. Patrick), 352–414 (kings after the Faith); no index.

The same, revised, provided with a chronology, and put into the form of annals, *The Annals of the Four Masters*, ed. John O'Donovan (1854) pp. 26–128 (kings before the Faith), pp. 128ff. (kings after the Faith, merged with genuine annalistic material); with indices, Vol. 7, and running annotation.

The same, revised and expanded with additional material, forming the major part of Geoffrey Keating's *Foras Feasa ar Éirinn* or "Foundation of Knowledge about Ireland" eds. David Comyn and Patrick Dinneen (1902–1914), Vol. 2, pp. 96–412 (kings before the Faith), Vol. 3, pp. 2–368 (kings after the Faith); with index, Vol. 4.

Early versions of many of the historical tales of the sort incorporated into the preceding work, translations of summaries only, in *The Cycles of the Kings* by Myles Dillon (1946).

3. Archbishop Florence Conry (O'Mulconaire) of Tuam was an Observantin Franciscan who died 18 November 1629 in Madrid, Spain. He was the founder of St. Anthony of Padua College in Louvain, Belgium, where he trained many of the Gaelic scholars who were Irish Franciscans. Archbishop Conry published in Gaelic the *Mirror of Religion*, a catechism, in Louvain. Edward O'Reilly, *Four Hundred Irish Writers*, rev. and ed. by Gearóid MacEoin (Dublin: Iberno-Celtic Society, 1820; rpt. New York: Barnes & Noble, 1970), clxxxii; Douglas Hyde, *Literary History of Ireland* (London: T. Fisher Unwin, 1899; rpt., London: Ernest Benn, Ltd., and New York: Barnes and Noble, 1967), p. 571.

4. "Goll chief of the heroes directed his sword against the king of Munster, so that the bones of his head were shattered thereby and the ground was gray with his brains," from the above named poem, *Contention* II.25, referring to the Battle of Moylena.

5. Warrior Band.

388. To Chevalier Thomas O'Gorman

BM, Add. MS 21121

Belanagare, 14 July 1784

I return you hearty thanks for the copy you sent me of my friend Dr. Campbell's[1] introductory discourse to his intended history of the revolutions in Ireland; like the authors of *The Universal History*[2] and other moderns of popular reputation, he puts a thorough slight on all transactions in this island anterior to the invasion and revolution under Henry II. Yet, after all, I think it will not be difficult to show that these writers are mistaken; and that they are I am laboring to prove, as far as the crazy state of my health will permit. Mr. Burke's idea relative to our antiquities is, I confess, just; and until we publish in literal translations our own authentic documents, the credit they merit will not be given nor allowed on our representation. Unfortunately, the taste of the public is unfavorable to such a publication, and in a few years the language of our old Annals will be as unintelligible as that of our law books. . . .

1. Thomas Campbell (1733–1795), Church of Ireland clergyman and miscellaneous writer, *Concise DNB*, 1:197. In 1787 Campbell borrowed from Burke four folio volumes of the papers of George Carew, first earl of Totnes (1555–1629). Campbell was still contemplating a history of the revolutions of Ireland. In 1792 Burke was still trying to get back these materials from Campbell. *Burke*, eds. P. J. Marshall and John A. Woods, 7:65, 104. Apparently Campbell never finished the work.

2. The authors of the *Universal History* were the famous imposter George Psalmanazar, George Sale, A. Bower, J. Campbell, and J. Sweaton. Faulkner printed the eight-volume work in February 1744. Catherine and Robert Ward, *Checklist and Census*, p. 31; *Concise DNB*, 1:1074.

389. To Chevalier Thomas O'Gorman

BM, Add. MS 21121

Belanagare, 22 July 1784

. . . I gratulate with you on the success you had with Dr. Wilson[1] and other heads of our University in approving of your idea that the documents still preserved in the ancient language of this country merit being published and translated. On this, as on every other subject, the judgment of Mr. Burke (in his letter of August last) to Colonel Vallancey is admirable: "I shall tell you," says he, "what a judicious antiquary about twenty years ago told me concerning the chronicles in verse and prose upon which the Irish histories and the discussions of antiquaries are founded: that he wondered that the learned of Ireland had never printed the originals of these pieces with literal translations in Latin or English by which they might become proper subjects of criticism and by a comparison with each other, as well as by an examination of each within itself, they might serve to show how much ought to be retained and how much rejected." He adds: "Until something of this kind is done, that ancient period of Irish history which precedes official records can not be said to stand upon any proper authority. A work of this kind, revised by the University and the Society of Antiquarians under your inspection, would do honor to the nation."[2] . . . Our translations, as Mr. Burke recommends, should be literal, and doubtless a misinterpretation of our ancient terms would not only disappoint the purpose of the undertaking but disgrace it. The compilations of Balimote, Lecan, and those of the O'Dugans contain many valuable documents and should be selected from others less authentic in these compilations. The same may be said of those procured by Mr. Burke from Sir John Seabright and now in the hands of Colonel Vallancey.[3] The Annals of Tigernach should be consulted in Oxford, for the copy I had from my worthy friend Colonel Vallancey is very defective and in some parts interpolated. The same I can say of the Annals of Inisfallen. As to the Annals of the Four Masters, they are as to the heathen part barren of facts, referring their readers to other works, not to remark on their intolerable chronology till they come to the age which immediately preceeded Christianity. Enough, however, is still left for obtaining a knowledge of the civil government, ancient manners and literature of our predecessors in this island. . . .

1. Thomas Wilson (c. 1727–99), a member of the governing board of Trinity College, Dublin. On 24 July O'Gorman wrote to O'Conor that Dr. Wilson was presenting O'Conor's letter of 22 July, presumably the letter to be "laid before the board." CFmH, Stowe Coll., O'Conor MS.
2. O'Reilly, p. iii, felt Burke's letter to General Vallancey so important that he quoted a large part of it in his *Transactions of the Iberno-Celtic Society for 1820*. An edition of the *Transactions . . .* was reprinted in 1970 and edited by Gearóid MacEoin in *A Chronological Account of Nearly Four Hundred Irish Writers*.
3. O'Reilly, pp. ii–iii. "That Gentleman [Mr. Burke] felt the matter of such vast moment to literature that he prevailed on Sir John Seabright to restore to this country many of her ancient records that had fallen into his hands and he accordingly presented to the library of Trinity College, Dublin, an invaluable treasure of Irish manuscripts. . . ."

390. To Chevalier Thomas O'Gorman

BM, Add. MS 21121

[Belanagare, 28 July 1784]

Nothing could be more gratifying to me than your information that the heads of one university have sent one of their respectable members[1] to Oxford to solicit for the temporary possession of their manuscripts relating to this country and should those manuscripts arrive, I would almost venture in the weak state I am in to fly up or rather to linger on to Dublin to take a view of them. I should be the more impelled to run the hazard as Colonel Vallancey assures me that my friend Dr. Campbell has laid himself out for demolishing all our ancient historical structures with a few well directed blows. He certainly will not find the task as easy as he imagines, or he must come to it with better attempered arms than fell into the hands of Mr. MacPherson[2] or of a much abler antiquary, Mr. Whitaker of Manchester. The more indeed the question about the origin, manners, and government of the old Milesians is agitated, the better the truth will be shifted and explored. . . . The discoveries of Ogham inscriptions on our ancient monuments (subterraneous or exposed in open air) will have their use, and if that said to be erected for *Conall Kearnach*[3] be genuine, we will be in possession of a very important point; I mean the chronology of that monument's erection. I yesterday received a large packet from Colonel Vallancey in which he enclosed me some curious drawings and inscriptions of the Cistercian Abbey of Knockmoy, endowed and built in 1190 by my ancestor. . . .

1. In his letter of 24 July O'Gorman wrote that Dr. Usher, chief lecturer at Trinity College, Dublin, had gone to Oxford to get permission for O'Gorman to use the Bodleian and to borrow Irish manuscripts which he will return with translations. CfmH, Stowe Coll., O'Conor MS.
2. The reference here is to James MacPherson.
3. Conall Cernach is an epic hero from the Saga, *Tain Bo Cuailgne*. O'Gorman wrote O'Conor of his intention of copying an Ogham inscription. However, this inscription must have been another Ogham stone than the one Theophilus O'Flanegan wrote about at Mt. Callan. See letter 385.

391. To Archbishop John Carpenter

OCD, 8.4 HS 141

From my Hermitage, 29 July 1784

Most Rev[eren]d Sir,

Parting with your Grace in a crazy state of health I had hopes of a speedy re-establishment in the country. I reckoned ill, not considering my great age. I am closed up in rheumatic chains with little prospect of being ever unbound. I receive it as a warning of my speedy dissolution, and a merciful one it is if I can make proper use of it. I had other and many pains to encounter and indeed some on your own account. You had physical and political evil to combat. Nature, I thank God, relieved you from the one, and your prudence freed you from the other. You have confined your great authority to spiritual government, as the Apostles have done, and took no other concern in Caesar's civil government than recommending it to your people to pay him his dues. May your people confine themselves to that duty and conduct themselves between contending parties so as to offend none; or if that be impossible, they should certainly stand to the consequence, nor can I bring myself to think that ultimately it will be a bad one after the present storm subsides. I recently suffered additional pain, the robbing of a worthy couple under whose roof I have been happy for several years. Were it of use to go into retrospects, I should blame my friend Tom[1] for leaving his house unguarded in one of the most dangerous cities on earth for an honest man to live in. I entertain hope that the account is not so bad as it has been represented to me in a private letter. But I shall be uneasy for a better account. I am uneasy for my dear children, as good and as promising as any I ever knew. My grandson in Rome conducts himself well. He reads incessantly and makes his studies subservient to his spiritual duty. In hope that your Grace may do it conveniently, his father remits you six guineas to remit to him, for doubtless such a succor to a youth of his temper will not be thrown away. It rather will be profitable. Another of Denis's sons[2] (who for a year past studies under Mr. Mulhall), having [the] same vocation with his Roman brother, is very urgent with his father and me to enable him to set off immediately for Rome where he may study with [more] advantage under his brother's eye than under his Dublin master. As [torn] differences of experience between Dublin and Rome can not be great, the father is willing to indulge him so that after a year's study of the *humaniora* there might be a vacancy for him in a Roman College. Of this your Grace's judgment shall be decisive to Denis, and he and I beg a thousand pardons for the trouble we give you.

As avocations and my crazy state permit, I am still laboring at the task your Grace has recommended to me under the title of *Revolutions,* etc. Dr. Campbell has taken up the same title and presented a prospectus of his intended work. I read it over. Of the ancient state of this island, he will have but very few pages to fill. He represents the people as the most uncultivated barbarians in Europe till the arrival of Henry II here in the twelfth century. He must be opposed; the more the question about the origin, the manners, the civil economy of the ancients of this century is agitated, the more the truth will appear, and the critical public will decide. I have more of my pain to communicate. I have been informed that my dear friend Dr. Sherlock has not been well for sometime past, and considering his time of life, and robust frame, I little dreaded such a change. I trust that by this time he is re-established, and I request you will present him with my affections. I remit the same to my dear friends in Pill Lane and to worthy Mrs. Troy. I crave your Grace's blessing.

1. Probably Thomas Lee, with whom Carpenter made his Dublin residence.
2. Matthew O'Conor (1773–1845). Although he began studies for the priesthood, Matthew turned to law. He wrote the *History of the Irish Catholics* and *Irish Brigades in the Service of Foreign States. The O'Conors of Connaught,* p. 320.

392. To Chevalier Thomas O'Gorman

BM, Add. MS 21121

From my Hermitage, 15 August 1784

... Mr. Burke's plan should be followed punctually. My learned friend Dr. Campbell is convinced, and he is now laboring to convince others that we have no authentic documents relative to the ancient state of Ireland, nay that those which treat of the times which precede the twelfth century contain little that is valuable. In a memoir I am now employed upon, I labor to show that he is mistaken, but *indirectly* without any application to the work he is preparing for the public. He is a worthy person, and I shall have no *direct* controversy with him. Indeed the more the matter between us is discussed the better; *ut ex conflictu et collisione rerum magis elucescat et eruatur veritas*.[1] By the way, the memoir I am writing is nearly at the extent I intend giving it, and had I the honour of the provost's permission, I would inscribe it to him. If you should think this application improper, I request you will inform me.[2] I purpose to put my memoir into the hands of Pat Byrne, a good young man in College Green who will take care to have it printed correctly; and yet I dread he will be a loser by the publication, as all our writings about Ireland, except such as are dictated by our present political frenzy, are neglected. I am in arrears to my very worthy friend Colonel Vallancey. Some articles in his last learned letter gave me great satisfaction, and God willing he shall soon have my grateful acknowledgments. . . .

1. St. Augustine. "So that from the conflict and collision of things the truth might shine forth the more and be brought to light."
2. The provost is the same John Hely-Hutchinson referred to in letter 402 as "our brother Milesian." He was born Hely (Ó hÉalaigh) and took the other surname, as commonly happened, to perpetuate the memory of a relative who made him a beneficiary. Letter 396 indicates that Hely had accepted the dedication.

393. To Chevalier Thomas O'Gorman, at Mr. Browne's, Kennedy's Lane, Dublin

BM, Add. MS 21121

1 September 1784

I warmly thank you for remitting me Astle's late publication[1] by the conveyance of Conor Flynn and assure Colonel Vallancey that it shall be thankfully returned to him but first to yourself without loss of time. I wrote lately to the Colonel, and I thank you for a copy of Sir James Foulis's[2] letter to him on the subject of our antiquities. The inclinations of those correspondents give the objects they see at a vast distance different colors. Each is satisfied with his own view and no doubt will remain so. Each will fall into mistakes, but in the mean and more important matter the Colonel will have the public on his side. I can get no satisfaction about the inscription in Donagall said to relate to the celebrated *Conall Cérnach*. None but a judicious inspector on the spot can give any satisfaction about it. . . .

1. Thomas Astle (1735–1803), antiquary and paleographer. Chief Clerk of the Record Office in the Tower of London. Editor of *The Antiquarian Repository* and contributor to *Archaeologia*. In 1784 in his *Origin and Progress of Writing*, he attacked the theory that the Irish had writing during pagan existence. *Concise DNB*, 1:36. On 19 August O'Gorman sent O'Conor a passage from his book in which Astle criticizes Keating, O'Flaherty, O'Halloran, O'Conor, and Vallancey. CFmH, Stowe Coll., O'Conor MS.

2. Sir James Foulis (1714–91), contributed to the *Transactions of the Antiquarian Society of Scotland* a dissertation on the origin of the Scots, 1781. *Concise DNB*, 1:458.

394. To Chevalier Thomas O'Gorman, at Mr. Browne's Attorney, Kennedy's Lane, Dublin

BM, Add. MS 21121

Belanagare, 16 October 1784

. . . The attention of our public is so much employed on the modern state of our island that it supersedes every thought on its ancient state. The latter subject is doubtless to us the least interesting; and yet it may afford some instructive lessons. I remain still in a feeble state and foresee I never will be re-established. I have been long working on the historical fragments that survived the Turgesian[1] devastations of the eighth century. From such scanty materials it is not easy to form an historical chain interesting to the public. . . .

1. Turgesius, the first Viking to attempt a kingdom in Ireland, drowned by Malachy, King of Meath, in 845. Curtis, p. 23.

395. To Chevalier Thomas O'Gorman, Kennedy's Lane, Dublin

BM, Add. MS 21121

From my Hermitage, 19 October 1784

... What conduct does the present state of things impose upon us?[1] Plainly this. To give no offense to either of our contending parties and acquiesce in the operation of laws which forbid our taking an active part in any matter relative to legislation. This submission to *things as they are* is our duty and out of that duty no man or party of men I [presume] will attempt to persuade us. Let those who have an eligible right to sit in Parliament labor to reform what is amiss in our civil constitution. We who are excluded from such a right should avail ourselves of the negative right left us, that of being silent and passive. It is true that no party in the nation wishes better to the prosperity of our country than the Roman Catholics, but that prosperity must come about (if it comes) through the virtue and prudence of men, *who are not* Roman Catholics. . . .

1. The Irish Parliament was granted independence from England in 1782, but it needed serious reforms. One of the most important issues was the makeup of parliament, which was unrepresentative and corrupt. Catholics, over two-thirds of the population, could not vote or hold office. Reformers were sharply divided on the question of extending the vote to Catholics. Only the most radical elements, headed by Napper Tandy, strongly supported Catholic inclusion. Many Catholic leaders, O'Conor included, strongly opposed this political radicalism. James Lydon and Margaret MacCurtain, gen. eds., *The Gill History of Ireland*. 11 Vols. (Dublin: Gill and MacMillan, 1972), vol. 9: *Ireland Before the Famine, 1798–1848*, by Gearóid Ó Tuathaigh, pp. 8–9.

396. To Chevalier Thomas O'Gorman, at Mr. Browne's, Kennedy Lane, Dublin

BM, Add. MS 21121

27 November 1784

... I must be thankful to the head of our university through his permission that I might inscribe my essay on the ancient state of this island to him. To render it the more acceptable I must transcribe it fair, make a better arrangement of my facts. Some new matter must be added and must be retrenched. This must be a distressing task to one in my valetudinary state; I am rather declining every day, for I gain no ground, and I am utterly unfit for a long journey to visit and enjoy my friends in our metropolis. When I finish the work in my hands, I shall commit it to the care of Mr. Brett, who has been so kind as to take the trouble of correcting the proof sheets as they come to him from the press. I speak conditionally, as I think that as my subject is far from being to the taste of the public no bookseller may be found hardy enough to undertake a work that, after considerable expense, would be left in his own hands....

397. To Charles Ryan

HL, STO 891

Belanagare, 22 December 1784

I longed for a letter from you, and yours of the 18th instant brought me particular gratification. The matter is important.[1] You detail it well, and it adds to my satisfaction that your reasonings and those of our friends upon it concur entirely with my own.... Even a general address after the many addresses presented for several years past appeared to myself no better than an useless act of political supererogation, in a word that nothing should be done in a matter of this consequence without taking the sense of our National Committee,[2] who live near the seat of information and are consequently in possession of the knowledge requisite to forward or postpone the act proposed....[3]

1. On 10 December Charles Ryan wrote to O'Conor that someone had proposed sending an address to the government of the viceroy, the duke of Rutland. The letter is a corrupt fragment. CFmH, Stowe Coll. O'Conor MS.

2. On 1 August 1784 the second Catholic Committee elected representatives from the major towns throughout Ireland for a term of three years, thus greatly expanding its membership. *Archivium Hibernicum,* 9:96–103.

3. In January Ryan responded to O'Conor's letter. Ryan was disturbed about "absurd Calumnies" against the Catholics, which had been propagated by "Court Followers-Men heretofore our sincerest Friends." Ryan asked O'Conor's aid in counteracting this propaganda before "the Parliament meets on the 20th." CFmH, Stowe Coll., O'Conor MS. There is no record of O'Conor's response. Lecky describes the false reports against Catholics that spread throughout Dublin in 1784. Lecky, 2:404–405.

398. To Joseph C. Walker[1]

PSPL, Gilbert MS 203

Belanagare, 23 March 1785

... I admire Mr. Flood's speech on the Question of Attachments.[2] I admire the powers of his elocution and think his argument in a constitutional light strong, but whether it applies to Mr. Reilly's case in particular, I pretend not to judge. . . . The question relating to our commercial adjustment with England is not of this nature. It will, I doubt not, be adopted in both houses of the British Parliament. It involves no ill consequences to the empire and the passions of some corporate bodies blown into a flame by Mr. Fox must speedily end like a dying taper.[3] Surely our countryman Mr. Burke must on this question desert that extraordinary demogogue.

I am very thankful to you for the copy you sent me of our friend Mr. Archdall's proposals for an *Irish Monasticon*.[4] He is equal to the work and to my knowledge has been long collecting and digesting the best materials for it. To fill the subscription, I doubt not but his friends, Lord Conyngham and his worthy brother, will be active, and I shall order Mr. White[5] to put down my name for one of his subscribers. It is to be regretted that of all subjects relating to the ancient state of this country, civil and ecclesiastic, it is the least regarded by Irish readers. Colonel Vallancey, an excellent antiquarian, has experienced this neglect; and though the slight put upon my own essays is not to be wondered at, yet as Dr. Johnson encouraged me to proceed on the subject, it would be a credit to me and it would indulge my vanity that that letter should come out in a publication of his epistolary correspondence—should any such be offered to the public. . . .

1. Joseph Cooper Walker (1761–1810) was a Dublin treasury official who wrote the *Historical Memoirs of the Irish Bards*. This book contained the first biography of Carolan, O'Conor's music teacher. *Concise DNB*, 1:1355.

2. Pursuant to a public notice in the Dublin newspapers, the high sheriff of Dublin sent notices to the sheriffs of the other counties to convene a session for the election of delegates to a parliamentary reform convention to be held in Dublin on 25 October. The Dublin committee chaired by Sir Edward Newenham passed several resolutions which the committee would present to the assembled congress. The committee asserted that "it is the inalienable right and indefeasible privilege of freeman and freeholders to assemble and deliberate on national grievances, and to adopt such constitutional measures as may remove those abuses. . . ." Furthermore, it maintained that any attempt to keep it from doing so was an attack "on the liberty of the subjects and an infringement of the *Magna Charta* and the *Bill of Rights*." The attorney general for Ireland, John Fitzgibbon (1749–1802), did not think so. He charged the delegates with contempt of the Court of Kings Bench and proceeded against the High Sheriff of County Dublin with a legal "attachment." Without jury, Fitzgibbon condemned the official and barred him. Flood and many Irish lawyers disputed the legality of Fitzgibbon's act. The congress met again in January 1785, but it accomplished little, and the reform congress died almost immediately, *DJ*, 12–14 October 1780. *Dictionary of Irish Biography*, p. 110; Lecky, 2:400–402, 440.

3. On 22 February both Charles James Fox and Lord North denounced William Pitt's bill that colonial goods might pass from Ireland to England and *vice-versa* without any increase of duty. Fox and North denounced the bill as "ruinous to English commerce." See Lecky, 2:432–450, for extensive commentary on the bill and its final defeat.

4. Mervyn Archdall (1723–91), Irish antiquary and Church of Ireland parson, who had the livings of Attanagh, the prebend of Cloneamary, 1762, and the prebend of

Mayne, 1764. Member of the Royal Irish Academy. *Concise DNB*, 1 : 28. *Monasticon Hibernicum* was published in Dublin in 1786.

5. Luke White, printer for the Royal Irish Academy.

399. To Joseph C. Walker

PSPL, Gilbert MS 203

Belanagare, 13 May 1785

I return you a thousand thanks for your last letters.—That which gave me the first notice of the establishment of an Irish Academy of *Sciences, Belle-lettres* and *Antiquities* gave me the highest pleasure.[1] I had the honor of receiving distinguished civilities under the roofs of the President and Treasurer and entertain the strongest ambition I ever had of being admitted a member of their society. It would be creditable to my family hereafter that my name was added to their learned list, and I shall request of my friend Colonel Vallancey to propose me as a member as soon as I remit him five guineas which (as the newspapers inform us) each gentleman advances on his admission.

I am so overcome with your kindness that I hardly have sufficient power to put proper estimate on it.—You think me an object of government bounty;[2] but, my dear friend, what merit have I to be entitled to any? . . .

One of your letters to me has miscarried; in one of mine I enclosed you the letter which Dr. Campbell brought me from Dr. Johnson.[3] I hope you received it, but in none of these letters I received from you is it acknowledged. . . .

1. On 18 April 1785 the original members of the Irish Academy of Sciences, Polite Literature, and Antiquities met at the home of Lord Charlemont (James Caulfield, first Earl Charlemont). A meeting followed at Colonel Conyngham's on 25 April for the submission of names of prospective members. These names were to be voted on on the 16th of May. John T. Gilbert, "The Streets of Dublin," pp. 37ff.

2. The inference here is that O'Conor would receive a government pension similar to those given to Thomas Sheridan and Dr. Johnson. When George Grenville, Marquis of Buckingham, became Lord Lieutenant for the second time, 1787–1789, he promised Colonel Vallancey that the government would give Charles O'Conor of Belanagare a pension of £100 per annum "with the possibility of continuing it subsequently in his family." Giovanni Costigan, "The Tragedy of Charles O'Conor, An Episode in Anglo-Irish Relations," *American Historical Review*, 49 (October 1943–July 1944), 35.

3. Walker received the letters and must have sent them to James Boswell for inclusion in his *Life of Johnson*. Boswell states:

"Mr. Joseph Cooper Walker of the Treasury Dublin, who obligingly communicated this to me and a former letter from Dr. Johnson to the same gentleman . . . writes to me as follows: 'Perhaps it would gratify you to have some account of Mr. O'Connor. He is an amiable, learned, venerable old gentleman, of an independent fortune who lives at

Belanagar, in the county of Roscommon; he is an admired writer and Member of the Irish Academy.' . . ." James Boswell, *Boswell's Life of Johnson* (London: Oxford University Press, 1966; Oxford Standard Authors Edition, 1969), p. 803n.

400. To Chevalier Thomas O'Gorman, No. 11 Castle Street, Dublin

BM, Add. MS 21121

Belanagare, 30 June 1785

My dear Chevalier,

In the middle of this month I made an excursion to my son's house[1] near Lough Allen on the confines of four counties (Roscommon, Sligo, Leitrim, and Cavan) with the hope of gaining some relief from a change of air and exercise; I thank God that I have obtained some, and at my time the smallest is an acquisition. The variety of views and prospects diverted me. The lake I mentioned, twenty miles in compass, is formed by a number of rivulets from the neighboring high mountains and drunk, as it were, with the excess it disgorges the Shannon out of its side mouth in a greater quantity of water than the Liffy discharges at Island Bridge. The mountains I mentioned offer a treasure to this nation yet almost untouched, coal and iron mines inexhaustible and the finest river surrounded with the finest lands in the three kingdoms for conveying the contents (by an improvement of our island navigation) to most parts of our island; but from causes too well known, our *natural advantages* have been hitherto neglected. Those causes now considerably removed, it is to be hoped that their effects will cease, and in this view no institution could be happier or more timely than that of our Academy of Arts, etc., lately planned by the first names of this nation when we consider their ability and patriotism. On this subject I presumed to write a letter to Colonel Vallancey, for undoubtedly the academists cannot begin better than by a display of our natural advantages. Of all other subjects it is at present the most important. The materials lie before us, and to obtain inerrable knowledge and durable profit from them, we have no more to do but to send skillful inspectors to consult and able artists to work on them. A memoir should immediately be prepared to show the inexhaustible benefits of the fishery begun on the coast of Dunagall and begun at the expense of Colonel Burton Conyngham, the greatest friend that Ireland has met with through the lapse of six centuries, for he has gone more than halves with the nation in that great undertaking! It gives me sensible pleasure that you are become an honorary member of our Irish Academy and that you made its members a present of the Collections of Balimote patronized by Mac Donogh of Coran in 1390. We want a skillful hand to copy the Annals of Tigernach and Inisfallen, etc., in the Bodleian Library. The copies I had from Colonel Vallancey are much corrupted, injured by interpolations from apocryphal hands and indeed very unskillful hands, particularly in the Annals of Inisfallen, where Cormac King of Ireland and Angus mac *Nad Fraoich* King of Munster are made contemporaries. The Annalists of that island (on Loughlein) could not be guilty of such a mistake, much less of some phrases which are defective in grammar, such as *Marbhúghadh* instead of *marghadh,* etc. The copy you go by, as taken from that of Oxford must be more correct and free from solecisms. Indeed too accurate care cannot be taken in restoring the genuine text of our ancient annals and rescuing them, so to speak, from the blunders of transcribers. An unskillful selection and bad translation would disgrace us on our first setting out and have only the effect of giving cause of ridicule as well as of triumph to our Irish and Scotish adversaries. I thank you warmly, my dear Chevalier, for the advice you give me. I do what I can to prevent my mind from preying on the crazy matter which envelopes it. Of my *Prospectus* on the origin, manners, and politics of the heathen inhabitants of this island, I have finished the first draft; in the second, it will want additions, castrations, and corrections, which I have not been for some time healthy enough to undertake but yet purpose to set about the task speedily in these long days and good weather. You see by my handwriting that writing must be painful to me. I should otherwise answer your letter immediately after my return to this place.

1. Charles of Mt. Allen.

401. To Joseph C. Walker, Treasury Chambers, Dublin

PSPL, Gilbert MS 203

Belanagare, 14 October 1785

I would enjoy you as my friend and as a man of letters, addressing yourself to my ears differently from the other companions about me who speak only to my eyes. Your observation is just that almost universally the blessings of nature in this country are thrown away on its inhabitants. We seem however of late to be roused from our lethargy. No man is now forbidden the benefits of our civil constitution; and united in one creed of politics, every member of society is sufficiently orthodox for the affairs of this world. Some men there are (I wish they may not be men in power) who heartily dislike this union; and to place us in our former discordant state, they can not succeed more effectually than by re-establishing the Penal Laws, which kept two-thirds of our people in a state of thralldom without the presence of any civil crime to justify civil punishment! I request you will present my respects, I should say my warm affection, to the lady[1] who paraphrased Carolan's "Monody" on his beloved Mary. She has improved on her original greatly; she caught and she adorned the poor blind man's feelings; and indeed she impressed myself with feelings which I had not before on the subject. Again I repeat the request that you will present her with my affection, nay with my commands that she will not omit cultivating the talent that nature endowed her with most bountifully. You inquire about Grace Nugent, a worthy lady the sister of the late worthy John Nugent of Ca[stle] Nugent Culambre.[2] She lived in our own neighborhood with her sister Mrs. Conmee when Carolan addressed her with the ode and piece of music you mention. I often listened to Carolan singing his ode on Miss Cruise in raptures. I thought the stanzas wildly enthusiastic and neglected preserving them."[3] . . .

1. Charlotte Brooke, Henry Brooke's daughter.
2. Walker is trying to get biographical data on Carolan from O'Conor. Carolan was born in 1670 in the village of Nobber in Westmeath on lands owned by the Nugents, the earls of Westmeath. Edmund Burke married a Nugent.
3. In Walker's biography of Carolan he quotes this passage. *Historical Memoirs of the Irish Bards*, p. 69.

402. To Chevalier Thomas O'Gorman, at Mr. Browne's, Kennedy's Lane, Dublin

BM, Add. MS 21121

From my Hermitage, 22 October 1785

Every line in your last letter to me brought the strongest proofs of your interesting yourself in whatever regards me and mine. I return you my hearty thanks. Last post I had a very friendly letter from Mr. O'Flanegan of Trinity College, and this day I expressed my gratitude in a long letter, though writing is painful to me from my rheumatic disorder which still oppresses me and gives me a warning which I should labor to turn to the best account. He was kind enough to send me a fair and elegant copy of the ogham inscription he found in the County of Clare. If he has deciphered it by a rule which must prove satisfactory to critics in that art, the discovery is a happy one, as it will come attended with a *Demonstration* that we had a cultivated literature in Ireland several ages before the introduction of Greek and Roman learning along with the Gospel.[1] I am gratified with the information you give me of your obtaining an unadulterated copy of the Inisfallen Annals, though for our setting out as academicians, I should wish that we began with Tigernach, the most learned annalist of the eleventh century and one who commences his accounts with a celebrated epoch, the building of Eamania six generations before the Christian era. It is hoped that the copy of these annals in the Bodleian Library is a genuine one, for that put into my hands by Colonel Vallancey is greatly corrupted in several places. The Annals of Inisfallen begin only seventy years antecedent to the introduction of Christianity into our island. . . .

1. Subsequent research has shown that genealogies appeared on ogham script. Written literature developed under Christian auspices. MacNeil, pp. 9, 45.

403. To Joseph C. Walker, Treasury Chambers, Dublin

PSPL, Gilbert MS 203

Belanagare, 20 November 1785

I return you a thousand thanks for Mr. Burke's speech on the affairs of the East India Company.[1] His eloquence charms, but it distresses at the same time. In his historical details we find a large kingdom turned into graves for human carcasses, desolation and silence through an extent of 300 miles; the mercy, so to speak, of killing men, women, and children all at once suspended for the unexampled cruelty of seeing them perish slowly by hunger! Good God! Can such wickedness be compatible with human, with British, feelings! A tear is filling my eye for the fate of the victims who were a majority and who certainly were innocent. God permitted the evil, and in *His own time* will dispense the punishment! . . .

I was gratified by a letter from your fair friend,[2] enclosed in one of yours of the last week. She is a poetess by hereditary right, and the daughter of my late worthy friend, the author of *Gustavus Vasa*. With the feelings of a man reminded of his speedy dissolution, I derive satisfaction from calling to mind the several happy evenings I spent in the company of Mr. Brooke and other gentlemen of virtue as well as learning, who admitted me into their society. Miss Charlotte Brooke, who gratefully acknowledges her obligations to the Walker family, is now, I apprehend, in the country. Give her my cordial respects. Her ode on *Carolan's Stafford* is elegant, but too paraphrastical. I would therefore wish that *Stafford* came out in your own version. . . .

    1. Burke's *Speech on Fox's India Bill,* delivered 1 December 1783 and published 22 January 1784, described oppressions committed by Wazir's revenue collectors. A violent controversy followed this speech. The brother of Colonel Alexander Hannay (c. 1742–82), Sir Samuel, took the publication as a personal insult. *Burke,* 5:129–130.
    2. Charlotte Brooke (c. 1740–93), who was translating Carolan's poems, published in 1789, *Reliques of Irish Poetry.* An unwise investment in 1783 reduced her to poverty, which she alleviated by her writing. *A Dictionary of Irish Biography,* pp. 37–38.

404. To James Clinch, 155 James Street, Dublin

OCD, 8.4 SP 145

                                      Belanagare, 14 December 1785

. . . We purpose to send off my grandson Matthew immediately for Rome.[1] If he be not in Dublin before you depart for Italy, he must wait for another opportunity and in the meantime attend Mr. Mulhall's school to be there instructed till that opportunity presents itself.

    May God bless and prosper you. Tell my grandson Charles (his true Christian name is Cathaldus) that I am highly pleased with some of his late letters and that he is making a progress in Hebrew and Greek literature. I say *highly pleased* because he makes all his studies subservient to his Christian duties and to his Christian vocation. To be learned to any other end would be a misfortune not an advantage. When we were children, our uncle O'Ruark, Bishop of Killala, gave us a preparatory prayer to our studies and pressed the following truth upon us—
    Sola salus servire Deo: sunt cetera fraudes.[2] . . .

    1. O'Conor's grandson Matthew never became a priest. He became a lawyer and historian.
    2. "The only safety is in service to God; all else is deception."

405. To Joseph C. Walker, Treasury Chambers, Dublin

PSPL, Gilbert MS 203

Belanagare, 10 January 1786

... Is Colonel Vallancey yet arrived from London? He is preparing or has prepared a learned memoir on the origin and cultivation of literature in this island before its inhabitants had any knowledge of Greek and Roman literature.[1] I am, as you know, preparing a memoir on the same subject; yet through the crazy state of my health and other avocations, I encounter frequent interruptions. I think that I will be able to put the last hand to it before the middle of March.[2] ...

... These terms *supremacy* and *subordination* will not please restless men who would wish for confusion as the only means to emerge from their present condition. But under good political regulations the discontents of such men will not be rewarded.[3] ...

Boswell entertained me highly, and I shall with pleasure purchase the improved duplicate of it.[4] Dr. Johnson, having a laudable passion for the discovery of every useful matter hitherto hid in the old language of Britain and Ireland, readily encouraged every attempt to throw light upon any such matter. He even condescended to encourage me in that study. On this principle I would be thankful to you if you prevailed on Mr. Boswell in his intended life of that great man to give a place to the two letters he wrote to me. It would be very gratifying to my family and indeed give myself more consideration hereafter than the possession of the power and property of my ancestors for some ages past. ...

    1. Perhaps O'Conor is referring to Vallancey's *A Vindication of the Ancient History of Ireland.* ... (Dublin: Luke White, 1786). *BMCPBCE*, 25:1049. Luke White became the printer for the Royal Irish Academy. See J. C. Walker to O'Conor, undated letter, CFmH, Stowe Coll., O'Conor MS.

    2. "Third Letter on the Pagan State of Ireland," *Collectanea* ... , 1786. *BMCPBCE*, 18:976.

    3. O'Conor is hoping that the revised Propositions to liberalize Irish trade, which were brought before the Irish parliament in August 1785 but were withdrawn on 15 August when it seemed unlikely that they would be accepted, would be reintroduced in the next session. See Edith Mary Johnston, *Ireland in the Eighteenth Century, The Gill History of Ireland*, vol. 8, p. 157–8.

    4. *The Journal of a Tour to the Hebrides with Samuel Johnson.*

406. To Chevalier Thomas O'Gorman

BM, Add. MS 21121

Belanagare, 21 January 1785–6

... In the succession of our Irish monarchs I formerly credited the lists (mostly indeed a catalog of proper names) given by Gilla Coeman and Flan, Lecturer of the Monastery of Bute.[1] In following such guides I should give our Milesian monarchy an earlier commencement by many hundred years than can be supported, or indeed admitted, by any credulity except Irish credulity. I found better guides in Tigernach and an anonymous antiquary quoted in the collections of Balimote, fol. 5.[2] They allow of an history of Ireland that can be depended on for any accuracy in date or facts till the commencement of the Eamanian era, six generations before the birth of our Saviour. Before that era Gilla Coeman and his followers give us a catalog of fifty-seven monarchs,[3] most of whom, they say, fell by the hands of their successors, but of whom no other act is recorded through the whole course of their reigns. This surely is not information, and had the writers invented history as they did proper names and years for reigns of kings, they would gain no credit in times of even less critical knowledge than the present. In following Tigernach and the Balimote antiquary,[4] I have the firmest support in Sir Isaac Newton and M. Goguet, the two most celebrated antiquarians of the present or any age.

P.S. . . . The recovery of King Cormac's Psalter of Cashel is a happy circumstance if the fact be certain.[5] If the quotations from it in the compilations of *Lecan* and *Balimote* be found in the book now discovered, it will be a good proof of its genuineness undoubtedly. Of that work (written mostly in verse) I apprehend that the King wrote no more than the Latin preface. Of the other parts it appears that he was only the patron. . . .

    1. For a discussion of the lists of Irish kings found in the writings of Gilla Coeman (d. 1072), Flann Mainistrech (d. 1056), and others see Eoin MacNeill, Chapter 3, "The Irish Synthetic Historians," and Chapter 4, "The Ancient Genealogies," in *Celtic Ireland* (Dublin: Martin Lester, Ltd.; London: Leonard Parson, Ltd., 1921), pp. 25–63.
    2. A reference to the synchronistic tract "A," ed. B. MacCarthy, *The Codex Palatino-Vaticanus No. 830* (1892), pp. 279–287.
    3. According to Gilla Coeman's poem *Ériu ard inis na ríg* "Noble Ireland island of the kings," ed. MacCarthy, *op. cit.*, pp. 142–213, there were in fact fifty-seven Milesian kings or rather kingships, prior to the founding of Emain Macha at the time of Cimbaeth.
    4. O'Conor surely has in mind the famous dictum *Omnia monumenta Scotorum usque Cimbaeth incerta erant* "Annals of Tigernach," *Revue Celtique*, 16:394; translated into

Irish in "A" *op. cit.* p. 281, "The Historical monuments of the Scots (i.e., the Irish) up to Cimbaeth were uncertain"; see further letter 410.

5. Unfortunately the original Psalter of Cashel manuscript no longer exists. Extracts from it do, however, appear in the major surviving genealogical compilations, including those of Lecan and Ballymote; ed. M. S. O'Brien, *Corpus Genealogiarum Hiberniae* (1962; 1976), pp. 192ff, and above all in Bodleian Laud 610, for which see Myles Dillon "Laud Misc 610," *Celtica*, 5 (1960), pp. 64–76.

407. To Joseph C. Walker

PSPL, Gilbert MS 203

From my Hermitage, 31 January 1786

From my bookseller Pat Wogan I yesterday received a letter informing me that you left in his hands for my use the London edition of Dr. Johnson's *Meditations*. You load me with benefactions. I make you returns in gratitude which, however sincere, I am far from thinking sufficient. I want the power of making better payments, and yet I am contracting new debts with you. In my last I informed you that I purpose making use of your friendship in handing over to Dr. Barnard[1] a *memoir* of mine on the state of Ireland before the establishment of Christianity here in the fifth century. I endeavor to show that we had a system of local civilization and local literature in this country for four centuries, at least, before the introduction of foreign literature along with the gospel. . . .

What I have collected on the subject should be previously laid before our learned Committee of Antiquities. They will see if the proofs I bring from domestic documents be well-founded. Should they find them defective, I would by no means intrude them on the time or patience of our academicians in their full meeting.—At this close of the eighteenth century when so much has profitably transpired from foreign academies, nothing discreditable to ours should appear. The natural history of our island (a subject almost untouched) is of all others the most important to us. Exploring its latent treasures under and over ground would excite a spirit of improvement through the whole kingdom. . . .

1. Dr. Thomas Barnard (1728–1806); Dean of Derry, 1769; afterwards the Bishop of Killaloe and Kilfenora, 1780. A member of Dr. Johnson's Literary Club. *Concise DNB*, 1:63.

408. To Joseph C. Walker

PSPL, Gilbert MS 203

Belanagare, 16 February 1786

... Let me here trouble you with a few facts as they may enable you to undeceive gentlemen of your acquaintance who may be prejudiced against us through representations lately made in the House of Commons of this kingdom from very bad information.[1] Our title to the estate of Ballintober is as well-founded as any other can be; that we were indolent and inactive in asserting it, I confess. In the year 1662 Hugh O'Conor Don of Ballintober made a last will and settlement devising his estate of Ballintober to his son Hugh: in failure of issue male on him to Charles his brother; in failure of said Charles to his cousin german, Daniel O'Conor of Clonalis; and in failure of issue male in the latter to his other cousin german, Charles O'Conor of Belanagare's elder son (of whom I am the representative.) Charles O'Conor Don, the brother of the aforesaid testator, was a simple man of a very weak capacity; and, notwithstanding the will and settlement which barred alienation of the family estate, he was prevailed on to will it to a kinsman of his of the name of Burke, nearly related to the Marquis of Clanrickard, formerly Lord Deputy of Ireland. Burke took immediate possession; Andrew O'Conor Don of Clonalis made an immediate claim to his just inheritance; on his death Daniel O'Conor Don, his eldest son, made a like claim; both kept the claim alive from time to time; and both from indolence and a constitutional inactivity fatal to their family made no further progress in the prosecution of their right.—Thus it was. The wound given by the aforesaid alienation rankled still. In the month of January last, Alexander O'Conor, brother to the present Dominic O'Conor Don applied to the persons residing on the lands of Ballintober to attorn to the legitimate heir, armed only with the aforesaid will and settlement; he used no other arms. And without menace or intimidation the persons gave up the possession to him. Whether he was right or wrong as to the part he acted, our common law will decide. ... The insinuations thrown out that the Roman Catholics of this country have countenanced an insurrection where there was none alarmed them to a degree which summoned up their grief and feelings. They think themselves under a necessity of testifying their loyalty in an address they are now framing. Like their brethren in the other counties of the kingdom, they look up to their sovereign and their Protestant fellow-subjects as legislative capacity. A different conduct they abhor as forbidden by the religion they profess and the interest they now have in our public prosperity under the best civil constitution. . . .

    1. O'Conor's cousin Alexander of the Clonalis branch of the family was attempting to regain Ballintober Castle, which the family had lost. See OCD, 8.4 HS 107 and 9.1 ES 393.

409. To Chevalier Thomas O'Gorman, Dublin

BM, Add. MS 21121

25 February 1786

. . . In several days past I could attend no business but the labor of removing the injury done us by a rash and wrongheaded kinsman,[1] who without taking advice of counsel or imparting any of his intentions to any of our family, prevailed on a herd to give him possession of the land of Ballintobber. Of this procedure a most exaggerated account was given in your capital, and a military corps was sent down to quell an insurrection where no insurrection exists. The Roman Catholics of the county took an alarm, a charge being made to them as favoring the lawless conduct of the silly man who alone was guilty. On Wednesday last, the principal Roman Catholics of the county assembled in the Sessions House of Roscommon where we put our several signatures to an address to the Lord Lieutenant expressive of our loyalty to his present Majesty and obedience to the laws. We immediately after drew up resolutions declaring our abhorrence of any attempts to disturb his Majesty's peace on any pretext whatever, etc. These resolves expressed in the strongest terms you will soon see in print. . . .

    1. Alexander O'Conor.

410. To Chevalier Thomas O'Gorman

BM, Add. MS 21121

7 March 1786

. . . The anxiety we suffered lately in this county through the rashness and folly of a kinsman of ours is now, I thank God, at an end. At a meeting of magistrates and some principal Protestants yesterday at Roscommon, resolutions have been entered into conformable to our own of the 22nd of February. O'Conor Don[1] and our family of Belanagare have been justly considered as entirely innocent of an act, of which certainly we knew nothing till the whole country had notice of it, and our subscriptions to an abhorrence of such an act has quieted or subdued all apprehensions on this silly conduct of a wrongheaded man. I confess to you that I derive great satisfaction from the conduct of the Roman Catholics of this county as they have been before hand with the gentlemen who assembled yesterday. They followed our example; we were not obliged to follow theirs. What they may do relative to the *culpable* man I know not, but as a weak man left alone and abandoned by every party I could wish that any further consideration about him was dropped. You'll, I trust, excuse so much on a subject which of late gave me great anxiety and which still hurts me through the memory of it. . . .

I should be very glad to contribute to the biographical work now under the press in Vienna, but as the work is in so forward a state, I am not prepared for furnishing (for it will take time to digest) the materials I possess in the dress I would wish. The late Count O'Gara and Colonel Daniel O'Conor,[2] governor of Ostend, should not be passed over slightly. I had the honor of a near kindred to both and I owed a particular obligation to the memory of the O'Gara, who left me in his last will and testament a legacy of ten thousand livres; to the worthy O'Conor I owed obligations also. I am now employed in finishing the prospectus of the heathen state of this country. I should not postpone it longer, though my health is in a very languid state. Denis, who gave you a favorable account of it, judged only by appearances, for I ski out every day and decline useless complaints.

Through your good offices with General D'Alton[3] for giving his protection to my grandson,[4] I am highly thankful to you. In my next I shall beg leave to write soon to you on this subject as this page is already full.

1. Dominick O'Conor Don of Clonalis. There is some discrepancy in the date of Dominick's death. Charles Owen O'Conor gives the date at 1785, but a letter in the Stowe Collection, O'Conor papers, at the Huntington Library includes a letter from Dominick O'Conor to Charles O'Conor dated 28 January 1788. *O'Conors of Connaught*, Table III; CFmH, Stowe Collection, STO 873.
2. O'Conor's brother Daniel.
3. Lieutenant General Edward Count Dalton (1737–1793) was colonel-commandant of the Fifteenth German Infantry Regiment of the Imperial Army. Dalton was related to Edmund Burke's wife, Jane Nugent Burke. For a situation similar to that of Roderick O'Conor's, see *Burke*, 7:379–382.
4. Roderick or Rory was Denis's fifth son.

411. To Joseph C. Walker

PSPL, Gilbert MS 203

Belanagare, 8 March 1786

My dear Friend,

In my last I have written to you in an anxious and querulous temper. I thank God that I can now write in a different state of mind. The conduct of a rash and silly man of our family grieved us; and the evil was complete before it came to our knowledge. It has been insinuated, however, to say no worse, that it had our approbation by a criminal and silent acquiescence; nay, this idea has been extended to a whole body of people. The principal Roman Catholics of the county, grieved and alarmed, met by appointment at Roscommon on the 22nd of February last. We there drew up an Address to the Lord Lieutenant expressive of our loyalty to our king and used as strong terms as [we] could offer in the declaration of a duty imposed upon us by gratitude as well as religion, the strongest sanctions that can bind honest men. We also drew up a number of resolves declaring our abhorrence of riots and tumults or the revival of any claims to lands or property not supportable by the laws of our country. It pleases us excessively that our conduct on this occasion had a good effect.

On Monday last there was a second meeting at Roscommon composed of magistrates and some principal Protestants. O'Conor of Clonalis[1] with several other R[oman] Catholics appeared there also. O'Conor in the most solemn manner expressed his concern at the wild and extravagant conduct of his brother[2] and hoped that in future he would have it in his power to prevent any of his illegal proceedings; and he pledged himself to his country that should his brother make a second attempt, he would himself appear foremost in having him apprehended and delivered up to the punishment of the laws; that the [deed] committed was without any knowledge of his till the neighborhood had it; that he had at all times approved himself a member of society peaceful by temper and in the good graces of all who knew him; and he hoped that in his old days he would be believed; and he concluded that he would die with an uniformity of character as a good subject and an honest man. His declarations were well received.

In this assembly resolutions were drawn up, testifying their abhorrence of tumults, illegal claims, etc. I thank God that we were beforehand with them, as it was incumbent on us to be.—What they will do with the unhappy criminal fool I know not. I wish that folly may plead for him, as indeed he is too insignificant for the severity of power. I remember a madman, one Daniel Ryan, who fancying himself a king, rushed into the Four Courts and sat in the Lord Chancellor's throne as his proper place. The fellow, on being apprehended and roughly handled, was dragged along to be punished according to law. The chancellor at the time entered the hall and was informed of the delinquency. He laughed and ordered that the poor fellow should be set at liberty.

When will our reverend friend Mr. Archdall's book[3] come out? Will it have the start of yours? I request you will present him with my respects. I should by this post write to my learned friend, Colonel Vallancey, but have been informed yesterday that he is not yet arrived. He stands well in the good graces of the King, and I hope that the young officer his son will be provided for at this time.

   1. Dominick O'Conor Don.   2. Alexander O'Conor.
   3. *The Irish Monasticon.*

412. To Chevalier Thomas O'Gorman

BM, Add. MS 21121

30 March 1786

. . . I have almost finished my *Prospectus* of the civil government and manners of the ancients of this island. It shall be laid before our *Committee of Antiquities,* and with them it shall stop if found defective of the instruction we want relative to this subject. It would be wrong to expose it in a learned academy, to whose attention I have perhaps no claim, *et sic,* to use Virgil's terms, *juvat ire sub umbras,*[1] and yet my vanity is made uneasy by taking in the word *juvat.*[2] . . . I gladly would have your judgment relative to a late information that my grandson, declined for the Austrian service, would study geometry and the principles of engineering at Douay as cheap or cheaper than in Dublin.[3] He might here have the better opportunity of learning the French language, and after a year's study be better qualified for receiving General D'Alton's protection. . . .

   1. Thus it helps to withdraw to the shadows (quiet and leisure).
   2. It helps.
   3. See Letter 410. Roderick or Rory was commissioned in France in Dillon's Regiment in 1791. It would appear he changed his plan of going into Austrian service; in-

stead, his studying at Douay put him in contact with Irishmen in Dillon's Regiment. Dunleavy and Dunleavy record a letter from Roderick in France in 1789 with a note on his commissioning in 1791, p. 38, 8.4 ES 036.

413. To John Pinkerton[1]

PSPL, Gilbert MS 203

From Belanagare near Roscommon, 4 April 1786

... Such was the art employed to gain the Scots a high antiquity, thoroughly inconsistent with the state of life in Europe before the commencement of the Persian Empire. The fabric, therefore, of technical genealogies and technical succession of ninety kings before the Christian era cannot stand, and your countryman Mr. Innes (a priest of the Scotch College in Paris) has sufficiently exposed its weak foundation, though in other respects a very mistaken writer. To Gilla Coman and Flan of Bute Abbey, we owe the publication of the regal list I mentioned. They were esteemed as able antiquaries by the majority of their contemporaries in the eleventh century, and the majority since their time (even our learned O'Flaherty) have adopted a popular error. I have done so in my youth, but on meeting with better guides I am not ashamed to retract.

In the Annals of Tigernach and the other ancient documents, I found that our more authentic notices are to be deduced from the building of Eamania in Ulster about two hundred years before the Christian era. The seven generations of Ultonian princes mentioned in the interval prove this calculation to be pretty exact. Of what passed in Ireland before this Eamanian Era little is known, except a few capital facts such as the expedition of the Scots from Spain to Ireland about five hundred years before the birth of our Saviour, the legislation of *Ollamh-Fodhla* and his erection of apartments for the College of Fileas at Teamor, where they continued undisturbed under every revolution and from then spread with equal immunities through the neighboring provinces. These were facts which were too big for oblivion in any country where the elements of literature were cultivated. These elements were imported from Spain, where the natives say the Celts held intercourse with Phoenicians and their Carthaginian posterity. It was in memory of these intercourses that the ancient Scots took occasionally and ostentatiously the name Phenii. Hence the dialect among them called the Phenian (the language of their jurisprudence preserved to this day, but not understood by me or any other

Irish scholar in this kingdom)—and hence the number of Phoenician terms discovered by Colonel Vallancey in our old intelligible writings.

... In the Book of Balimote I find our antiquaries concurring with Bede in the establishment of Carbry Riada as the leader of the first colony of Scots in Britain, supported there partly by the indulgence of the Picts and partly by the negotiating power of the wisest of our monarchs, Cormac Ulfada, Carbry's cousin german.[2] The second great colony was established by Carbry's posterity, the sons of Erk, about the year 503. The succession of the Dalriada kings from that period, with the years of reigns down to Malcolm Canmor has been preserved in the poem[3] quoted by Mr. O'Flaherty, a copy of which I possess and the original with a translation shall be remitted to you as soon as I recover a little from my present languid state, bound by rheumatic pain. That the Tuatha De Danann arrived in Ireland from North Britain and subjected the Belgians, all our documents aver. ...

1. John Pinkerton (1758–1826), Scottish antiquarian and historian, was beginning his *History of Scotland from the Accession of the House of Stuart to that of Mary*, published in 1797. He requested from O'Conor information in the Irish Annals concerning Scotland. *Concise DNB*, 1:1044.

2. Cormac son of Art son of Cónn Cétchathach; Cairbre son of (Conaire and) Sárait daughter of Conn. The foundation of the story of this Cairbre is set out in *De Shíl Chonairi Móir* "Of the Race of Conaire Mór," ed. L. Gwynn, *Ériu* 6 (1912), pp. 130–143 (and see *ibid.* 144–153), which does occur in the Book of Ballymote: but it is not clear where O'Conor found such details as he records in Letters 422 and 433 below.

3. That beginning *A eolcha Alban uile* "Oh all (you) learned of Scotland" generally known as the *Duan Albanach* or "Scottish Poem" or simply the *Duan* or "Poem"; ed. Kenneth Jackson, *Celtica*, 3 (1956), pp. 149–167, with a detailed account of all extant versions, manuscript and printed, the latter including those of O'Flaherty, Pinkerton, and Rev. Charles O'Conor. All the references O'Conor makes in subsequent letters to a poem (or regnal list) ending with Malcolm Canmore (Mael Coluim III Ceannmhór "Great-head") seem to be to this one item.

414. To Dr. Charles O'Conor

OCD, 8.4 HL 163

12 April 1786

... In the course of the last year I have written to you at several times, and it is evident that my letters miscarried as you acknowledged none. I have received but some of your books, and you must be more careful hereafter in the choice of your messengers. Through my ignorance of the present language of Italy, I am in the case of an American Indian by possessing a treasure of which I do not know the value. It shall, however, be carefully reserved for yourself. Some essays of *Argaroti* I have perused in English, and I found him a profound thinker as well as a learned man. Italy has given us Transalpines the best models of writing and thinking; nor could we pretend to excell our masters, except perhaps in license, a license of great use, when kept within proper bounds. As no intellectual subject is yet inherited, the more any is agitated by Frenchmen, Englishmen, Germans, etc., the more will the sum of attainable knowledge be increased. Even heretics and Deists contribute instrumentally to this sum by rousing all the powers that truth seldom supplies till it is attacked, as steel elicits the fire which would otherwise lie dormant in the flint. . . .

415. To Chevalier Thomas O'Gorman, No. 18 Peter Street, Dublin

BM, Add. MS 21121

From my Hermitage and from a weak arm, 20 April 1786

The interest you take in the cultivation of my grandson puts me under obligations that demand a more than ordinary return of gratitude. The plan you laid down for him must doubtless be the best as it met with the approbation of General D'Alton to whom I request that you will present my profound respects. My brother in St. Omer (a proficient in mathematical learning) will, I am confident, be active in the improvement of this youth in the branches of knowledge necessary for induction into the École at Douay in October next. These preparatory steps strike my mind so forcibly that I cannot but prefer them to his setting off immediately to Hungary in company with Messrs. De Lacy, O'Reilly, and Plunkett. In the year which will succeed to the present, he will be prepared for meeting those gentlemen with some advantage, and he will profit of your letter of recommendation to them and other friends of yours in the Austrian service; families who for ages displayed celebrity in this country must now re-establish it in foreign lands. By reflection the fact grieves me, but by anticipation I enjoy the future effects of a spirit that no hardships at home could subdue. To a spirit like this no soil can be barren, and it will often thrive best by transplantation. General D'Alton and many others I could mention will prove this truth for me. . . .

416. To Joseph C. Walker, Treasury Chambers, Dublin

PSPL, Gilbert MS 203

Belanagare, 14 June 1786

... Mr. Beaufort[1] has given me satisfaction in his tract on our ancient literature published in the *Collectanea,* and yet in his ancient *Topography of Ireland,* a book as large as his own might be written to detect his mistakes. In casting an eye over Carolan's *Life,* I find that your anonymous correspondent trusted too much to informers who were ill-informed themselves; for being himself a child when Carolan died, he could furnish you with a nothing from his knowledge.[2] I very warmly thank you for a quotation from one of Dr. Johnson's letters to me. A letter from one of the first writers of his age or any age to such as I am does honor to his heart by wishing well to the studies of a person who he knew meant well, however unequal to the task he undertook. ...

    1. William Beauford of Athy had contributed some musical information for Walker's book. See Walker, "Acknowledgements."

    2. The "Anonymous correspondent" who contributed the anecdote of "Carolan's (or Stafford's) Receipt," was O'Conor's apothecary, Mr. Stafford of Elphin. Walker, p. 84.

417. To Chevalier Thomas O'Gorman

BM, Add. MS 21121

From my Hermitage, 16 July 1786

... More outlines from Colonel Vallancey are coming out. He has honored me with the perusal of his introduction. I found in it some excellent matter, which (through the want of our knowledge in oriental literature) had escaped us, the domestic writers, on this subject. Such assistance is come to us very opportunely; but in his multifarious researches, commencing from the *more remote* and consequently the *darker* periods of antiquity, mistakes can hardly be avoided. I ventured to mark out one in the *introduction before me,* and probably he is satisfied still that the mistake is on my side, not on his. In these differences relative to the assertions of Dr. Campbell that we have no ancient facts to produce but that our predecessors before the introduction of the Gospel were ignorant and unlettered savages, the public I think will not be content with the bare negative arguments and plausible objections of Mr. Innes, retailed with additions in two quarto volumes by two learned gentlemen of the name of MacPherson. . . .

. . . The information you received that O'Reilly, prince of eastern Breffny was hereditary marshall of the royal army of Ireland and had the office of placing the crown on the head of each monarch proves nothing but the ignorance of your informer. The surname of O'Reilly was not imposed or known before the eleventh century. It was so with the O'Briens, O'Conors, O'Ruarks, etc. How could the O'Reillys have the privilege of crowning Irish monarchs where no Irish monarchs existed since the death of Malachy II, for the few princes who assumed the title of Kings since Malachy's time were not generally acknowledged? . . .

418. To Joseph C. Walker, Treasury Chambers, Dublin

PSPL, Gilbert MS 203

Belanagare, 15 August 1786

My dear Sir,

This letter will not be worth the sixteenth part of what it will cost you, yet I must send you some expression of my gratitude for repeated favors. Your last was extremely acceptable as it brought me a detail of our sovereign's escape from the hands of mad women. His condescension in letting strangers approach too near his person, however exalting to his character, cannot certainly be justified by prudence; and the late attack upon him will, we hope, be a good lesson to a great and amiable prince who owes the highest care of his life to his subjects as well as to his family.[1] I thank you for Mr. Pinkerton's letter and shall remit him a document relating to the kings of Scotland which has been preserved in Ireland though lost in his own country. For sixteen days past I have been in the parish of Kilronan in my younger son's house on the brink of Lough Allen. I am now in my old place of confinement without hope of other prisoners who sooner or later expect to shake off their chains. I am, however, still able to discharge one part of my obligations to you by perusing again and again your printed book and offering such corrections on the blank leaves as some good documents in my possession will justify. You indeed took care that my labor will not be great. In my late excursion I enjoyed one of the noblest landscapes in this province, intersected by a deep lake of more than thirty miles in compass. Mr. Wilson of Dame Street, the son of my old friend Peter, is printing a book on the natural history of Ireland. He applied to me, though a very bad naturalist, for some assistance; and this day I remitted him a description of the place I lately left, as well as I could give it. The mountains which environ the lake are high and contain within their bowels coal and iron mines that are inexhaustible, treasures within our reach almost in the center of the kingdom, but in a great degree useless through the neglect of opening a communication by water between the Shannon and Liffey. One of the richest veins of coal lies near the lake on Mr. Tennison's estate; and as far as the efforts of a single gentleman can reach, he has been active in extending the benefits of his colliery. He has encouraged Mr. Thomas Reilly of Thomas Street to erect an iron manufactury near the lake.[2] The work is begun, is conducted with great spirit, but must be attended with great expense, and will (it is hoped) meet parliamentary encouragement, as an earnest of the great future work of a canal through the level country between the Shannon and Liffey. I detailed this matter as well as I could in a hasty letter to Mr. Wilson, and I wish you could peruse and correct what I have written, should it be shown to any of our parliamentary patriots. You'll please to present my best respects to our friend the Reverend Mr. Archdall. The two half-guinea receipts for his *Monasticon* I'll remit, soon I hope, to Mr. Luke White. Through my son's hands I received Colonel Vallancey's yet unpublished book.[3] The extent of his oriental learning and skill in modern languages is vast. In my last to him I ventured to predict that his last performance will draw on him the attention of all the academics in Europe and divide those learned bodies into applauders and opposers. It is from the conflict and collision of authorities and opinions that the truth will come out at last on every question.—You inquire about the dramatic performances of the Irish; they had ludicrous farces at their entertainments, such I suppose as satisfied an ill-cultivated taste. I never met with any in writing, and such as were exhibited at wakes were wrecked performances indeed.

1. Although George III had a "pathological hatred of the Roman Catholics," the Catholic Committee on 7 September 1786 moved that a "congratulatory address from the Catholics of Ireland be presented to his Majesty on his late providential escape from the attempt on his sacred life." A committee of seven was appointed to write the address: Lord Killeen, John and Michael Keogh, D. T. O'Brien, Charles Ryan, John Comerford, and Frances McDermott. The address was presented and accepted the next evening, 8 September. On 5 October Chief Secretary Hamiliton wrote Lord Killeen that his Majesty "was pleased to receive the same [the address] in the most gracious manner." Alvin Redman, *The House of Hanover* (New York: Coward McCann, Inc., 1961), p. 131; "The Catholic Committee Minute Book 1773–92," pp. 104–106.

2. Throughout his life, O'Conor was an advocate for developing the iron and coal deposits. His pamphlet on *Working and Manufacturing Mines and Minerals* published in 1753 was, no doubt, one of the reasons why coal and iron deposits were first developed

in the Roscommon Triangle (Roscommon, Sligo, Leitrim). The *DJ*, 31 May–3 June 1760 mentions the continuation of the iron works at Boyle, Co. Roscommon, after the death of its proprietor William Rutledge. Again, the *DJ*, 26–29 May 1778 asks that iron mines of Ireland be developed rather than import Swedish iron.

3. Probably *A Vindication of the Ancient History of Ireland*, published in Dublin by Luke White 1786. *BMCPBCE*, 25:1049.

419. To Charles Kelly

OCD, 8.4 SH 150

[Belanagare, 22 August 1786]¹

Rev[eren]d Father,

In our survey of human affairs we derive much comfort from the fact that while moral evil prevails so much in the world, while the governors of states spread the disorder they should repress, providence raises up some men who, without human power, stop the progress and arrest the influence of human evils, civil and ecclesiastical. You'll give my leave, Rev. Father, to count you one in the number. You have done service. Roman cardinals and Irish prelates you have set right in matter relating to your native country, for your zeal was seconded by knowledge. They follow you into your enclosure to receive your judgment on matters to be settled hereafter. When you seek them, it is for the good of others; you do not want them for your own. You enjoy comforts which seldom enter the palaces of the Roman princes who surround you. In the services you have rendered your country, I have received an ample share. In the services you have rendered my grandson in the Ludovician college, that youth has been impressed with every duty of his vocation in divinity and literature. I trust that he has made a good progress. The knowledge of Church history and languages is more requisite in these kingdoms than in those which are thoroughly orthodox.

Arianism is at present making a progress in England and Deism is making a greater. The established religion is only (for political ends) preserved by external forms and by the acts of Parliament on which it has been established. The anarchy in religion has become so great that the late Protestant Bishop Berkeley declared it must necessarily end in Popery, by which term all Protestants mean the Catholic religion. Though no prophet, his prediction will, I hope, be fulfilled when equal zeal and piety on our side unite with knowledge on the eradication of religious error.

My grandson's term in the Ludovician College is now expired unless the Cardinal Protector can dispense with the statutes for another year in his favor. If not, he must set out for Paris to improve himself further in his theological studies and learn to converse in the language of that country. Through the kindness of our worthy A[rch] B[ishop] of Tuam[2] and of our worthy Dr. Fallon,[3] we have obtained for another of my grandsons a succession to his brother in the aforesaid seminary. He is there at present, I hope, and as he will be received at a period of life when our human passions do not encroach upon innocence, the example before him will, I trust in God, secure him against their evil effects in a more advanced period and make active virtue succeed to the absence of vice. It would be happy for him if in the first year of his studies his progress should be made under the inspection of his brother.

Our dear Dr. Fallon is arrived at the seventy-seventh year of his age, and we are anxious because we are informed that interest is made for another prelate to succeed to him on his demise. The translation, I can assure you, would be highly grievous to our clergy and laity in the diocese of Elphin. We all wish for an episcopal coadjutor to prevent such a translation, a measure to which Dr. Fallon himself is not averse. Dr. O'Conor of Roscommon, in whose favor I have written to you many years since, is now past seventy years. A younger gentleman is now deemed the fittest for the episcopal office, and some of our diocesan canon have declared for Mr. Flyn of Sligo. He is certainly a learned gentleman whose zeal and knowledge are recommended by his prudent conduct in a town of Presbyterians, whose virulence is so far abated as to permit Mr. Flyn to erect a chapel in that town, one of the best at present in this kingdom. You'll have soon full testimonies of the merits of this excellent pastor and to them I refer. Through a life checkered with crosses and afflictions, I am now in my old age confined by rheumatic pains without the hope of other prisoners who expect one day or other to shake off their chains. May I make the proper use of the warnings I receive and the sentence of death I lie under. Excepting yourself and a few others, I have outlived all my contemporaries. My dear father, my friend, and my kinsman, let me have a share in your prayers. I need not give you here an assurance that living or dying, I shall remain your grateful and faithful servant.

Belanagare, 22 August 1786
[In another hand]

1. There is an earlier draft of this letter, dated 18 August 1786 in CFmH, Stowe Collection, STO. 889.
2. Dr. Philip Philips, *HBC*, p. 406.

3. James O'Fallon was bishop of Elphin. O'Conor was correct in his worry about the bishop's health. O'Fallon died on 2 December 1786 and Edward French was translated to the bishopric. *HBC*, p. 409.

420. To Joseph C. Walker

HL, STO 1346

[c. 1 October 1786]¹

I sent to Colonel Vallancey the chronological poem composed in the reign of Malcolm Keanmore, King of Scots; it relates to the succession of the kings of Scotland from Fergus, the son of *Erk* to Malcolm. I have added a literal English translation for the use of Mr. Pinkerton and hope that the Colonel has even now transmitted it *with the original* to him. The second great colony of Irish in Scotland was established by Carbry Riada, A.D. 503.² The succession of the Dalriada kings from that period with the years of their origins down to Malcolm is preserved in the poem quoted by O'Flaherty, a copy of which I possess, and the original with my translation shall be translated to you.

1. This undated letter is enclosed in a letter from Vallancey to O'Conor. In another hand is written, "The next letter to this in order of time is one from Mr. O'Conor to Mr. Walker dated October 1, 1786."
2. Some confusion here; see the end of Letter 413.

421. To Joseph C. Walker, Treasury Chambers, Dublin

PSPL, Gilbert MS 203

21 October 1786

My Dear Sir,

Yesterday I received your letter of the 5th instant, and I heartily thank you for the contents. The concern of my friends about me at this time brings me consolation amidst my bodily pains. They think me a well-meaning member of society; to be a useful one was always my wish. At present I resemble a town besieged; for three years past the enemy has been making slow but sure advances against me. In the close of the last month, I have been attacked in the citadel. The pains in my bowels confined and alarmed me. I am now (in this good weather) tolerably re-established, and I stir out to attend my poor laborers in finishing my harvest business. Poor indeed they are, and I strive, as far as I am able, to alleviate their condition. —Here, as in the south, our laborers exist in a state of invincible distress and must do so till legislative wisdom comes to their relief. Landlords, were they willing, are not equal to the business. On 170 acres of mountain that I subdued by drains, removing stones, and lime-stone gravel, I have planted seventeen seulages. Each of these occupants pays hearth money for a smoking fire and tithes on ground which, till my own time, paid neither and which to myself paid next to nothing. I now have good interest arising out of the money I laid out, but how are the laborers benefited? In two years of scarcity, I have made my poor people some abatement. The worthy representative of our county in Parliament, Mr. French, has laid out great sums for the relief of the indigent on his estate in these two seasons. At this time those creatures are not pressed by hunger. They have plenty of potatoes, plenty of water, and plenty of naked brats; they are moreover happy in the insensibility of which their southern brethren are destitute. I spare you the pain of having more on this subject from my weak arm.

The profound researches, extensive reading, and oriental erudition of Colonel Vallancey are almost without example in the present time. On one part of ancient history he has thrown irresistible light.[1] He has shown the swarms of the primevil [unreadable] (bordering on the Euxine and Caspian Seas) have spread themselves over Asia and in their progress westward made settlements in Egypt, Libya and Spain; that instructed in the elements of literature and arts, they had the name of *Pano-Scuit,* ventured upon voyages into Britain and Ireland, and made a settlement in the latter island, where they remained undisturbed till long after the introduction of Christianity among them. Here then is a *lux in tenebris.*[2] He shows that though the southern and northern Scythians were descendants from the same stock, yet that the latter remained long in a rude state, while the former picked up the rudiments and employed the means of civilization in their several Asiatic migrations. Other facts depending on his principal argument may and, I believe, will be contested with him relative to time and the scene of a[ction]. Mistakes in such relative matters are hardly avoidable, and when detected, the Colonel will be no great loser. I beg you'll present him with my affection. I sent him as he desired the chronological poem composed in the reign of Malcolm Kanmore K[ing] of Scots. It relat[es] to the regal succession of the kings of Scotland from Fergus the son of Erk to the time of the aforesaid Malcolm. I have added a literal English translation for the satisfaction of Mr. Pinkerton, and I hope that the Colonel has before this time remitted the original with the translation to that gentleman.³ Be by no means concerned [with] the *critique* of the critical reviewers on your book. They are n[ot] just in censuring your quotations from ancient and modern writers. Without such authorities how could you support many of your facts? Would they not censure you for omitting them? Why did I not commend you for the lights you have cast on a subject never att[empted] before you by an antiquary of our island? In many instances it [should] be shown that the reviewers of France, England, and Germany have been hurtful to true knowledge by giving but too often a wrong direction to the public judgments.

Burke, the great Burke,⁴ is now among you. If you do not distinguish him by the honors due to him from his countrymen, you will transmit to posterity a stain and an indelible one on Irish history.

P.S. My best respects to Dr. Young. He treated me kindly in his own chambers in the university. His grandfather proved very kind to me in a money dealing. On that very account, I should entertain the best wishes for his grandson, independent of any other merit.

    1. *A Vindication of the Ancient History of Ireland Wherein is Shown: I The Descent of the Old Inhabitants from the Pheno-Scythians of the East; II The Early Skill of the Pheno-Scythians etc.; III Accounts of the Ancient Bards.* BMCPBCE, 25:1049.
    2. Light in darkness.   3. See note 6, Letter 413.
    4. Edmund Burke.

422. To [John Pinkerton]¹

PSPL, Gilbert MS 203

[24 October 1786]

In one of your letters you make inquiry about *Carbry Eochad Riada*,² employed in his wars by Cormac Ulfada, Monarch of Ireland and Carbry's cousin german. That Cormac, the best of our heathen monarchs, had obtained the ill will of the druids by opposing the religion of nature and the adoration of our God alone to their pantheism and superstitious theology. He labored to introduce a good system of legislation against which the provincial oligarchs had at several times revolted. . . .

    1. The editors believe that this letter was to John Pinkerton, but that O'Conor enclosed it with a letter to Joseph Cooper Walker to be transmitted to Pinkerton in Scotland. See Pinkerton's letter to O'Conor for 4 April 1786 in which Pinkerton asks about Corman Ulfada and Carbry Riada. This letter is written in another hand and has a note, "copied from his own handwriting."

2. Evidently a conflation of two names, Cairbre Riada (also Righfhoda) and Eochaidh or Eochu Riada, both of which refer, according to some medieval sources, to the same individual.

423. To Denis O'Conor, No. 115, Capel Street, Dublin

OCD, 8.4 SE 148

15 November 1786

... Mr. Peter Plunkett was with us at Mass last Sunday. I suspected that his taking Belanagare in his way was with a view to money dealings. As you might obtain the turn you wanted through another channel, I did not open a word to him on my side; and he was silent on *his*. Cathy invited him to take some refreshment with her, but he interposed the necessity he had to proceed to another place and took his leave of us. Your brother informs me that Mr. O'Berne of Carrick is ready to serve you but would wish that the sum you want should be specified.

I went over this morning to Frenchpark to learn from Mr. French whether he purposed to meet you soon on the affair which [delays] you in town or postpone the matter to another time. Mr. French assured he would get off tomorrow morning for Dublin and meet you on Friday next. Mr. Martin Browne is now in Belanagare so extremely and unnecessarily anxious about the payment of our rent charge of £79.10. If Mr. French and you agree about the purchase of that sum, it is surely understood that you'll owe but £39 on the fees of November instant, a little more if the rest was payable on the 29th of September last. . . .

424. To Joseph C. Walker, Treasury Chambers, Dublin

PSPL, Gilbert MS 203

22 November 1786

... I am sorry that the Great Burke has left your city without any recognition of the credit he has done to his native country by his talents and, let me add, some services also. Why do the insurgents in Munster escape with impunity? . . . You have opened a subject long neglected by ourselves. You have said enough already to show that it is important by proving that the ancients of this island (long unknown and long uninvaded by foreign nations) had yet patronized customs and some arts also which humanize society and render the history of a cultivated people, called barbarians, an object of profitable inquiry. I have offered some corrections historical and chronological in the blank book you sent me and shall add a few more before a new edition of your work is prepared. The works of Tacitus and Gibbon are not free from mistakes, and a reviewer who should expose them without enlarging on the great merit of the chief parts of their writings would be contemptible indeed. By the way, I look upon Gibbon to be equal to Tacitus in talents and perhaps superior in composition. But like the late Mr. Hume, Mr. Gibbon is unfortunately and, I believe, irreclaimably a sceptic relative to revealed religion; and Providence permits the employment of great genius in an attack upon Christianity as a spur to great genius on the other side to demonstrate its coming to us from God himself. . . .

425. To Denis O'Conor, Capel Street, Dublin

OCD, 8.4 SE 148

22 November 1786

Dear Denis,

Premature as your journey to Dublin was, yet as you prepared the means of finishing or breaking off the treaty you write upon, you will be enabled the sooner to quit the town and meet your family at home. Of your proceeding I expect an account by the post tomorrow. You are at present at extraordinary expense, and by Pat Hart I sent you five guineas to buy some groceries and other little articles for me and in particular a [not clear] for Ally whose mind is restless to have one. Who would not gratify such a lady, who already has distinguished herself from most other ladies, by minding her knitting! Mr. Browne is now in Belanagare and sends your son Martin up to make an affidavit which [corrupt] I know not the purport of it. After dry weather of more than thirty days we had last Sunday an incessant rain which left [not clear] a great flood. But Owen husbanded the dry bogs so well that he supplied your own care effectually. Your potatoes are all housed, and you have great bulk of them. Your hay cocks and reeks are thatched. I have men at work preparing new lodgments for Owen's young trees. Thus are your affairs at home well-conducted. I had a letter here from a worthy friend, Father John O'Conor, requesting me to write to Father O'Kelly at the Minerva recommending Dr. Troy of Ossory for the see of Dublin. I replied that he was late in his application, for that already I wrote in favor of a gentleman long beloved and long in the confidence of the late Archbishop,[1] that at present I could not recall what I have done without disgracing myself with Father O'Kelly and every other friend, and that Father O'Conor himself upon reflection would not consent [rest of letter faded].

1. Archbishop Carpenter died 29 October. Dr. John Thomas Troy was translated from the see of Ossory to the archbishopric of Dublin. *HBC*, p. 402.

426. To Denis O'Conor, 115 Capel Street, Dublin

OCD, 8.4 SE 148

8 December 1786

Dear Denis,

I write this on the anniversary of my junction with your mother fifty-five years ago. This whole period I have had many frequent rubs in life. They were things hereditary to my family. You had a share in the inheritance. Your present situation is an instance, but what is unavoidable as a grievance should be submitted to as a duty; and a compliance with that makes every burden supportable. You should civilly dismiss Mr. Reilly. You, your brother, and I have been expensive on his account here in Belanagare and that expenditure was enough and more than enough for his friendship. I think you must be soon at liberty to return to your family. I have this week been in sorrow for the loss of our dear Dr. Fallon, who died on the third instant. He was a warm friend to you and to me; so was the late worthy Metropolitan of Leinster. We can not expect equal kindness from superiors who probably will be strangers to us. You forgot that you bought some tea and coffee for me when you were in town in the last harvest. What I wanted was sugar to season those articles. Have you bought the linen I bespoke for two pair of sheets? If my friend Mr. William Wilson of Dame Street sends to your lodging some books for me, I request you will give him my thanks and pay him the contents of his bill containing two copies of his *Post Chaise Companion,* a Watson's Almanack, and the *English Lists for the Year 1787.* I pity Tom Lee for his late conduct relative to Dr. Carpenter's will. He will only expose himself to censure by it. You are acquainted with my intimate friends in the capital. I request you will present them with my service. I had this week a packet from the Castle enclosing a letter from Mr. Burke to Colonel Vallancey and another from the Colonel himself. My mind and hand are in too infirm a state to thank the latter on this day; I am indeed unfit for writing on any subject but the present.

427. To Joseph C. Walker, Treasury Chambers, Dublin

PSPL, Gilbert MS 203

Belanagare, 18 or 19 December 1786

My dear Friend,

To my happiness, in the correspondence of some worthy persons there is a counterweight of misfortune that throws me greatly in arrears to them. My rheumatic pains and rapid decline prevent the speedy acknowledgment of their favors or (I should say) retard the activity of any little service I could render them; I have, however, a consolation in their indulgence to me, as well as in the warmth of my own grateful mind. I lately in pain and weakness wrote to our learned and worthy friend Colonel Vallancey, who with other favors sent me a copy of Mr. Burke's letter to him on the subject of his *Vindication* of the earlier parts of our insular history.[1] Like every other intellectual performance of that great man (for he is great) his letter to our friend is highly judicious. To such men we owe chiefly the cultivation of the human mind, relatively to the legislation and knowledge we stand most in need of; and yet Mr. B[urke] arrived here lately and in the capital of his native country, as little noticed as if he had landed on the coast of Kamchatka—Oh Dublin! O frigidity! In the historical fragments we have (as you know) employed a considerable part of my time. Of my studies on the subject I purpose (if life permits) to give an account and publish therein my obligations to Colonel Vallancey. You'll soon, I hope, see him and present *inter alia*[2] with my affections. He is to set off for [Thessaly] in his royal master's service, and on the business brought to him our sovereign could not employ an abler servant. Besides the matter recommended in his commission, the Colonel, by perusal of the documents laid before him, will pick up many things relating to this island that have been long secreted from the public; and on his return, he will come back to us like Virgil's great but flattered patron *spoliis orientis onustus*.[3]

I am this moment interrupted by friends who are come in to me and till my next must postpone some things I want to communicate to you. I shall, as little as I can, be an insolvent debtor, and I request you will put me in this light with Mr. Luke W[hite][4] and Mr. William Wilson.[5] I am under strong obligations to [them], and I shall soon with this weak hand remit them my acknowledgments.

P.S. By sending you these lines on a scrip of paper you have a proof that I have not leisure to transcribe them. I know you'll pardon an impropriety that is unavoidable, without a [word] to others that I am not capable of.

1. Burke admired Vallancey's activity but was suspicious of his scholarship. Burke's editor Holden Furber wrote, "Vallancey apparently overlooked the large number of cautious reservations in Burke's letter, and imagining it to be a nearly unqualified approval of his own conclusions, sent it to Charles O'Conor and to others of his friends." *Burke* 5:292–93.
2. Among other things.
3. Laden with spoils of the East.
4. Luke White is the Dublin publisher for the Royal Irish Academy. John C. Walker, to Charles O'Conor, n.d., 1785 or '86. HL, Stowe Coll., O'Conor MS. STO 47.
5. Peter Wilson took William Wilson into partnership in 1769. Whether William was Peter Wilson's son or a relative is unknown. On Peter Wilson's death, c. 1771, William became publisher of the *Dublin Directory*. Plomer, pp. 407–408.

428. To Joseph C. Walker, Treasury Chambers, Dublin

PSPL, Gilbert MS 203

Belanagare, 13 January 1787

My Dear Friend,

By the last post I have made an effort to acquit myself of an epistolary debt to Colonel Vallancey. I now sit down to discharge some part of my arrears to yourself. Painful days and restless nights make me almost an insolvent, and yet I trust that lengthening days and good weather may so far re-establish me as not to be thoroughly useless to my friends. My grandson in Rome assures me that your *Memoirs* on our *Irish Bards* is much approved of. The literate of that capital do you justice, and they will do more on the next edition of your book. Be assured of my forwardness to serve you as far as the documents I have been long collecting will enable me. Your third and fourth sections are very important, yet you have fallen into some mistakes historical and chronological, which I shall point out in your blank book but which can not be comprised in a miscellaneous half-sheet like the present. I request that you will inform our dear and learned friend Colonel Vallancey that I have written to one of our titular bishops who has sufficient influence on the superiors of the Lombard College to throw their collection of Old Irish manuscripts open to him and pay him respectful attention during his stay in Paris. I trust Dr. Brady (that titular prelate)[1] will soon remit me the recommendation I requested of him; if he does it speedily, I hope that Dr. Brady's letter will fall into the Colonel's hands before he quits Dublin. Here we suffer by the loss of Dr. Carpenter, the Colonel's and my own fast friend. I purposed to write on this subject to Dr. Philips, the titular A[rch] Bishop of Tuam, but I desisted on being informed that between the latter prelate and the superiors of Lombard some coldness subsists at present. I trouble you with no more on this head till I hear from Dr. Brady. The salary obtained by Colonel Vallancey for Mr. O'Flanegan gives me great pleasure, as I hope that the latter gentleman is qualified by his knowledge of our classical language to translate as Mr. Burke requires of our historical documents. My infirmity is a very great obstacle to my own historical researches, and when I sit down to them I am arrested by various interruptions. I am doing what I can but my letter is short, and I am prudent enough to burn my papers if I can not put them into any tolerable order. It is very seldom that any posthumous work merits public approbation. I yesterday received a very kind letter from our worthy friend Mr. Will Wilson. I request you will present him with my warm thanks and inform him I shall soon reply to his letter. I believe that you are assured of my affection and therefore conclude in a few words.

1. Dr. James Brady was bishop of Ardagh and Clonmacnois. *HBC*, p. 385.

429. To Fr. Brett, Rosemary Lane Chapel, Dublin

OCD, 8.4 HL 163

From my Hermitage, 23 January 1787

I return you my warmest thanks for your letter of the 20th instant and for the papers you enclosed therein of my grandson's letter to you from Rome. Your judgment is just, and it is a fortunate circumstance that whatever fell from him indiscreetly has been communicated to a discreet correspondent who has been so kind to return him instructions which I trust will guard him for the future against committing (to paper especially) too free a judgment against men and things.[1] When you write next to him, I request you will repeat your correction to him as he appears to forget what he learned here at school from old

Lily:[2] "*quid de quoque viro [et cui viro] dicat valde cavendum est.*"[3] In his style he is too diffuse and, in my opinion, verbose to a degree of affectation. He should take Cicero and the younger Pliny for his models in the epistolary style. . . . From the extracts I have seen from the Bishop of Cloyne's book I do not desire to know more of him.[4] . . .

    1. Unfortunately, Dr. Charles allowed this undisciplined forthrightness to appear in his *Columbanus* pamphlets against the Irish hierarchy. Such pamphlets caused his suspension from his priestly duties in England and Ireland. See Costigan, "The Tragedy of Charles O'Conor," pp. 44–46.
    2. William Lily (1468?–1522), high master of St. Paul's School, London, and author of a short Latin Syntax with rules in English, *Grammatices Rudimenta*. *Concise DNB*, 1:776.
    3. "One must be very careful what he says to any man [and to whom he says it]."
    4. Dr. Richard Woodward, Protestant bishop of Cloyne, *HBC*, p. 364.

430. To John Pinkerton

CFmH, STO 890

10 February 1787

. . . The part of my letter to the Colonel which related to this subject[1] has, I find, been copied by a careless transcriber. He puts *orior* for *iarthar* and consequently *eastern* for *western*.[2] For *Da Righ for chaogad,* he writes *Deich Righ for chogad,* and consequently instead of giving as the true number of fifty-two kings, he gives the false one of sixty.[3] When such mistakes are committed by transcribers almost under our eye, we may judge how little this poem of Kings of Albany[4] could escape being vitiated in the long course of 700 years. . . .

    1. A list of the kings of Albany.
    2. *Iarthar* "west(ern)", but *orior,* not "east(ern)" (*oirthear*); rather "shore" or "border" (*oirear*), the proper reading. See Jackson's apparatus, *art. cit.* p. 161 n. 4, Pinkerton's divergent text reflecting O'Conor's "correction."
    3. O'Conor is correcting a mistranslation by John Pinkerton.
    4. I.e., Scotland.

431. To Charles Ryan

CFmH, STO 892

Belanagare, 28 March 1787

If you should think that what I have expressed to you in my last packet of any use, you must think also that I have finished it a little abruptly. I have therefore added the enclosed paper to complete my argument and take a respectful leave of my Lord Bishop of Cloyne. If you think the whole should be suppressed, be it so. I shall be happy in finding that the little assistance I could give is not wanted. I have not yet seen our friend's Mr. O'Leary's book.[1] I expect much from it and hope that he has exhausted the subject that has made me uneasy on the perusal of Dr. Woodward's book.

In my last I have poured out to you my anxiety at the censure put on me as the publisher of Dr. Curry's *Historical Memoirs.* Our dear friend, Mr. Braughall will inform you how groundless that charge is. Some parts not proper to be exposed to the public at present, we both agree, should be rescinded. I was positive that our friend Mr. Gaven would have done so, and the more as it required little labor. What must be done, I shall be determined by Mr. Braughall's judgment and your own.

On this unlucky affair I am under great obligation to Mr. Walker of Dublin Castle, who assured Dr. Browne of the College that I had no hand in the late publication as an editor and that I only remitted a sketch of the author's life.[2] With his true representation, Dr. Browne seemed satisfied. . . .

1. Mr. O'Leary's Defense Containing a Vindication of his Conduct and Writings during the Late Disturbances in Munster. With a Full Justification of the Catholics . . . In Answer to the False Accusations of Theophilus (i.e. Right Honourable P. Duigenan in His Pamphlet "An Address to the Nobility and Gentry of the Church of Ireland") and the ill-grounded Insinuations of . . . Dr. Woodward, Lord Bishop of Cloyne (Dublin: P. Byrne, 1787) BMPCBCE 18: 1065. There is no indication that O'Conor published an answer to Bishop Woodward's attacks.

2. A reprint of Curry's *Historical and Critical Review* . . . did appear in 1786 with a life of Curry by O'Conor; however, a historical introduction by O'Conor was dropped after the 1775 edition and not included until the 1810 edition. *An Historical and Critical Review of the Civil Wars in Ireland from the Reign of Queen Elizabeth to the Settlement under King William. A new and Improved Edition,* ed. Dr. Charles O'Conor (Dublin: P. Connolly, 1810), iiin.

432. To Joseph C. Walker

PSPL, Gilbert MS 203

Belanagare, 31 July 1787

. . . What were the contents of the papers you enclosed to me from Colonel Vallancey? I am singularly unhappy in the miscarriage of the letter which enclosed that paper. My dear friend, I have many wrongs to subjoin here, but I must finish abruptly as the decorum of attention to friends just come in requires. It will expose more trouble hereafter.

I am glad that you can count Lady Moira in the number of your friends. I had the honor one morning of being presented to her Ladyship in her dressing room by her Lord.[1] Of all the women of great rank I ever knew, I never met with any that had made such a rank more easy to every person about her. In viewing the pictures in the great dining room, I cried out on seeing that of Cardinal Pole there at full length[2]—"Madam, I am happy in finding here your kinsman's the Cardinal's picture." "Sir," said her Ladyship, "the memory of good men and particularly of such a kinsman as the Cardinal is dear to me. He was a good man who acted from a principle that he thought conducive to virtue, and what is man without such a principle?" . . .

    1. Elizabeth Hastings, Lady Moira. O'Conor was calling at Moira House on Usher's Quay, home of John Rawdon Hastings, first earl of Moira. Lord Moira was a founding member of the Royal Irish Academy. Maxwell, p. 344; Craig, p. 233; Gilbert, "Streets of Dublin," p. 38.
    2. Reginald, Cardinal Pole (1500–1558), archbishop of Canterbury under Queen Mary. His ambition was to bring the Anglican Church back to the Roman Church and reestablish the Roman Catholic ecclesiastical system in England. *Concise DNB*, 1 : 1054.

433. To Joseph C. Walker, Treasury Chambers, Dublin

PSPL, Gilbert MS 203

Belanagare House, 24 October 1787

This minute your friend and mine, Mr. Beauford, parted this house for Elphin. He called on me yesterday at my Hermitage. He dined with me and slept in an apartment I prepared for him. He is a gentleman of knowledge and communicative of it in a most pleasing manner. My eldest son and MacDermot (a physician from Paris and Edinburgh and my grandson) dined with us. In our quaffing we toasted our friends at home and abroad. I showed Mr. Beauford some paragraphs related to Colonel Vallancey and yourself; your book has had a good reception from such Roman readers as understand our language, and one gentleman in particular wants a copy of your *Bards*, which I could wish that you forwarded to Rome by the first opportunity. On my grandson's waiting on Cardinal Boncompagni with a set of Vallancey's books, he met with a gracious reception; and from the beginning to the end of their conversation the Cardinal spoke to him the English language, an uncommon and pleasing instance of attention to foreign literature by an Italian prelate. It is the more pleasing as it brings a proof of a liberal correspondence between nations formerly divided by principles, ill directed because ill understood. I thank you for the good account you give me of Mr. Johnstone.[1] To the shame of our countrymen only seven copies of his book have been disposed of in Dublin. The impression made on our countrymen that this island was formerly (in its heathen state) the habitation of the most ferocious savages can not be easily worn away. . . .

1. James Johnstone (d. 1798), was a Church of England clergyman and chaplain to the English envoy to Denmark. He translated Danish and Norwegian classics and published his *Antiquitates Celto-Scandicae* in 1784, and his *Antiquitates Celto-Normannicae* in 1786. O'Conor was writing about the latter book. *Concise DNB,* 1:698.

434. To Edmund Malone

RIA, Stowe MS B1a

24 December 1787

Sir,

With sensible pleasure I sit down to answer your letter of the 12th[1] instant as I can give you some good information on the subject of it, but you must be content with dry facts which, however justly slighted by persons who put the proper estimate on things, are yet found of some use to men who can show that their consequence in the world is not single but partly derived from a line of ancestors who once had great consequence in their country.

In a former letter which you have seen I made mention of Murry, nicknamed Mullethan (i.e. longhead). He was a celebrated King of Conaght who died A.D. 701. From his son Inraghtach descended the O'Conors, O'Malones, MacDermots, and other reputable families. All bore the general name of Clan Murrey or Siol Murray until the introduction of surnames in the eleventh century. These surnames were taken from a grandfather or father by the prepositive monosyllables *O* or *Mac,* the former signifying grandson, the latter son. Then it was that Teig (of the white steed) K[ing] of Conaght took to the surname O'Conor, from Conor his grandfather; then was also the surname of O'Malone imposed and indeed the chief surnames of the kingdom.

In the eleventh century Ireland, without a controlling monarch or controlling legislation, was torn by hostile factions. In the wars between Conaght and Meath the O'Conors, who bore the chief power in the latter province, obtained a good settlement for the O'Malone family, their kinsmen in the country of Breaghmary, bordering on the Termon of Clonmacnois, a celebrated city under the monastic rule of St. Kiarnan, an order to which the O'Malones were protectors and who ornamented the city with some of its principal buildings, as our annals testify. In the territory of Breaghmary the O'Malones remained in full possession of their part of it for more than five hundred years down to the days of Philip and Mary, with which my annals end. To this day a property of 2,000 a year, a part of the ancient estate, is still in the possession of your kinsmen, the O'Malones of Balinahown. Of the state of your family from the days of the aforesaid Philip and Mary, I doubt not your grandfather has left good documents.

You observe that the name of Murrey is Scotch. It is so; there was another Clan Murrey in the part of Leinster, now called the county of Wicklow, but though the names are identic the families are from different stocks. You need not being told that the Scots of the highlands were a people of the same blood, language, and manners with our old Irish; that they should in several families bear similar names and surnames is not to be wondered. You would wish to know what was meant by the word "termon." It derives from the Latin words *terra immunes*,[2] contracted into our compound "termon," a landed property set apart by princes for the endowment of our monastic houses. These termons were exempted from all taxes. The institution was good in its principle, but noxious in its abuse.

The name Maol-Eoin (Malone) signifies a man tonsured in honor of St. John, like Malcolm, one tonsured for St. Columb. Instances of this custom would be endless. It arose from the devotion of persons who devoted themselves to a patron saint, to have his daily petitions to God for their salvation. *Maol* in a liberal sense signifies *bald* undoubtedly, but in an extended sense it signifies a tonsure, which had a resemblance to baldness. The French and English had a custom similar to this in the surnames St. John, St. Aubin, St. Leger, St. Lawrence, etc.

I often listened with great attention to your grandfather, a great man in his profession and, what is better, a man of great virtue. To the fame and talents of his three sons I have been long a witness. They threw luster back on their ancestors, but you, sir have done so without deriving any from them. Your natural powers under the highest cultivation constitute a singularity of eminence independent [and] self-derived. [Two lines crossed out]

[On a separate sheet: a scrawled genealogy of Teig of the Tower A.D. 954.]

1. On 12 December Edmund Malone wrote to O'Conor. Malone, in England, had seen a letter O'Conor had written to someone in Dublin in which O'Conor discussed the Malone's genealogy. Edmund Malone wanted more details as he was submitting his brother Lord Sunderlin's genealogy for a new edition of Lodge's *Irish Peerage*. Malone wanted O'Conor to explain the term *termon*. He also asked if the Clan Murray were not

originally "Scotch" and if the name Malone did not come from the word *moil*, meaning *bald*. CFmH, Stowe Coll., O'Conor MS.

2. More likely simply from Latin *terminus*.

435. To Chevalier Thomas O'Gorman, 49 Bride Street, Dublin

BM, Add. MS 21121

[Belanagare, 24 December 1787]

My dear Chevalier,

You are welcome to your native country, and you are in an eminent manner welcome to me as my dear fellow laborer in historical collections relative to the ancient state of this island. My essays are still a *rudis* and *indigesta moles;*[1] I am retarded by my rheumatic infirmity and indeed by domestic avocations, but, if God spares me life, I strongly purpose to throw my deranged notes into some form. I want help greatly and I depend much on your sedulity in procuring the Book of Munster so highly extolled by Bishop O'Brien; but more of this hereafter. I have formerly corresponded with a friend on the pedigree of the O'Hagans, corrupted in the name Fagan. My father-in-law, John Fagan, told me that he was of the family of Feltrim. He knew no more. In my documents I find that the O'Hagans were descended from Niall the great, that their estate by the denomination of Tully og was in Tirone, and that they were the hereditary chieftains who assisted at the inauguration of O'Neill of Tirone when elected to provincial dignity. In the filiations of the genealogy, the generations most wanted are not to be found out of this authentic account, defective as it is. Some pedigree may be formed, by *genealogical prudence*, for your friend in France, such as may satisfy the persons with whom Mr. O'Hagan would wish to ally by matrimonial bonds. May you enjoy many happy new years; mine are elapsed, being now completely at the end of seventy-eight years.

1. Ovid, *Metamorphoses*, 1:7. *Rudis indigestaque moles.* "Unformed, disordered mass"; "a chaotic condition."

436. To Edmund Malone

RIA, Stowe MS B1 1a

[February 1788][1]

Sir,

I have your favor of the 28th of January last before me. In the documents I have perused I found that the O'Malones and O'Conors of Conaght were branches of the same family and that the former were established in a part of Breagh Many, an extensive territory in West Meath, of which the country now called King's County formed a part. In that country they continued in power from age to age till the revolutions of latter times (that particularly under Cromwell) had reduced them and the O'Conors to the ranks of private gentlemen. My documents ended with the reign of James I, and I hoped that from the profession of your grandfather and his knowledge consequently from the records in the old rolls he might have supplied by taking notes what related to his own and other families since the period I mentioned. I cannot think but he did so, and more diligent search should be made among his papers. The late Mr. Lodge[2] assured myself of his having a number of documents relating to those latter times in his hands and that he intended to insert the more important transactions of those times in his intended history of the attainted peers; Lodge's papers therefore should be consulted. You notice that the O'Conors who had great property in the country of Roscommon and Sligo on the commencement of the seventh century had [not been rewarded] by titles of nobility from the crown. Among chieftains, who were elective, to an indivisible [unreadable] of domain and therefore [barely?] tenants for life, titles by patent were not admissible nor desirable. The O'Neills of Tyrone and O'Briens of Thom[ond], it is true, accepted titles from the crown, but the former event gave so much offense to the Tyrone clan that Hugh O'Neill to qualify for the Gael of Tyrone was obliged to lay aside the title of Earl, and the creation of the first Earl of Thomond gave so much offense to the O'Briens that it produced tragical events which are specified in the Irish Annals.

In the *Annals of the Four Masters*, the first mention of the recent surname of O'Malone occurs in 1124. He is represented as a chief of great wealth and piety; that he built the noble tower of hewn stone yet standing in Clonmacnois, entered into the monastic order, and died abbot of that city 1127. The surname of O'Malone must begin with his grandfather or great grandfather, for the surnames included were not earlier than the eleventh century. For 500 years at least that family continued in the chieftainship of their territory in Breagh Mowr, and since the succession of James I they continued possessed of good estates in their country to this day.

[Hand almost unreadable—rheumatic?]

    1. This letter is an undated fragment, but it answers Edmund Malone's letter of 28 January 1788. CFmH, Stowe Coll., O'Conor MS. Malone asked where the name O'Malone first appeared in the Irish annals; this letter is obviously O'Conor's answer.
    2. John Lodge (d. 1774), archivist.

437. To Joseph C. Walker, Treasury Chambers, Dublin Castle

PSPL, Gilbert MS 203

From my Hermitage, 16 February 1788

... I now, as well as I can, discharge the debt of gratitude I owe you both for recommending my grandson in Rome (to the principals of our Royal Academy) as one qualified to make a search in the Vatican and other Roman archives relative to some parts of the history of this island which lie still in the dark and may involve some useful information, if discovered....

... I shall punctually observe your directions as to the receipt you require, and relative to the two guineas I trouble you with you'll, by inspection into the Academy register, learn when the time of payment will become due....

438. To Joseph C. Walker, Treasury Chambers, Dublin Castle

PSPL, Gilbert MS 203

28 February 1788

... Of the defaced monument in Roscommon I can satisfy you with a faithful account. The Abbey was built in 1253 by Felim O'Conor, King of Conaght, the son of Cathal Crovedarg and nephew of unfortunate Roderic. After a very active life he died in 1265. Over his place of interrment on the Gospel side of the great altar, he is represented in marble stretched horizontally in a monastic habit with the figure of an otter at his feet. His guard stood about him in the military habit of the times, not unlike our Battleax Guards of Dublin Castle. In a drunken quarrel those guards were pulled down lately and scattered about as remains of Popish superstition, but a good draft may still be taken of those figures, as a few are entire. I have not heard a word of our learned friend the Reverend Mr. Beauford since he parted this country. In his topography he will be much assisted by Mr. Archdall's *Monasticon.* When you meet those gentlemen, I request of you to present them with my affection. I thank you warmly for discharging the annual debt I owe to our Royal Academy. I trust that no member is in arrears to it. . . .

439. To Joseph C. Walker, Treasury Chambers, Dublin Castle

PSPL, Gilbert MS 203

[c. March 1788][1]

. . . By the statutes of his College my grandson cannot remain in Rome longer than the ensuing month of July next unless licensed by the Roman court, a dispensation which would doubtless be granted by the smallest application from the President of our Academy, formerly much esteemed when resident in Rome. Colonel Vallancey has been kind enough to represent me to our popular Lord Lieutenant as one not unworthy of his Excellency's patronage.[2] His recommendation had weight; and yet as I know that several suitors among the learned had a much better right to his Excellency's bounty than I could pretend to and that I am enfeebled by age and infirmity, I have in a grateful letter to our friend besought him to think again on this matter before I should hereafter, from my inability, bring any discredit on his recommendation. Let me have your judgment, my dear friend, on the subject; and when you meet the Colonel, you'll please to expose my fears to him. I lately received from my friend Dr. Archer of Stephen's Street the first volume of the *Transactions* of our Academy. The mathematical and medical parts are, I doubt not, very excellent. In the parts relating to polite literature, Dr. Slack has acquitted himself admirably on *sublimity in writing.* Dr. Burrows makes objections to some parts of Dr. Johnson's style of writing. The instances he uses are, I think, just; but I can not but think also that the spots which the telescopical eye of criticism discovers in his style are lost in the blaze of his perfections as a phraseologist and a philosopher. —I am much pleased with my Lord

Bishop of Killala's *Enquirey into the Original of the Scots*.³ It will help greatly to recommend the essays now in my hands on that subject. . . .

    1. No date. However, the editors believe this letter to Walker was written near the date of a letter from Charles Vallancey to Charles O'Conor, 28 February 1788, CFmH, Stowe Coll. O'Conor MS. Both letters discuss Vallancey's proposal to the Lord Lieutenant that he grant O'Conor a pension.
    2. The Lord Lieutenant, the Marquis of Buckingham, Vallancey wrote, "was ready to comply with cheerfulness to any reasonable proposal I should make. 'Then, my Lord, give him instantly a pension of one hundred pounds per annum'—'You may this night assure your friend that if he will secure to you or the Irish Academy in case of death, etc., his papers, that I will settle the pension on him without delay—advise him to pack them up and come to town as soon [he can] and I shall be glad to confirm with my own lips what I have said.'"
    3. Dr. Thomas Barnard (See letter 407) was a former Dean of Derry and a longtime friend of O'Conor's. The full title of Barnard's book was *Enquirey into the Origin (al) of the Scots in Britain*. O'Conor should have written bishop of *Killaloe*, not Killala.

440. To Colonel Charles Vallancey

OCD, 8.4 HL 164

27 March 1788

. . . Your friendship is surely boundless, and my gratitude is equally so for the favorable impression you gave of me to our worthy chief Governor, who happily has brought halcyon days along with him into our island. To merit his Excellency's patronage would be my first ambition; my next would be to do some justice to your partiality. This species of merit derived from intellectual abilities would be superior under good direction to the advantages of power and fortune, such as my ancestors were formerly possessed of in this western province.

I trust that good weather will enable me to shake off some of my rheumatic chains and that before the end of the ensuing month I may have the pleasure of paying you a visit at Milltown at the seventy-ninth year of my age. I have but a short time to live; when the event of my dissolution comes about, I shall leave you all my Irish manuscripts in trust for the library of our Royal Irish Academy. . . .

441. To Chevalier Thomas O'Gorman, No. 9 Jervas Street, Dublin

BM, Add. MS 21121

9 May 1788

... The book you mention (the work of an ancient Greek historian) would be a valuable acquisition and a decisive proof that our earliest traditions are not (as to material points) the fictions of senachies after the establishment of the Gospel among us. You (a fortunate collector of perishing or unknown documents) will, I am positive, procure us a copy of old *Scymnus Chius*.[1] ...

> 1. Scymnus of Chio. Hyde, p. 6n. quotes a passage from Scymnus in Greek. Hyde further says, "Greek writers of the fourth century speak of Celts as practicing justice, of having nearly the same manners and customs as the Greeks. . . ."

442. To Joseph C. Walker, Treasury Chambers, Dublin Castle

PSPL, Gilbert MS 203

From my Hermitage, 16 July 1788

... My grandson makes mention of a countryman of ours of the name of Heutson, one of the best sculptors now alive and now employed on a statue in marble of the celebrated philosopher *Leibnitz*. It would be a credit to his country if our nobility and gentry invited this native home and gave him employment. You had a letter from Salviati (a Roman Academist, I suppose). My grandson would wish to know if you published that letter. He asks also some intelligence about Ferrar, who published the history of Limerick, and whether anything has transpired about the Pope's letter to him? In the history of the Papacy such a correspondence is truly singular from a Roman Pontiff to a Protestant bookseller, little known at home. Such a humiliation is edifying, though to others it will perhaps appear ridiculous. . . .

443. To Joseph C. Walker, Treasury Chambers, Dublin Castle

PSPL, Gilbert MS 203

From my Hermitage, 30 October 1788

... To think honestly and at the same time erroneously may be, and often must be, the lot of numbers; but error and/or the correction of universal benevolence can never harm society; under the direction of knowledge, benevolence forms the sublime in life, especially when attended with power such as the late Earl Nugent proposed.[1] Through a course of sixty years I have attended to him from his first motions as Bob Nugent of Carlonstown to the last as a noble man of the first distinction. He threw luster back on an illustrious ancestry, often, however, ill treated by English and Irish through a course of 350 years. They placed their glory in moderation between two jealous parties, each claiming and each rejecting their best friends, occasionally, through the vicissitudes of domestic animosities. One of his Lordships's ancestors lamented the public misfortune in a fine Irish couplet. Between these parties, said he, we the Nugents are sufferers by both. We resemble an apple tossed on the sea surges. But this apple braved the waves, and no storm could sink it. To do good, public and private, was Earl Nugent's passion through life; genius under the spur of activity supplied him with the means; he was one of the best friends to his native country that this island ever produced, and he left us a legacy in our most excellent Viceroy to operate as it were posthumously for the good of a people now united in a single creed of loyalty and constitutional politics. . . .

1. Robert Nugent (1702–1788). Born in Westmeath, he was brought up as a Roman Catholic but conformed to the Established Church. Created Earl Nugent 1776. *Concise DNB* 1:958; Crone, p. 170.

444. To Denis O'Conor

OCD, 8.4 SE 148

[c. November 1788][1]

Your intended *letter* of this date to Mr. D[olphi]n[2] is as polite as the subject can bear. In my mind, it virtually implies a departure or rather a dismiss of the treaty concluded upon between you and him. To justify this conduct on your part, you assign intricate matters which occurred. Such articles agreed upon were put into a form of law. Are those intricate points to be found in your lawyer's draft. If they are obvious in that draft, Mr. D[olphi]n will probably consent to remove the difficulty to your satisfaction, etc. I say this because Mr. D[olphin] may inform you by letter that he will thus satisfy you. . . .

1. See Dunleavy and Dunleavy, p. 37, OCD SE 0239.
2. Mr. John Dolphin. In letters to his father Denis, Owen refers to the prospects of marriage to Miss Dolphin and to Miss Byrne, but he tells his father that he has decided to marry Miss Jane Moore. The marriage took place on 20 June 1792. Charles is obviously advising his son Denis on a diplomatic way to break off the engagement for which Heads of Matrimonial Treaty had been prepared. Dunleavy and Dunleavy, pp. 33, 37, 41; OCD SE 8.4 004, SE 029, SE 048.

445. To Chevalier Thomas O'Gorman, No. 9 Jervas Street, Dublin

BM, Add. MS 21121

26 May 1789

My dear Chevalier,

Your late kind letter found me in the worst situation I have experienced in the course of sixty years; since Palm Sunday I have been confined to my cell, laboring under acute pains and fatigued by restless nights; my rheumatic complaints descended into my legs, ankles and feet. Wholly deprived of the power of standing up or walking, it is only by a continuance of taking Peruvian bark that within a few days I have had the power of walking a little. But thrown out of my own habits of life, my appetite is gone, nor can I digest any animal food but in very small quantities; writing is very painful to me from weakness in my right arm. It is a warning, my dear Chevalier, and God grant I may make the proper use of it.

I once had a good drawing of the arms and inscriptions of the monument of O'Conor of Sligo in the Dominican Abbey of that town. It is now in the hands of the Reverend Mr. Mervin Archdall, author of the *Irish Monasticon,* and if that gentleman has not mislaid it, he can furnish you with a copy of it. At present I know not of any man in Sligo skilled in taking a copy of the original.

Relative to the family of Castleplunket, I could give you (were I not idle) a good account as I was intimate with the owner of that place, the worthy Captain James Plunkett, with his brother, Counselor John

Plunkett, the father of the late general with whom I was also well acquainted. The Captain was first married to Elizabeth MacGennis, the Lord Iveagh's daughter; and his brother the Counselor was married to Briget Fitzgerald, the daughter of—Fitzgerald of Skullockstown in the county of Kildare; that lady (General Plunkett's mother) I knew well, but I knew not in what year she and her husband died. I had like to forget informing you that Captain James Plunkett and his brother John were the sons of Patrick Plunkett of Castleplunkett Esquire and of—Talbot of Castleruby in the County of Roscommon, a near kinsman of the noble family of Talbot. This is a meager account, but you'll find a much fuller one from documents, collected I believe by General Plunkett himself in his last visit to Ireland.

If I can recover my spirits, I shall sit down to finish the arrangement I have been making of the materials I have been long collecting relative to the ancient state of politics, manners, and religion in this island. Personal avocations have much retarded my progress, and the time before me is rather too short for one now in his eightieth year.

446. To Ralph Owsley[1]

OCD, 8.4 SO 165

[?1789]

Sir,

The crazy state of my health and the increase of my rheumatic pains for six days past prevented a grateful reply immediately to your very kind letter of the 27th of September.[2] I now with a shaking hand, recognize my singular obligation to you, for singular it is, undoubtedly, from your inquiry about my family and studies. I should not have a stronger proof of your kindness, for it is such as must supersede the reluctance one ought to have in mentioning his ancestors but himself in particular.

My great grandfather Charles was the third son of Sir Hugh O'Conor Don of Ballintobber, a chieftain, who for his activity in the service of Queen Elizabeth received from her the honor of military knighthood and who with the other chiefs of Conaght had in 1535 compounded by indenture for their estates with Lord Deputy Perrot.[3] Of these compositions the originals are still to be found in our [unreadable] office. Said Hugh O'Conor Don married Mary O'Rouark, the daughter of Bryan naMurtha O'Rouark, chieftain of the western Brefny, now called the county of Letrim, and said O'Ruark, being accused of high treason was tried and condemned by a London jury. For his trial, condemnation, and execution in 1591, I refer you to Camden's *History of Queen Elizabeth*. Hugh O'Conor Don died in Ballintobber in 1632 in the ninety-first year of his age. He willed his estates to his four sons by Mary O'Ruark, but through the several revolutions since his time, little now remains except about nine hundred acres now in possession of Dominick O'Conor Don of Clonalis and nearly as much by myself here in Belanagare. This is surely too much on this subject, but relative to a meager subject I must be brief. I was born on the 1st of January 1709/10. To the best of fathers, Denis O'Conor, I owe my being instructed in grammar, learning by such school-masters as this country could afford. At the age of seventeen I had better fortune by being sent to Dublin and put to the care of Mr. Walter Skelton, a learned and worthy man. In his academy I was instructed in the Latin tongue and initiated in the elements of mathematical learning. Under this same master I also picked up as much French as enabled me to understand that language in books; but I was never in the habit of conversing in it. My father was married in 1706 to Mary, daughter of Colonel Dermot O'Ruark, grand nephew to Brian naMurtha, above mentioned, who followed the fortunes of the late King James, entered into the French service, and was killed at the Battle of Luzara, July 1702. This daughter, my mother, died in Belanagare, December 22, 1760, and was buried in our family tomb in Ballintobber. My father died in 1750, aged seventy-six. I am the eldest of his sons and was bred a farmer. I was myself married to Catherine O'Hagan the daughter of John O'Hagan of Abbey Boyle, merchant, and of the family Hagan of Tullyboy in the county of Tirone. My dear wife died November 11, 1741, and was buried at Ballintobber. She left me two sons, Denis and Charles. The former is in possession of Belanagare, [and] is the father of six sons by Catherine Browne of Galway. My second is a farmer of good property.

    1. Ralph Owsley of Limerick. See "Dedication" in J. C. Walker's *Historical Memoirs of the Irish Bards* (1786).
    2. Incorrectly dated in another hand 22 October 1729. Internal evidence indicates that this letter was probably written in 1789.
    3. O'Conor is mistaken here. The Composition of Connacht took place in 1585. John Perrot was Lord Deputy of Ireland from 1584 to 1588.

447. To Brigadier Thomas O'Conor[1]

OCD, 8.4 SO 166

Belanagare, 14 November 1789

My Dear Cousin,

The share you ever had in my affections was what it should be and indeed it increased gradually; with your own fame you brought credit to our whole family through a series of honorable and unwearied conduct, and you received nothing from the family but a name which a different conduct from yours would have disgraced. I am happy in hearing that you enjoy good health in your honorable retreat. On my side I am worn out by rheumatic pains which stuck to me with very little intermission for five years past. And as I have completed the eightieth year of my age, the time before me must be very short. This probably may be my last letter to any friend of mine on the continent. Before I conclude I have the pleasure of informing you that your nephew, the present O'Conor Don, is a very worthy and religious person and a fast friend to me, but it grieves me to tell you that his health for some time past has been on the decline. This letter may possibly be put into your hands by my grandson Roderick O'Conor, a youth who lately took on in Dillon's Regiment. His intentions are good and his morals blameless. How fortune will dispose of him cannot be foreseen, but your recommendation of him and acknowledging him one of your family will doubly render him very important service in France or Spain or Austria. We are informed here that the foreign troops in the French service will be dismissed as soon as the perfect reform of political legislation in France is completed. May God preserve you for doing good in this world as the best preparation for the next.

1. Brigadier O'Conor was the brother of Daniel O'Conor Don of Clonalis and uncle of Dominick. See Charles Owen O'Conor, *O'Conors of Connaught*, Table IV. See also Dunleavy and Dunleavy, p. 59, OCD 8.4 SE 182.

448. To Bishop Edward French[1]

RIA, Stowe MS B1 1a

1 May 1790

Most Reverend Sir,

After passing the eightieth year of a life checkered with many crosses well-known, I at length found consolation in my present solitude from the apparent good conduct of my children and grandchildren. Such a blessing threw a ray of comfort in the few days I have to life. This comfort has been greatly abated by your Lordship's letter of the 26th ultimo, importing that the pastor you lately inducted into the parish of Killkevin has not acquitted himself entirely to your satisfaction.[2] I rest, however, satisfied that your Lordship was ill informed in regard to him. He has good wishes and indeed the affection of most reputable persons of every denomination in that parish. He knows his duty and happily keeps that duty under the government of Christian humility, obedience to his superiors, and an attention to giving good example to all persons. I trust that through your own inspiration he will every day more and more make the impression on you which is so requisite to a minister and which you expect from a teacher of the gospel. By uniting my hopes to my wishes and under the aid of knowledge as far as I could obtain it, your Lordship will not disapprove.

R.M.D., a youth of little knowledge of the world, may be unguarded like other youths, by publishing or repeating those tales he hears in the world; folly is here joined with ignorance, what is worse a charge that can not be supported becomes criminal. Even the most ignorant who fear dying wish good from God. An untruth injurious to your Lordship's character and dignity can not be dropped lightly, and exemplary reparations should be made and that as soon as possible by confronting and examining the party or parties making the several charges and the parties on whom it is incumbent to refute those charges. MacDermot is ready to go in his defense as soon as your Lordship calls upon him to do it.

As to what you heard of Father Clarke and myself, your informer deceived you or was perhaps deceived himself. Mr. C[larke] served me with Mass for a short time. He was called to a more urgent duty and he complied as he ought to do, and I (thanks to the Almighty) have been able since that time to walk or rather creep afoot to the chapel of Belanagare to attend at Mass on Sundays and H[oly] days.

I desist from writing more on subjects disagreeable to your Lordship and extremely disagreeable to myself (who write with a paralytic hand) till we meet, God willing, soon and shift the contents of your Lordship's letter of the 26th of April last from controversy to a fair detection of facts.

 1. Bishop Edward French, bishop of Elphin 13 February 1787 to 29 April 1810. *HBC*, p. 409.
 2. If Giovanni Costigan is correct, the unsatisfactory curate was Dr. French's nephew, a Mr. Tonry. See Costigan, pp. 34ff.

449. To Joseph C. Walker, Treasury Chambers, Dublin

PSPL, Gilbert MS 203

From my Hermitage, 5 May 1790

My dear Sir,

It pains me that you are obliged at present to fly to the mountains for the physic of goats, but I rejoice that you are benefited by it. Happily you live in the prime of life, and I am satisfied that air and exercise will share with those physicians in your re-establishment. My malady is incurable after a course of eighty years, and the attacks upon me are so severe that I am confident the thread of life is nearly spun out. For six weeks past I have been so racked by acute rheumatic pains that (from a disability in my right shoulder) I could not write with a legible hand to acknowledge the favors of friends to whom I am bound by lasting obligations. You are one of the number, and I now remit you my warmest thanks for your kind letter of the 24th ultimo and for the envelope wherein you enclosed the celebrated parliamentary speeches of our two countrymen, Mr. Flood and Mr. Burke. The reasonings of the former can not be overturned; those of the latter may be just, but they are not on the popular side of the question; and it may be possible that the French National Assembly may form a salutary Code of legislation before the end of their session. Enough of this.

To consider a more interesting subject to an Irishman, some of our elections here and in Ulster are carried on with some animosity; but I hope that our apprehensions and jealousies will not continue and that our new House of Commons will chiefly consult the good of their country preferable to all other considerations, for the means of our prosperity are obvious. Other points of no immediate concern to us yet deserve a retrospect, and I confess to you that I have been pained and ashamed at the ungenerous attacks on my learned friend Colonel Vallancey, who by his writings has opened new and effulgent lights on the antiquities of this country. His adversaries have nibbled at some of his etymologies of oriental and Irish terms, some of which may not stand the test as in some etymologies of the learned Selden[1] and learned Bochart[2] In a great number of such outworks some may not be tenable, but some are strong and particularly the interior forts in respect to those two great antiquaries are impregnable; at least no artillery of criticism has hitherto made any impression upon them. The interior forts erected by Colonel Vallancey have not been yet attacked, and to demolish them should be the task of his adversaries. Indeed they will find it a hard one and must understand the old language of this country and old writings still preserved in it before they can be admitted to a hearing at the bar of criticism. What has the Colonel done? He has shown that the first colonies who took possession of this island were of Scythian extraction, not from the wild Hyperborean Scythians who roamed through the countries bordering on the Baltic Sea but from the oriental Scythians who in early times roamed from the confines of the Euxine sea and spread themselves in several hordes over the countries of Persia, Chaldea, Phoenicia, Egypt, Libya and, skilled in the art of sailing, made some establishments in the west of Spain and from thence emitted some swarms which obtained a recess on the western coasts of Gaul, Germany, and eastern coasts of Britain, from whence some of their hordes by the names of Nemedes, Belgian, and DeDanans[3] entered Ireland and settled here. Finally, the Colonel has shown that a fresh colony of Scythians from Spain subdued this island to their power and continued in power here before the Christian era and for more than eleven hundred years after that. Those Scythians imported hither the elements of literature and arts; and instead of being lost or neglected as in other northern countries, the natives have improved them in favorable conjunctures. Unacquainted with Greek or Roman science, they became a singular people among the northern nations by the improvement of their mental faculties, of which we have a demonstrable proof in the copiousness, regularity, and vigor of their language, replete with terms for their abstract ideas and mixed modes, while the other northern countries were indebted to the Greeks and Romans for such terms on their conversion to Christianity. Those vernacular terms continue in our old writings to the present time and defeat the gratuituous assertion that the heathens of Ireland were savages till the fifth century of Christianity. With great labor Colonel Vallancey has paralleled the earliest tradition of the old Irish with oriental documents. He found the former corresponding in many striking instances with the latter, and he justly rejected the fabulous parts incorporated by the vanity of Irish bards with our more genuine traditions after the introduction of Christianity. I call the traditions genuine because the Colonel has for the greater number supported them by foreign authorities; the other heathen traditions till the erection of the court of Eamania in Ulster are mixed with uncertainty. I could add a great deal more on this subject, but before you come to this last line you must be tired with what I have done, as in truth I am myself heartily tired. I request you'll present my respects to your father and brother, to the Chevalier O'Gorman also when you see him.

P.S. Colonel Vallancey comes frequently to the Castle. I request you'll show him this letter; and should he think it would be any use as a precursor to his intended publication, he may make any alteration he pleases before he sends it to the printer of some newspaper.

 1. John Selden (1584–1654), jurist and orientalist. Wrote *De Diis Syris*, 1617. *Concise DNB*, 1:1176.
 2. Samuel Bochart (1599–1667), French orientalist and divine. Published *Geographia Sacra*, 1746; *Hierozoicon sive de Animalibus Scripturae Sacrae*, 1652. *Chambers Biographical Dictionary*, eds. Wm. Geddie and J. Liddell Geddie. (Edinburgh: W. & R. Chambers, Ltd., 1897), p. 108.
 3. Clann Nemid, FirBolg, Tuatha Dé Danann.

450. To Colonel Charles Vallancey

OCD, 8.4 HS 164

6 August 1790

 I return you my warmest thanks for serving me with a complete copy of the 5th volume of your *Collectanae* under envelopes from Dublin Castle; but I must inform you that your very learned present found me in so languid a state that I was unable to write at the time and that I received much alleviation of my pains from the perusal of your last book. You have exhibited so many proofs of the establishment of an oriental Colony of Scythians in Ireland in early times as must attract the attention of our ablest European antiquaries and quicken their labors on new researches. They will work on the foundations you have laid, benefit by the works you have reared thereon, and close this eighteenth century with a new fabric equally curious and instructive. All this we must owe to your knowledge in oriental literature as well as in our insular writings which have preserved some oriental traits, but which have been lost in Britain and on the continent exposed to many revolutions, while Ireland was exposed to none through a course of many ages. The collection and collation of these forces must distress and oppress your adversaries; but possibly, like other discomfited combatants in literary warfare, they will return to the charge and scratch with their nails when deprived of every other weapon.

Such writers, no doubt, will derive some advantages from negative arguments. Antiquaries, from the nature of their object, must sometimes work in a kind of visible darkness, and many will lose their way even in the twilight. It is only when they confront foreign languages and compare the facts [discovered] in those languages (without any communications between the speakers and recorders for a great number of ages) that modern antiquaries will be enabled to battle the combatants I speak of. Thus Bochart, thus you, sir, have had successes, though in a multitude of facts of little consequence; each of you will be found to mistake in a few particulars. But this is losing nothing as your facts are impregnable.

THE KNOWN WORKS OF CHARLES O'CONOR

"An Account of the Author," in John Curry's *An Historical and Critical Review of the Civil Wars in Ireland from the Reign of Queen Elizabeth to the Settlement under King William. With the State of Irish Catholics from That Settlement to the Relaxation of the Popery Laws in 1778*. London: G. G. J. and J. Robinson; J. Murray, 1786. 2 vols. KU.
———. Dublin: Luke White, 1786. 2 vols. BMCPBCE, 6:745.
———. A New and Improved Edition, ed. Charles O'Conor, with Notes by the Duke of Sussex. Dublin: R. Connolly, 1810. BMCPBCE, 6:745.
An Account of the Nature and Conditions of a Charter to be Granted for the Working and Manufacturing Mines and Minerals in Ireland; Together with Some General Heads Relating to the Advantages That Must Necessarily Result from that Laudable Establishment. In a Letter to the Honourable Lord Southwell. London: n.p., 1754. GM, 61:776.
The Case of the Roman Catholics. Dublin: Patrick Lord, 1755. DJ, 21/6/55.
The Cottager's Remarks on "The Spirit of Party." Dublin: n.p., 1754. IU.
A Counter-Appeal to the People of Ireland. Dublin: n.p., 1749. ICN.
The Dangers of Popery to the Present Government Examined. Dublin: George Faulkner, 1761. DJ, 15/12/61.
Dedication: "To the Lords and Gentlemen of the Volunteer Associations of Ireland." in Thomas Sheridan's *A General Dictionary of the English Language*. Dublin: Pat Wogan, 1784. IU.
Dissertations on the Antient History of Ireland. Dublin: James Hoey, 1753. IU.
Dissertations on the History of Ireland. To Which is Subjoined a Dissertation on the Irish Colonies Established in Britain with Some Remarks on Mr. MacPherson's Translation of "Fingal" and "Temora." Dublin: George Faulkner, 1766. IaU.
———. 3rd edition. Dublin: J. Christie, 1812. IU, KU.
Essay on the Ancient and Modern State of Ireland with the Various Important Advantages Thereunto Derived under the Auspicious Reign of His Most Sacred Majesty, King George the Second. Dublin: Patrick Lord, 1760. DJ, 1/3/60; BMCPBCE, 13:27.
"A Letter to David Hume, on Some Misrepresentations in His History of Great Britain," *Gentleman's Museum* (April–May, 1763), pp. 55–64; pp. 65–78. CtY.
Maxims Relative to the Present State of Ireland. Humbly Submitted to the Legislative Powers. Dublin: n.p., 1757. BMCPBCE, 13:29.
With John Curry. *Observations on the Popery Laws*. Dublin: Thomas Ewing, 1771. IU.
———. Dublin: n.p., 1772. BMCPBCE, 18:976.

O'Flaherty, Roderick. *Ogygia Vindicated against the Objections of Sir George MacKenzie* . . . , ed. Charles O'Conor. Dublin: George Faulkner, 1775. IU.

"On the Heathen State and Ancient Topography of Ireland," in Vol. 4, *Collectanea de Rebus Hibernicis*, ed. Charles Vallancey. Dublin: Charles Vallancey, 1783. *BMCPBCE*, 18:976.

"Preface" to John Curry's *Historical Memoirs*. . . . Dublin: n.p., 1758. RCHM-8a, 450.

"Preface," to *The Speech Delivered by R. Jephson . . . In the Debate on the Committing of Heads of a Bill for the 'Better Encouragement of Persons Professing the Popish Religion to Become Protestants.'* Dublin: n.p., 1774. *BMCPBCE*, 18:976.

The Principles of the Roman Catholics, Exhibited. Dublin: Patrick Lord, 1756. *DJ*, 6/7/56.

"To the Printer of the *London Chronicle*," *London Chronicle* (30 August 1763). RIA, Stowe MS. Bil.

Proposals for the Printing by Subscription, Ogygian Tales, or a Curious Collection of Irish Fables, Allegories, and Histories. Dublin: Oliver Nelson, 1743. RIA, Stowe MS. Bil.

The Protestant Interest Considered Relatively to the Operation of the Popery Laws in Ireland. Dublin: Patrick Lord, 1756. *BMCPBCE*, 13:30; *DJ*, 29/10/57.

Reflexions on Our Present Critical Situation in a Letter from a Landed Proprietor. Dublin: Pat Wogan, 1777. *LCOC*, 4/10/77.

———. London: T. Caddell, 1777. *BMCPBCE*, 21:299; *LCOC*, 10/6/77.

"Reflexions on the History of Ireland during the Times of Heathenism, with Observations on Some Publications on that Subject," in *Collectanea de Rebus Hibernicis*, ed. Charles Vallancey. Dublin: Charles Vallancey, 1770. *BMCPBCE*, 18:976.

———. Reprinted in Vol. 4, *Collectanea de Rebus Hibernicis*, ed. Charles Vallancey, Dublin: Charles Vallancey, 1783. *BMCPBCE*, 18:976.

"Remarks on an *Essay on the Antiquity of the Irish Language* . . . Addressed to the Printer of the *London Chronicle* . . . in 1772," printed with Charles Vallancey's *An Essay on the Antiquity of the Irish Language*. 3rd ed. London, n.p., 1818. *BMCPBCE*, 25:1049.

Seasonable Thoughts Relating to Our Civil and Ecclesiastical Constitution. Wherein Is Considered the Case of the Professors of Popery. Dublin: George Faulkner, 1751. *DJ*, 12/10/51.

———. Dublin: George Faulkner, 1754. Cul Bradshaw; *DJ*, 2/2/54.

"A Short View of the Ancient State of Ireland from the Earliest Times to the Establishment of the Tuathalian Constitution." Publication unknown. Internal evidence in the correspondence leads the editors to believe this article became part of Charles Vallancey's *Collectanea de Rebus Hibernicis* for either 1773 or 1774. *LCOC*, 25/9/73.

Statistical Account of the Parish of Kilronan in Ireland and of the Neighbouring District. Dublin: n.p., 1773. *BMCPBCE*, 18:976.

———. Edinburgh, n.p., 1798. *BMCPBCE*, 18:976.

"Third Letter on the Pagan State of Ireland . . . ," In *Collectanea de Rebus Hibernicis*, ed. Charles Vallancey. Dublin: Charles Vallancey, 1786. *BMCPBCE*, 18:976.

Touchet, James, Lord Audley and Earl of Castlehaven. *Memoirs*, ed. Charles O'Conor. London, n.p., 1753. *BMCPBCE*, 18:976.

Vindication of Lord Taaffe's Civil Principles in a Letter to the Author of the Pamphlet Entitled "Lord Taaffe's Observations on the Affairs of Ireland Examined and Confuted." Dublin: George Faulkner, 1768. *DJ*, 26/12/67.

A Vindication of a Pamphlet Lately Entitled "The Case of the Roman Catholics of Ireland." Dublin: Patrick Lord, 1755. *DJ*. 7/10/55; See CFmH, MS. 1346.

BIBLIOGRAPHY

Primary Sources

Manuscripts

Dublin. Royal Irish Academy. Ashburnham Collection, Stowe MSS. Bi1, Bi1a, Bi2, Bi2a; Sheehan, Catherine, "Charles O'Conor of Belanagare," MS. 13 W 36.
Dublin. Dublin Public Libraries, Central Department, Pearse. Gilbert MS. 203.
Castlerea, County Roscommon. Clonalis House. The O'Conor Don Papers.
London. The British Library, Department of Manuscripts. Additional MS. 21121; Egerton MS. 201, ff. 31–61.
San Marino, California. The Henry Huntington Library and Art Gallery. Stowe Collection, O'Conor MSS. STO 887–892, 1346.
Sheffield, England. Sheffield City Libraries. Wentworth-Woodhouse Muniments, Bk. 1/43.

Published

"Accounts of the Genealogy of Count O'Rourke." *Hibernian Magazine,* 11 (March 1782): 144–148.
Dublin Journal. Irish Newspapers in Dublin Libraries before 1750. Ann Arbor, Michigan: University Microfilms, 1953.
Dublin Journal. Irish Newspapers in Dublin Libraries. Vol. 2. Ann Arbor, Michigan: University Microfilms, 1958.
Edwards, R. Dudley, ed. "Minute Book of the Catholic Association (1770–1793)." *Archivum Hibernicum,* 9 (1942): 3–172.
"A List of the Peers of Ireland with Their Titles-at-Large, Dates of Their Respective Creations, the Blazon of Their Arms and Mottos . . ." *Gentleman's Magazine,* 19 (1749): 587–594.
Ní Chinnéide, Síle. "Dhá Leabhar Nótaí le Séarlas Ó Conchubhair." *Galvia* 1 (1954): 32–41.
O'Conor, Reverend Charles, D.D. *Memoirs of the Life and Writings of the Late Charles O'Conor of Belanagare, Esq., M.R.I.A.* Dublin: J. Mehain, 1796.
The Public Register: Freeman's Journal. Irish Newspapers in Dublin Libraries. Vol. 2. Ann Arbor, Michigan: University Microfilms, 1958.
Ward, Robert E., and Catherine Coogan Ward. *The Letters of Charles O'Conor of Belanagare.* 2 vols. Ann Arbor: University Microfilms International, 1980.

Secondary Sources

Boylan, Henry, ed. *A Dictionary of Irish Biography.* New York: Barnes and Noble, 1978.

British Museum General Catalogue of Printed Books to 1955. Compact ed., 26 vols. New York: Readex Microprint Corporation, 1967.
Burke, Edmund. *Political Miscellanies.* Vol. 3. *The Works of Edmund Burke.* Bohn's Libraries Edition, 8 vols. London: G. Bell and Sons, 1899–1917.
Byrne, Francis. *Irish Kings and High-Kings.* New York: St. Martin's Press, 1973.
Cleeve, Brian, ed. *Dictionary of Irish Writers.* 2nd Series. Vol. 2. Cork: Mercier Press, 1969.
Cochrane, Eric. "Caesar Baronius and the Counter-Reformation." *The Catholic Historical Review,* 66 (January 1980): 55–58.
Cokayne, George Edward. *The Complete Peerage* . . . , rev. Vicary Gibbs *et al.* 2nd ed. 13 vols. Exeter: G. Pollard, 1910–1959.
Copeland, Thomas W., gen. ed. *The Correspondence of Edmund Burke.* 10 vols. Cambridge: The University Press and Chicago: University of Chicago Press, 1928.
Corish, Patrick J. *The Catholic Community in the Seventeenth and Eighteen Centuries.* Dublin: Helicon Limited, 1981.
Costigan, Giovanni. "The Tragedy of Charles O'Conor, an Episode in Anglo-Irish Relations." *American Historical Review,* 49 (October 1943–July 1944): 32–54.
Craig, Maurice, *Dublin 1660–1860.* Dublin: Allen Figgis, 1960; Riverrun Books, 1969.
Crone, John S., ed. *A Concise Dictionary of Irish Biography.* Dublin: Talbot Press, 1928.
Curtis, Edmund. *A History of Ireland.* New York: D. Nostrand, 1936.
Daniel, Stephen H. *John Toland, His Methods, Manners, and Mind.* Montreal: McGill–Queens University Press, 1984.
Dolley, Michael. *Anglo-Norman Ireland.* The Gill History of Ireland. Vol. 3. Gen. eds. James Lydon and Margaret MacCurtain. Dublin: Gill and Macmillan, 1972.
Dunleavy, Gareth and Janet. *The O'Conor Papers, A Descriptive Catalog and Surname Register of the Materials at Clonalis House.* Madison: University of Wisconsin Press, 1977.
Edwards, Ruth Dudley. *An Atlas of Irish History.* London: Methuen, 1973.
Ellis, Peter Berresford. *Hell or Connaught! The Cromwellian Colonisation of Ireland 1652–1660.* New York: St. Martin's Press, 1975.
Enciclopedia Italiana di Scienze, Lettere, ed Arti. 35 vols. Roma: Instituto della Enciclopedia Italiana, 1949.
Gallagher, Seán F. *The Life and Works of Henry Brooke (1703–1783).* Ph.D. dissertation. National University of Ireland. 1966.
Gilbert, John T. "Correspondence and Mss. of Charles O'Conor of Belanagare, Co. Roscommon, The O'Conor Don, D.L., Clonalis, Co. Roscommon." *Appendix to the Eighth Report.* London: Royal Commission on Historical Manuscripts, 1881.
———. "The Streets of Dublin." *Irish Quarterly Review,* 2 (June 1852): 284–347.
———. "The Streets of Dublin." *Irish Quarterly Review,* 3 (March 1853): 17–50.
———. "The Streets of Dublin." *Irish Quarterly Review,* 3 (September 1853): 541–625.
Hayes, Richard. *Biographical Dictionary of Irishmen in France.* Dublin: M. H. Gill, 1949.

Hoefer, M. Le Dr., ed. *Nouvelle Biographie Générale depuis les Temps le Plus Récules jusqu'à nos Jours*. 46 vols. Paris: Firmin Didot Frères, Editeurs, 1855.
Horace. *Satire and Epistles*, trans. Smith Palmer Bovie. Chicago: University of Chicago Press, 1959; Phoenix Books, 1963.
Hume, David. *The History of England*. . . . 6 vols. New York: Harper Brothers, 1855.
Hyde Douglas. *Literary History of Ireland*. London: Fischer and Unwin, 1899; rpt. London: Ernest Benn, Ltd. and New York: Barnes and Noble, 1967.
Johnston, Edith Mary. *The Eighteenth Century*. The Gill History of Ireland, vol. 8. Dublin: Gill and Macmillan, 1974.
Lecky, William Edward Hartpole. *A History of Ireland in the Eighteenth Century*. 5 vols. London: Longmans, Green, 1892; rpt. New York: AMS Press, 1969.
Lee, Sir Sidney, ed. *The Concise Dictionary of National Biography*. vol. 1 2nd ed. London: Oxford University Press, 1969.
Love, Walter. "Charles O'Conor of Belanagare and Thomas Leland's 'Philosophical' History of Ireland." *Irish Historical Studies* 12 (1962); 1–25.
———. "Edmund Burke and an Irish Historiographical Controversy." *History and Theory* 2 (1962): 180–198.
MacEoin, Gearóid, ed. Edward O'Reilly. *A Chronological Account of Nearly Four Hundred Irish Writers*. . . . Dublin: Iberno-Celtic Society, 1820; rpt. New York: Barnes and Noble, 1970.
MacLysacht, Edward. *Irish Families*. New York: Crown Publishers, 1972.
MacNeill, Eoin. *Celtic Ireland*. Dublin: Martin Lester, Ltd., and London: Leonard Parsons, Ltd., 1921.
Madden, Richard Robert. *The History of Irish Periodical Literature from the End of the Seventeenth Century to the Middle of the Nineteenth Century*. 2 vols. Dublin: T. C. Newby, 1867; rpt. New York: Johnson Reprint Corporation, 1968.
Maxwell, Constantia. *Dublin under the Georges 1714–1830*. London: George Harrap, 1936; rpt. London: Faber and Faber, 1956.
O'Connell, Maurice R. *Irish Politics and Social Conflict in the Age of the American Revolution*. Philadelphia: University of Pennsylvania Press, 1965.
O'Conor Don, Charles Owen. *The O'Conors of Connaught, an Historical Memoir*. Dublin: Hodges, Figgis, 1891.
O'Conor, Charles, S.J. *The Early Life of Charles O'Conor (1710–1791) of Belanagare, the Beginning of the Catholic Revival in Ireland in the Eighteenth Century*. M.A. Thesis. University College Dublin, (1934).
———. "Charles O'Conor of Belanagare: An Irish Scholar's Education" and "An Irish Scholar's Education, Part Two: A Visit to Dublin." *Studies* (Dublin) 23 (1934): 124–43, 455–469.
———. "Origins of the Royal Irish Academy." *Studies* 38 (1949): 325–337.
Ó Corráin, Donncha. *Ireland Before the Normans*. The Gill History of Ireland, vol. 2. Gen. eds. James Lydon and Margaret MacCurtain. Dublin: Gill and Macmillan, 1972.
O'Halloran, Sylvester. *A General History of Ireland*. 2 vols. London: A. Hamilton, 1778.
O'Hart, John. *The Irish and Anglo-Irish Landed Gentry*. Dublin: M. H. Gill and Son, 1884; rpt. New York: Barnes and Noble, 1969.
Ó Raifeartaigh, T. *The Royal Irish Academy: A Bicentennial History, 1785–1985*. Dublin: The Royal Irish Academy, 1985.
O'Sullivan, Donal. *Carolan, the Life, Times, and Music of an Irish Harper*. 2 vols. London: Routledge and Kegan Paul, 1958.

Peardon, Thomas Preston. *The Transition in English Historical Writings, 1760–1830.* New York: Columbia University Press, 1933.
Peerage Chart for 1821: Scotch and Irish Peers. London: Shackell and Arrowsmith, 1821.
Plomer, H. R., G. H. Bushnell, and E. R. McC. Dix, eds. *A Dictionary of the Printers and Booksellers Who Were at Work in England, Scotland, and Ireland from 1726 to 1775.* Oxford: The Bibliographical Society, 1933; rpt. Oxford: The Bibliographical Society, 1968.
Powicke, Sir F. Maurice, and E. B. Fryde, eds. *Handbook of British Chronology.* 2nd ed. London: Offices of the Royal Historical Society, 1961.
Redman, Alvin. *The House of Hanover.* New York: Coward-McCann, 1961.
Roche, Richard. *The Norman Invasion of Ireland.* Tralee, Ireland: Anvil Books, 1970.
Ruvigny, Melvill Henry Massue, Marquis de. *The Jacobite Peerage, Baronetage, Knightage, and Grants of Honor.* Edinburgh: T. C. and E. C. Jack, 1904; rpt. London and Edinburgh: Charles Skilton, Ltd., 1974.
Simms, J. G. *The Williamite Confiscations in Ireland, 1690–1703.* Westport, CT; Greenwood Press, 1976.
Sullivan, W. K., ed. *On the Manners and Customs of the Ancient Irish.* Eugene O'Curry, gen. ed. vol. I: *On the Manners and Customs of the Ancient Irish,* 3 vols. Dublin: W. B. Kelly, 1873; rpt. New York: Lemma Publishing Corporation, 1971.
Townsend, Peter, ed. *Burke's Genealogical and Heraldic History of the Peerage, Baronetage, and Knightage.* London: Burke's Peerage, 1967.
Valentine, Alan. *The British Establishment, 1760–1784.* Vol. 2. *The British Establishment.* 2 vols. Norman: University of Oklahoma Press, 1970.
Walker, Joseph Cooper. *Historical Memoirs of the Irish Bards.* Dublin: Luke White, 1786; rpt. New York: Garland Publishing, Inc., 1971.
Wall, Maureen. "The Rise of a Catholic Middle Class in Eighteenth-Century Ireland." *Irish Historical Studies,* 11 (September 1958): 91–115; rpt. J. McCaffrey and Emmet Larkin, gen. eds. Reprints in Irish Studies, History Series, No. 2, from the American Committee for Irish Studies. Chicago: University of Chicago, 1971.
Walsh, Reverend Paul, P.P. "The Ua Maelechlainn Kings of Meath." *The Irish Ecclesiastical Record,* 57 (January–June 1941), 5th Series: 165–183.
Ward, Catherine Coogan and Robert E. *Checklist and Census of 400 Imprints of the Irish Printer and Bookseller, George Faulkner, from 1725–1775.* Sioux City, Iowa: Ragnarok Press, 1973.
———. "The Catholic Pamphlets of Charles O'Conor (1710–1791)." *Studies,* 68 (Winter 1979): 259–264.
———. "The Ordeal of O'Conor of Belanagare." *Eire-Ireland,* 14 (Summer 1979): 6–14.
Ward, Robert. *Prince of Dublin Printers, the Letters of George Faulkner.* Lexington: The University Press of Kentucky, 1972.
Williams, Basil. *The Whig Supremacy.* 2nd ed. Oxford: The Clarendon Press, 1962.
Wrynn, John F., S.J. "Silvester O'Halloran, 1728–1807." *Irish Literary Supplement* III, 2 (Fall, 1984): 59.

INDEX

Numbers in italics indicate that the person is the recipient of the letter. All numerical references are to letter number.

Abbey of Knockmoy, drawings of, 390
"An Account of the Author" (1786), see O'Conor, Charles, Works
An Account of the Nature and Conditions of Charter . . . for the Working and Manufacturing Mines . . . in Ireland . . . (1754), see O'Conor, Charles, Works
Achonry, bishop of, see Kirwan, Patrick Robert, and Egan, Boethius
Adam and Eve's, Franciscan chapel, 231
Addison, Joseph (1672–1719), revised the *Spectator* during publication, 38
An Address . . . to Buckinghamshire (1776), 280; (1779), 324n
An Address . . . to Harcourt (1773), 239; (1775), O'C's criticism of, 280–282
An Address to the King (1727), 64; (1757), 7; (1759), 64, 66, 68; (1760), 79, subscription list for, 80; (1761, the Remonstrance), 81, 82, 85, 86, 88, 111, opposed by Trimleston, 82; (1779), 324; (1786), 418, written by Lord Killeen, John and Michael Keogh, D. T. O'Brien, Charles Ryan, John Comerford, and Frances McDermott, 418n
An Address to the King from Meath, (1761), 88
An Address to the Lord Lieutenant (1772), 237, 239
Admonitions to the Papists of Ireland, O'C throws it aside, 55
Adrian IV, Pope, claims to Ireland treated with contempt even in the twelfth century, 20; claims not to be exculpated, 256
Agriculture, suggestions for reform, 207
Alexander III, King of Scots, senachy's role in coronation, 194
American Revolution, absorbs the public's attention, 207; causes depression in Ireland, 302, 303, 310, 311; Irish Catholics should be regranted Maryland in exchange for their loyalty to England, 295, 297
Andrews, Dr. Francis, Provost of Trinity College; kindness to O'C, 161
Annals of Connacht, contain history of Co. Clare before the Reformation, 166, see O'Conor, Charles, Historical Activities
Annals of the Four Masters, 186, 349, 383, 436; abundant materials for a history of Co. Clare, 166; barren of facts on pagan history, chronology intolerable, 389; see O'Conor, Charles, Historical Activities
Annals of Inisfallen, O'Gorman obtains an unadulterated copy of, 402; Vallencey's copy mangled and interpolated, 384, 389, 400, 402; see O'Conor, Charles, Historical Activities
Annals of Tigernach,. 186, 413; Vallencey's copy defective, Oxford copy to be consulted, 383, 389, 400, 402; see O'Conor, Charles, Historical Activities
Anne, Queen (1665–1714), schemes for the good of Ireland, 213
An Appeal to His Grace the Lord Primate . . . see Curry, John, Works
Aodh Balbh macInreachtaigh, 202
Apostasy, of clergy, 220; of O'C's sister's daughter, 313
Archbold, Curry's uncle, death, the worthiest of men, 55
Archbold, Richard, Curry's cousin, a Jesuit who conformed, Dr. Traill's eulogy for, 180
Archdall, Mervyn (1723–91), antiquarian, Irish *Monasticon,* 398, 411, 418, 438; has O'C's copy of the O'C arms, 445

514   INDEX

Argaroti, a profound thinker, 414
Arran, earl of, Sir Arthur Gore, introduced to O'C by Faulkner, 154
Ascendency, prejudice of, 73
Astle, Thomas (1735–1803), paleographer, O'C's criticism of, 393
Attacolic Wars, 87

Balaam, O'C compares Hume to Balaam's ass, 103
Ballinatown, 334
Ballintober Castle, Alexander O'Conor attempts to regain, 408, 409; O'C family title traced from 1662, 408; Roscommon Catholics censure A. O'C and draw up an address to the viceroy, 408–411
Barnewall, Lord Trimleston's son, conforms to the Church of Ireland, 115
Barnewall, George, see Kingsland, Lord
Barnewall, Nicholas, see Kingsland, viscount
Barnard, Dr. Thomas (1726–1806), Dean of Derry, bishop of Killaloe and Kilfenora, and later of Limerick, Ardfert, and Aghadoe, 407
Baronius, Caesar, historian, 354, 381
Bayle, Pierre (1647–1708), encyclopedist, compared to the bishop of Clogher, 23
Beauford, William of Athy, antiquarian, 416, 433, 438; O'C answers his false representations, 370
Becanus, Martinus, lost himself in the "wilds of etymology," 193
Beccari, unidentified, 343
Bedford, fourth duke of, see Russell, John
Belanagare, 281, 312
Bellew, Sir Patrick, member of the Catholic Committee, 115
Bellewstown Meeting (1781), 351n, 352
Benedict XIV, Pope, 256
Bennett, Tom, 273
Beranger, Gabriel, antiquarian, 343
Beresford, John (1738–1805), Irish M.P., supposed heir to Duggan's manuscripts, 180n
Berkeley, George (1685–1753), bishop of Cloyne, predicts Protestantism will return to Catholicism, 419; his *Querist:* 22; a model for O'C's *Observations on the Popery Laws*, 210n, 211, 213, 219
Bessborough, second earl of, see Ponsonby, William

Bier, witness in the trial of Nicholas Sheeby, 148n
Bingham, Sir Charles, seventh baronet (1735–99), later (1776) first baron and (1795) first earl of Lucan, presents bill for long leases, 221
Birmingham, Roscommon postmaster, shot himself dead, 74
Birmingham, Mrs., boarded Fr. Fitzgerald, 83
Blackstone, Judge, on oaths of allegiance, 270
Blake, Francis Xavier, 380
Bochart, Samuel (1599–1677), 449, 450
Bogland Act, arguments for, 222
Bolingbroke, first viscount (1678–1751), O'C reads his *Dissertations on Parties* . . . , 46
Book of Ballymote, 370, 383, 389, 406, 413; disappearance of, 351; O'C annotates, 351; presented to the Royal Irish Academy by O'Gorman, 400
Book of Lecan, 370, 383, 389, 406; O'Flaherty takes his account from, 87
Book of Munster, 435
Book of Rights, Lebor na cert, 351, 352
Borlase, Sir John, his administration contributed to the Rebellion of 1641, 242
Boswell, James (1740–95), 401; *Tour to the Hebrides*, 405
Bowden, John, chaplain to the lord chancellor, Warner sent him copies of his history, 121
Bowyer, William, Jr., printer, Faulkner contracted with for the Irish rights to Lord Lyttleton's history, 168n; Faulkner received books from, 169n
Brady, James, bishop of Ardagh and Clonmacnoise, 428
Braughall, Thomas (c. 1730–1803), member of the Catholic Committee, 295, 305, 308, 320, 431
Breithe Nemhe, 252
Brett, John, book to be published, 200; frankness of, 199; O'More corresponds with, 197
Brett, Fr., of Rosemary Lane Chapel, 429; a very worthy gentleman, 384
Brian Borovey (Boru, Boramha), 166
Bridge, John, murdered in Munster uprising, 148n
A Brief Account . . . of the Irish Rebellion . . . 1641, see Curry, John, Works, also called *Dialogue*
Brooke, Charlotte, (c. 1740–93), daugh-

INDEX 515

ter of Henry Brooke, captured the spirit of Carolan's "Monody" on Mary, 401, 403
Brooke, Henry (c. 1703–83), the Farmer, bias of the *Freeman's Journal*, 132; discontinues work for the Catholic Committee, 121; discouraged about finishing the *Farmer's Letters*, 77; employed by Wyse for the Catholic Committee, 68; established the *Freeman's Journal*, 130, 132; finishing the *Farmer's Letters*, 77; a hired pen, 94; invites O'C to co-author a history of Ireland, 74, 84; O'C defends Brooke's approach, 70; O'C praises, 403; proposes that the Catholic Committee hire lobbyists, 72; should be paid no matter the price, 81; should be retained by the Catholic Committee, 82, 83; struggling with want, 104; suspected author of *A Counter-Appeal*, 2; a useful tool, 197; Works: *Anthony and Cleopatra*, 97, 104; *Farmer's Letters*, 69, 71, 73, 74, 76, 77; *The Tryal . . .* , 97, 105, 129
Brown, John (1715–66), Whig preacher, 121
Brown, Col. William, may help obtain commissions for O'C's and Curry's sons, 100
Browne, Martin (Denis's father-in-law), his opinion on son Charles's marriage contract, 142; signs an address to the king (1760), 80; 267, 425
Browne, Pat, 267
Browne, Thomas, see Kenmare, fourth viscount
Buckinghamshire, second earl of, see Hobart, John
Bullet, Jean Baptiste, O'C longs to see his *Celtic Dictionary*, 138; Vallancey should encourage him to revise the dictionary, 248
Burke, Edmund (1727–97), *145;* disappointed in Leland's history, 247; a friend of John Ridge, 173n; in favor of Catholic relief, 301; letter to Vallancey sent to O'C, 426, 427; must desert Fox on the question of free trade, 398; parliamentary speech just but unpopular, 449; praises O'C, 377; praises Vesey, 185n; readers extoll in Burke what they would censure in their best friends, 130; receives a pension of £300 a year, 134; refuses the offer of money from the Catholic Committee, 328n; should be recognized in Dublin for his service to Ireland, 421, 424, 427; suggests printing the *Annals* with translations in English and Latin, 388, 389, 392, 428; visits O'C in Dublin, 152; Works: *History of America*, 295; *Speech on Fox's India Bill*, charms but distresses, 403
Burne, Mr., pastor of Castledermot, conforms to the Established Church, 225
Burnet, Gilbert (1643–1715), bishop of Salisbury, Catholics should counter his history, 62; made history subservient to his passions, 230
Burton-Conyngham (Col. Burton), member of Royal Irish Academy, 315, 398, 405; the greatest friend of Ireland in 600 years, 400; O'C's patron, 341, 343; and Seabright's manuscripts, 352
Butler, James, archbishop of Cashel, signs the Parliamentary Test (1774), 274
Butler, *Life of St. Lawrence*, 331; *Lives of the Saints*, subscriptions for, 275
Buxton, James, executed for murder, 148, 149
Byrne, Pat, 386, 392

Caddell, Hugh O'C's landlord, 267
Caddell, Robert, member of the Catholic Committee, 313n, 315
Caddell, Thomas (1742–1802), bookseller, 286, 289
Calmet, Augustin, 354
Campbell, Mr., Catholic priest, death, 165
Campbell, Dr. Thomas (1733–95), historian, 351; claims early Irish are savages, 417; determined to attack ancient Irish manuscripts, 390, 392; discredits history of pre-Norman Ireland, 388; represents the ancient Irish as "the most uncultivated barbarians in Europe," 391; unbiased history of Ireland from the 12th century on, 388
A Candid Inquiry . . . , see Curry, John, Works
Cairbre Riada (Carby), 413, 420, 422
Carolan, Turlogh (1670–1738), "Monody" on Mary, 401; taught O'C to play the harp, 220
Carpenter, Dr. John, archbishop of Dublin, *180, 183, 184, 204, 206, 220, 223, 231, 237, 241, 250, 251, 253, 277, 283, 331, 337–339, 342, 346, 371, 380, 391;* agrees to sign the Parliamentary Test (1774), 310, 311; becomes arch-

Carpenter, Dr. John (*continued*)
bishop of Dublin, 203 n; chides O'C for not writing a history of Ireland, 200; compared to Laurence O'Toole, 237; confined his authority to spiritual government, 391; death, 425 n; desires a better assignment, 168; disrespectful treatment by Catholic Committee, 309; does not visit the Hermitage, 198; elected to the Select Committee, Dublin Society, 243; failure to get advancement, 155, 171, 179, 180; my fast friend, 428; health, 217, 221; illness, 217, 219, 220; instructions on Parliamentary Test (1774), 309; invited to be a corresponding member of the Select Committee, Dublin Society, 240, 241; letters to O'C, 183, 270; O'C expects Carpenter to attend a book sale for him, 179, 201; O'C invites to Belanagare, 177; O'C negotiates with Irish bishops for Carpenter's appointment, 187; O'C writes recommendations for, 185; position on the Parliamentary Test (1774), 270; received at Court, 338; received with great respect by the Select Committee ("in my own days such a man would only be spoken to through the medium of a warrant and constable"), 243, 244; recommends Bishop Egan, 342; recommends grandson Charles for Propaganda Fide, 301; reconciled with Curry, 266; recovering from a dangerous fever, 380; sends O'C trimmings for chest and bookcase, 183, 184; Taaffe requests him as secretary, 165 n; testimonies for Bishop Egan, 274; tries to have established Irish educational centers in Spain and Portugal, 301; virtues entitle him to his office, 205; visits the Hermitage, 199

Carte, Thomas (1686–1752), historian, O'C charmed with his honesty, 52

The Case of the Roman Catholics . . ., see O'C, Charles, Works

Cath Mhaigh Lena, O'C possesses a copy, 385

Catholic Clergy, conformity case, 223, 225; conformity of 241; unlikely to speak out against the Parliamentary Test (1774), 265

Catholic Committee, the first, An Address to Buckinghamshire, 324; An Address to King George II (1756), 7; Address to the King (1759), 63, 64, 66, 68; (1760), 79; subscription list for, 80; (1761, Remonstrance): 81, 82, 85, 86, 88; opposed by Lord Trimleston, 85 n; supported by Taaffe, 82 n; Address to King George III (1779), 324; all-Ireland collection (1762), 101, 116, 117, 121; apathy of, 33, 35, 64, 68, 84; Brooke's proposal to lobby before the Privy Council, 72 n; Curry's and O'C's influence lessens, 132; deserts Curry, 132; denounced by Archbishop Lincoln, 65; despair of, 104; disapproval of Curry's proposal for a test, 15; disintegration of, 130; dissension of, 7, 14, 15, 31, 37, 38, 64, 66–68, 72, 123; dissension caused by Trimleston, 111; disunity of, 63, 66, 83, 95 n, 100, 239; divided over An Address to the King (1761), 81, 82; does not support an address to Townshend (1772), 239; financial affairs: 72, 105 n; causes Lord to lose money, 71; cost of Trimleston's negotiations in London, 111; debts for the *Farmer's Letters,* 73; cannot pay Brooke, 84, 85; Howard requests payment, 132; Daniel O'C requests payment, 135; lack of support by hierarchy, 82; hires Henry Brooke, 69, 83, 140; opposition of Trimleston, 72, 84; perverseness of, 86; response to the Elegit Bill, 97; retains Counselor McNamara, 181; sends Trimleston and Killeen to London, 108; statement of allegiance (1762), 95; Wyse proposes a petition to Parliament, 93

Catholic Committee, the second, foundation under Kenmare (1772), 240; maintains a resident agent in England, 315; National Committee formed, 397; O'C approves of Curry's address to Townshend (1772), 239; an unnamed person proposes an address to the duke of Rutland, 397

Catholic hierarchy, disagrees about an oath (1773), 246; rejects the all-Ireland collection, 116 n

Catholics, disunity of, 266; divided over Parliamentary Test (1774), 270, 271, 274, 279; meet to sign the Test (1774), 269

Case of the Roman Catholics, see O'Conor, Charles, Works

Cashel, archbishop of, see Butler, James

Charlemont, first earl of, James Caulfield (1728–1799), 232 n

INDEX

Chamberlain, Dillon, publisher, listed O'C as the author of the *Third Appeal*, 105; published Curry's *Third Appeal*, 73, 296

Cheevers, Augustine, bishop of Meath, Taaffe writes to, 89

Chesterfield, fourth earl of, Philip Dormer Stanhope (1674–1773), viceroy, his administration bitter, 107; O'C expects Chesterfield to censure the *Dissertations*, 149; O'C improving his land as Chesterfield improved Phoenix Park, 86; said Catholics' principles justified restraint, 66

Chrysostum, St., 246, 249

Church reform, need for, 277

Cicero, 3, 19, 56, 62, 86, 429

Clanbrassil, Lord, James Hamilton, approved publishing regulations for Catholics of Holland, 30; death, 40; negotiates with the Catholic Committee, 34 n

Clanricard, earl of, Smyth Burke, O'C pleased with Dr. Reddy's freedom in his company, 155

Clare, Co., notes for its history, 166

Clarendon, first earl of, Edward Hyde (1609–74), an able and popular adversary, 83; prejudiced against Catholics, 28; took notice of Rinuccini, 60

Clarke, Fr., O'C defends to Bishop French, 448

Clayton, Robert, bishop of Clogher, death, 40; gave O'C a "commission," 8; Faulkner introduced O'C to, 23; negotiates with the Catholic Committee, 34; O'C's *Case of the Roman Catholics* groundwork for Clogher's *Matter of Fact*, 10

Clement VI, Pope, "All stipulations made . . . by Catholics in favor of Protestants are utterly null and void," 158 n

Clement XIV, Pope, correspondence of, 281; disclaims all jurisdiction over temporal rights of princes, 281

Clinch, James, schoolmate of grandson Charles, 404

Clinch, Dr. John, vicar to Archbishop Lincoln, 17; death, 32; free from partiality, 16; in the right, did more than predecessors to soften our masters, 19; O'C sends affection to, 11; worth and probity of, 18

Clogher, bishop of, see Clayton, Dr. Robert

Clogher, dean of, author of the Ulster Annals, 186

Clonalis, 274

Cloyne and Ross, bishop of, see O'Brien, John

Coal and iron industry, 418

Cocking vs. O'Conor, 312, 318

Colgan, Fr. John, 13 n

Comerford, John, Dublin merchant, member of the Catholic Committee, O'C suggests that Comerford assist with Curry's publications, 46, 47, 103, 129; letter to O'C, 239; writes An Address to George III, 418 n

Comyn, Andrew of Elphin, signs An Address to the King (1780), 80

Conall Cernach (Kernach), 390, 393

Concovar MacNessa, 254

Coner Monroy, 236

Conor of Bridge Street, unidentified, 204

Connor, Bernard, *History of Poland*, 56

Conry (Conery, Ó Maolchonaire), Archbishop Florence, 387

Conry, (Ó Maolchonaire), John, 1

Contention of the Bards, 385 n, 387 n

Copernicus, 218

Cork macLuighdheach, not mentioned in Vallancey's *Inisfallen Annals*, 384

Cormac Ulfada, 413, 422

Corr, Edmond of Roscommon, signs An Address to the King (1760), 80

Cotter, Thomas, bookseller and publisher, 96 n

The Cottager's Remarks . . . , see O'Conor, Charles, Works

A Counter-Appeal to the People of Ireland, see O'Conor, Charles, Works

Cousin of Shrule, a MacDermot, 10

Cox, Sir Richard, O'C refutes his history of Ireland, 2

Croften, Edward, M.P. for Roscommon, 279 n, 299

Croughan, John of Roscommon, signs An Address to the King (1760), 80

Cumberland, Richard (1732–1811), Ulster Secretary, a man of fine talents and amiable manners, 97

Cunningham, O'C's London agent, 104, 107–111, 129

Curraghnahivry, 320

Curry, Frank, 185, 199, 200, 207, 216, 249, 250, 281, 292

Curry, Dr. John, *11–16, 18–22, 26–38, 40–57, 59, 61–67, 69–86, 88–94,*

Curry, Dr. John (*continued*)
100–121, 123, 124, 128–141, 146–149, 151, 153, 155–160, 162, 164, 165, 168, 171, 172, 174–179, 181, 182, 185, 187, 195–201, 203, 205, 207, 208, 210–217, 219, 221, 222, 224–230, 233–236, 238–240, 242, 246, 247, 249, 259, 261, 262, 265, 266, 269–272, 279, 281, 282, 292, 297, 310, 328; his accomplishments, 253; champion for Catholicity, 241; criticized for "breaking silence," 43; criticized for signing the Address (1759), 66, 67; declining fast, 231; death and small estate, 334; difficulty with fellow physicians, 53; editing O'C's *Reflexions* . . . , 291; edits O'C's *Vindication* . . . , 174; first to break silence, 310; illness, 253; ill-treated by Brooke, 83; letters to O'C, 226n; opinion of Stone's rejection of an address to the king (1761), 90; preparing an address to Harcourt (1773), with James Reynolds, 239; prepares an address to Townshend with James Reynolds, 239; reconciled with Carpenter, 266; spurs Irish Catholics to act, 93, 108; subscribes to Warner's history, 117; thinks Leland's history is biased, 247n; trial of (1772), 237; with O'C draws up a circular letter for the Catholic Committee, 313; Works: see O'Conor, Charles, *Observations on the Popery Laws; An Appeal to the Lord Primate* (1757), 37; *A Second Appeal* (1760), 73, 93, 105; *Appeals* . . . , (1757–60), 77; *A Brief Account* . . . , or *Dialogue* (1747), 19, 45, 48, 93; *A Candid Inquiry* . . . , (1766), 155, 156, 158; *An Essay towards . . . the Gunpowder Plot* (1765), 139, 140; *An Historical and Critical Review* or *Memoirs* (1775), 162, 195, 198, 200, 233, 253, 259, 262n, 266–269, 271, 272, 292; Supplements to *An Historical* . . . , 205; *Historical Memoirs* or *A Letter* (1758), 19, 22, 26, 28, 36, 38, 42, 46, 48, 50; *Historical Memoirs*, Reilly's 1760 edition, 51, 52, 54–57, 59–61, 75, 83, 103, 104, 129, 135; criticism of O'C's part in, 431; review of, 102n; *Occasional Remarks on Leland's History* . . . (1773), 247, 249, 265; *Some Thoughts on the Natures of Fevers* . . . (1774), the "medical work," 266
Curry, Martin, 156, 160, 171, 199, 200, 216
Curry, Thady, 110, 111, 114, 119, 128, 139, 160n, 171, 185, 199, 200, 207, 216, 269, 170
Cusack, unidentified, 52

Dalton, Lt. Gen. Edward, count (1737–93), 410, 415
Dál Riata, kings of, 413
Davidson, Joseph, editions of Virgil and Horace, 3
Davis, Jefferson, President of the United States, Charles O'C of New York defends, 216n
Davis, Lockyer, Faulkner contracts with, 168n
Dease, Pat, 305
de Burgo, Thomas, bishop of Ossory, see Parliamentary Test (1774); *Hibernia Dominicana*, cost of, 272; opposes an oath, 246, 249, 250; letter of recommendation requested to, 143; letter to O'C, 246, 250
de Courcy, John, 236
de Fleury, André, Cardinal (1653–1743), 354
de Lacy, Hugh, viceroy under Henry II, 415
Delane, Dennis (d. 1750), actor, 56
Delany, Dr. Patrick (1685–1768), Senior Fellow, Trinity College, praises O'C's *Dissertations*, 149
Dermot, Anthony, secretary to the Catholic Committee dines with O'C, 7; gives Curry an account of a party, 156; has influence with Trimleston, 110; Howard requests funds from, 132; letter to O'C, 66n; O'C asks him to report to Curry, 64; O'C writes to, 124; presents an address (1759) to the Speaker, 63n; releases the funds withheld by Trimleston, 72n, 105
Dermott, Anne O'Conor (daughter, "Nancy"), family difficulties, 255
Derry, bishop of, and earl of Bristol, see Hervey, Frederick Augustus
Dervorgilla, 191
de Tillemont, Louis, 354
Digby, Richard, letter to O'C, 84n
Dillon, Dr., unidentified, 118
Dillon, James, Catholic priest, trial of, 206
Dillon, John of Francis Street (son Charles's father-in-law), *340;* 150, 181, 258, 267, 302, 321, 326, 345, 360, 423
Dillon, Lord of Dillon's Regiment, 111
Dioscorides Pedanius, 166
Dolabella, 19

INDEX 519

Dol-Cas, Rari of, see Rari of Dol-Cas (Dáil Cais)
Dolphin, John, failed marriage arrangements with Denis O'C for son Owen, 444
Domville, Protestant cleric, appointment, 247
Doran, Catholic priest, O'C requests Carpenter's protection for, 204; promoted, 206
Dowdall, Nicholas, bookkeeper for A. Dermot, 198
Dowell, unidentified, 202
Down, bishop of, see Traill, James
Dromore, bishop of, see Hawkins, James, and Percy, Thomas
Druid festivals, 193
Druid temples, 194
Druid worship, 189, 190
Duane, Matthew (1707–85), antiquarian, 181
Duany, Francis, Dublin surgeon, 11–13, 22, 74
Dublin, archbishop of, see Carpenter, John; Fitzsimons, Patrick; Lincoln, Richard; Troy, John
Dublin Society, Select Committee, creation and purpose of, 233; invites Carpenter and O'Halloran to be corresponding members, 240, 241; membership list, 232 n; president O'Brien writes to O'C, 231, 233; searching for manuscripts in private collections, 233; sponsors the publication of *Ogygia Vindicated*, 227, 240; invites O'C to edit *Ogygia*, 240, 241
Duggan, Michael, Dublin auctioneer; book forwarded to, 13; did not forward *Cambrensis* to Curry, 16; death, 179, 180; disposal of his manuscripts, 181, 183, 184; "a good angler" for rare 201
Du Hamil, M. DuMonceau, *Husbandry*, 169, 170
Duigenan, Dr., Roscommon physician, 43, 50, 53, 181, 321
Dunk, George Montagu, see Halifax, second earl of

The Earl of Strafford's Letters . . . , 172
Ecclesiastical censure, 63–65, 69
Egan, Boethius, bishop of Achonry and Tuam, to join Curry on a Committee, 104; O'C recommends for an appointment, 274; recommended by Carpenter, 342

Egan, John, letter to O'C, 274 n
Egan, Sam, letter to O'C, 274 n
Elegit Bill (1762), 97, 100, 102; (1763), 130, 133–135
Ellis on Sheep, 244
Elphin, bishop of, see Synge, Edward, and O'Fallon, James
Emigration, 252, 261, 272
English Ministry (1763), 131
Enquiry into the Authenticity of the Poems Ascribed to Ossian, 350
Eochy Feylugh, 90
Eochaidh (Eochu) Riada, 422 n
Erasmus, 13, 55, 94
Essai sur l'Histoire de l'Ireland, 160
Ewing, George, good publisher of O'C's *Observations*, 212–214; reveals O'C's authorship, 217–221

Fagan, Jack (cousin), 268
Fagan, John (father-in-law), 435
Falkland, Lord, 107
Farrell, James, patriot, executed, 148 n, 149
Faulkner, George (1699–1775), printer, 23–25, 96, 98, 127, 152, 154, 161, 163, 167, 169, 170, 173; advertised books for sale, 52 n, 145 n; asks O'C to annotate Lord Lyttleton's history, 163; Chesterfield's letter to, 149; dines with O'C, 167; letter to O'C, 224, 227 n; neglected Warner, 121; Faulkner's obituary for Dr. Clinch, 32 n; O'C asks Faulkner to contact Dr. Johnson, 24; O'C fears he may not print a paper of Clinch's, 17; O'C pays for *Dublin Journal*, 82; O'C reads Faulkner's publications, 46; O'C writes to, 124; prints *Case of the Roman Catholics*, 10 n; prints Leland's history, 247 n; publishes *The Dangers of Popery*, 93 n, and publication of the *Annals of the Four Masters*, 130; reads O'C's letters in public, 156; sends sheets of Lord Lyttleton's history to O'C, 226; wants a new edition of *Dissertations*, 135
Fergus, Dr. John (d. 1763), *1:* O'C asks Curry about, 56; O'C tells Denis to "give him my service," 4; quarrel with O'C, 12, 13, 32, 45
Fergus, king of Ulster, 6
Ferns, bishop of, see French, Nicholas
Ferral, Dr. Charles, death, 292
Ferral, James, O'C's lawyer, 299, 314, 318–322, 348, 386
Ferral, Luke, O'C's lawyer, issues a writ

Ferral, Luke (*continued*)
of outlawry against Kelly of Springfield, 258, 267; handles the discovery suit with James, 283, 319–321, 345, 348, 359
Field, Mr., of Rosemary Lane, priest, 296
Fingall, earl of, see Plunkett, Arthur James
Fitzgerald, Edmund, Fr., O'C's confessor, 83, 136, 180, 204, 220, 241, 383
Fitzgerald, William Robert (1749–1804), earl and marquis of Kildare and duke of Leinster, 328
Fitzgibbon, John (1749–1802), first earl of Clare, Attorney General, 398 n
Fitzsimons, Patrick, archbishop of Dublin, does not give Carpenter the appointment he requests, 155 n; every possible effort should be made to have him appointed archbishop, 123, 124; helps Taaffe apply for a dispensation, 168; ignores O'C's request for Carpenter's advancement, 200; in the right, 19; a man of excellent sense, 33; misunderstanding with O'C, 200; O'C asks him to edit an article, 17; O'C pleased with his appointment, 133; O'C sends affection to, 11; O'C shares a secret with, 63; sympathetic to O'C's and Curry's efforts, 16 n; Taaffe wants him to sign a testimonial to Taaffe's son's character, 168; visits Curry, 165 n; wisdom of, 18
Flann Mainistrech, 406, 413
Fleury, Rev. Claude, 182 n, 354 n
Flyn, Fr., of Sligo, O'C recommends to become bishop of Elphin, 419
Flynn, Conor, 393
Flynn, Michael, signs An Address (1760), 80
Flynn, Roger, signs An Address (1760), 80
Flood, Henry (1732–91), speech (1790), 449; speech on the Question of Attachments, 398
Forchern (Forlkern), 252
Forrester, Mr., parish priest, 143
Foulis, Sir James (1714–91), antiquarian, letter to Vallancey, 393
Fox, Charles James (1749–1806), 398; in favor of Catholic relief, 301 n
Freeman's Journal, 282
French, Arthur, 279, 305, 312, 314, 364, 423; laid out great sums for the relief of the indigent, 421
French, Col. Arthur, 10

French, Edmund, signs An Address, (1760), 80
French, Edward, bishop of Elphin, *448*
French, John, O'C's landlord, 80, 312–314
French National Assembly, 449
French, Nicholas, bishop of Ferns, O'C searching for his *Iphigenia* for the bishop of Elphin, 27, 59–62
French, Patrick, 51, 53, 54, 64
French, Judge Robert, 4, 5, 130 n, 149, 208; handles O'C's dicovery suit, 312, 314, 318, 319, 348, 360
French, William, 18

Gardiner, Charles, brings manuscript to Vallancey, 248
Gardiner, Luke (1745–98), Catholic Relief Bill, 354 n
Gaven, Martin, secretary to the Catholic Committee under Kenmare; assists O'C with the publication of the *Reflexions* . . . , 293, 296; O'C suggests that Gaven transcribe Curry's *An Historical and Critical Review*, 249
Geoghegan, Abbé James (1702–63), imitated by the Abbé Kelly of Mons, 201; recommends the *Dissertations*, 53, 54
George III, King, 198, 215; escapes from the hands of a mad woman, 418
Ghillini, Tommaso (1718–87), papal nuncio to Brussels, rejects Hervey's proposal for an oath of allegiance, 246; O'C's opposition to, 249, 250, 253, 265, 266
Gilla Coemain, list of Irish kings, 406, 413
Giraldus Cambrensis (1146?–1220?), annalists reconciled with, 191; indifferent as to the facts, 230
Goldsmith, Oliver, 173 n
Gore, Sir Arthur, see Arran, earl of
Gorman, Maurice, scribe for O'C and O'Gorman, 349
Gormanston, tenth viscount, Jenico Preston (1707–57), 324 n
Gortnaggan, 312
Grandison, fifth viscount (1699) and earl (1721) (d. 1776), John Villiers, 107
Gunpowder Plot, 109
Grenville, George Nugent (1753–1813), first marquess of Buckingham, viceroy, receives Count O'Rourke, 356
Grotius, 151, 193
Guicciardini, Francesco, (1483–1540), O'C reads his history, 34

INDEX 521

Guthrie, William (1708–70), geographer, 252
Guy, Roscommon postmaster, intercepts O'C's mail, 328

Halifax, second earl of, George Montagu Dunk (1716–71), viceroy, favors lenient action, 95n; gives Trimleston and Killeen cold reception, 108n; no viceroy was ever more popular, 97; O'C addresses the *Dangers of Popery* to, 91; O'C not acquainted with, 89; proposes encouragement of agriculture and linen manufacture, 92; receives Trimleston coldly, 114
Hamilton, William Gerard (1729–96), "Single Speech," giddy over his elevation (chief secretary for Ireland), 114; the public would condemn in a friend what they extoll in Hamilton, 130; a young lively man of great parts, 97
Hanley, William, herald-at-arms, 143
Harcourt, Simon, first earl Harcourt (1714–77), viceroy, administration; favorable for reform, 240, 241; should not be distressed by the printed libels against Catholics, 239; Address from the Roman Catholics of Ireland to, 239, 280, 281
Harris, Walter (1686–1761), historian, bookseller, loses money on his works, 29; Curry searching for his "reams," 13; ignorance of the language causes him to make many mistakes, 54; O'C's evaluation of his *Dialogue*, 12; O'C puns on *Fiction Unmasked*, 19; a scribbler, 26; threatens O'C's printer with imprisonment, 2n
Hart, Pat, servant, 425
Hastings, Elizabeth, Lady Moira, 432
Hely-Hutchinson, John, Provost of Trinity, 392n, 396, 402
Henigan, Mr., son Charles's clerk, 180
Hennessy, Richard, 111
Henry II, King, 20, 163, 167, 184, 185
Henry, Mr., Presbyterian minister, 94
Henry, William, 73n, 94
Herbert, witness in the trial of Nicholas Sheehy, 148n
Herring, Thomas, archbishop of Canterbury, 127
Hervey, Frederick Augustus (1730–1803), bishop of Derry, later (1779) fourth earl of Bristol, 256; proposed an oath of allegiance for Irish Catholics, 246, see Parliamentary Test (1774)

Hesdin, William, 4
Hewitt, James (c. 1709–89) first baron Lifford, lord chancellor of Ireland, 307, 319–321
Hibernia Dominicana, 272
Hibernian Journal, 281
Hobart, John, second earl of Buckinghamshire (1723–93), viceroy, An Address to, 280
Hoey, James, printing Curry's *Historical Memoirs*, 198n, 200n, 212, 214, 217
Hogan, Owen, agent of the Catholic Committee, 237n
Horace, 3, 6, 50, 56, 77, 205n, 217n, 222, 223
Howard, Gorges Edmund (1715–86), Dublin solicitor, 122, 368; Catholic Committee hires Howard, 115; demands payment of the Catholic Committee, 132; intends us good, 123; thinks favorably of O'C, 127
Hughes, Lambert, Rev., 117, 121
Hughes, Martin, O'C's scribe, trained in Gaelic, copying the *Annals of the Four Masters* for O'C, 343, 344
Hume, David (1711–76), a careless historian, 129; Curry's answer to, 271; excels all our ablest historians in one particular, 169; Leland could equal, 161; O'C's "Letter to Hume" finished, 106–108; O'C suggests sending Curry's *Historical Memoirs* to Hume, 53, 83; prejudice of, 104; thinks the old Irish were barbarians, 103, 167
Hunter, John, 93n
Hunter, William, 93n
Hyde, Edward, see Clarendon, Lord
Hyper-doctor, see Lincoln, Richard

Innes, Fr. Thomas (1622–1744), historian, 338; a very mistaken writer, 413
Iphigenia, see French, Nicholas
Ireland, economic conditions (1756), 11; (1757), 23; (1758), beef embargo, 48; (1765), 155; (1770), bankruptcies, 204, 207; famine, 203; (1771), the public is undone, 208; (1773), 254; caused by trade restrictions and the penal laws, 222; compared to 1763, 252; (1777), crop failures, 296; (1778), bankruptcies, 302, 303; prices falling, 310, 311; (1783), (1786), 421
Ireland, history of, chronology of princes, 387, 406; genealogies of Irish kings, 406, 413, 417; list of surnames not known before the eleventh century,

Ireland (*continued*)
417; Milesian period, 385; O'C's notes from the annals, 188; see O'Conor, Charles, Historical Activities
Irish, perverseness of, 73; industriousness of, 170
Irish drama, ludicrous farces, ill-cultivated, unwritten, 418
Irish manuscripts, 413

James I, King, 242
James III, King, the Pretender, 94
Jamestown, fortifications of, 61, 81
Jamestown Meeting (6 August 1650), 52
Jennings, Dr. David, will assist Faulkner, 24
Jephson, Robert (1736–1803), master of horse to the lord lieutenant, O'C gives copies of *Reflexions . . .* to, 291, 296
Jocelyn, Robert, first earl of Roden, possesses the MacFirbis treatise on genealogy, 383
Johnson, Samuel (1709–84), encouraged O'C to write on Irish antiquities, 398, 405; Faulkner brings O'C and Johnson together, 23; Faulkner reads O'C's letters to Johnson, 156 n; letters to O'C, 416; O'C wants Faulkner to offer money from the Catholic Committee to Johnson so he will write for their cause, 24; praises Leland's history, 247
Johnstone, James (d. 1798), 433
Jordan, of School-house Lane, tailor, 138, 139

Kaldraugh, 355
Keating, Geoffrey (1570?–1644?), "Foundations of Knowledge of Ireland," 222
Kelbourne, printer, threatened by Harris, 2 n
Kelly, Abbé of Mons, letter to O'C, 228; plan for a history of Ireland, 228; writing a history of Ireland, 201
Kelly, Fr., 326
Kelly (O'Kelly), Fr., at the Minerva, 425
Kelly (O'Kelly), Charles, of Rome, 274, 325, *419;* not well treated, 342; O'C wants Kelly to help Carpenter get advancement, 180, 181; O'C wants Kelly to place his grandsons in Rome, 313, 317, 326; praises grandson Charles, 372
Kelly, Dr. John, Dublin physician, 53, 101, 108

Kelly, Robert, signs An Address (1760), 80
Kelly of Springfield, 258, 267
Kelly, O'C's lawyer in the discovery suit, 287, 290
Kenmare, fourth viscount, Browne, Thomas, chairs the Select Committee, 313; rebuffed by Halifax, 114; suggests the "Roman Legion," 100 n
Kennicott, Benjamin, *The Ten Annual Accounts . . .* , 327
Keogh, John, writes An Address to George III, 418 n
Keogh, Michael, writes An Address to George III, 418 n
Keon, Ambrose, Dublin woolen merchant, 272
Kildare and Leighlin, bishop of, see O'Keefe, James
Killala, bishop of, see Philips, Philip
Killeen, Lord, cold reception by Halifax, 108 n; O'C dedicates *Lives of the Martyrs* to, 339; writes An Address to George III, 418 n
Kingsland, Lady, Reilly might ask for money, 73
Kingsland, fifth viscount of and baron of Turvey (d. 1800), George Barnewall, might aid Reilly, 73; suggested the "Roman Legion," 100 n
Kirwan, Patrick Robert, bishop of Achonry, death, 274; visits O'C, 123
Knockroe, 312
Knox, O'C's son Charles's landlord, 273, 317

Langrishe, Sir Hercules, first baronet (1731–1811), speech in the House (1772), 227
LaTouche, David, Dublin banker, 305
Laurence O'Toole, St., interposed for Roderic O'Conor, 342
Lawless, Pat, banker, 326
Lawson, John, Lecturer at Trinity College (1712–59), Faulkner sends a copy of Lawson's *Lectures* to O'C, 52
Lee, Thomas, Carpenter's landlord, *280;* 277, censurable conduct in regard to Carpenter's will, 426; robbed, 391
Ledwich, Edward (1738–1832), antiquarian, accepted O'C's criticism of his mistakes, 361; O'C answers his false representations, 370
Leeds, duke of, see Osborne, Thomas
Le Hunte, Thomas, M.P. for Newton,

INDEX 523

151, 169; casts the deciding vote in the Elegit Bill, 226 n
Leighlin, bishop of, see O'Keefe, James
Leland, Dr. Thomas (1722–85) Trinity College, *188;* allows O'C access to Trinity College manuscripts, 154, 161, 166; anniversary sermon biased, 207; fails to get the appointment he desires, 247; letters to O'C, 188 n, 227 n, 247; O'C wants Faulkner to persuade Leland to write a history of Ireland, 163, 167, 169, 170, 197; response to Curry's *Occasional Remarks,* 249; dines at his home, 152; wants to be in Curry's good graces, 228; will publish state tracts and records hard to come by, 222; *History of Ireland:* 236, 247; has disappointed booksellers, 259
Leslie, Charles, 12, 13
Lily, William (c. 1468–1522), 429
Lincoln, Richard, archbishop of Dublin, the Hyper-doctor, *95;* Catholic Committee's business can be done without his assistance or concurrence, 18; death, 123 n; declares Bishop O'Keefe schismatic, 31; directive to the clergy, 19; exhortation to the Catholics of Dublin, 30, 63, 64, 69; illness, 121; inconstancy of, 16; Fitzgerald asks Lincoln's permission to be O'C's confessor, 83; opposition to An Address (1759), 64, 65; pastoral letter (1759), 65; O'C surprised that Lincoln is complimented, 22; succeeded John Linegar, 11 n
Linen manufacture, 170
Lismore, bishop of, see Creagh, Peter
Lismore, Lady, Maria Josepha O'Brien, widow of Daniel O'Brien, baron of Castle Lyons and earl of Lismore, *126;* O'C traces her genealogy, 121, 124
Literary piracy, 163, 169
Lodge, John, (d. 1774), archivist, O'C first presumed that Duggan had willed his manuscripts to Lodge, 180 n, 183 n, 188; 436
Lord, Patrick, printer, bills Catholic Committee for the *Farmer's Letters,* 72; not paid, 73, 74, 76; publishes *Farmer's Letters,* 69, 71; publishes O'C's *The Principles . . . ,* 11; O'C purchases books from, 34
Lough Allen, description of, 400, 418
Luby, O'Conor, 277, 331
Lucas, Charles, collaborates with Brooke in *Freeman's Journal,* 130; O'C disgusted with, 2
Lucky, a servant, 4
Lynch, John, archdeacon of Tuam, a learned and zealous writer, but not a genius, 13
Lynch, Pat of Roscommon, signs An Address (1760), 80
Lyster, O'Dwyer, O'C's lawyer, *347;* 283, 284, 287, 345, 348; O'C sends legal document to, 347
Lyttleton, George, first baron (1709–73), *186, 191, 192;* asks O'C about Henry II's conquest of Ireland, 184; letter to O'C, 186, 187; Faulkner sends O'C Lord Lyttleton's history in sheets as it comes from the press, 167, 168, 170; Faulkner slow in publishing Lord Lyttleton's continuation of his history, 207; his history, able, judicious, but prejudiced, 168; his history free from prejudice, 167; O'C agrees to send notes on *Annals* to Vesey for Lord Lyttleton, 185; O'C answers Lord Lyttleton's objection to *Dissertations,* 98; O'C provides Leland and possibly Lord Lyttleton with notes about the Revolution of 1170, 188; O'C sends notes from *Annals* to Vallancey for Lord Lyttleton, 186; O'C sends notes to Lord Lyttleton, 191, 192; O'C waiting to see Leland's and Lord Lyttleton's histories, 197; O'C willing to supply notes for Lord Lyttleton's history, 163; praises O'C, 224, 226; questions O'C about tribal warfare before the invasion of Henry II, 191; Works: *History of Ireland,* pre-Norman period weak, Norman period "the best I have hitherto seen," 226; prolix and digressive, 230

Mac Broudin, Conor, 349
Macaria, 73, 76, 82
MacCartney, Sir George, 223 n
MacCarthy More of Desmond, 6
MacDáire, Tadhg, 223 n; O'C's criticism of, 385, 387
MacDermot, Dr., 142
MacDermot, Brigid O'Conor (daughter), 335; death, 285; her home life has disagreeable circumstances, 136; requires prudence and good nature, 8; requires reason and religious dictates, 10; requires resignation, 209; lives at Cool-

MacDermot, Brigid O'Conor (*continued*)
avin, 151 n; O'C decides not to live with, 136; visits Belanagare, 162
MacDermot, Charles, not a prince, 294
MacDermot, Charles (grandson), bound for the Austrian Netherlands, 344
MacDermot, Denis (grandson), 275, 317, 333; "let him be an instructor" to Denis O'C's sons, 302; O'C attempts to place him in European schools, 301, 302
MacDermot, Francis, of Usher's Quay, provision merchant, 106 n; writes An Address to George III, 418 n
MacDermot, Hugh (grandson), 276, 357; inheritance of, 357; squanders funds in Paris and London, 357 n
MacDermot, James, signs An Address (1760), 80
MacDermot, Michael of Roscommon, signs An Address (1760), 80
MacDermot, Myles (son-in-law), *294*, *333*; affairs not in a good way, 8; brings is family to live with O'C, 147; illness, 43; O'Conor visits, 80
MacDermot, Owen (grandson), 301
MacDermot, Owen of Roscommon, Curry's efforts collect his bill from, 101, 107, 108, 116; inheritance, 49 n; insanity leads to his arrest, 51; jealous of Duigenan, 53; treated by Curry, 51, 55
MacDermot, Owen, member of the Catholic Committee, 106 n
MacDermot, Capt. Peter (cousin), 126
MacDermot, Rody (grandson), a youth who tells an untruth injurious to Bishop French, 448
MacDermot-Roe, Charles (cousin), 8, 344
MacDermot-Roe, Mrs. Terence, husband left her in a desperate way, 49
MacDonough, Major Owen (cousin), 4
MacEgan, Flan, 349 n
MacEgans, lawyers of Tipperary, 252
MacFirbis, Duald (1585–1670), historian, 351; his genealogy in the hands of the earl of Roden, 383, 384
MacGeoghegan, Abbé James, see Geoghegan, Abbé James
MacKenzie, Sir George, 227, 241
MacLagan, James, a worthy gentleman, 209
McManus, Arthur, O'C recommends to Carpenter, 337, 338
MacMurrough Dermot, or MacMurchad, king of Leinster, 191, 192, 230

Macnamara, Daniel (1720–1800), agent for the Catholic Committee, 257; paid by the Catholic Committee, 181, 295
MacPherson, James (1736–96), 227, 241; Campbell will fall into his hands, 390; declared war on O'C, 240; resembles the cuddlefish, 147; O'C's treatment of, 189; O'Halloran preparing an answer to, 193; *Ossian*, 350, 351, 352
Macpherson, John, D.D. (1710–1765), 227, 241, declared war on O'Conor, 240; *Caledonian Dissertations*, 189
MacPherson, John (c. 1745–1821), resents O'C's treatment of James MacPherson, 189
Magee, massacre of, 236
Mahon, Charles of Strokestown, 80, 158, 267
Mahon, Dominick, 80, 108
Mahon, Patrick, signs An Address (1760), 80
Mahon, young Mr., death, 320
Malcolm Canmor, 413
Malone, printer, should be employed by Sullivan, 125
Malone, Edmund (1741–1812), *434*, *436*; letter to O'C, 434 n, 436 n
Malone, family history, 434, 436
Maria Theresa of Austria, 164
Marshall, Judge Robert, 154, 169
Martin, Andrew of Elphin, signs an address (1760), 80
Mason, John Monck (1726–1809), speaks for the Elegit Bill, 130 n, 233 n
Matt, unidentified, 171
Maeba's Carn, 90
Member of the House of Commons, early draft, *260*, final draft, *263*, on the Parliamentary Test, 1774
Moira, earl of, see Rawdon, Sir John
Moncrief, R., printer, 281 n
Moore, Jane, marries Owen O'Conor, Denis's son, 444 n
Moran, letter in *Freeman's Journal*, 226
Morris, Mr., Catholic priest, apostasy of, 241
Morris, Mr., of Galway, owns *Ogygia Vindicated*, 227
Morris, Mr., printer, 338, 339; compositor to Ewing, 213, 214; printing the *Observations*, 250, 269, 271
Moryson or Morrison, Fynes (1566–1630), 98
Mount Callan ogham, 390 n
Mulhall, Mr., holds a school, 391
Mulvihily, Denis, servant, death, 302

INDEX

Mulvy, A Catholic priest, 206
Munster uprising, see also Whiteboy uprisings, and Sheehy, Nicholas, 108, 116; O'C's apology to Burke, 145
Murphy, David, letter to O'C, 113n

Nary, Cornelius (1660–1738), priest, 174
Navigation Board, 304
Neidhe (Neid), 252
Netterville, Catholic provincial, 204
Newton, Sir Isaac, 406
Nicholson, servant, 273
Normans, invasions of Ireland, 192; ninth-century treaties with the Irish, 351
North, Frederick (1732–92), in favor of Catholic relief, 301n
Northumberland, second earl of, Hugh Percy, viceroy, Taaffe well received by, 134; who is Northumberland, 120
Nugent, Grace, 401
Nugent, Robert (1702–88), a noble man of the first distinction, 443
Nugent, Thomas, 86

Oakboy and Steelboy uprisings (1763), 128
O'Brian, Donall, (Dónal Mór Ó Briain), 192, 236
O'Brian, Murkertach, or Murcertach Ó Briain, high king, 192
O'Brien, Charles, see Thomond, Marshal
O'Brien, D.T., writes An Address to George III, 418n
O'Brien, of George's Hill, 204
O'Brien, John, Roman Catholic bishop of Cloyne and Ross, 338
O'Brien, Sir Lucius Henry, third Baronet (1731–95), M.P., disapproved of the Elegit Bill, 135; kindness to O'C, 349; letter to O'C, 233; president of the Select Committee of the Dublin Society, 232n, 233
O'Brien, Margaret, 350
O'Brien, Maria Josepha, see Lismore, Lady
Occasional Remarks on Certain Passages in Dr. Leland's History . . . , see Curry, John, Works
O'Clery, Cúcoigriche, 13n
O'Cléirigh, Lughaidh, O'C's criticism of, 385, 387
O'Clery, Michael, compiler of the *Annals*, 13n, 349
O'Conor, "Molly" or Maud (sister), 8; death, 245

O'Conor, sisters, 55
O'Conor, Alexander (cousin), attempts to regain Ballintober Castle, 408n, see Ballintober Castle; a rash and silly man, 411
O'Conor arms, 445
O'Conor (Conor), Bernard, 56n
O'Conor, Bryan of Kerry, 6

O'CONOR, CHARLES (1710–91)

General

despairs of reforming men's minds, 151; devotion to Ireland, 149; loyalty to his religion, 149; response to criticism, 14

Activities in Behalf of Family Members

brother, Daniel, 109–13, 115, 137, 138, 313, 415; grandsons, 313, 317, 336 (provision for son Charles's children after their mother's death); grandson, Denis MacDermott, 301 (tries to place in Spain), 302, 313, 317; grandson, Roderick O'Conor, 447; grandson, Charles O'Conor, 301, 302 (helps to place him in the Irish College in Rome), 313, 391 (asks Carpenter to convey money to him in Rome), 419; grandson, Matthew O'Conor, 391 (asks Carpenter to place in a seminary in Rome)

Advice

to Curry about *Hist. Mem.*, 27; to brother Daniel, 9; to son Denis, 376; to grandson Charles, 381

Biographical Details

Lough Allan, 400, 418 (his son, Charles, there); assizes of Roscommon, O'C attends, 54, 118, 119; Belanagare, 10 (affairs of), 43 (isolation of), 79 (O'C moves from), 138 (arrived back in); 169 ("enjoys" 800 acres, reclaiming 300 more), 170 (O'C encourages linen manufacturing in the town), 446 (in possession of Denis; mother died there); birthdays, 159, 331, 440; Brooke invites O'C to co-author history of Ireland, 84; brothers-in-law, 55 (death of three in 1759), 216; Burke visits, 152; Burton-Coyngham, 343 (O'C visits), 400 ("greatest" friend of Ireland); Carolan taught him to play

526 INDEX

O'Conor, Charles (*continued*)
the harp, 220; Archbishop Carpenter, O'C in Kildare with, 275; Connacht, isolation in, 137; correspondence, O'C keeping his for descendants, 331; criticism of O'C, 43 (for "breaking silence"), 81; Curry's *Hist. Mem.*, O'C censured for publishing, 431; Dillon, J., O'C thanks for clothes for grandchildren, 340; Dublin, 147 (stays with son-in-law there), 136–38 (will divide his time between there and the Hermitage), 426 (O'C orders books from); Elphin, 157, 165, 218, 226, 246; Faulkner, 167 (O'C dines with), 156 (O'C disturbed that Faulkner read his letters in public); Dr. Fergus, quarrel with, 12, 13, 32; Fingall, earl of, 345; Fitzgerald becomes his confessor, 83; great-grandmother, chalice in O'C's keeping sent to her from Rome, 350; genealogy of O'Conors to 1525, 446; government pension for O'C proposed, 399, 440; grand jury of Roscommon, testifies before, 13; his health, 11, 12, 148, 149, 191, 396, 400, 405, 421, 426, 428 (general), 96 (ankle sprained), 117–19 (eye injury, fall from horse), 11 (shin injury, fall from horse), 382, 384, 391, 402, 427, 435, 440, 445–447, 449, 450 (rheumatic pains), 449 (thread of "my life is nearly spun out"), 445 (wholly deprived of the power of standing or walking); Hermitage, 136 (built), 137 (O'C moves in), 136–38 (will divide his time between there and Dublin), 149, 178 (description); History of Ireland, 77 (O'C burns a draft), 84 (invitation from Brooke to co-author history); Kileen, Lord, 345; King, Sir Edward, 90; land, 40; mail, 105, 169 (possibly opened); Matthew, his brother, death of, 120; Moira, presented to lady, 432; O'Briens, O'Conors intermarried with, 350; O'Gara, O'C's relationship to, 202; O'More, 153, 275; Royal Irish Academy, O'C entertained by President and Treasurer of, 399; school, O'C quit at fifteen, 301; Sligo, 44, 48, 80, 89, 104, 121, 133, 141, 151, 163, 164, 272; son-in-law, O'C will live with in Dublin during winter, 147; Count Taaffe visits O'C, 89; Trinity College Library, well treated in, 209; Vallancey, 399 (O'C asks him to propose name for Royal Irish Academy, 405 (inquires about arrival), 426 (letter from), 440 (recommends O'C for pension); viceroy, O'C sends address to, 13; Walker, 401 (assists Walker in his biography of Carolan), 405 (asks Walker to encourage Boswell to print Johnson's letters to O'C), 437, 438 (asks Walker to pay his dues to the Royal Irish Academy); Whalker, duchess of, relationship to, 111; wedding anniversary, fifty-fifth, 426; the western Province, several counties in, 119.

Discovery Suit
(1777), filed by Hugh, 281, 283; lease for Belanagare, 281, 282; a maiden case, 285; O'C argues under Statute of Limitations, 285, 286, 290; Statute of Limitations may not apply to Catholics, 285–287; times favorable for Charles's side, 284, 285, 287, 290; O'C levies a fine in Common Pleas, 286; O'C may take an appeal to London, 287, 290; John O'Conor agrees to plea gratis, 289; O'C and Denis called to appear before a Parliamentary committee, 299; (1778), answer and plea to be filed this term, 302; tactics of delay, 206, 307; now in a quiescent state, 305, 308; plea will not be received by the Lord Chancellor till November, 306; will appeal in London if he loses his case in Ireland, 306, 307; plea entered in Chancery, 307; (1779), Cocking vs. O'Conor, 312, 318; Hugh sues under a gavel clause, 312; bill filed against French, 313; O'C defers answering the Cocking vs. O'C suit, 312, 318; O'C will move for a hearing if Hugh does not, 312; tactics of delay, 313; O'C claims his father was not a lessee by an heir-at-law, 314; out-of-court settlement suggested by Hugh, 317; Ferral neglects answering Cocking's bill, 318; O'C put under house arrest, 318–320; released, 321; Hugh's verbal charges, 323; (1780), continues, 331, 336; (1781), O'C subpoenaed, 344; Bill of

INDEX 527

Exceptions filed by Hugh, 345; O'C's answer, 347; costs, 353; Denis's anxiety over, 359; French thinks no injury will come this term, 360; French suggests applying for a dismissal next term, 361; Hugh sends someone to suggest Chancery, 364; Hugh appeals to Equity, 364; farm rents to pay court costs, 364; Hugh serving notice to Denis for hearing evidence, 366; Hugh claims that O'C detained a lease from him, 367; O'C traces the history of the case for Howard, 368; Scott and Yelverton argued the case for O'C, 368

Ecclesiastical Appointments

Achonry, 274; Blake, Francis Xavier, 380; Carpenter, 187 (negotiates with Irish bishops for), 180 (enlists Kelly's aid), 425 (replacement for); Bishop Egan recommended for Achonry to Kelly, 274; Fitzsimmons suggested as Archbishop of Dublin, 123, 133; Kelly, Mr. Charles, 180 (enlists aid), 274 (recommends Bishop Egan to), 419 (recommends Flyn of Sligo to); McManus, Arthur, recommended, 338; Teige, Mr., 143.

Educational Advice

to son Charles, 4; to son Denis, 3–5, 39; for grandchildren, 268, 276, 301, 327; to grandson Charles, 327, 354, 414

Estate Affairs

10, 144, 170, 204, 258, 267, 268, 273, 275, 287, 289, 302, 323, 324, 345, 360, 363, 364, 421, 423, 425, 426; reclaiming wasteland, 51, 56, 86

Financial Affairs

4, 5, 7, 55, 56, 136, 137, 200, 207, 216, 227, 273; funds for Luke Wallis, 143, 150; O'Gara's bequest, 287; pays son Charles's debts, 215–217, 220, 273, 315

Friendship

for Curry, 29, 43, 54, 72, 102, 159, 165, 175, 241, 242, 253; with Curry threatened by Curry's signing the Parliamentary Test (1774), 270, 279

Historical Activities

Annals [of the Four Masters], 12, 13, 55, 78, 161 (O'C studying), 124, 125, 130 (proposes the publication of), 166 (recommends them to O'Gorman, 186 (history of his manuscript of), 191 (O'C justifies to Lord Lyttleton), 343, 349 (directs the translating of), 350 (annotating directing the copying of), 389 (on authenticity and suggestions for editing, transcribing, and publishing); other annals, 77, 87, 400; astronomical manuscripts in Gaelic, 218; annalists' accuracy, 191; *Bleeding Iphigenia*, 59, 60, 62; *Book of Ballymote*, 400, 413, 351 (annotating); Butler's *Life of Saint Lawrence*, editing, 331; Campbell's attack on the authenticity of the Irish manuscripts, 391, 392; *Connacht, Annals of*, 166, 377 (has annotated them); Curry, 26 (O'C offers to translate and annotate *Annals* for), 175 (O'C suggests outline for history), 188 (O'C sends books for *Hist. and Crit. Rev.*); 195, 249, 259 (O'C pressures him to finish history and writes preface to); Duggan's Manuscripts, asks Carpenter to bid on, 201; Faulkner, O'C praises O'Gorman's scholarship to, 167; genealogical researches, 294 (MacDermotts), 121, 126 (Lady Lismore), 143 (O'Conors), 329, 300 (O'Donnells), 383, 384 (O'Dowds), 435 (O'Hagans), 434 (O'Malones), 358, 365 (O'Rourkes); 445 (Plunketts); Harris 19; *History of the Holy Fathers and Martyrs*, writes the notes for, 334; history of Ireland, 6, 13, 20, 27, 45, 88, 331, 338, 341, 349, 350 (in general), 353 (has suspended work on), 373, 377, 382, 384, 388 (fears it will have a poor sale), 394, 396 (O'C working on, but the subject is not popular), 440, 445 (still at work); Hume, 83 (sending *Hist. Mem.* to), 103 (refutes to Warner); Johnson, Samuel, encourages O'C, 403; Abbé Kelly of Mons, 201 (O'C agrees to assist), 228 (receives letter from); Leland, 161, 163, 167, 169 (O'C suggests to Faulkner that Leland write history), 166 (suggests to O'Gorman that

528 INDEX

O'Conor, Charles (*continued*)
Leland write history), 188 (on Revolution of 1170), 197 (O'C waiting to see his history), 247 (Leland praised by Lord Lyttleton, Burke, and Dr. Johnson); Lyttleton, 186 (notes via Vessey to), 188 (notes via Leland on Revolution of 1170), 191, 192 (O'C sends notes on pre-Norman Irish warfare), 197 (O'C waiting to see his history); Abbé MacGeoghegan's history recommended to O'C, 76; manuscripts, 1, 13, 133, 179, 180, 183 (collecting), 99 (locates a mislaid manuscript); Milesian period, comments on, 133, 154 (O'C studying the Trinity College manuscripts), 385; O'Brien's *Dictionary*, makes additions to and corrections of, 232; O'Flaherty, 387 (O'C criticized), 413, 420; O'Flanagan, O'C helps with research on ogham characters, 385; O'Gorman, 166 (O'C assists him with his history of Clare), 167, O'C praises his scholarship to Faulkner, 382 (agrees to defend him if critics attack his work), 341–43 (O'C assists with genealogies); *Ogygia Vindicated*, 227 (O'C proposes translation of), 241 (a means of answering the MacPhersons); Ossian, 102 (fraud exposed), 350 (refutation of); Pinkerton, O'C assists, 413, 422, 430, 420–21 (O'C sends poem composed in the time of Malcolm Kenmore via Walker to); Pownall, 342 (O'C assists), 248 (on writings of Moses); Royal Irish Academy, 399 (founding of), 400 (O'C preparing a memorial for), 440 (O'C's manuscripts in trust for); Select Committee, 233, 240 (invites O'C to translate *Ogygia Vindicated*), 243 (meets with and introduces Carpenter), 407 (presents the manuscript of the "Third Letter ..." to for their comment); "A Short View . . . ," O'C sends to Carpenter, Vallancey, and Leland for comments, 407; Smollett, 42 (sending him Curry's *Hist. Mem.*), 84 (tries to influence); Sullivan, O'C send manuscripts to, 133; Taaffe's *Observations*, O'C supplies notes for, 150; *Teagusg Flatha*, 316; topography of the second and eleventh centuries, 351; Vallancey, 221 (O'C will provide him with material), 232, 236, 242 (*Essay on the Antiquity of the Irish Language*), 330 (translates the Petersburg fragment for), 405 (*A Vindication of the Ancient History of Ireland*), 428 (O'C seeks permission for Vallancey to use manuscripts at the Lombard College); Vesey, 185, 186; Walker's *Irish Bards*, corrects, 416; Warner, 86 (O'C agrees to assist), 93, 94 (O'C answers his objections to the *Dangers* . . .), 104 (critical of Hume and Voltaire), 121 (O'C gets subscriptions for his history); Woodward, answers, 431

Opinions

An Address to the King (1761, Remonstrance), 85; arguments in favor of the Address (1759), 66, 67; An Address to the lord lieutenant (1772), 237; Arianism, 419; artifice, necessity of, 70; Bedford, 30; Berkeley, 354; books, well attended, our best masters, 301; Brigid, daughter, 8, 10; Brooke, 69, 70, 104, 129; Brooke's *Freeman's Journal*, 132, 133; Burke, 134; *Cambrensis Eversus*, 19; Campbell's history, 387, 388; Carpenter, 179, 205; Carte's history, 52; Catholic Committee causes for disunity, 15, disaffection with, 132, hopes for, 85, inactivity of, 128; Catholic hierarchy, 82; Catholics may find repose in Canada, 261; Catholics should submit to things as they are (1784), 395; Charles, son, 8, 143; Chesterfield, 149; Church reform, need for, 204, 205; Clarendon, 28; Clinch, 11, 18, 19, 32; bishop of Clogher, 23; compromise, necessity of, 9; contemporary Irish have lost virtues and principles of ancestors, 202; Cumberland, 97; Curry, 11, 12, 43, 157; Curry's *An Appeal*, 37; *Second Appeal*, 41; *Dialogue, Brief Account*, 19; *Hist. Mem.*, 19, 27, 48, 52, 57, 75; *Historical and Critical Review*, a mere compilation, not history, biased, 268; Daniel, brother, 7, 137; Deism, 381; difficulty of translating the *Annals*, 370, 373, 377, 378; discretion, importance of, 89; Divine Providence, 283; Duany, 22; Duggan, 179, 180; early Irish not barbarians, 416, 433; early use of letters in Ireland, 402, 406, 407, 417; ecclesiastical contentions may be necessary, 381; Elegit Bill (1772), 222, 234; *Farmer's Letters*, 69, 71; fisheries should be begun in Donegal, 400; Fergus, 12, 45; Fitzgerald, 183; French of Ferns, 60; A. French, 10; funding Brooke, 121; Gibbon equal to Tacitus, 424; Gunpowder Plot, 109; The Golden Mean, 212; history, 161; history, importance of an accurate one, 388; history of Ireland from Henry II, importance of, 166, 167; history of Ireland, unbiased version, importance of, 162; honesty not enough, 89; hostility, 171; Irish, not barbarians, 167, 188; Irish Catholic hierarchy, 187; Irish Catholics, baseness of, 55; Irish Catholic clergy, 30, 121; Irish House of Commons (1763), 135; Irish Parliament of 1756, 15; Irish Parliament (1771), 208; Irwin, 29; Dr. Johnson, 23; W. King, 12; laughter better than tears, 221; Leland, 152, 163; Leland's *History of Ireland*, 236, biased, 247; letters in Ireland, early use of, 147, 193, 218; Le Hunte, 169; literary merit alone stands man in little stead, 247; Lodge's *Desiderata*, 188; Lyttleton's history, 167–170, 230; McNamara, 181; military career, 112, 128; Leslie, 12, 13; Archbishop Lincoln, 16, 18, 19, 121; his exhortation (1759), 64; Lucas, 2; mining in Roscommon, 400; morality and power, 54; his mother, 80; Nature can do no more than lay foundations, 276; oath of allegiance (1756), 15; oaths of allegiance, inefficiency of, 234; obedience to the government, necessity of, 62, 93, 95; obedience to the Pope reconcilable with obedience to secular authority, 246; O'Brien, 135; O'Halloran, 217; opposes Catholics' joining the Volunteers until it is legal, 351; Dan O'Rourke, 7; papal authority, 31; Parliamentary Test (1774), 259–263, 265, 266; asks Curry to delay signing, 269; Catholics should delay signing, 269; party interest prevents unbiased history, 207; party strife, 200; party writers, 62, 242, 247; patience and resignation, 90; penal laws, 13, 15, 203; arguments against, 122, 170, 207; cause of religious indifference, 204; effects of, 30, 204, 218; an evil without remedy, 205; ruinous to the economy, 208; Phillip's biography of Pole, 146; position of a Catholic in Ireland, 5; power, importance of, 41; prejudice, 70, 85, 88, 115, 134, 157, 239; compared to an elm, 199; Protestantism, no central theology, 354; public good vs. private gain, 91; public service, 94; the Pretender, 93, 94; Registry Bill, 33–35; M. Reilly, 22; religion, its effect on manners and politics, 189, 190, 194; religious duty, 3, 150; resignation, 162, 209; resignation to Providence, 176; role of the gentry in the Catholic Committee, 240; Roman theologians, 354; the Royal Irish Academy and promotion of Ireland's natural resources, 407; scholars, 113; secrecy, about Curry's *Hist. Mem.*, 52; secrecy, necessity of, 22, 56, 58, 89, 212–214, 216, 217; secrecy, not immoral, 58; *Serious Thoughts*, 32; Sheehy *et al*, 149, 151; speaking out, necessity of, 61, 62, 83, 103; Archbishop Stone, 82; submitting to unjust laws vs. approving of them, 208; supporting Brooke, importance of, 85; Synge, 47, 60; Taaffe, 200; Taaffe's application for a dispensation for his son, 164, 168; taking men in their way, 157; tactics for handling the Ascendency, 22; time, proper use of, 106; times favorable for reform, 68, 83, 85, 92, 210, 308, 312; times unfavorable for reform, 131; *Transactions* of the Royal Irish Academy, 438; Trimleston, 83, 84, 105, 115; Trimleston's negotiations with Halifax, 111; truth, 155; *Universal History*, 388; J. Ussher, 124; virtue, 73; Voltaire's *General History*, 176; Walker's history, 124, 129

Participation in the First Catholic Committee

(1755) founding of, 7; (1756) proposes a Test, 14; writes to Clinch and Fitzsimmons, 16; edits paper for Clinch, 17; importance of the laity in, 18; (1757) Clinch and Fitzsimmons have published some good instructions, 19; lack of support of hierarchy, 19; argument for repeal of the penal laws, 20; attempts to hire Dr. Johnson to write pamphlets, 24; response to the Registry

O'Conor Charles (*continued*)
Bill, 33–35; (1759) writes a defense of the Address to the King (1759), 64; (1760) supplies materials to Brooke, 68; contributes money to, 72; writes an Address to George III (1760), 79; (1762) defends the statement of allegiance and seeks Archbishop Lincoln's approval for it, 95; debates the Elegit Bill, 97; proposes an all-Ireland collection (1762), 100; encourages Curry to revive Catholic Committee, 104; addresses the Committee on behalf of Curry and suggests making Curry its negotiator with the government, 111; (1763) contributes to subscription for Howard, 115; outlines all-Ireland collection, 116; all-Ireland collection, 117; encourages Curry to stir up Catholic Committee, 120, 121; placed in a subordinate position by new officers, 128; O'C's participation lessened, 134, 135; (1766) suggests collecting evidence about the trial of Sheehy *et al.*, 148, 151; (1767) suggests to Faulkner codification of the penal laws, 173; suggests the possibility of a new test, 174; (1769) first to break silence, 197; (1770) supports Carpenter's rejection of the idea of an address to the Townshend administration, 203; suggests to Faulkner relaxation of restrictions in agriculture, 207

Participation in the Second Catholic Committee

(1773) approves of the formation, 240; objects to Ossory's opposition to an oath, 246; does not expect the government to propose a test oath, does not favor Catholics' presenting an oath of allegiance, 249, 250; (1774) defends Carpenter to Curry, 262; (1777) criticism of the address to Harcourt, 280; proposes a Select Committee, 292, 293; proposes that the king regrant Maryland to the Catholics for their loyalty during the American Revolution, 295, 297, 298; (1779) invited to join the Select Committee, 313; draws up a circular letter with Curry proposing an all-Ireland collection, 313–315; attempts to legalize Catholics' entry into the military, 324, 328; (1784) disapproves of an address to Rutland, 397

O'Conor, Charles (1736–1808, son), *4;* accused of withholding money from uncle, Daniel, 205; compared with Denis, 306; doing well, 8; debts, 181, 182, 215, 216, 267, 273, 302; dines with A. Dermot, 7; fit for no business, 336; finances, 143, 146; has brought disappointment from the beginning and grief in end to his family, 335; has gone too far in his own undoing, 244; health, 180, 181; in Dublin, 104, 105; lives near the colliery of Munterkeney, 371; marriage contract to Mary Dillon, 142, 144; O'C asks Faulkner to send a book to, 169; O'C writes to, 171, 201; provided for, 136

O'Conor, Charles (1764–1828, grandson), *327, 354, 381, 414;* 331, 439; blocks out sections of his grandfather's letters, 88; conducts himself well, excessive freedom in expressing himself in ecclesiastical matters, 380; indiscreet correspondence of, 429; O'C pleased with his progress in Hebrew and Greek, 404; recommended for Propaganda Fide, 301; sends letter to Carpenter, 342, 380; success, 342, 372; writing style, verbose to a degree of affectation, 429

O'Conor, Charles, of New York (1804–84, great-grandson), success in the United States, 216n

O'Conor, Counselor, 318

O'Conor, Daniel (b. 1727, brother), *9, 353;* 114, 115, 117, 302, 313, 410, 415; demands rents in advance from Charles's son, 205; desires and attempts to return to Ireland after serving in a foreign army, 112, 113; falsely accuses Charles of trying to cheat him, 205; gives daily instances of imprudence, 273; going to Dublin, 135; has he left Dublin? 4; in the Netherlands, 53; leaves Ireland for Dunkirk, 137, letter to O'C, 8; marriage, 143; needs money to get to Paris, 138; O'C doubts he will be useful to the Catholic Committee, 119; O'C writes to, 105, 109, 111; severe in his letters, 7; suggestions for revising the *Dissertations*, 54; works for a London bookseller, 147; writes like a madman, 137

O'Conor, Denis (d. 1804, son), *3, 5, 7, 8, 10, 39, 97, 142–144, 209, 243–245,*

INDEX 531

255, 258, 267, 268, 273, 275, 284–287, 289, 290, 299, 301–303, 305–308, 312–315, 317–323, 326, 334–336, 344, 345, 348, 355, 356, 358–364, 366, 367, 369, 372, 376, 386, 423, 425, 426, 444; anxiety over the discovery suit, 345; compared with Charles, 306; did not receive as much property as Charles, 306; finances, 217; gives O'Gorman favorable account of O'C's research, 410; health, 39, 40, 42, 44, 49–51, 53, 55, 56, 64, 65, 78; marriage to Catherine Browne, 78; O'C gives up Belanagare to, 79n; O'C writes P.S. to, 4; shares O'C's fate in the discovery suit, 283; thanks to Carpenter for news of Charles in Rome, 342; well provided for, 136
O'Conor, Denis (grandson), 340, 372
O'Conor, Dennis of Balaghnadarn, signs An Address (1760), 80
O'Conor, Dermot, 202n
O'Conor, Dr. of Roscommon, once recommended by O'C to become bishop of Elphin, now too old, 419
O'Conor Don, Dominick, 408, 410, 411; signs An Address (1760), 80; a very worthy and religious person, 447
O'Conor, Dorothy (great aunt), 202
O'Conor, Felim, 194; tomb, 438
O'Conor genealogy, 446
O'Conor, Hugh (b. 1729, brother), discovery suit, 281, 283, 290, 312, 313, 317, 323, 364; signs An Address (1760), 80; O'C asks Hugh to send money to Daniel, 8; O'C sends affection to, 7; weak, 273
O'Conor, Hugh (cousin), 4
O'Conor, Sir Hugh, son of Brig Thomas O'C, 202n
O'Conor, John, Dublin lawyer, 289, 312
O'Conor, John, Fr., 425
O'Conor, Luby, Carpenter's nephew, 342, 380
O'Conor, Martin (grandson), 425
O'Conor, Mary Dillon (daughter-in-law), death, 335; illness, 155, 156
O'Conor, Mary O'Rourke (d. 1760, mother), death, a good mother, an honest woman, 80; O'C intends to have a document for his mother to sign which would enable him to live at home, 8
O'Conor, Matthew (d. 1763, brother), parish priest of Roscommon, 13, 231, 367
O'Conor, Matthew (grandson), attends Mulhall's school, 391, 404, 419; to begin study in Rome, 391, 404, 418
O'Conor, Owen (brother), signs An Address (1760), 80
O'Conor, Major Owen (great uncle), 4n
O'Conor, Owen (grandson), 136n, 334; administering Belanagare, 425; diligent, 372; marriage negotiations for, 444; should begin to help run Belanagare, 301
O'Conor, Roderick (Rory), 230; O'C's defense of, 188, 192
O'Conor, Roderick (grandson), 410, 412, 415; in Dillon's Regiment, 447
O'Conor, Roger (brother-in-law), health, 21, signs an address (1760), 80
O'Conor, T., of Belaghnadarn, signs An Address (1760), 80
O'Conor, Brig Thomas (cousin), 202, 447, 4
O'Conor, Thomas (1770–1855, grandson), 340
O'Conor, Turlough, 191
O'Cuinn, Cormac, 248; *Teagusg Flatha*, 316
O'Domhnaill, Ruairí (1575–1608), earl of Tirconnell, 300n
O'Dowd family, 384
O'Duigenan, Cúcoigriche, 13n
O'Fallon (Fallon), James, Catholic bishop of Elphin, 372; death, 426; O'C solicits an appointment for a cleric, 143; recommends Bishop Egan, 274; recommends Denis MacDermot, 275; suggestions for his successor, 419
O'Fallon (Fallon), John, the bishop's nephew, 324; 328
O'Faolan, Malachlyn, 191
O'Flaherty, Roderic (1629–1718), *Ogygia*, 87, 241; confidence in its accuracy plunged O'C into mistakes, 224; errors in lists of Irish kings, 413
O'Flanegan, Theophilus, Gaelic specialist, letter to Vallancey, 385; Royal Irish Academy hires to translate, 428; sends O'C copy of an ogham inscription, 402
O'Gara, Count Charles, leaves a legacy to O'C, 308, 353, 410
O'Gara, John, not a prince, 294
O'Gara, Fergal, lord of Moy O'Gara and Coolavin, 186
O'Gara, Col. Oliver (cousin), death, 202; O'C writes to, 13; protector of Abbé O'Kelly, 228
Ogham inscriptions, 390, 393
O'Gorman, Chevalier Thomas (1732–1809), 166, 341, 343, 349–352, 370,

O'Gorman, Chevalier Thomas (*continued*) 373–375, 377–379, 382–385, 387–390, 392–396, 400, 402, 406, 409, 410, 412, 415, 417, 435, 441, 445; asked to become an honorary member, Royal Irish Academy, 400; dines with Faulkner, 167; leaves France in disgust (1783), 377; letters to O'C, 351, 383, 390; a man of honor, 272; obtains an unadulterated copy of the *Inisfallen Annals*, 402; presents the Royal Irish Academy with a copy of the *Book of Ballymote*, 400; procuring a copy of Scymnus, 441; returns to France with transcriptions of the *Annals*, 353; writing the genealogies of the Munster families, 341, 342, 343, 344

O'Hagan (Fagan) genealogy, 435

O'Halloran, Sylvester (1729–1807), *189, 190, 193, 194*; asks O'C about Druid worship, 189; invited to join the Select Committee of the Dublin Society, 241n; O'C loans book to, 144; *Introduction to the History of Ireland*, 217

O'Keefe, James, bishop of Kildare and Leighlin, declaration of principles, 31; disagrees with bishop of Ossory, 249

O'Kelly, Comte John James (1749–1800), French minister at Mainz, 281

O'Lachlyn, Muirchertach, king of the North Ui-Neill, 186n, 191

O'Leary, Arthur (1727–1802), Catholic priest, 292, 431

O'Malley, William of Aughtertire, 294

O'Malachlyn, Malachlyn, 191

O'Malrony, 191

Ó Maolchonaire, Flaithrí, see Conery, Florence

Ó Maolchonaire, Torna, 194

O'Melaghlin (Malachlin), Murchad, 186, 191

O'Malaghlin (O'Malachlin), Dermod, 191

O'Melaghlin (O'Malachlin), Donall, 191

O'More, James of Ballina, *300, 329*; Curry's correspondence with, 199, 200; letter to O'C, 300n; O'C's correspondence with, 198; O'C visits, 153

O'Mulchonry, Farfassa, 13n

O'Mulloy, Rev. Francis, *Irish Grammar*, 222

O'Neal, Charles, 1

O'Neaghtan, Teige (Ó Neachtain, Tadhg), 232n

O'Neill, Capt. (Daniel O'Conor's father-in-law), 143

O'Neill, Maria Theresa, see Wharton, duchess of

O'Neill, Sir Phelim, 242

O'Reilly, 415

O'Reilly, Michael, archbishop of Armagh, pastoral letter, 30

Orleans, duke of, memorial for Irish Catholics presented to, 160

O'Rourke, Countess (grandmother), 4n

O'Rourke, Con, 356

O'Rourke, Count Daniel (cousin), his invectives are more useful than his friendship, 7; letter to Charles of Mt. Allen, 4; O'C proposes putting Taaffe in possession of O'Rourke's papers and memoirs, 150

O'Rourke, James, 150

O'Rourke, Count (cousin), *365;* ill-treated in the *Evening Post*, 365; lobbied with Gardiner for Catholic Relief, 365; O'C preparing a genealogy for, 358; well received by the viceroy, 356

O'Rourke, Bishop Thadeus (uncle), 4; in 1734 made early manuscripts available to O'C, 13; prayer before studies, 404

O'Rourke, Col. Tiernan (grandfather), 4n

O'Ruark, Tiernan, 191

Orsi, Giuseppe, 354

Ortelius, 169

Osborne, Thomas, Duke of Leeds, 127

Ossian poems, 102

Ossory, bishop of, see de Burgo, Thomas

O'Sullivan, unidentified, death, 166

Owsley, Ralph, *446*

Parker, George, *see* MacClesfield, second earl of

Parlan, Patrick, tenant, 319

Parliament, English (1778), Catholic Relief, 301, 306, 308; (1780), free trade legislation, 332

Parliament, Irish (1756), imposes no bondage on us, 15; (1763), hopes men of good sense will prove the majority, 135; (1771), will not remedy the ills of the country, 208; bill for long leases presented, 221; something will be done, but little, 209; (1772), will not act on reform of the penal laws, 234; Elegit Bill, 222, 226, 233, 234; (1774), see parliamentary Test; (1775), Bill for the Better Encouragement for Papists, 269, 271; (1778), to consider relaxation of the penal laws, 301, 302; Gardiner's Relief Act, 306, 308; (1783), our first constitutional parliament, 377, 378; (1784), Catholics should stay out of the contention, 395; (1785), de-

bates on free trade, 398; reform measure, 398; (1786), O'C hopes for economic relief from, 405
Parliamentary Test (1774), see de Burgo, Thomas; Butler signs, 274; Carpenter signs, 309–311; Galway prelates meet, 309n; O'C hesitates, 309; O'C's objections to 309; Troy signs, 309; an insult linked to an absurdity, 259; O'C's arguments against, 259–263, 265, 266, 269–271; O'C's version, a veiled attempt to divide Catholics, 266, 274
Parsons, Sir William (1570?–1650), his administration contributed to the Rebellion of 1641, 242
Paul, St., 9, 32
Penal laws, see O'Conor, Charles, Opinions, arguments against presented to Burke, 145; arguments against, 278; effects of, 226, 272, 296, 303, 401
Percy, Sir Hugh, see Northumberland, second earl of
Pery, Edmund Sexton, Speaker, 301n
Petit, Peter, 231
Pezron, Paul Yves, lost himself in the wilds of etymology, 193
Philips, Philip, bishop of Killala, helped place grandson Matthew in Roman seminary, 419; poor relationship with Brady, 428; recommends Bishop Egan, 274; recommends D. MacDermot to leave for Rome, 317; to sign the MacDermot genealogy, 294
Phillips, Thomas (1708–74), English priest, letter to O'C, 146
A Philosophical Survey of the South of Ireland, mentions O'C's discovery suit, 302
Pinkerton, John (1758–1826), Scottish antiquarian, *413, 422, 430;* writes to O'C through Wharton, 418
Pitt, William, the Elder (1708–78), free from prejudice, religious and national, 83
Pitt, William, the Younger (1759–1806), 398n
Plautus, 232
Pliny, 429
Pluche, Noel Antoine, his defense of Moses an antidote to Bolingbroke, 46
Plunkett, Arthur James, eighth earl of Fingall (1759–1836), Catholic Peer, 324, 339; law suit, 346
Plunkett, genealogy, 445
Plunkett, Counselor John, 345
Plunkett, Michael of Ardkenna, signs An Address (1760), 80
Plunkett, Michael of Ox-hill, signs An Address (1760), 80
Plunkett, Robert, signs An Address (1760), 80
Pole, Reginald (1500–58), cardinal, 432
Ponsonby, John (1713–87), Speaker, Irish Commons asked to intercede for Daniel O'Conor, 114n; Catholics present an address to, 64n, 68; replies to the Catholics for the viceroy, 67n
Ponsonby, William, second earl of Bessborough (1704–93), Warner writes to in behalf of Daniel O'Conor, 114n
Pope, Alexander (1688–1745), 23, 172
Pownall, Thomas (1722–1805), 248, writes to O'C, 342
Poyning's law, 332
The Pretender, 93, 94
Psalter of Cashel, 406
Purcell, unidentified, 104
Purcell, John of Roscommon, signs An Address (1760), 80

Quebec Act, 261n, 272n

Rafodagh, 144
Rari of Cormac Cas, 166
Rari of Dol-Cas (Dáil Cais), 166
Rawdon, Sir John, earl of Moira, Faulkner introduced to, 154; on the Select Committee, Dublin Society, 232n; chairs it, 244
Rebellion of 1641, defense of, 242
Reddy, Dr. Richard, encourages O'C to write history, 74; matchmaking for his son with Mahon of Strokestown, 158; O'C offers to send his historical material to, 75
Reflecions on our Present . . . Situation, see O'Conor, Charles, Works
Reginald, 191
Registry Bill (1757), 30, 33–35, 37
Reilly, servant, 426
Reilly, Michael (Civicus, cousin), 2; Activities as O'C's and Curry's publishing agent, 3, 5, 12, 19, 20, 22, 34, 38, 44–46, 48, 49, 56, 57, 62, 69, 73, 92, 93, 101, 104, 107–111, 115, 129, 130, 132, 135, 139, 149, 151; copying *Ogygia Vindicated,* 249; embezzles funds from the Foundling Hospital, 73; financial difficulties of, 22, 134, 135; plans a weekly paper, 116, 117, 119
Reilly, Thomas, encourages mining at Lough Allen, 418
"Remarks upon the New Test . . . ," see O'Conor, Charles, Works

Remonstrance, see Address to the King (1761)
Reymer, Charles, printer, 169n
Reynolds, James, silk merchant, member of the Catholic Committee, 74; to form a committee with Curry and Bishop Egan, 104; Curry to discontinue working with on the Catholic Committee, 130; treasurer of the Catholic Committee, death, 310
Reynolds, Thomas, member of the Catholic Committee, 272
Rice, Councilor, 286
Richard, Earl, 192
Richard of Cirencester (1401?), an eighteenth century forgery like MacPherson's *Ossian*, unmasked in 1866, 254
Ridge, John (c. 1728–76), lawyer, told O'C about a plan to codify the penal laws, 173; visits O'C, 177; a worthy gentleman, Curry's friend, gave Smollett the *Hist. Mem.*, 177
Rinuccini, Archbishop Giovanni Battista (1592–1653), conduct condemned by the Pope, 60
Robertson, Dr. William (1721–93), historian, 161; unfair historian, 107
Robinson, Thomas, praises Curry's *Candid Inquiry*, 156
Roderic, 188n, 191, 192
Rollin, Charles, 46
"Roman Legion," 100, 103, 104
Rooth, author of *Analecta Sacra*, 43
Roscommon Abbey, 438
Roscommon Castle, 343
Roscommon triangle, coal and iron deposits, 400
Ross, William, bookseller, auctioneer, 13
Ross and Cloyne, bishop of, see O'Brien, John
Rowlands, Henry, 193
Royal Irish Academy, foundation of, 399; O'C invited to be a member, 414; O'C promises Vallancey to leave all his manuscripts to, 440; O'C proposes that it study the best use of the natural resources of Ireland, 400
Russell, John, fourth duke of Bedford (1710–71), viceroy, his administration has never supported or opposed Catholics' efforts to obtain long leases, 222; O'C pleased with his speech to Parliament (1757), 30; Ponsonby presents an address from the Catholic Committee to, 67; Stone preached before him in favor of the Catholics, 68

Ryan, Charles, member of the Catholic Committee, 291, 293, 295, 296, 298, 311, 397, 431; assists O'C with the publication of *Reflexions*, 291–293, 295, 296, 298; letters to O'C, 397; O'C's letter is lost, 328; writes an address to George III, 418n
Ryan, Dan, madman, sat in the Lord Chancellor's throne, 411

Salviati, 442
Sanadon, O'C recommends his editions to Denis, 3
Scottish history, O'C's notes to Pinkerton, 413, 420, 421
Scottish Kings, list of, 430
Scott, John (1739–98), earl of Clonmel, 306
Seabright, Sir John, manuscripts, 389
Selden, John (1582–1654), 449
Sérent, Count, 167
Serious Thoughts Concerning the True Interest and Exigencies of the State of Ireland, 30
Sheehy, Nicholas (1728–66), Catholic priest, hanged, drawn, and quartered, see Munster uprisings and Whiteboys; O'C suggests documenting the case and publishing the true facts, 148n, 149, 151n
Sheridan, Thomas (1719–88), *Dictionary*, O'C's subscription to, 386; O'C writes dedication for, 358
Sherlock, Mr., Dublin priest, 309; 202, 223, 231, 296
"A Short View of the Ancient State of Ireland . . . ," see O'Conor, Charles, Works
Skerrett, Michael, archbishop of Tuam, 250, 274, 301, 302
Slingsby, member of the Catholic Committee; jealous temper, 281; praises *Dissertations*, 149
Smith, Charles (1715?–62), O'Gorman follows Smith's plan for his history of Clare, 166
Smith, Samuel, Faulkner's nephew, 167
Smollett, Tobias, collecting materials for a history of Ireland, 104; informs Hume of the *Hist. Mem.*, 86; O'C not displeased with his review, 13n; O'C would like him to write a history of Ireland, 88; review of Warner's history, 127, 129
Some Thoughts on the Natures of Fevers, see Curry, John, Works

INDEX   535

Stafford, Hugh, 58, 60, 68, 99; O'C sends *Hist. Mem.* to Synge through Stafford, 59, 61; signs An Address (1760), 80

Stone, George (c. 1708–64), archbishop of Armagh, Primate, a most worthy person, 82; O'C asks Taaffe to solicit Stone's help for Daniel, 110; opposition to the Registry Bill, 37; preaches in favor of Catholics, 68; refuses to present an address to the king (1761), 88, 89

Strongbow, 188 n

Stuart, Charles (1720–88), the Young Pretender abuses his wife in public, 342

Subscriptions, An Address to George III (1760), 80; Curry's *Hist. Mem.*, 56, 57; *Ogygia Vindicated*, 240

Sullivan, Dr. Francis (1719–76), Fellow of Trinity College, 125; O'C proposes editing and publishing *Annals of the Four Masters*, 125, 130, 131; refused to translate parts of the *Annals*, 351

Swift, Jonathan (1667–1745), 252, 317; little inclined to think favorably of court chaplains, 127 n; saw the danger of Presbyterians in Northern Ireland, 130 n

Synge, Edward, bishop of Elphin, O'C compares his reputation to a pope's, 47; O'C has Stafford give Synge the *Hist. Mem.*, 58, 59, 60; one of the ablest men in our nation, 60; suspects O'C wrote the *Hist. Mem.*, 61; searching for *The Bleeding Iphigenia*, 27; John Taylor contradicts, 76

Taaffe, Francis Count, dispensation to marry his sister-in-law, 164 n, 168; smuggles money into Ireland, 143

Taaffe, Major, obtains permission to return to Ireland after having served in the Austrian Army, 111, 113 n

Taaffe, Nicholas Viscount: 150; application for marriage dispensation for his son, 164, 168, 171; asked to help Curry's son in Austria, 160 n; asks Stone to present an address to the king, 88, 90; assists Daniel O'Conor, 111; displeased with Martin Curry, 199, 200; funds channeled through O'C, 143, 151; gives book to O'C, 93; legacy of his zeal for Catholics, 149; letter to O'C, 139; letter to Trimleston, requesting return of Catholic Committee funds, 72 n; reception at Court, 155; reports to O'C on his visit with Stone, 89; turns over affairs of the Catholic Committee to a young inexperienced man, 128; supports An Address to the King (1761), 82; visits Belanagare, 89; well-received by Northumberland, 134; to arrive in Dublin, 198; *Observations on Affairs in Ireland*, 150, 152, 155, 157, 158, criticism of, 164, 171

Tacitus, 220, 237

Talbot, William, 88, 267

Tanistry Laws, 106, 107

Taylor, John, oculist, drunk with vanity, 76

Teagusg Flatha, abstract of the manuscript, 248

Teige, Mr., priest, 143

Tennison, Thomas, coal deposits on his estate, 418

Thomond, Marshal, Charles O'Brien (1699–1761), dispute with the Lady Lismore over titles, 121

Thurot, Francois, attack on Carrickfergus, 69

Tiernan, Edmund, signs An Address (1761), 80

Tiernan, James of Strokestown, signs An Address (1761), 80

Tigernach, 186; accuracy of, 406; the most learned annalist of the eleventh century, 402

Tillotson, Archbishop J., reputation compared to Synge's, 47

Tisdal, Philip (1703–77), Irish attorney general, agrees to present the Elegit Bill a second time, 130; death, 292

Todd, Thomas, 167

Tonry, Fr., Bishop French's nephew, improper conduct of, 448

Toland, John, *History of the Druids*, 193, 194

Torna Éigeas, spurious, 385 n, *Dáil Chatha*, 387

Totnes, earl of, George Carew (1555–1629), *Pacata Hibernia*, 196, 198

Touchet, third earl of Castlehaven (1617?–84), *Memoirs*, edited by O'C, 242

Townshend, George, fourth viscount (1724–1807), viceroy, anecdote about his departure, 239; argues for Catholic relief, 301 n; reaction to his administration, 173; speech, 200

Traill, James, bishop of Down and Conor, anniversary sermon, 200; funeral sermon on Dr. Archbold, 180

Trade restrictions, effect of, 377; petition against importation of corn, 222
Trebatius Testa, 86
Trimleston, Lord, Nicholas Barnewall (1726–1813), leads Catholics signing the Parliamentary Test (1774), 269n; negotiates with Halifax, 108, 109, 111; O'C has no acquaintance nor influence with, 110; opposition to the Address to King George III (1761), 85; opposition to the Catholic Committee, 83; rebuffed by Halifax, 114; son conforms to the Established Church, 115, 222n; thinks and acts by others, 104; withholds the funds of the Catholic Committee, 72, 84, 105
Troy, Dr. John, bishop of Ossory, 309n, 425n
Tuatha Dé Dannan, inaccuracy of accounts of regal succession, 254; 413
Tuam, titular archbishop of, see Skerrett, Michael
Tuamond, 166
Turgesius, Viking invader, 394n

Ufford, Robert de, 343
Universal History, 388; piracy of, 163
Ulster, elections (1790), 449
Usher, Dr., Chief Lecturer, Trinity, goes to Oxford to borrow Irish manuscripts, 390
Usher, Mr., a Catholic priest, death, 225
Ussher, James, archbishop of Armagh (1581–1656), claims the Irish Catholics are not in conformity to Rome, 124

Vallancey, Colonel Charles (1721–1812), *218, 232, 248, 252, 254, 264, 304, 316, 330, 332, 440, 450;* 342, 370, 373, 375, 377, 378, 390, 392, 393, 417, 433; asks O'C about the antiquity of Irish literature, 221; attack on his linguistic theories, 382; disturbed about Ewing's disclosure of the authorship of the *Observations*, 221; entertains Ledwick, Carpenter, and O'C, 361; essays not appreciated, 398; hopes Parliament (1771) will relax the penal laws, 217; in good graces of the king, 411; introduces O'C to Col. Burton, 315; letters to O'C, 223, 233, 240, 241, 248n, 420, 428; O'C praises his research, 421; O'C suspects "Moran" is Vallancey, 226; on a royal commission, 427; proposes publication on *Ogygia Vindicated*, 227n; recommends O'C's grandson Charles, 437, 439; recommends O'C for a pension, 438; research attacked, 449; research praised by O'C, 449, 450; research, 389; sends O'C a copy of the *Tigernach Annals*, 383; sends O'C MacPherson's book and O'Halloran's answer to it, 217; shows O'C's letter to Ewing, 217, 219, 220; Works: *Collectanea*, 343, first 3 volumes have had hardly any sale, 374; *Essay on the antiquity of the Irish language*, 229, 231, 232, 235, 236; European response to, 248; *A Vindication of the ancient History of Ireland*, 405, 418
Vesey, Agmondesham (d. 1785), 185, 186
Villiers, John, see Grandison, Lord
Virgil, 3, 208, 238
Voltaire, 248; *General History*, 176
Volunteers, Bellewstown Meeting (1781), 351, 352; national convention, 378
von Mosheim, Johann, 354
von Stolberg, Louisa, abused by her husband, the Young Pretender, 342

Wagstaffe, George, bookseller, 199
Walker, Joseph Cooper (1761–1810), Dublin treasury official, *398, 399, 401, 403, 405, 407, 408, 411, 416, 418, 420, 421, 424, 427, 428, 432, 433, 437–439, 442, 443, 449;* defends O'C, 431; recommends grandson Charles, 437, 439; sends Johnson's letter to O'C to Boswell, 399; Works, *History of Irish Bards*: O'C's correction of, 428; O'C defends against hostile reviewers, 421; reputation in Rome, 433
Wallis, Luke, 143, 144, 150, 151
Wallis, Patrick, 143n
Walsh, Fr. Peter (1618–88), criticized the *Iphigenia*, 62; *History of the Irish Remonstrance*, 196, 198
Ward, Fr. Hugh, 186
Ware, Sir James, 12
Warner, Ferdinado (1703–68), *87;* asks O'C's assistance in his history, 86; believes Ossian poems authentic, 102; criticism of *The Dangers of Popery ...*, 93; ill treatment of, 127, 129; letters to O'C, 89, 114; O'C fears his discouragement, 148; O'C sends Warner's letter to Lyttleton, 98; O'C sends material to, 96; O'C suggests using Warner to ask the Viceroy to help Daniel, 111, 113, 114; recognizes O'C authorship of *The Dangers of Popery ...*, 93; refutes

Archbishop Ussher, 124; requests Curry's *Hist. Mem.*, 104; *History of Ireland*, 102, 117, 121, 124; *Remarks on the History of Fingal*, 102
Watt, O'C's servant, 136, 201
Weldon, Kitt, 108
Welsh, Mary, 277
Wentworth Parliament, defense of Catholic members in, 242
Wentworth, Thomas, see Stafford, earl of
Wharton, duchess of, Maria Theresa O'Neill O'Beirne, "cousin" to O'C, 202; possible source of help for Daniel O'Conor, 111
William, King, 22, 94, 211, 213
Wilson, Peter, printer, 141
Whitaker, John (1735–1808), antiquarian, 254, 338, 374, 390
White, Luke, printer for the Royal Irish Academy, 398, 418, 427
Whiteboy uprisings (1762), 95, 102, 106, 148, 151; see Sheehy, Nicholas; Buxton, James; Farrell, James: Munster insurrections
Whitten, Edward, herald, 300, 329
Wilson, Thomas (c. 1727–99), approves publishing *Annals*, 389
Wilson, William, bookseller, 418, 426–428
Wogan, Pat, printer, 290, 291, 296, 386, 407
Woodward, Richard, bishop of Cloyne, 429, 431
Wyse, Thomas, 72n; O'C wants Wyse to "spur Dublin indolence," 83; proposes a petition to Parliament and it is approved, 93

Yelverton, Barry (1736–1805), 306, 368
Young, Rev. Matthew, Trinity College, treated O'C well, 421